ATLANTA 1996

OFFICIAL

PUBLICATION

OF THE U.S.

OLYMPIC

COMMITTEE

WITHDRAWN

ALLSPORT / STEPHEN DUNN

COMMEMORATIVE PUBLICATIONS, INC.

SALT LAKE CITY, UTAH

publisher
Mikko Laitinen
Commemorative Publications, Inc.

corporate manager
Judd L. Parr

managing editor
Lisa H. Albertson

USOC editor
Frank Zang

profiles
Lee Benson

typesetting
Marjo Peltonen

computer input
Teresa Jones

ALLSPORT / AL BELLO

special thanks

Karin Adolf, Orris E. Albertson, Atlanta Chamber of Commerce, Sue Baldus, Banta Spanish Fork staff, Duane Carter, Barry King, Director of USOC Marketing and Fundraising Communications, Tom Kupka, Tarja Laitinen, Lee Martin, Mike Moran, Director, USOC Public Information and Media Relations Division, Sharon Parr, Richard Smith, Edgar Spallek, Steve Stolba, Jeff N. Walker, Gigi Zvonkovich.

printing
Banta ISG
Bushman Press, Inc.
Provo, Utah

binding
Lincoln & Allen
Portland, Oregon

color separations
Pre Press Services, Inc.
Salt Lake City

paper
International Paper
Coated Miraweb II® Gloss

ink
Flint Ink Corporation
Detroit, Salt Lake City

ALLSPORT / SIMON BRUTY

photographers

Allsport / Los Angeles, London, Mexico
Allsport / Vandystadt
Al Bello, Nathan Bilow, Simon Bruty, David Cannon, Michael Cooper, Tony Duffy, Stephen Dunn, Stu Forster, John Gichigi, Mike Hewitt, Jed Jacobsohn, Rusty Jarrett, Ross Kinnaird, David Leah, Gray Mortimore, Doug Pensinger, Mike Powell, Gary M. Prior, Edward Rio Roda, Pascal Rondeau, Jamie Squire, Rick Stewart, Billy Stickland, Matthew Stockman, David Taylor, Peter Thompson, Gerard Vandystadt, Martin Venegas
AP Photo / Katsumi Kasahara
Hamilton McDonald
Atlanta Chamber of Commerce

Published under license from the U.S. Olympic Committee by:

Commemorative Publications
P.O. Box 71038
Salt Lake City, UT 84171
tel (801) 288-9668
fax (801) 262-6883

ISBN 0-918883-08-3

ALLSPORT / MATTHEW STOCKMAN

Supporting Our Athletes

The U.S. Olympic Committee supports its athletes in the pursuit of excellence, and is committed to providing financial, career and education assistance to enable them to achieve greater successes in their personal lives and athletic endeavors. These programs are designed to prolong competitive careers, improve athletic performance and better prepare for life after sport.

During the four-year period leading up to the 1996 Olympic Games, the USOC awarded about 10,000 grants in direct aid to athletes, totaling upward of $30 million. A full menu of personal and professional development services was also available so athletes could keep pace with their non-athlete peers.

The USOC administers five types of athlete grants: Basic, Special Assistance, Tuition, Olympic Job Opportunities and Operation Gold.

A typical Basic Grant is for $2,500 and is designed to help high-performance athletes defray basic living and training expenses. Special Assistance Grants, up to $5,000, are available to Basic Grant recipients who have additional financial need and show meritorious circumstances. Tuition Grants, up to $5,000 are available to those athletes enrolled in a degree- or certificate-granting program of study and who have financial need.

Employment opportunities that provide financial help and work schedule flexibility are coordinated through the Olympic Job Opportunities Program, which is a partnership between the U.S. Olympic Committee, Ernst & Young and The Olsten Corporation. More than 450 athletes have been placed in jobs through OJOP.

Operation Gold Grants of $1,000 to $15,000 based on performances at the Olympic Games, Pan American Games and World Championships, or an equivalent competition, are available to athletes who achieve top performances at these events. At the 1996 Olympic Games in Atlanta, the top four places earned Operation Gold awards of $15,000, $12,500, $10,000 and $7,500, respectively. The award amounts are reduced in non-Olympic years.

The USOC, through a variety of programs, assists its high-performance athletes in exploring areas of career and education opportunities. A one-day workshop program, conducted by Drake Beam Morin, Inc., has been developed for active and retired athletes to address issues related to sports experiences, sports retirement planning, career exploration and planning, and education. The Athlete Support Division staff is also available to counsel athletes, regarding individual education and career issues.

About 1,500 elite athletes per year are eligible for a special health insurance program with the premium paid for by the USOC. In 1995, 1,100 athletes and dependents submitted medical claims totaling more than $1.2 million. In 1996, the USOC allocated almost $1.8 million to cover the premium for this program.

Finally, Hometeam '96 was a series of supplemental performance-enhancing programs and services to augment preparations for the 1996 Olympic Games. About $4.25 million was set aside for these athletes and teams that were considered top-medal prospects in Atlanta. ▼

White House Welcome

About 650 delegation members of the 1996 U.S. Olympic and Paralympic Teams, including more than 100 Olympic medalists, traveled to Washington, D.C., on Aug. 6-7 in recognition of their efforts at the Centennial Olympic Games and Paralympic Games in Atlanta.

President Clinton, the honorary president of the U.S. Olympic Committee, and First Lady Hillary Rodham Clinton greeted the athletes and staff on the South Lawn of the White House. Delegation members toured the White House and had individual portraits taken with the First Family.

Gold medalist high jumper Charles Austin and synchronized swimmer Becky Dyroen-Lancer presented President Clinton with a commemorative pin set from the 1996 U.S. Olympic Team.

The group was treated to a dinner, hosted by NationsBank, and a concert with Tracy Chapman and the Charley Hunter Quartet for "Olympic Night at Wolf Trap" on the night prior to the White House visit.

The McLean Hilton in McLean, VA., hosted the Olympic Team, holding a send-off celebration and a luncheon with about 70 local youth from the Amateur Athletic Union.

Following the White House visit, about 300 athletes departed for Williamsburg, VA., and "Victory Lap '96" as Busch Gardens saluted Team USA. ▼

CONTENTS

ATLANTA

Atlanta the brave

BY DOUG ROBINSON

ATLANTA CHAMBER OF COMMERCE / TERYL JACKSON

RIGHT / *The city of Atlanta formed the backdrop of the Olympic Stadium where the Games of the XXVIth Olympiad officially opened and were watched on television by 3.5 billion people – two-thirds of the world's population.*
ALLSPORT / MIKE POWELL

AFTER ALL WAS SAID AND DONE, AFTER the last race was run and the last medal presented, after they said goodbye at the Closing Ceremonies and turned out the lights, the Centennial Olympic Games left a trail of lasting images ...

The Olympics were Kenny Harrison filling a sandwich bag with sand from the triple jump pit moments after his winning jump.

The Olympics were the entire world — 197 countries, 10,700 athletes — present and accounted for, a first in the history of the Games.

The Olympics were a curtain call for Mary Slaney, Carl Lewis, Janet Evans and Jackie Joyner-Kersee. All but Lewis left quietly.

The Olympics were little girls: Amanda Beard and her teddy bear and Kerri Strug in Bela's arms and Dominique Moceanu, "who owns two-thirds of the world's known supply of cuteness," wrote humorist Dave Barry.

The Olympics were Namibian sprinter Frank Fredericks playing the role of peacemaker and ambassador of goodwill. He separated Linford Christie and Ato Boldon before they could come to blows, and after each race went out of his way to shake hands with every one of his competitors before leaving the track.

The Olympics were a bomb in the night.

The Olympics were the black and white hands of strangers intertwined at the reopening of Centennial Park.

The Olympics were Martin Luther King's I-Have-a-Dream speech echoing through Olympic Stadium in the Opening Ceremony, and believing for a moment that it had been realized.

The Olympics were Josia Thugwane of South Africa, Ghada Shouaa of South Africa, Armen Nazaryan of Armenia, Jefferson Perez of Ecuador and Claudia Poll of Costa Rica proudly winning their country's first Olympic gold medals.

The Olympics were a Paris runway model named Marie-Jose Perec, a.k.a. La Gazelle, eating up the home stretch with

her graceful, long-legged stride.

The Olympics were Janet Evans doing Amanda Beard's laundry.

The Olympics were Angel Martino giving her bronze medal to a sick friend and wishing she could give her a gold.

The Olympics were America's Scott Shipley giving Bosnia's Samir Karabasid his custom-made kayak after Karabasid's boat, patched with duct tape, fell apart and sank during a practice run.

The Olympics were Dikembe Mutombo spending more than $10,000 to buy sneakers, uniforms, personal gifts and clothing for his native Zaire's basketball team.

The Olympics were Americans cheering other nations like the home team.

The Olympics were Holyfield to Evans to Ali. What a relay team.

The Olympics were Svetlana Masterkova sprinting around the track after winning the 800-meter run, proving there were no bounds to her kick or joy. Her radiant smile and tears dispelled the image of the stoic Russian.

The Olympics were unfathomable pressure and Fredericks saying flat out that he couldn't handle it before his 100-meter race.

The Olympics were Shannon Miller winning her first gold medal on the 30th and final routine of her long career.

The Olympics were American women, the first generation of Title IX girls, winning the team gold medals in softball, basketball, soccer and gymnastics. They took home 19 of America's 44 gold medals.

The Olympics were Dan O'Brien, kneeling and crying at the finish line of the 1,500 meters — the final event of the decathlon — and his four-year bid for redemption.

The Olympics were Andre Agassi playing for his country, no charge.

The Olympics were miles of booths and vendors hoping for their own Olympic gold on the streets of Atlanta.

TOP / *From Athens to Atlanta: Greece's Voula Patoulidou, the 1992 gold medalist in 100-meter hurdles, rounded the track with Atlanta's own Evander Holyfield, a boxing bronze medalist in Los Angeles, in a symbolic celebration of the 100 years of the modern Olympic Games.* ALLSPORT / DAVID TAYLOR

.... ABOVE / *The duo handed the torch to Janet Evans, the greatest female distance swimmer of all-time, who first appeared in the Olympic spotlight in Seoul as a 16-year-old teenager and came to Atlanta for her third consecutive Games as a 24-year-old woman with a mission to have fun.* ALLSPORT / DOUG PENSINGER

ABOVE / *An Olympic moment: The mystery of who would light the torch unfolded when Janet Evans handed the torch to one of the most beloved athletes in the history of sport, Muhammad Ali. Ali stood proudly and trembled slightly, an affliction of Parkinson's disease, and saluted the roaring crowd.* ALLSPORT / MICHAEL COOPER

The Olympics were a man selling key chains on International Boulevard with this promise: "Michael Jordan touched them."

The Olympics were a menagerie of cultures, dress, languages and personalities.

The Olympics were overkill and Dan O'Brien's dad telling him, "I'm Danned out, son." His son said, "I know what you mean, Dad. I'm Danned out, too."

The Olympics were NBC zooming in for tear shots.

The Olympics were wrestler Derrick Waldroup leaving his shoes on the mat after his final match, marking the end of his wrestling career.

The Olympics were celebrity sightings at Planet Hollywood, music at the House of Blues and greasy burgers at The Varsity.

The Olympics were getting lost in a maze of streets named Peachtree.

The Olympics were a cop sympathizing with the thousands of fans waiting at a MARTA subway station. "We're here, we might as well have fun," she said, and then she started a mass wave, going back and forth with fans on both sides of the track.

The Olympics were traffic gridlock and sweltering heat and human causeways of people flowing through the narrow Atlanta streets, teeming with a vigor and life that was only temporary.

The Olympics were long lines.

The Olympics were security searches and x-ray machines.

The Olympics were millions of people wearing Olympic pins and trying to score a trade.

The Olympics were hundreds of people standing in the fountain in Centennial Park, and guys with water-filled backpacks spraying overheated visitors on the street.

The Olympics were Southern Hospitality and Georgians setting Olympic records for friendliness and old world manners.

The Olympics were a reporter stopping at a house to ask for directions and being

TOP / Billy Payne, who breathed life into the dream of Atlanta hosting the Centennial Olympic Games, stood tall with President Bill Clinton and International Olympic Committee President Juan Antonio Samaranch at the Opening Ceremonies. ALLSPORT / DAVID TAYLOR

ABOVE / From dog-day heat to nonstop action, Atlanta lived up to its nickname "Hotlanta." ALLSPORT / STU FORSTER

TOP AND ABOVE / The popular AT&T Global Village in Centennial Olympic Park overcame the horror of the bomb in the night and after three days of closure resumed its popularity with Olympic revelers, who cooled their heels in the nearby Olympic ring fountain. ALLSPORT / NATHAN BILOW

invited to come into the house ("You look hot. Would you like a cold drink?")

The Olympics were Muhammad Ali sightings and presenting him with another gold medal to replace the one "he lost." No one seemed to mind that he lost the medal by throwing it into a river.

The Olympics were a whoooosh in the night, running 19.32.

The Olympics were Kerri Strug landing a one-legged vault to win the gold.

The Olympics were a day at the man-made beach.

The Olympics were Amy Van Dyken hauling four gold medals from the pool.

The Olympics were Carl Lewis atop the medal stand for old times' sake, one last time.

The Olympics were four more years and hoping for another chance in Sydney.

The Olympics were remembering 100 years of Olympic Games.

The Olympics were a MARTA driver telling passengers over the PA system in a deep, slow drawl, "I've seen a whole lot of people tonight. It's been real nice. I've always wanted to travel the world and

ABOVE / *MARTA's Olympic performance.* HAMIL-TON MCDONALD

meet people from far away places. Thanks to y'all, I don't have to. I've had a great time." ▼

MARTA MAGIC

ER REAL NAME IS METROPOLITAN Atlanta Rapid Transit Authority, but she's just plain MARTA to those who know her, and who didn't by the end of the Olympic Games. The world came to Atlanta ... and rode MARTA together.

MARTA, Atlanta's mass transit system, literally carried the Olympics. For 17 days, back and forth to and from Olympic venues, MARTA delivered 17.8 million passengers — a mark that normally requires a month and a half to achieve. Using buses and a subway, she averaged more than one million passengers a day — almost three times her normal daily deliveries of 475,000.

On Day 1 of the Olympics, MARTA delivered 850,000 passengers, breaking her previous record of 790,000 that was set during the Atlanta Braves World Series championship parade in 1991. That record was broken several times during the Olympics, peaking on Aug. 2 with 1.3 million passengers — 380,000 by bus and 920,000 by rail.

MARTA also must have set some kind of Olympic record for endurance. From July 19 to Aug. 4, MARTA trains and buses operated 24 hours a day.

If nothing else, MARTA's success underscored the benefits of mass transit. By vastly reducing the number of automobiles driven into downtown Atlanta, air pollution and traffic congestion were significantly diminished during the Olympics.

Proponents of mass transit hope that the Olympics increased public awareness enough that MARTA will continue to be fully utilized long after the Games are gone. ▼

LEFT / *After 16 days of athletic competitions, after 1,800-plus medals had been handed out, after a score of magnificent performances and a trail of lasting images, the Atlanta Games ended in a burst of color.* ALLSPORT / NATHAN BILOW

ALLSPORT / NATHAN BILOW

ALLSPORT / SIMON BRUTY

ALLSPORT / NATHAN BILOW

ALLSPORT / SIMON BRUTY

ALLSPORT / NATHAN BILOW

ALLSPORT / GARY M. PRIOR

Olympic Gallery

ALLSPORT / AL BELLO

ALLSPORT / ROSS KINNAIRD

ALLSPORT / GARY M. PRIOR

ALLSPORT / SIMON BRUTY

Guardian Of The Olympic Movement

In 1978, the passage of the Amateur Sports Act as federal law appointed the U.S. Olympic Committee as the coordinating body for Olympic-related athletic activity in the United States. The vision of the USOC has been to assist in finding opportunity for every American to participate in sport, regardless of gender, race, age, geography or physical ability.

Thus, the U.S. Olympic Committee, a multi-faceted organization headquartered in Colorado Springs, Colo., and its 73 member organizations have continued to provide leadership and guidance for the Olympic movement in this country and around the world as recognized by the International Olympic Committee.

America is unique in the Olympic world to the extent that the nation's Olympic effort is propelled by its individual citizens, and by major support from the corporate community. The USOC is one of only a few National Olympic Committees in the world that does not receive continuous support from the federal government.

Therefore the USA's Olympic teams are truly representative of the free enterprise system, and the USOC is proud to say, "America doesn't send its athletes to the Olympic Games, Americans do."

In the past 20 years, the USOC's quadrennial budget has grown from $13 million to $426 million. The USOC is continually ranked among the top 100 non-profit organizations in America. The USOC budget allocates 80 cents of every dollar spent on its programs, at an increase of 32 percent since 1976.

The mission to provide opportunities has resulted in the USOC hosting more than 25,000 athletes each year at its Olympic Training Centers in Colorado Springs, Lake Placid, N.Y., Chula Vista, Calif., and the Olympic Education Center in Marquette, Mich. The USOC also allocates more than 10,000 grants worth $30 million in direct athlete programs, awards $115 million in grants to member organizations in the recent quadrennium, and underwrites the full expenses of U.S. teams at the Olympic, Pan American and World University Games.

In addition to a staff of almost 500 employees, the USOC relies heavily on the expertise of its volunteer leadership. The USOC's Officers, Executive Committee, Board of Directors and various committees are comprised of the leaders of sport in America.

The athletes have an important voice in the U.S. Olympic Movement as well through the Athletes' Advisory Council. All governance councils of the USOC and the NGBs have at least 20 percent membership and voting power held by recent or active athletes representing each sport.

The USOC supports the bid of U.S. cities to host the winter and summer Olympic Games or Pan American Games. The USOC endorsed Atlanta as the host of the 1996 Games and the successful effort of Salt Lake City to welcome the world in 2002 for the Olympic Winter Games.

The USOC is also a leadership organization in administration. From sports medicine to sports science and technology to coaching, the USOC continually strives for excellence in all areas. ▼

OLYMPIC AND PAN AMERICAN GAMES SPORT ORGANIZATIONS

Olympic Division

National Archery Association
U.S. Badminton Association
USA Baseball
USA Basketball
U.S. Biathlon Association
U.S. Bobsled and Skeleton Federation
USA Boxing
American Canoe Association
USA Curling
USA Cycling, Inc.
United States Diving, Inc.
American Horse Shows Association
U.S. Fencing Association
U.S. Field Hockey Association
U.S. Figure Skating Association
USA Gymnastics
USA Hockey, Inc.
United States Judo, Inc.
U.S. Luge Association
U.S. Modern Pentathlon Association
United States Rowing Association
United States Sailing Association
USA Shooting
U.S. Skiing
U.S. Soccer Federation
Amateur Softball Association
U.S. Speedskating
U.S. Swimming, Inc.
U.S. Synchronized Swimming, Inc.
USA Table Tennis
U.S. Team Handball Federation
U.S. Tennis Association
USA Track & Field
USA Volleyball
United States Water Polo
U.S. Weightlifting Federation
USA Wrestling

Pan American Division

USA Bowling
American Amateur Racquetball Association
U.S. Amateur Confederation of Roller Skating
U.S. Taekwondo Union

ALLSPORT / SIMON BRUTY

DR. LEROY T. WALKER RICHARD D. SCHULTZ

USOC Officers

Dr. LeRoy T. Walker, President
Dr. Ralph W. Hale, Vice President
Michael B. Lenard, Vice President
George M. Steinbrenner III, Vice President
Charles U. Foster, Secretary
Sandra Baldwin, Treasurer

USOC Executive Office

Richard D. Schultz, Executive Director / Secretary General
John Krimsky Jr., Deputy Secretary General / Managing Director, Business Affairs
Tom Wilkinson, Assistant Executive Director
Jim Page, Deputy Executive Director for Programs

Affiliated Sport Organizations

USA National Karate-Do Federation, Inc.
U.S. Orienteering Federation
United States Sports Acrobatics Federation
U.S. Squash Racquets Association
USA Trampoline and Tumbling
Triathlon Federation USA
Underwater Society of America
American Water Ski Association

Community-Based Multisport Organizations

Amateur Athletic Union
American Alliance for Health, Physical Education, Recreation and Dance
Boys and Girls Clubs of America
Catholic Youth Organization
Jewish Community Centers Association
National Association of Police Athletic Leagues
National Congress of State Games
National Exploring Division, Boy Scouts of America
Native American Sports Council
U.S. National Senior Sport Organization
YMCA of the USA
YWCA of the USA

Education-Based Multisport Organizations

National Association of Intercollegiate Athletics
National Collegiate Athletic Association
National Federation of State High School Associations
National Junior College Athletic Association

Armed Forces

U.S. Armed Forces Sports

Disabled in Sports

American Athletic Association of the Deaf, Inc.
United States Cerebral Palsy Athletic Association
Disabled Sports USA
Dwarf Athletic Association of America
Wheelchair Sports USA
Special Olympics International
U.S. Association for Blind Athletes

Vaulting Into History

Kerri Strug

The signature event of the Centennial Games came on Day Four when a barefoot 90-pound gymnast performed a two-legged vault on one leg.

With that vault:

■ The United States women's gymnastics team clinched its first Olympic gold medal ever.

■ Kerri Strug passed her character test.

■ And the Games of Atlanta, destined to follow a script of adversity followed by resiliency throughout their 17-day run, had their defining moment.

In many ways, the fix the women's team found themselves in as Strug faced her moment of truth was a microcosm of the Atlanta Games. When it came down to the wire, the 18-year-old Strug, a middle-of-the-pack member of the team used to competing in the estimable superstar shadow of the Dominiques (Dawes and Moceanu) and Shannon Miller, made her own permanent mark in history. The fact that she'd sprained her ankle on her first vault and should be in an x-ray room dissuaded her not a bit. Neither did the fact that they might not need her second vault. Might not wouldn't cut it. All that meant was they might need it, too.

She ran, she vaulted, she landed, and then she winced. By that point, she had company. All of America was wincing along with her. But it was a happy wince. Across the land there was a collective sense that now this was the epitome of the going-getting-tough and the tough-getting-going.

Not that there weren't the usual critics who wondered if it was wise for her to have gone back out for that second vault.

Yeah, right. And Kirk Gibson shouldn't have stepped up to the plate and Willis Reed shouldn't have taken the court for Game Seven, and ...

Kerri Strug had 75 seconds to decide her fate — 45 seconds to get back to the top of the runway for her second vault and 30 seconds to complete that vault. History will show that by the time she landed vault No. 2 she still had about 15 seconds to spare. She took one for the team, and she didn't have to even think about it. She took one for Atlanta, too. There are worse ways to be remembered. ❏

RIGHT / Kerri Strug, along with Carl Lewis, won the Olympic Spirit Award, an award recognizing the best in athletic performance, determination and sportsmanship. They received $10,000 in cash and an original sculpture created by BMW, the sponsor of the award. ALLSPORT / TONY DUFFY

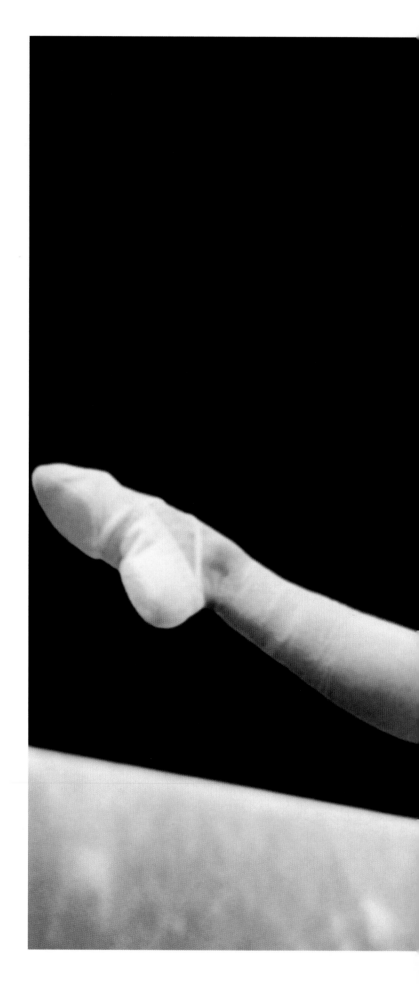

New Zealand's Toni Hodgkinson and the USA's Meredith Rainey ran strongly in their heat of the 800-meter run. Hodgkinson advanced to the final, but Rainey faded to seventh in the semifinals and didn't advance.
ALLSPORT / MIKE POWELL

Carl's Kingdom

Carl Lewis

If there were any doubts as to just exactly where Carl Lewis stood in the Olympic pantheon, they were all cleared up during the final flight of Air Lewis.

It took place, in case you missed it — and chances are, you didn't — on a windy night in Centennial Stadium as, oh, about a billion people looked on.

Now that he had everyone's attention...

The long jump was far from the longest in Lewis's storied career, but the timing was, as usual, perfect. Into a stiff headwind and late in the program, he flew 27 feet, 10 3/4 inches, eight inches farther than anyone else, including Mike Powell, the world record-holder. In so doing, the indefatigable Lewis joined the company of these Olympic track and field legends:

■ He joined U.S. discus thrower Al Oerter as the only track and field athlete to ever win the same event in four consecutive Olympic Games.

■ He joined Finnish distance runner Paavo Nurmi as the only athlete to win nine gold medals.

Of course, he'd already joined the company of Jesse Owens, the only man in history to win four track and field gold medals in one Games until Lewis came along and matched him in 1984.

Oerter, Nurmi and Owens.

Only Lewis can say he did what they did.

And none of them can say they did all that he did.

Lewis' knack was always knowing "when" as well as knowing "how." His final jump in Atlanta was a climactic example. On a night when Michael Johnson, the emerging superstar of the Atlanta Games, won the 400 to produce the first leg of his 200-400 double, there came Lewis, stirring up the fresh sand at the far end of the long jump pit.

He could have easily stepped aside with no dishonor. He was 35 years old. He'd won his share. He'd won more than his share. The curtain was closing. Nobody said he had to trump Johnson. Nobody said he had to trump them all.

But these were the Olympic Games, and there were more elite clubs to join, so F. Carlton Lewis did what he'd always done in just such a situation. He joined. ❑

LEFT / *Five-time Olympian Carl Lewis proved he still had the fire burning at age 35 by claiming his ninth Olympic gold medal in Atlanta.* ALLSPORT / MIKE POWELL

'For All the Nerds'

Amy Van Dyken

After Amy Van Dyken collapsed on the deck following her very first Olympic race, her legs severely cramped because of her furious kick in a desperate, fourth-place, out-of-the-medal finish in the women's 100-meter freestyle, the U.S. coach, Richard Quick, had an explanation.

"Amy hates to lose," he said.

He had that right.

She did not lose again. Four times Van Dyken dove in the pool in four more finals, and every time she got out wearing a gold medal. She became the first American woman to win four gold medals in one Games. From cramp to champ.

The 23-year-old Van Dyken, who began swimming as a child when a doctor told her it would be good therapy for her asthma, just would not be denied. Two days after her nationally televised "collapse" she was swimming the second fastest 100-meter freestyle split in history (53.91) to pace the winning U.S. 400-meter freestyle relay team. The next day she edged Liu Limin of China in the 100-meter butterfly. The day after that she was part of the winning U.S. 400-meter medley relay squad. And on the last day of the swimming competition, she won the 50-meter freestyle over world record-holder Le Jingyi of China, who had won the 100-meter freestyle to begin the week.

In the process, Van Dyken became a one-woman thrill-of-victory Kodak Moment. She led group hugs after the relays, she gleefully threw her bouquet of flowers into the stands after her triumph in the butterfly, and after she made history with her fourth gold in the 50-meter freestyle she let out a scream they could hear all the way back to Englewood, Colo., where she grew up just trying to make the swim team, used to being picked last. "This is a victory for all the nerds out there," she shouted. "To all the girls who gave me a hard time in high school, I say, 'Thank you.'"

Not only did Amy hate to lose. She loved to win. ❑

LEFT / *The irrepressible Amy Van Dyken punctuated her string of victories with unabashed glee.* ALLSPORT / AL BELLO

Double Trouble
Michael Johnson

The noted perfectionist had it his way. The man who hates flaws — the man who never met a bed that couldn't be made better, a day that couldn't be planned tighter, a race that couldn't be run faster — had a flawless Olympic Games. Everything went exactly as planned: Blurry and, well, perfect.

It was like a moon launching, only smoother and with a faster start. He set it up, and then he pulled it off. Without a hitch. First, he successfully petitioned the International Olympic Committee to change the track and field schedule so he could attempt to go where no man had ever gone before — namely, to gold-medal finishes at both 200 meters and 400 meters. Then, on a Monday night in the kind of heat and humidity only a sprinter born in Texas could love, he won the 400 in an Olympic record 43.49 seconds; and he followed that up 72 hours with his history-making win in the 200, which, for good measure, lowered the world record by over three-tenths of a second.

As the week got longer, he got quicker.

Michael Johnson's 19.32 was so fast that if Canada's Donovan Bailey, who five days earlier had set a world record at 100 meters with a 9.84 second clocking, had kept running at full throttle he'd have finished second in the 200.

If Johnson had been equipped with a speedometer, it would have registered 23 miles an hour.

In all, a performance for the record books and the history books. To find an Olympic multiple track performance its equal, you have to use names like Carl Lewis and Jesse Owens.

And to think it had been set up on an upset stomach four years earlier, in Barcelona, when Johnson, weakened after a bout of suspected food poisoning, failed to qualify into the finals of the 200 and to even make it to the starting blocks in the 400.

In Barcelona, much to Johnson's chagrin, absolutely nothing went according to plan. In Atlanta, he made certain absolutely everything did. ❏

RIGHT / *Michael Johnson cooly completed an unprecedented Olympic double in the men's 200- and 400-meter races, setting a mind-boggling, world-record time of 19.32 in the 200.* ALLSPORT / MIKE POWELL

Smack in the pack, Imelda Chiappa of Italy broke free to take second place behind France's legend Jeannie Longo-Ciprelli in the women's road race. ALLSPORT / MIKE POWELL

Stuff of Dreams

Dot Richardson

ABOVE / *When Dot Richardson finally heard the International Olympic Committee say "play softball," her dream to play in the Olympic Games came true.* ALLSPORT / JED JACOBSOHN

Say this for Dorothy "Dot" Richardson, she knows how to hang on to a dream. When she was 15 years old she turned down an offer to play softball for money so she could one day play in the Olympics.

That was in 1976 — 20 years ago. The Olympics didn't even play baseball at the time, let alone the version with the bigger ball.

No matter. Richardson stuck with her fantasy and refused to let it go, declining to retire from competitive softball even after she became a resident in orthopedic surgery at the University of Southern California Medical Center in Los Angeles and they wondered if what she was doing was good for her hands.

Through more than two decades she played her game, winning everything you could win. Fourteen times she was named American Softball Association All-American. Seven times she was named Outstanding Defensive Player at the national championships. She played on four Pan American championship teams and another three world championship teams. At UCLA she was a four-time All-American. The NCAA named her Player of the Decade for the '80s. She was part of Team America's 106-game international winning streak that lasted nine years; part of the 1995 Pan American squad that outscored the opposition a combined 118-0.

Then, after all that, her dream came true. The International Olympic Committee finally said what she'd been waiting to hear — "play softball" — and Richardson and her teammates reported to Atlanta.

Normally no power hitter, Richardson hit three home runs in the nine games the United States played in Atlanta. In the 61 games prior to that, she'd hit two.

The third of those home runs couldn't have come at a more opportune time — a two-run shot in the third inning of the gold medal game against China, with the score tied 1-1. Thus powered by their 34-year-old all-time shortstop, the U.S. went on to win, 3-1. Just as she'd always dreamed they would, Dot Richardson and softball had arrived at the Olympics. ❏

Long jumper Chioma Ajunwa takes a golden leap for Nigeria.
ALLSPORT / TONY DUFFY

On the Beach

Karch Kiraly

Memo to sports making Olympic debuts: It doesn't hurt having the king handle your introduction. With none other than Karch Kiraly teaming with partner Kent Steffes to win the gold medal on Atlanta Beach in Jonesboro, Ga., beach volleyball, competing in the Olympic Games for the first time, got instant credibility, TV coverage and sellout crowds.

There have been worse entrances.

Getting Karch Kiraly to compete was like baseball showing up with Babe Ruth, soccer with Pele, golf with Arnold Palmer, basketball with Michael Jordan, politics with Abraham Lincoln.

Getting Kiraly to win was the icing on the cake.

It wasn't easy. Just to qualify, Kiraly and Steffes had to survive a loss at the double-elimination Olympic Trials in Baltimore. And in the preliminary rounds, they had to survive an overtime scare from the forerunner to Karch, 39-year-old Sinjin Smith, and his partner Randy Stoklos. But when the gold-medal finals came along, there were Kiraly and Steffes, poised to defeat fellow Americans Mike Dodd and Mike Whitmarsh, 12-5, 12-8, and win one for the beach.

For Kiraly, it was the continuation of a gold-medal habit that began when he was a fresh-out-of-college 23-year-old who led the United States to its first-ever indoor volleyball medal in the Los Angeles Games of 1984. Four years later, in the Seoul Games, Kiraly and the U.S. made it two golds in a row.

He "retired" from the indoor game after that, preferring to play volleyball's two-man beach version. He and Steffes formed a partnership that emerged as the best in the world, at one time winning 13 consecutive matches.

Since beach volleyball wasn't an Olympic sport, it appeared Kiraly would not add again to his medal collection. But, as fate would have it, the beach game's coming-out party was added to the Atlanta schedule.

And as fate would also have it, there was Karch Kiraly, taking care of the introductions. ❑

ABOVE / *Volleyball legend Karch Kiraly added a gold in the new discipline of beach volleyball to his cache of indoor volleyball gold.* ALLSPORT / PETER THOMPSON

Andrzej Chylinski of the USA took a cool, on-the-go sponge bath during the 50-kilometer walk, finding temporary relief on a muggy August day.

Kazakhstan's Igor Pota-povich sur-vived the bar but placed fourth in the pole vault.
ALLSPORT / MIKE HEWITT

A Model Player

Lisa Leslie

ABOVE / *Sometimes Lisa Leslie couldn't get the Aussies out of her hair, but she managed 16 points against them anyway. A 6-foot-5 fashion model, Leslie was a model performer during America's run for the gold medal, scoring 29 points and making 12 of 14 shots in the gold-medal game.* ALLSPORT / DOUG PENSINGER

Not only did Lisa Leslie know how to win a gold medal, she knew how to wear one. After scoring 29 points, blocking two shots and grabbing six rebounds in the USA's 111-87 win over Brazil in the championship game of the Olympic women's basketball tournament, Leslie — six-foot-five even in flats — walked to the top of the winner's peristyle with posture so poised and erect they could have put the medal on top of her head. Then, after she'd had a chance to shower and change, she emerged from the locker room wearing a sleek tropical floral print, its colors of green, orange and blue perfectly complementing the gold medal on its deep-green ribbon hanging around her neck. Talk about knowing how to accessorize.

It was quite a year for the three-time All-American and 1994 NCAA Player of the Year from the University of Southern California. She got to indulge both of her loves — basketball and modeling. On the modeling front, she did a layout for Vogue, a cover for Sports Illustrated and signed with the prestigious Wilhelmina modeling agency. And on the basketball front, she starred on a team that never lost.

With Leslie doing her share and then some, the best U.S. women's team in history followed up an unblemished 52-0 pre-Olympic exhibition tour with an unblemished 8-0 run through the Olympics. In the three medal-round games in Atlanta, against Japan, Australia and Brazil, Leslie averaged 28.7 points and nine rebounds while making 38 of her 51 shots for a shooting percentage of 74.5 percent.

When asked what she planned to do following that, Leslie didn't miss a beat. "Well," she said. "I plan to model first."

She didn't rule out eventually playing some more ball, possibly with one of the two new professional leagues starting up in the United States, but after 10 years of full-time basketball — including a year in a professional league in Italy directly after her graduation from USC — the 24-year-old decided what she wanted to do next was see about being the next Kate Moss. She already was Lisa Leslie. ❑

La Gazelle: Marie-Jose Perec of France strode to a double 200- and 400-meter victory. ALLSPORT / DAVID LEAH

ALLSPORT / SIMON BRUTY

Rock On
Justin Huish

When he was a kid growing up in California and his dad would drag him along to practice field archery, Justin Huish would shoot at rocks on purpose. As soon as he'd broken enough arrows they had to go home, and he could play with his friends.

The thing is, he could hit those rocks.

A natural — even when he didn't want to be.

With time, enmity turned to downright affection, however. While his friends developed addictive relationships with their surfboards, Huish did the same with his bow. By the time he was 14 all he wanted to do was shoot arrows. Well, that and hang out.

His archery skills and his social skills grew exponentially — to the point that, at age 21, not only did he take the Olympic Games by storm, winning two gold medals in Atlanta, but the ponytailed, baseball-cap-on-backwards free spirit from the Golden State pulled the capacity crowds at Stone Mountain Park right along with him.

Suddenly, archery had its own Andre Agassi, its answer to Dennis Rodman.

As the Olympic tournament progressed, Huish's encouragement to the crowd seemed to take on an energy all its own. He got stronger as the Games grew longer. In the men's individual competition, he routed Belgium's Paul Vermeiren in the semifinals by a whopping nine points — the archery equivalent of, say, four touchdowns — and then he semi-routed Magnus Petersson of Sweden in the gold-medal match by five points, 112 (out of a possible 120) to 107. Only in the quarterfinals did Huish face real trouble, when France's Michele Frangilli, a pre-meet medal favorite, forced the young American into a tiebreaker. But Huish, and the crowd, came through with two consecutive 10's to move on.

In the team competition that followed, Huish scored two 10's and a nine on his last three arrows to move he and his teammates — Butch Johnson, 40, and 19-year-old Rod White — ahead of Korea for good. As with the rocks, he knew once he'd hit enough targets, he could go home to his friends. ❏

LEFT / *Justin Huish used an innovative training routine letting his arrow fly from across the street, through his front yard and his garage to a bull's-eye in the backyard.*

ALLSPORT / RICK STEWART

Pause for the cause: Hector Vinent, Cuba's light welterweight gold medalist. ALLSPORT / JOHN GICHIGI

Sweet Feat

Mia Hamm

ABOVE / *Mia Hamm and the U.S. women cemented their claim as the best in the sport with a gold-medal performance in front of 76,000 fans.* ALLSPORT / DAVID CANNON

When it was finally over, when the referee blew her whistle and the first-ever Olympic women's soccer gold medal was in America's bag, the star of the team just sat there. Mia Hamm couldn't move.

She wasn't frozen by shock. She was frozen by the ankle she'd sprained, again. Just minutes earlier, they'd had to carry her off the field on a stretcher. She'd had to miss the final minutes of Team USA's 2-1 victory over China. And now, worse yet, she was missing the celebratory pile-on at midfield.

But just as the 24-year-old forward known as "the best soccer player in the world" had somehow managed to assist on both of America's goals before that ankle finally gave out, she also managed to make it to that pile. Motioning to two members of the U.S. medical staff, Hamm got them to lift her off her feet and carry her out to her teammates.

For Hamm, America's win represented the high point of a nine-year run with the national team that began when she joined up at the age of 15 (the youngest ever) in 1987. She'd seen it all — the world championship in 1991, the U.S. Cup championship in 1995, and now this, the ultimate, the Olympic gold medal as women's soccer made its debut.

She'd gotten the U.S. off to a good start in the Olympic tournament with a goal in its opening win, a 3-0 shutout of Denmark. But in the next game, a 2-1 win over Sweden, a collision with the goalkeeper knocked her out for not only the rest of that game, but the following match against China as well. After a scoreless tie with the Chinese, the obvious was even more obvious: The U.S. needed Hamm.

She hobbled back into action against Norway, the defending world champs, who did their best to apply pressure to her ailing ankle. But Hamm's teammates were able to use the distraction to their advantage in the resulting 2-1 win. In the gold-medal final, China, too, kept hammering at Hamm's ankle, but in the end, it was too little, too late. She made sure she was on the field when it counted. During the game — and after. ❑

ALLSPORT / NATHAN BILOW

Horse Sense

Karen and David O'Connor

ABOVE / Straight from the horse's mouth: "To win a medal and to be able to share that experience with my husband (OPPOSITE – ALLSPORT /JED JACOBSOHN), *to actually stand with him on the medal stand, is certainly a highlight we'll both remember for the rest of our lives," said Karen O'Connor.* ALLSPORT /PASCAL RONDEAU

It isn't hard to guess where David and Karen O'Connor of The Plains, Va., will celebrate their silver wedding anniversary on June 26, 2018. Odds are off the charts that they'll be at the Georgia International Horse Park in Conyers, Ga.

That's where they won their silver medal in 1996 — together.

The O'Connors took the notion of an Olympic "family" literal, striding together as husband-and-wife to the medal podium as part of the four-person U.S. team that placed second in equestrian's three-day team event.

They met, they married, they medaled.

Odds are also very good that the O'Connors, who were wed in 1993 after meeting — of course — at an equestrian event, will still be together for their 25th. Their Olympic year allowed the relative newlyweds to show off an uncommon amount of compatibility. Before they competed with each other at the Games, they competed against each other in the tryouts to make the U.S. team.

Now there's a marital test.

But not only did they both survive the selection process and make the team — David aboard his horse, Giltedge, and Karen aboard her horse, Biko — but they made it strong enough to survive all but the Australians in Atlanta.

Afterward, Karen said she considers competing alongside each other to be a big plus. "It enhances the whole relationship," she said. "If you are going to do horse sport, you have to have somebody you can relate to. This is a very specialized sport. You need somebody who understands completely what you are going through."

Preferably, that somebody isn't your horse.

For proof of what she was saying, Karen could point to her only previous Olympic experience, in 1988, when she represented the United States Equestrian Team in Seoul — as a single woman.

She did not medal.

Case closed. ❏

In Memoriam
Kurt Angle

Proudly wearing the red, white, and blue USA uniform with a black band in memory of Dave Schultz, would-be actor Kurt Angle of Pittsburgh, Pa., fell to his knees, put his palms together, closed his eyes, and cried. Only this was no act. Anyone who knew Kurt Angle knew that. Anyone who knew Dave Schultz, too.

It had been a crazy year. Who would have ever thought that Schultz would be murdered in January — allegedly by eccentric millionaire John E. duPont who funded the Foxcatcher Wrestling Club of which Schultz, Angle and others were members? Who'd have ever thought the Olympics would roll around and Angle would be there and Schultz, a gold medalist in 1984, wouldn't? Who'd have ever thought Nancy Schultz, in spite of her grief, would put together a grass-roots wrestling club for many of her late husband's buddies?

And who would have thought that Kurt Angle would be the only member of the Dave Schultz Wrestling Club who would have a chance to pay a gold-medal tribute to their fallen mentor, friend, and inspiration?

It wasn't easy. In wrestling it never is. With hundreds of family members, friends and club teammates in the stands, Angle made it to the 220-pound finals against 1995 world bronze medalist Abbas Jadidi of Iran. Together, Angle and Jadidi staggered through what Angle was sure was the longest match in history. First they tied 1-1 through five minutes of regulation. Then they stayed tied through another three minutes of overtime. After that, like a couple of boxers, they had to wait for a judge's decision.

As they stood at bay in the center of the ring, Jadidi, a picture of arrogance, kept trying to get the referee to raise the Iranian's hand as the victor. For his part, Angle just stood there, not looking one way or the other. Finally, after they'd been taught the definition of eternity, the decision was reached.

The referee raised the American's hand.

That's when Kurt Angle went to his knees. Finally, some good tears. The tough guy from Pittsburgh had his medal, and so did his buddy, Dave Schultz. ❑

RIGHT / *Kurt Angle held fast to his Olympic dream in memoriam of his friend Dave Schultz and of his father, who died in a construction accident.* ALLSPORT / JED JACOBSOHN

As if their race were perfectly choreographed, a chorus line of sprinters broke from the blocks in near mirror image of each other in a heat of the women's 100-meter dash, with eventual winner Gail Devers sandwiched in the crowd. ALLSPORT / TONY DUFFY

From a Distance

Janet Evans

As the world watched, it was Muhammad Ali who prepared her for what was to come. When Janet Evans, the queen of American distance swimming, handed the torch to a stooped and bent Ali so he could light the flame and begin the Atlanta Olympic Games, it was a poignant reminder that no one remains the greatest forever. Indeed, by handing over that flame to Ali, the boxing pride of the Rome Games of 1960, Evans was lighting the fuse that would end her own career.

She had hoped to go out on the highest note possible, of course, perhaps do a "Bonnie Blair" and match the speed skater's Olympic women's record of five individual gold medals. At 24 (the fourth oldest member of the U.S. swim team), she'd defied the odds by making her third straight Games, qualifying alongside the teenagers at both the 400- and 800-meter freestyle distances. If she won both events that would make a record six individual gold medals for her Olympic career. As a bubbly 101-pound high school junior, she won three in Seoul in 1988. As a seasoned veteran in Barcelona — by now old enough to vote — she added another gold and a silver.

But despite the fact she held the world record in both events — at times laughingly beyond anything she or anyone else would swim in Atlanta — she was not favored at either distance. The years take their toll. In distance swimming especially, it's what you've done lately.

In the 400, she failed to make it out of the qualifying. In the 800, a distance she'd ruled in two straight Games, she made it to the finals but finished sixth, 11 seconds behind the victor — her 16-year-old American teammate, Brooke Bennett — and some 23 seconds behind her own world mark.

When the race was over, Evans swam across three lanes to give Bennett a congratulatory hug. Then, her place in history, if not the Atlanta victory stand, secured, she waved to the crowd and disappeared. But she'll be back, no one doubts that. Like Ali, Janet Evans has more Olympics to ignite. Prime time may not last forever, but once you've picked it up, you'll always carry the flame. ❏

RIGHT / *Janet Evans, despite not winning any medals, called the Atlanta Games her most memorable, capping a golden Olympic career.* ALLSPORT / SIMON BRUTY

Arthemon Hatungimana of Burundi leads Andrea Benvenuti of Italy and David Strang of Great Britain past the packed stands of Olympic Stadium in their first-round heat of the 800-meter run. ALLSPORT / GARY M. PRIOR

Simply Smashing!

Kim Rhode

ABOVE / On the wild side: Kim Rhode, the girl who accompanied her parents on a safari in Africa, became the first-ever double trap gold medalist at age 17. ALLSPORT / RICK STEWART

With the final two clay targets about to be launched, Kim Rhode carefully sized up her situation. This was her last shot. The competition was still not decided. If she hit both targets, smashed them to smithereens, she would be Olympic champion; if not, well, she could feel the German and the Australian breathing down her neck, just waiting for her to collapse under all the pressure ...

Oh, sorry, wrong script.

By point of fact, one week after her 17th birthday and one month prior to the start of her senior year at Arroyo High School in El Monte, Calif., Rhode (pronounced Road-ee) wasn't thinking about much of anything beyond aiming her shotgun when they released those final two targets with a gold medal attached. She merely raised her gun, sighted in on the first of those four-inch flying saucers, blew it away, and then sighted in on the other, and blew it away too.

"I wasn't really paying any attention to anything else," said Rhode afterward. Or anyone else, either. In all, she and her shotgun broke 141 targets — out of 160 — to finish two hits in front of Germany's Susanne Kiermayer and Australia's Deserie Huddleston and become the first-ever Olympic champion in double trap.

A nonchalant, unperturbable teenager who admitted to fitness training that consisted mainly of "line dancing" and who'd colored her braces red-white-and-blue in anticipating of making the Olympic team, Rhode and her shotgun took the Wolf Creek shooting venue more by charm than by storm. A competitive shooter since she was 10, she'd already won a national championship and the U.S. Olympic Festival title prior to Atlanta, but she was better known for the 400-pound black bear she dropped while hunting in the California mountains when she was 15.

Even after winning in Atlanta, they still wanted to know about shooting that bear. How did it compare to winning the gold medal, she was asked.

"Oh, the gold medal outweighs the bear," said Kim, "most definitely." She didn't even have to think about it. ❏

Super heavyweight Andrey Chemerkin of Russia celebrates the gold. ALLSPORT / SIMON BRUTY

A Heart of Gold

Matt Ghaffari

ABOVE / *A man with a heart of gold, Matt Ghaffari (right) lost the gold to Russia's Alexander Karelin but won the respect of everyone when he, on his own, went on a goodwill tour of Atlanta to help salve the wounds caused by the bomb explosion in Centennial Olympic Park.* ALLSPORT / ROSS KINNAIRD

Going into the Games of Atlanta it did not figure that Matt Ghaffari would leave much of an impression. For one thing, he was entered in Greco-Roman, the brand of wrestling that prohibits the use of the legs and is largely unpracticed in the United States. For another thing, he was in the same division as Russia's Alexander Karelin, known as Alexander the Great, a man who hadn't lost in 10 years.

Who was to know that this 286-pound naturalized American who spent the first 16 years of his life in Iran would not only take the great Karelin to the wire before losing, 1-0, but would then take his silver medal on a goodwill tour of Atlanta right when Atlanta needed it most.

If they'd given medals to ambassadors, Ghaffari would have won the gold.

He was a one-man gang of good. Acting completely on his own volition, with no accompanying entourage, no press officers, no tabloid TV cameras trailing behind, Ghaffari took it upon himself to do what he could to salve the wounds caused by a madman's bomb that had gone off in Centennial Olympic Park halfway through the Games, wounding more than a hundred and directly killing one.

As Atlanta struggled to get back on its feet and the world held its breath, Ghaffari first went to the Georgia Baptist Hospital, where he visited the injured, among them Fallom Stubbs, the daughter of bomb victim Alice Hawthorne, and Alice's widower, John Hawthorne. Ghaffari hung his silver medal around John's neck. "You've got to be the hero now, man," he said.

Two days later, when Centennial Park reopened, there was Ghaffari waiting for the gates to be unlocked, to walk with the crowd and share with them that medal.

Two days after that, while sitting in the wrestling arena next to yet another bombing victim, Christian Sobb, Ghaffari helped Sobb walk on his crutches to the center of the mat as the crowd paid tribute.

"There is power in that medal," the 34-year-old Ghaffari.

Power in the man wearing it, too. ❑

ABOVE / *Spirits were dampened, but not extinguished by the bomb explosion: the Games continued but flags flew at half mast in honor of the victims.* ALLSPORT / NATHAN BILOW

In the fastest 1-2-3 finish in Olympic history, Donovan Bailey of Canada won the gold medal in the 100 meters with a late burst in a world-record 9.84 seconds. ALLSPORT /
GERARD VANDYSTADT

All-American Honor

Teresa Edwards, Oathtaker. ALLSPORT / ROSS KINNAIRD

Bruce Baumgartner, Opening Ceremonies, Flagbearer. ALLSPORT / ROSS KINNAIRD

Michael Matz, Closing Ceremonies, Flagbearer. ALLSPORT / PASCAL RONDEAU

(OPPOSITE - ALLSPORT / PASCAL RONDEAU)

They came from the corners of the athletic universe, a wrestler, a basketball player and an equestrian rider, connected by a decree from their peers to represent them. The wrestler, four times an Olympian, carried the United States flag into the Opening Ceremonies. The basketball player, another four-timer, recited the athletes' oath. The equestrian rider, in his third Games, carried the flag into the Closing Ceremonies.

Each also carried a history that made their duty all the more meaningful.

Bruce Baumgartner, the wrestler, carried the memory of he and his good friend Dave Schultz gawking openly at the 90,000 people going berserk during the Opening Ceremonies in 1984. He and Schultz both went on to win gold medals. They were going to go for more gold in Atlanta, too, until Schultz was killed in January. Holding the flag in his big right hand, the 286-pound Baumgartner carried a silent tribute to his friend as he led 667 U.S. athletes into the Games.

Teresa Edwards, the basketball player, also remembered those '84 Games in L.A. She flashed on her memories of Edwin Moses, the American hurdler, as he attempted with difficulty to repeat the athletes' oath from memory. Edwards went on to win a gold medal with the U.S. women's team in '84. She added another gold in '88, a silver in '92, (and, in two weeks, would add yet another gold). The Olympics were always good to her. She read the oath from her heart — and a printout she held in her hand.

Michael Matz, the equestrian rider, carried the flag into the Closing Ceremonies only days after winning his first Olympic medal, a silver. But it was too trite to trace his flag-carrying election to his horse-riding skills alone. In 1989, Matz was on an airliner that crash landed in Iowa. Before he saved himself, he made sure the two children next to him had gotten to safety. As the Games of Atlanta — marred by a bomb blast that took a life — marched to their conclusion, Matz represented the good guys, not the bad. They had a hero lead them. It made for a much better ending. ❏

ARCHERY

Totally cool, totally golden

BY COLLEEN WALKER MAR

ALLSPORT / PASCAL RONDEAU

CLOCKWISE (FROM TOP) / *Justin Huish, Rod White and Butch Johnson (left to right) set their sights high and their arrows straight to claim the gold in the team event, outshooting the Koreans, 251-249.* ALLSPORT / NATHAN BILOW

Silver medalist He Ying of China is a picture of calm and concentration, a fitting combination in the sport of archery. ALLSPORT / NATHAN BILOW

With the help of the big-screen video, record crowds got an up-close and personal look at the archers. American Butch Johnson placed 11th in the men's individual event. ALLSPORT / NATHAN BILOW

At 42, Janet Dykman doesn't rule out the possibility of Sydney. Dykman placed 16th in the individual competition, the best finish for the U.S. women. ALLSPORT / NATHAN BILOW

THANKS TO A TONE ESTABLISHED early by a 21-year-old free spirit from California, archery enjoyed its most entertaining Olympic Games ever in Atlanta. Justin Huish's outgoing personality coupled with the recently installed head-to-head direct elimination competitive format combined to draw sellout crowd after sellout crowd to the archery complex at Stone Mountain Park.

The homegrown Huish, from Simi Valley, Calif., was the star of the show as he exuberantly marched toward the gold medal in the men's competition and, along with U.S. teammates Butch Johnson and Rod White, also marched to the gold medal in the men's team competition.

In the more sedate women's division, Korea's Kim Kyung-wook won the individual gold medal, He Ying of China took the silver and Olena Sadovnycha claimed the bronze, defeating Turkey's Elif Altinkaynak. In the women's team competition, Korea won gold, Germany silver and Poland bronze. The United States team of Janet Dykman, Lindsay Langston and Judi Adams lost in the first round to Kazakhstan, 235-226.

Individually, Dykman carried the U.S. colors highest, winning two matches before being eliminated in the round of 16 by Wang Xiaozhu of China. Langston finished 22nd and Adams, also a 1980 Olympian, claimed 39th.

With his historic double, Huish became the first American to win two gold archery medals in one Games; he also joined Darrell Pace, who won in 1976 and 1984, as the U.S.'s only multiple gold medalists. His singles victory marked the fifth time in seven tries that an American man has won the Olympic crown since archery's readmittance to the Games in 1972.

Huish defeated Sweden's Magnus Petersson in the gold-medal showdown, 112-107. In the semifinals, he defeated Paul Vermeiren of Belgium, 112-103, and in the quarterfinals he won in a sudden-death shootout with France's Michele Frangilli after they tied in regulation, 112-112. In the bronze-medal match, Oh Kyo-moon of Korea defeated Vermeiren, 115-110.

"I'm stoked," said Huish. "Every arrow I shot had a lot of pressure. I was just trying to hit the 10 every time. I was just trying to give it my all. I was in a fog, just trying to see gold in my sight and let it rip."

> "I'm stoked."
> Justin Huish,
> the free-spirited
> California kid,
> gave U.S. archery
> a shot in the arm with
> his two gold medals and
> crowd-pleasing style.

Huish, who repeatedly turned to the pro-American crowd and urged them to scream and cheer, led the men's team to the same kind of consistency he enjoyed in singles. The U.S. men scored four straight 251's (out of possible 270) en route to the gold medal. They defeated India in the opening round, 251-235, then got past Ukraine by a 251-240 score and Italy by a 251-247 count in the quarterfinals and semifinals, respectively. In the gold-medal match, Team USA defeated Korea 251-249. At first it appeared the countries had tied at 250-250. But once the judges had officially checked the targets it was clear that one U.S. arrow was a nine instead of an eight and one Korean arrow was actually a nine instead of a 10.

The team victory was America's first gold-medal effort since team play was instituted in the Seoul Games in 1988 when the U.S. men won a silver medal in Seoul and the U.S. women won a bronze.

"I feel totally thrilled," said Johnson, who led the U.S. team effort with six 10's. "It's a great feeling. It doesn't get much better than this." ▼

ATHLETICS

A star-studded field

BY DOUG ROBINSON

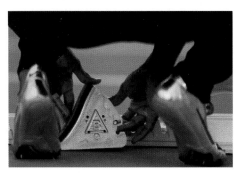

ALLSPORT / GARY M. PRIOR

RIGHT / Michael Johnson's feet were golden when he pulled away from Frank Fredericks in the 200-meter dash, running faster than any man has ever run at any distance. His world record of 19.32 was so fast that bronze medalist Ato Boldon thought the stadium timer was broken. Johnson covered the second 100 meters of the race in a mind-boggling 9.20. ALLSPORT / GARY M. PRIOR

LOOKING BACK ON THE TRACK AND field competition of the Centennial Olympic Games, where will historians begin?

There was Michael Johnson's fuel-injected sprinting that defied belief. There was Dan O'Brien's long-awaited coronation as World's Greatest Athlete. There was Carl Lewis' and Jackie Joyner-Kersee's curtain calls. There was Gail Devers, writing another scene for her made-for-TV movie. There were the 11th-hour victories by Randy Barnes and Charles Austin.

Those were just a few of America's stars. Everyone seemed to get in on the act in Atlanta. A model from Paris beat Michael Johnson to his double. A stockbroker from Canada claimed the 100. A Russian mother came from nowhere to win the middle-distance races. A janitor won the marathon. The farmer's daughter won the other marathon.

In the end, the competition provided another dazzling display of speed, strength and endurance ...

THE SUPERSONICS

A NUMBER OF ATHLETES CAME TO Atlanta seeking redemption, and Johnson was one of them. He was a prohibitive favorite to win the 200-meter dash in 1992, but food poisoning rendered him so weak that he couldn't even make the final. He came to Atlanta burning to erase that disappointment, and this time he wouldn't try for one gold medal; he'd try for two.

For added inspiration, he carried a note from Jesse Owens' widow around with him to each of his races. She had written to him after watching his performance in the Olympic trials, noting, as others had, that his short, choppy, low-kneed running form recalled Owens' style.

Johnson's first Olympic final was a mere formality. No one was a match for him in the 400-meter dash, a race he hadn't lost since 1989. After dawdling through the heats, he blasted the final in an Olympic-record 43.49, a second ahead of his nearest rival.

That race was only an hors d' oeuvre. Johnson was thought to be more vulnerable in the 200 than in the 400. A month earlier, Namibia's Frank Fredericks had ended his 21-race winning streak in Oslo. But Johnson came to Atlanta with a new gear. Johnson's coach, Clyde Hart, knew as much while watching Johnson warm up for the semifinals on the practice track. He was running so fast that Hart ran across the track to tell him to slow down.

As Johnson climbed into the starting blocks for the final, he told himself, 'This is the one I want. The one I wanted in Barcelona.' He blasted the turn and entered the homestretch virtually even with Fredericks and Ato Boldon. It seemed Johnson finally would be challenged. But then he seemed to shift gears and explode.

"I knew I was running faster than I ever had in my life," said Johnson, who seemed to run seemingly faster and faster down the homestretch until one half expected his muscles and tendons to blow from the exertion (as it turned out, they did). As he reached the finish line, the digital timer on the infield stopped at a number that caused observers to gasp.

Gosh, it's broken, thought Boldon when he saw the clock. Fredericks clapped and then embraced Johnson. Cuba's Ivan Garcia bowed at the waist toward the winner.

The clock read: 19.32.

Every Games produces one or two performances that stand above the rest; every 50 years or so, there is a feat that stands above all of those and forces men to rethink their limitations. This was one of those. A buzz swept through the stadium. Sports writers, coaches and athletes shook their heads and invoked words such as unbelievable.

Gosh, it's broken, thought Boldon when he saw the clock. Fredericks clapped and then embraced Johnson. Cuba's Ivan Garcia bowed at the waist toward the winner. The clock read: 19.32.

They had just witnessed the equivalent of Beamon's 29-foot jump, or Babe Ruth's 60 homers, or Wilt's 100 points, or maybe something greater. Time will tell. Consider this: From 1968 to June of 1996, the world record in the 200 improved .11 of a second, from 19.83 to 19.72. In a single night, Johnson lowered it .34.

More numbers: In 1979, Italy's Pietro Mennea ran a world record of 19.72 with the aid of altitude. That record stood for 17 years until Johnson ran 19.66 in the June Olympic trials. In a matter of two months, he lowered the record .4 of a second.

It's not that it was considered impossible to run 19.3 seconds; it's that it wasn't considered at all. It's a time ahead of its time. Something from another generation. Johnson ran the first 100 meters in 10.12, the second 100 in a mind-boggling 9.20.

"I saw Beamon's jump (in the '68 Olympic Games), and before they measured it one of the coaches I was sitting near said, 'I think we just saw something special,'" said Hart. "That's what it was like tonight. I knew it was special at 100 meters. But I thought maybe it would be 19.59 of 19.5-something."

More remarkably, Johnson did it with virtually no wind (.4 meters per second), in heavy humid air, at sea level, after running a total of 1 1/2 miles of sprints in six days. Oh, yes, and he said he stumbled at the start of the race. And strained a hamstring muscle late in the race, which forced him to withdraw from the relay.

Fredericks had run a dazzling 19.68, and he wasn't even in the race. Some struggled to explain the time, suggesting it was the fast track surface, but why then did only three of the runners break 20.1?

In the end, even Johnson was stunned by his performance. Asked what it felt like to

ALLSPORT / MARTIN VENEGAS

TOP AND ABOVE / *A time to remember: Michael Johnson didn't just settle for medal. He set two Olympic records and a stunning world record, making good on his stated goal to make history.* ALLSPORT / GARY M. PRIOR

OPPOSITE / *Donovan Bailey was pumped after his victory in the 100-meter dash, in which he established a world record of 9.84, well below his previous best of 9.91.* ALLSPORT / GRAY MORTIMORE

run so fast, he said the only thing he could compare it to was an experience he had as a kid: he used to ride a go-cart down a hill.

"I said before that the fastest man in the world is the winner of the 100, but I've changed my mind," said Boldon. "The fastest man in the world (is Johnson)."

THE CARIBBEAN CRUISERS

DONOVAN BAILEY, A FORMER BASKETBALL player, was already a successful stockbroker when he decided to take sprinting seriously in 1994. He hadn't even been good enough to be included on Canada's team for the '92 Olympics and '93 world championships, but he packed up and moved to the U.S. to train. Eighteen months later, he won the 100-meter dash in the '95 world championships.

For all that, he was not the favorite in the Olympics. That burden fell to Fredericks, who had beaten Bailey soundly in two races and produced the second and third fastest times in history, 9.86 and 9.87.

They lined up for the 100-meter dash finals and what happened next was one of the strangest dramas in Olympic history. There were three false starts, each one raising the tension another notch. The first one was by Linford Christie, the second by Boldon and the third by Christie. Thus, Christie, the 36-year-old defending Olympic champion and grandfather, was disqualified.

Told to leave the track, he refused. Finally, the meet referee was summoned and repeated the request. This time Christie complied, but by then the race had been delayed several minutes, anger-

LEFT / *Frank Fredericks, who came to the Olympics unbeaten, appeared to be on his way to victory midway through the 100-meter dash, but a moment later Donovan Bailey surged past him to claim the gold medal. For the second straight Olympics, Fredericks was the silver medalist.* ALLSPORT / AL BELLO

ing many of the contestants.

Finally, they got a clean start. Fredericks opened a slight lead midway through the race, but seemingly from nowhere Bailey charged past him, hitting the finish line in 9.84, a world record. Fredericks was second in 9.89 and Boldon third in 9.90. The Olympic record had been 9.92.

The race was further proof of what many had suspected for some time. America's dominance of the sprints was finished. For the first time in 20 years, they failed to medal in the 100 in an Olympics in which they attended.

Africans and Caribbean athletes were taking charge. Bailey, Christie and Boldon were all born in the Caribbean. Canada's 4x100-meter relay, composed entirely of Jamaican-born sprinters, delivered the coup de grace, winning the Olympic final in 37.69, with the U.S. a well-beaten second. It marked the first time the U.S. has lost that race being disqualified.

The U.S. restored some of its pride by winning the other three relays. The men's 4x400 team prevailed even without the injured Johnson and Butch Reynolds, as did the women's 4x100 and 4x400 squads. But Caribbean countries claimed three more medals in the relays.

THE MODEL AND
THE BRIDESMAID

WITH LITTLE PRE-RACE HYPE, FRANCE'S elegant Marie-Jose Perec actually beat Johnson to completing the 200-400 by a few minutes. A runway model from Paris, she is so popular in France that she actual-

RIGHT / *While other teams gave chase in the rough-and-tumble 4 x 400-meter relay, the Americans ran safely from the front, with Derek Mills making a quick getaway after receiving the handoff from Alvin Harrison. Even without their top guns, Olympic champion Michael Johnson and world record-holder Butch Reynolds (both sidelined with injuries), the Americans won the relay, as usual.* ALLSPORT / MIKE HEWITT

ly moved to Hollywood, of all places, to escape the pre-Olympic crush.

"I'm quite famous in my country," she explained to Olympic media. "I'm the equivalent of Michael Jordan. I can't walk down the street without being recognized. I think it's going to get even worse."

No doubt it will after her Olympic performance. Perec, whose graceful, long-legged stride has won her the nickname La Gazelle, defended her Olympic title in the 400-meter. She clocked an Olympic-record time of 48.25, which some consider to be the "real world record," based on the drug revelations made about Eastern Bloc athletes since the Iron Curtain came down. It was the fastest 400-meter race in history, with six runners under 50 seconds. America's Jearl Miles, a former world champion, ran a personal best 49.55 and placed only fifth.

Perec returned for the 200-meter dash and won again by running down the early leaders in the homestretch. In the process, she relegated another elegant athlete to second place, Jamaica's Merlene Ottey, the quintessential bridesmaid.

"When I passed the finish line I was quite happy, but also a little bit sad," said Perec. "I think you could see on my face I was not overjoyed because I admire Merlene a lot."

The race capped a brilliant, if not star-struck 16-year career for the 36-year-old Ottey. She competed in five Olympic Games and won four bronze medals in the 100 and 200, but never a gold. "Ms. Bronze," they call her. In Atlanta, she upgraded to a pair of silver medals in the 100 and 200, missing a gold by maybe an inch in the 100. She will retire, having won eight bronze, four silver and two gold

LEFT / Marie-Jose Perec, the French model, used her long runway stride to run down Merlene Ottey (3478) in the homestretch of the 200. It gave her a second gold medal, but she found little joy in leaving the 36-year-old Ottey second and short of the gold once again.

ALLSPORT / ROSS KINNAIRD

LEFT / Gail Devers, Chryste Gaines, Inger Miller and Gwen Torrence were beaming during the medal ceremony following their victory in the 4x100-meter relay. ALLSPORT / SIMON BRUTY

BELOW / Deon Hemmings celebrated the first gold medal ever won by a Jamaican woman as she crossed the finish in the 400-meter intermediate hurdles, leaving Americans Kim Batten (left) and Tonja Buford-Bailey with silver and bronze, respectively. ALLSPORT / MIKE HEWITT

medals in Olympic and world championship competitions.

It seemed almost unfair when Deon Hemmings, all of 27 years old, became the first Jamaican woman to win a gold medal. She relegated American favorites Kim Batten and Tonja Buford-Bailey to second and third while winning the 400-meter hurdles in 52.82.

THE REDEMPTION

LIKE JOHNSON, NOUREDDINE MORCELI, the greatest middle distance runner in history, came to Atlanta seeking to erase the memory of a bitter experience at the '92 Olympics. He had set world records, won world championships and gone unbeaten for three years, but he had no Olympic medal. In the '92 Games, he was a heavy favorite, but he ran poorly and finished seventh in the 1,500.

And then in Atlanta he nearly experienced disaster again. With a lap to go, he was running from the front when Morocco's Hicham El Guerrouj tripped on Morceli's leg. He crashed to the track and rolled into the Algerian's right leg, but Morceli managed to keep his feet while the rest of the field hurdled El Guerrouj. With a spike wound in his leg, Morceli launched his kick, covering the last lap in 53 seconds to finish in 3:35.78, and then pronounced himself, "The happiest man in Atlanta."

O'Brien could've staked the same claim. For four years he had lived with failure, despite the fact that, like Morceli, he had claimed world records, world championships and an unbeaten record. All anyone knew was that in the '92 Olympic trials he had failed to clear a height in the pole vault, which meant the world's greatest decathlete couldn't participate in the Olympics.

In Atlanta, the outcome was never really in doubt, especially after O'Brien cleared 16-4 3/4 in the pole vault. He scored 8,824 points to clinch the gold medal. At the conclusion of the 1,500-meter run, the final event, he knelt at the finish line and cried.

LEFT / *No one could collar Noureddine Morceli until the finish of the 1,500-meter run, where Ali Hakimi, (2294) the eighth-place finisher, and runner-up Fermin Cacho, the defending Olympic champ, offered their congratulations.*
ALLSPORT / GRAY MORTIMORE

BELOW / *Decathlete Dan O'Brien waited four years for redemption after his famous failure in '92. He found it at the finish line in Atlanta, where first he cried and then he smiled.* ALLSPORT /
MIKE HEWITT

"It's the hardest two days of my life," said O'Brien, the event's first American winner since '76. "I've thought about this every day for four years."

Others sought redemption, as well. In 1992, Kenny Harrison and Derrick Adkins, like O'Brien, failed to make the U.S. Olympic team. And like O'Brien, they made amends in a dramatic way.

Competing in his hometown, Adkins won the 400-meter intermediate hurdles, clocking 47.54, while American teammate Calvin Davis, who had run his first hurdles race on April 13, closed fast to take the bronze. Combined with the victory by Allen Johnson in the 110-meter high hurdles, in which he ran an Olympic-record 12.95 despite knocking down several hurdles, and Mark Crear's runner-up performance, U.S. men won four of six medals in the two hurdle races.

Harrison, who missed making the '88 Olympic team by three inches and was injured before the '92 Games, came to the Atlanta having taken only three competi-

TOP / *Allen Johnson left a lane littered with fallen hurdles en route to a big victory in the 110-meter high hurdles. Despite running through, rather than over, a number of hurdles, he set an Olympic record of 12.95* (ALLSPORT / GARY M. PRIOR).

ABOVE / *American Derrick Adkins breezed to a first-place finish in the 400-meter hurdles. Teammate Calvin Davis (right) leaned hard enough for the bronze while Zambia's Samuel Matete (not pictured) claimed the silver.* (ALLSPORT / SIMON BRUTY)

tive jumps all year because of injuries — all of them in the Olympic trials. He faced a field that included world record-holder and world champion Jonathan Edwards of Great Britain, the only man to leap 60 feet, and defending Olympic champ Mike Conley of the U.S.

On Harrison's first attempt, he leaped an Olympic-record 59-0 1/2. While waiting for another attempt, he walked onto the track to hug his girlfriend and training partner, Gail Devers, as she took a victory lap following the 100-meter dash. When Edwards, leaped 58-8 on his fourth attempt, Harrison answered with a leap of 59-4 1/2, the second best jump in history. Edwards, who scratched four of his six attempts, had to settle for second place.

As a memento, Harrison filled a plastic bag with sand from the pit, then he went off to share the moment with Devers — in drug testing.

THE HEARTBREAKS

EDWARDS WAS NOT THE ONLY FAVORITE to fall in Atlanta. There was an epidemic of it. To be a favorite in Atlanta was to invite trouble. As Michael Johnson discovered in 1992, the greatest athlete in the world is only a germ or pulled muscle away from failure. Sergei Bubka, 32, the greatest pole vaulter ever, withdrew from the competition with an injury. Javier Sotomayor, history's greatest high jumper, placed 11th, having missed training because of a virus.

Ireland's Sonia O'Sullivan, the best distance runner in this decade, was weakened by a virus. She dropped out of the 5,000 and failed to qualify for the 1,500 final. Maria Mutola, winner of 49 straight races, also struggled with a virus. She was third in the 800 and withdrew from the 1,500.

Hassiba Boulmerka, the defending world and Olympic 1,500-meter champ, failed to make the 1,500 final. Earlier in the year, world champion Gwen Torrence of the U.S. was a good bet to win the 100 and 200, but an injury in the Olympic trials cost her a spot on the team in the 200 and she was third in the 100.

ABOVE / Kenny Harrison, having taken just three competitive jumps all year before the Olympics, bounded to the second best triple jump mark in history to upset the world record-holder Jonathan Edwards. ALLSPORT / GARY M. PRIOR

ABOVE / At the age of 37, Mary Slaney, the greatest distance runner America has ever produced, failed to make the final in the 5,000. She won world titles and set world records, but she never has won an Olympic medal during her star-crossed career. ALLSPORT / DAVID LEAH

ABOVE (RIGHT) / The Olympics proved to be hazardous duty for big-name, thirtysomething athletes. World record-holder Butch Reynolds fell to the track with a pulled muscle in the semifinals of the 400-meter dash. ALLSPORT / GARY M. PRIOR

RIGHT / Jackie Joyner-Kersee, 34, had to reach high and dig deep in the long jump. Stuck in sixth place with an injured leg and one jump to go, Kersee told herself "Forget the leg ... this is your last shot." She leaped 22-11 3/4 to claim the bronze medal on the final leap of her final Olympics. ALLSPORT / MIKE HEWITT

OPPOSITE / For world record-holder Mike Powell, the long jump was no day at the beach. He could place no better than fifth and was hindered by an injury on his last two attempts. ALLSPORT / MIKE POWELL

The Games also were hard on many of America's long-time greats, now thirty something and showing their ages. World record-holder Butch Reynolds pulled up lame in the semifinals of the 400. Johnny Gray, 36 and running in his fourth Olympics, finished seventh in the 800. Lynn Jennings, 36, was ninth in the 5,000.

Jackie Joyner-Kersee, 34, the greatest female athlete of her generation, withdrew from the heptathlon after one event, having aggravated a hamstring injury. She returned a few days later for the long jump, an event she won in the '88 Games while setting a still-standing Olympic record. Finding herself in sixth place with one attempt remaining, she told herself, "Forget about the leg ... This is your last shot." She leaped 22-11 3/4 to take the bronze medal.

Meanwhile, Mary Slaney, 37 and the greatest middle distance runner America has ever produced, failed to make the final in the 5,000. Great careers do not guarantee the sport's most coveted prize. Jim Ryun never won a gold medal. Slaney never won a medal of any color.

Some athletes have an uncanny knack for rallying their forces when the Olympic Games are on the line. Al Oerter was one. Lewis is another.

THE KING

LEWIS, ARGUABLY THE GREATEST TRACK and field athlete of all time, showed up for his fifth and final Olympics at the age of 35, his haired flecked with gray, his legs betraying him a little more each day. His decline could be tracked in the Olympics. He won four gold medals in 1984, two golds and a silver in '88, and two golds in '92.

Since the Barcelona Olympics, he hadn't won a major championship in any event. He slipped annually in the world rankings and rarely even contested the long jump.

At the 1996 Olympic trials, he failed to make the team in the sprints, and claimed the third and final spot in the long jump by one inch. He aspired to win the Olympic long jump for the fourth consecutive time, but he seemed to be running out of time. In a pre-Olympic meet, he leaped only 26-3 — the worst performance of his 17-year career. In the Olympic qualifying round, he faced elimination after two attempts, but on his final attempt he sailed from 15th place to first to make the next day's final.

In the final, he took only three jumps all night; only one of them was good enough

to medal. On his third attempt he leaped 27-10 3/4 into a slight headwind, then collapsed on the track in relief, realizing even before the jump was measured that it was big. With everything on the line, he had produced his best jump in two years.

"27-10!" gushed U.S. bronze medalist Joe Greene. "That's almost a first down, and he did it at 35, into a headwind. He's a legend."

If not for that one jump, Lewis would have finished fifth. Fate conspired to help him. There were 23 fouls in the competition, some of them nullifying big jumps. World champion Ivan Pedroso of Cuba was still recovering from surgery and world record-holder Mike Powell pulled a muscle on his next to last attempt. But even if they had jumped well, one suspects Lewis, the great clutch performer, would have found a way to win.

The victory gave Lewis his 10th Olympic medal and his ninth gold, tying the record held by distance runner Paavo Nurmi, swimmer Mark Spitz and gymnast Larissa Latynina. He also joined Oerter as the only men to win the same event four times.

"This one," said Lewis, "is the most special."

It was Lewis' last Olympics. His Olympic career came full circle. It began in front of an American crowd at the Olympics in 1984, and it ended in front of an American crowd a dozen years later in Atlanta. Five decades passed between Jesse Owens and Lewis; probably another 50 years will pass before another sprinter-jumper like them comes along again.

THE SEQUELS

DEVERS PROVED TO BE ANOTHER CLUTCH performer. She had been rather quiet since the last Olympics because of injuries. She missed most of the '94 season with a hamstring injury and concentrated on the hurdles in '95 fearing the sprints would strain her hamstring. She returned to the sprints in the Olympic year, but was always a step behind Gwen Torrence at the finish, most

ABOVE / *Joe Greene won the bronze medal in the long jump, but his celebration looked golden.*
ALLSPORT / PASCAL RONDEAU

OPPOSITE / *Carl Lewis made the Olympic team by an inch, then made the Olympic final on his last attempt, and produced only one jump good enough to medal, but it was good enough to win his fourth gold medal in the long jump at the age of 35.* ALLSPORT / MIKE POWELL

notably at the Olympic trials.

But she'd done this before. Leading up to the 1992 Olympics she had never won an international race in the 100 and finished second to Torrence at the Olympic trials. Yet she won the gold medal in Barcelona, and afterward, her story was told and retold. Years earlier she had been diagnosed with Graves' disease, her condition becoming so severe that doctors recommended amputating her feet. But she made a miraculous recovery, culminating with her Olympic performance. It read like a made-for-TV movie, which is exactly what it became.

Atlanta will be the sequel. Once again, she delivered when it counted most. Devers burst into the lead and then held off a late charge by Ottey and Torrence, the next two finishers. The finish was so close that for a time no one was certain who had won between Devers and Ottey. Finally it was determined Devers was the winner — only the second repeat winner in the 100 ever. Both were timed in 10.94.

Devers had more unfinished business. In Barcelona, she held a clear lead in the 100-meter hurdles but tripped over the last hurdle and staggered to a fifth-place finish. This time she hoped to complete the double, but, as she said later, "It just wasn't meant to be."

Devers fell victim to someone else's sequel. In 1992, Ludmilla Narozhilenko, the '91 world champ from Russia, was favored to win the Olympic hurdle race but had to withdraw because of a pulled hamstring. Then her life turned into a made-for-TV movie. Two years later she tested positive for steroids and was given a four-year suspension. She claimed innocence and was finally reinstated in 1995 when her ex-husband confessed that he had spiked her protein powder.

She came to Atlanta at 32 with a new husband, a new name (Enquist) and a new country, having been adopted by her husband's homeland of Sweden in June.

Like the 100-meter dash, the hurdle race was a photo finish, but Devers wasn't in the picture this time. She was in fourth

place. Enquist and Brigita Bukovec of Slovakia hit the finish line together. "Who won?" asked Enquist.

"I think you did," said Bukovec, who was right.

Enquist, who clocked 12.57, .01 ahead of Bukovec, became the first "Swede" to win a gold medal in 20 years.

THE SURPRISES

BEFORE THESE OLYMPICS, ONLY ONE Norwegian had claimed a gold medal in track and that was 40 years ago. Then Vebjoern Rodal came along and won the 800 in Atlanta. Rodal, relatively unknown, clocked an Olympic-record time of 1:42.58, as four runners ran under 1:43, making it the fastest race in history.

If you're wondering why Norway and Sweden don't fare better in track, look at Rodal's training. Because of the cold, he was unable to run outdoors much of the year, so he trained for the Olympics by running back and forth in a tunnel that was only 350 meters long.

ABOVE / *After narrowly winning the 100-meter hurdles, Ludmila Enquist proudly carried the colors of her newly adopted country of Sweden while leading the other medalists – Brigita Bukovec of Slovakia (middle) and Patricia Girard-Leno of France – on a victory lap.* ALLSPORT / MIKE HEWITT

OPPOSITE (TOP AND BOTTOM) / *American Gail Devers bolted to an early lead in the 100-meter dash, but Merlene Ottey closed quickly in the last 20 meters, producing a finish so close that a photo had to determine the winner. Both were given identical times of 10.94 but Devers was the winner again.* ALLSPORT / JOHN GICHIGI

The women's 800 produced another surprise winner, as well. All the pre-race hype was directed at Mutola and Ana Quirot, who had come back to win the '95 world championships two years after a kerosene cooker explosion left her with burns over 40 percent of her body. And the winner is ...

... Somebody named Svetlana Masterkova, who had laid off running for three years to have a baby and recover from injuries. She sprinted away from the field in the homestretch to clock 1:57.73. Quirot and Mutola were second and third, respectively. Masterkova had so much energy and kick left that she sprinted much of her victory lap.

A few days later, Masterkova repeated her performance by winning the 1,500 in 4:00.83. "I want to shout and sing, and I feel a little bit dizzy," she said.

THE JANITOR AND THE FARMER'S DAUGHTER

IF THE U.S. IS LOSING ITS GRIP ON THE sprints, the Africans are not relinquishing their hold on distance events. They won every men's race from 1,500 meters through the marathon, plus the women's marathon. In the seven distance races, Africans claimed 13 of 21 medals, five of them gold.

Before the women's marathon, few had heard of Fatuma Roba, the 22-year-old farmer's daughter from Ethiopia who grew up running six miles to and from school every day. She won by such a large margin that she had time to kneel at the finish, kiss the track and take a victory lap before the runner-up even appeared in the stadium. Her time: 2:26:05.

"This is not only a special thing for me, but also for my country," she said.

ABOVE / Johnny Gray towed the 800-meter field through the first 600 meters at a record pace, but Norway's Vebjoern Rodal (running second here) was just waiting to pounce and carried the field to a record finish. Rodal burst past Gray and sprinted to an Olympic record of 1:42.58. It was the fastest 800 in history, with four runners running under 1:43. Gray faded to seventh. ALLSPORT / STEPHEN DUNN

Another unknown, Josia Thugwane, a 5-foot-2, 99-pound janitor from South Africa, won the men's marathon, becoming the first black South African to win a gold medal. It was one of the closest marathons in Olympic history, with Thugwane clocking 2:12:36, three seconds ahead of Korea's Lee Bong-ju and eight seconds ahead of Kenya's Eric Wainaina.

"He is our golden boy, and he has reinforced our pride and confidence as a nation," said no less than Nelson Mandela, president of South Africa.

More African pride. Ethiopia's 5-foot-3 world record-holder Haile Gebrselassie, who grew up on a farm 9,000 feet above sea level, running 10 kilometers to school, 10 kilometers to pasture cattle and 10 kilometers to get water, ran 10 kilometers to win the gold medal. His time: an Olympic record 27:07.34. Incredibly, he ran the second 5,000 meters of the race faster than the winning time in all but one Olympic 5,000-meter race.

ABOVE / *Maria Mutola (3569) and Ana Quirot (left) were heavily favored to take the top two spots in the 800-meter run, but while everyone was waiting for them to make a late kick entering the homestretch, Russia's Svetlana Masterkova (3700) beat them to it. She sprinted to the finish first, and still had a sprint left for her victory celebration.*
ALLSPORT / GRAY MORTIMORE

LEFT / *Ethiopia's Fatuma Roba had reason to smile. She won the marathon by such a large margin that she had time to kneel at the finish, kiss the track and run a victory lap before the runner-up even entered Olympic Stadium.*
ALLSPORT / MIKE HEWITT

Weary of losing to Morceli in the 1,500, Burundi's Venuste Niyongabo moved up to the 5,000 in Atlanta hoping finally to win. He did, clocking 13:07.96. American Bob Kennedy gamely took the lead with two laps to go, but finished sixth.

THE BREAKTHROUGHS

EUROPEANS STILL RULE THE THROWING events. Their men won nine of a possible 12 medals in four throwing events; the women won seven of 21 medals in three throwing events.

There were American breakthroughs. Shot putter Randy Barnes moved from sixth place to first on his final throw, with a mark of 70-11 1/4, and countryman John Godina was second at 68-2 1/2.

Lance Deal, became the first America to medal in the hammer since 1956. After the qualifying round, he thought he had failed to make the final and had removed his shoes and singlet when it was announced that he had qualified. He threw 266-2 on his final attempt, moving from eighth place to second.

LEFT / *Josia Thugwane, a 5-foot-2, 99-pound janitor from South Africa, led marathoners through the streets of Atlanta and was still leading when they reached the finish line in Olympic Stadium, but not by much. In one of the closest finishes in Olympic marathon history, Thugwane beat silver medalist Lee Bong-ju by three seconds and and bronze medalist Eric Wainaina by eight seconds. Thus, Thugwane became the first black ever to win a gold medal for South Africa. "He is our golden boy," said President Nelson Mandela.* ALLSPORT / GARY M. PRIOR

OPPOSITE (TOP) / *Kenyan teammates Moses Kiptanui (1803) and Joseph Keter ran in tandem in the steeplechase, at least until it came to decide the winner. As usual, Kenyans dominated the race, but there was one surprise: Kiptanui, the world record-holder, was outkicked by Keter for the gold medal.* ALLSPORT / MIKE POWELL

(BOTTOM) / *Haile Gebrselassie shouldered the burden of his countrymen's hopes in the 10,000-meter run, then he shouldered their flag.* ALLSPORT / GARY M. PRIOR

There was another U.S. breakthrough in the high jump. Charles Austin became the first American to win the high jump since 1968, leaping an Olympic-record 7-10. ▼

ABOVE / *Balasz Kiss of Hungary held the lead in the hammer throw when American Lance Deal stepped into the ring for his last throw. "When he made his final throw, you had to restart my heart," said Kiss. Deal's throw was a good one (266-2), but it was four inches shy of Kiss's mark. Kiss won the gold, Deal the silver.* ALLSPORT / GARY M. PRIOR

RIGHT / *Charles Austin spread his wings and flew to clear an Olympic-record height of 7-10, becoming the first American to win the high jump since 1968.* ALLSPORT / MIKE HEWITT

TOP / With the Olympic flame burning in the background, Great Britain's Steve Backley heaved the javelin skyward and won a silver medal. ALLSPORT /MIKE POWELL

ABOVE / Bronze medalist Trine Hattestad of Norway shares the joy of Finland's Heli Rantanen after she clinched the gold medal in the javelin. ALLSPORT / DAVID CANNON

RIGHT / American Randy Barnes stood alone in the end, moving from sixth to first on his last throw to give the U.S. a 1-2 finish in the shot put. ALLSPORT / MIKE POWELL

BADMINTON

World's fastest racquet sport

BY PAUL PAWLACZYK

ALLSPORT / SIMON BRUTY

OPPOSITE (TOP) / *American Kevin Han, ranked No. 63 coming into the Olympic Games, was eliminated by Great Britain's Peter Knowles, the Scottish Open champion.* ALLSPORT / SIMON BRUTY

(BOTTOM) / *The mixed doubles match was a battle between the South Koreans. The odds-on favorite Park Joo-bong, considered one of the game's greatest players, and his partner Ra Kyung-min fell to Kim Dong-moon and Gil Young-ah (pictured).* ALLSPORT / STU FORSTER

BADMINTON MADE ITS SECOND appearance on the Olympic stage after debuting in Barcelona in 1992. As was the case four years ago, the Atlanta tournament, held at Georgia State University, still featured very much an Asian flavor as 14 of the 15 medals went to competitors from Indonesia, South Korea, Malaysia and China. But there was one significant breakthrough as Denmark's Poul-Erik Hoyer-Larsen became the first European — and non-Asian — to win an Olympic gold medal.

Using his height to good advantage, the 6-foot-2 Hoyer-Larsen prevailed in men's singles over 5-foot-10 Dong Jiong of China in the gold-medal match, 15-12, 15-10. In the semifinals, Hoyer-Larsen, who'd finished fifth in Barcelona and was beaten by Heryanto Arbi at the world championships, got past the Indonesian in straight games, 15-11, 15-6. It was a sweet victory for the Dane who made no bones about being out for revenge.

South Korea, Indonesia and China all won four medals apiece, while Malaysia won two. With two, South Korea had the most golds — they came in mixed doubles, where Gil Young-ah and Kim Dong-moon defeated Korean teammates Ra Kyung-min and Park Joo-bong, and in women's singles, where Ban Soo-hyun defeated Mia Audina of Indonesia 11-6, 11-7. Indonesia and China each had one gold, one silver and two bronze medals. Indonesia's gold came in men's doubles, as the top-seeded tandem of Ricky Subagja and Rexy Mainaky needed three games to get past Malaysia's Cheah Soon Kit and Yap Kim Hok, 5-15, 15-13 and 15-12, in a nail-biting match that lasted one hour and 29 minutes. China's gold came in women's doubles, as Ge Fei and Gu Jun defeated Gil and her partner Jang Hye-ock, 15-5, 15-5. The Chinese duo dispatched the No. 1 seeds in 36 minutes.

Malaysia got one silver and one bronze medal. When the men's doubles tandem of Kit and Hok finished second they accounted for Malaysia's first-ever Olympic silver medal.

Despite high expectations, the United States team was largely disappointed with its production at the Games, where the crowd was partisan and continually chanted "U-S-A." Hopes rode especially high on the shoulders of Kevin Han, whose runnerup performance in the 1995 Bulgarian Open had the badminton world talking.

But Han, ranked No. 63 in the world, drew 27th-ranked Peter Knowles of Great Britain in the opening round and, after scaring the British champion, fell in three games, 2-15, 15-10, 15-7. Han made spirited comebacks in the latter two games. He was down 9-0 in game two and fought back to 14-10 before succumbing. In game three he dropped behind 11-1 to the defending Scottish Open champion before using improved net play to come within the 15-7 final score.

"In the first game I was really aggressive and executed my strategy very well," said Han. "Peter came out very aggressive off my serve in the second and third games and it's really difficult to catch up when you are down 10-1."

There was also disappointment on the U.S. women's side as 89th-ranked Erika Von Heiland, playing on knees that had been operated on five times, fell to 44th-ranked Jeng Shwu-Zen of Chinese Taipei in the first round of women's singles, 11-2, 11-6. In women's doubles, Von Heiland and partner Linda French drew a pair of Danes ranked third in the world — Lisbet Stuer-Lauridsen and Marlene Thomsen — in the opening round. After taking a 4-3 lead, the Americans quickly came to earth and fell in two games, 15-4 and 15-1. ▼

> **Between 1949-67, the United States dominated the sport of badminton, winning 23 world championships.**

BASEBALL

Smoking the field like a fine cigar

BY LEE BENSON

ALLSPORT / MIKE HEWITT

OPPOSITE / *Louisiana State's Jason Williams turns a double play on defense against Japan.*
ALLSPORT / MIKE HEWITT

WITH WHAT MAY WELL HAVE BEEN the final flex of its international amateur muscles, Cuba won its second straight Olympic baseball gold medal in Atlanta. The Cubans were undefeated in the nine-game tournament as they ran their winning streak in official international competition to 143 games.

Amid speculation that baseball would open its doors to professionals in upcoming Olympic Games, the Cubans — perpetual amateurs who are supported by the state — played as if there were no tomorrow. Despite the fact their best pitcher, Rolando Arrojo, defected to the United States just a week before the Opening Ceremonies; despite the fact they'd lost six of nine exhibition games against the American national team the past two summers; and despite the fact everybody was gunning for them in Atlanta, they still made sure everyone else played for second place.

Japan, a 13-9 loser to Cuba in the gold-medal game, took home the silver medal, while Team USA won the bronze.

While it was the first medal for the U.S. since baseball became a medal sport in Barcelona, third place was nonetheless a disappointment for a team that had legitimate reasons to think it could unseat the Cubans, not the least of which was the home field advantage.

The 20-man all-amateur U.S. team, representing 14 different colleges and universities and including no less than eight first-round selections from the June major league baseball draft, came into the Games riding the momentum of a 28-3 record amassed during a pre-Olympic tour that included tests against each of the seven opponents that qualified for Atlanta, except for the Netherlands. Against Cuba, the U.S. was 2-3 on that tour. Against everyone else, it was a perfect 26-0.

And indeed, paced by hitters Warren Morris, who led the team in Atlanta with a .409 batting average, Jacque Jones (.395), Matt LeCroy (.394), Travis Lee (.382), Chad Allen (.375), Jason Williams (.367) and Mark Kotsay (.303), and by pitchers Kris Benson, R.A. Dickey and Seth Greisinger, the United States actually picked up the pace in Atlanta. After averaging nine runs and 2.4 home runs per game in exhibition play, the U.S. averaged 10.3 runs and 3.6 home runs in the Olympics. Overall, coach Skip Bertman's squad clobbered the opposition 93-41 and hit a collective .332 while winning seven games and losing two.

Those two losses made all the difference, however. The first loss came in game six of the preliminary round-robin tournament, when Cuba survived a five home-run U.S. assault and still prevailed, 10-8. That win sent Cuba into the four-team medal round tournament as the top seed and sent the United States into a much tougher semifinal against Japan.

Which was the second loss.

In a game where nothing went according to the book, the U.S. fell, 11-2, to a Japanese team it had beaten twice on the pre-Olympic tour and once in the round-robin portion of the tournament by an aggregate 40-14 score. In their first Olympic meeting the week before, the Americans won 15-5 in a game that was called early because of the 10-run mercy rule (it was the second of four mercy-rule verdicts produced by the U.S. in the round-robin). Benson, the Clemson University pitcher chosen first in the big league draft and unbeaten in two previous Olympic outings, was suddenly shelled. He gave up eight hits and five earned runs in just four innings. In all, a Japanese squad

> **While it was the first medal for the U.S. since baseball became a medal sport in Barcelona, third place was nonetheless a disappointment for a team that had legitimate reasons to think it could unseat the Cubans.**

not noted for its power hit five home runs and 15 hits. A U.S. team that was noted for its power — it would hit 32 in nine Olympic games, second only to Cuba's record 38 — had just one home run, by LeCroy, as righthander Masanori Sugiura shut out the U.S. for the first five innings.

The United States returned to form in the bronze-medal game the next afternoon against Nicaragua, winning by a comfortable 10-3 margin. There were four home runs (by LeCroy, Williams, Glaus and Lee) and 12 hits as Greisinger won his third game of the tournament while limiting the Nicaraguans to two hits in seven innings.

Meanwhile, in the game the United States coveted, Cuba was winning the gold medal over Japan with a power display of eight home runs, including three by legendary third baseman Omar Linares and another by Orestes Kindelan, his ninth of the Games. Curiously, Japanese manager Katsuji Kawashima elected to start Sugiura, the pitcher who had mastered the U.S. bats. That was the good news. The bad news was that he'd mastered them less than 24 hours ago. The Cubans lit him up like a fine cigar. They had a double and two home runs after four batters. What was left of Sugiura's arm lasted barely over an inning.

The 13-run, 14-hit finale served as a fitting climax for the longtime dictators of the "amateur" game. The Cubans didn't just win, and they didn't just win convincingly; above all, they won when they needed to. ▼

ABOVE / *Orestes Kindelan, who hammered nine home runs in the Olympic tournament, has plenty to give thanks for. The Cubans' prayers were answered when they smoked Japan in the gold-medal game, 13-9.* ALLSPORT / JED JACOBSOHN

OPPOSITE (TOP) / *The U.S. rolled over Japan in its first meeting, 15-5, with Warren Morris and A.J. Hinch (bottom) joining in the slugfest. The tables turned one week later when Japan dusted a disheartened U.S. team, 11-2. The Americans bounced back in their finale against Nicaragua to capture the bronze medal.* ALLSPORT / RICK STEWART

BASKETBALL

Double gold for American basketball

BY LEE BENSON

ALLSPORT / STU FORSTER

RIGHT / *The USA women's basketball team celebrated to some music at the end of its gold-medal winning Olympic tournament.*
ALLSPORT / RICK STEWART

SUCCEEDING PAGES (LEFT) / *Zaire's Lukengu Ngalula couldn't stop the U.S. and Katrina McClain at the basket. The Americans averaged 102 points while winning all eight of their games.* ALLSPORT / MIKE POWELL

(RIGHT) / *Like everyone else, Venus Lacey found the crowds in Atlanta difficult to deal with at times.* ALLSPORT / TONY DUFFY

NOT ONE BUT TWO DREAM TEAMS surfaced for the United States of America at the Centennial Olympic Games, where men's basketball was again dominated by the latest dreamy U.S. edition, and where the U.S. women not only dominated their field, but actually tended to overshadow the men's play as well.

Four years ago in Barcelona the world got its first look at a men's dream team; in Atlanta, they saw the first edition of a women's dream team.

Those U.S. women rolled through eight games, and victories, in Atlanta, winning by an average of 28.6 points. They were never seriously threatened as they played night after night to record crowds, including the largest gathering ever for women's basketball in the world at 33,952.

Coupled with the U.S. men's similar 8-0 undefeated romp, the result was double gold for American basketball. And it you think it had been awhile, you're right. Not since 1984, when Michael Jordan, on loan from the North Carolina Tar Heels, led the men's team to gold in Los Angeles, and Cheryl Miller and Lynette Woodard, on her way to becoming a two-time Olympian, led the women's team to gold, had the United States or any country completely ruled the Olympic roundball world. No other country has ever managed such an Olympic double.

The women had done their part in Seoul in 1988, but that was the year the men were gunned down in the semis by a Soviet team that had prepared by playing against NBA teams. Then, in Barcelona, the men did their part, fielding the original Dream Team, but alas the women stumbled, losing to the Unified Team (read: Soviet Union) in the semifinals and having to settle for the bronze.

By the time the Atlanta Games rolled around, however, USA Basketball was well prepared to return to the glory of '84. Not only did it field another Dream Team consisting of the NBA's best players on the men's side of the draw, but for the women it offered a unique opportunity to showcase their talents at home with the best

ABOVE / *Clearly in control: Charles Barkley brushes off Rima Kurtinaitis, leading the USA to a 22-point victory over Lithuania (104-82). Barkley scored 16 points and nabbed five rebounds, both team highs.* ALLSPORT / DOUG PENSINGER

OPPOSITE / *Ruthie Bolton, a first lieutenant in the Army Reserves, was a fierce leader on the floor for the USA. In the final, she had 15 points, five assists and five steals.* ALLSPORT / AL BELLO

American pros from Europe and the country's emerging college stars for the formation of a historic women's national team.

Because of the absence of a women's professional league in America, USA Basketball formed the women's national team early, so it could have an opportunity to come together as it traveled around the world. For nearly 10 months the national team prepared for the Atlanta Games by playing the best collection of collegiate and national teams. Tara VanDerveer, one of the most successful college coaches and a veteran coach of six previous USA

squads, took a leave of absence from her duties at Stanford University to guide the team.

Ranging in age from 32-year-old Teresa Edwards, who became the first U.S. basketball Olympian, male or female, to play in four Olympics (and to win three gold medals), to 22-year-old Rebecca Lobo, who a year earlier was helping Connecticut to the 1995 NCAA title, the women went 52-0 while outscoring the opposition by an average of 31 points per game — in getting ready for Atlanta.

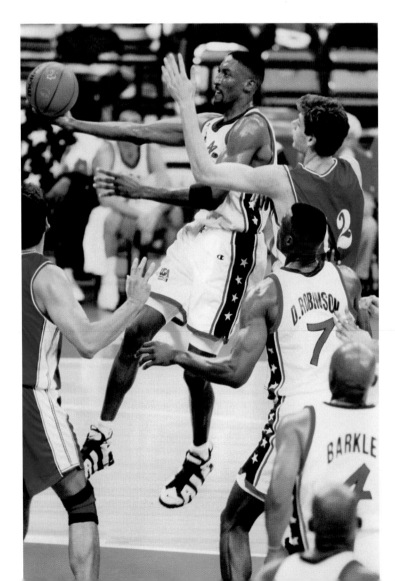

Meanwhile, the members of the men's team were preparing in their usual way — by spending the winter playing for their respective NBA teams and then coming together less than a month before Atlanta to get ready to take on the world.

With five holdovers from the original Dream Team, including Charles Barkley, Karl Malone, Scottie Pippen, David Robinson and John Stockton, the men's team in Atlanta bore a strong resemblance to the gang that wowed Barcelona. But Larry, Michael and Magic were gone, replaced by Penny Hardaway, Shaquille O'Neal and Grant Hill — and for good measure, Hakeem Olajuwon — and it wasn't really all that difficult to tell the new dream from the old one. Other new-comers were Reggie Miller, Mitch Richmond and Gary Payton, while Lenny Wilkens, the winningest coach in NBA history, took over on the sidelines from Chuck Daly, and while Daly made it a point to never call a timeout during an Olympic game, Wilkens took a different approach, standing up when he felt like it.

OPPOSITE (TOP LEFT) / *David Robinson, with 18 points and seven rebounds, helped the U.S. shake off a sluggish first half against Argentina to rally the USA to a 96-68 win in its Olympic opener.* ALLSPORT / DOUG PENSINGER

(TOP RIGHT) / *One big guy: Dream Team's Shaquille O'Neal takes center stage. Shaq averaged 9.3 points in the Olympic tourna-ment, scoring 13 points in this game against Argentina.* ALLSPORT / MIKE POWELL

(BOTTOM LEFT) / *It didn't take any stretch of the imagination to know Scottie Pippen's second gold medal was in easy reach; the question from the start was the degree of Dream Team's dominance. The U.S. rolled over Argentina, 96-68, Angola, 87-54, Lithuania, 104-82, China, 133-70, Croatia, 102-71, Brazil, 98-75, Australia, 101-73 and Yugoslavia, 95-69.*
ALLSPORT / JED JACOBSOHN

(BOTTOM RIGHT) / *Game high scorer Karl Malone shoots past the Angolan defense. Malone finished with 12 points and while Angola narrowed the U.S. margin of victory from 68 points in Barcelona to 33 points in Atlanta, the U.S. was simply beyond reach.*
ALLSPORT / DOUG PENSINGER

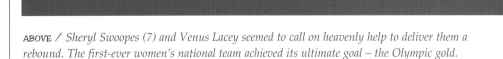

ABOVE / *Sheryl Swoopes (7) and Venus Lacey seemed to call on heavenly help to deliver them a rebound. The first-ever women's national team achieved its ultimate goal – the Olympic gold.*
ALLSPORT / JED JACOBSOHN

In its two-week, eight-game Atlanta romp, six different players (Barkley, Malone, Robinson, Pippen, Richmond and Hardaway) led the U.S. team in scoring, and only three times did anyone score more than 20. The closest anyone got was Brazil when it lost by 23, 98-75, and the only semi-serious threat to the Americans came from Yugoslavia in the gold-medal game. Featuring a number of players with NBA experience, including Vlade Divac, Zavko Paspalj and Sasha Danilovic, Yugoslavia actually led by seven points nearing intermission, before the U.S. got on track and won going away, 95-69.

The scores in the sequel Dream Team's games were slightly closer than in Barcelona. Thus, the average margin of victory was 43.8 points while in Atlanta it was 31.6.

Capturing the men's bronze medal was Lithuania, still featuring Arvydas Sabonis, Rimas Kurtinaitis and Sarunas Marciulionis, the big three who shot down the Americans in Seoul in '88. Australia, paced by former Seton Hall shooting star Andrew Gaze and point guard Shane Heal, lost to Lithuania by six, 80-74, to finish fourth while Brazil, led yet again by scoring machine Oscar Schmidt — who passed the 1,000 point scoring plateau in Atlanta, the first player, male or female, in Olympic history to reach that milestone — beat Croatia (featuring Toni Kukoc and Dino Radja) to place fifth.

The American women beat Australia by 22 points in the semifinal game and beat Brazil by 24 points in the gold-medal game. The win over Brazil avenged a loss in the semifinals of the 1994 World Championships when the Brazilians upset a USA squad comprised largely of future 1996 Olympic team members. Forward Lisa Leslie and Katrina McClain emerged as the brightest stars on the U.S. team. In the semifinal win over the Aussies, Leslie had 22 points and 13 rebounds while McClain had 18 points and 15 boards. In the gold-medal game, Leslie had 29 points and six rebounds and McClain a dozen points and five rebounds. Edwards, the U.S. women's floor leader who led the Olympics in assists averaging nearly eight per game, had nine points and 10 assists against the Brazilians. In a memorable performance earlier in the tournament she had 20 points, 15 assists and seven boards against Australia. Sheryl Swoopes and Ruthie Bolton had 16 and 15 points, respectively, in the championship game — indicative of their steady play all tournament long.

In the women's bronze medal match, Australia beat Ukraine, 66-56.

Almost every game in Atlanta was a sell-out, for both genders, and that's no idle statement since most of the action took place in the spacious Georgia Dome. Night after night, as the men's and women's tournaments alternated play, crowds in excess of 30,000 came to see the best players in the world. ▼

OPPOSITE / Teresa Edwards, a four-time Olympian playing in her hometown, looked right at home while threading her way through the Australian defense. She became the first basketball player, male or female, to win three gold medals. ALLSPORT / MIKE POWELL

ABOVE / Penny Hardaway joined the Dream Teamers in Atlanta, having played on a USA Basketball Developmental Team that scrimmaged the original Dream Team daily in practice in 1992. ALLSPORT / DOUG PENSINGER

BOXING

USA doubles medal count from '92

BY LEE BENSON

ALLSPORT / AL BELLO

RIGHT / *A thinking man's boxer known for speed and a solid jab, American David Reid ended his bout to become Olympic champion with a knockout.* ALLSPORT / AL BELLO

I T WAS OLYMPIC BUSINESS AS USUAL IN the boxing arena, dominated, as always, by the "professional amateurs" from Cuba; but for the American amateurs, along with a golden breakthrough, there was an ample collection of bronze.

There was also considerable "debate" over the Olympic computerized scoring, a system that continues to meet with animated controversy. It calls for the five judges surrounding the ring to press a button on the computer console in front of them within one second each time they see what they consider a scoring punch. Whenever at least three of the judges are in agreement, the boxer gets a point. Too often, however, the resulting final score reflects an outcome not in accordance with what many eyewitnesses have just seen.

By the time they finally shut down the computerized scoring system in Atlanta, Cuba had four gold medals, three silver and no bronze, while the U.S. had one gold, no silver, and five bronze. That gave Cuba a Games-high of seven medals and the USA a next-best six. Nobody else came close. Russia, Kazakhstan and Germany had four medals each, Bulgaria had three, and Ukraine, Thailand, Algeria and Romania had two apiece. Another 12 nations had one medal each.

Indeed, fits of indignity about the computer scoring system were universal in Atlanta. Even the Cubans joined in. When welterweight Juan Hernandez lost by a 14-9 decision to Russia's Oleg Saitov in the gold-medal bout, legendary Cuban coach Alcides Sagarra threw Hernandez's gloves to the mat in disgust and turned his back to the ring.

The biggest fuss, however, belonged to the American camp following featherweight Floyd Mayweather's 10-9 loss to Bulgaria's Serafim Todorv in the semifinals. Even referee Hamadi Hafez Shouman of Egypt, who prematurely began to raise Mayweather's hand as the victor, was fooled by a computer-generated result that was in contradiction of the one-sided fight everyone had just seen live. But a decision is a decision, and as Mayweather took his place alongside other shortchanged U.S.

LEFT / *A favorite to win the light heavyweight title, American Antonio Tarver's gold-medal hopes were ended by Vasili Jirov of Kazakhstan, who went on to win the gold. The 1995 world champion took home the bronze.* ALLSPORT / JOHN GICHIGI

OPPOSITE (TOP) / *Hard-hitting Juan Hernandez of Cuba received the biggest blow when he lost to Russia's Oleg Saitov by a 14-9 decision in the gold-medal welterweight bout.* ALLSPORT / AL BELLO

(BOTTOM) / *Defending Olympic heavyweight champion Felix Savon (in blue) waits for his chance to strike gold. The indomitable Cuban overwhelmed Canadian David Defiagbon in a 20-2 decision.* ALLSPORT / AL BELLO

boxers from earlier Games — Roy Jones Jr. in 1988, Eric Griffin in 1992 — there was nothing left to lose but a few tempers, and that didn't reverse his verdict, either.

Mayweather's loss was especially tough to take because just two days earlier the 19-year-old, 125-pounder from Grand Rapids, Mich., had qualified for the medal round by doing what no American boxer had done since before he was born. He'd beaten a Cuban in the Olympic Games.

Mayweather's 12-11 verdict over Cuba's Lorenzo Aragon marked the first head-to-head win for a U.S. fighter over a Cuban since the Montreal Games in 1976. Despite the fact Aragon was a last-minute replacement in the Cuban lineup for Joel Casamayor — who, along with light heavyweight Ramon Garbey, had defected to the United States from the team's training camp in Mexico — the U.S. wasn't about to put an asterisk on the break-

through. With no Cubans left in his path, Mayweather suddenly became America's best bet for a gold medal.

Until the Bulgarian and the computer came along.

Still, Mayweather's loss was able to help produce American gold anyway, as teammate David Reid, who fought directly after Mayweather, used his teammate's computerized setback to alter his mindset. "I decided I wasn't going to leave it in the

judges' hands," said Reid, who proceeded to completely obliterate Karim Tulaganov of Uzbekistan in the semifinals, winning 12-4.

In the gold-medal match, Reid's opponent was Alfredo Duvergel of, you guessed it, Cuba. Duvergel, the defending Pan American champion, was the heavy favorite, and looked it. He held a 15-5 scoring advantage entering the third and final round, when Reid, once again, decided to shun any compatibility with conventional scoring. With U.S. coach Al Mitchell, Reid's "second father," telling him to "forget about trying to outbox him, go for the knockout," Reid threw a short but powerful overhand right just as the third round started and caught Duvergel near the right eye and knocked him to his hands and knees.

The Cuban got up at seven, but he was staggering, and Bulgarian referee Simeon Stojadinov stopped the bout 36 seconds into the third round. Not only had America scored its second win in Atlanta over a Cuban (against three losses — flyweight Maikro Romero had beaten Eric Morel of Madison, Wis., in the opening round; bantamweight Arnaldo Mesa had beaten highly-regarded Zahir Raheem of Philadelphia in the second round; and in the semifinals, middleweight Ariel Hernandez, the defending Olympic champion, had defeated Roshii Wells of Riverdale, Ga.), but Team USA had also successfully avoided being shut out of the boxing gold medals, something that last happened in London in 1948.

The total U.S. medal haul of six doubled the three medals won in Barcelona (where Oscar De La Hoya got the gold). Besides Reid's gold and the bronze finishes by Mayweather and Wells, the other three U.S. bronzes were collected by lightweight Terrance Cauthen, who lost to Bulgaria's

RIGHT / *He has had enough hard knocks to last a lifetime, but American Nate Jones dealt out a few hard knocks himself in the Olympic ring before bowing out to hard-hitting David Defiagbon (right) of Canada in the heavyweight semis.* ALLSPORT / JOHN GICHIGI

Tontcho Tontchev in the semis; heavyweight Nate Jones, whose semifinal loss was to Canada's David Defiagbon; and highly-regarded light heavyweight Antonio Tarver, the 1995 world champion who made the mistake of coming on too strong in the semis and tired and lost — amid some controversy after a most impressive second-round flurry — to Vasili Jirov of Kazakhstan.

In addition to welterweight Fernando Vargas, who lost in a hotly-disputed 8-7 second-round contest to Marian Simion of Romania, other American casualties in the preliminaries were light welterweight David Diaz, who lost in the second round to Oktay Urkal of Germany; light flyweight Albert Guardado Jr., who lost in the quarterfinals to Oleg Kiryukhin of Ukraine; and super heavyweight Lawrence Clay-Bey, who had the misfortune of meeting eventual gold medalist Vladimir Klichko in the second round.

As it turned out, every fighter in Atlanta who defeated an American went on to place in the medals, including four gold medalists — besides Ukraine's Klichko, there was Kazakhstan's Jirov and the two Cubans, Romero and Hernandez.

Cuba's other gold medalists included Hector Vinent at light welterweight and, at heavyweight, the indomitable Felix Savon, the defending Olympic champion and four-time world champion who beat Canada's Defiagbon 20-2 in the finals.

Paea Wolfgram of Tonga, at a massive 309 pounds, attracted a large following at the Alexander Memorial Coliseum as he captured his nation's first-ever Olympic medal, a silver in the super heavyweight division. After pulling off the upset of the tournament by defeating heavily-favored Alexis Rubalcaba of Cuba in the quarterfinals, 17-12, Wolfgram edged Nigeria's Duncan Dokiwari in the semifinals, 7-6. That set up the gold-medal bout with Ukraine's Klichko. Despite a broken wrist, sustained in the fight with Dokiwari, Wolfgram insisted on boxing in the final anyway. Amazingly, he actually led after two rounds. The computer. It just had to get in one final shot. ▼

CANOE / KAYAK

Go with the flow

BY CRAIG BOHNERT

ALLSPORT / PASCAL RONDEAU

RIGHT / *The course at Tennessee's Ocoee River was fast with some make-or-break gates (18,19, 20!) to trip up even the favorites, which they did. Cathy Hearn of the USA placed seventh in the women's slalom kayak race.* ALLSPORT / PASCAL RONDEAU

IT WAS HARD TO FIND ANY COMPETItion in Atlanta more balanced than on the waters of Tennessee's Ocoee River and Georgia's Lake Lanier. When it comes to canoe and kayak racing, the Olympic field is incredibly level.

No less than 18 countries divided up the 48 medals given out in whitewater and flatwater racing, with nine countries accounting for the 16 gold medals awarded. Germany was the most prevalent medalist, with nine (five gold), followed by Hungary with six (two gold), the Czech Republic with five (three gold), and Italy with five (two gold). The United States was one of six nations to win one medal in the competition.

The most decorated individuals in the water were Antonio Rossi of Italy, who won gold medals in both the 500-meter single kayak race and in the 1,000-meter double kayak competition, where he teamed with countryman Daniel Scarpa; and Martin Doktor of the Czech Republic, also a double gold medalist after wins in both the 500-meter and 1,000-meter single canoe races.

The lone American medal came in dramatic fashion as kayaker Dana Chladek of Kensington, Md., the bronze medalist in whitewater women's slalom in Barcelona, flipped her boat almost as soon as she slipped into the waters of the Ocoee River.

She missed four gates before she could right herself and her boat. The result: 205 penalty points. And this in a sport where the five-point penalty for a single gate touch can be the difference between a gold medal and finishing out of the top 10.

But Chladek bounced back by going for broke on her second run, vaulting into an early tie for first place with Stephanka Hilgertova of the Czech Republic. As Chladek and Hilgertova watched from the bank, 29 athletes entered the Ocoee and failed to surpass their scores. Since the tiebreaker compared first run results, the gold went to Hilgertova, giving Chladek the silver.

"Sitting as the first boat, then having to wait an hour and a half and expecting that

run to get beaten by three to five people made it a shock," said Chladek of the result. "When I saw Lynn (Simpson of Great Britain) 50 that gate, I thought 'I've got a medal.'" Simpson, a favorite entering the competition, was assessed a 50-point penalty for missing gate 11 on her second run, assuring Chladek no worse than the bronze.

Chladek's silver medal provided the lining to an otherwise gray performance for the United States. In whitewater slalom, two world championship medalists were considered favorites in their classes. However, neither David Hearn, in single canoe, nor Scott Shipley, in men's kayak, could jump onto the medal podium. Shipley was virtually a unanimous pick for gold but he faded to 12th as Rich Weiss, who placed sixth, took honors as the top U.S. finisher.

"I was pretty happy with the way I paddled and I was extremely happy to come into the race ranked No. 1 in the world," said Shipley. "Kayak races are hard to win, and today I wasn't the man. I've had better days, a lot better days."

THE UNITED STATES HAD SEEN BETTER days, too, in flatwater sprint racing. The retirement of gold medalists Greg Barton and Norman Bellingham following the Barcelona Games left a void that was not filled in Atlanta. Of the 10 American entries at Lake Lanier in Gainesville, Ga., not one advanced to the finals. Just two, the men's double kayak at 500- and 1,000-meters, came close. In the 500, John Mooney and Stein Jorgensen had a close finish in the semifinals, and in the 1,000, Mooney teamed with Peter Newton to also come close to qualifying out of the semifinal round.

Three-time Olympian Traci Phillips of Honolulu, who finished ninth in the semifinals in the 500-meter women's single kayak, pointed out that the breakup of the Soviet bloc flooded the competition in Atlanta with athletes who would have been left at home before, unable to find a spot when there were fewer teams to make. "There are so many good girls now," said Phillips. "It makes it hard to make the finals."

Several bright young stars held out hope for a rebound of American fortunes. Flatwater saw the introduction of Lia Rousset, who at 19 holds promise for a return to form in women's kayak, while the kayak doubles tandem of Mooney and Jorgensen also shows promise, as does Cliff Meidl, who made his first Olympic team after only three years of competitive training.

In slalom, Shipley and fellow men's kayaker Eric Giddens are expected to maintain the level of excellence the U.S. has enjoyed in that class in recent years, while Adam Clawson is expected to continue a strong career in single canoe. ▼

Uh-oh! ALLSPORT / SIMON BRUTY

David Hearn, USA. ALLSPORT / PASCAL RONDEAU

Geronimo! ALLSPORT / NATHAN BILOW

RIGHT / *Scott Shipley, a favorite going into the slalom competition, didn't win a medal, but he won many a heart, Bosnia's Samir Karasbasid in particular. After the Bosnian's boat, patched with duct tape, sank during a training run, Shipley gave him one of his custom-made kayaks.* ALLSPORT / NATHAN BILOW

▲ *Negotiating the Ocoee.*
ALLSPORT / PASCAL RONDEAU

wet 'n wild

▼ *Stephanka Hilgertova, gold.*
ALLSPORT / PASCAL RONDEAU

▼ *Oliver Fix, gold.* ALLSPORT / PASCAL RONDEAU   ▲ *Port!* ALLSPORT / SIMON BRUTY   ▼ *Whoa!* ALLSPORT / NATHAN BILOW

CYCLING

Professionals, mountain biking debut in Atlanta

BY LEE BENSON

ALLSPORT / PASCAL RONDEAU

OPPOSITE (CLOCKWISE) / *After 137.7 miles and five hours of intense cycling, Switzerland's Pascal Richard came out ahead in the men's road race, but just barely. He and Rolf Sorenson recorded identical times but the Swiss edged the Dane by less than a wheel length.* ALLSPORT / PASCAL RONDEAU

Italian Andreas Collinelli's world-record pace, twice over, set the stage early in the men's individual pursuit for his gold-medal performance a day later. ALLSPORT / MIKE POWELL

Thomas Frischknecht of Switzerland raced through the trees and over the 30.272-mile dirt course to a second-place finish among a field of 44 men where, for many, the heat and humidity proved tougher than the course itself. ALLSPORT / NATHAN BILOW

The 64.87 mile women's road race began with a 75-degree temperature and 88 percent humidity and was plagued by rain, conditions which took their toll on many of the riders. ALLSPORT / NATHAN BILOW

Erin Hartwell bettered his Barcelona bronze to take silver in Atlanta in the one-kilometer time trial. ALLSPORT / ROSS KINNAIRD

THERE WAS A LEGENDARY FEEL AT THE Olympic cycling venues, where two of the greatest performers ever — France's Jeannie Longo-Ciprelli and Spain's Miguel Indurain — led a Who's Who procession of gold medalists.

The 37-year-old Longo-Ciprelli, competing in her fourth Olympic Games, got the cycling competition started by winning the women's road race. In securing her first gold medal, Longo-Ciprelli put the cap on an 18-year career dotted with virtually every major women's cycling trophy. Fourteen days later, as the Games of Atlanta were about to close, Indurain won the 14th and final cycling event with a 12-second margin of victory in the men's individual time trial. The 32-year-old Indurain, winner of the Tour de France five consecutive times in the '90s, had competed in one previous Games, as a 20-year-old amateur in Los Angeles in 1984, where he placed well down in the standings. It was shortly thereafter that he turned professional and his career erupted. Until Atlanta, professionals were not allowed to compete in Olympic cycling.

At rest, his heart beats 28 times a minute. The superbly conditioned Miguel Indurain of Spain beat the clock and the rest of the 37-man field in the individual time trial.

Indurain was just the top of the iceberg as the professionals took Atlanta by siege. In their own, understated way, the world's best cyclists, particularly the men, staged their own "Dream Team" performance on the streets of Atlanta and at the Stone Mountain velodrome. In the men's road race, for example, the medalist podium was shared by a trio of riders with Tour de France credentials. The winner was Pascal Richard of Switzerland, who'd won the 12th stage of the 1996 2,400-mile Tour de France. He was followed by Rolf Sorensen of Denmark, who'd won the 13th stage, and by Maximilian Sciandri of Britain, who had won a stage in the 1995 Tour.

The mildly undulating 138-mile men's road race course wound through the neigh-borhoods of Buckhead, an Atlanta suburb. The terrain favored one-day racing specialists over the endurance champions, helping explain why Bjarne Riis, the Danish cyclist who two weeks earlier had won the Tour de France, finished 87th, and why Indurain was 26th.

In the women's road race, contested along the same mildly undulating suburban roads, rain added an additional element of adversity. France's Longo-Ciprelli covered the 64.8 miles 25 seconds faster than silver medalist Imelda Chiappa of Italy and 31 seconds ahead of bronze medalist Clara Hughes of Canada. Immediately after the race, Longo-Ciprelli, a sports legend in her homeland, received a phone call from French president Jacques Chirac. She closed out her Games in the women's time trial, where she finished second by 20 seconds to Russia's Zuifiya Zabirova.

French riders dominated in Atlanta by winning nine medals overall, including five golds, three silvers and a bronze. Italy won four golds and a silver for a total of five medals, while Canada and Australia also won five medals each, but no golds. Germany, Switzerland, Netherlands, Spain and Russia captured one gold medal apiece.

The United States team finished fifth in overall medals with three, including two silvers and one bronze. Frankie Andreu had the closest medal near-miss for the U.S., finishing fourth in the men's road race, about a minute behind Switzerland's Richard. America's top-rated cyclist, Lance Armstrong, finished 12th in the road race and sixth in the men's 32.4-mile individual time trial, two minutes and 23 seconds off Indurain's winning time.

America's silver medalists included sprint veterans Marty Nothstein, 25, in men's sprint and Erin Hartwell, 27, in men's one-kilometer time trial. Hartwell, a bronze medalist in the same event in

Barcelona, took advantage of a bad start by world record-holder Shane Kelly, who was disqualified after slipping on the start. France's Florian Rousseau was the one-kilometer gold medalist and Takanobu Jumonji followed Hartwell with the bronze.

Nothstein missed winning his first race in the best-of-three sprint finals by less than an inch to Germany's Jens Fiedler, who used that momentum to win the next race and successfully defend the Olympic title he had won in Barcelona. The bronze medalist was Curt Harnett of Canada, who also won the bronze in Barcelona. In the early rounds, Nothstein not only swept past Harnett, but also world champion Darryn Hill of Australia.

MOUNTAIN BIKING TAKES TO THE HILLS

Susan DeMattei claimed a bronze medal in the inaugural women's mountain bike race, held at the Georgia International Horse Park, an equestrian facility 30 miles east of Atlanta. The rolling hills plus heat and humidity produced a challenging course that spread out the field. A Dutchman, Bart Jan Brentjens, won the men's gold medal and Italy's Paolo Pezzo won the women's gold. DeMattei was one minute and forty-five seconds behind Pezzo's winning pace on the women's 19.8-mile course. Juliana Furtado, the American favorite, finished almost eight minutes back in 10th place. Among the American men, David "Tinker" Juarez and Don Myrah placed 19th and 20th.

CENTER / *When Paola Pezzo of Italy (center) breezed past the pack, finishing the 19.8-mile course in 1:50:51, the race became one for second place. It was two-time world champion Alison Sydor (left) of Canada who crossed the line second, 38 seconds before 33-year-old Susan DeMattei of the U.S.* ALLSPORT / MIKE POWELL

SUPERSTAR AND SUPERBIKE

ATLANTA MARKED THE LIKELY END OF THE competitive road for Connie Paraskevin-Young, a veteran of five Olympic Games, two as a speedskater (Lake Placid in 1980 and 1984 in Sarajevo) and three as a cyclist (Seoul in 1988, Barcelona in 1992 and Atlanta). A bronze medalist in women's sprint in Seoul, the four-time world champion was eliminated in the preliminary sprint rounds in Atlanta.

The Atlanta Games also marked the culmination of USA Cycling's Project '96, a U.S. Olympic Committee-endorsed program with the mission of combining the best athletes with the most advanced technology in equipment, apparel and training. Project '96 produced the most aerodynamic bicycles in the world with SuperBike II (used in only four of the 14 events) along with breakthroughs in physiological testing, rider biomechanics, sport science and sport psychology. Although the expectations were higher, the three medals for the United States in Atlanta marked an improvement over Seoul and Barcelona. ▼

OPPOSITE (TOP) / *American Marty Nothstein and German Jans Fiedler went head-to-head for the gold in the men's sprint, with Fiedler inching Nothstein for the honors.* ALLSPORT / PASCAL RONDEAU

TOP RIGHT / *With the entry of professional cyclists in Atlanta, the spotlight was on Spain's Miguel Indurain, five-time consecutive winner of the Tour de France. He won the individual time trial in 1:04:05.* ALLSPORT / NATHAN BILOW

RIGHT / *Italy claimed four golds in the cycling events, including the men's point race won by Silvio Martinello.* ALLSPORT / PASCAL RONDEAU

DIVING

Recovery from the deep end

ALLSPORT / MIKE HEWITT

OPPOSITE / *With the platform gold already in hand, Fu Mingxia concentrated on diving for the double. When she won the gold in spring-board, she joined six other divers who had won both Olympic events: Greg Louganis, USA, in 1984 and 1988; East German Ingrid Kramer in 1960; Pat McCormick, USA, in 1952 and 1956; Vicki Draves, USA, in 1948; Ulise "Pete" Desjardins, USA, 1928; and Al White, USA, in 1924.* ALLSPORT / JED JACOBSOHN

IN A DIVING COMPETITION DOMINATED at the top by the Chinese, it was a trio of American divers who provided the drama. While 17-year-old Fu Mingxia became the first woman in 36 years to win gold medals in both the platform and springboard divisions and Xiong Ni and Yu Zhuocheng gave the Chinese a one-two finish in men's springboard, the made-in-America stories of Mary Ellen Clark, Mark Lenzi and Scott Donie were equally as compelling.

Clark won a bronze medal in women's platform, Lenzi a bronze in men's spring-board, and Donie finished fourth in men's springboard — in each case, the achieve-ment capped stirring comebacks from adversity that hit each diver after the Games in Barcelona.

In the aftermath of those '92 Games, Clark, who won bronze at Barcelona in platform, came down with a severe case of vertigo that rendered her unable to even climb to the top of the ladder; Donie, the winner of platform silver in Barcelona, suf-fered a case of post-Olympic depression and took six months off in 1993; and Lenzi, the springboard gold medalist in Barcelona, suffered burnout and depression and retired in 1994.

Each athlete, however, was able to find a way back. Clark's vertigo was finally cured by CranialSacral therapy. Donie got a job teaching children with learning disabili-ties, giving him a healthy perspective that altered his depression; and Lenzi spent a year in flight school before a couple of flips into his apartment pool had him back on the diving board.

The three comeback kids regrouped in time to qualify for the U.S. Olympic diving team along with 1988 Olympian Patrick Jeffrey and first-time Olympians David Pichler, Jenny Keim, Melisa Moses and Becky Ruehl.

The medals from Lenzi and Clark, who at age 33 became the oldest diving medal-ist in history, led a team performance by the Americans that was, if not spectacular, very steady. There were also three fourth-place finishes — in addition to Donie's

ABOVE / *Coming out of retirement to compete in Atlanta, Mark Lenzi made his final dive, a reverse 3 1/2 somersault, of his career count. It secured him a bronze medal in springboard and even opened the door to trade places with the Chinese divers Xiong Ni and Yu Zhoucheng. But Xiong and Yu closed the door and the evening with the same display of precision and grace they maintained throughout the competition to give China the gold and silver, respectively.* ALLSPORT / JED JACOBSOHN

OPPOSITE / *With a bag of good-luck charms poolside, Mary Ellen Clark turned on the magic to turn around a diving career stopped by vertigo to win her second Olympic bronze in platform.* ALLSPORT / JED JACOBSOHN

United States for runner-up honors, while Canada collected the remaining medal.

The inimitable Fu, just 13 when she won her first diving gold medal in Barcelona, did a double for her encore act four years later, becoming the first woman to win both diving medals since East Germany's Ingrid Kramer did it in Rome in 1960. In the springboard competition she prevailed over silver medalist Irina Lashko of Russia, who repeated her placement in Barcelona, and bronze medalist Annie Pelletier, who won just the third diving medal in Canadian history. In the platform division, Fu outlasted silver medalist Annika Walter of Germany and the USA's Clark, who needed a comeback to complete her comeback. She was in sixth place, well out of the medals, until she nailed her final two dives to secure the bronze.

Xiong Ni and Yu Zhuocheng held Lenzi and Donie at bay in men's springboard to continue China's mastery. In men's platform, however, Russia's Dmitry Sautin, the early favorite on the board, broke through to take the gold and Jan Hempel of Germany grabbed the silver. Xiao Hailiang hung on for the bronze medal, making sure a Chinese diver was represented on every award peristyle.

Like Clark, Lenzi made a comeback after a shaky opening. He closed his career with nines on his final dive, a reverse three and a half tuck. Donie, too, aced his last dives, but couldn't make up enough ground to overtake either the Chinese or his teammate to get into the springboard medals.

"I knew either Mark or I was going to win a medal," said Donie. "So I'm happy we got an American in the medals. It's important for our sport and for our history. I'm just real happy with my performance."

Lenzi dedicated his bronze medal to coach Hobie Billingsley, while Clark presented her father, Gene, with her bronze medal. "This means a lot for my dad," said Clark, whose father was unable to travel to Barcelona after surgery but made it to Atlanta despite an April bout with cancer. "I'm glad he was here. He was my first coach and he is really my hero." ▼

fourth, Melisa Moses placed fourth in women's springboard and Becky Ruehl finished fourth in women's platform — as well as a sixth-place finish by Pichler in men's platform and ninth-place efforts by Jeffrey in men's platform and Keim in women's springboard. Even though Atlanta marked the first time an American diver hadn't won Olympic gold since 1912, every U.S. diver made the finals and none finished out of the top 10, a claim no other nation in Atlanta could make.

Then again, no other nation beyond China could claim three of four gold medals, a silver, and a bronze, making it a total of five medals in all. Russia and Germany had two medals each, tying the

EQUESTRIAN

U.S. medals in all three disciplines

BY MARTY BAUMAN

ALLSPORT / MIKE HEWITT

OPPOSITE / *Former racehorse Out and About and Kerry Millikin, who came to Atlanta as an alternate on the U.S. equestrian team, held their own to win the bronze medal in the individual three-day event.* ALLSPORT / RICK STEWART

IN AN EQUESTRIAN SETTING THAT WAS decidedly cosmopolitan, the host team from the United States more than held its own in Atlanta. Along with Germany, which topped the gold-medal count with four, the U.S. was co-star of the Games, the only country to win medals in all three equestrian disciplines — three-day eventing, dressage and show jumping.

In enjoying its best Olympics since 1984, the U.S. equestrian team won four medals, two silver and two bronze, tying the Germans for overall medals. New Zealand, with a gold, a silver and a bronze, and the Netherlands, with two silvers and a bronze, also had good showings at the Georgia International Horse Park in Conyers.

"Our success here is extremely rewarding," said U.S. show jumping chef d'equipe (coach) Frank Chapot. "We have spent four years preparing for these Games on U.S. soil and our expectations were to win medals in all three disciplines. To be the only country to achieve that shows where the U.S. ranks on the world equestrian scene."

The U.S. started its medal run in the first competition, the team three-day event. Led by the husband-and-wife duo of Karen and David O'Connor of The Plains, Va., along with five-time Olympic Bruce Davidson of Unionville, Pa., and 21-year-old Jill Henneberg of Vorhees, N.J., the U.S. won the team silver medal behind 1992 Olympic champion Australia.

Karen O'Conner competed on Biko, a 12-year-old Thoroughbred owned by Mr. and Mrs. Richard Thompson, and David competed on Giltedge, a 10-year-old Irish Thoroughbred owned by Jacqueline Mars. Davidson, who earned his fourth Olympic medal, rode Heyday, a nine-year-old Thoroughbred owned by Dr. Elinor Jenny, while Henneberg rode her Nirvana II, an 11-year-old Thoroughbred mare which she purchased for $600.

Two days after the team event ended, Kerry Millikin of Westport, Mass., a registered nurse, rode her former racehorse Out and About to the bronze medal in the individual three-day event. Along with a fifth-place finish by David O'Connor on Custom Made, a 10-year-old Thoroughbred owned by Joseph Zada, and a sixth-place finish by Mara DePuy of South Stafford, Vt., on Hopper, her 13-year-old Thoroughbred, the U.S. placed three riders among the top six finishers. The two three-day event medals were the first for the U.S. since 1984.

The U.S. continued its medal parade with a team bronze in dressage. The final standings of Germany first, the Netherlands second and the U.S. third matched the final standings from the 1992 Games in Barcelona and the 1994 World Championships in The Hague.

The U.S. team was led by Michelle Gibson of Roswell, Ga., whose Grand Prix score of 75.20 percent on Peron TSF, an 11-year-old Trakehner stallion owned by Dr. Carole Meyer-Webster, was the highest ever achieved by a U.S. rider in Olympic competition. Joining her on the medal stand were teammates Guenter Seidel of Encinitas, Calif., riding Graf George, a 13-year-old Hanoverian gelding owned by Mr. and Mrs. Richard Brown; Steffen Peters of Escondido, Calif., riding Udon, an 18-year-old Dutch Warmblood gelding owned by Lila Kommerstad, and four-time Olympian Robert Dover of Flemington, N.J., riding Metallic, a 12-year-old Dutch Warmblood gelding owned by Mr. and Mrs. David Gribbons and Jane Forbes Clark.

Not to be outdone by its three-day and dressage teammates, the U.S. show jumping squad rode to a dramatic silver-medal performance in the Nations' Cup team competition. A veteran team of Peter Leone of Greenwich, Conn., on Legato, a 10-year-old French/German Cross gelding owned by Lionshare Farm, and Olympic veterans Leslie Burr-Howard (1984 team gold medalist) of Westport, Conn., on Extreme, a nine-year-old Dutch-bred mare owned by Janes Forbes Clark; Anne Kursinski (1988 team silver medalist) of Flemington, N.J., on Eros, a nine-year-old Australian Thoroughbred gelding owned by the Eros Group; and Michael Matz of Collegeville, Pa., on Rhum IV, a 13-year-old Selle Français gelding owned by Mr.

and Mrs. F. Eugene Dixon, Jr., challenged the powerhouse German team and earned a place on the medal stand for the first time since 1988.

After sitting third with eight faults following round one, the U.S. came back strong with only four faults in the second round to move ahead of bronze-medal winner Brazil. Burr-Howard, Kursinski and Leone each posted one clear round while Matz scored just four faults in each of the two rounds.

While the U.S. did not win an individual medal in either dressage or show jumping, the team's riders were unanimous in their feelings of pride and accomplishment for winning medals in all three team competitions. "Not one rider came here thinking about an individual medal," said U.S. team captain Robert Dover, who rode in his fourth consecutive Olympic Games. "We all looked at individual medals as icing on the cake. Each and every one of us had a goal of helping the United States of America win a team medal and all three of our squads were able to achieve that." ▼

ABOVE / *Husband-and-wife team David and Karen O'Connor join Jill Henneberg and Bruce Davidson to celebrate the USA's silver-medal finish in the team three-day event.* ALLSPORT / MIKE HEWITT

BELOW / *The U.S. equestrian team made its mark in Atlanta: It was the only country to place in the medals in all three team events – dressage (bronze), three-day (silver), and jumping (silver).* ALLSPORT / STU FORSTER

OPPOSITE / *Three-time Olympian Anne Kursinski riding Eros left Atlanta with more than memories. She was part of the USA's silver-medal jumping team.* ALLSPORT / DAVID CANNON

FENCING

Where tradition still reigns

BY COLLEEN WALKER MAR

ALLSPORT / JED JACOBSOHN

OPPOSITE (TOP) / *Giovanna Trillini, bronze medalist in foil, celebrates her victory. The Italian teamed with silver foil medalist Valentina Vezzali and Francesca Bortolozzi Borella to win the women's team foil over Russia.* ALLSPORT / STU FORSTER

(BOTTOM) /*The traditional super powers of fencing vied for the top three positions in men's team epee. Italy came out on top, followed by Russia in second and France in third.* ALLSPORT / STU FORSTER

ALTHOUGH THE VENUE WAS ON American turf, there was no mistaking fencing's European flavor in Atlanta, where the medals parade favored the customary traditional power from Russia, Italy, France and Romania, with the occasional Pole, Cuban and Hungarian thrown in for good measure.

Despite holding the home strip advantage, the U.S. fencing team failed to secure any medals in Atlanta; but no less than five top 10 finishes in the team events and a seventh-place finish by Ann Marsh in women's foil — the first top eight finish by an American female fencer in 40 years — did give rise to some optimism for the Sydney Games of 2000.

The 25-year-old Marsh, a foil specialist, had entered her second straight Olympic Games as America's best hope for an individual medal, while she, Suzanne Paxton and Felicia Zimmermann — who all live together in Rochester, N.Y. — were considered medal contenders in team foil after briefly sitting atop the World Cup standings earlier in the season. But while Marsh's seventh-place individual finish at least left her within sniffing distance of a medal, the team's 10th-place finish — in a field of 11 — was a major disappointment.

It took a furious rally by Poland, however, to keep the Americans at bay. In that memorable opening match, Marsh put the U.S. ahead 40-38 entering the final round. With the U.S. still ahead, 42-40, Poland's Anna Rybicka tallied three straight touches against Zimmermann for a 43-42 advantage. Zimmermann rallied with two touches of her own, however, to regain the lead for the Americans, but Rybicka came right back, scoring the last two touches to give Team Poland a 45-44 triumph.

In the individual foil competition, besides Marsh's seventh-place effort, Zimmermann placed 21st and Paxton claimed 33rd. The medalists were, in order, Romania's Laura Badea, Italy's Valentina Vezzali and Giovanna Trillini of Italy, the defending champion from the Barcelona Games.

The highest finish for an American team came when the women's epee team of Elaine Cheris, Nhi Lan Le and Leslie Marx placed seventh. In men's epee, the U.S. men's team of Tamir Bloom, James Carpenter and Michael Marx placed eighth, defending Korea 45-41 in the round of 16 before giving top-seed Italy a major scare in a 45-44 overtime loss. Italy went on to win the gold medal, followed by Russia and France.

In men's team foil, Cliff Bayer, Nick Bravin and Peter Devine finished 10th as Russia, Poland and Cuba won the medals. In men's team sabre, Peter Cox Jr., Thomas Strzalkowski and Peter Westbrook placed ninth, a result that sent the 44-year-old Westbrook into retirement. Atlanta was Westbrook's sixth Olympic team. He'd qualified for every U.S. team since Montreal in 1976. In the 1984 Games in Los Angeles he won a bronze medal in men's individual sabre — still the only medal won by an American fencer in the last 36 years. In Barcelona he carried the U.S. flag in the Opening Ceremonies.

Besides Marsh's seventh-place finish in foil and Leslie Marx's 16th-place finish in epee, U.S. fencers had a difficult time in Atlanta's individual events. Eliminations in the round of 64 were common. In men's epee, however, all three American entrants made it into the round of 32, with James Carpenter finishing the highest, in 25th place. Aleksandr Beketov of Russia won the gold medal in that event, followed by Ivan Trevejo Perez of Cuba and Geza Imre of Hungary.

In men's individual sabre, Peter Cox Jr. finished highest among the Americans, in 28th place, while in men's individual foil, Cliff Bayer's 34th place was the highest U.S. finish. In sabre, Russia's Stanislav Pozdnyakov defeated teammate Sergey Sharikov for the gold medal and Damien Touya of France won the bronze medal. In foil, Italy's Alessandro Puccini won the gold while a pair of Frenchmen, Lionel Plumenail and Franck Boidin, took the silver and bronze, respectively. ▼

FIELD HOCKEY

Aussie women set the stage for Sydney

BY MARC WHITNEY

ALLSPORT / STU FORSTER

OPPOSITE (TOP) / The U.S. women fell to Great Britain, 1-0, in their third game of the tournament, unable to convert against the stalwart British defense. ALLSPORT / RICK STEWART

(BOTTOM LEFT) / All of five-feet, two-inches, Katrina Powell packed plenty of power in her swings. She was the leading scorer for Australia's gold-medal winning team. ALLSPORT / AL BELLO

(BOTTOM RIGHT) / Great Britain's Mandy Davies puts the pressure on the U.S., who finished in fifth place in the tournament, one place behind Great Britain. ALLSPORT / ROSS KINNAIRD

TEAMS FROM THE NETHERLANDS AND Australia enjoyed Southern hospitality, field hockey style, as they captured the men's and women's gold medals, respectively, in the field hockey tournament at the Centennial Games in Atlanta. In the men's gold-medal match, the Netherlands, behind a pair of goals from Floris-Jan Bovslander, defeated Spain 3-1, while in the women's title match, Australia's Alyson Annan scored twice in a 3-1 win over Korea. In a gender reversal, the Australia men's team and the women's team from the Netherlands finished with bronze medals.

Overall, the Australian women and Netherlands men managed to thoroughly dominate the tournament. Australia ran its unbeaten streak in international competition to 40 straight matches, dating back more than a year, with its two-goal win in the gold-medal match over the Koreans. During the Games, the Aussies went 7-0-1. The Dutch men finished 6-0-1 en route to their gold medal while runner-up Spain compiled a 5-2 record.

But if the medalists came from oceans away, it was the local women's team that attracted the biggest crowds and caused the most excitement. The United States women's team, which had practiced in residence in Atlanta for a year to get ready for the Games, routinely drew large crowds — including more than 14,000 to Morris Brown College stadium to watch a 2-0 win over Spain — and, in the tournament's second game, produced the most thrilling victory when it defeated the eventual silver medalists from Korea with a game-winning goal 10 seconds before the finish.

"The most exciting game of my career," team captain Barb Marois said of the Korea match, which was televised live throughout northern Georgia. It was Marois who scored from a penalty corner to give the U.S. its 3-2 win. Earlier, Tracey Fuchs and Marcia Pankratz had scored to give the Americans a 2-0 first-half lead. Korea, the second-ranked team in the world, roared back with two goals of its own after intermission, but then Marois put the Americans back on top for good.

The round robin wins over Korea and defending Olympic champion Spain showed that the Americans could play with anyone. Unfortunately, they were the only wins for the Americans in the tournament, and the resulting 2-3-2 record kept the "home" team from making it into the medal games. In a pair of one-goal losses to Great Britain and Argentina, it was a case of an offensive shortage. Still, the fifth-place finish by Team USA was its second-highest in Olympic history, exceeded only by the bronze-medal team from the Los Angeles Games of 1984.

The U.S. men's team didn't fare as well as the women in Atlanta, failing to get a win in seven games. It has been tough sledding, trying to get the men's program up to Olympic-level caliber.

The U.S. men did record some good wins in the months leading up to the Games, giving cause for optimism. But the glare of the Olympic spotlight seemed to reel them in. In the end, the losses tended to take away from the strong performance of 21-year-old Nick Butcher, the team's youngest member and leading scorer. Goalie Steve Wagner also had an excellent tournament. ▼

Vice President Al Gore and Tipper Gore, who FAXed personal messages of good luck to the players on White House stationery, made a special trip to Atlanta to watch the U.S. women's team.

GYMNASTICS

Vaulting to gold

BY LEE BENSON

ALLSPORT / SIMON BRUTY

OPPOSITE / *Standout Kerri Strug, who landed the team gold for the U.S. – the first ever for the women's gymnastics team – savors the moment with her teammates Amanda Borden, Dominique Dawes, Amy Chow, Jaycie Phelps, Dominique Moceanu, and Shannon Miller.* ALLSPORT / DOUG PENSINGER

SUCCEEDING PAGES / *Emotional rollercoaster: Few could have foreseen a sequence of events as dramatic as Kerri Strug's final vault – which clinched the team gold for the U.S. – and landing – which abruptly ended her Olympic competition.* ALLSPORT / MIKE POWELL

THAT WAS SOME ROLLER COASTER RIDE they took us on, the men and women gymnasts of America. Up one minute, down the next, then up again. It was like holding the remote and hitting quick-view between "Mission: Impossible" and "ER."

And as soon as it was over, there was an incredible urge to do it all again.

The United States has had more decorated Olympic quests and it has certainly crowned more individual champions, but when they finally rolled up the mats and packed away the rings and the bars in the Georgia Dome, no one was asking for their money back. Just seeing "The Vault" was in itself worth the price of admission.

"The Vault," of course, refers to Kerri Strug's moment of high drama, when, on the altar of the horse, she sacrificed her ankle for her team. In the 100-year history of the modern Olympic Games, few, if any, moments have featured a more complete blend of all the components that make the Games what they are. Here was suspense, intrigue, pain, exhilaration, selflessness, and skill — and a deadline — all symmetrically rolled into one.

It was a climax that rose up quickly, like a white squall. For most of the night the women's team from the United States was riding high and confident. The team title was at stake, and the Americans, in second place behind Russia after compulsories, quickly took charge in optionals. As more than 32,000 partisan fans warmed up their vocal chords, each superlative U.S. routine gave way to another.

As they moved from rotation to rotation, the team's superstars, appropriately enough, took turns leading the way. On the uneven parallel bars, 19-year-old

> **In the 100-year history of the modern Olympic Games, few, if any, moments have featured a more complete blend of all the components that make the Games what they are.**
> **That moment was, of course, Kerri Strug's vault.**

Dominique Dawes, the 1994 U.S. national champion, reeled off a routine with a degree of difficulty to make even the best of gymnasts blanch. By the time she was through successfully pulling off a "reverse Hecht" and a "Hindorff," she'd scored a 9.850, the team's best, and suddenly Team USA was in front of the Russians by nearly half-a-point and the Romanians by almost a full point.

The next stop was the balance beam, where it was 19-year-old Shannon Miller's turn to show off. It was Miller who came within twelve thousandths of a point of the individual all-around gold medal at the Olympic Games in Barcelona in 1992, a close call that kept her on the mats and gearing for Atlanta four years later. After a nearly flawless routine that included a full-twisting double back dismount, only a small hop on her landing that cost her a tenth of a point kept Miller from "10" territory. At that, she scored a team-high 9.862. Team America's lead over the Russians was extended further.

On floor exercise, 14-year-old Dominique Moceanu, a.k.a. "the next Nadia," made her presence felt. Moceanu's coach, Bela Karolyi, often said she reminded him of the great Nadia Comaneci, and on the floor, Dominique showed why. Performing to the Charlie Daniels Band ballad "Devil Went Down to Georgia," she sailed through a series of double saltos, full twists, and flic-flacs, finally ending with a flawless two-and-a-half twisting salto. Her score: 9.837. With just one event to go, the U.S. team was now up on the Russians by nearly a full point (.897).

As the Russians moved to the floor for their final rotation and the Americans

moved to the vault for theirs, everyone in the Georgia Dome knew it was all over but the bursting. But in gymnastics, where gravity is the supreme judge, disaster is never more than a misstep away. The Americans needed five solid scores — out of six competitors — to keep ahead of the Russians. Spectacular they could do without, but solid was still a requirement.

They got four solids from the first four vaulters — in order, a 9.662 from Jaycie Phelps, a 9.712 from Amy Chow, a 9.7 from Miller and from Dawes a 9.762.

They only needed one more.

This is where it got interesting.

Improbably, Moceanu, the next American to compete, fell backward on both of her landings. She probably hadn't done that since she was nine, but she did it now. Her highest score was a 9.2. Obviously, hers would be the non-counting score on vault. The U.S. would obviously use the highest of the two vaults upcoming from their anchor woman, Kerri Strug.

This seemed appropriate, too. For two days now, throughout the optionals and the compulsories, Strug had been the team's steadiest player. Now, she could make the difference while the whole world

$1996

watched; and as a nice bonus, virtually any score at all would qualify her into the all-around competition two days later. (A maximum of three gymnasts per team are eligible to move on to the all-around, and coming into the vault, Strug was America's No. 3, just in back of Miller and Dawes, and ahead of Moceanu).

Certainly Strug had some individual glory coming. She'd been a team player her entire career. Along with Miller and Dawes, as a 14-year-old in Barcelona she'd helped the U.S. women to their bronze medal there. Now, she could be the one to put the icing on an upgrade to gold.

But on her first vault Strug, too, slipped backward. Her score: 9.162. Not enough. Over on the floor, where the routines typically take longer, the Russians still had two routines to go and there was no telling what they might do. If they popped a couple of 9.95's, and the U.S. had to use a 9.2 vault, well, there went the .897 lead. They

needed Strug to stick her final vault. They needed at least a 9.5.

That wasn't the only problem. On her landing, Strug had rolled over on her left ankle and felt it snap. When she stood up she couldn't put her weight on her left foot. Tears came to her eyes. Instinctively, she knew she was in no condition to vault again. "Do I have to?" she asked her coach, Karolyi, standing beyond the boards.

His non-answer was an answer.

"You can do it!" he shouted back.

"One more vault!"

Strug had only seconds to make her way back to the top of the runway, then another 30 seconds once the flag was raised to complete her second vault. There was no time to have a conference on this; no chance for a TV timeout. Certainly there was no time to get out a calculator and add up all the possibilities and decide if it was

absolutely necessary. As her parents sat in the stands, an arena away, Strug knew this was her decision and her decision alone.

Once she'd made it, she did not hesitate.

She limped to the top of the runway, turned, and sprinted for all she was worth. She placed both hands on the horse and soared into her vault, a "Yurchenko 1 1/2 twist in the layout position" that she'd done at least a thousand times. Her turns through the air were clean and tight. She landed softly yet solidly, like an alley cat, looking over at the judges as if to say, "satisfied!"

Then, her duty done (and a 9.712 vault safely in the books), she lifted her left foot off the ground and screwed her face into a painful grimace.

If those 32,040 people hadn't been there, and if a hundred million or so hadn't been watching on television, she might have also said a choice word or two.

ABOVE AND OPPOSITE / *Shannon Miller, who won the silver in the uneven bars in Barcelona, finally garnered an individual gold in Atlanta. She capped her Olympic career with a stunning beam performance and then, along with the rest of America, had to watch competitor after competitor try to match her performance. None did and Miller won the gold that eluded her in Barcelona.* ALLSPORT / TONY DUFFY

ALLSPORT / SIMON BRUTY

Fifteen minutes later, when it was time for the medal ceremony, Karolyi carried Strug, her ankle already encased in a soft cast, into the arena. The ovation she got was deafening.

It would turn out later that they didn't need her vault after all. The final two Russians underachieved on the floor with scores of 9.725 and 9.5. Even if they had used Moceanu's 9.2 vault, America's "Magnificent Seven" (Dawes, Miller, Moceanu, Strug, Phelps, Chow and Amanda Borden) would have beaten the Russians by .309. It would also turn out later that Strug had two torn ligaments in her left ankle — torn them enough to keep her out of the all-around finals as well as two individual apparatus finals for which she'd qualified (floor exercise and, ironically, vault).

In hindsight, she could have skipped that second vault. Also in hindsight, she never would have.

SUCH A DRAMATIC TRIUMPH — THE first team gold medal ever in Olympic history for women's gymnastics — seemed to bode well for the American women as the competition moved to the individual all-around finals. Such did not prove to be the case, however, as each of the three U.S. finalists — Miller, Dawes and, as Strug's replacement, Moceanu had problems. Dawes was in first place when she fell on the floor exercise; Miller was in second place when she landed low on tumbling; and Moceanu's mistake on the beam kept her from getting anywhere near the medals in the first place. Miller wound up finishing eighth overall, Moceanu ninth and Dawes 18th. Taking the gold medal was Ukraine's Lilia Podkopayeva, while Gina Gogean of Romania won the silver, ahead of teammates Simona Amanar and Lavinia Milosovici, who tied for the bronze medal.

ON THE MEN'S SIDE, LI XIAOSHUANG of China became the first Olympic champion from that traditional gymnastics power as he captured the all-around gold medal, followed in the silver position by Alexei Nemov of Russia and, in the bronze position, the dominator of Barcelona himself, Vitaly Scherbo of Belarus. In Barcelona, Scherbo won gold in every event he touched, six of them in all. In Atlanta, his touch turned to bronze as he finished third in four events, adding bronze-medal apparatus finishes on horizontal bars, parallel bars and vault to his similar placing in the all-around.

In the men's team competition, Nemov led a strong Russian team that finished in first place more than a point ahead of the Chinese and more than five points ahead of the bronze medalists from Ukraine. Belarus finished fourth, followed by the United States in fifth. The American squad, consisting of Mihai Bagiu, Jair Lynch, John Macready, John Roethlisberger, Kip Simons, Chainey Umphrey, and Blaine Wilson, could at least take solace in the fact that in the old Cold War days — when first-place Russia, third-place Ukraine and fourth-place Belarus were all part of Team USSR — they would have won the bronze medal.

Five falls in optionals, including one each by Bagiu and Roethlisberger during aggressive pommel horse routines at the last rotation, effectively kept the men from getting into the medals. But, at that, a fifth-place finish was a considerable improvement for a team that finished ninth in the world championships in both 1994 and 1995.

In the individual all-around finals, both Roethlisberger and Wilson managed top 10 finishes — Roethlisberger seventh, Wilson 10th — while Macready placed 29th.

But just when it appeared the U.S. men were skidding into a no-medals Olympics, Lynch came to the rescue in the individual apparatus finals, winning silver on the parallel bars. The 24-year-old Lynch, a Stanford University graduate, came within twelve thousandths of a point of the gold,

ALLSPORT / DOUG PENSINGER

ALLSPORT / DOUG BRUTY

ALLSPORT / DOUG PENSINGER

ALLSPORT / JAMIE SQUIRE

his score of 9.825 just behind the 9.837 given to gold medalist Rustam Sharipov of Ukraine.

In a truly international display, other men's apparatus winners included Andreas Wecker of Germany on horizontal bars, Russia's Nemov in the vault, Yuri Chechi of Italy on rings, Donghua Li of Switzerland on the pommel horse, and Ioannis Melissanidis of Greece in floor exercise. Li, a Chinese native, emigrated to Switzerland in 1989 after marrying a Swiss gymnast; Chechi extended his unbeaten streak on the rings to four years; and Melissanidis made history by becoming the first Greek to win an Olympic gymnastics gold medal in a century. The only other Greek medal in men's gymnastics came in the first modern Games, held in Athens in 1896.

By adding bronze medals in floor exercise, pommel horse and horizontal bars to his silver medal in the all-around and his gold medals in vault and team competi-

tion, Russia's Nemov clearly emerged as the most decorated of Atlanta's gymnasts. China's Xiaoshuang, the all-around champ, wasn't as prominent in the individual competitions; he added a silver medal in floor exercise to go along with his all-around gold and his team silver.

BESIDES GIVING ALL-AROUND ACES Podkopayeva and Amanar a chance to further show off (the Russian and Romanian won on floor and vault, respectively), the women's apparatus finals also gave the U.S. women a final fling at Georgia Dome glory and redemption. On the first night, Amy Chow produced an uneven bars routine that her coach, Mary Young, termed "pretty close to the best she's ever done" and won a silver medal, in back of Russia's Svetlana Chorkina and in a tie with China's Bi Wenjiing. Then, on the final night of competition, first it was Dominique Dawes who shook off any demons remaining from her all-around disaster by nailing a solid floor routine and

ABOVE / *In what was perhaps the best peformance of her gymnastics career, American Amy Chow came out from the shadows and into the limelight to share the silver medal with Bi Wenjiing of China in the uneven bars.*
ALLSPORT / PASCAL RONDEAU

OPPOSITE / *Vitaly Scherbo, whose six golds were unparalled in Barcelona, had dreams of repeating his performance in Atlanta. Still a crowd favorite with a touching comeback story, the man from Belarus who lives in the United States took home four bronzes, but no gold.*
ALLSPORT / PASCAL RONDEAU

finishing with the bronze medal, in fast company right behind Podkopayeva and Amanar. After that it was Shannon Miller's turn. The two-time Olympic veteran went out in style by beating Podkopayeva for the gold medal on the balance beam. In the process, she ran her career medal haul to seven overall (two gold, two silver, three bronze), ranking her second all-time among all American women Olympians, trailing only swimmer Shirley Babashoff, who won eight.

THE BATTLE FOR THE RHYTHMIC gymnastics medals was an intra-country affair between Russia and Ukraine, with Ukraine getting the upper hand. Ukraine's Ekaterina Serebryanskaya prevailed for the gold medal while Russia's Ianina Batyrchina finished with the silver medal and Ukraine's Elena Vitrichenko finished with the bronze. Another Russian, Amina Zaripova, was fourth. Six of the top eight finishers represented countries from the former Soviet Union.

Jessica Davis, the lone American in the individual competition, did not make it out of the qualifying round and finished 30th. In the group competition, the six-member team of Aliane Baquerot, Mandy James, Kate Nelson, Brandi Siegel, Challen Sievers and Becky Turner, which had trained together in Downers Grove, Ill., finished ninth in the first-ever Olympic team event. ▼

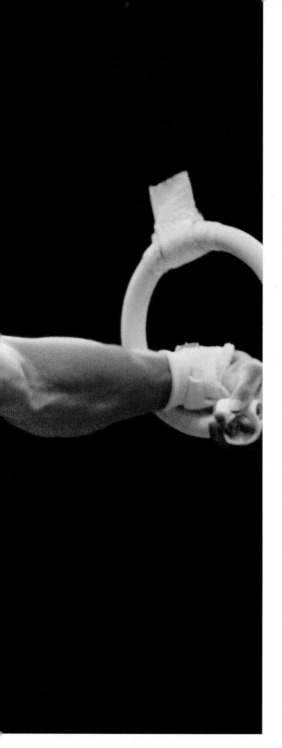

ABOVE / John Roethlisberger's seventh place in the all-around event was the U.S.'s best showing since 1984. ALLSPORT / DOUG PENSINGER

ABOVE (RIGHT) / Despite blisters affecting his grip, Jair Lynch was America's hands-on favorite to medal in the parallel bars. Competing last, Lynch came through with a clutch performance that bumped Vitaly Scherbo into third and gave Ukraine's Rustam Sharipov a good scare. ALLSPORT / DOUG PENSINGER

LEFT / *China's Li Xiaoshuang, back from Barcelona, became the first Chinese man to win the all-around title in a closely-battled competition; the spread between Li and silver medalist Alexi Nemov was a scant .049.* ALLSPORT / PASCAL RONDEAU

SUCCEEDING PAGES (LEFT) / *Years of training, and not a magic wand, allow rhythmic gymnasts like Romania's Alina Stoica to perform wondrous feats of flexibility.* ALLSPORT / PASCAL RONDEAU

(RIGHT) / *Ianina Batyrchina of Russia, the silver medalist in rhythmic gymnastics, stretched everyone's imagination with her performance.* ALLSPORT / PASCAL RONDEAU

JUDO

The gentle way of the warrior

BY DAVE SHATKOWSKI

ALLSPORT / SIMON BRUTY

OPPOSITE (TOP LEFT) / *While it seems Ryoko Tamura has the upper hand, Japan's darling and Barcelona's silver medalist was again defeated in the final, this time by People's Republic of Korea upstart Kye Sun-hi in the 106-pound class.* ALLSPORT / DOUG PENSINGER

(TOP RIGHT) / *Marissa Pedulla of Pittsburgh threw Venezuela's Kathy Santaella to score an ippon victory in her half lightweight match. She lost to eventual gold medalist Marie-Claire Restoux to finish seventh overall.* ALLSPORT / DOUG PENSINGER

(BOTTOM LEFT) / *One of three brothers on Japan's 1996 Olympic judo team, Yukimasa Nakamura claimed silver in the 143-pound class. Brother Kenzo (156 lbs) struck gold while brother Yukio (209 lbs) struck out.*
ALLSPORT / DOUG PENSINGER

(BOTTOM RIGHT) / *Thrown off-guard and for an ippon, Sebastian Pereira of Brazil lost his lead in the 156-pound bronze-medal match to American Jim Pedro (on top), who claimed the eighth Olympic medal in U.S. judo history.*
ALLSPORT / GARY M. PRIOR

JIM PEDRO DIDN'T COME TO ATLANTA just happy to be there. The national champion — a son of judo instructor and 1976 U.S. Olympic Team alternate James Pedro Sr. — had already taken that approach, as a 21-year-old first-time Olympian at Barcelona in 1992, and it just hadn't felt right when he came home without a medal to show for it.

"I knew coming in that this wasn't going to be the same," said Pedro, who began playing the sport at the age of six under his father's tutelage. "You dream your whole life about making the Olympics, and it seems like the end of the world if you don't win any medals."

So even though an early-round loss placed him in the repechage bracket in the lightweight division, Pedro determinedly clawed his way back, staging a magnificent display of judo prowess in the process. By soundly defeating three consecutive opponents, throwing two of them for match-winning ippons, he was able to make it into the bronze-medal match.

In the battle for that medal against Brazil's Sebastian Pereira, Pedro was not to be denied. He thrilled the capacity crowd at the Georgia World Congress Center when he recorded an ippon at the 3:38 mark.

Pedro's dream come true was also the eighth U.S. judo medal in Olympic history.

"I had a stellar day," Pedro, the holder of numerous international medals, would say later about his performance. "It was the best day of my life as far as judo goes. The bronze medal ... I'd been dreaming about gold all week, but I'm definitely happy with the bronze."

Though Pedro's bronze was the lone medal for the U.S. judo team, outstanding efforts were turned in by all 14 team members. Jason Morris, the half-middleweight who won a silver medal in Barcelona, became the first U.S. judo player to win a match in three consecutive Olympic Games.

Morris won his opening bout before bowing out to Turkey's Iralko Uznadze. When asked about his future in the sport, Morris, 29, was uncertain if he would continue. He admitted, however, that he would have to change his style if he decides to remain in competitive judo. "Technically," he said, "I'm still one of the top guys in the division. It's just that the new styles make it difficult for me. I can't just win with good judo anymore."

Other U.S. victories were recorded by Liliko Ogasawara, Marissa Pedulla, Hillary Wolf, Brian Olson and Orlando Fuentes. Rounding out the team were Sandra Bacher, Corrina West, Colleen Rosensteel, Celita Schultz, Rene Capo, Damon Keeve and Cliff Sunada.

Leaving no doubt that judo is truly a global sport, the 14 gold medals up for grabs in Atlanta were divided among eight nations. Japan and France led the way with three each, while South Korea and Belgium earned two apiece and Germany, Cuba, Poland and People's Republic of Korea had one each. A total of 17 countries were represented on the awards stand.

Upsets and surprises were the norm. For instance, defending Olympic men's heavyweight champion David Khakhaleichvili of Georgia was disqualified when he mistakenly went to the venue instead of the athlete's village for his pre-match weigh-in. Another defending champion, Hidehiko Yoshida of Japan, was thrown for ippon in his opening fight against Romania's Adrian Croitoru. One of the unexpected medalists was Marisabel Lomba of Belgium, who captured a bronze in women's middleweight.

Despite the international flavor on the medals stand, chants of "U-S-A, U-S-A" provided a constant reminder that these Games were on home turf. Never before had a judo crowd in America been as large and as vocal. Pedulla, who scored a second-round ippon in her half-lightweight division, summed up the feelings of all U.S. judo players about the appreciative fans.

"I had the support of the crowd," she said. "It made it so exciting. I'm happy the Olympics are in the United States and I had the opportunity to fight in front of that crowd." ▼

MODERN PENTATHLON

Crossed off the endangered list

BY MARGARET MARSHALL BROWN

ALLSPORT / DAVID LEAH

IN AN EFFORT TO KEEP THE FIVE-EVENT sport — originally introduced to the Olympics by Pierre de Coubertin, the founder of the modern Games — up to date, and, more importantly, away from the elimination list, the International Federation of the Modern Pentathlon and Biathlon streamlined the schedule for Atlanta. For the first time in Olympic history, all five events that make up the modern pentathlon — shooting, fencing, swimming, riding and running — were scheduled on the same day.

The competition began at 7 a.m. and ended more than 23 hours later as the competitors traveled by bus among three world-class venues — the Georgia World Congress Center, the Georgia Tech Aquatics Center and the Georgia International Horse Park. Prevailing for the gold medal was Aleksandr Parygin of Kazakhstan with a score of 5,551 points, barely 21 points ahead of second-place finisher Eduard Zenovka of Russia.

Parygin's victory wasn't secured until the last event, the 2.5-mile cross-country run, when he surged ahead of Zenovka after the Russian fell while sprinting down the final straightaway. Zenovka recovered to cross the finish line before medical personnel carried him away off the course.

Janos Martinek of Hungary took the bronze medal, 50 points behind the leader. Two-time world champion Dmitry Svatkovsky of Russia, the favorite, placed fourth.

Three-time Olympian Michael Gostigian of the United States finished 16th, precisely in the middle of the field of 32 finalists. He totaled 5,305 points.

Philipp Waeffler of Switzerland opened the competition by winning the shooting event. America's Gostigian finished 27th.

Fencing came next, with aggressive play marking the one-touch-bout format. Kazakhstan's Parygin won the competition ahead of Ukraine's Heorhiy Chymerys. Gostigian won 15 of his 31 bouts and improved his overall placing from 27th to 24th.

In the swimming competition, Kim Mi-sub of Korea and Vakhtang Yagorashvili of Georgia finished one-two and Gostigian wasn't far behind, in fourth, after covering the 300-meter distance in 3:16.38. Still on the climb, the American used his best event to move to 19th-place overall.

The successful swim boosted Gostigian's confidence as he went to the riding event in the late afternoon, where he drew a 10-year-old horse named "Warren" for his second-round ride. With a ride aboard Warren that was almost flawless, the 33-year-old Gostigian scored 1,043 points and continued to move up in the standings, to 15th overall.

He slipped one spot after the final event, the cross-country run, however, as he covered the course in 14:21.66, placing 16th.

Gostigian was disappointed with his overall performance, but pleased with the new format.

"The modern pentathlon is an ancient sport and it's a beautiful sport," he said. "Having it in one day is best because it offers more continuity for the spectators. We put on a great show today. The venues are world-class and the modern pentathlon is an Olympic event at its best."

"Our sport is going to be fine," Gostigian continued. "The modern pentathlon rightfully belongs in the Olympic movement and we proved it today. Baron de Coubertin would be proud of the event he created." ▼

> "The modern pentathlon rightfully belongs in the Olympic movement and we proved it today. Baron de Coubertin would be proud of the event he created."
>
> – Michael Gostigian

BELOW / *Three-time Olympian Michael Gostigian, the sole modern pentathlete for Team USA, assesses the competition in fencing, the second of five events in an all-day affair.* ALLSPORT / STU FORSTER

LEFT / *With the end in sight and leading the competition coming into the final event, the 4,000-meter cross country run, Russian Eduard Zenovka breaks away from Aleksandr Parygin, only to collapse moments later, giving the man from Kazakhstan a date with the gold. The exhausted Zenovka crept across the finish line to claim silver before he was carried away.* ALLSPORT / STU FORSTER

ROWING

Silver linings glitter on Lake Lanier

BY TERESE FRIEL

ALLSPORT / ROSS KINNAIRD

RIGHT / *The U.S. men's quad of Tim Young, Brian Jamieson, Eric Mueller and Jason Gailes rowed their way into the record books, earning a first-ever Olympic medal – the silver – at Lake Lanier.* JOEL ROGERS

WITH LAKE LANIER PROVIDING A spectacular setting, rowers from around the world came to Atlanta, where a record 606 athletes from 45 countries competed in 14 events and 139 races. Of the 42 medals awarded, Australia and Canada topped the country medal count, with six each, but the Aussies, with two, had the most gold.

It was a man from Great Britain, however, who made the most indelible impression. When England's Steven Redgrave earned his fourth gold medal in as many Olympic Games he joined a small club of just three other Olympians who managed the feat (American discus thrower Al Oerter, Danish yachtsman Paul Elvstrom and Hungarian fencer Aladar Gerevich; less than a week later, American long jumper Carl Lewis also added his name to the list). Redgrave and partner Matthew Pinsent held off an Australian boat to win the pair without coxswain. Other highlights from the lake:

■ Marnie McBean and Kathleen Heddle, two of Canada's double gold medalists from Barcelona, added another gold to their tally in double sculls and a bronze in women's quad — and they may have become the first rowers in history to win four Olympic medals in four different boats.

■ Three of the four "Awesome Foursome" from Australia's gold medal men's four from Barcelona returned to Olympic competition and repeated their performance.

■ In the single sculls, Switzerland's Xeno Muller, who was educated in the U.S., claimed the men's title and Yekaterina Khodotovich of Belarus pulled out a sprint to remember to win the women's title.

■ And in the always eagerly anticipated eights, the Dutch men and Romanian women wore the king's and queen's crowns. A few excited Netherlands fans even jumped into Lake Lanier after their men crossed the finish line. The Romanian women, twice world champions in 1990 and 1993 and bridesmaids in the past three

Games, centered themselves between the Canadians and Belarussians on the awards dock. The U.S. women's and men's eights finished fourth and fifth, respectively, after three straight years of trips to the world medal stage.

But if the eights were a disappointment for the Americans, in general, it was a good

week for the host nation, as:

■ Four medals were won overall, more than any non-boycotted Games since 1964.

■ Two medals were captured in the newly-added lightweight events.

■ In over half of the finals, American crews were represented.

■ No U.S. crew finished lower than 11th place.

■ And in men's quadruple sculls, America won a medal for the first time in history.

■ Ruth Davidon and Cyrus Beasley stepped into the mantle reserved for the single sculls and emerged with strong performances which unfortunately yielded no medals.

Indeed, the silver-medal finish by the quadruple sculls team of Jason Gailes, Eric Mueller, Brian Jamieson and Tim Young was all the more impressive because the

LEFT / *American women's pair Karen Kraft (left) and Missy Schwen, who went from national team alternates in 1994 to world championship silver medalists in 1995, missed the gold by a sliver to Megan Still and Kate Slatter of Australia, the defending world champions.* ALLSPORT / DAVID CANNON

BELOW / *Great Britain's Steven Redgrave, who won the coxless pairs with Matthew Pinsent, became the fourth Olympian and first rower to win gold medals in four consecutive Olympic Games.* ALLSPORT / DAVID CANNON

and Kate Slatter of Australia, 7:01.39 to 7:01.78. It was the smallest gap separating first and second place in all of Atlanta's rowing finals. Although in previous confrontations, Schwen and Kraft had a history of overtaking them with a strong kick, the Australians, defending world champions, grabbed an early lead and maintained it throughout the race. It was the first loss all week for the disappointed American pair. "We wanted gold and nothing less," said Kraft. "We didn't even have a seed of doubt that we wouldn't do it." ▼

LEFT / *Bill Carlucci, Marc Schneider, Jeff Pfaendtner and David Collins took the field by surprise and force when they turned in the fastest time in the semifinals in the lightweight men's four. The Americans won the bronze medal in the final behind Denmark and Canada.* ALLSPORT / JED JACOBSOHN

BELOW / *When the three-time defending champions from Canada didn't advance to the finals in the women's lightweight double sculls, they opened the door for another pair – Teresa Z. Bell (right) and Lindsay Burns – to contend for the gold. The Americans, overpowered by the Romanians, held on for second to win their first Olympic medal.* ALLSPORT / JED JACOBSOHN

U.S. team defeated, among others, the defending world championship team from Italy. Despite the fact no American quadruple sculls crew had ever won a medal in either the Olympic Games or the world championships, the U.S. crew rowed with medals on its mind. At the finish, the American boat was closing fast on the German boat crew that wound up winning gold with a strong wire-to-wire performance. What had been a 3.79 second Germany advantage was whittled to 2.17 seconds at the end, barely more than a boat length. Australia finished third to take the bronze medal. On the awards dock at Lake Lanier, Anita DeFrantz, a 1976 Olympic bronze-medal rower in the women's eight for the United States and now a member of the International Olympic Committee, bestowed the silver medals around the necks of the Americans.

The quadruple sculls medal came on the final day of the competition, capping an American effort that accounted for three silver medals and one bronze medal.

American rowing benefited especially from the addition of lightweight divisions,

introduced for the first time in Atlanta. In the lightweight women's double sculls, Lindsay Burns and Teresa Z. Bell rowed to a silver medal, and in lightweight men's four, which replaced men's four with coxswain, the team of Bill Carlucci, Marc Schneider, David Collins and Jeff Pfaendtner won a bronze medal. Burns and Bell, who vaulted out of the semifinals with the fastest time of the day, tracked a fast-starting Romanian crew the length of the course. They never caught up, but nobody caught the Americans either. Australia finished third. For the Burns-Bell team, it was a repeat of their second-place finish at the world championships in 1991.

Barely 10 minutes after Burns and Bell won their silver medal, the men's lightweight four team rowed to its surprising medal. In the year previous, at the 1995 world championships, the Americans had finished just seventh. Denmark won the Olympic gold medal.

In women's pair without coxswain, Missy Schwen and Karen Kraft missed gold by the narrowest of margins. They lost by less than four-tenths of a second to Megan Still

SHOOTING

Atlanta's shooting stars

BY NANCY MOORE

ALLSPORT / SIMON BRUTY

OPPOSITE (TOP) / *In the men's trap event, Australia's Michael Diamond (center) handily shot 149 out of 150 for the gold, but the silver-medal position was still up for grabs when U.S. teammates Josh Lakatos (left) and Lance Bade tied for second. Lakotos won the sudden-death shootout and the silver when Bade missed his 28th target.* ALLSPORT / RUSTY JARRETT

(BOTTOM) / *Forty-three-year-old Bill Meek shot 698.9 out of 709 points to finish eighth in the men's 50-meter prone rifle.* ALLSPORT / RUSTY JARRETT

LED BY ESTABLISHED CHAMPIONS SUCH as Germany's Christian Klees, who fired a perfect 600 in a prone rifle qualifying round, and Italy's Roberto Di Donna, whose air pistol gold medal came by a tenth of a point when China's Yifu Wang blinked and missed on his final shot, the shooting stars in Atlanta were an international cast.

But the brightest of the newcomers was an American teenager, 17-year-old Kim Rhode, who won the first-ever gold medal in women's double trap; and, as far as the crowd at the Wolf Creek shooting center was concerned, the most thrilling of all the competitions was between American trap-shooting buddies Josh Lakatos and Lance Bade.

After finishing the two-day, 125-target qualifying round and the 25-target final round tied at 147 targets each — behind Australia's Michael Diamond, who took the gold medal while setting an Olympic record with 149 hits — Lakatos and Bade squared off to decide who would get silver and who would get bronze. Throughout an on-and-off rain, the capacity crowd was on the edge of its chairs as Bade's methodical style provided a stark counterpoint to Lakatos' quick, first-barrel responses. Through 27 targets the American team-mates and friends matched strike for strike, but on No. 28 Bade finally missed and Lakatos ended the showdown with the winning shot.

"I think it showed how relaxed we are shooting against each other," said Bade. "We made a decision four or five years ago that we were going to train hard and make the Olympic team and we were going to do it together."

In all, U.S. shooters snagged three medals — one better than in Barcelona — as eight Americans made the finals in six of the 15 shooting events. All three U.S. medals came in shotgun, the best U.S. shotgun medal haul since 1920. Rhode, who shattered 141 targets on her way to the gold, was followed in women's double trap by teammate Terri DeWitt, who finished just four targets behind in fourth.

Rifle shooter Rob Harbison made the finals in both of his events. He finished sixth in men's three-position rifle after a shoot-off for fifth place with Slovakia's Joseph Gonci. Jean-Pierre Amat of France shot a 1,273.9 for the gold. Harbison also finished seventh in men's air rifle as Artem Khadzhibekov of Russia took the gold.

Seventh-place Elizabeth Bourland turned in the highest U.S. finish in women's three-position rifle. Yugoslavia's Aleksandra Ivosev claimed the gold. Bourland missed the women's air rifle finals by a single point as Poland's Renata Mauer overcame a three-point deficit to take the gold medal.

In men's prone rifle, U.S. shooter Bill Meek finished in eighth place after qualifying for the final with 597 hits out of 600.

Four more U.S. shooters were shut out of the finals by three points or less. In men's double trap, another new event for 1996, David Alcoriza finished the qualifier in a three-way tie for sixth place. He dropped his second bird in the tie-breaker shoot-off to place eighth. The gold and two Olympic records went to Australia's Russell Mark.

Bill Roy tied for ninth place in men's skeet but was only a point down from the sixth place cutoff for the final. Ennio Falco of Italy was golden at 149 targets. In women's sport pistol, two-time Olympian Connie Petracek fell two points short of the final while John McNally missed the rapid fire pistol final by three points. China's Duihong Li won in women's sport pistol while Germany's Ralf Schumann struck gold in rapid fire pistol.

Junior shooter Rebecca Snyder finished 32nd in women's air pistol as Russia's Olga Klochneva claimed the gold. Ben Amonette shot his way to 25th place in men's free pistol while Neal Caloia was 41st in men's free pistol. Russia took another gold with Boris Kokorev's free pistol score.

After only six months of training with new U.S. shooting coach Sergey Luzov, Adam Saathoff finished 20th in men's running target. ▼

SOCCER

USA's golden gooooal!

BY DOUG ROBINSON

ALLSPORT / DAVID CANNON

OPPOSITE / *Like the U.S. women's softball team in its Olympic debut, the women's soccer team dazzled the crowds, then joined in the hoopla after finishing off China, 2-1, in the gold-medal match.* ALLSPORT / DAVID CANNON

F OR YEARS, THE BEST KEPT SECRET IN the United States has been its football team, which was hard to understand because a) all they had done was win a world championship and b) they were women. You don't see that everyday. Then again, it wasn't that kind of football. What the world calls football, America calls soccer, but maybe not everyone was clear on that point judging from the scene in football-crazy Georgia.

It sure looked like the other kind of football. Lines of cars stretched for miles down Highway 316, their windows covered with soap-scrawled go-team graffiti and filled with faces painted the colors of their favorite team. Nearly 80,000 people packed Sanford Stadium in Athens and watched a game that featured ball control,

Hamm, a former middle school quarterback, so frustrated her opponents with her quick dashes through the defense that opponents resorted to tripping and tackling her.

a strong running attack and stingy defense. In the end, the star player was carried off the field on a stretcher, but the home team prevailed anyway.

By then, the U.S. team was a secret no longer. Americans finally knew what the rest of the world already knew: Mia Hamm, Michelle Akers, Shannon MacMillan, Julie Foudy, Kristine Lilly, Carla Overbeck, Joy Fawcett, etc., are the best football team in the world.

Some 76,481 fans showed up for the final — the largest crowd ever to see a women's soccer game anywhere — as the U.S. defeated China, 2-1, to capture the gold medal, touching off victory laps, standing ovations, flag waving, hugging and a little streaking (goalie Briana Scurry later lived up to a pre-game promise and ran naked down an Athens street).

For the record, the Americans are 92-16-5 in the 1990s, and 64-5-4 since early 1993. They came to the Olympics as co-favorites with archrival Norway. They beat Norway, 2-1, to win the 1991 World Championship and lost to Norway, 1-0, en route to a third-place finish in the '95 World Championship.

In the Olympic Games, the U.S. had to survive a series of close games and injuries to their two star players. Hamm had a sprained ankle that forced her to miss one game and finally gave out at the end of the finale when she was carried off the field on a stretcher. It was bound to happen. Hamm, a former middle school quarterback, so frustrated her opponents with her quick dashes through the defense that opponents resorted to tripping and tackling her.

Then there was Akers, who played five games in 12 days despite having her knee drained five times and coping with the Epstein-Barr virus she has struggled with for three years.

The Americans began their Olympic stand with a 3-0 victory over Denmark and a 2-1 defeat of Sweden to clinch a berth in the semifinals.

The American men weren't so fortunate. For the 11th consecutive time, they failed to survive the first round, losing to powerful Argentina, beating Tunisia and tying Portugal (Nigeria upset Argentina in the final to win the gold).

Meanwhile, the U.S. women played China to a scoreless tie in their final first-round game. Hamm, who sprained her left ankle in the previous game, didn't play.

Both China and the U.S. advanced to the semifinals with identical 2-0-1 records, but China was awarded first place because it had scored two more goals than the U.S. in its three games. That meant the U.S. had to play Norway — the winner of the other group — in the semifinals; the meeting between rival soccer superpowers would not be in the finals.

Their Olympic showdown was as good as it was billed, and by the end of regulation the score was 1-1. Enter Shannon

ABOVE / *Wang Liping and Tisha Venturini battle for the ball and the gold medal in the showdown game between China and the U.S. Final score: USA 2, China 1.* ALLSPORT / DAVID CANNON

MacMillan in overtime to save the day for the U.S., although a more unlikely heroine couldn't have been found. MacMillan was originally cut from the team the previous December when the roster was trimmed to 25 players. But when a dozen players went on strike to protest their bonus payment structure, Coach Tony DiCicco needed players for the Brazil Cup and called MacMillan back. She played so well that she was retained even when the striking players returned. When the roster was cut to 16 players for the Olympics, she was still on the team.

MacMillan started the entire Olympic tournament until the semifinal. DiCicco benched her in favor of a stronger defensive lineup against Norway. During the game he told her to warm up on several occasions, but then changed his mind and told her to return to the bench. Six minutes into overtime, he sent her into the game. Three minutes after entering the game, touching the ball for only the second time all day, she gathered in a pass from Foudy, dribbled once and kicked the ball from 20 yards out into the net.

"Obviously, it was a great coaching move," joked DiCicco of subbing MacMillan.

The victory set up a rematch between the U.S. and China, which beat Brazil, 3-2, in the other semifinal game. Once again, the score was tied 1-1 late in the game, thanks to another goal by MacMillan, which she scored when a shot by Hamm ricocheted off the post.

In the 68th minute, Hamm and Fawcett teamed on a give-and-go to set up the winning shot. Fawcett intercepted a pass and raced down right sideline and then passed to Hamm at midfield. Fawcett kept running and Hamm sent the ball back to her. Fawcett drew one defender to her, then sent a crossing pass past a diving goalkeeper to Tiffeny Milbrett, who had arrived at the far post for an easy shot. That was enough to give the U.S. the first Olympic gold medal in women's football.

"Oh, my gosh, it's the best feeling in the world," said MacMillan. ▼

ABOVE / *In the last tangle with Norway, the U.S. lost and finished third in the '95 World Championship. In Atlanta, the tables turned when the U.S. beat Norway, 2-1, in the semifinals, relegating Norway to the bronze-medal match.* ALLSPORT / DAVID CANNON

ABOVE / *Kristine Lilly of the U.S. puts the pressure on Malin Andersson of Sweden. The United States' 2-1 win over Sweden clinched a berth in the semifinals.* ALLSPORT / STEPHEN DUNN

OPPOSITE (TOP AND BOTTOM RIGHT) / *It was tough going for the perennial favorites, Brazil and Argentina, as Nigeria tipped the axis of power. Nigeria squeezed past Brazil in the semifinals, relegating the Brazilians to a bronze-medal consolation prize and then went on to spoil the party for another tournament favorite, Argentina, to win the gold medal.* ALLSPORT / DAVID CANNON

(BOTTOM LEFT) / *Despite a goal scored by Claudio Reyna in the first 30 seconds of the game, gold-medal contender Argentina controlled the midfield and beat the Americans, 3-1, in the opening game of the Olympic tournament.* ALLSPORT / MARTIN VENEGAS

SOFTBALL

Historic homer delivers gold to USA

BY RONALD A. BABB

ALLSPORT / RUSTY JARRETT

OPPOSITE (TOP) / *The end of a long journey: Team USA celebrates its gold-medal win over China, 3-1, to earn the first Olympic softball gold medal in history.* ALLSPORT / MIKE HEWITT

(BOTTOM LEFT) / *The U.S. faced its toughest loss in the round-robin game against Australia. The 2-1 setback was only the USA's second international loss in more than 100 games. Australia finished the tournament with the bronze.* ALLSPORT / JED JACOBSOHN

(BOTTOM RIGHT) / *Thirty-five-year-old Dot Richardson, USA's team captain and short-stop, put her medical career on temporary hold to live her Olympic dream.* ALLSPORT / JEB JACOBSOHN

IT WAS THE SHOT HEARD 'ROUND THE softball world. In the bottom of the third inning, Laura Berg was on base. Her gaze focused intently on American teammate Dot Richardson who was bouncing and stretching before stepping into the box to take her swings against Chinese pitcher Liu Yaji.

And then it came, a jolting right field rope that sent right fielder Wei Qiang scurrying to the fence in time to witness the ball slicing past her as it completed its destination into the stands and into history.

Berg and Richardson rounded the bases as a deafening chorus of "U-S-A, U-S-A" resonated from a raucous crowd of supporters who had waited hours, days and, for some, decades to live this moment.

With arms raised in triumph they crossed the plate. Berg first, then Richardson. They were greeted by a swarming host of teammates, sensing that their dreams were about to be realized.

The Chinese never recovered from that home run. On the strength of its three third-inning runs, the USA went on to win, 3-1, in what could arguably be called the most important softball game in history. In so doing, it permanently etched its name as the first to ever earn an Olympic gold medal.

The win punctuated the sport's triumphant run to Olympic recognition. For softball the road to the Games spanned more than 29 years, from 1965 to its debut in the 1996 Centennial Olympic Games.

Despite three consecutive world championship titles and an international record of 110-1 over the past decade, the USA understood going in that the Olympics would be no walkover. They understood right. After a pair of lopsided opening wins — 10-0 over Puerto Rico and 9-0 over the Netherlands — no margin of victory would be more than four runs. En route to the semifinals, the U.S. defeated Japan, 4-1, Chinese Taipei, 4-0, Canada, 4-2, lost to Australia, 1-0, in extra innings, and beat China, 3-2.

The loss to the Aussies had more than its share of drama, controversy, and outright weirdness. U.S. pitcher Lisa Fernandez threw a perfect game through nine straight innings. That would have been enough if a home run by USA teammate Dani Tyler had counted. But it hadn't counted because Tyler failed to stop on home plate. In the 10th inning, Joanne Brown hit a home run for Australia to give the Aussies the win.

In the semifinals, the U.S. met China again, and didn't prevail until Sheila Cornell hit a game-winning single in the bottom of the 10th inning for a 1-0 win. That sent the Americans into the gold-medal game, against whoever survived a loser's (and bronze medal) bracket game between China and Australia.

It turned out to be the Chinese, setting up the stage for a third USA-China game in four days ... and for Richardson's curling, historic, home run.

Capacity audiences at each contest created an electric atmosphere at Golden Park in Columbus, Ga., site of all the Olympic games. By the medal rounds, softball had become one of the hottest tickets at the Games, with demand far exceeding supply on the street outside the stadium. The Olympics unquestionably marshaled in a new era for the sport of softball. "It was like we stepped through a doorway from the past into the future," said USA pitcher Michele Smith.

And the future for the sport of softball has never looked better. ▼

> **After a three-decade struggle to get fastpitch women's softball in the Olympics, the Atlanta Games had a hit: softball and the USA team were the hottest tickets in town.**

SWIMMING

Breathtaking success in pool

BY LEE BENSON

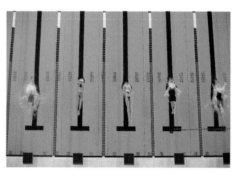

ALLSPORT / EDWARD PIO RODA

OPPOSITE / *For the record – and in order – Amy Van Dyken's week in the Olympic pool that brought her four golds came in the 4x100-meter freestyle relay, where she swam the second leg; the 100-meter butterfly, in which she won in a time of 59.13; the 4x100-meter medley relay, in which she swam the final, freestyle leg; and the 50-meter freestyle, where she edged China's Le Jingyi with a time of 24.87.* ALLSPORT / SIMON BRUTY

L ED AND INSPIRED BY A PAIR OF ASTH-matics, United States swimming took a deep breath after the water had settled at the Georgia Tech Aquatic Center. It turned out that the rumors of its demise were not well anchored after all. Instead of descending into Olympic mediocrity, as many experts had predicted, the U.S. led all countries in Atlanta with a total of 26 swimming medals, including 13 gold, 11 silver, and two bronze. No other nation won even half as many. Indeed, the U.S. team exceeded both its gold and silver medal efforts in Barcelona, when it won 11 gold, nine silver and seven bronze medals.

The stage was set early when Tom Dolan, an asthmatic since boyhood, won the men's 400-meter individual medley over his old Club Wolverine training rival, Eric Namesnik, on the second day of the competition. It was America's first gold medal. Its 13th and final gold came five days later, on the last day of competition, when Amy Van Dyken, who'd had asthma since birth and sometimes had trouble breathing after races, defeated China's Le Jingyi, the world record-holder, in the women's 50-meter freestyle final. It was Van Dyken's fourth gold medal in Atlanta, making her the most decorated U.S. woman gold medalist in any sport in a single Olympic Games.

In between Dolan's medley gold and Van Dyken's 50-meter freestyle gold, Americans beat a steady path to the top step of the medal peristyle. Van Dyken added her second individual gold medal in the women's 100-meter butterfly, while 16-year-old Brooke Bennett took over the mantle from Janet Evans in the women's 800-meter freestyle, 15-year-old Beth Botsford edged her mentor Whitney Hedgepeth in the women's 100-meter backstroke, Brad Bridgewater won the men's 200-meter backstroke, and Jeff Rouse won the men's 100-meter backstroke. Beyond that, the United States won every relay contested, six of them in all, women's and men's — a run that was capped on the final day by a world-record performance in the men's 400-meter medley relay.

And that's to say nothing of 14-year-old

Amanda Beard's near-golden efforts in both the women's 100- and 200-meter-breaststroke races — behind South Africa's vaunted Penelope Heyns; or of Allison Wagner's silver-medal finish in the women's 400-meter individual medley, behind the surprising Irish ironwoman, Michelle Smith; or of Gary Hall Jr.'s close calls in both the 50- and 100-meter men's freestyle races, behind Russia's great Alexander Popov, the reigning Olympic sprint champion; or of Tom Malchow's gallant effort in the 200-meter butterfly behind Russia's Denis Pankratov, the world record-holder; or of Jeremy Linn's American record and silver medal in the 100-meter breaststroke; or of 29-year-old Angel Martino's two gold relay medals and two bronze medals in the 100-meter freestyle and 100-meter butterfly, bringing her total Olympic haul to a nicely balanced three golds and three bronzes in two Games' appearances. Not only did Martino, at 29, become the oldest U.S. female swimming medalist ever, but her six Olympic medals tied her with 1996 teammate Jenny Thompson, a triple relay gold medalist, for second place in most career U.S. women's Olympic swimming medals — behind only Shirley Babashoff, who had eight.

It was Dolan who got the wave rolling. The 20-year-old with a well-documented history of health problems became the first American in any sport to win a gold medal in Atlanta when he edged Namesnik in the 400-meter individual medley final on Day Two of the Games. Dolan was introduced to irony early in life when his doctor explained to him that he had "exercise-induced asthma." The very things he loved to do — swim and compete — were the very things that were making it difficult to breathe.

A lot of people might have gotten out of the pool then and there. Not Dolan. Also afflicted with a variety of allergies and a restricted windpipe, he decided to turn the problem in a cure. His doctor customized his inhaler — by "watering it down" enough so it would qualify under allowable medication — and Dolan dove back in the

ABOVE AND TOP / *Beth Botsford (left) and Whitney Hedgepeth finished 1-2 in the women's 100-meter backstroke. The 15-year-old Botsford exclaimed, "We wanted to do what the guys did last night," referring to the 1-2 finish of Tom Dolan and Eric Namesnik in the 400-meter individual medley.* ALLSPORT / DAVID CANNON

… Four days later, the U.S. men produced another 1-2 finish when Brad Bridgewater (right) and Tripp Schwenk won gold and silver in the men's 200-meter backstroke. ALLSPORT / AL BELLO

water, determined that fitness would overcome.

He and Namesnik's one-two finish set the stage for the men's 800-meter freestyle relay later that same day, as Josh Davis, Joe Hudepohl, Brad Schumacher and Ryan Berube finished more than three seconds ahead of second-place Sweden. Also a gold medalist in Barcelona, where he was part of the winning U.S. freestyle relay team at 400 meters, Hudepohl made it two golds in two Games, while Schumacher and Davis warmed up for yet more gold later on in the 400-meter freestyle relay.

That same day, the 14-day-old Beard nearly equaled Dolan's individual gold. Closing with a furious kick in the 100-meter breaststroke, she almost caught South Africa's Heyns, the reigning world record-holder. Beard settled for a silver

the distinction as youngest individual gold medalist, albeit briefly. Two day's earlier, when she won the 100-meter backstroke in front of Hedgepeth, it was Botsford — all of 15 years, two months and one day — who was "youngest" as she edged Hedgepeth, a former sixth-grade teacher who un-retired from competition to come to Atlanta, by barely more than a quarter of a second.

Botsford and Hedgepeth's strong one-two performance set the stage for the U.S. women's 400-meter freestyle relay team, who later that day held off China and Germany to win gold. The team consisted of Van Dyken, Martino, Catherine Fox and the ever-present Thompson, who swam the anchor leg. Later on, Thompson would team with three more U.S. teammates — Trina Jackson, Cristina Teuscher

medal and a new American record of 1:08.09. Heyns, who became South Africa's first gold medalist since the Helsinki Games of 1952, won in 1:07.73, barely off her own world-record time of 1:07.46.

Two days later, in the 200-meter breaststroke, it was once again Heyns-Beard in a one-two finish, with Heyns needing an Olympic record time of 2:25.41 to hold off the fast-closing Beard, who finished in 2:25.75. The effervescent Beard gave Heyns a huge hug after the race and a day later was getting a gold medal hug herself, after teaming with a bunch of older women — the 15-year-old Botsford, the 23-year-old Van Dyken and the 29-year-old Martino — to win the women's 400-meter medley relay. At 14 years, eight months and 27 days, Beard became one of the youngest American female swimmers ever to win a gold medal (in 1964, Lillian "Pokey" Watson, at 14 years, 96 days, won a gold medal as a member of the winning 400-meter freestyle relay team).

Until Beard's triumph, Botsford had held

and Sheila Taormina — to win the women's 800-meter freestyle relay. Along with the gold she won for swimming in the preliminary portion of the women's medley relay, that gave the 23-year-old Stanford graduate three relay golds in Atlanta to go along with the two relay golds and the relay silver she'd won four years earlier in Barcelona. Not only did her six overall medals make her, along with Martino, the second-most decorated U.S. woman Olympian in history, but her five gold medals tied her with speed skater Bonnie Blair for most golds of all-time for any U.S. female Olympian.

It all made for a surprising and unexpected fast start for the U.S. women, who were supposed to struggle to win more than one gold medal in Atlanta. Going in, their best hopes were thought to be with distance specialist Brooke Bennett of Plant City, Fla., who the summer before, as a precocious 15-year-old, had ended Janet Evans' eight-year winning streak in the 800-meter freestyle at the Summer Nationals. As it turned out, by the time Bennett — and

ABOVE / *Jeff Rouse won the 100-meter backstroke race, giving the U.S. gold-medal finishes in both backstroke races.* ALLSPORT / DAVID CANNON

PAGE 137 (CLOCKWISE) / *Russia's great Alexander Popov laid claim to being the world's fastest human ... in water, that is.* ALLSPORT / TONY DUFFY

In the morning heats, Fred DeBurghgraeve of Belgium set a world record in the 100-meter breaststroke and capped the evening with the gold medal. ALLSPORT / MIKE HEWITT

Twenty-one-year-old Krisztina Egerszegi of Hungary was back for more gold, winning the same event – the 200-meter backstroke – in three consecutive Olympic Games. ALLSPORT / MIKE HEWITT

South Africa's Penelope Heyns burst on the Olympic scene with a sweep of the breaststroke events. ALLSPORT / SIMON BRUTY

Australia's Kieren Perkins was unmatched in the pool, where he defended his Barcelona title in the 1500 meters. ALLSPORT / DAVID CANNON

Susan O'Neill, gold medalist in the 200-meter butterfly, was a classic reflection of Australia's growing prominence in swimming. ALLSPORT / SIMON BRUTY

ABOVE / *Amanda Beard, all of 14, belied her age by taking home two silvers, one gold, oh, and her teddy bear.* ALLSPORT / AL BELLO

BELOW / *Critics tried to put a tarnish on Michelle Smith's three golds, but the Irish swimmer kept her poise in and out of the pool.* ALLSPORT / DAVID CANNON

Evans — lined up for the 800 final on Day Six of the Games, American women had already won three gold medals and, in general, were regulars on the victory stand. Bennett quickly made it four golds as she lived up to expectations and handily won the 800, finishing a second and a half ahead of Dagmar Hase of Germany and more than two seconds ahead of Kirsten Vlieghuis of the Netherlands. Evans, the only woman to win the 800 in back-to-back Olympics (Seoul-Barcelona) and generally regarded as the greatest-ever female distance swimmer, finished in sixth place, leaving her Olympic legacy at four gold medals and one silver.

While America's women were thriving in the waters at Atlanta, the same could not be said of the Chinese women. In three of Van Dyken's four wins, for example, she place in front of Chinese swimmers – yet another telling turn of events for a nation that had dominated the competition at the short course World Championships in Mallorca in 1993 and again at the World Championships in Rome in 1994. In Mallorca, Chinese women won 10 of 15 events with nine world records. In Rome, they won 12 gold medals in 16 finals, adding another five world records.

It was just a month after the World Championships, however, that three of China's top women tested positive for performance-enhancing drugs, resulting in a ban on Chinese swimmers at the 1995 Pan Pacifics.

In Atlanta, China's Le Jingyi, the world record-holder at both 50 and 100 meters, started out fast, winning the 100-meter freestyle gold medal on opening day, well ahead of Martino, who was third, and Van Dyken, who was fourth. But the Chinese women would experience few highlights thereafter. And when Van Dyken got another chance at Le, in the 50-meter freestyle, she reeled her in down the stretch, winning in a U.S. record 24.87

seconds compared to Le's 24.90.

Among the U.S. men, if Dolan's win represented a victory over the physical, the individual triumphs by backstrokers Jeff Rouse and Brad Bridgewater represented victories over the mental. With his win at 100 meters, Rouse effectively lost the runner-up tag he'd carried after failing to win gold medals in either the 1992 Barcelona Games or the 1994 World Championships. In both those races, Rouse was the heavy favorite. In both, he took second. But those second-place finishes, "put my life in perspective," he said. When he finally won the race he'd been expected to win for four long years, one of the first people to congratulate him was Mark Tewksbury, the Canadian swimmer who beat him by six-hundredths of a second in Barcelona. Now retired and a broadcaster for a Canadian television station, Tewksbury interviewed

Rouse immediately after the race. "I thanked him for beating me," Rouse said. "I wouldn't be here without him beating me. That experience taught me a lot about myself. It made me what I am today."

As for the 23-year-old Bridgewater, his was a potential unfulfilled. Prior to Atlanta, he'd shown great promise as a swimmer, but few results. The Dallas, Texas, native first went to the University of Texas on a swimming scholarship, but flunked out. As a participant at the '94 Worlds he failed to even make the final.

But with the '96 Games looming as a goal, Bridgewater made up enough credits to get into the University of Southern California, where he eventually became eligible to swim for the Trojans. In the Olympic final he edged his good friend and teammate, Tripp Schwenk, also a 1992 Olympian, who grabbed the silver medal.

Rouse added to his gold-medal collection in the 400-meter men's medley relay, where he teamed with Jeremy Linn, Mark Henderson and Hall to not only win the race but set a world record. In doing so, the American men upheld a longstanding Olympic tradition. In every Games since the medley relay was introduced in 1960, the United States has either set or tied the world record in the event.

In lowering that world mark to 3:34.84, Rouse, the backstroker, went out first, followed by Linn, who produced the fastest breaststroke leg in history. Then came Henderson, a butterfly specialist, and finally, Hall — whose father, Gary Sr., was a three-time Olympian and carried the flag in the Opening Ceremonies in the 1976 Games — dove in the water, keeping Russia's Popov at bay on the anchor freestyle leg. The second-place Russians

OPPOSITE / *An unobstructed view, or breath, is a luxury for asthma sufferer Tom Dolan, gold medalist and world record-holder in the 400-meter individual medley.* ALLSPORT / SIMON BRUTY

RIGHT / *Nineteen-year-old Tom Malchow finished second in the 200-meter butterfly, chasing world record-holder Denis Pankratov of Russia down to the wire.* ALLSPORT / SIMON BRUTY

LEFT / *Erik Namesnik, Barcelona's silver medalist in the 400-meter IM, wasn't able to escape the shadow of Tom Dolan in Atlanta. The 26-year-old ended his swimming career with another silver-medal finish.* ALLSPORT / AL BELLO

RIGHT / *Allison Wagner won the silver in the 400-meter individual medley race, a race dominated by Michelle Smith of Ireland.* ALLSPORT / AL BELLO

were nearly three seconds slower than the Americans.

In both the medley and freestyle relays, Hall exacted at least a measure of revenge on his nemesis, Popov, after losing to the Russian in both individual freestyle sprints, duplicating identical results from the 1994 World Championships. In the freestyle relay, Hall's anchor split of 47.45 eclipsed Matt Biondi's 47.66 split in 1985 as the fastest in history.

In winning the 100-meter individual freestyle — by seven-hundredths of a second over Hall — Popov became the first man to repeat in that signature Olympic event since American Johnny Weissmuller managed the double in 1924 and 1928.

Popov's equally famous teammate, Pankratov, was also at his best individually as he dominated both individual butterfly events, becoming the first man to win both fly events since Mark Spitz in 1972. The noted practitioner of the dolphin kick shaved five-hundredths of a second off his own world record in winning the 100. Scott Miller of Australia came close to world-record time himself in the 100, finishing a close second, 52.27 to 52.53.

Two more Australians, Kieren Perkins and Daniel Kowalski, finished one-two in the men's 1500-meter freestyle final. That made it two golds in a row for Perkins at 1500 meters. In Barcelona in 1992 he set a world record of 14:43.48, a mark he lowered to 14:41.66 two years later. He was well off that pace in Atlanta, with a 14:56.40 clocking, but still won by more than six seconds over his countrymate.

The first world record of the Atlanta Games came early in the competition, when a Belgian with a short first name and a long second name — Fred Deburghgraeve — broke a three-year-old mark in the 100-meter breaststroke during a qualifying race the first morning of the competition. The Belgian swimmer's time of 1:00.60 bettered a mark of 1:00.95 set in 1993 by Hungary's Karoly Guttler. In the finals that evening, as he towed Linn to his American record, Deburghgraeve bettered Guttler's mark yet again, but not his own,

as he swam 1:00.65 to win the gold medal. It was quite a reversal for Deburghgraeve, a homespun swimmer coached by his father in a backyard pool. In the 1992 Olympic Games in Barcelona he finished 34th in the same event after slipping off the starting block. The disappointment and embarrassment he felt kept him out of swimming for a year, but then he got back in the pool and, as a result, gave Belgium its first-ever swimming gold medal.

Among other record performances in Atlanta, Hungary's Krisztina Egerszegi earned her third straight triumph in the 200-meter backstroke, tying Australian swimmer Dawn Fraser's record of winning the same individual event at three consecutive Olympic Games. Like Evans, Egerszegi bounded on the Olympic stage as a teenager in Seoul in 1988 at age 14.

Atlanta's most decorated individual swimmer was Michelle Smith of Ireland, who won three gold medals — in the 400-meter individual medley, the 400-meter freestyle, and the 200-meter individual medley — and a bronze medal in the 200-meter butterfly, where goggle problems slowed her down. No woman had so dominated the Games since Kristin Otto of East Germany won four individual golds in 1988. Smith came close to that kind of domination. Her triumphs were diluted, although hardly denied, by the number of eyebrows raised about a woman whose times in all events except the 400-freestyle weren't ranked in the top 20 in the world coming into the Games. Such rapid improvement by a 26-year-old brought on the usual suspicions of performance-enhancing drugs, but Smith categorically denied any such involvement. "No, I have never used performance-enhancing drugs," she said when a reporter asked her the question point-blank. "Every time I'm tested, it's always negative and I can assure you, I've been tested again and again." ▼

LEFT / *Angel Martino capped her bronze-medal swim in the pool with a gold-medal performance on deck. She gave her medal to her friend Trisha Henry, diagnosed with cancer, saying, 'She's the hero.'* ALLSPORT / MIKE HEWITT

ABOVE / *Awesome foursome – Angel Martino, Catherine Fox, Amy Van Dyken and Jenny Thompson – show their mettle ... gold!* ALLSPORT / MIKE HEWITT

USA's world-record medley relay team. ALLSPORT / DAVID CANNON

Advantage USA ... 4x100 medley relay race. ALLSPORT / NATHAN BILOW

RIGHT / *Josh Davis, Joe Hudepohl, Ryan Berube and Bradley Schumacher got that gold-medal glow.* ALLSPORT / AL BELLO

SYNCHRONIZED SWIMMING

USA perfectly in sync for the gold medal

BY LAURA LAMARCA

ALLSPORT / DAVID LEAH

OPPOSITE / *An exuberant Team USA waved to the crowd after earning the top score in the technical program that put them in perfect position to capture the gold three days later.*
ALLSPORT / EDWARD PIO RODA

THE U.S. OLYMPIC SYNCHRONIZED swimming team called itself "A Team With a Dream" with just one dream in mind — to win the Olympic gold medal.

The 1996 Olympics marked a new era for synchronized swimming. Gone were the solo and duet events that introduced the sport in the Games in 1984. Appearing for the first time was the team competition, featuring eight swimmers in the water.

For a number of very good reasons, high expectations rested on Team USA heading into the Games. It was a team that had gone undefeated in the last quadrennium and had been ranked No. 1 in the world since 1991. Also, the team was coming off a perfect performance of straight 10 scores at the 1995 Olympic qualifying event, a competition that sent the top eight countries on to Atlanta.

In the technical program — the opening phase of the competition that requires teams to perform a series of required elements in a prescribed order — Team USA had a near flawless swim while performing to music from "When the Saints Go Marching In" and the "Hallelujah Chorus." The U.S. earned a score of 99.200, including two 10's in technical merit and one 10 in artistic impression. Canada, which had a few small execution errors, scored 97.933 and Japan was a close third at 97.667.

Swimming in the technical routine for the U.S. were Tammy Cleland, Becky Dyroen-Lancer, Heather Pease, Emily LeSueur, Jill Savery, Nathalie Schneyder, Jill Sudduth and Margot Thien. For the free routine, LeSueur and Thien were replaced by Suzannah Bianco and Heather Simmons-Carrasco.

Of the top three countries, Japan swam first in the free routine. Its routine exhibited traditional artistic flair and expression in a most unusual portrayal of the "Four Seasons," scoring 97.800. Canada, swimming next, demonstrated precision and energy to an original arrangement of its national anthem, "Oh Canada!," and totaled 98.600.

Swimming last, the USA's "Fantasia on an Orchestra" captivated the crowd and the judges. From the sound of the orchestra warming up to the final whole note, the team members were in perfect control, executing lifts and intricate precision moves with power and perfection. The routine was brought to an exciting climax as two swimmers were catapulted through the air while executing parallel back layout somersaults immediately followed by a third swimmer who was standing on the shoulders of another being lifted and spun high above the water surface.

> **The USA's routine was brought to an exciting climax as two swimmers were catapulted through the air while executing parallel back layout somersaults ...**

To a roaring hometown crowd of nearly 15,000, the judges awarded Team USA straight 10s in technical merit and four out of five 10s in artistic impression. Dropping the high and low scores, it was a perfect score of 100 — the first time in Olympic synchro history a routine had earned a perfect score.

Team USA's cumulative total of 99.720 easily claimed the gold medal, with Canada a distant second at 98.367 and Japan in bronze position at 97.753.

"I think after the technical program we all felt very confident," said Dyroen-Lancer, the U.S. captain. "We didn't focus on scores. We just went along with the plan that we had from the beginning. We focused on the task at hand and everything else took care of itself."

With the prospect of all 10 members of the U.S. team retiring, co-captain Emily LeSueur summed up the team's feelings: "I think for us tonight, it was a perfect swim and we'll always remember this moment as being a perfect moment." ▼

TABLE TENNIS

Scaling the great wall of China

BY TRICIA DOWNING

ALLSPORT / DOUG PENSINGER

OPPOSITE (TOP) / *Twenty-year-old Liu Guoliang, noted for his foot speed and well-disguised spin serves, defeated Chinese team-mate Wang Tao in five games to add another gold to his collection. Earlier, he had won the doubles gold with partner Kong Linghui.*
ALLSPORT / NATHAN BILOW

(BOTTOM) / *Two-time Olympian Jim Butler from Augusta, Ga., rallied behind the support of the hometown crowd to win a key game before being eliminated in the preliminaries.*
AP PHOTO / KATSUMI KASAHARA

BECAUSE ANY SLIGHT DRAFT COULD cause the 2.5 gram ball to be set off course, table tennis made its Olympic home in an air-locked chamber in Hall D of the Georgia World Congress Center. But not even the special air-control system could keep the Chinese team from breezing past the competition.

Not only did the Chinese claim all the gold in Atlanta, but nearly all the silver, too. With the exception of women's singles, the finals saw one Chinese athlete against another. Even in the semifinals, only competitors from Germany, Korea, the Czech Republic and Chinese Taipei were able to join the Chinese.

China's Liu Guoliang and Deng Yaping came away the big winners with gold medals in both singles and doubles. In the men's doubles, Liu was assisted by team-mate Kong Linghui; in women's doubles, Deng teamed up with Qiao Hong.

With the Chinese in such uncommon top form, even top world players such as Jan-Ove Waldner of Sweden, Jean-Philippe Gatien of France and Johnny Huang of Canada couldn't keep up. Each was eliminated before reaching the medals rounds.

The home team ran into problems as well. Going into the Games, the feeling was positive for Team USA, buoyed by a bronze-medal showing by the U.S. men's team in the 1995 World Team Cup, held in Atlanta as an Olympic test event. That medal was the first the United States had earned in a major international table tennis competition in 48 years.

Led by two-time Olympians Jim Butler and Lily Yip, the U.S. team did manage to walk away with some key wins. Another plus was the enthusiasm and support showed by the hometown crowds. But the losses were also a reminder that there is still ground to cover.

In women's singles, Yip and Amy Feng fell just short of qualifying for the single-elimination medal tournament. Feng, the highest ranked U.S. player at No. 44, got past Valentina Poplva of Slovakia and Berta Rodriguez of Chili in straight games before losing in three games to Liu Wei of China, the No. 4 ranked player in the world who was eliminated by country-woman Yaping in the semifinals. Yip, ranked 95th in the world entering the Olympics, defeated 30th-ranked Krisztina Toth of Hungary and Monica Doti of Brazil in straight-game matches before losing to Tan Lui Chan of Hong Kong in a tight match.

In men's singles, both Butler and David Zhuang failed to make it to the medal round after posting 1-2 marks in the preliminary round-robin. Butler scored a victory over Tarik Hodzic of Bosnia-Herzegovina after losses to Dimitriy Mazunov of Russia and, in a three-set thriller, to his former practice partner Peter Karlsson of Sweden. Zhuang defeated Sule Olaleye of Nigeria in straight games after losses to Johnny Huang of Canada and Xinhua Chen of China.

In doubles, Yip and Wei Wang won games over Emily Noor and Hunberta Vriesehoop of the Netherlands and Bose Kaffo and Olufunke Oshonaike of Nigeria before falling in straight games to the Russian team of Irina Palina and Yelena Timina. Butler and Todd Sweeris had a tougher time in doubles, losing three straight. ▼

Of the 12 medals awarded, China won eight: golds in all four singles and doubles events, three silvers and one bronze.

TEAM HANDBALL

Favorites fall to Croatia and Denmark

BY MAUREEN STONE

ALLSPORT / MIKE HEWITT

OPPOSITE (TOP) / *In a tournament that featured one of the USA's tougher Olympic squads, the men still had to contend with some disappointing moments, like this 31-16 loss against Russia.* ALLSPORT / MIKE POWELL

(BOTTOM LEFT) / *Darrick Heath was the second leading scorer for the U.S., firing in 23 goals during the six-game tournament.* ALLSPORT / MIKE POWELL

(BOTTOM RIGHT) / *On the women's side, veteran Sharon Cain was one of the USA's leading game scorers, totaling 22 goals in the tournament.* ALLSPORT / DOUG PENSINGER

TEAMS FROM CROATIA AND DENMARK won first-ever gold medals in team handball at the Games of Atlanta, where narrow wins dominated perhaps the most exciting Olympic tournament ever.

The men's and women's respective gold-medal matches served as a good example of just how close the competition was in Atlanta, as Croatia won the men's gold medal by a single point, 27-26, over Sweden; and, in the women's championship match, Denmark prevailed in overtime over the two-time defending Olympic champions from Korea.

For other examples, there were the scores from virtually every game involving a team from the United States. Although neither the men's or women's U.S. teams medaled, both played the best teams in the world almost to a standstill. The men's team's opening 23-19 loss to eventual silver medalist Sweden was a harbinger of things to come, as was the women's team's 29-19 opening game loss to eventual gold medalist Denmark. Indeed, with the exception of a 31-16 loss by the men to a powerful Russian squad that shot 67.4 percent, no U.S. verdict was separated by more than 10 goals.

In a preliminary round game following its losses to Sweden and Russia, the U.S. men outscored the eventual gold medalists from Croatia in the second half before falling by a hard-fought 35-27 verdict. Another loss followed, this one by a 29-20 margin to Switzerland, which got 13 goals from Marc Baumgartner. But after that the men did not lose, taking a 29-24 verdict over Kuwait and finally, behind superb goalkeeping from Cliff Mannon and a game-winning penalty shot by David DeGraaf, a 27-26 double overtime victory over Algeria. That brought their Olympic record to 2-4 and gave them a ninth-place finish, tying the men's best finish ever. The two wins marked the first-ever multiple-

Gold-medal winner Denmark was the Cinderella squad that had never before qualified for the Olympic Games.

win Olympic competition for the men, who were led in scoring by Derek Brown, who had 26 goals for the six games of the tournament, Darrick Heath, who had 23, and DeGraaf, who chipped in 19.

Top scorers for the U.S. women's team were Chryssandra Hires with 26 goals, Sharon Cain with 22 and Toni Jameson with 10. Loaded with veterans from both the 1988 Games in Seoul and the 1992 Games in Barcelona, where they finished sixth, the women had high hopes for Atlanta. But drawing opening games against eventual medalists Denmark and Hungary, who would go on to win the bronze medal, did not make for a fast start.

After the 29-19 loss to Denmark — a Cinderella squad that had never before qualified for the Olympic Games — came a 30-24 setback to Hungary. In that match, the U.S. staged a spirited rally in the second half, cutting the deficit to just four goals before a series of two-minute penalties late in the match enabled Hungary to hang on for the victory.

The loss to Hungary was a costly one as it eliminated the U.S. of any medal hopes. Next came a 31-21 loss to China and, finally, in the last game for a large group of veterans, came a heartbreaking 24-23 loss for seventh-place against Angola.

As a consolation prize for the women, they could watch the medal-deciding games knowing they had given both Denmark, which won the gold medal match over Korea, and Hungary, which defeated Norway in the bronze-medal match, all they wanted.

The same went for the U.S. men, who watched Croatia and Sweden, two teams they'd lost to by a combined 12 goals, battle it out for the gold medal. In the men's bronze match, Spain upset defending world champion France. ▼

TENNIS

Agassi's true colors

BY DOUG ROBINSON

ALLSPORT / GARY M. PRIOR

OPPOSITE / *Double duty: Andre Agassi showed true grit and true Olympic spirit when he eagerly substituted for the doubles team when the U.S. was one man down due to Richey Reneberg's injury, in effect jeopardizing his chances for the gold in the singles.* ALLSPORT / GARY M. PRIOR

MAYBE IT WASN'T A COINCIDENCE that the Olympic singles champions ultimately were two Americans who grew up with fathers who had competed in the Olympics and held a sort of reverence for the Games.

That's what it seemed to require to play and win in Atlanta: passion and deep-seated respect for the Games. Andre Agassi and Lindsay Davenport had all of that.

For once, money took a back seat to things Olympian, little things such as wanting to hear the National Anthem from atop the podium, representing one's country, owning an Olympic medal and marching in the Opening Ceremonies.

Agassi had won Wimbledon and the U.S. and Australian Opens. He had won millions of dollars in prize money. Yet he came to Atlanta, where the prize money was zero and the only thing they gave you was a uniform and a few gifts and the opportunity to participate.

That wasn't enough for his rivals. Only three of the world's top 10 male players could play in the Olympics; the rest said they were injured like Pete Sampras and Boris Becker or resting for other tournaments.

"I can't get into the heads of athletes who chose not to be here," said Agassi. "I can't comprehend the feeling of being inconvenienced by the Olympics."

Agassi yearned to play in the Games. His father, Mike, had boxed in the Olympics for Iran in 1948 and 1952. He didn't medal, but he knew what it meant to compete in the Olympic Games.

"My father is as proud, if not prouder, of my being at the Olympics than anything I have ever accomplished," said Agassi.

Agassi's personal coach, Brad Gilbert, who won a bronze medal in tennis at the 1988 Games, realized what it meant to Agassi even before he came to Atlanta. "He'd be at my home, and he'd look at my bronze medal in the case," recalled Gilbert. "And then he'd say, 'I don't want one of those.'"

Wrong color.

Tennis is one of the rare sports in which the Olympic Games is not considered to be the ultimate event, at least partly because the sport was absent from the Games from 1928 until 1988 and partly because of the riches and prestige that other tournaments offer. But some, such, as Agassi, Arantxa Sanchez Vicario, Monica Seles and MaliVai Washington, among others, saw things differently.

"To win a Grand Slam in tennis is the biggest thing you can accomplish inside your sport," said Agassi. "But the Olympics is the biggest thing you can do in all of sports ... If you can't come in here and give everything to win the medal for your country, then you're really missing out."

Agassi became so wrapped up in patriotism and the Olympic spirit that he volunteered for double duty. The American doubles team of Washington and Richey Reneberg was undermined when Reneberg aggravated an old groin muscle injury during a singles match. That left Washington with no partner unless Agassi stepped forward, since injuries to Reneberg and Sampras left the U.S. with only a two-man squad.

"Andre Agassi is here to do well in singles," said Reneberg. "Unfortunately, it may end up being we just don't have a doubles team."

Agassi wouldn't hear of it. "The team took a hit, and we have to adjust," he said. "I'm not going to not play just to give myself a chance in singles. Even if it costs me a medal, it's something I've got to do."

Agassi and Washington, paired for the first time, won their first-round match, but lost in the second round to Ellis Ferreira and Wayne Ferreira of South Africa, 7-5, 6-7 (2-7), 6-0.

An injury also threatened the women's doubles team, but there Agassi could not help. Davenport was originally scheduled to play with Gigi Fernandez but volunteered to be taken out of doubles so Mary Joe Fernandez, who had been added as a fifth player to the Olympic roster by the International Tennis Federation, could defend their doubles gold from 1992. Four

But in Atlanta, Davenport, whose father Wink played on the U.S. volleyball team in the 1968 Olympic Games, was a different player.

"When you grow up in a culture where a family member has been in the Olympics," said U.S. coach Billie Jean King, "it gives you more of a sense of what it can mean and the depth of meaning."

Davenport faced a stiff field that included all of the world's best players except for an injured Steffi Graf. But while big names such as Seles and Gabriela Sabatini fell along the way, Davenport rolled on, beating a string of players with bigger reputations and higher seedings. She took No. 5 Anke Huber of Germany in the third round and No. 4 Iva Majoli of Croatia in the quarterfinals. Then she beat her best friend, No. 7 Mary Joe Fernandez, in the semifinals, after which she told her at the net, "Sorry."

That sent Fernandez, who was playing singles after a wrist injury knocked American Chanda Rubin out of the Games, to the bronze-medal match, where she lost to Jana Novotna of the Czech Republic, and put Davenport into the final against the world's third-ranked player, Spain's Sanchez Vicario. Davenport had lost five straight matches to Sanchez Vicario while winning just one set, but she overpowered her this time, winning 7-6 (8-6), 6-2.

"I thought I'd like to hear the National Anthem," explained Davenport, who celebrated the family's first Olympic medal with her father, mother and sisters. "No matter what happens in my life, I'll always be a gold medalist ... That was definitely the proudest I've ever been — for myself, my family and my country." ▼

years later, the unrelated Fernandez duo won gold again, beating Jana Novotna and Helena Sukova, 7-6 (8-6), 6-4, in the final.

As for Agassi, his Olympic zeal seemed to bring him out of a long slump. He came to the Olympics playing some of the worst tennis of his career, having failed to win a tournament since March. Some observers wondered if his best tennis was behind him, at the age of 26, after he was knocked out of the French Open in the second round and Wimbledon in the first round.

Yet he played his best tennis in a year at the Games, particularly when his back was to the wall. Against Wayne Ferreira of South Africa in the quarterfinals, he trailed 5-3 in the third and final set before he won four straight games to advance.

In the semifinals, he claimed a 7-6 (7-5), 6-3 win over India's Leander Paes, the eventual bronze medalist whose father and mother had both competed in the Olympics.

Agassi saved his best for last, taking just one hour and 17 minutes to dispatch two-time French Open champion Sergi Bruguera of Spain, 6-2, 6-3, 6-1. Then he tossed his racquet in the air, hugged his father and cried as he stood on the medals stand.

"It was a memorable embrace we'll have forever," said Agassi, the first American gold medalist in 72 years. "To me, this is the greatest thing I've accomplished in this sport."

Undoubtedly, Davenport, a tall (6-foot-2) 20-year-old, can make the same claim. She had never so much as gotten past the quarterfinals in a Grand Slam event and entered the tournament as the No. 9 seed.

ABOVE / *Meant to be: Gigi Fernandez (right)*
and Mary Joe Fernandez teamed up again in
women's doubles to successfully defend their
Barcelona title. ALLSPORT / ROSS KINNAIRD

155
TENNIS

VOLLEYBALL

Beach bragging rights

BY DOUG ROBINSON

ALLSPORT / STU FORSTER

OPPOSITE / USA star Tara Cross-Battle (#13), who led the team with 146 kills during its eight Olympic matches, watches while Teee Williams sets up the play. With a veteran and talented lineup, the Americans looked like medal contenders, especially after winning four of their five preliminary matches, but they fell victim to Cuba and left Atlanta without a medal. ALLSPORT / STU FORSTER

WHEN IT CAME TO VOLLEYBALL, the U.S. men put their hopes in two thirtysomething guys with funny names who already had Olympic hardware in their trophy case. The new beach game boasted old Karch Kiraly, the son of Laszlo, a former Hungarian freedom fighter who threw Molotov cocktails at Soviet tanks in 1956 before escaping to California. The traditional indoor game had Bob Ctvrtlik, the son of Josef, who escaped from Czechoslovakia in 1948 by hiding under a train in a blizzard and then skiing to Austria, never stopping until he reached California.

Kiraly, a living legend in the volleyball world, led the U.S. to gold medals in the 1984 and '88 Olympic Games; Ctvrtlik won gold in '88 with Kiraly and then bronze in '92. Since then, both had become wealthy businessmen and professional volleyball players, but they returned for their third Olympic Games looking for another gold medal.

Kiraly, 35, found it. Returning to "his roots," as he called it — he played in his first beach volleyball tournament when he was 11, with his father as his partner — he teamed with Kent Steffes to play in the first Olympic beach volleyball competition. California claimed gold and silver. Kiraly and Steffes met Mike Dodd and Mike Whitmarsh for the gold medal and California beach bragging rights and won, 12-5, 12-8, giving Kiraly his third gold medal. The third American men's duo of Sinjin Smith and Carl Henkel placed fifth in the final standings after barely losing to Kiraly and Steffes in the quarterfinals.

Afterward, the usually cool and controlled duo cried. Kiraly's father, Las, who had taught the game to Karch, received a late phone call from his son the previous night informing him that he had made a plane reservation to Atlanta and would he come? Las caught a redeye and arrived 13 hours later in time to see the final.

"Beach volleyball was Karch's first love," said Las.

Even Kiraly's rivals were happy for him. "He has done more for volleyball than any-

one," said Whitmarsh. "I'm very happy for both him and Kent."

Said Kiraly, "What I'm most proud of is having won gold medals in both forms of volleyball."

Ctvrtlik, 33, wasn't so fortunate. Playing on a team that had just two starters with Olympic experience, the U.S. men's indoor team won its first two matches in straight sets, but then lost its next three to exit in ninth place. He was crushed.

"This is about as painful a thing as you can have," said Ctvrtlik, the intense, take-charge team captain who was dubbed "Four Star" (as in general) by his teammates. "I can't find a bright side. I hope the sun comes up tomorrow."

The Italians knew how he felt. They came to Atlanta looking for revenge and their first Olympic gold medal. They found neither. They had won every major championship in this decade except the Olympics, losing to the Netherlands in the quarterfinals of the 1992 Games. As a prelude to the '96 Olympics, the Netherlands won the World League Championship — a league Italy had dominated.

Italy met the Netherlands in the Olympic preliminary round and won in straight sets, but afterward, losing coach Joop Alberda noted, "I'm remembering 1984, when the U.S. lost to Brazil in the preliminaries. There was a different result in the finals."

Italy and the Netherlands met again in the Olympic final and played a match to remember. The Netherlands won the first set, Italy won the second; the Netherlands won the third set, Italy the fourth. That forced a fifth and deciding set.

It came down to this: Italian star Andrea Giani spiked the ball off the arm of Dutch star Bas van de Goor to give Italy match point. But van de Goor, a 6-foot-11 middle blocker, responded with a spike down the middle to tie the score at 15.

Ron Zwerver's kill made it match point for the Dutch, who wrapped up the gold by winning the next rally. Final score: 15-12, 9-15, 16-14, 9-15, 17-15.

ies. But in the quarterfinals, they beat the U.S. in straight sets, 15-1, 15-10, 15-12.

The Americans then dropped another match to Korea in three sets before rallying to defeat Germany for seventh place and a 5-3 record in the Olympic tournament.

Meanwhile, back on the beach, the final consisted of four women from Brazil. The legendary Jackie Silva, 34, the so-called Queen of the Beach, teamed with Sandra Pires to win the gold medal, beating Adriana Samuel Ramos and Monica Rodrigues, 12-11, 12-6, in an all-Brazilian final that produced their country's first two Olympic medals for women.

Once again, Americans had high hopes for medals in the beach game — after all, they invented the sport — but they came away empty handed. The top-seeded American team of Holly McPeak and Nancy Reno received more attention for their feuding than for their playing. Once an unbeatable duo, they broke up twice before reuniting just before the Olympics.

"The soap opera has ended," McPeak said, but they were knocked out of the tournament by the American team of Linda Hanley and Barbara Fontana, 15-10, and had to settle for fifth place.

The victory sent Hanley and Fontana to the semifinals, where they lost to the eventual champions. That done, they faced Australia's Kerry Pottharst and Natalie Cook in the bronze-medal match and lost, 12-11, 12-7.

But if it wasn't a particularly good Olympics for American volleyball players, it was a good Olympics for volleyball. Beach volleyball's Olympic debut was a big hit, drawing large crowds and regular TV coverage. Expect the sport to return in Sydney. Maybe Kiraly will be there, too. ▼

The Italians settled for the silver medal, and Yugoslavia won the bronze by beating Russia in four sets.

AS EXPECTED, CUBA WON THE GOLD medal in the women's indoor competition for the second straight Olympic Games. Mireya Luis, who at 28 had played on the national team for half her life, delivered 31 kills in Cuba's four-set win over China in the finals, and then retired from the team.

One of Cuba's earlier victims was the Olympic bronze medalists in 1992. The Americans looked like medal contenders again after winning the 1995 World Cup tournament — the program's first major title ever. They brought a group of experienced and talented players to Atlanta — Paula Weishoff (a three-time Olympian and a member of the '84 Olympic silver-medal team), Tara Cross-Battle (the 1995 world MVP), Caren Kemner, Elaina and Bev Oden, Lori Endicott and Tammy Liley.

Record crowds witnessed the women's team with 14,750 in attendance against Ukraine and 15,100 versus China. The American women were on a roll.

Their hopes for a medal looked even more promising after they won four of five preliminary matches, losing only to China. Cuba, meanwhile, looked vulnerable, losing to Brazil and Russia in the preliminar-

ABOVE (LEFT) / *Holly McPeak (1) and Nancy Reno were once unbeatable, but on Atlanta Beach they were just undone. They finished fifth, as American women finished out of the medals in volleyball.* ALLSPORT / STU FORSTER

ABOVE / *Mike Dodd digs deep to bury Portugal in the semifinals. Dodd and teammate Mike Whitmarsh then played fellow Americans Karch Kiraly and Kent Steffes for the gold medal, losing 12-5, 12-8.* ALLSPORT / DOUG PENSINGER

LEFT / *Jeff Nygaard and Mike Lambert smother a spike attempt during a straight-set victory over Poland. The Americans had high hopes after winning their first two matches in the preliminaries, but then they dropped the next three and failed to advance to medal competition.* ALLSPORT / NATHAN BILOW

WATER POLO

Spain's splashy comeback

BY MARY ANN RINEHART

ALLSPORT / AL BELLO

OPPOSITE (TOP LEFT) / *A goal slips by Croatia which beat Ukraine nonetheless, paving the way for a rousing win – tinged with political overtones – over Yugoslavia in the semifinals.* ALLSPORT / AL BELLO

(TOP RIGHT) / *Romania couldn't stop Italy, the 1992 Olympic champions, losing 10-8, but neither could Italy live up to a repeat performance, ending up instead with the bronze.* ALLSPORT / AL BELLO

(BOTTOM) / *The water churned as the U.S. battled Spain in the quarterfinals. The 5-4 loss delivered a sharp blow to the U.S. as it was washed out of medal contention and, in the end, settled for seventh overall.* ALLSPORT / AL BELLO

DEVASTATION OVERWHELMED THE Spanish water polo team when it lost the gold medal to Italy in its homeland four years ago in Barcelona. But redemption, as it turned out, was just four years and 5,000 miles around the corner, as Spain conquered the water polo pool in Atlanta to win the gold medal at the Centennial Olympic Games.

Ironically, in order to avenge their heartbreak, the Spaniards had to deal out a little pain and suffering to the host team from the United States, a hometown gold-medal hopeful in its own right.

It was a 5-4 defeat of the Americans in the quarterfinals that sent Spain hurtling toward its gold and eliminated the U.S. from medal consideration. When that game was over, all the Spaniards could do was tell the Americans they knew how they felt.

Spain moved quickly in front in that quarterfinal match, taking a 4-0 lead that the Americans were never able to overcome. U.S. scoring leader Chris Humbert was ejected in the fourth quarter for unsportsmanlike conduct (he splashed a referee and then swam away), but even without Humbert, Team USA managed a valiant comeback. Fourth-quarter goals by Jeremy Laster and Chris Oeding brought the U.S. within two of Spain and yet another goal by Gavin Arroyo closed the gap to one, but Arroyo's score came with just two seconds remaining.

For Spain's senior statesman Manuel Estiarte, appearing in his fifth Olympic Games, Spain's gold medal ended a personal quest that spanned from Moscow 1980 to Atlanta 1996. In the gold-medal match against Croatia, it was the 35-year-old veteran who led the Spanish attack with three goals. In addition, Spain got excellent goalkeeping from Jesus Rollan, who recorded eight saves to preserve the 7-5 victory. Croatia provided the upset of the tournament in the semifinals when Dubravko Simenc and Perica Bukic led a 7-6 triumph over defending Olympic champion Italy.

Italy managed to hang on and win the bronze medal, but first it had to survive two overtimes against Hungary. Italy had only itself to blame for the extra periods. With just seconds remaining in regulation, and the Italians ahead by a goal, members of the Italian team, in a hurry to celebrate, jumped off the bench and into the pool. Hungary's appeal for a penalty throw was granted, the shot was made, and Italy went back to work. The Italians finally prevailed 20-18.

The United States, coached by Richard Corso, opened preliminary competition with a 10-7 loss to the Italians but defeated Greece, Romania, Ukraine and Croatia to finish the preliminary round 4-1. Then came the ill-timed, one-goal loss to Spain, just as the medal round-robin began. After yet another loss, this one to Greece, 7-6, Team USA ended the tournament by defeating Yugoslavia, 12-8, and officially finishing seventh.

Two-time Olympian Humbert led the United States in scoring with 14 goals while Oeding added 11 goals in his first Olympic appearance. Goalkeeper Chris Duplanty, a reserve goalkeeper for both the 1988 U.S. silver-medal team and the 1992 team that placed fourth, recorded 77 saves for the Americans for a 58.3 percent save ratio.

Troy Barnhart, Mike Evans, Kirk Everist, Kyle Kopp, Rick McNair, Alex Rousseau, Wolf Wigo and reserve goalkeeper Dan Hackett all contributed to the U.S. effort.

Although the outcome was far less than anticipated, many young members of the United States team could take solace in the realization that they can carry their Atlanta experience to Sydney in 2000. The 24-year-old Arroyo, for one, plans to remain in the U.S. Water Polo training camp in California to prepare for the first Games of the 21st century.

"I'm just more hungry now," Arroyo said. "This is my first Olympics. It was a great experience. I can't imagine what it would be like with a medal. I'm in this through Sydney."

If he needs further encouragement, he can always talk to the guys from Spain. ▼

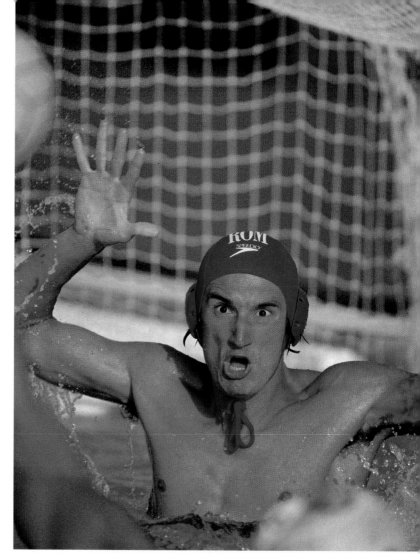

WEIGHTLIFTING

Iron men with steely resolve

BY ANTHONY BARTKOWSKI

ALLSPORT / BILLY STICKLAND

RIGHT / *When the dust settled, Wes Barnett had broken four American records and turned in a 870 3/4-pound total for sixth place in the 238-pound weight class. The event was won by Timur Raimazov of Ukraine with a total lift of 947 3/4 pounds.* ALLSPORT / DOUG PENSINGER

AS FAR AS WEIGHTLIFTING IS CONcerned, the 1996 Centennial Olympic Games will be remembered as record-setting. No less than 25 Olympic records and 19 world records were established at the Georgia World Congress Center in Atlanta, with at least one record set in nine of the 10 official categories.

Of course, the mandate by the International Weightlifting Federation to change all the weight classes in Atlanta and re-establish Olympic records had a lot to do with all the record-smashing going on. Nonetheless, it made for an exciting competition, an excitement that extended to the U.S. team, which, despite failing to account for any medals, did manage to account for 15 new American records, the most for any U.S. Olympic team.

Highlighting the show was Turkey's Naim Suleymanoglu, known as the "Pocket Hercules," who jumped into the Olympic history books by becoming the first weightlifter to win three Olympic gold medals. The 141-pound Suleymanoglu, who waged a tight battle with Valerios Leonidis of Greece, totaled 738 1/2 pounds to qualify for his third gold medal while establishing Olympic and world records and staking a claim as maybe the greatest weightlifter ever.

Suleymanoglu, who was successful in five-of-six attempts, completed his lifts before three-time world silver medalist Leonidis attempted his last lift. The Greek had a chance to write some history of his own, but when Leonidis failed in his 418 3/4 pound clean-and-jerk, Suleymanoglu, who had won convincingly in both Seoul and Barcelona, was able to claim his third straight gold by a slim 5 1/2-pound margin.

The United States was led by two-time Olympians Wes Barnett and Bryan Jacob. Barnett, of St. Joseph, Mo., went five-for-six in his attempts and broke four American records en route to a sixth-place finish in the 238-pound division. Barnett set American records in the clean-and-jerk (485 pounds) and total (870 3/4 pounds), missing only on a 496-pound clean-and-jerk.

the national team, broke two American records. He hoisted 435 1/4 pounds in the clean-and-jerk to break a U.S. record set by Barnett in the 218-pound division in 1993. With a total of 788 pounds, Kelley broke the record he had set in April.

Super heavyweight and hometown favorite Tom Ingalsbe of Powder Springs, Ga., was also sidelined by injury. He was three-for-three in the snatch with a high mark of 374 3/4 pounds, but in the clean-and-jerk, the 335-pound lifter pulled an abdominal muscle and succeeded only with 440 3/4 pounds for a total of 804 1/2 pounds.

The final two athletes on the U.S. team, Vernon Patao of Wailuku, Hawaii and Thanh Nguyen of Pacifica, Calif., competed in the 141-pound division and finished 22nd and 32nd, respectively. Patao, a 1992 Olympian, totaled 622 3/4 pounds with a 270-pound snatch and a 352 1/2-pound clean-and-jerk. Nguyen totaled 567 1/2 pounds after managing one lift in the snatch and clean-and-jerk. ▼

Jacob, a resident of nearby Alpharetta, Ga., was surrounded by friends and family as he finished ninth overall in the 130-pound division. He totaled 600 3/4 pounds for an American record. In the two lifts, he matched his American marks of 270 pounds in the snatch and 330 1/2 pounds in the clean-and-jerk.

"My family alone bought 34 tickets," said Jacob. "I work here in Atlanta too, so my boss is here and a lot of my co-workers, as well as my wife's office. Then everybody out there is cheering for the U.S. guys. To me, whatever the attendance is, that is what's out there for me."

Konstantine Starikovitch of White Plains, N.Y., turned in a 14th-place finish for the U.S. in the 238-pound division after going three-for-six in his attempts. The Russian native, who made the U.S. Olympic team 16 days after becoming a U.S. citizen, totaled 854 1/4 pounds. He set an American record with a snatch of 391 1/4 pounds.

Mark Henry of Silsbee, Texas, who finished in 10th place in the unlimited divi-

sion in his Olympic debut four years earlier in Barcelona, was plagued by a back injury and finished 14th after having to withdraw after a total of just 832 pounds. Henry set another record for heaviest weightlifter, weighing in at 407 pounds. "I'm mostly disappointed for my team," Henry said. "Because a high finish would have shut up our critics, as far as the United States being a lesser country."

Three other United States national team members placed 14th in the competition — 1992 Olympian Tim McRae of Daytona Beach, Fla., Tom Gough of Fairfax, Fla., and Pete Kelley of St. Joseph, Mo.

The 154-pound McRae broke three American records as he snatched 440 3/4 pounds, clean-and-jerked 391 1/4 pounds and totaled 710 3/4 pounds.

Gough, a corporal in the United States Marine Corps, made a clean sweep with American records in the 200 1/2 pound division, snatching 369 1/4 pounds, clean-and-jerking 440 3/4 pounds and totaling 810 pounds.

Kelley, at 22, the youngest member of

WRESTLING

Memories on and off the mat

BY GARY ABBOTT

ALLSPORT / ROSS KINNAIRD

RIGHT / *Tête-à-tête: This private conversation ended with Russia's Alexander Karelin (in red) on top when he scored the lone point of the match against American Matt Ghaffari. Ghaffari, who has wrestled Karelin over a dozen times without a victory, had to settle for second place in the 286-pound weight class.*
ALLSPORT / PASCAL RONDEAU

THE 1996 CENTENNIAL OLYMPIC Games wrestling tournament was among the most competitive in history as many veteran stars collided headlong into just as many young challengers eager to create history of their own.

Poland won the most medals in the Greco-Roman competition with five, including three golds, while Russia, the United States and Belarus each won three medals. In the freestyle competition, the United States led the way with five medals, while Russia had four and Iran and Korea captured three each.

Russia's Alexander Karelin carried the banner highest for the old guard. The massive super heavyweight Greco-Roman specialist from Siberia, a six-time world champion, remained unbeaten in international competition as he won his third straight Olympic gold medal, joining freestyle great Alexander Medved of the Soviet Union as the only wrestlers to win gold medals in three Games. Poland's Andrzej Wronski, who won at 100 kilograms (220 pounds), was another repeat Olympic Greco-Roman gold medalist. He'd also topped that division in the 1988 Games in Seoul.

In the freestyle competition, Kim Il of the People's Republic of Korea won his second straight gold medal at 48 kilograms (105.5 pounds), while Bulgaria's Valentin Jordanov, a seven-time world champion, finally wrested away an elusive Olympic gold medal in the 52 kilogram (114.5 pounds) division. It took a while. Jordanov placed eighth in the Seoul Games in 1988 because of injury and could only manage a bronze-medal finish in the Barcelona Games in 1992.

With a Games-leading eight medals overall, the host team from the United States enjoyed consistent success throughout both the Greco-Roman and freestyle competitions. The three silver medals won by Brandon Paulson at 52 kilograms (114.5 pounds), Dennis Hall at 57 kilograms (125.5 pounds) and Matt Ghaffari at 130 kilograms (286 pounds) in Greco-Roman represented one of the best U.S. performances ever in that discipline.

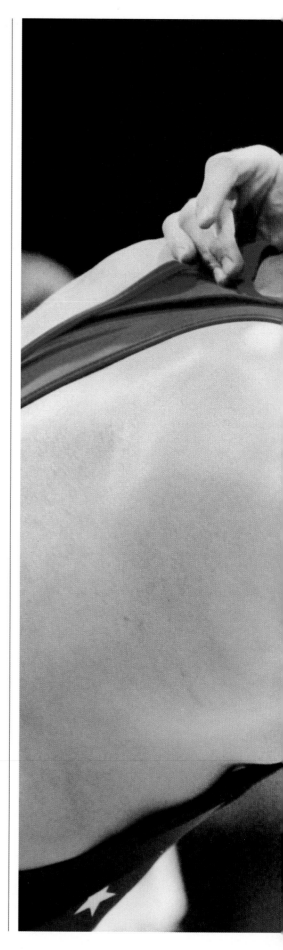

Paulson's medal was the biggest surprise of the three. The 22-year-old wrestler took a year off from his studies at the University of Minnesota to prepare for the Games with the support of his father, Doug. He won three matches to reach the finals, where he lost to two-time world silver medalist Armen Nezaryan of Armenia, 5-1.

Hall, a 1995 world champion, met the person he defeated for that world title, Yurij Melnichenko of Kazakhstan, for the Olympic gold medal. This time, however, Melnichenko, the 1994 world champ, prevailed, winning 4-1. To get to the title match, Hall defeated 1992 Olympic bronze medalist Zetian Sheng by a 1-0 referee's decision.

Ghaffari was edged 1-0 in the gold-medal super heavyweight final by Russia's Karelin, who was tested more than in any international match the past 10 years. Karelin scored the lone point 1:51 into the bout.

Three Americans captured gold medals in freestyle bouts. They included Kendall Cross at 57 kilograms (125.5 pounds), Tom Brands at 62 kilograms (136.5 pounds) and Kurt Angle at 100 kilograms (220 pounds). In addition, two-time Olympian Townsend Saunders won a silver medal at 68 kilograms (149.5 pounds) and veteran Bruce Baumgartner rewrote the history books with his fourth career Olympic freestyle medal, a bronze, in the 130 kilogram (286 pounds) division.

Cross, competing in his second Olympic Games, swept all four of his matches, including a 5-3 victory over 1995 world silver medalist Giuvi Sisanouri of Canada in the gold-medal match. It was a three-point double overhook throw 30 seconds

ABOVE / *Yurij Melnichenko of Kazakhstan jumped to an early 4-0 lead with a lift and an appreciation point over American Dennis Hall, who gamely attacked the remainder of the match trying to wear down his opponent. Hall scored one point with 15 seconds left in the match, giving Melnichenko the gold in the 125.5-pound class.* ALLSPORT / DOUG PENSINGER

into the match that made the difference.

"It's a very comforting feeling to finally realize a lifelong dream," said Cross. "I was in a throw position. I decided to throw ... and it came out golden."

Brands, the 1993 world champion, combined a fierce intensity with a strong offensive attack to defeat four straight opponents. He gave up just one point in the entire Olympic competition. In the final he shutout Jang Jae-sung of Korea, 7-0.

"The final match was my best of the tournament," Brands said. "I felt good in all my previous matches but the final was the best. You want to go out that way." Tom's twin brother Terry, an alternate to the U.S. team, helped Tom prepare for each match.

Angle, the 1995 world champion, remained the world's best with five victories. His gold-medal triumph was a dramatic referee's decision over 1995 world bronze medalist Abbas Jadidi of Iran. The match was tied 1-1 at the end of the five-minute regulation, forcing the bout into a three-minute overtime. Both wrestlers had the same number of passivity warnings — two each — so the winner was determined by the three officials.

"It was up to the officials," said Angle. "I think the last shot I took really helped me. I was more aggressive the whole match. I'm the proudest man in the world."

Saunders was on the other end of a tie-breaking decision. After battling Vadim Bogiyev of Russia to a 1-1 draw through overtime, he was edged out of the gold because Bogiyev had fewer passivity warnings. Saunders' wife, Tricia, a 1992 world champion in women's wrestling, was on hand to share his silver-medal finish.

Baumgartner's quest for a third super heavyweight Olympic gold medal — to go alongside those he captured in 1984 in Los Angeles and 1992 in Barcelona — was derailed by a 6-1 setback to Andrey Shumlin of Russia in the second round. But Baumgartner came back through the consolation rounds to qualify for a bronze-medal bout against, as fate would have it, Shumlin. In the rematch the American prevailed on a referee's decision after a 1-1 tie.

The bronze finish gave Baumgartner — who was selected by his U.S. teammates to carry the flag in Atlanta's Opening Ceremonies — each color medal from his four Olympics appearances (he won silver in Seoul in 1988). He is the only freestyle wrestler to ever win four Olympic medals and his 13 international-level medals ranks as the most of all-time. ▼

YACHTING

Savannah hosts Olympic regatta

BY BARBY MACGOWAN

ALLSPORT / VANDYSTADT

OPPOSITE / *Hong Kong celebrated its first-ever gold medal when world champion boarder Lee Lai-shan won the women's Mistral.* ALLSPORT / VANDYSTADT

THERE WAS AN UPROAR WHEN Savannah was originally chosen as site of the 1996 Olympic Regatta. Beautiful protected wetlands and sparse marine facilities combined to make ominous political and logistical hurdles for organizers and skepticism, at best, for critics. The international sailing community had little faith that something — in this case, a regatta site capable of hosting the most important yachting event in the world — could be made of nothing.

But perseverance prevailed, and by the time the Olympic spotlight fell on Savannah it revealed a 150,000 square foot "dry marina" constructed on the edge of Wassaw Sound. As well, the site of an abandoned hotel had been brought to life as the Olympic's regatta headquarters. Seven miles by water, traveled in 45 minutes by high-speed shuttle, separated these two focal point facilities.

The fact that logistics would play an important role in this regatta was not lost on any of the national teams. Germany, Great Britain and several other countries joined the USA in setting up home bases in Savannah years before the event, to familiarize themselves with the lay of the land, the currents, the wind. The Savannah community, in typical hospitable southern fashion, embraced their visitors and turned every resource over to hosting the yachting event.

Appropriately, the Olympic torch first touched Georgia soil in Savannah after being carried up the Savannah River to the city's waterfront by the schooner *America*. The USA's returning 1992 Star gold medalists Mark Reynolds and Hal Haenel were awarded the honor of transferring the flame from the historic vessel to land, where a structure similar but smaller than the one in Atlanta, 256 miles away, was lit to symbolize Savannah's part of the Centennial Games. Olympic fans came in droves to witness yachting's own opening ceremony, which took place on the waterfront soon after the torch relay passed through town.

Once the competition began, mastering the logistical nuances figured heavily in team performances. Competitors who best adapted to the challenging and changing conditions, including shifty light winds and nearly daily thunderstorms, were the ones who succeeded.

The USA, with representation in all 10 Olympic divisions, started off surprisingly empty-handed when Reynolds and Haenel, two-time Olympic medalists and the favorites on home waters, were confused by lighter than usual winds and placed just eighth in the Star division.

Indeed, the winds throughout the regatta never matched up with those the USA had trained in over the years. "Someone who doesn't know the place and hasn't practiced here could do well by using plain instinct," said Mike Gebhardt, also a returning medalist who wound up eighth in the men's Mistral class. "It's frustrating because we've invested so much in figuring it all out, but that's sailboat racing."

As the competition wore on, however, the USA improved its position, either medaling or knocking at the door in seven of the 10 divisions. The last bit of execution could swing either way and it swung in favor of bronze for first-time Olympians Courtenay Becker-Dey in Europe and the trio of Jeff Madrigali, Kent Massey and Jim Barton in Soling.

After the final awards ceremony, the USA could claim, along with its two medals, top-eight finishes in seven of 10 disciplines, a performance to be commend-

> **Competitors who best adapted to the challenging and changing conditions, including shifty light winds and nearly daily thunderstorms, were the ones who succeeded.**

ed but overshadowed by the team's 1992 performance in Barcelona, where sailors took home nine medals from 10 events.

Brazil won the most medals in Savannah with three, while five nations matched the USA's record with two apiece and over a dozen claimed one medal each. Included in memorable moments was Hong Kong's first-ever Olympic medal won by Lee Lai-shan in the women's Mistral division and Theresa Zabell's successful defense of her Spanish gold from '92 in women's 470. Brazil's Robert Scheidt handily topped the men's Laser class, the event's largest with 56 entrants, while Poland's Mateusz Kusznierewicz won the first gold medal of the regatta when he clinched his Finn series one day early.

The 1996 Olympic regatta was a huge event, and success, by every measure. While the '92 event hosted 68 nations, this one hosted 78. Records were set for numbers of sailors participating (458) and numbers of nations medaling for the first time (five). While 12 nations claimed 30 medals in 1992, 22 nations took the 30 top-three spots this year. Savannah, an eager, persistent and gracious host, proved that if you build a world-class event, world-class sailors will come. ▼

RIGHT / *The USA's Tornado team of Charlie Ogletree and John Lovell placed eighth.*
ALLSPORT / VANDYSTADT

RESULTS

1 9 9 6 MEDAL COUNT

Amy Van Dyken's medal haul. ALLSPORT / MATTHEW STOCKMAN

	G	S	B	T
United States	44	32	26	101
Germany	20	18	27	65
Russia	26	21	16	63
China	16	22	12	50
Australia	9	9	23	41
France	15	7	15	37
Italy	13	10	12	35
Korea	7	15	5	27
Cuba	9	8	8	25
Ukraine	9	2	12	23
Canada	3	11	8	22
Hungary	7	4	10	21
Romania	4	7	9	20
Netherlands	4	5	10	19
Poland	7	5	5	17
Spain	5	6	6	17
Bulgaria	3	7	5	15
Brazil	3	3	9	15
Great Britain	1	8	6	15
Belarus	1	6	8	15
Japan	3	6	5	14
Czech Republic	4	3	4	11
Kazakhstan	3	4	4	11
Greece	4	4	0	8
Sweden	2	4	2	8
Kenya	1	4	3	8
Switzerland	4	3	0	7
Norway	2	2	3	7
Denmark	4	1	1	6
Turkey	4	1	1	6
New Zealand	3	2	1	6
Belgium	2	2	2	6
Nigeria	2	1	3	6
Jamaica	1	3	2	6
South Africa	3	1	1	5
DPR Korea	2	1	2	5
Ireland	3	0	1	4
Finland	1	2	1	4
Indonesia	1	1	2	4

	G	S	B	T
Yugoslavia	1	1	2	4
Algeria	2	0	1	3
Ethiopia	2	0	1	3
Iran	1	1	1	3
Slovakia	1	1	1	3
Argentina	0	2	1	3
Austria	0	1	2	3
Armenia	1	1	0	2
Croatia	1	1	0	2
Portugal	1	0	1	2
Thailand	1	0	1	2
Namibia	0	2	0	2
Slovenia	0	2	0	2
Malaysia	0	1	1	2
Republic of Moldova	0	1	1	2
Uzbekistan	0	1	1	2
Georgia	0	0	2	2
Morocco	0	0	2	2
Trinidad and Tobago	0	0	2	2
Burundi	1	0	0	1
Costa Rica	1	0	0	1
Ecuador	1	0	0	1
Hong Kong	1	0	0	1
Syrian Arab Republic	1	0	0	1
Azerbaijan	0	1	0	1
Bahamas	0	1	0	1
Chinese Taipei	0	1	0	1
Latvia	0	1	0	1
Philippines	0	1	0	1
Tonga	0	1	0	1
Zambia	0	1	0	1
India	0	0	1	1
Israel	0	0	1	1
Lithuania	0	0	1	1
Mexico	0	0	1	1
Mongolia	0	0	1	1
Mozambique	0	0	1	1
Puerto Rico	0	0	1	1
Tunisia	0	0	1	1
Uganda	0	0	1	1

PARTICIPATING NATIONS

AFG	Afghanistan	GAB	Gabon	NOR	Norway
ALB	Albania	GAM	Gambia	OMA	Oman
ALG	Algeria	GEO	Georgia	PAK	Pakistan
ASA	American Samoa	GER	Germany	PLE	Palestine
AND	Andorra	GHA	Ghana	PAN	Panama
ANG	Angola	GBR	Great Britain	PNG	Papua New Guinea
ANT	Antigua and Barbuda	GRE	Greece	PAR	Paraguay
ARG	Argentina	GRN	Grenada	PRK	Democratic People's Republic of Korea
ARM	Armenia	GUM	Guam	PER	Peru
ARU	Aruba	GUA	Guatemala	PHI	Philippines
AUS	Australia	GUI	Guinea	POL	Poland
AUT	Austria	GBS	Guinea-Bissau	POR	Portugal
AZE	Azerbaijan	GUY	Guyana	PUR	Puerto Rico
BAH	Bahamas	HAI	Haiti	QAT	Qatar
BRN	Bahrain	HON	Honduras	ROM	Romania
BAN	Bangladesh	HKG	Hong Kong	RUS	Russian Federation
BAR	Barbados	HUN	Hungary	RWA	Rwanda
BLR	Belarus	ISL	Iceland	SKN	Saint Kitts and Nevis
BEL	Belgium	IND	India	LCA	Saint Lucia
BIZ	Belize	INA	Indonesia	VIN	Saint Vincent and The Grenadines
BEN	Benin	IRI	Islamic Republic of Iran	SMR	San Marino
BER	Bermuda	IRQ	Iraq	STP	Sao Tome and Principe
BHU	Bhutan	IRL	Ireland	KSA	Saudi Arabia
BOL	Bolivia	ISR	Israel	SEN	Senegal
BIH	Bosnia and Herzegovina	ITA	Italy	SEY	Seychelles
BOT	Botswana	JAM	Jamaica	SLE	Sierra Leone
BRA	Brazil	JPN	Japan	SIN	Singapore
IVB	British Virgin Islands	JOR	Jordan	SVK	Slovakia
BRU	Brunei Darussalam	KAZ	Kazakhstan	SLO	Slovenia
BUL	Bulgaria	KEN	Kenya	SOL	Solomon Islands
BUR	Burkina Faso	KOR	Korea	SOM	Somalia
BDI	Burundi	KUW	Kuwait	RSA	South Africa
CAM	Cambodia	KGZ	Kyrgyzstan	ESP	Spain
CMR	Cameroon	LAO	Lao People's Democratic Republic	SRI	Sri Lanka
CAN	Canada	LAT	Latvia	SUD	Sudan
CPV	Cape Verde	LIB	Lebanon	SUR	Suriname
CAY	Cayman Islands	LES	Lesotho	SWZ	Swaziland
CAF	Central African Republic	LBR	Liberia	SWE	Sweden
CHA	Chad	LBA	Libyan Arab Jamahiriya	SUI	Switzerland
CHI	Chile	LIE	Liechtenstein	SYR	Syrian Arab Republic
CHN	People's Republic of China	LTU	Lithuania	TPE	Chinese Taipei
COL	Colombia	LUX	Luxembourg	TJK	Tajikistan
COM	Comoros	MAD	Madagascar	TAN	United Republic of Tanzania
CGO	Congo	MAW	Malawi	THA	Thailand
COK	Cook Islands	MAS	Malaysia	TOG	Togo
CRC	Costa Rica	MDV	Maldives	TGA	Tonga
CIV	Côte d'Ivoire	MLI	Mali	TRI	Trinidad and Tobago
CRO	Croatia	MLT	Malta	TUN	Tunisia
CUB	Cuba	MTN	Mauritania	TUR	Turkey
CYP	Cyprus	MRI	Mauritius	TKM	Turkmenistan
CZE	Czech Republic	MEX	Mexico	UGA	Uganda
DEN	Denmark	MDA	Republic of Moldova	UKR	Ukraine
DJI	Djibouti	MON	Monaco	UAE	United Arab Emirates
DMA	Dominica	MGL	Mongolia	USA	United States of America
DOM	Dominican Republic	MAR	Morocco	URU	Uruguay
ECU	Ecuador	MOZ	Mozambique	UZB	Uzbekistan
EGY	Egypt	MYA	Myanmar	VAN	Vanuatu
ESA	El Salvador	NAM	Namibia	VEN	Venezuela
GEQ	Equatorial Guinea	NRU	Nauru	VIE	Vietnam
EST	Estonia	NEP	Nepal	ISV	Virgin Islands
ETH	Ethiopia	NED	Netherlands	SAM	Western Samoa
FIJ	Fiji	AHO	Netherlands Antilles	YEM	Yemen
FIN	Finland	NZL	New Zealand	YUG	Yugoslavia
MKD	Former Yugoslav Republic of Macedonia	NCA	Nicaragua	ZAI	Zaire
		NIG	Niger	ZAM	Zambia
FRA	France	NGR	Nigeria	ZIM	Zimbabwe

ARCHERY

MEN'S INDIVIDUAL
Final: August 1

RANK	CTRY	ATHLETE
1	USA	Justin Huish
2	SWE	Magnus Petersson
3	KOR	Oh Kyo-moon
4	BEL	Paul Vermeiren
5	KOR	Kim Bo-ram
6	ITA	Michele Frangilli
7	KOR	Jang Yong-ho
8	FRA	Lionel Torres
11	USA	Richard "Butch" Johnson
24	USA	Rod White

MEN'S TEAM
Final: August 2

RANK	CTRY	ATHLETES
1	USA	Justin Huish / Butch Johnson / Rod White
2	KOR	Jang Yong-ho / Kim Bo-ram / Oh Kyo-moon
3	ITA	Matteo Bisiani / Michele Frangilli / Andrea Parenti
4	AUS	Simon Fairweather / Jackson Fear / Mathew Gray
5	SLO	Peter Koprivnikar / Matevz Krumpestar / Samo Medved
6	SWE	Goran Bjerendal / Mikael Larsson / Magnus Petersson
7	UKR	Oleksandr Yatsenko / Valeriy Yevetsky / Stanyslav Zabrodsky
8	FIN	Jari Lipponen / Tomi Poikolainen / Tommi Tuovila

WOMEN'S INDIVIDUAL
Final: July 31

RANK	CTRY	ATHLETE
1	KOR	Kim Kyung-wook
2	CHN	He Ying
3	UKR	Olena Sadovnycha
4	TUR	Elif Altinkaynak
5	BLR	Olga Yakusheva
6	KOR	Kim Jo-sun
7	CHN	Wang Xiaozhu
8	GER	Barbara Mensing
16	USA	Janet Dykman
22	USA	Lindsay Langston
39	USA	Judi Adams

WOMEN'S TEAM
Final: August 2

RANK	CTRY	ATHLETES
1	KOR	Kim Jo-sun / Kim Kyung-wook / Yoon Hye-young
2	GER	Barbara Mensing / Cornelia Pfohl / Sandra Wagner
3	POL	Iwona Dzieciol / Katarzyna Klata / Joanna Nowicka
4	TUR	Elif Altinkaynak / Elif Eksi / Natalia Nazaridze
5	UKR	Natalya Bilukha / Lina Herasymenko / Olena Sadovnycha
6	CHN	Ye Ying / Wang Xiaozhu / Yang Jianping
7	SWE	Christa Backman / Kristina Persson / Jenny Sjovall
8	KAZ	Irina Leonova / Anna Mozhar / Yana Tuniyants
13	USA	Judi Adams / Janet Dykman / Lindsay Langston

ATHLETICS

MEN'S 100 METERS
Final: July 27
Wind: +0.7

RANK	CTRY	ATHLETE	TIME	
1	CAN	Donovan Bailey	9.84	WR
2	NAM	Frank Fredericks	9.89	
3	TRI	Ato Boldon	9.90	
4	USA	Dennis Mitchell	9.99	
5	USA	Michael Marsh	10.00	
6	NGR	Davidson Ezinwa	10.14	
7	JAM	Michael Green	10.16	
—	GBR	Linford Christie	DQ	
10T	USA	Jon Drummond	10.16	(semi)

MEN'S 200 METERS
Final: August 1
Wind: +0.4

RANK	CTRY	ATHLETE	TIME	
1	USA	Michael Johnson	19.32	WR
2	NAM	Frank Fredericks	19.68	
3	TRI	Ato Boldon	19.80	
4	BAR	Obadele Thompson	26.14	
5	USA	Jeff Williams	20.17	
6	CUB	Ivan Garcia	20.21	
7	BEL	Patrick Stevens	20.27	
8	USA	Michael Marsh	20.48	

MEN'S 400 METERS
Final: July 29

RANK	CTRY	ATHLETE	TIME	
1	USA	Michael Johnson	43.49	OR
2	GBR	Roger Black	44.41	
3	UGA	Davis Kamoga	44.53	
4	USA	Alvin Harrison	44.62	
5	GBR	Iwan Thomas	44.70	
6	JAM	Roxbert Martin	44.83	
7	JAM	Davian Clarke	44.99	
8	QAT	Ibrahim Ismail	DNF	
16	USA	Butch Reynolds	DNF	(semi)

MEN'S 800 METERS
Final: July 31

RANK	CTRY	ATHLETE	TIME	
1	NOR	Vebjoern Rodal	1:42.58	OR
2	RSA	Hezekiel Sepeng	1:42.74	
3	KEN	Fred Onyancha	1:42.79	
4	CUB	Norberto Tellez	1:42.85	
5	GER	Nico Motchebon	1:43.91	
6	KEN	David Kiptoo	1:44.19	
7	USA	Johnny Gray	1:44.21	
8	MAR	Benyounes Lahlou	1:45.52	
39	USA	Brandon Rock	1:48.47	
47	USA	Jose Parrilla	1:49.99	

MEN'S 1,500 METERS
Final: August 3

RANK	CTRY	ATHLETE	TIME
1	ALG	Noureddine Morceli	3:35.78
2	ESP	Fermin Cacho	3:36.40
3	KEN	Stephen Kipkorir	3:36.72
4	KEN	Laban Rotich	3:37.39
5	KEN	William Tanui	3:37.42
6	SOM	Abdi Bile	3:38.03
7	NED	Marko Koers	3:38.18
8	TUN	Ali Hakimi	3:38.19
19	USA	Paul McMullen	3:37.81
29	USA	Jason Pyrah	3:39.91
48	USA	Brian Hyde	3:48.20

MEN'S WHEELCHAIR 1,500 METERS
Final: August 1

RANK	CTRY	ATHLETE	TIME
1	FRA	Claude Issorat	3:15.18
2	USA	Scot Hollonbeck	3:15.30
3	SUI	Franz Nietlispach	3:16.41
4	FRA	Philippe Couprie	3:16.45
5	MEX	Saul Mendoza	3:16.58
6	MEX	Jorge Luna	3:16.78
7	AUS	Paul Wiggins	3:16.86
8	USA	Jacob Heiveil	3:16.90

MEN'S 5,000 METERS
Final: August 3

RANK	CTRY	ATHLETE	TIME
1	BDI	Venuste Niyongabo	13:07.96
2	KEN	Paul Bitok	13:08.16
3	MAR	Khalid Boulami	13:08.37
4	GER	Dieter Baumann	13:08.81
5	KEN	Tom Nyariki	13:12.29
6	USA	Bob Kennedy	13:12.35
7	ESP	Enrique Molina	13:12.91
8	MAR	Brahim Lahlafi	13:13.26
28	USA	Jim Spivey	14:27.72
34	USA	Matt Giusto	14:30.76

MEN'S 10,000 METERS
Final: July 29

RANK	CTRY	ATHLETE	TIME	
1	ETH	Haile Gebrselassie	27:07.34	OR
2	KEN	Paul Tergat	27:08.17	
3	MAR	Salah Hissou	27:24.67	
4	BDI	Aloys Nizigama	27:33.79	
5	KEN	Josphat Machuka	27:35.08	
6	KEN	Paul Koech	27:35.19	
7	MAR	Khalid Skah	27:46.98	
8	RWA	Mathias Ntawulikura	27:50.73	
30	USA	Brad Barquist	29:11.20	

| 38 | USA | Dan Middleman | 29:50.72 |
| — | USA | Todd Williams | DNF |

MEN'S 110-METER HURDLES
Final: July 29
Wind: +0.6

RANK	CTRY	ATHLETE	TIME	
1	USA	Allen Johnson	12.95	OR
2	USA	Mark Crear	13.09	
3	GER	Florian Schwarthoff	13.17	
4	GBR	Colin Jackson	13.19	
5	CUB	Emilio Valle	13.20	
6	USA	Eugene Swift	13.23	
7	AUS	Kyle Vander-Kuyp	13.40	
8	CUB	Erick Batte	13.43	

MEN'S 400-METER HURDLES
Final: August 1

RANK	CTRY	ATHLETE	TIME
1	USA	Derrick Adkins	47.54
2	ZAM	Samuel Matete	47.78
3	USA	Calvin Davis	47.96
4	SWE	Sven Nylander	47.98
5	AUS	Rohan Robinson	48.30
6	ITA	Fabrizio Mori	48.41
7	BRA	Everson Teixeira	48.57
8	BRA	Eronilde de Araujo	48.78
16	USA	Bryan Bronson	50.32

3,000-METER STEEPLECHASE
Final: August 2

RANK	CTRY	ATHLETE	TIME
1	KEN	Joseph Keter	8:07.12
2	KEN	Moses Kiptanui	8:08.33
3	ITA	Alessandro Lambruschini	8:11.28
4	KEN	Matthew Birir	8:17.18
5	USA	Mark Croghan	8:17.84
6	GER	Steffen Brand	8:18.52
7	MAR	Brahim Boulami	8:23.13
8	NOR	Jim Svenoey	8:23.39
12	USA	Marc Davis	9:51.96
33	USA	Robert Gary	8:49.68

MEN'S 20-KILOMETER WALK
Final: July 26

RANK	CTRY	ATHLETE	TIME
1	ECU	Jefferson Perez	1:20.07
2	RUS	Ilya Markov	1:20.16
3	MEX	Bernardo Segura	1:20.23
4	AUS	Nick A'Hern	1:20.31
5	RUS	Rishat Shafikov	1:20.41
6	LAT	Aigars Fadejevs	1:20.47
7	RUS	Mikhail Shchennikov	1:21.09
8	POL	Robert Korzeniowski	1:21.13
50	USA	Curt Clausen	1:32.11

MEN'S 50-KILOMETER WALK
Final: August 2

RANK	CTRY	ATHLETE	TIME
1	POL	Robert Korzeniowski	3:43.30
2	RUS	Mikhail Shchennikov	3:43.46
3	ESP	Valentin Massana	3:44.19
4	ITA	Arturo Di Mezza	3:44.52
5	BLR	Viktor Ginko	3:45.27
6	MEX	Ignacio Zamudio	3:46.07
7	FIN	Valentin Kononen	3:47.40
8	KAZ	Sergey Korepanov	3:48.42
24	USA	Allen James	4:01.18
26	USA	Andrzej Chylinski	4:03.13
—	USA	Herman Nelson	DQ

MEN'S 4x100-METER RELAY
Final: August 3

RANK	CTRY	ATHLETES	TIME
1	CAN	Robert Esmie / Glenroy Gilbert / Bruny Surin / Donovan Bailey	37.69
2	USA	Jon Drummond / Tim Harden / Michael Marsh / Dennis Mitchell / Tim Montgomery (prelim)	38.05
3	BRA	Arnaldo Silva / Robson da Silva / Edson Ribeiro / Andre Silva	38.41
4	UKR	Kostya Rurak / Serhiy Osovych / Oleh Kramarenko / Slava Dologodin	38.55
5	SWE	Peter Karlsson / Torbjorn Martensson / Lars Hedner / Patrik Strenius	38.67
6	CUB	Andres Simon / Joel Lamela / Joel Isasi / Luis Alberto Perez	39.39
7	FRA	Hermann Lomba / Regis Groisard / Pascal Theophile / Needy Guims	DNF
8	GHA	Zakari Aziz / Christian Nsiah / Albert Agyemang / Emmanuel Tuffuor	DNS

MEN'S 4x400-METER RELAY — Final: August 3

RANK	CTRY	ATHLETES	TIME
1	USA	LaMont Smith / Alvin Harrison / Derek Mills / Anthuan Maybank / Jason Rouser (prelim)	2:55.99
2	GBR	Iwan Thomas / Jamie Baulch / Mark Richardson / Roger Black	2:56.60
3	JAM	Michael McDonald / Roxbert Martin / Greg Haughton / Davian Clarke	2:59.42
4	SEN	Moustapha Diarra / Aboubakry Dia / Hachim Ndiaye / Ibou Faye	3:00.64
5	JPN	Shunji Karube / Koji Ito / Jun Osakada / Shigekazu Omori	3:00.76
6	POL	Piotr Rysiukiewicz / Tomasz Jedrusik / Piotr Haczek / Robert Mackowiak	3:00.96
7	BAH	Carl Oliver / Troy McIntosh / Dennis Darling / Timothy Munnings	3:02.71
8	KEN		DNS

MEN'S MARATHON — Final: August 4

RANK	CTRY	ATHLETE	TIME
1	RSA	Josia Thugwane	2:12.36
2	KOR	Lee Bong-ju	2:12.39
3	KEN	Eric Wainaina	2:12.44
4	ESP	Martin Fiz	2:13.20
5	GBR	Richard Nerurkar	2:13.39
6	MEX	German Silva	2:14.29
7	AUS	Steve Moneghetti	2:14.35
8	MEX	Benjamin Paredes	2:14.55
28	USA	Keith Brantly	2:18.17
31	USA	Bob Kempainen	2:18.38
41	USA	Mark Coogan	2:20.27

MEN'S HIGH JUMP — Final: July 28

RANK	CTRY	ATHLETE	METERS	FT/IN	
1	USA	Charles Austin	2.39	7-10	OR
2	POL	Artur Partyka	2.37	7-9 1/4	
3	GBR	Steve Smith	2.35	7-8 1/2	
4	YUG	Dragutin Topic	2.32	7-7 1/4	
5	NOR	steinar Hoen	2.32	7-7 1/4	
6	GRE	Lambros Papakostas	2.32	7-7 1/4	
7	AUS	Tim Forsyth	2.32	7-7 1/4	
8	KOR	Lee Jin-taek	2.29	7-6	
26	USA	Cameron Wright	2.20	7-2 1/2	
31	USA	Ed Broxterman	2.15	7-0 1/2	

MEN'S LONG JUMP — Final: July 29

RANK	CTRY	ATHLETE	METERS	FT/IN
1	USA	Carl Lewis	8.50	27-10 3/4
2	JAM	James Beckford	8.29	27-2 1/2
3	USA	Joe Greene	8.24	27-0 1/2
4	FRA	Emmanuel Bangue	8.19	26-10 1/2
5	USA	Mike Powell	8.17	26-9 3/4
6	SLO	Gregor Cankar	8.11	26-7 1/4
7	BLR	Aleksandr Glovatskiy	8.07	26-5 3/4
8	SWE	Mattias Sunneborn	8.06	26-5 1/2

MEN'S TRIPLE JUMP — Final: July 27

RANK	CTRY	ATHLETE	METERS	FT/IN	
1	USA	Kenny Harrison	18.09	59-4 1/4	OR
2	GBR	Jonathan Edwards	17.88	58-8	
3	CUB	Yoelbi Quesada	17.44	57-2 3/4	
4	USA	Mike Conley	17.40	57-1	
5	ARM	Armen Martirosyan	16.97	55-8 1/4	
6	BER	Brian Wellman	16.95	55-7 1/4	
7	BUL	Galin Georgiev	16.92	55-6 1/4	
8	USA	Robert Howard	16.90	55-5 1/2	

MEN'S POLE VAULT — Final: August 2

RANK	CTRY	ATHLETE	METERS	FT/IN	
1	FRA	Jean Galfione	5.92	19-5	OR
2	RUS	Igor Trandenkov	5.92	19-5	OR
3	GER	Andrei Tivontchik	5.92	19-5	OR
4	KAZ	Igor Potapovich	5.86	19-2 3/4	
5	RUS	Pyotr Bochkaryov	5.86	19-2 3/4	
6	BLR	Dmitriy Markov	5.86	19-2 3/4	
7	GER	Tim Lobinger	5.80	19-0 1/4	
8	USA	Lawrence Johnson	5.70	18-8 1/4	
11	USA	Jeff Hartwig	5.60	18-4 1/2	
13	USA	Scott Huffman	5.60	18-4 1/2	

MEN'S SHOT PUT — Final: July 26

RANK	CTRY	ATHLETE	METERS	FT/IN
1	USA	Randy Barnes	21.62	70-11 1/4
2	USA	John Godina	20.79	68-2 1/2
3	UKR	Oleksandr Bagach	20.75	68-1
4	ITA	Paolo Dal Soglio	20.74	68-0 1/2
5	GER	Oliver-Sven Buder	20.51	67-3 1/2
6	UKR	Roman Virastyuk	20.45	67-1 1/4
7	USA	C.J. Hunter	20.39	66-10 3/4
8	YUG	Dragan Peric	20.07	65-10 1/4

MEN'S DISCUS — Final: July 31

RANK	CTRY	ATHLETE	METERS	FT/IN	
1	GER	Lars Riedel	69.40	227-8	OR
2	BLR	Vladimir Dubrovshchik	66.60	218-6	
3	BLR	Vasiliy Kaptyukh	65.80	215-10	
4	USA	Anthony Washington	65.42	214-7	
5	LTU	Virgilijus Alekna	65.30	214-3	
6	GER	Juergen Schult	64.62	212-0	
7	UKR	Vitaliy Sidorov	63.78	209-3	
8	LTU	Vaclovas Kidykas	62.78	206-0	
12	USA	Adam Setliff	56.30	184-8	
14	USA	John Godina	61.82	202-10	

MEN'S JAVELIN — Final: August 3

RANK	CTRY	ATHLETE	METERS	FT/IN
1	CZE	Jan Zelezny	88.16	289-3
2	GBR	Steve Backley	87.44	286-10
3	FIN	Seppo Raty	86.98	285-4
4	GER	Raymond Hecht	86.88	285-0
5	GER	Boris Henry	85.68	281-1
6	RUS	Sergey Makarov	85.30	279-10
7	FIN	Kimmo Kinnunen	84.02	275-8
8	USA	Tom Pukstys	83.58	274-2
15	USA	Dave Stephens	79.18	259-9
17	USA	Todd Riech	78.02	255-11

MEN'S HAMMER — Final: July 28

RANK	CTRY	ATHLETE	METERS	FT/IN
1	HUN	Balasz Kiss	81.24	266-6
2	USA	Lance Deal	81.12	266-2
3	UKR	Oleksiy Krykum	80.02	262-6
4	UKR	Andriy Skvaruk	79.92	262-2
5	GER	Heinz Weis	79.78	261-9
6	RUS	Ilya Konovalov	78.72	258-3
7	BLR	Igor Astapkovich	78.20	256-7
8	BLR	Sergey Alay	77.38	253-10
24	USA	Kevin McMahon	73.46	241-0
29	USA	Dave Popejoy	72.46	237-9

DECATHLON — Final: August 1

RANK	CTRY	ATHLETE	POINTS
1	USA	Dan O'Brien	8824
2	GER	Frank Busemann	8706
3	CZE	Tomas Dvorak	8664
4	USA	Steve Fritz	8644
5	BLR	Eduard Hamalainen	8613
6	EST	Erki Nool	8543
7	CZE	Robert Zmelik	8422
8	UZB	Ramil Ganiyev	8318
10	USA	Chris Huffins	8300

WOMEN'S 100 METERS — Final: July 27
Wind: -0.7

RANK	CTRY	ATHLETE	TIME	
1	USA	Gail Devers	10.94	
2	JAM	Merlene Ottey	10.94	
3	USA	Gwen Torrence	10.96	
4	BAH	Chandra Sturrup	11.00	
5	RUS	Marina Trandenkova	11.06	
6	RUS	Natalya Voronova	11.10	
7	NGR	Mary Onyali	11.13	
8	UKR	Zhanna Pintusevych	11.14	
11	USA	D'Andre Hill	11.20	(semi)

WOMEN'S 200 METERS — Final: July 31
Wind: +0.3

RANK	CTRY	ATHLETE	TIME	
1	FRA	Marie-Jose Perec	22.12	
2	JAM	Merlene Ottey	22.24	
3	NIG	Mary Onyali	22.38	
4	USA	Inger Miller	22.41	
5	RUS	Galina Malchugina	22.45	
6	BAH	Chandra Sturrup	22.54	
7	JAM	Juliet Cuthberg	22.60	
8	USA	Carlette Guidry	22.61	
9	USA	Dannette Young-Stone	22.49	(semi)

WOMEN'S 400 METERS — Final: July 29

RANK	CTRY	ATHLETE	TIME	
1	FRA	Marie-Jose Perec	48.25	OR
2	AUS	Cathy Freeman	48.63	
3	NGR	Falilat Ogunkoya	49.10	
4	BAH	Pauline Davis	49.28	
5	USA	Jearl Miles	49.55	
6	NGR	Fatima Yusuf	49.77	
7	JAM	Sandie Richards	50.45	
8	GER	Grit Breuer	50.71	
10	USA	Kim Graham	51.13	
11	USA	Maicel Malone	51.16	

WOMEN'S 800 METERS — Final: July 29

RANK	CTRY	ATHLETE	TIME
1	RUS	Svetlana Masterkova	1:57.73
2	CUB	Ana Fidelia Quirot	1:58.11
3	MOZ	Maria Lurdes Mutola	1:58.71
4	GBR	Kelly Holmes	1:58.81
5	RUS	Yelena Afanasyeva	1:59.57
6	FRA	Patricia Djate-Taillard	1:59.61
7	BLR	Natasha Dukhnova	2:00.32
8	NZL	Toni Hodgkinson	2:00.47
13	USA	Meredith Rainey	1:59.36
19	USA	Joetta Clark	2:00.38
20	USA	Suzy Hamilton	2:00.47

WOMEN'S WHEELCHAIR 800 METERS — Final: August 1

RANK	CTRY	ATHLETE	TIME
1	AUS	Alix Sauvage	1:54.90
2	USA	Jean Driscoll	1:55.19
3	USA	Cheri Becerra	1:55.49
4	GBR	Tanni Grey	1:55.55
5	CAN	Chantal Petitclerc	1:55.61
6	USA	Leann Shannon	1:55.82
7	SWE	Monica Wetterstrom	1:56.83
8	GER	Lily Anggreny	2:05.33

WOMEN'S 1,500 METERS — Final: August 3

RANK	CTRY	ATHLETE	TIME
1	RUS	Svetlana Masterkova	4:00.83
2	ROM	Gabriela Szabo	4:01.54
3	AUT	Theresia Kiesl	4:03.02
4	CAN	Leah Pells	4:03.56
5	AUS	Margaret Crowley	4:03.79
6	POR	Carla Sacramento	4:03.91
7	RUS	Lyudmila Borisova	4:05.90
8	POL	Malgorzata Rydz	4:05.92
10	USA	Regina Jacobs	4:07.21
25	USA	Vicki Huber	4:14.82
30	USA	Juli Henner	4:27.14

WOMEN'S 5,000 METERS — Final: July 28

RANK	CTRY	ATHLETE	TIME
1	CHN	Wang Junxia	14:59.88
2	KEN	Pauline Konga	15:03.49
3	ITA	Roberta Brunet	15:07.52
4	JPN	Michiko Shimizu	15:09.05
5	GBR	Paula Radcliffe	15:13.11
6	RUS	Yelena Romanova	15:14.09
7	ROM	Elena Fidatov	15:16.71
8	KEN	Rose Cheruiyot	15:17.33
9	USA	Lynn Jennings	15:17.50
10	USA	Amy Rudolph	15:19.77
21	USA	Mary Slaney	15:41.30

WOMEN'S 10,000 METERS — Final: August 2

RANK	CTRY	ATHLETE	TIME	
1	POR	Fernanda Ribeiro	31:01.63	OR
2	CHN	Wang Junxia	31:02.58	
3	ETH	Gete Wami	31:06.65	
4	ETH	Derartu Tulu	31:10.46	
5	JPN	Masako Chiba	31:20.62	
6	KEN	Tecla Loroupe	31:23.22	
7	JPN	Yuko Kawakami	31:23.23	
8	ROM	Iulia Negura	31:26.46	
21	USA	Joan Nesbit	32:33.48	
23	USA	Kate Fonshell	32:48.05	
31	USA	Olga Appell	34:12.54	

WOMEN'S 100-METER HURDLES — Final: July 31
Wind: +0.2

RANK	CTRY	ATHLETE	TIME
1	SWE	Ludmila Engquist	12.58
2	SLO	Britiga Bukovec	12.59
3	FRA	Patricia Girard-Leno	12.65
4	USA	Gail Devers	12.66
5	JAM	Dione Rose	12.74
6	JAM	Michelle Freeman	12.76
7	RUS	Natalya Shekhodanova	12.80
8	USA	Lynda Goode	13.11
20	USA	Cheryl Dickey	12.92

WOMEN'S 400-METER HURDLES — Final: July 31

RANK	CTRY	ATHLETE	TIME	
1	JAM	Deon Hemmings	52.85	OR
2	USA	Kim Batten	53.08	
3	USA	Tonja Buford-Bailey	53.22	
4	JAM	Debbie Parris	53.97	
5	GER	Heike Meissner	54.03	
6	CAN	Rosey Edeh	54.39	
7	ROM	Ionela Tirlea	54.40	
8	GER	Silvia Rieger	54.57	
9	USA	Sandra Farmer-Patrick	54.73	

WOMEN'S 10-KILOMETER WALK — Final: July 29

RANK	CTRY	ATHLETE	TIME
1	RUS	Yelena Nikolayeva	41:49
2	ITA	Elisabetta Perrone	42:12
3	CHN	Wang Yan	42:19
4	CHN	Gu Yan	42:34
5	ITA	Rossella Giordano	42:43
6	BLR	Olya Kardapoltseva	43:02
7	POL	Katarzyna Radtke	43:05
8	BLR	Valya Tsybulskaya	43:21
14	USA	Michelle Rohl	44:29
20	USA	Debbi Lawrence	45:32
—	USA	Victoria Herazo	DQ

WOMEN'S 4x100-METER RELAY — Final: August 3

RANK	CTRY	ATHLETES	TIME
1	USA	Chryste Gaines / Gail Devers / Inger Miller / Gwen Torrence / Carlette Guidry (prelim)	41.95
2	BAH	Eldece Clarke / Chandra Sturrup / Sevatheda Fynes / Pauline Davis	42.14
3	JAM	Michelle Freeman / Juliet Cuthbert / Nikole Mitchell / Merlene Ottey	42.24
4	RUS	Yekaterina Leshchova / Galina Malchugina / Natalya Voronova / Irina Privalova	42.27
5	NGR	Chioma Ajunway / Mary Tombiri-Shirey / Christy Opara-Thompson / Mary Onyali	42.56
6	FRA	Sandra Citte / Odiah Sidibe / Patricia Girard-Leno / Marie-Jose Perec	42.76
7	AUS	Sharon Cripps / Kylie Hanigan / Lauren Hewitt / Jodi Lambert	43.70
8	GBR	Angie Thorp / Marcia Richardson / Simmone Jacobs / Katharine Merry	43.93

WOMEN'S 4x400-METER RELAY — Final: August 3

RANK	CTRY	ATHLETES	TIME
1	USA	Rochelle Stevens / Maicel Malone / Kim Graham / Jearl Miles / Linetta Wilson (prelim)	3:20.91
2	NGR	Bisi Afolabi / Fatima Yusuf / Charity Opara / Falilat Ogunkoya	3:21.04
3	GER	Uta Rohlaender / Linda Kisabaka / Anja Ruecker / Grit Breuer	3:21.14
4	JAM	Merlene Frazer / Sandie Richards / Juliet Campbell / Deon Hemmings	3:31.69
5	RUS	Tatyana Chebykina / Svetlana Goncharenko / Yekaterina Kulikova / Olga Kotlyarova	3:22.22
6	CUB	Idalmis Bonne / Julia Duporty / Surella Morales / Ana Fidelia Quirot	3:25.85
7	CZE	Nadezda Kostovalova / Ludmila Formanova / Helena Fuchsova / Hana Benesova	3:26.99
8	FRA	Francine Landre / Viviane Dorsile / Evelyne Elien / Elsa De Vassoigne	3:28.46

WOMEN'S MARATHON — Final: July 28

RANK	CTRY	ATHLETE	TIME
1	ETH	Fatuma Roba	2:26:05
2	RUS	Valentina Yegorova	2:28:05
3	JPN	Yuko Arimori	2:28:39
4	GER	Katrin Doerre-Heinig	2:28:45
5	ESP	Rocio Rios	2:30:50
6	ROM	Lidia Simon	2:31:04
7	POR	Maria Machado	2:31:11
8	GER	Sonja Krolik	2:31:16
10	USA	Anne Marie Lauck	2:31:30
31	USA	Linda Somers	2:36:58
—	USA	Jenny Spangler	DNF

WOMEN'S HIGH JUMP — Final: August 3

RANK	CTRY	ATHLETE	METERS	FT/IN	
1	BUL	Stefka Kostadinova	2.05	6-8 3/4	OR
2	GRE	Niki Bakogianni	2.03	6-8	
3	UKR	Inha Babakova	2.01	6-7	
4	ITA	Antonella Bevilacqua	1.99	6-6 1/4	
5	RUS	Yelena Gulyayeva	1.99	6-6 1/4	
6	GER	Alina Astafei	1.96	6-5	
7	RUS	Tatyana Motkova	1.96	6-5	
8	LTU	Nele Zilinskiene	1.96	6-5	
11	USA	Tisha Waller	1.93	6-4	
19	USA	Connie Teaberry	1.90	6-2 3/4	
25	USA	Amy Acuff	1.85	6-0 3/4	

WOMEN'S LONG JUMP — Final: August 2

RANK	CTRY	ATHLETE	METERS	FT/IN
1	NGR	Chioma Ajunwa	7.12	23-4 1/2
2	ITA	Fiona May	7.02	23-0 1/2
3	USA	Jackie Joyner-Kersee	7.00	22-11 3/4
4	GRE	Niki Xanthou	6.97	22-10 1/2
5	UKR	Iryna Chekhovtsova	6.97	22-10 1/2
6	POL	Agata Karczmarek	6.90	22-7 3/4
7	BUL	Iva Prandzheva	6.82	22-4 1/2
8	AUS	Nicole Boegman	6.73	22-1
17	USA	Marieke Veltman	6.49	21-3 1/2
—	USA	Shana Williams	no mark	

WOMEN'S TRIPLE JUMP — Final: July 31

RANK	CTRY	ATHLETE	METERS	FT/IN
1	UKR	Inessa Kravets	15.33	50-3 1/2
2	RUS	Inna Lasovskaya	14.98	49-1 3/4
3	CZE	Sarka Kasparkova	14.98	49-1 3/4
4	BUL	Iva Prandzheva	14.92	48-11 1/2
5	GBR	Ashia Hansen	14.49	47-6 1/2
6	GRE	Olga Vasdeki	14.44	47-4 1/2
7	CHN	Ren Ruiping	14.30	46-11
8	ROM	Rodica Mateescu	14.21	46-7 1/4
11	USA	Sheila Hudson	14.02	46-0
16	USA	Cynthea Rhodes	13.95	45-9 1/4
—	USA	Diana Orrange	no mark	

WOMEN'S SHOT PUT — Final: August 2

RANK	CTRY	ATHLETE	METERS	FT/IN
1	GER	Astrid Kumbernuss	20.56	67-5 1/2
2	CHN	Sui Xinmei	19.88	65-2 3/4
3	RUS	Irina Khudorozhkina	19.35	63-6
4	UKR	Vita Pavlysh	19.30	63-4
5	USA	Connie Price-Smith	19.22	63-0 3/4
6	GER	Stephanie Storp	19.06	62-6 1/2
7	GER	Kathrin Neimke	18.92	62-1
8	RUS	Irina Korzhanenko	18.68	61-3 1/2
9	USA	Ramona Pagel	18.48	60-7 3/4
16	USA	Valeyta Althouse	18.16	59-7

WOMEN'S DISCUS — Final: July 29

RANK	CTRY	ATHLETE	METERS	FT/IN
1	GER	Ilke Wyludda	69.66	228-6
2	RUS	Natalya Sadova	66.48	218-1
3	BLR	Elya Zvereva	65.64	215-4
4	GER	Franka Dietzsch	65.48	214-10
5	CHN	Xiao Yanling	64.72	212-4
6	RUS	Olga Chernyavskaya	64.70	212-3
7	ROM	Nicole Grasu	63.28	207-7
8	AUS	Lisa-Marie Vizaniari	62.48	205-0
30	USA	Lacy Barnes-Mileham	57.48	188-7
33	USA	Suzy Powell	56.24	184-6
34	USA	Aretha Hill	56.04	183-9

WOMEN'S JAVELIN — Final: July 27

RANK	CTRY	ATHLETE	METERS	FT/IN
1	FIN	Heli Rantanen	67.94	222-11
2	AUS	Louise McPaul	65.54	215-0
3	NOR	Trine Hattestad	64.98	213-2
4	CUB	Isel Lopez	64.68	212-2
5	CUB	Xiomara Rivero	64.48	211-6
6	GER	Karen Forkel	64.18	210-7
7	FIN	Mikaela Ingberg	61.52	201-10
8	CHN	Li Lei	60.74	199-3
26	USA	Nicole Carroll	54.74	179-7
30	USA	Erica Wheeler	53.34	175-0

HEPTATHLON — Final: July 28

RANK	CTRY	ATHLETE	POINTS
1	SYR	Ghada Shouaa	6780
2	BEL	Natasha Sazanovich	6563
3	GBR	Denise Lewis	6489
4	POL	Urszula Wlodarczyk	6484
5	SLE	Eunice Barber	6342
6	HUN	Rita Inancsi	6336
7	GER	Sabine Braun	6317
8	USA	Kelly Blair	6307
9	USA	Sharon Hanson	6292
—	USA	Jackie Joyner-Kersee	DNF (injury)

BADMINTON

MEN'S SINGLES — Final: July 31

RANK	CTRY	ATHLETE	GAME SCORES
1	DEN	Poul-Erik Hoyer-Larsen	15-12, 15-10
2	CHN	Dong Jiong	
3	MAS	Rashid Sidek	15-5, 11-15, 15-6
4	INA	Heryanto Arbi	
5T	INA	Joko Suprianto	
5T	KOR	Lee Kwang jin	
5T	KOR	Park Sung woo	
5T	INA	Alan Budi Kusuma	
—	USA	Kevin Han	elim. 1st rd

MEN'S DOUBLES — Final: July 31

RANK	CTRY	ATHLETES	GAME SCORES
1	INA	Rexy Mainaky / Ricky Subagja	5-15, 15-13, 15-12
2	MAS	Cheah Soon Kit / Yap Kim Hock	
3	INA	S. Antonius / Denny Kantono	15-4, 12-15, 15-8
4	MAS	Soo Beng Kiang / Tan Kim Her	
5T	RUS	Andreij Antropov / Nickolaj Zuev	
5T	GBR	Simon Archer / Chris Hunt	
5T	KOR	Ha Tae kwon / Kang Kyung jin	
5T	CHN	Huang Zhanzhong / Jiang Xin	

no USA entry

WOMEN'S SINGLES — Final: July 31

RANK	CTRY	ATHLETE	GAME SCORES
1	KOR	Bang Soo hyun	11-6, 11-7
2	INA	Mia Audina	
3	INA	Susi Susanti	11-4, 11-1
4	KOR	Kim Ji hyun	
5T	DEN	Camilla Martin	
5T	CHN	Yao Yan	
5T	CHN	Ye Zhaoying	
5T	CHN	Han Jingna	
—	USA	Erika Von Heiland	elim. 1st rd.

WOMEN'S DOUBLES — Final: July 31

RANK	CTRY	ATHLETES	GAME SCORES
1	CHN	Ge Fei / Gu Jun	15-5, 15-5
2	KOR	Gil Young ah / Jang Hye ock	
3	CHN	Qin Yiyuan / Tang Yongshu	7-15, 15-4, 15-8
4	DEN	Helene Kirkegaard / Rikke Olsen	
5T	CHN	Chen Xingdong / Peng Xingyong	
5T	INA	Eliza / Rosiana Zelin	
5T	DEN	Ann Jorgensen / Lotte Olsen	
5T	DEN	Lisbet Stuer-Lauridsen / Marlene Thomsen	
—	USA	Linda French / Erika Von Heiland	elim. 1st rd.

MIXED DOUBLES

RANK	CTRY	ATHLETES	GAME SCORES
1	KOR	Gil Young ah / Kim Dong moon	15-13, 4-15, 12-15
2	KOR	Park Joo bong / Ra Kyung-min	
3	CHN	Liu Jianjun / Sun Man	13-15, 17-15, 15-4
4	CHN	Chen Xingdong / Peng Xingyong	
5T	CHN	Tao Xiaoqiang / Wang Xiaoyuan	
5T	DEN	Rikke Olsen / Michael Sogaard	
5T	INA	Nimpele Flandy / Rosalina Riseu	
5T	INA	Trikus Heryanto / Minarti Timur	

Final: August 1

no USA entry

BASEBALL

FINAL STANDINGS

Final: August 2

RANK	CTRY	RECORD	SCORE	USA GAME SCORES	
1	CUB	9-0	13-9	USA vs NCA	4-1
2	JPN	5-4	(final)	USA vs KOR	7-2
3	USA	7-2	10-3	USA vs ITA	15-3
4	NCA	4-5	(3rd-4th)	USA vs JPN	15-5
5	NED	2-5		USA vs AUS	15-5
6	ITA	2-5		USA vs CUB	8-10
7	AUS	2-5		USA vs NED	17-1
8	KOR	1-6		USA vs JPN	2-11
				USA vs NCA	10-3

USA TEAM: Chad Allen / Kris Benson / R.A. Dickey / Troy Glaus / Chad Green / Seth Greisinger / Kip Harkrider / A.J Hinch / Jacque Jones / Billy Koch / Mark Kotsay / Matt LeCroy / Travis Lee / Braden Looper / Brian Loyd / Warren Morris / Augie Ojeda / Jim Parque / Jeff Weaver / Jason Williams / Head Coach: Skip Bertman / Assistant Coaches: Ron Polk / Ray Tanner / Jerry Weinstein

BASKETBALL

MEN

Final: August 3

RANK	CTRY	RECORD	SCORE	USA GAME SCORES	
1	USA	8-0	95-69	USA vs ARG	96-60
2	YUG	7-1	(final)	USA vs ANG	87-54
3	LTU	5-3	80-74	USA vs LTU	104-82
4	AUS	5-3	(3rd-4th)	USA vs CHN	133-70
5	GRE	5-3		USA vs CRO	102-71
6	BRA	3-5		USA vs BRA	98-75
7	CRO	4-4		USA vs AUS	101-73
8	CHN	2-6		USA vs YUG	95-69

USA TEAM: Charles Barkley / Anfernee Hardaway / Grant Hill / Karl Malone / Reggie Miller / Shaquille O'Neal / Hakeem Olajuwon /Gary Payton / Scottie Pippen / Mitch Richmond / David Robinson / John Stockton / Head Coach: Lenny Wilkens / Assistant Coaches: Jerry Sloan / Bobby Cremins / Clem Haskins

WOMEN

Final: August 4

RANK	CTRY	RECORD	SCORE	USA GAME SCORES	
1	USA	8-0	111-87	USA vs CUB	101-84
2	BRA	7-1	(final)	USA vs KOR	98-65
3	AUS	5-3	66-56	USA vs ZAI	107-47
4	UKR	4-4	(3rd-4th)	USA vs AUS	96-79
5	RUS	6-2		USA vs KOR	105-64
6	CUB	3-5		USA vs JPN	108-93
7	JPN	3-5		USA vs AUS	93-71
8	ITA	3-5		USA vs BRA	111-87

USA TEAM: Jennifer Azzi / Ruthie Bolton / Teresa Edwards / Venus Lacey / Lisa Leslie / Rebecca Lobo / Katrina McClain / Nikki McCray / Carla McGhee / Dawn Staley / Katy Steding / Sheryl Swoopes / Head Coach: Tara VanDerveer / Assistant Coaches: Ceal Barry / Nancy Darsch / Marian Washington

BOXING

LIGHT FLYWEIGHT - (48 KG/106 LBS)

Final: August 3

RANK	CTRY	ATHLETE	DECISION
1	BUL	Daniel Petrov Bojilov	19-6
2	PHI	Mansueto Velasco	
3T	ESP	Rafael Lozano	
3T	UKR	Oleg Kiryukhin	
—	USA	Albert Guardado	elim. qtr finals

FLYWEIGHT - (51 KG/112 LBS)

Final: August 4

RANK	CTRY	ATHLETE	DECISION
1	CUB	Maikro Romero	12-11
2	KAZ	Bolat Djumadilov	
3T	GER	Zoltan Lunka	
3T	RUS	Albert Pakeev	
—	USA	Eric Morel	elim. 1st rd.

BANTAMWEIGHT - (54 KG/119 LBS)

Final: August 3

RANK	CTRY	ATHLETE	DECISION
1	HUN	Istvan Kovacs	14-7
2	CUB	Arnaldo Mesa	
3T	THA	Vichairachanon Khadpo	
3T	RUS	Raimkul Malakhbekov	
—	USA	Zahir Raheem	elim. 2nd rd.

FEATHERWEIGHT - (57 KG/125 LBS)

Final: August 4

RANK	CTRY	ATHLETE	DECISION
1	THA	Somluck Kamsing	8-5
2	BUL	Serafim Todorov	
3T	USA	Floyd Mayweather	
3T	ARG	Pablo Chacon	

LIGHTWEIGHT - (60 KG/132 LBS)

Final: August 3

RANK	CTRY	ATHLETE	DECISION
1	ALG	Hocine Soltani	3-3
2	BUL	Tontcho Tontchev	
3T	USA	Terrance Cauthen	
3T	ROM	Leonard Doroftei	

LIGHT WELTERWEIGHT - (63.5 KG/139 LBS)

Final: August 4

RANK	CTRY	ATHLETE	DECISION
1	CUB	Hector Vinent	20-13
2	GER	Oktay Urkal	
3T	KAZ	Bolat Niyazmybetov	
3T	TUN	Fathi Missaoui	
—	USA	David Diaz	elim. 2nd rd.

WELTERWEIGHT - (67 KG/147 LBS)

Final: August 3

RANK	CTRY	ATHLETE	DECISION
1	RUS	Oleg Saitov	14-9
2	CUB	Juan Hernandez	
3T	PUR	Daniel Santos	
3T	ROM	Marian Simion	
—	USA	Fernando Vargas	elim. 2nd rd.

LIGHT MIDDLEWEIGHT - (71 KG/156 LBS)

Final: August 4

RANK	CTRY	ATHLETE	DECISION
1	USA	David Reid	KO-3, 0:36
2	CUB	Alfredo Duvergel	
3T	UZB	Karim Tulaganov	
3T	KAZ	Ezmouhan Ibzaimov	

MIDDLEWEIGHT - (75 KG/165 LBS)

Final: August 3

RANK	CTRY	ATHLETE	DECISION
1	CUB	Ariel Hernandez	11-3
2	TUR	Malik Beyleroglu	
3T	USA	Roshii Wells	
3T	ALG	Mohamed Bahari	

LIGHT HEAVYWEIGHT - (81 KG/178 LBS)

Final: August 4

RANK	CTRY	ATHLETE	DECISION
1	KAZ	Vassili Jirov	17-4
2	KOR	Lee Seung-bae	
3T	USA	Antonio Tarver	
3T	GER	Thomas Ulrich	

HEAVYWEIGHT - (91 KG/201 LBS)

Final: August 3

RANK	CTRY	ATHLETE	DECISION
1	CUB	Felix Savon	20-2
2	CAN	David Defiagbon	
3T	GER	Luan Krasniqi	
3T	USA	Nate Jones	

SUPER HEAVYWEIGHT - (+91 KG/+201 LBS)

Final: August 4

RANK	CTRY	ATHLETE	DECISION
1	UKR	Vladimir Klichko	7-3
2	TGA	Paea Wolfgram	
3T	RUS	Alexei Lezin	
3T	NGR	Duncan Dokiwari	
—	USA	Lawrence Clay-Bey	elim. 2nd rd.

CANOE/KAYAK

MEN'S C-1, WHITEWATER SLALOM

Final: July 27

RANK	CTRY	ATHLETE	POINTS
1	SVK	Michal Martikan	151.03
2	CZE	Lukas Pollert	151.17
3	FRA	Patrice Estanguet	152.84
4	GBR	Gareth Marriott	155.83
5	FRA	Herve Delamarre	155.98
6	FRA	Emmanuel Brugvin	156.71
7	GER	Martin Lang	159.91
8	POL	Ryszard Mordarski	161.00
9	USA	David Hearn	162.51
19	USA	Adam Clawson	172.53

MEN'S C-2, WHITEWATER SLALOM

Final: July 28

RANK	CTRY	ATHLETE	POINTS
1	FRA	Frank Adisson / Wilfrid Forgues	158.82
2	CZE	Miroslav Simek / Jiri Rohan	160.16
3	GER	Michael Senft / Andre Ehrenberg	163.72
4	GER	Michael Trummer / Manfred Berro	163.72
5	FRA	Thierry Saidi / Emmnuel Del Rey	165.47
6	CZE	Pavel Stercl / Petr Stercl	168.45
7	POL	Krzysztof Kolomanski / Michal Staniszewski	169.95
8	CAN	Benoit Gauthier / Francois Letourneau	172.67
11	USA	Horace Holden / Wayne Dickert	180.90

MEN'S K-1, WHITEWATER SLALOM

Final: July 28

RANK	CTRY	ATHLETE	POINTS
1	GER	Oliver Fix	141.22
2	SLO	Andraz Vehovar	141.65
3	GER	Thomas Becker	142.79
4	FRA	Laurent Burtz	144.33
5	IRL	Ian Wiley	145.21
6	USA	Rich Weiss	145.78
7	SLO	Jernej Abramic	145.81
8	GER	Jochen Lettmann	145.99
12	USA	Scott Shipley	148.31
20	USA	Eric Giddens	151.65

WOMEN'S K-1, WHITEWATER SLALOM

Final: July 27

RANK	CTRY	ATHLETE	POINTS
1	CZE	Stepanka Hilgertova	169.49
2	USA	Dana Chladek	169.49
3	FRA	Myriam Fox-Jerusalmi	171.00
4	ITA	Christina Giai Pron	171.84
5	SVK	Gabriela Broskova	172.57
6	FRA	Anne Boixel	172.79
7	USA	Cathy Hearn	173.03
8	CAN	Margaret Langford	173.59

MEN'S C-1, FLATWATER 500 METERS

Final: August 4

RANK	CTRY	ATHLETE	TIME
1	CZE	Martin Doktor	1:49.93
2	SVK	Slavomir Knazovicky	1:50.51
3	HUN	Imre Pulai	1:50.75
4	UKR	Mykhaylo Slivinskiyy	1:51.71
5	GER	Thomas Zereske	1:52.35
6	DEN	Christian Fredriksen	1:52.84
7	KAZ	Konstantin Negodyayev	1:53.15
8	CAN	Steve Giles	1:53.32
—	USA	Jim Terrell	elim. semis

MEN'S C-1, FLATWATER 1,000 METERS

Final: August 3

RANK	CTRY	ATHLETE	TIME
1	CZE	Martin Doktor	3:54.418
2	LAT	Ivan Klementyev	3:54.954
3	HUN	Gyorgy Zala	3:56.366
4	GER	Patrick Schulze	3:57.778
5	FRA	Pascal Sylvoz	3:59.014
6	ROM	Victor Partnoi	3:59.858
7	UKR	Roman Bundz	4:02.078
8	CRO	Ivan Sabjan	4:04.066
—	USA	Joseph Harper	elim. semis

MEN'S C-2, FLATWATER 500 METERS

Final: August 4

RANK	CTRY	ATHLETE	TIME
1	HUN	Csaba Horvath / Gyorgy Kolonics	1:40.42
2	MOL	Nikolai Juravschi / Victor Reneischi	1:40.45
3	ROM	Gheorghe Andriev / Grigore Obreja	1:41.33
4	GER	Andreas Dittmer / Gunar Kirchbach	1:41.76
5	BUL	Martin Marinov / Blagovest Stoyanov	1:42.20
6	RUS	Andrey Kabanov / Pavel Konovalov	1:42.49
7	ESP	Jose Alfredo Bea / Oleg Shelestenko	1:43.57
8	SVK	Csaba Orosz / Peter Pales	1:44.11

no USA entry

MEN'S C-2, FLATWATER 1,000 METERS

Final: August 3

RANK	CTRY	ATHLETE	TIME
1	GER	Andreas Dittmer / Gunar Kirchbach	3:31.870
2	ROM	Antonel Borsan / Marcel Glavan	3:32.294
3	HUN	Csaba Horvath / Gyorgy Kolonics	3:32.514
4	BUL	Martin Marinov / Blagovest Stoyanov	3:34.382
5	MDA	Nikolai Juravschi / Victor Reneyskiy	3:35.198
6	GBR	Andrew Train / Stephen Train	3:36.694
7	SVK	Csaba Orosz / Peter Pales	3:36.938
8	ESP	Jose Alfredo Bea / Oleg Shelestenko	3:37.154

no USA entry

MEN'S K-1, FLATWATER 500 METERS — Final: August 4

RANK	CTRY	ATHLETE	TIME
1	ITA	Antonio Rossi	1:37.42
2	NOR	Holmann Knut	1:38.33
3	POL	Piotr Markiewicz	1:38.61
4	ROM	Geza Magyar	1:38.97
5	GER	Lutz Liwowski	1:39.30
6	ESP	Miguel Garcia	1:40.04
7	FIN	Mikko Kolehmainen	1:40.33
8	SVK	Robert Erban	1:40.40
—	**USA**	**Mike Herbert**	**elim. semis**

MEN'S K-1, FLATWATER 1,000 METERS — Final: August 3

RANK	CTRY	ATHLETE	TIME
1	NOR	Knut Holmann	3:25.785
2	ITA	Beniamino Bonomi	3:27.073
3	AUS	Clint Robinson	3:29.713
4	GER	Lutz Liwowski	3:30.025
5	ESP	Agustin Calderon	3:31.397
6	POL	Andrzej Gajewski	3:32.521
7	ROM	Marin Popescu	3:34.549
8	BRA	Sebastian Cuattrin	3:34.669
—	**USA**	**Michael Harbold**	**elim. semis**

MEN'S K-2, FLATWATER 500 METERS — Final: August 4

RANK	CTRY	ATHLETE	TIME
1	GER	Kay Bluhm / Torsten Gutsche	1:28.69
2	ITA	Beniamino Bonomi / Daniele Scarpa	1:28.72
3	AUS	Danny Collins / Andrew Trim	1:29.40
4	RUS	Oleg Gorobiy / Anatoliy Tishchenko	1:29.67
5	POL	Maciej Freimut / Adam Wysocki	1:29.93
6	HUN	Krisztian Bartfai / Zsolt Gyulay	1:30.00
7	ROM	Daniel Stoian / Romica Serban	1:30.05
8	BUL	Milko Kazanov / Andrian Dushev	1:30.51
—	**USA**	**Stein Jorgensen / John Mooney**	**elim. semis**

MEN'S K-2, FLATWATER 1,000 METERS — Final: August 3

RANK	CTRY	ATHLETES	TIME
1	ITA	Antonio Rossi / Daniele Scarpa	3:09.190
2	GER	Kay Bluhm / Torsten Gutsche	3:10.518
3	BUL	Andrian Dushev / Milko Kazanov	3:11.206
4	POL	Dariusz Bialkowski / Grzegorz Kotowicz	3:11.262
5	FRA	Patrick Lancereau / Pierre Lubac	3:11.402
6	DEN	Thor Nielsen / Jesper Staal	3:12.054
7	AUS	Grant Leury / Peter Scott	3:13.054
8	SWE	Staffan Malmsten / Markus Oscarsson	3:14.182
—	**USA**	**John Mooney / Peter Newton**	**elim. semis**

MEN'S K-4, FLATWATER 1,000 METERS — Final: August 3

RANK	CTRY	ATHLETES	TIME
1	GER	Detlef Hofmann / Thomas Reineck / Olaf Winter / Mark Zabel	2:51.528
2	HUN	Attila Adrovicz / Ferenc Csipes / Gabor Horvath / Andras Rajna	2:53.184
3	RUS	Oleg Gorobiy / Anatoliy Tishchenko / Georgiy Tsybulnikov / Sergey Verlin	2:53.996
4	POL	Grzegorz Kaleta / Piotr Markiewicz / Marek Witkowski / Adam Wysocki	2:54.772
5	ESP	Miguel Garcia / Jovino Gonzalez / Emilio Merchan / Gregorio Vicente	2:55.884
6	SWE	Jonas Fager / Paw Madsen / Henrik Nilsson / Mattias Oscarsson	2:55.908
7	CAN	Mihai Apostol / Renn Crichlow / Peter Giles / Liam Jewell	2:56.664
8	BUL	Georgi Choykov / Petar Karadzhov / Petar Merkov / Nikolay Yordanov	2:56.696
—	**USA**	**Curt Bader / Philippe Boccara / Mark Hamilton / Cliff Meidl**	**elim. semis**

WOMEN'S K-1, FLATWATER 500 METERS — Final: August 4

RANK	CTRY	ATHLETE	TIME
1	HUN	Rita Koban	1:47.65
2	CAN	Caroline Brunet	1:47.89
3	ITA	Josefa Idem	1:48.73
4	GER	Birgit Fischer	1:49.38
5	SWE	Susanne Gunnarsson	1:49.59
6	AUS	Ursula Profanter	1:50.27
7	AUS	Katrin Borcher	1:50.81
8	SUI	Ingrid Haralamow	1:50.87
—	**USA**	**Traci Phillips**	**elim. semis**

WOMEN'S K-2, FLATWATER 500 METERS — Final: August 4

RANK	CTRY	ATHLETES	TIME
1	SWE	Agneta Andersson / Susanne Gunnarsson	1:39.32
2	GER	Ramona Portwich / Birgit Fischer	1:39.68
3	AUS	Katrin Borchert / Anna Wood	1:40.64
4	HUN	Rita Koban / Szilvia Mednyanszki	1:40.89
5	CAN	Marie-Josee Gibeau / Corrina Kennedy	1:41.31
6	ESP	Izaskun Aramburu / Beatriz Manchon	1:42.62
7	POL	Izabela Dylewska-Swiatowiak / Elzbieta Urbanczyk	1:42.75
8	RUS	Larisa Kosorukova / Natalya Guliy	1:43.23
—	**USA**	**DeAnne Hemmens / Lia Rousset**	**elim. semis**

WOMEN'S K-4, FLATWATER 500 METERS — Final: August 3

RANK	CTRY	ATHLETES	TIME
1	GER	Birgit Fischer / Manuela Mucke / Ramona Portwich / Anett Schuck	1:31.077
2	SUI	Daniela Baumer / Sabine Eichenberger / Ingrid Haralamow / Gabi Mueller	1:32.701
3	SWE	Agneta Andersson / Ingela Ericsson / Anna Olsson / Susanne Rosenqvist	1:32.917
4	CHN	Dong Ying / Gao Beibel / Xian Bangdi / Zhang Qin	1:33.089
5	CAN	Marie-Josee Gibeau / Alison Herst / Corrina Kennedy / Klari MacAskill	1:33.093
6	ESP	Izaskun Aramburu / Beatriz Manchon / Ana Maria Penas / Belen Sanchez	1:33.577
7	RUS	Natalya Guliy / Larisa Kosorukova / Olga Tishchenko / Tatyana Tishchenko	1:34.345
8	AUS	Natalie Hunter / Lynda Lehmann / Yanda Nossiter / Shelley Oates	1:34.673
—	**USA**	**Alexandra Harbold / DeAnne Hemmens / Lia Rousset / Drusilla van Hengel**	**elim. semis**

CYCLING

MEN'S INDIVIDUAL CROSS COUNTRY MOUNTAIN BIKING — Final: July 30

RANK	CTRY	ATHLETE	TIME
1	NED	Bart Jan Brentjens	2:17:38
2	SUI	Thomas Frischknecht	2:20:14
3	FRA	Miguel Martinez	2:20:36
4	FRA	Christophe Dupouey	2:25:03
5	ITA	Daniele Pontoni	2:25:08
6	CRC	Jose Andres Brenes	2:25:51
7	DEN	Lennie Kristensen	2:26:02
8	ITA	Luca Bramati	2:26:05
19	**USA**	**David Juarez**	**2:35:15**
20	**USA**	**Don Myrah**	**2:35:50**

WOMEN'S INDIVIDUAL CROSS COUNTRY MOUNTAIN BIKING — Final: July 30

RANK	CTRY	ATHLETE	TIME
1	ITA	Paola Pezzo	1:50:51
2	CAN	Alison Sydor	1:51:58
3	**USA**	**Susan DeMattei**	**1:52:36**
4	NOR	Gunn-Rita Dahle	1:53:50
5	NED	Elsbeth Vink	1:54:38
6	ITA	Annabella Stropparo	1:55:56
7	GER	Regina Marunde	1:57:21
8	NZL	Kathy Lynch	1:57:40
10	**USA**	**Juliana Furtado**	**1:58:32**

MEN'S ROAD RACE — Final: July 31

RANK	CTRY	ATHLETE	TIME
1	SUI	Pascal Richard	4:53:56
2	DEN	Rolf Soerensen	4:53:56
3	GBR	Max Sciandri	4:53:58
4	**USA**	**Frankie Andreu**	**4:55:10**
5	FRA	Richard Virenque	4:55:10
6	ESP	Melchor Mauri	4:55:11
7	ITA	Fabio Baldato	4:55:24
8	ITA	Michele Bartoli	4:55:24
12	**USA**	**Lance Armstrong**	**4:55:25**
74	**USA**	**Greg Randolph**	**4:56:49**
76	**USA**	**George Hincapie**	**4:56:49**
93	**USA**	**Steve Hegg**	**4:56:51**

MEN'S INDIVIDUAL TIME TRIAL — Final: August 3

RANK	CTRY	ATHLETE	TIME
1	ESP	Miguel Indurain	1:04.05
2	ESP	Abraham Olano	1:04.17
3	GBR	Chris Boardman	1:04.36
4	ITA	Michele Fondriest	1:05.01
5	SUI	Tony Rominger	1:06.05
6	**USA**	**Lance Armstrong**	**1:06.28**
7	SUI	Alex Zuelle	1:06.33
8	AUS	Patrick Jonker	1:06.54
16	**USA**	**Steve Hegg**	**1:08.29**

WOMEN'S ROAD RACE — Final: July 21

RANK	CTRY	ATHLETE	TIME
1	FRA	Jeannie Longo-Ciprelli	2:36.13
2	ITA	Imelda Chiappa	2:26.38
3	CAN	Clara Hughes	2:35.44
4	GER	Vera Hohlfeld	2:37.06
5	LTU	Jolanta Polikeviciute	2:37.06
6	RUS	Zulfiya Zabirova	2:37.06
7	ITA	Alessandra Cappellotto	2:37.06
8	SUI	Barbara Heeb	2:37.06
29	**USA**	**Jeanne Golay**	**2:37.06**
36	**USA**	**Linda Brenneman**	**2:40.27**
37	**USA**	**Allison Dunlap**	**2:41.21**

WOMEN'S INDIVIDUAL TIME TRIAL — Final: August 3

RANK	CTRY	ATHLETE	TIME
1	RUS	Zulfiya Zabirova	36:40
2	FRA	Jeannie Longo-Ciprelli	37:00
3	CAN	Clara Hughes	37:13
4	AUS	Kathryn Watt	37:53
5	FRA	Marion Clignet	38:14
6	FIN	Tea Vikstedt-Nyman	38:24
7	LTU	Jolanta Polikeviciute	38:27
8	ITA	Imelda Chiappa	38:47
11	**USA**	**Linda Brenneman**	**38:52**
16	**USA**	**Jeanne Golay**	**39:36**

MEN'S KILOMETER TIME TRIAL — Final: July 24

RANK	CTRY	ATHLETE	TIME	
1	FRA	Florian Rousseau	1:02.712	OR
2	**USA**	**Erin Hartwell**	**1:02.940**	
3	JPN	Takanobu Jumonji	1:03.261	
4	GER	Soren Lausberg	1:03.514	
5	RSA	Jean-Pierre van Zyl	1:04.214	
6	POL	Grzegorz Krejner	1:04.697	
7	GRE	Dimitrios Georgalis	1:04.995	
8	LAT	Ainars Kiksis	1:05.497	

MEN'S MATCH SPRINT — Final: July 28

RANK	CTRY	ATHLETE	
1	GER	Jens Fiedler	
2	**USA**	**Marty Nothstein**	
3	CAN	Curtis Harnett	
4	AUS	Gary Neiwand	
5	AUS	Darryn Hill	
6	FRA	Frederic Magne	
7	GER	Eyk Pokorny	
8	FRA	Florian Rousseau	
—	**USA**	**Bill Clay**	**elim. 2nd rd repechage**

MEN'S 4,000-METER INDIVIDUAL PURSUIT — Final: July 25

RANK	CTRY	ATHLETE	TIME
1	ITA	Andrea Collinelli	4:20.893
2	FRA	Philippe Ermenault	4:22.714
3	AUS	Bradley McGee	4:26.121
4	RUS	Aleksey Markov	4:26.828
5	ESP	Juan Martinez	4:28.310
6	GER	Heiko Szonn	4:31.583
7	UKR	Andriy Yatsekno	caught
8	ARG	Walter Perez	caught
9	**USA**	**Kent Bostick**	**4:33.008**

MEN'S 4,000-METER TEAM PURSUIT — Final: July 27

RANK	CTRY	ATHLETES	TIME	
1	FRA	Christophe Capelle / Philippe Ermenault / Jean-Michel Monin / Francis Moreau	4:05.930	OR
2	RUS	Anton Chantyr / Eduard Gritsun / Nikolay Kuznetsov / Aleksey Markov	4:07.730	
3	AUS	Bradley McGee / Stuart O'Grady / Timothy O'Shannessey / Dean Woods / Brett Aitken	4:07.535	
4	ITA	Adler Capelli / Andrea Collinelli / Mauro Trentini / Cristiano Citton	4:08.317	
5	ESP	Juan Llaneras / Bernardo Gonzalez / Adolfo Alper. Plaza	4:11.324	
6	**USA**	**Dirk Copeland / Mariano Friedick / Adam Laurent / Michael McCarthy**	**4:12.510**	
7	UKR	Oleksandr Fedenko / Serhiy Matveyev / Bodyan Bondaryev / Andriy Yatsenko / Alexander Simonenko	4:12.794	
8	NZL	Gregory Henderson / Julian Dean / Timothy Carswell / Brendon Cameron	4:15.635	

MEN'S 50 KM POINTS RACE — Final: July 28

RANK	CTRY	ATHLETE	POINTS
1	ITA	Silvio Martinello	37
2	CAN	Brian Walton	29
3	AUS	Stuart O'Grady	27
4	UKR	Vasyl Yakovlev	24
5	FRA	Francis Moreau	21
6	ESP	Juan Llaneras	17
7	KOR	Cho Ho-sung	15
8	NZL	Glenn McLeay	8
19	USA	**Brian McDonough**	5

WOMEN'S MATCH SPRINT — Final: July 27

RANK	CTRY	ATHLETE
1	FRA	Felicia Ballanger
2	AUS	Michelle Ferris
3	NED	Ingrid Haringa
4	GER	Annett Neumann
5	RUS	Oksana Grishina
6	EST	Erika Salumae
7	CHN	Wang Yan
8	CAN	Tanya Dubnicoff
—	USA	**Connie Paraskevin-Young** elim. 1/8 finals rep.

WOMEN'S 3,000-METER INDIVIDUAL PURSUIT — Final: July 28

RANK	CTRY	ATHLETE	TIME
1	ITA	Antonella Bellutti	3:33.595
2	FRA	Marion Clignet	3:38.571
3	GER	Judith Arndt	3:38.744
4	GBR	Yvonne McGregor	3:40.885
5	USA	**Rebecca Twigg**	3:41.611
6	LTU	Rasa Mazeiktyte	3:42.129
7	NZL	Sarah Ulmer	3:45.761
8	AUS	Kathryn Watt	caught

WOMEN'S POINTS RACE — Final: July 28

RANK	CTRY	ATHLETE	POINTS
1	FRA	Nathalie Lancien	24
2	NED	Ingrid Haringa	23
3	AUS	Lucy Tyler Sharman	17
4	RUS	Svetlana Samokhvalova	14
5	ESA	Maureen Kaila Vergara	11
6	BLR	Lyudmila Gorozhanskaya	11
7	FIN	Tea Vikstedt-Nyman	9
8	NZL	Jacqueline Nelson	8
17	USA	**Jeanne Golay**	0

DIVING

MEN'S 10-METER PLATFORM — Final: August 2

RANK	CTRY	ATHLETE	TOTAL
1	RUS	Dmitri Saoutine	692.34
2	GER	Jan Hempel	663.27
3	CHN	Xiao Hailiang	658.20
4	CHN	Tian Liang	648.18
5	RUS	Vladimir Timoshinin	628.59
6	USA	**David Pichler**	607.11
7	MEX	Fernando Platas	603.03
8	GER	Michael Kuehne	583.98
9	USA	**Patrick Jeffrey**	560.22

MEN'S 3-METER SPRINGBOARD — Final: July 29

RANK	CTRY	ATHLETE	TOTAL
1	CHN	Xiong Ni	701.46
2	CHN	Yu Zhuocheng	690.93
3	USA	**Mark Lenzi**	686.49
4	USA	**Scott Donie**	666.93
5	RUS	Dmitri Saoutine	644.67
6	AUS	Michael Murphy	640.95
7	GER	Jan Hempel	622.32
8	MEX	Fernando Platas	619.98

WOMEN'S 10-METER PLATFORM — Final: July 27

RANK	CTRY	ATHLETE	TOTAL
1	CHN	Fu Mingxia	521.58
2	GER	Annika Walter	479.22
3	USA	**Mary Ellen Clark**	472.95
4	USA	**Becky Ruehl**	455.19
5	CHN	Guo Jingjing	447.21
6	UKR	Olena Zhupyna	437.01
7	KAZ	Irina Vygouzova	432.60
8	RUS	Olga Khristoforova	426.12

WOMEN'S 3-METER SPRINGBOARD — Final: July 31

RANK	CTRY	ATHLETE	TOTAL
1	CHN	Fu Mingxia	547.68
2	RUS	Irina Lashko	512.19
3	CAN	Annie Pelletier	509.64
4	USA	**Melisa Moses**	507.99
5	UKR	Olena Zhupyna	507.27
6	JPN	Yuki Motobuchi	506.04
7	RUS	Vera Ilyina	493.56
8	SWE	Anna Lindbereg	489.81
9	USA	**Jenny Keim**	486.63

EQUESTRIAN

INDIVIDUAL JUMPING — Final: August 4

RANK	CTRY	ATHLETE/HORSE	TOTAL
1	GER	Ulrich Kirchhoff / Jus De Pommes	1.00
2	SUI	Willi Melliger / Calvaro	4.00
3	FRA	Alexandra Ledermann / Rochet M	4.00
4	AUT	Hugo Simon / ET	4.00
5	SUI	Urs Fah / Jeremia	4.00
6	GBR	Geoff Billington / It's Otto	4.00
7	NED	Jan Tops / Top Gun	4.00
8	BRA	Alvaro Miranda Neto / Aspen	4.00
11T	USA	**Leslie Burr-Howard / Extreme**	8.00
20T	USA	**Anne Kursinski / Eros**	16.00
30T	USA	**Michael Matz / Rhum IV**	12.00 (semi)
—	USA	**Peter Leone / Legato**	

TEAM JUMPING — Final: August 1

RANK	CTRY	ATHLETE/HORSE	TOTAL
1	GER	Ulrich Kirchhoff / Jus De Pommes	1.75
		Lars Nieberg / For Pleasure	
		Franke Sloothaak / Joly	
		Ludger Beerbaum / Ratina	
2	USA	**Anne Kursinski / Eros**	12.00
		Michael Matz / Rhum IV	
		Peter Leone / Legato	
		Leslie Burr-Howard / Extreme	
3	BRA	Rodrigo Pessoa / Tomboy	17.25
		Andre Johannpeter / Calei	
		Luiz Felipe Azevedo / Cassiana	
		Alvaro Miranda Neto / Aspen	
4	FRA	Alexandra Ledermann / Rochet M	20.25
		Patrice Delaveau / Roxanne de Gruchy	
		Roger Yves-Bost / Souviens Toi	
		Herve Godignon / Viking du Tillard	
5	ESP	Fernando Sarasola / Ennio	29.75
		Rutherford Lathan / Sourire d'Aze	
		Alenjandro Jorda / Hernando du Sablon	
		Pedro Sanchez / Riccarda	
6	SUI	Willi Melliger / Calvaro	32.00
		Beat Mandli / City Banking	
		Markus Fuchs / Adelfos	
		Urs Fah / Jeremia	
7	NED	Jos Lansink / Carthago	32.25
		Emile Hendrix / Finesse	
		Bert Romp / Samantha	
		Jan Tops / Top Gun	
8	IRL	Damian Gardner / Arthos	34.50
		Peter Charles / Beneton	
		Eddie Macken / Schalkhaar	
		Jessica Chesney / Diamond Exchange	

INDIVIDUAL DRESSAGE — Final: August 3

RANK	CTRY	ATHLETE/HORSE	TOTAL
1	GER	Isabell Werth / Gigolo	235.09
2	NED	Anky Van Grunsven / Bonfire	233.02
3	NED	Sven Rothenberger / Weyden	224.94
4	GER	Monica Theodorescu / Grunox	224.56
5	USA	**Michelle Gibson / Peron**	222.83
6	GER	Klaus Balkenhol / Goldstern	221.81
7	FRA	Margit Otto-Crepin / Lucky Lord	219.80
8	USA	**Guenter Seidel / Graf George**	215.02

TEAM DRESSAGE — Final: July 28

RANK	CTRY	ATHLETE/HORSE	TOTAL
1	GER	Isabell Werth / Gigolo	5553
		Klaus Balkenhol / Goldstern	
		Monica Theodorescu / Grunox	
		Martin Schaudt / Durgo	
2	NED	Tineke Bartels-De Vries / Barbria	5437
		Sven Rothenberger / Weyden	
		Anky Van Grunsven / Bonfire	
		Gonnelien Rothenberger / Dondolo	
3	USA	**Robert Dover / Metallic**	5309
		Michelle Gibson / Peron	
		Steffen Peters / Udon	
		Guenter Seidel / Graf George	
4	FRA	Dominique D'Esme / Arnoldo	5045
		Margit Otto-Crepin / Lucky Lord	
		Dominique Brieussel / Akazie	
		Marie-Helene Syre / Marlon	
5	SWE	Tinne Wilhelmsson / Caprice	4996
		Annette Solmell / Strauss	
		Ulla Hakansson / Bobby	
		Louise Nathhorst / Walk on Top	
6	SUI	Eva Senn / Renzo	4893
		Hans Staub / Dukaat	
		Christine Stueckelberger / Aquamarin	
		Barbara von Grebel Schiendorfer / Ramar	
7	ESP	Rafael Soto / Invasor	4875
		Beatriz Ferrer Salat / Brillant	
		Juan Matute / Hermes	
		Ignacio Rambla / Evento	
8	GBR	Joanna Jackson / Mester Mouse	4761
		Jane Bredin / Cupido	
		Vicky Thompson / Enfant	
		Richard Davison / Askari	

INDIVIDUAL THREE-DAY EVENT — Final: July 26

RANK	CTRY	ATHLETE/HORSE	TOTAL
1	NZL	Blyth Tait / Ready Teddy	56.80
2	NZL	Sally Clark / Squirrel Hil	60.40
3	USA	**Kerry Millikin / Out and About**	73.70
4	FRA	Jean Teulere / Rodosto	77.20
5	USA	**David O'Connor / Custom Made**	80.15
6	USA	**Mara Depuy / Hopper**	85.00
7	GER	Hendrik Von Paepcke / Amadeus	87.20
8	BEL	Constantin Van Rijckevorsel / Otis	87.40

TEAM THREE-DAY EVENT — Final: July 24

RANK	CTRY	ATHLETE/HORSE	TOTAL
1	AUS	Andrew Hoy / Darien Powers	203.85
		Wendy Schaeffer / Sunburst	
		Phillip Dutton / True Blue Girdwood	
		Gillian Rolton / Peppermint Grove	
2	USA	**Karen O'Connor / Biko**	261.10
		David O'Connor / Giltedge	
		Bruce Davidson / Heyday	
		Jill Henneberg / Nirvana II	
3	NZL	Andrew Nicholson / Jagermeister II	268.55
		Vaughn Jefferis / Bounce	
		Blyth Tait / Chesterfield	
		Vicky Latta / Broadcast News	
4	FRA	Koris Vieules / Tandresse De Canta	307.65
		Rodolphe Scherer / Urane Des Pins	
		Jacques Dulcy / Upont	
		Marie-Christine Duroy /	
		Yarlands Summer Song	
5	GBR	Ian Stark / Stanwick Ghost	312.90
		William Fox-Pitt / Cosmopolitan II	
		Gary Parsonage / Magic Rogue	
		Karen Dixon / Too Smart	
6	JPN	Masaru Fuse / Talisman De Jarry	326.15
		Yoshihiko Kowata / Hell at Dawn	
		Takeaki Tsuchiya / Right on Time	
		Kazuhiro Iwatani / Sejane De Vozerier	
7	SWE	Therese Olavsson / Hector T	345.25
		Paula Tornqvist / Monaghan	
		Linda Algotsson / Lafayette	
		Dag Albert / Nice N' Easy	
8	ESP	Luis Alvarez-Cervera / Pico's Nippur	621.65
		Javier Revuelta / Toby	
		Santiago Centenara / Just Dixon	
		Enrique Sarasola / New Venture	

FENCING

MEN'S INDIVIDUAL FOIL
Final: July 22

RANK	CTRY	ATHLETE
1	ITA	Alessandro Puccini
2	FRA	Lionel Plumenail
3	FRA	Franck Boidin
4	GER	Wolfgang Wienand
5	CUB	Rolando Samuel Tucker Leon
6	UKR	Serhiy Golubytsky
7	FRA	Philippe Omnes
8	KOR	Kim Young-ho
34	USA	**Cliff Bayer**
37	USA	**Peter Devine**
39	USA	**Eric "Nick" Bravin**

MEN'S TEAM FOIL
Final: July 25

RANK	CTRY	ATHLETES
1	RUS	Dmitriy Shevchenko / Ilgar Mamedov / Vladislav Pavlovich
2	POL	Piotr Kielpikowski / Adam Krzesinski / Ryszard Sobczak
3	CUB	Elvis Gregory / Rolando Samuel Tucker Leon / Oscar Manuel Garcia Perez
4	AUT	Marco Falchetto / Michael Ludwig / Joachim Wendt
5	HUN	Zsolt Ersek / Robert Kiss / Mark Marsi
6	GER	Alexander Koch / Uwe Romer / Wolfgang Wienand
7	KOR	Chang Soo-ki / Kim Yong-kook / Kim Young-ho
8	ITA	Marco Arpeno / Stefano Cerioni / Alessandro Puccini
10	USA	**Cliff Bayer / Eric "Nick" Bravin / Peter Devine**

MEN'S INDIVIDUAL SABRE
Final: July 21

RANK	CTRY	ATHLETE
1	RUS	Stanislav Pozdnyakov
2	RUS	Sergey Sharikov
3	FRA	Damien Touya
4	HUN	Jozsef Navarrete
5	GER	Felix Becker
6	UKR	Vadym Guttsayt
7	POL	Rafal Sznajder
8	GER	Steffen Wiesinger
28	USA	**Peter Cox, Jr.**
34	USA	**Thomas Strzalkowski**
37	USA	**Peter Westbrook**

MEN'S TEAM SABRE
Final: July 24

RANK	CTRY	ATHLETES
1	RUS	Sergey Sharikov / Stanislav Pozdnyakov / Grigoriy Kiriyenko
2	HUN	Csaba Koves / Jozsef Navarrete / Bence Szabo
3	ITA	Luigi Tarantino / Tonhi Terenzi / Raffaello Caserta
4	POL	Rafal Sznajder / Janusz Olech / Norbert Jaskot
5	FRA	Jean Daurelle / Franck Ducheix / Damien Touya
6	ESP	Antonio Garcia / Fernando Medina / Raul Peinador
7	ROM	Mihai Covaliu / Florin Lupeica / Filmos Szabo
8	GER	Felix Becker / Frank Bleckmann / Steffen Wiesinger
9	USA	**Peter Cox, Jr. / Thomas Strzalkowski / Peter Westbrook**

MEN'S INDIVIDUAL EPEE
Final: July 20

RANK	CTRY	ATHLETE
1	RUS	Aleksandr Beketov
2	CUB	Ivan Trevejo Perez
3	HUN	Geza Imre
4	HUN	Ivan Kovacs
5	ITA	Sandro Cuomo
6	FRA	Jean-Michel Henry
7	EST	Kaido Kaaberma
8	GER	Mariusz Strzalka
25	USA	**James Carpenter**
28	USA	**Michael Marx**
31	USA	**Tamir Bloom**

MEN'S TEAM EPEE
Final: July 23

RANK	CTRY	ATHLETES
1	ITA	Sandro Cuomo / Angelo Mazzoni / Maurizio Randazzo
2	RUS	Aleksandr Beketov / Pavel Kolobkov / Valeriy Zakharevich
3	FRA	Jean-Michel Henry / Robert Leroux / Eric Srecki
4	GER	Elmar Borrmann / Arnd Schmitt / Mariusz Strzalka
5	EST	Kaido Kaaberma / Andrus Kajak / Meelis Loit
6	HUN	Geza Imre / Ivan Kovacs / Krisztian Kulcsar
7	ESP	Oscar Albarracin / Cesar Gonzalez / Raul Maroto
8	USA	**Tamir Bloom / James Carpenter / Michael Marx**

WOMEN'S INDIVIDUAL FOIL
Final: July 22

RANK	CTRY	ATHLETE
1	ROM	Laura Badea
2	ITA	Valentina Vezzali
3	ITA	Giovanna Trillini
4	FRA	Laurence Modaine-Cessac
5	GER	Monika Weber-Koszto
6	CHN	Xiao Aihua
7	USA	**Ann Marsh**
8	HUN	Aida Mohamed
21	USA	**Felicia Zimmermann**
33	USA	**Suzanne Paxton**

WOMEN'S TEAM FOIL
Final: July 24

RANK	CTRY	ATHLETES
1	ITA	Francesca Bortolozzi Borella / Valentina Vezzali / Giovanna Trillini
2	ROM	Laura Badea / Roxana Scarlat / Reka Szabo - Lazar
3	GER	Sabine Bau / Anja Fichtel Mauritz / Monika Weber-Koszto
4	HUN	Aida Mohamed / Zsuzsa Nemethne Janosi / Gabriella Romaczne Lantos
5	FRA	Clothilde Magnan / Laurence Modaine-Cessac / Adeline Wuilleme
6	RUS	Svetlana Boyko / Olga Sharkova / Olga Velitchko
7	CHN	Liang Jun / Wang Huifeng / Xiao Aihua
8	POL	Barbara Szewczyk / Anna Rybicka / Katarzyna Felusiak
10	USA	**Ann Marsh / Suzanne Paxton / Felicia Zimmermann**

WOMEN'S INDIVIDUAL EPEE
Final: July 21

RANK	CTRY	ATHLETE
1	FRA	Laura Flessel
2	FRA	Valerie Barlois
3	HUN	Gyoengyi Szalay Horvathne
4	ITA	Margherita Zalaffi
5	HUN	Timea Nagy
6	HUN	Adrienn Hormay
7	GER	Eva-Maria Ittner
8	KOR	Ko Jung-sun
16	USA	**Leslie Marx**
37	USA	**Nhi Lan Le**
39	USA	**Elaine Cheris**

WOMEN'S TEAM EPEE
Final: July 24

RANK	CTRY	ATHLETES
1	FRA	Laura Flessel / Sophie Moresee-Pichot / Valerie Barlois
2	ITA	Margherita Zalaffi / Laura Chiesa / Elisa Uga
3	RUS	Karina Aznavuryan / Yuliya Garayeva / Mariya Mazina
4	HUN	Gyoengyi Szalay Horvathne / Adrienn Hormay / Timea Nagy
5	EST	Maarika Vosu / Oksana Jermakova / Heidi Rohi
6	CUB	Milagros Palma Gonzales / Tamara Esteri Almeida / Mirayda Garcia
7	GER	Katja Nass / Eva-Maria Ittner / Claudia Bokel
8	USA	**Nhi Lan Le / Leslie Marx / Elaine Cheris**

FIELD HOCKEY

MEN
Final: August 2

RANK	CTRY	RECORD	SCORE	USA GAME SCORES	
1	NED	6-0-1	3-1	USA vs PAK	0-4
2	ESP	5-2-0	(final)	USA vs ARG	2-5
3	AUS	4-2-1	3-2	USA vs IND	0-4
4	GER	3-3-1	(3rd-4th)	USA vs ESP	1-7
5	KOR	3-2-2		USA vs GER	0-3
6	PAK	3-3-1		USA vs RSA	0-3
7	GBR	2-2-3		USA vs MAS	1-4
8	IND	2-3-2			
12	USA	0-7-0			

USA TEAM: Larry Amar / Nick Butcher / Steve Danielson / Ahmed Elmaghraby / Steve Jennings / Ben Maruquin / Marq Mellor / John O'Neill / Otto Steffers / Phil Sykes / Steven Van Randwijck / Tom Vano / Steve Wagner / Eelco Wassenaar / Mark Wentges / Scott Williams / Head Coach: Jon Clark / Assistant Coaches: Lenny McCaigue / Dave McMichael

WOMEN
Final: August 1

RANK	CTRY	RECORD	SCORE	USA GAME SCORES	
1	AUS	6-0-1	3-1	USA vs NED	1-1
2	KOR	4-1-2	(final)	USA vs KOR	3-2
3	NED	3-2-2	4-3	USA vs GBR	0-1
4	GBR	3-2-2	(3rd-4th)	USA vs ARG	1-2
5	USA	2-3-2		USA vs GER	1-1
6	GER	2-4-1		USA vs AUS	0-4
7	ARG	2-4-1		USA vs ESP	2-0
8	ESP	0-6-1			

USA TEAM: Pamela Bustin / Kris Fillat / Tracey Fuchs / Kelli James / Katie Kauffman / Antoinette Lucas / Leslie Lyness / Diane Madl / Barb Marois / Laurel Martin / Marcia Pankratz / Jill Reeve / Patty Shea / Liz Tchou / Cindy Werley / Andrea Wieland / Head Coach: Pam Hixon / Assistant Coach: Missy Meharg

GYMNASTICS

MEN'S TEAM COMPETITION
Final: July 22

RANK	CTRY	ATHLETES	TOTAL
1	RUS	Alexei Nemov / Alexei Voropaev / Eugeni Podgorni / Dmitri Vasilenko / Sergei Charkov / Nikolay Krukov / Dmitriy Trush	576.778
2	CHN	Li Xiaoshuang / Zhang Jingjing / Shen Jian / Fan Bin / Huang Huadong / Huang Liping / Fan Hongbin	575.539
3	UKR	Rustam Sharipov / Alexandre Svetlichnyi / Vladimir Shamenko / Igor Korobchinski / Oleg Kosiak / Yuri Yermakov / Grigory Misutin	571.541
4	BLR	Vitaly Scherbo / Andrei Kan / Vitaly Rudnitski / Alexander Belanovski / Alexander Shostak / Ivan Pavlovski / Aleksey Sinkevich	571.381
5	USA	**John Roethlisberger / Blaine Wilson / John Macready / Jair Lynch / Kip Simons / Chainey Umphrey / Mihai Bagiu**	**570.618**
6	BUL	Jordan Jovtchev / Krasimir Dounev / Dimitar Lunchev / Kalofer Hristozov / Deyan Tordanov / Ivan Ivanov / Vassil Vetzev	567.567
7	GER	Andreas Wecker / Valeri Belenki / Jan-Peter Nikiferow / Oliver Walther / Karsten Oelsch / Uwe Billerbeck / Marius Toba	567.405
8	KOR	Lee Joo-hyung / Han Yoon-soo / Kim Dong-hwa / Jung Jin-soo / Yeo Hong-chul / Cho Seong-min / Kim Bong-hyun	567.054

MEN'S INDIVIDUAL ALL-AROUND
Final: July 24

RANK	CTRY	ATHLETE	TOTAL
1	CHN	Li Xiaoshuang	58.423
2	RUS	Alexei Nemov	58.374
3	BLR	Vitaly Scherbo	58.197
4	CHN	Zhang Jinjing	58.148
5	CHN	Shen Jian	57.861
6	GER	Valeri Belenki	57.848
7	USA	**John Roethlisberger**	**57.762**
8	UKR	Rustam Sharipov	57.712
10	USA	**Blaine Wilson**	**57.686**
29	USA	**John Macready**	**56.210**

MEN'S FLOOR EXERCISE — Final: July 28

RANK	CTRY	ATHLETE	TOTAL
1	GRE	Ioannis Melissanidis	9.850
2	CHN	Li Xiaoshuang	9.837
3	RUS	Alexei Nemov	9.800
4T	BUL	Ivan Ivanov	9.750
4T	FRA	Thierry Aymes	9.750
6	RUS	Eugeni Podgorni	9.550
7	BLR	Vitaly Scherbo	9.275
8	UKR	Grigory Misutin	9.100

no USA entry

MEN'S HORIZONTAL BAR — Final: July 29

RANK	CTRY	ATHLETE	TOTAL
1	GER	Andreas Wecker	9.850
2	BUL	Krasimir Dounev	9.825
3T	BLR	Vitaly Scherbo	9.800
3T	CHN	Fan Bin	9.800
3T	RUS	Alexei Nemov	9.800
6	RUS	Alexei Voropaev	9.712
7	ESP	Jesus Carballo	9.350
8	KOR	Lee Joo-hyung	8.525

no USA entry

MEN'S VAULT — Final: July 29

RANK	CTRY	ATHLETE	TOTAL
1	RUS	Alexei Nemov	9.787
2	KOR	Yeo Hong-chul	9.756
3	BLR	Vitaly Scherbo	9.724
4T	BUL	Ivan Ivanov	9.643
4T	CHN	Li Xiaoshuang	9.643
6	RUS	Alexei Voropaev	9.618
7	UKR	Igor Korobchinski	9.568
8	BLR	Ivan Pavlovski	9.493

no USA entry

MEN'S PARALLEL BARS — Final: July 29

RANK	CTRY	ATHLETE	TOTAL
1	UKR	Rustam Sharipov	9.837
2	USA	Jair Lynch	9.825
3	BLR	Vitaly Scherbo	9.800
4T	CHN	Zhang Jinjing	9.750
4T	RUS	Alexei Nemov	9.750
6	CHN	Huang Liping	9.737
7	KOR	Lee Joo-hyung	9.687
8	RUS	Sergei Charkov	9.650

MEN'S POMMEL HORSE — Final: July 28

RANK	CTRY	ATHLETE	TOTAL
1	SUI	Donghua Li	9.875
2	ROM	Marius Urzica	9.825
3	RUS	Alexei Nemov	9.787
4	FRA	Patrice Casimir	9.762
5T	JPN	Yoshiaki Hatakeda	9.712
5T	CHN	Huang Huadong	9.712
7	FRA	Eric Poujade	9.350
8	CHN	Fan Bin	9.300

no USA entry

MEN'S STILL RINGS — Final: July 28

RANK	CTRY	ATHLETE	TOTAL
1	ITA	Yuri Chechi	9.887
2T	HUN	Szilveszter Csollany	9.812
2T	ROM	Dan Burinca	9.812
4	BUL	Jordan Jovtchev	9.800
5T	GER	Andreas Wecker	9.762
5T	CHN	Fan Hongbin	9.762
7T	GER	Marius Toba	9.737
7T	USA	Blaine Wilson	9.737

WOMEN'S TEAM COMPETITION — Final: July 23

RANK	CTRY	ATHLETES	TOTAL
1	USA	Shannon Miller / Dominique Dawes / Kerri Strug / Dominique Moceanu / Jaycie Phelps / Amy Chow / Amanda Borden	389.225
2	RUS	Dina Kochetkova / Rozalia Galiyeva / Svetlana Chorkina / Elena Grosheva / Elena Dolgopolova / Eugenia Kuznetsova / Oksana Liapina	388.404
3	ROM	Lavinia Milosovici / Gina Gogean / Alexandra Marinescu / Simona Amanar / Mirela Tugurlan / Ionela Loaies	388.246
4	CHN	Mo Huilan / Mao Yanling / Qiao Ya / Liu Xuan / Ji Liya / Kui Yuanyuan / Bi Wenjiing	385.867
5	UKR	Lilia Podkopayeva / Svetlana Zelepoukina / Lioubov Sheremeta / Anna Mirgorodskaia / Oksana Knijnik / Olena Shaparna / Olga Teslenko	385.841
6	BLR	Yelena Piskun / Alena Polozkova / Svetlana Boguinskaia / Olga Yurkina / Ludmila Vitiukova / Svetlana Tarasevich / Tatiana Zharganova	381.263
7	ESP	Monica Martin / Joana Juarez / Mercedes Pacheco / Diana Plaza / Elisabeth Valle / Veronica Castro / Gemma Paz	378.081
8	FRA	Isabelle Severino / Elvire Teza / Ludivine Furnon / Emilie Volle / Cecile Canqueteau / Orelie Troscompt / Laure Gely	377.715

WOMEN'S INDIVIDUAL ALL-AROUND — Final: July 25

RANK	CTRY	ATHLETE	TOTAL
1	UKR	Lilia Podkopayeva	39.255
2	ROM	Gina Gogean	39.075
3T	ROM	Simona Amanar	39.067
3T	ROM	Lavinia Milosovici	39.067
5	CHN	Mo Huilan	39.049
6	RUS	Dina Kochetkova	38.980
7	RUS	Rozalia Galiyeva	38.905
8	USA	Shannon Miller	38.811
9	USA	Dominique Moceanu	38.755
17	USA	Dominique Dawes	38.318

WOMEN'S BALANCE BEAM — Final: July 29

RANK	CTRY	ATHLETE	TOTAL
1	USA	Shannon Miller	9.862
2	UKR	Lilia Podkopayeva	9.825
3	ROM	Gina Gogean	9.787
4	RUS	Dina Kochetkova	9.737
5	UKR	Olga Teslenko	9.625
6	USA	Dominique Moceanu	9.125
7	RUS	Rozalia Galiyeva	9.112
8	ROM	Alexandra Marinescu	8.462

WOMEN'S FLOOR EXERCISE — Final: July 29

RANK	CTRY	ATHLETE	TOTAL
1	UKR	Lilia Podkopayeva	9.887
2	ROM	Simona Amanar	9.850
3	USA	Dominique Dawes	9.837
4	USA	Dominique Moceanu	9.825
5	RUS	Dina Kochetkova	9.800
6	CHN	Mo Huilan	9.700
7	ROM	Gina Gogean	9.662
8	CHN	Ji Liya	9.637

WOMEN'S UNEVEN BARS — Final: July 28

RANK	CTRY	ATHLETE	TOTAL
1	RUS	Svetlana Chorkina	9.850
2T	CHN	Bi Wenjiing	9.873
2T	USA	Amy Chow	9.837
4	USA	Dominique Dawes	9.800
5T	ROM	Simona Amanar	9.787
5T	RUS	Dina Kochetkova	9.787
5T	UKR	Lilia Podkopayeva	9.787
8	ROM	Lavinia Milosovici	9.750

WOMEN'S VAULT — Final: July 28

RANK	CTRY	ATHLETE	TOTAL
1	ROM	Simona Amanar	9.825
2	CHN	Mo Huilan	9.768
3	ROM	Gina Gogean	9.750
4	RUS	Rozalia Galiyeva	9.743
5	BLR	Svetlana Boguinskaia	9.712
6	USA	Dominique Dawes	9.649
7	RUS	Elena Grosheva	9.637
8	USA	Shannon Miller	9.350

RHYTHMIC ALL-AROUND INDIVIDUAL — Final: August 4

RANK	CTRY	ATHLETE	TOTAL
1	UKR	Ekaterina Serebryanskaya	39.683
2	RUS	Ianina Batyrchina	39.382
3	UKR	Elena Vitrichenko	39.331
4	RUS	Amina Zarlpova	39.264
5	BUL	Maria Petrova	38.999
6	FRA	Eva Serrano	38.816
7	BEL	Laris Loukianenko	38.666
8	BEL	Tatiana Ogryzko	38.530
30	USA	Jessica Davis	36.564

RHYTHMIC ALL-AROUND TEAM — Final: August 2

RANK	CTRY	ATHLETE	TOTAL
1	ESP	Marta Baldo / Nuria Cabanillas / Estela Gimenez / Lorena Gurendez / Tania Lamarca / Estibaliz Martinez	38.933
2	BUL	Ivelina Taleva / Valentina Kevlian / Ina Deltcheva / Maja Tabakova / Maria Koleva / Vjara Vatachka	38.866
3	RUS	Evguenia Botchkareva / Irina Dziouba / Angelina Iouchkova / Olga Chtyrenko / Elena Krivochei / Ioulia Ivanova	38.365
4	FRA	Charlotte Camboulives / Caroline Chimot / Sylvie Didone / Audrey Grosclaude / Frederique Lehon / Nadia Mimoun	38.199
5	CHN	Zheng Ni / Zhong Li / Cai Yingying / Huang Ting / Huang Ying	37.999
6	BLR	Natalia Boudilo / Oxana Jdanovitch / Alesija Pohodina / Svetlana Louzanova / Olga Demskaia / Galina Malachenko	37.982
9	USA	Aliane Baquerot / Mandy James / Kate Nelson / Brandi Siegel / Challen Sievers / Becky Turner	36.633

JUDO

MEN'S EXTRA LIGHTWEIGHT (60 KG/132 LBS) — Final: July 26

RANK	CTRY	ATHLETE
1	JPN	Tadahiro Nomura
2	ITA	Girolamo Giovinazzo
3T	GER	Richard Trautmann
3T	MGL	Dorjpalam Narmandakh
5T	RUS	Nikolay Oyegin
5T	BLR	Natik Bagirov
7T	GBR	Nigel Donohue
7T	GEO	Giorgi Vazagashvili
—	USA	Clifton Sunada	elim. 2nd rd.

MEN'S HALF LIGHTWEIGHT (65 KG/143 LBS) — Final: July 24

RANK	CTRY	ATHLETE
1	GER	Udo Quellmalz
2	JPN	Yukimasa Nakamura
3T	BRA	Henrique Guimaraes
3T	CUB	Israel Hernandez Plana
5T	BEL	Philip Laats
5T	HUN	Jozsef Csak
7T	BUL	Ivan Netov
7T	GEO	Giorgi Revazishvili
—	USA	Orlando Fuentes	elim. 3rd rd.

MEN'S LIGHTWEIGHT (71 KG/156 LBS) — Final: July 24

RANK	CTRY	ATHLETE
1	JPN	Kenzo Nakamura
2	KOR	Kwak Dae-sung
3T	USA	James Pedro
3T	FRA	Christophe Gagliano
5T	BRA	Sebastian Pereira
5T	MGL	Khaliun Boldbaatar
7T	UZB	Audrey Shturbabin
7T	GER	Martin Schmidt

MEN'S HALF MIDDLEWEIGHT (78 KG/172 LBS) — Final: July 23

RANK	CTRY	ATHLETE
1	FRA	Djamel Bouras
2	JPN	Toshihiko Koga
3T	KOR	Cho In-chul
3T	GEO	Soso Liparteliani
5T	GER	Stefan Dott
5T	ARG	Dario Garcia
7T	BRA	Flavio Canto
7T	TUR	Irakli Uznadze
—	USA	Jason Morris	elim. 3rd rd.

MEN'S MIDDLEWEIGHT (86 KG/189 LBS)   Final: July 22

RANK	CTRY	ATHLETE	
1	KOR	Jeon Ki-young	
2	UZB	Armen Bagdasarov	
3T	NED	Mark Huizinga	
3T	GER	Marko Spittka	
5T	JPN	Hidehiko Yoshida	
5T	ROM	Adrian Croitoru	
7T	RUS	Oleg Maltsev	
7T	CAN	Nicolas Gill	
—	USA	Brian Olson	elim. 3rd rd.

MEN'S HALF HEAVYWEIGHT (95 KG/209 LBS)   Final: July 21

RANK	CTRY	ATHLETE	
1	POL	Pawel Nastula	
2	KOR	Kim Min-soo	
3T	BRA	Miguel Fernandes	
3T	FRA	Stephane Traineau	
5T	NED	Benardus Sonnemans	
5T	HUN	Antal Kovacs	
7T	ARG	Alejandro Bender	
7T	JPN	Yoshio Nakamura	
—	USA	Rene Capo	elim. 2nd rd.

MEN'S HEAVYWEIGHT (+95 KG/+209 LBS)   Final: July 20

RANK	CTRY	ATHLETE	
1	FRA	David Douillet	
2	ESP	Ernesto Perez	
3T	BEL	Harry van Barneveld	
3T	GER	Frank Moeller	
5T	CHN	Liu Shenggang	
5T	JPN	Naoya Ogawa	
7T	GRE	Harris Papaioannou	
7T	RUS	Sergey Kosorotov	
—	USA	Damon Keeve	elim. 2nd rd.

WOMEN'S EXTRA LIGHTWEIGHT (48 KG/106 LBS)   Final: July 26

RANK	CTRY	ATHLETE	
1	PRK	Sun-Hi Kye	
2	JPN	Ryoko Tamura	
3T	ESP	Yolanda Soler	
3T	CUB	Amarilis Savon	
5T	ALG	Salima Souakri	
5T	FRA	Sarah Nichilo	
7T	BLR	Tatyana Moskvina	
7T	POL	Malgorzata Roszkowska	
—	USA	Hillary Wolf	elim. quarterfinals

WOMEN'S HALF LIGHTWEIGHT (52 KG/114 LBS)   Final: July 25

RANK	CTRY	ATHLETE	
1	FRA	Marie-Claire Restoux	
2	KOR	Hyun Sook-hee	
3T	JPN	Noriko Sugawara	
3T	CUB	Legna Verdecia	
5T	POL	Larysa Krause	
5T	ESP	Almudena Munoz	
7T	USA	Marisa Pedulla	
7T	ARG	Carolina Mariani	

WOMEN'S LIGHTWEIGHT (56 KG/123 LBS)   Final: July 24

RANK	CTRY	ATHLETE	
1	CUB	Driulis Gonzalez	
2	KOR	Jung Sun-yong	
3T	BEL	Marisabel Lomba	
3T	ESP	Isabel Fernandez	
5T	CHN	Liu Chuang	
5T	GBR	Nicola Fairbrother	
7T	AZE	Zulfiya Guseynova	
7T	RUS	Zulfiya Garipova	
—	USA	Corinna Broz West	elim. 1st rd.

WOMEN'S HALF MIDDLEWEIGHT (61 KG/134 LBS)   Final: July 23

RANK	CTRY	ATHLETE	
1	JPN	Yuko Emoto	
2	BEL	Gella Vandecaveye	
3T	NED	Jenny Gal	
3T	KOR	Jung Sung-sook	
5T	TUR	Ilknur Kobas	
5T	ISR	Yael Arad	
7T	ESP	Sara Alvarez	
7T	VEN	Xiomara Griffith	
—	USA	Celita Schutz	elim. 1st rd.

WOMEN'S MIDDLEWEIGHT (66 KG/145 LBS)   Final: July 22

RANK	CTRY	ATHLETE	
1	KOR	Cho Min-sun	
2	POL	Aneta Szczepanska	
3T	CHN	Wang Xianbo	
3T	NED	Claudia Zwiers	
5T	FRA	Alice Dubois	
5T	CUB	Odalis Reve	
7T	USA	Liliko Ogasawara	
7T	GBR	Rowena Sweatman	

WOMEN'S HALF-HEAVYWEIGHT (72 KG/158 LBS)   Final: July 21

RANK	CTRY	ATHLETE	
1	BEL	Ulla Werbrouck	
2	JPN	Yoko Tanabe	
3T	CUB	Diadenis Luna Castellano	
3T	ITA	Ylenia Scapin	
5T	UKR	Tatiana Beliaeva	
5T	FRA	Estha Essombe	
7T	RUS	Svetlana Galante	
7T	GER	Hannah Ertel	
—	USA	Sandra Bacher	elim. 1st rd.

WOMEN'S HEAVYWEIGHT (+72 KG/+158 LBS)   Final: July 20

RANK	CTRY	ATHLETE	
1	CHN	Sun Fuming	
2	CUB	Estela Rodriguez	
3T	GER	Johanna Hagn	
3T	FRA	Christine Cicot	
5T	RUS	Svetlana Gundarenko	
5T	POL	Beata Maksymowa	
7T	KOR	Shon Hyun-me	
7T	BRA	Edinanci Da Silva	
—	USA	Colleen Rosensteel	elim. 1st rd.

MODERN PENTATHLON

INDIVIDUAL   Final: July 30

RANK	CTRY	ATHLETE	FENCE	SWIM	SHOOT	RUN	RIDE	TOTAL
1	KAZ	Aleksandr Parygin	970	1196	1072	1273	1040	5551
2	RUS	Eduard Zenovka	820	1268	1084	1342	1016	5530
3	HUN	Janos Martinek	910	1248	1000	1243	1100	5501
4	RUS	Dmitriy Svatkovskiy	880	1248	1012	1339	1010	5489
5	POL	Igor Warabida	790	1208	1072	1282	1100	5452
6	HUN	Akos Hanzely	940	1236	1084	1228	947	5435
7	EST	Imre Tiidemann	820	1212	1144	1288	950	5414
8	ITA	Cesare Toraldo	880	1296	1108	1078	1040	5402
16	USA	Michael Gostigian	790	1304	976	1192	1043	5305

ROWING

MEN'S SINGLE SCULLS   Final: July 27

RANK	CTRY	ATHLETE	TIME
1	SUI	Xeno Mueller	6:44.85
2	CAN	Derek Porter	6:47.45
3	GER	Thomas Lange	6:47.72
4	SLO	Iztok Cop	6:51.71
5	CZE	Vaclav Chalupa	6:55.65
6	NOR	Fredrik Bekken	6:59.51
10	USA	Cyrus Beasley	6:54.17#

#B Final

MEN'S LIGHTWEIGHT DOUBLE SCULLS   Final: July 28

RANK	CTRY	ATHLETES	TIME
1	SUI	Markus Gier / Michael Gier	6:23.47
2	NED	Maarten van der Linden / Pepijn Aardewijn	6:26.48
3	AUS	Anthony Edwards / Bruce Hick	6:26.69
4	ESP	Jose Maria de Marco / Juan Carlos Saez	6:28.09
5	AUT	Wolfgang Sigl / Walter Rantasa	6:30.85
6	SWE	Mattias Tichy / Anders Christensson	6:34.78
9	USA	Thomas Auth / Stephen Peterson	6:25.89#

#B Final

MEN'S DOUBLE SCULLS   Final: July 27

RANK	CTRY	ATHLETES	TIME
1	ITA	Davide Tizzano / Agostino Abbagnale	6:16.98
2	NOR	Kjetil Undset / Steffen Stoerseth	6:18.42
3	FRA	Frederic Kowal / Samuel Barathay	6:19.85
4	DEN	Lars Christensen / Martin Haldbo Hansen	6:24.77
5	AUT	Arnold Jonke / Christoph Zerbst	6:25.17
6	GER	Sebastian Mayer / Roland Opfer	6:29.32

no USA entry

MEN'S QUADRUPLE SCULLS   Final: July 28

RANK	CTRY	ATHLETES	TIME
1	GER	Andre Steiner / Andreas Hajek / Stephan Volkert / Andre Willms	5:56.93
2	USA	Tim Young / Brian Jamieson / Eric Mueller / Jason Gailes	5:59.10
3	AUS	Janusz Hooker / Duncan Free / Ronald Snook / Boden Hanson	6:01.65
4	ITA	Massimo Paradiso / Alessio Sartori / Rossano Galtarossa / Alessandro Corona	6:02.12
5	SUI	Rene Benguerel / Michael Erdlen / Ueli Bodenmann / Simon Stuerm	6:04.52
6	SWE	Johan Flodin / Pontus Ek / Fredrik Hulten / Henrik Nilsson	6:07.75

MEN'S PAIR WITHOUT COXSWAIN   Final: July 27

RANK	CTRY	ATHLETES	TIME
1	GBR	Steven Redgrave / Matthew Pinsent	6:20.09
2	AUS	David Weightman / Robert Scott	6:21.02
3	FRA	Michel Andrieux / Jean-Christophe Rolland	6:22.15
4	ITA	Marco Penna / Walter Bottega	6:28.61
5	NZL	Toni Dunlop / David Schaper	6:29.24
6	CRO	Marko Banovic / Ninoslav Saraga	6:30.48
7	USA	Michael Peterson / Adam Holland	6:33.81#

#B Final

MEN'S FOUR WITHOUT COXSWAIN   Final: July 27

RANK	CTRY	ATHLETES	TIME
1	AUS	Drew Ginn / James Tomkins / Nicholas Green / Michael McKay	6:06.37
2	FRA	Gilles Bosquet / Daniel Fauche / Bertrand Vecten / Olivier Moncelet	6:07.03
3	GBR	Rupert Obholzer / Jonny Searle / Gregory Searle / Timothy Foster	6:07.28
4	SLO	Denis Svegelj / Jani Klemencic / Milan Jansa / Sadik Mujkic	6:07.87
5	ROM	Claudiu Marin / Dorin Alupei / Dimitrie Popescu / Vasile Mastacan	6:08.97
6	ITA	Valter Molea / Riccardo Del Rossi / Raffaello Leonardo / Carlo Mornati	6:10.60
11	USA	Jason Scott / Sean Hall / Jeff Klepacki / Tom Murray	5:59.91#

#B Final

MEN'S LIGHTWEIGHT FOUR WITHOUT COXSWAIN   Final: July 28

RANK	CTRY	ATHLETES	TIME
1	DEN	Niels Henriksen / Thomas Poulsen / Eskild Ebbesen / Victor Feddersen	6:09.58
2	CAN	Jeffrey Lay / Dave Boyes / Gavin Hassett / Brian Peaker	6:10.13
3	USA	David Collins / Jeff Pfaendtner / Marc Schneider / William Carlucci	6:12.29
4	IRL	Derek Holland / Samuel Lynch / Neville Maxwell / Anthony O'Connor	6:13.51
5	GER	Tobias Rose / Martin Weis / Michael Buchheit / Bernhard Stomporowski	6:14.79
6	AUS	Haimish Karrasch / Gary Lynagh / David Belcher / Simon Burgess	6:18.16

MEN'S EIGHT

Final: July 28

RANK	CTRY	ATHLETE	TIME
1	NED	Henk-Jan Zwolle / Diederik Simon / Michiel Bartman / Koos Maasdijk / Niels van der Swan / Niels van Steenis / Ronald Florijn / Nico Rienks / Jeroen Duyster	5:42.74
2	GER	Frank Richter / Mark Kleinschmidt / Wolfram Huhn / Marc Weber / Detlef Kirchhoff / Thorsten Streppelhoff / Ulrich Viefers / Ronald Baar / Peter Thiede	5:44.58
3	RUS	Anton Chermashentsev / Andrey Glukhov / Dmitriy Rozinkevich / Vladimir Volodenkov / Nikolay Aksyonov / Roman Monchenko / Pavel Melnikov / Sergey Matveyev / Aleksandr Lukyanov	5:45.77
4	CAN	Gregory Stevenson / Philip Graham / Henry Hering / Mark Platt / Darren Barber / Andrew Crosby / Scott Brodie / Adam Parfitt / Patrick Newman	5:46.54
5	USA	**Doug Burden / Bob Kaehler / Porter Collins / Edward Murphy / Jamie Koven / Jonathan Brown / Donald Smith / Fred Honebein / Steven Segaloff**	**5:48.45**
6	AUS	James Stewart / Geoffrey Stewart / Robert Jahrling / Nicholas Porzig / Jaime Fernandez / Benjamin Dodwell / Robert Walker / Richard Wearne / Brett Hayman	5:58.82

WOMEN'S SINGLE SCULLS

Final: July 27

RANK	CTRY	ATHLETE	TIME
1	BLR	Yekaterina Khodotovich	7:32.21
2	CAN	Silken Laumann	7:35.15
3	DEN	Trine Hansen	7:37.20
4	SWE	Maria Brandin	7:42.58
5	GBR	Guin Batten	7:45.08
6	USA	**Ruth Davidon**	**7:46.47**

WOMEN'S DOUBLE SCULLS

Final: July 27

RANK	CTRY	ATHLETE	TIME
1	CAN	Marnie McBean / Kathleen Heddle	6:56.84
2	CHN	Cao Mianying / Zhang Xiuyun	6:58.35
3	NED	Irene Eijs / Eeke van Nes	6:58.72
4	AUS	Marina Hatzakis / Bronwyn Roye	7:01.26
5	GER	Jana Thieme / Manuela Lutze	7:04.14
6	NZL	Philippa Baker / Brenda Lawson	7:09.92
9	USA	**Michelle Knox Zaloom / Jennifer Devine**	**6:58.78#**

#B Final

WOMEN'S LIGHTWEIGHT DOUBLE SCULLS

Final: July 28

RANK	CTRY	ATHLETE	TIME
1	ROM	Constanta Burcica / Camelia Macoviciuc	7:12.78
2	USA	**Teresa Z. Bell / Lindsay Burns**	**7:14.65**
3	AUS	Rebecca Joyce / Virginia Lee	7:16.56
4	ITA	Lisa Bertini / Martina Orzan	7:16.83
5	DEN	Berit Christoffersen / Lene Andersson	7:18.20
6	NED	Laurien Vermulst / Ellen Meliesie	7:21.92

WOMEN'S QUADRUPLE SCULLS

Final: July 28

RANK	CTRY	ATHLETE	TIME
1	GER	Jana Sorgers / Katrin Rutschow / Kathrin Boron / Kerstin Koeppen	6:27.44
2	UKR	Olena Ronzhina / Inna Frolova / Svitlana Maziy / Diana Miftakhutdinova	6:30.36
3	CAN	Laryssa Biesenthal / Marnie McBean / Diane O'Grady / Kathleen Heddle	6:30.38
4	DEN	Inger Pors / Ulla Hansen / Sarah Lauritzen / Dorthe Pedersen	6:30.92
5	CHN	Cao Mianying / Zhang Xiuyun / Liu Xirong / Gu Xiaoli	6:31.10
7	NED	Irene Eijs / Meike van Driel / Nelleke Penninx / Eeke van Nes	6:35.54
8	USA	**Cecile Tucker / Catherine Symon / Andrea Thies / Julia Chilicki**	**6:24.49#**

#B Final

WOMEN'S PAIR WITHOUT COXSWAIN

Final: July 27

RANK	CTRY	ATHLETES	TIME
1	AUS	Megan Still / Kate Slatter	7:01.39
2	USA	**Missy Schwen / Karen Kraft**	**7:01.78**
3	FRA	Christine Gosse / Helene Cortin	7:03.82
4	GER	Katherin Haacker / Stefani Werremeier	7:08.49
5	CAN	Emma Robinson / Anna van der Kamp	7:12.27
—	RUS	Albina Ligachova / Vera Pochitayeva	DQ

WOMEN'S EIGHT

Final: July 28

RANK	CTRY	ATHLETES	TIME
1	ROM	Anca Tanase / Vera Cochelea / Liliana Gafencu / Doina Spircu / Ioana Olteanu / Elisabeta Lipa / Marioara Popescu / Doina Ignat / Elena Georgescu	6:19.73
2	CAN	Heather McDermid / Tosha Tsang / Maria Maunder / Alison Korn / Emma Robinson / Anna van der Kamp / Jessica Monroe / Theresa Luke / Lesley Thompson	6:24.05
3	BLR	Natalya Lavrinenko / Aleksandra Pankina / Natalya Volchek / Tamara Davydenko / Valentina Skrabatun / Yelena Mikulich / Natalya Stasyuk / Marina Znak / Yaroslava Pavlovich	6:24.44
4	USA	**Anne Kakela / Mary McCagg / Laurel Korholz / Catriona Fallon / Betsy McCagg / Monica Tranel Michini / Amy Fuller / Jennifer Dore / Yasmin Farooq**	**6:26.19**
5	AUS	Jennifer Luff / Georgina Douglas / Amy Safe / Anna Ozolins / Karina Wieland / Alison Davies / Carmen Klomp / Bronwyn Thompson / Kaylynn Hick	6:30.10
6	NED	Femke Boelen / Marleen van der Velden / Astrid van Koert / Marieke Westerhof / Rita de Jong / Tessa Knaven / Tessa Appeldoorn / Muriel van Schilfgaarde / Jissy de Wolf	6:31.11

SHOOTING

MEN'S 10-METER AIR PISTOL

Final: July 20

RANK	CTRY	ATHLETE	PRELIM	FINAL
1	ITA	Roberto Di Donna	585	684.2
2	CHN	Wang Yifu	587 OR	684.1
3	BUL	Tanu Kiriakov	584	683.8
4	RUS	Sergey Pyzhyanov	583	683.5
5	POL	Jerzy Pietrzak	585	682.7
6	CHN	Tan Zongliang	581	682.0
7	BLR	Igor Basinski	582	681.8
8	NAM	Friedhelm Sack	583	680.2
41T	USA	**Neal Caloia**	571	
44T	USA	**Ben Amonette**	569	

MEN'S 50M FREE PISTOL

Final: July 23

RANK	CTRY	ATHLETE	PRELIM	FINAL	
1	RUS	Boris Kokorev	570	666.4	FOR
2	BLR	Igor Basinski	565	662.0	
3	ITA	Roberto Di Donna	569	661.8	
4	BLR	Konstantin Loukachik	564	660.1	
5	ITA	Vigilio Fait	569	659.8	
6	CHN	Wang Yifu	564	659.3	
7	CZE	Martin Tenk	564	657.7	
8	GUA	Sergio Sanchez	563	657.1	
25T	USA	**Ben Amonette**	555		
39	USA	**Neal Caloia**	544		

MEN'S 25M RAPID-FIRE PISTOL

Final: July 25

RANK	CTRY	ATHLETE	PRELIM	FINAL	
1	GER	Ralf Schumann	596 OR	698.0	FOR
2	BUL	Emil Milev	590	692.1	
3	KAZ	Vladimir Vokhmyanin	589	691.5	
4	POL	Krzysztof Kucharczyk	589	690.5	
5	CHN	Meng Gang	587	687.1	
6	MDA	Ghenadie Lisoconi	586	687.0	
7	HUN	Lajos Palinkas	586	685.9	
8	GER	Daniel Leonhard	586	683.6	
12T	USA	**John McNally**	583		
18	USA	**Roger Mar**	581		

MEN'S RUNNING GAME TARGET

Final: July 26

RANK	CTRY	ATHLETE	PRELIM	FINAL	
1	CHN	Yang Ling	585 OR	685.8	FOR
2	CHN	Xiao Jun	577	679.8	
3	CZE	Miroslav Janus	580	678.4	
4	HUN	Jozsef Sike	579	677.1	
5	RUS	Dmitri Lykin	581	676.7	
6	FIN	Krister Holmberg	578	672.4	
7	GER	Jens Zimmermann	574	672.2	
8	GUA	Attila Solti	570	667.0	
20	USA	**Adam Saathoff**	555		

MEN'S 10M AIR RIFLE

Final: July 22

RANK	CTRY	ATHLETE	PRELIM	FINAL	
1	RUS	Artem Khadzhibekov	594	695.7	FOR
2	AUT	Wolfram Waibel, Jr.	596 OR	695.2	
3	FRA	Jean-Pierre Amat	591	693.1	
4	RUS	Evgeni Aleinikov	591	692.9	
5	NOR	Leif Steinar Rolland	591	692.5	
6	SLO	Rajmond Debevec	591	692.1	
7	USA	**Rob Harbison**	594	**691.8**	
8	CZE	Milan Bakes	591	690.5	
41	USA	**Glenn Dubis**	576		

MEN'S 50M THREE POSITION RIFLE

Final: July 27

RANK	CTRY	ATHLETE	PRELIM	FINAL	
1	FRA	Jean-Pierre Amat	1175 OR	1273.9	FOR
2	KAZ	Sergey Beliaev	1175 EOR	1272.3	
3	AUT	Wolfram Waibel Jr	1170	1269.6	
4	YUG	Goran Maksimovic	1173	1268.8	
5	SVK	Jozef Gonci	1166	1267.7 10.0#	
6	USA	**Rob Harbison**	1170	**1267.7 8.5#**	
7	CZE	Vaclav Becvar	1168	1264.0	
8	BLR	Serguei Martynov	1166	1263.9	
10	USA	**Glenn Dubis**	1165		

#shoot-off

MEN'S 50M FREE RIFLE, PRONE

Final: July 25

RANK	CTRY	ATHLETE	PRELIM	FINAL	
1	GER	Christian Klees	600 EWR, OR	704.8 FWR, FOR	
2	KAZ	Sergey Beliaev	598	703.3	
3	SVK	Jozef Gonci	599	701.9	
4	ESP	Jorge Gonzalez	597	701.7	
5	CZE	Milan Mach	596	700.9	
6	BLR	Serguei Martynov	598	699.6	
7	KOR	Lee Eun-chul	596	699.1	
8	USA	**Bill Meek**	597	**698.9**	
30T	USA	**Eric Uptagrafft**	592		

MEN'S TRAP

Final: July 21

RANK	CTRY	ATHLETE	PRELIM	FINAL	
1	AUS	Michael Diamond	124 OR	149	FOR
2	USA	**Josh Lakatos**	123	**147**	**28#**
3	USA	**Lance Bade**	123	**147**	**27#**
4	AUS	John Maxwell	123	146	7#
5	CHN	Zhang Bing	122	146	6#
6	SVK	Vladimir Slamka	122	145	
7	POR	Manuel Vieira	122		
8	CAN	George Leary	121		
20T	USA	**Bret Erickson**	119		

#shoot-off

MEN'S DOUBLE TRAP

Final: July 24

RANK	CTRY	ATHLETE	PRELIM	FINAL	
1	AUS	Russell Mark	141 OR	189	FOR
2	ITA	Albano Pera	139	183	7#
3	CHN	Zhang Bing	140	183	6#
4	KOR	Park Chul-sung	138	183	2#
5	GBR	Richard Faulds	139	180	
6	TPE	I-Chien Huang	141 EOR	178	
7	CHN	Li Bo	138		
8	USA	**David Alcoriza**	138		
10	USA	**Lance Bade**	136		

#shoot-off

MEN'S SKEET

Final: July 27

RANK	CTRY	ATHLETE	PRELIM	FINAL	
1	ITA	Ennio Falco	125 EWR, OR	149	FOR
2	POL	Miroslaw Rzepkowski	123	148	
3	ITA	Andrea Benelli	123	147	6#
4	DEN	Ole Rasmussen	122	147	5#
5	RUS	Nikolai Tiopliy	122	146	
6	LAT	Boriss Timofejevs	122	145	
7	EST	Andrey Ineshin	121		
8	CUB	Juan Rodriguez	121		
9T	USA	**Bill Roy**	121		
15T	USA	**Todd Graves**	120		
26T	USA	**George Quigley**	118		

#shoot-off

WOMEN'S 10M AIR PISTOL
Final: July 21

RANK	CTRY	ATHLETE	PRELIM	FINAL	
1	RUS	Olga Klochneva	389	490.1	FOR
2	RUS	Marina Logvinenko	390 OR	488.5 10.1#	
3	BUL	Mariya Grozdeva	389	488.5 9.9#	
4	YUG	Jasna Sekaric	384	487.1	
5	GEO	Nino Salukvadze	385	484.0	
6	KAZ	Galina BEliaeva	384	481.7	
7	KAZ	Yuliya Bondareva	383	479.3	
8	BLR	Lolita Milchina	382	479.1	
30T	USA	Rebecca Snyder	372		
32T	USA	JoAnn Sevin	371		

#shoot-off

WOMEN'S 25M SPORT PISTOL
Final: July 26

RANK	CTRY	ATHLETE	PRELIM	FINAL	
1	CHN	Li Duihong	589	687.9	FOR
2	BUL	Diana Yorgova	585	684.8	
3	RUS	Marina Logvinenko	583	684.2	
4	KOR	Boo Soon-hee	583	683.9	
5	MGL	Gundegmaa Otryad	580	681.3	
6	YUG	Jasna Sekaric	580	680.4	
7	GEO	Nino Salukvadze	586	677.6	
8	POL	Julita Macur	580	677.4	
9T	USA	Connie Petracek	288	578.0	
23T	USA	Libby Callahan	284	573.0	

WOMEN'S AIR RIFLE
Final: July 20

RANK	CTRY	ATHLETE	PRELIM	FINAL
1	POL	Renata Mauer	395	497.6
2	GER	Petra Horneber	397 OR	497.4
3	YUG	Aleksandra Ivosev	395	497.2
4	FRA	Valerie Bellenoue	395	496.6
5	BLR	Olga Pogrebniak	394	496.4
6	CZE	Marta Nedvedova	395	495.1
7	HUN	Eva Joo	393	494.5
8	UKR	Lesya Leskiv	394	494.2
13T	USA	Elizabeth Bourland	392	
36T	USA	Nancy Napolski	386	

WOMEN'S THREE-POSITION RIFLE
Final: July 24

RANK	CTRY	ATHLETE	PRELIM	FINAL	
1	YUG	Aleksandra Ivosev	587	686.1	FOR
2	RUS	Irina Gerasimenok	585	680.1	
3	POL	Renata Mauer	589 OR	679.8	
4	GER	Kirsten Obel	584	679.2	
5	BUL	Nonka Matova	584	678.8	
6	KOR	Kong Hyun-ah	583	675.8	
7	USA	Elizabeth Bourland	583	674.0	
8	UKR	Tetyana Nesterova	581	673.3	
12	USA	Jean Foster	578		

WOMEN'S DOUBLE TRAP
Final: July 23

RANK	CTRY	ATHLETE	PRELIM	FINAL	
1	USA	Kim Rhode	108 OR	141	FOR
2	GER	Susanne Kiermayer	105	139	2#
3	AUS	Deserie Huddleston	103	139	1#
4	USA	Terry Dewitt	105	137	
5	FIN	Riitta-Mari Murtoniemi	107	133	
6	JPN	Yoshiko Kira	105	132	
7	AUS	Annmaree Roberts	103		
8	CHN	Gao E	103		

#shoot-off

SOCCER

MEN
Final: August 3

RANK	CTRY	RECORD	SCORE	USA GAME SCORES	
1	NGR	5-1-0	3-2	USA vs ARG	1-3
2	ARG	3-1-2	(final)	USA vs TUN	2-0
3	BRA	4-2-0	5-0	USA vs POR	1-1
4	POR	2-2-2	(3rd-4th)		
5	FRA	2-1-1			
6	ESP	2-1-1			
7	MEX	1-1-2			
8	GHA	1-2-1			
10	USA	1-1-1			

USA TEAM: Imad Baba / Frankie Hejduk / Miles Joseph / Kasey Keller / Jovan Kirovski / Alexi Lalas / Brian Maisonneuve / Matthew McKeon / Clint Peay / Brandon Pollard / Eddie Pope / Claudio Reyna / Damian Silvera / Rob Smith / Chris Snitko / Nelson Vargas / Billy Walsh / A.J. Wood / Head Coach: Bruce Arena / Assistant Coach: Glenn Myernick

WOMEN
Final: August 2

RANK	CTRY	RECORD	SCORE	USA GAME SCORES	
1	USA	4-0-1	2-1	USA vs DEN	3-0
2	CHN	3-1-1	(final)	USA vs SWE	2-1
3	NOR	3-1-1	2-0	USA vs CHN	0-0
4	BRA	2-2-2	(3rd-4th)	USA vs NOR	2-1
5	GER	1-1-1		USA vs CHN	2-1
6	SWE	1-2-0			
7	JPN	0-3-0			
8	DEN	0-3-0			

USA TEAM: Michelle Akers / Brandi Chastain / Joy Fawcett / Julie Foudy / Carin Gabarra / Mia Hamm / Mary Harvey / Kristine Lilly / Shannon MacMillan / Tiffeny Milbrett / Carla Overbeck / Cindy Parlow / Tiffany Roberts / Briana Scurry / Tisha Venturini / Staci Wilson / Head Coach: Tony DiCicco / Assistant Coaches: Lauren Gregg / April Heinrichs

SOFTBALL
Final: July 30

RANK	CTRY	RECORD	SCORE	USA GAME SCORES	
1	USA	8-1	3-1	USA vs PUR	10-0
2	CHN	6-4	(Final)	USA vs NED	9-0
3	AUS	6-3	3-0	USA vs JPN	6-1
4	JPN	5-3	(3rd-4th)	USA vs TPE	4-0
5	CAN	3-4		USA vs CAN	4-2
6	TPE	2-5		USA vs AUS	1-2
7	NED	1-6		USA vs CHN	3-2
8	PUR	1-6		USA vs CHN	1-0
				USA vs CHN	3-1

USA TEAM: Laura Berg / Gillian Boxx / Sheila Cornell / Lisa Fernandez / Michele Granger / Lori Harrigan / Dionna Harris / Kim Ly Maher / Leah O'Brien / Dot Richardson / Julie Smith / Michele Smith / Shelly Stokes / Dani Tyler / Christa Williams / Head Coach: Ralph Raymond / Assistant Coaches: Ralph Weekly Jr. / Margie Wright

SWIMMING

MEN'S 50-METER FREESTYLE
Final: July 25

RANK	CTRY	ATHLETE	TIME
1	RUS	Aleksandr Popov	22.13
2	USA	Gary Hall Jr.	22.26
3	BRA	Fernando Scherer	22.29
4	CHN	Jiang Chengji	22.33
5	RSA	Brendon Dedekind	22.59
6	USA	David Fox	22.68
7	VEN	Francisco Sanchez	22.72
8	PUR	Ricardo Busquets	22.73

MEN'S 100-METER FREESTYLE
Final: July 22

RANK	CTRY	ATHLETE	TIME
1	RUS	Aleksandr Popov	48.74
2	USA	Gary Hall Jr.	48.81
3	BRA	Gustavo Borges	49.02
4	NED	Pieter van den Hoogenband	49.13
5	BRA	Fernando Scherer	49.57
6	UKR	Pavlo Khnykin	49.65
7	PUR	Ricardo Busquets	49.68
8	VEN	Francisco Sanchez	49.84
9	USA	Jon Olsen	49.80#

#B Final

MEN'S 200-METER FREESTYLE
Final: July 20

RANK	CTRY	ATHLETE	TIME
1	NZL	Danyon Loader	1:47.63
2	BRA	Gustavo Borges	1:48.08
3	AUS	Daniel Kowalski	1:48.25
4	NED	Pieter van den Hoogenband	1:48.36
5	SWE	Anders Holmertz	1:48.42
6	ITA	Massimiliano Rosolino	1:48.50
7	USA	Josh Davis	1:48.54
8	GBR	Paul Palmer	1:49.39
12	USA	John Piersma	1:49:90#

#B Final

MEN'S 400-METER FREESTYLE
Final: July 23

RANK	CTRY	ATHLETE	TIME
1	NZL	Danyon Loader	3:47.97
2	GBR	Paul Palmer	3:49.00
3	AUS	Daniel Kowalski	3:49.39
4	ITA	Emiliano Brembille	3:49.87
5	SWE	Anders Holmertz	3:50.68
6	ITA	Massimiliano Rosolino	3:51.04
7	GER	Jorg Hoffmann	3:52.15
8	DEN	Jacob Carstensen	3:54.45
9	USA	John Piersma	3:50.69#
—	USA	Tom Dolan	scratched B final

#B Final

MEN'S 1500-METER FREESTYLE
Final: July 26

RANK	CTRY	ATHLETE	TIME
1	AUS	Kieren Perkins	14:56.40
2	AUS	Daniel Kowalski	15:02.43
3	GBR	Graeme Smith	15:02.48
4	ITA	Emiliano Brembilla	15:08.58
5	RSA	Ryk Neethling	15:14.63
6	JPN	Masato Hirano	15:17.28
7	GER	Jorg Hoffmann	15:18.86
8	RUS	Aleksey Akatyev	15:21.68
12	USA	Peter Wright	15:25.43#
13	USA	Carlton Bruner	15:25.82#

#B Final

MEN'S 100-METER BACKSTROKE
Final: July 23

RANK	CTRY	ATHLETE	TIME
1	USA	Jeff Rouse	54.10
2	CUB	Rodolfo Falcon	54.98
3	CUB	Neisser Bent	55.02
4	ESP	Martin Lopez-Zubero	55.22
5	USA	Tripp Schwenk	55.30
6	ITA	Emanuele Merisi	55.53
7	GER	Ralf Braun	55.56
8	FRA	Franck Schott	55.76

MEN'S 200-METER BACKSTROKE
Final: July 26

RANK	CTRY	ATHLETE	TIME
1	USA	Brad Bridgewater	1:58.54
2	USA	Tripp Schwenk	1:58.99
3	ITA	Emanuele Merisi	1:59.18
4	POL	Bartosz Sikora	2:00.05
5	JPN	Hajime Itoi	2:00.10
6	ESP	Martin Lopez-Zubero	2:00.74
7	ITA	Mirko Mazzari	2:01.27
8	CUB	Rodolfo Falcon	2:08.14

MEN'S 100-METER BREASTSTROKE
Final: July 20

RANK	CTRY	ATHLETE	TIME
1	BEL	Fred DeBurghgraeve	1:00.65
2	USA	Jeremy Linn	1:00.77
3	GER	Mark Warnecke	1:01.33
4	HUN	Karoly Guttler	1:01.49
5	AUS	Philip Rogers	1:01.64
6	USA	Kurt Grote	1:01.69
7	CHN	Zeng Qiliang	1:02.01
8	RUS	Stanislav Lopukhov	1:02.13

MEN'S 200-METER BREASTSTROKE
Final: July 24

RANK	CTRY	ATHLETE	TIME
1	HUN	Norbert Rozsa	2:12.57
2	HUN	Karoly Guttler	2:13.03
3	RUS	Andrey Korneyev	2:13.17
4	GBR	Nick Gillingham	2:14.37
5	AUS	Philip Rogers	2:14.79
6	POL	Marek Krawczyk	2:14.84
7	USA	Eric Wunderlich	2:15.69
8	USA	Kurt Grote	2:16.05

MEN'S 100-METER BUTTERFLY
Final: July 24

RANK	CTRY	ATHLETE	TIME	
1	RUS	Denis Pankratov	52.27	WR
2	AUS	Scott Miller	52.53	
3	RUS	Vladislav Kulikov	53.13	
4	CHN	Jiang Chengji	53.20	
5	POL	Rafal Szukala	53.29	
6	AUS	Michael Klim	53.30	
7	CAN	Stephen Clarke	53.33	
8	UKR	Pavlo Khnykin	53.58	
10	USA	Mark Henderson	53.23#	
16	USA	John Hargis	54.29#	

#B Final

MEN'S 200-METER BUTTERFLY
Final: July 22

RANK	CTRY	ATHLETE	TIME
1	RUS	Denis Pankratov	1:56.51
2	USA	Tom Malchow	1:57.44
3	AUS	Scott Goodman	1:57.48
4	FRA	Franck Esposito	1:58.10
5	AUS	Scott Miller	1:58.28
6	UKR	Denys Sylantyev	1:58.37
7	GBR	James Hickman	1:58.47
8	HUN	Peter Horvath	1:59.12
21	USA	Ray Carey	2:01.10

MEN'S 200-METER IND. MEDLEY — Final: July 25

RANK	CTRY	ATHLETE	TIME
1	HUN	Attila Czene	1:59.91 OR
2	FIN	Jani Sievinen	2:00.13
3	CAN	Curtis Myden	2:01.13
4	NED	Marcel Wouda	2:01.45
5	AUS	Matthew Dunn	2:01.57
6	USA	**Greg Burgess**	**2:02.56**
7	USA	**Tom Dolan**	**2:03.89**
8	FRA	Xavier Marchand	2:04.29

MEN'S 400-METER IND. MEDLEY — Final: July 21

RANK	CTRY	ATHLETE	TIME
1	USA	**Tom Dolan**	**4:14.90**
2	USA	**Eric Namesnik**	**4:15.25**
3	CAN	Curtis Myden	4:16.28
4	AUS	Matthew Dunn	4:16.66
5	NED	Marcel Wouda	4:17.71
6	ITA	Luca Sacchi	4:18.31
7	POL	Marcin Malinski	4:20.50
8	MDA	Serguei Mariniouk	4:21.15

MEN'S 4x100-METER FREESTYLE RELAY — Final: July 23

RANK	CTRY	ATHLETES	TIME
1	USA	**Jon Olsen / Josh Davis / Bradley Schumacher / Gary Hall Jr.** (prelims: David Fox / Scott Tucker)	**3:15.41 OR**
2	RUS	Roman Yegorov / Aleksandr Popov / Vladimir Predkin / Vladimir Pyshnenko	3:17.06
3	GER	Christian Troger / Bengt Zikarsky / Bjorn Zikarsky / Mark Pinger	3:17.20
4	BRA	Fernando Scherer / Alexandre Massura / Andre Cordeiro / Gustavo Borges	3:18.30
5	NED	Mark Hermanus Veens / Pie Geelen / Martin van der Spoel / Pieter van den Hoogenband	3:19.02
6	AUS	Michael Klim / Matthew Dunn / Scott Logan / Chris Fydler	3:20.13
7	SWE	Lars Frolander / Fredrik Letsler / Anders Holmertz / Christer Wallin	3:20.16
8	GBR	Nicholas Shackell / Alan Rapley / Mark Stevens / Michael Fibbens	3:21.52

MEN'S 4X200-METER FREESTYLE RELAY — Final: July 21

RANK	CTRY	ATHLETES	TIME
1	USA	**Josh Davis / Joe Hudepohl / Bradley Schumacher / Ryan Berube** (prelims: Jon Olsen)	**7:14.84**
2	SWE	Christer Wallin / Anders Holmertz / Lars Frolander / Anders Lyrbring	7:17.56
3	GER	Aimo Heilmann / Christian Keller / Christian Troeger / Steffen Zesner	7:17.71
4	AUS	Daniel Kowalski / Michael Klim / Malcolm Allen / Matthew Dunn	7:18.47
5	GBR	Paul Palmer / Andrew Clayton / Mark Stevens / James Salter	7:18.74
6	ITA	Massimiliano Rosolino / Emanuele Idini / Emanuele Merisi / Piermaria Siciliano	7:19.92
7	NED	Marcel Wouda / Mark van der Zijden / Martin van der Spoel / Pieter van den Hoogenband	7:21.96
8	FRA	Yann de Fabrique / Lionel Poirot / Bruno Orsoni / Christophe Bordeau	7:24.85

MEN'S 4x100-METER MEDLEY RELAY — Final: July 24

RANK	CTRY	ATHLETES	TIME
1	USA	**Jeff Rouse / Jeremy Linn / Mark Henderson / Gary Hall Jr.** (prelims: Tripp Schwenk / Kurt Grote / John Hargis / Josh Davis)	**3:34.84 WR**
2	RUS	Vladimir Selkov / Stanislav Lopukhov / Denis Pankratov / Aleksandr Popov	3:37.55
3	AUS	Steven Dewick / Philip Rogers / Scott Miller / Michael Kim / Toby Haenen	3:39.56
4	GER	Ralf Braun / Mark Warnecke / Christian Keller / Bjorn Zikarsky	3:39.64
5	JPN	Keitaro Konn Al / Akira Hayashi / Takashi Yamamoto / Shunsuke Ito	3:40.51
6	HUN	Tamas Deutsch / Karoly Guttler / Peter Horvath / Attila Czene	3:40.84
7	POL	Mariusz Siembida / Marek Krawczyk / Rafal Szukala / Bartosz Kizierowski	3:41.94
8	ISR	Eithan Urbach, Vadim Alekseyev / Dan Kutler / Yoav Bruck	3:42.90

WOMEN'S 50-METER FREESTYLE — Final: July 26

RANK	CTRY	ATHLETE	TIME
1	USA	**Amy Van Dyken**	**24.87**
2	CHN	Le Jingyi	24.90
3	GER	Sandra Volker	25.14
4	USA	**Angel Martino**	**25.31**
5	BAR	Leah Martindale	25.49
6	SWE	Linda Olofsson	25.63
7	CHN	Shan Ying	25.70
8	RUS	Natalya Meshcheryakova	25.88

WOMEN'S 100-METER FREESTYLE — Final: July 20

RANK	CTRY	ATHLETE	TIME
1	CHN	Le Jingyi	54.50 OR
2	GER	Sandra Volker	54.88
3	USA	**Angel Martino**	**54.93**
4	USA	**Amy Van Dyken**	**55.11**
5	GER	Franziska van Almsick	55.59
6	AUS	Sarah Ryan	55.85
7	DEN	Mette Jacobsen	56.01
8	NED	Karin Brienesse	56.12

WOMEN'S 200-METER FREESTYLE — Final: July 21

RANK	CTRY	ATHLETE	TIME
1	CRC	Claudia Poll	1:58.16
2	GER	Franziska van Almsick	1:58.57
3	GER	Dagmar Hase	1:59.56
4	USA	**Trina Jackson**	**1:59.57**
5	AUS	Susan O'Neill	1:59.87
6	USA	**Cristina Teuscher**	**2:00.79**
7	AUS	Julia Greville	2:01.46
8	ROM	Liliana Dobrescu	2:01.63

WOMEN'S 400-METER FREESTYLE — Final: July 22

RANK	CTRY	ATHLETE	TIME
1	IRL	Michelle Smith	4:07.25
2	GER	Dagmar Hase	4:08.30
3	NED	Kirsten Vlieghuis	4:08.70
4	GER	Kerstin Kielgass	4:09.83
5	CRC	Claudia Poll	4:10.00
6	NED	Carla Louise Geurts	4:10.06
7	JPN	Eri Yamanoi	4:11.68
8	USA	**Cristina Teuscher**	**4:14.21**
—	USA	**Janet Evans**	scratched B final

WOMEN'S 800-METER FREESTYLE — Final: July 25

RANK	CTRY	ATHLETE	TIME
1	USA	**Brooke Bennett**	**8:27.89**
2	GER	Dagmar Hase	8:29.91
3	NED	Kirsten Vlieghuis	8:30.84
4	GER	Kerstin Kielgass	8:31.06
5	NOR	Irene Dalby	8:38.34
6	USA	**Janet Evans**	**8:38.91**
7	NED	Carla Louise Geurts	8:40.43
8	GBR	Sarah Hardcastle	8:41.75

WOMEN'S 100-METER BACKSTROKE — Final: July 22

RANK	CTRY	ATHLETE	TIME
1	USA	**Beth Botsford**	**1:01.19**
2	USA	**Whitney Hedgepeth**	**1:01.47**
3	RSA	Marianne Kriel	1:02.12
4	JPN	Mai Nakamura	1:02.33
5	CHN	Chen Yan	1:02.50
6	GER	Antje Buschschulte	1:02.52
7	AUS	Nicole Stevenson	1:02.70
8	JPN	Miki Nakao	1:02.78

WOMEN'S 200-METER BACKSTROKE — Final: July 25

RANK	CTRY	ATHLETE	TIME
1	HUN	Krisztina Egerszegi	2:07.83
2	USA	**Whitney Hedgepeth**	**2:11.98**
3	GER	Cathleen Rund	2:12.06
4	GER	Anke Scholz	2:12.90
5	JPN	Miki Nakao	2:13.57
6	NZL	Anna Simcic	2:14.04
7	ITA	Lorenza Vigarani	2:14.56
—	RUS	Nina Zhivanevskaya	DQ
10	USA	**Beth Botsford**	**2:13.48#**

#B Final

WOMEN'S 100-METER BREASTSTROKE — Final: July 21

RANK	CTRY	ATHLETE	TIME
1	RSA	Penelope Heyns	1:07.73
2	USA	**Amanda Beard**	**1:08.09**
3	AUS	Samantha Riley	1:09.18
4	UKR	Svitlana Bondarenko	1:09.21
5	AUT	Vera Lischka	1:09.24
6	CAN	Guylaine Cloutier	1:09.40
7	HUN	Agnes Kovacs	1:09.55
8	BEL	Brigitte Becue	1:09.79
19	USA	**Kristine Quance**	**1:10.92**

WOMEN'S 200-METER BREASTSTROKE — Final: July 23

RANK	CTRY	ATHLETE	TIME
1	RSA	Penelope Heyns	2:25.41 OR
2	USA	**Amanda Beard**	**2:25.75**
3	HUN	Agnes Kovacs	2:26.57
4	AUS	Samantha Riley	2:27.91
5	JPN	Masami Tanaka	2:28.05
6	AUS	Nadine Neumann	2:28.34
7	BEL	Brigitte Becue	2:28.36
8	CAN	Christin Petelski	2:31.45
15	USA	**Jilen Siroky**	**2:33.43#**

#B Final

WOMEN'S 100-METER BUTTERFLY — Final: July 23

RANK	CTRY	ATHLETE	TIME
1	USA	**Amy Van Dyken**	**59.13**
2	CHN	Liu Limin	59.14
3	USA	**Angel Martino**	**59.23**
4	JPN	Hitomi Kashima	1:00.11
5	AUS	Susan O'Neill	1:00.17
6	JPN	Ayari Aoyama	1:00.18
7	CHN	Cai Huijue	1:00.46
8	DEN	Mette Jacobsen	1:00.76

WOMEN'S 200-METER BUTTERFLY — Final: July 26

RANK	CTRY	ATHLETE	TIME
1	AUS	Susan O'Neill	2:07.76
2	AUS	Petria Thomas	2:09.82
3	IRL	Michelle Smith	2:09.91
4	CHN	Qu Yun	2:10.26
5	CHN	Liu Limin	2:10.70
6	CAN	Jessica Deglau	2:11.40
7	JPN	Mika Haruna	2:11.93
8	USA	**Trina Jackson**	**2:11.96**
12	USA	**Annette Salmeen**	**2:13.64#**

#B Final

WOMEN'S 200-METER IND. MEDLEY — Final: July 24

RANK	CTRY	ATHLETE	TIME
1	IRL	Michelle Smith	2:13.93
2	CAN	Marianne Limpert	2:14.35
3	CHN	Lin Li	2:14.74
4	CAN	Joanne Malar	2:15.30
5	AUS	Elli Overton	2:16.04
6	USA	**Allison Wagner**	**2:16.43**
7	NED	Minouche Smit	2:16.73
8	SWE	Louise Karlsson	2:17.25
9	USA	**Kristine Quance**	**2:15.24#**

#B Final

WOMEN'S 400-METER IND. MEDLEY — Final: July 20

RANK	CTRY	ATHLETE	TIME
1	IRL	Michelle Smith	4:39.19
2	USA	**Allison Wagner**	**4:42.03**
3	HUN	Krisztina Egerszegi	4:42.53
4	GER	Sabine Herbst	4:43.78
5	AUS	Emma Johnson	4:44.02
6	ROM	Beatrice Coada	4:44.91
7	ESP	Lourdes Becerra	4:45.17
8	USA	**Whitney Metzler**	**4:46.20**

WOMEN'S 4x100-METER FREESTYLE RELAY — Final: July 22

RANK	CTRY	ATHLETES	TIME
1	USA	**Angel Martino / Amy Van Dyken / Catherine Fox / Jenny Thompson** (prelims: Lisa Jacob / Melanie Valerio)	**3:39.29 OR**
2	CHN	Le Jingyi / Chao Na / Nian Yun / Shan Ying	3:40.48
3	GER	Sandra Volker / Simone Osygus / Antje Buschschulte / Franziska van Almsick	3:41.48
4	NED	Marianne Muis / Minouche Smit / Willemina van Hofwegen / Karin Brienesse	3:42.40
5	SWE	Linda Olofsson / Louise Johncke / Louise Karlsson / Johanna Sjoberg	3:44.91
6	AUS	Sarah Ryan / Julia Greville / Lise Mackie / Susan O'Neill	3:45.31
7	CAN	Shannon Shakespeare / Julie Howard / Andrea Moody / Marianne Limpert	3:46.27
—	RUS	Yelena Nazemnova / Svetlana Leshukova / Natalya Meshcheryakova / Natalya Sorokina	

WOMEN'S 4x200-METER FREESTYLE RELAY — Final: July 25

RANK	CTRY	ATHLETES	TIME
1	USA	Trina Jackson / Cristina Teuscher / Sheila Taormina / Jenny Thompson (prelims: Lisa Jacob / Ashley Whitney / Annette Salmeen)	7:59.87 OR
2	GER	Franziska van Almsick / Kerstin Kielgass / Anke Scholz / Dagmar Hase	8:01.55
3	AUS	Julia Greville / Nicole Stevenson / Emma Johnson / Susan O'Neill	8:05.47
4	JPN	Eri Yamanoi / Naoko Imoto / Aiko Miyake / Suzu Chiba	8:07.46
5	CAN	Marianne Limpert / Shannon Shakespeare / Andrea Schwartz / Jessica Deglau	8:08.16
6	NED	Carla Louise Geurts / Patricia Stokkers / Minouche Smit / Kirsten Vlieghuis	8:08.48
7	ROM	Liliana Dobrescu / Loredana Zisu / Ioana Diaconescu / Carla Negrea	8:10.02
8	CHN	Nian Yun / Wang Luna / Chen Yan / Shan Ying	8:15.38

WOMEN'S 4x100-METER MEDLEY RELAY — Final: July 24

RANK	CTRY	ATHLETES	TIME
1	USA	Beth Botsford / Amanda Beard / Angel Martino / Amy Van Dyken (prelims: Whitney Hedgepeth / Kristin Quance / Jenny Thompson / Catherine Fox)	4:02.88
2	AUS	Nicole Stevenson / Samantha Riley / Susan O'Neill / Sarah Ryan	4:05.08
3	CHN	Chen Yan / Han Xue / Cai Huijue / Shan Ying	4:07.34
4	RSA	Marianne Kriel / Penelope Heyns / Amanda Loots / Helene Muller	4:08.16
5	CAN	Julie Howard / Guylaine Cloutier / Sarah Evanetz / Shannon Shakespeare	4:08.29
6	GER	Antje Buschschulte / Kathrin Dimitru / Franziska van Almsick / Sandra Volker	4:09.22
7	RUS	Nina Zhivanevskaya / Yelene Makarova / Yelena Nazemnova / Natalya Mescheryakova	4:10.56
8	ITA	Lorenza Vigarani / Manuela Dalla Valle / Ilaria Tocchini / Cecilia Vianini	4:10.59

SYNCHRONIZED SWIMMING
TEAM COMPETITION — Final: August 2

RANK	CTRY	TECHNICAL	FREE	POINTS
1	USA	99.200	100.000	99.720
2	CAN	97.933	98.600	98.367
3	JPN	97.667	97.800	97.753
4	RUS	97.000	97.400	97.260
5	FRA	95.600	96.333	96.076
6	ITA	93.733	94.533	94.253
7	CHN	94.600	93.867	94.124
8	MEX	94.400	93.533	93.836

USA TEAM: Suzannah Bianco / Tammy Cleland / Becky Dyroen-Lancer / Emily Porter LeSueur / Heather Pease / Jill Savery / Nathalie Schneyder / Heather Simmons-Carrasco / Jill Sudduth / Margot Thien / Coaches: Gail Emery / Chris Carver

TABLE TENNIS
MEN'S SINGLES — Final: August 1

RANK	CTRY	ATHLETE	
1	CHN	Liu Guoliang	
2	CHN	Wang Tao	
3	GER	Joerg Rosskopf	
4	CZE	Petr Korbel	
5T	BLR	Vladimir Samsonov	
5T	BEL	Jean-Michel Saive	
5T	CAN	Johnny Huang	
5T	KOR	Kim Taek-soo	
—	USA	Jim Butler	elim. (1-2)
—	USA	David Zhuang	elim. (1-2)

MEN'S DOUBLES — Final: July 30

RANK	CTRY	ATHLETES	
1	CHN	Kong Linghui / Liu Guoliang	
2	CHN	Lu Lin / Wang Tao	
3	KOR	Lee Chul-seung / Yoo Nam-kyu	
4	GER	Steffen Fetzner / Joerg Rosskopf	
5T	FRA	Damien Eloi / Jean-Philippe Gatien	
5T	KOR	Kang Hee-chan / Kim Taek-soo	
5T	JPN	Koji Matsushita / Hiroshi Shibutani	
5T	SWE	Jorgen Persson / Jan-Ove Waldner	
—	USA	Jim Butler / Todd Sweeris	elim. (0-3)

WOMEN'S SINGLES — Final: July 31

RANK	CTRY	ATHLETE	
1	CHN	Deng Yaping	
2	TPE	Jing Chen	
3	CHN	Qiao Hong	
4	CHN	Liu Wei	
5T	HKG	Tan Lui Chan	
5T	PRK	Hyon Kim	
5T	JPN	Chire Koyama	
5T	GER	Nicole Struse	
17T	USA	Amy Feng	elim. (2-1)
17T	USA	Lily Yip	elim. (2-1)

WOMEN'S DOUBLES — Final: July 30

RANK	CTRY	ATHLETES	
1	CHN	Deng Yaping / Qial Hong	
2	CHN	Liu Wei / Qiao Yunping	
3	KOR	Park Hae-jung / Ryu Ji-hae	
4	KOR	Kim Moo-kyo / Park Kyoung-ae	
5T	HKG	Po Wa Chai / Tan Lui Chan	
5T	TPE	Chiu-Tan Chen / Jing Chen	
5T	JPN	Chire Koyama / Taeko Todo	
5T	RUS	Irina Palina / Yelena Timina	
—	USA	Wei Wang / Lily Yip	elim. (2-1)

TEAM HANDBALL
MEN — Final: August 4

RANK	CTRY	RECORD	SCORE	USA GAME SCORES	
1	CRO	6-1	27-26	USA vs SWE	19-23
2	SWE	6-1	(final)	USA vs RUS	16-31
3	ESP	5-2	27-25	USA vs SUI	20-29
4	FRA	4-3	(3rd-4th)	USA vs CRO	27-35
5	RUS	4-2		USA vs KUW	29-24
6	EGY	3-3		USA vs ALG	27-26
7	GER	4-2			
8	SUI	2-4			
9	USA	2-4			

USA TEAM: Derek Brown / Greg Caccia / Yaro Dachniwsky / Dave DeGraaf / Robert Dunn / Denny Fercho / Joseph Fitzgerald / Thomas Fitzgerald / Darrick Heath / John Keller Jr. / Cliff Mannon / Steven Penn / Matt Ryan / Mark Schmocker / Michael Thornberry / Chip Van Os Jr. / Head Coach: Rick Oleksyk / Assistant Coach: Rhett Nichol

WOMEN — Final: August 3

RANK	CTRY	RECORD	SCORE	USA GAME SCORES	
1	DEN	5-0	37-33	USA vs DEN	19-29
2	KOR	4-1	(final)	USA vs HUN	24-30
3	HUN	3-2	20-18	USA vs CHN	21-31
4	NOR	2-3	(3rd-4th)	USA vs ANG	23-24
5	CHN	2-2			
6	GER	1-3			
7	ANG	1-3			
8	USA	0-4			

USA TEAM: Cheryl Abplanalp / Dawn Allinger / Sharon Cain / Kim Clarke / Laura Coenen / Kristen Danihy / Lisa Eagen / Laurie Fellner / Chryssandra Hires / Jennifer Horton / Tami Jameson / Toni Jameson / Dannette Leininger / Dawn Marple / Pat Neder / Carol Peterka / Head Coach: Claes Hellgren / Assistant Coach: Reita Clanton

TENNIS
MEN'S SINGLES — Final: August 3

RANK	CTRY	ATHLETE	
1	USA	Andre Agassi	
2	ESP	Sergi Bruguera	
3	IND	Leander Paes	
4	BRA	Fernando Meligeni	
5T	USA	MaliVai Washington	
5T	RSA	Wayne Ferreira	
5T	ITA	Renzo Furlan	
5T	RUS	Andrei Olhovskiy	
—	USA	Richey Reneberg	withdrew injury

MEN'S DOUBLES — Final: August 1

RANK	CTRY	ATHLETES	
1	AUS	Todd Woodbridge / Mark Woodforde	
2	GBR	Neil Broad / Tim Henman	
3	GER	Marc-Kevin Goellner / David Prinosil	
4	NED	Jacco Eltingh / Paul Haarhuis	
5T	CRO	Sasa Hirszon / Goran Ivanisevic	
5T	ESP	Sergi Bruguera / Tomas Carbonell	
5T	RSA	Ellis Ferreira / Wayne Ferreira	
5T	CZE	Jiri Novak / Daniel Vacek	
—	USA	Andre Agassi / MaliVai Washington	elim. 2nd rd.

WOMEN'S SINGLES — Final: August 3

RANK	CTRY	ATHLETE	
1	USA	Lindsay Davenport	
2	ESP	Arantxa Sanchez Vicario	
3	CZE	Jana Novotna	
4	USA	Mary Joe Fernandez	
5T	USA	Monica Seles	
5T	JPN	Kimiko Date	
5T	CRO	Iva Majoli	
5T	ESP	Conchita Martinez	
—	USA	Chanda Rubin	withdrew injury

WOMEN'S DOUBLES — Final: August 1

RANK	CTRY	ATHLETES	
1	USA	Gigi Fernandez / Mary Joe Fernandez	
2	CZE	Jana Novotna / Helena Sukova	
3	ESP	Conchita Martinez / Arantxa Sanchez Vicario	
4	NED	Manon Bollegraf / Brenda Schultz-McCarthy	
5T	GBR	Valda Lake / Clare Wood	
5T	CAN	Jill Hetherington / Patricia Hy-Boulais	
5T	THA	Benjamas Sangaram / Tamarine Tanasugarn	
5T	SUI	Martina Hingis / Patty Schnyder	

VOLLEYBALL
MEN'S INDOOR — Final: August 4

RANK	CTRY	RECORD	SCORE	USA MATCH SCORES	
1	NED		3-2	USA vs POL	3-0
2	ITA		(final)	USA vs ARG	3-0
3	YUG		3-1	USA vs CUB	2-3
4	RUS		(3rd-4th)	USA vs BRA	0-3
5	BRA			USA vs BUL	2-3
6	CHN				
7	BUL				
8	ARG				
9	USA	2-3			

USA TEAM: Lloy Ball / Bob Ctvrtlik / Scott Fortune / John Hyden / Bryan Ivie / Mike Lambert / Dan Landry / Jeff Nygaard / Tom Sorensen / Jeff Stork / Ethan Watts / Brett Winslow / Head Coach: Fred Sturm / Assistant Coaches: Rudy Suwara / Rod Wilde

MEN'S BEACH — Final: July 28

RANK	CTRY	ATHLETES
1	USA	Karch Kiraly / Kent Steffes
2	USA	Michael Dodd / Mike Whitmarsh
3	CAN	John Child / Mark Heese
4	POR	Luis Miguel Barbosa Maia / Joao Carlos Pereira Brenha Alves
5	USA	Carl Henkel / Christopher St. John "Sinjin" Smith
6	ESP	Javier Bosma Minguez / Sixto Jimenez Galan

WOMEN'S INDOOR — Final: August 4

RANK	CTRY	RECORD	SCORE	USA MATCH SCORES	
1	CUB		3-1	USA vs UKR	3-0
2	CHN		(final)	USA vs NED	3-1
3	BRA		3-2	USA vs CHN	1-3
4	RUS		(3rd-4th)	USA vs JPN	3-0
5	NED			USA vs KOR	3-1
6	KOR			USA vs CUB	0-3
7	USA	5-3		USA vs KOR	0-3
8	GER			USA vs GER	3-1

USA TEAM: Tara Cross-Battle / Lori Endicott / Caren Kemner / Kristin Klein / Tammy Liley / Bev Oden / Elaina Oden / Danielle Scott / Paula Weishoff / Teee Williams / Elaine Youngs / Yoko Zetterlund / Head Coach: Terry Liskevych / Assistant Coaches: Aldis Berzins / Jeanne Reeves

WOMEN'S BEACH — Final: July 27

RANK	CTRY	ATHLETES
1	BRA	Jackie Silva Cruz / Sandra Pires Tavares
2	BRA	Monica Rodrigues / Adriana Samuel Ramos
3	AUS	Natalie Cook / Kerri Ann Pottharst
4	USA	Barbara Fontana Harris / Linda Hanley
5T	USA	Holly McPeak / Nancy Reno
5T	JPN	Sachiko Fujita / Yukiko Takahashi
7T	AUS	Liane Fenwick / Anita Spring (Palm)
7T	GER	Beate Bühler / Danja Müsch
9	USA	Gail Castro / Debra Richardson

WATER POLO

Final: July 28

RANK	CTRY	RECORD	SCORE	USA GAME SCORES	
1	ESP	6-2	7-5	USA vs ITA	7-10
2	CRO	5-3	(Final)	USA vs GRE	9-7
3	ITA	7-1	20-18	USA vs UKR	9-7
4	HUN	6-2	(3rd-4th)	USA vs ROM	10-5
5	RUS	4-3-1	10-8	USA vs CRO	10-8
6	GRE	3-5	(5th-6th)	USA vs ESP	4-5
7	USA	5-3	12-8	USA vs GRE	6-7
8	YUG	3-4-1	(7th-8th)	USA vs YUG	12-8

USA TEAM: Gavin Arroyo / Troy Barnhart, Jr. / Chris Duplanty / Mike Evans / Kirk Everist / Dan Hackett / Chris Humbert / Kyle Kopp / Jeremy Laster / Rick McNair / Chris Oeding / Alex Rousseau / Wolf Wigo / Head Coach: Rich Corso / Assistant Coaches: Ricardo Azevedo / John Vargas

WEIGHTLIFTING

54 KG (119 LBS)

Final: July 20

RANK	CTRY	ATHLETE	SNATCH	C & J	TOTAL KG
1	TUR	Halil Mutlu	132.5 WR/OR	155.0	287.5 OR
2	CHN	Xiangsen Zhang	130.0	150.0	280.0
3	BUL	Sevdalín Minchev	125.0	152.5	277.5
4	CHN	Lan Shizhang	125.0	150.0	275.0
5	ROM	Tráian Ciharean	120.0	145.0	265.0
6	BUL	Ivan Ivanov	112.5	145.0	257.5
7	KOR	Ko Kwang-ku	115.0	140.0	255.0
8	COL	Juan Fernandez	110.0	145.0	255.0

no USA entry

59 KG (130 LBS)

Final: July 21

RANK	CTRY	ATHLETE	SNATCH	C & J	TOTAL KG
1	CHN	Tang Ningsheng	137.5	170.0 OR	307.5 WR/OR
2	GRE	Leonidas Sabanis	137.5	167.5	305.0
3	BUL	Nikolay Pechalov	137.5	165.0	302.5
4	JPN	Hiroshi Ikehata	132.5	165.0	297.5
5	CUB	William Vargas	135.0	162.5	297.5
6	CHN	Xu Dong	132.5	162.5	295.0
7	AUS	Yurik Sarkisian	125.0	155.0	280.0
8	HUN	Zoltan Farkas	130.0	150.0	280.0
9	USA	Bryan Jacob	122.5	150.0*	272.5

64 KG (141 LBS)

Final: July 22

RANK	CTRY	ATHLETE	SNATCH	C & J	TOTAL KG
1	TUR	Naim Suleymanoglu	147.5	187.5	335.0 WR/OR
2	GRE	Valerios Leonidis	145.0	187.5 WR/OR	332.5
3	CHN	Xiao Jiangang	145.0	177.5	322.5
4	GRE	Yorgos Tzelilis	145.0	177.5	322.5
5	HUN	Adrian Popa	135.0	172.5	307.5
6	BUL	Ilian Iliev	142.5	162.5	305.0
7	TUR	Mucahit Yagci	135.0	167.5	302.5
8	HUN	Zoltan Kecskes	135.0	167.5	302.5
22	USA	Vernon Patao	122.5	160.0	282.5
32	USA	Thanh Nguyen	112.5	145.0	257.5

70 KG (154 LBS)

Final: July 23

RANK	CTRY	ATHLETE	SNATCH	C & J	TOTAL KG
1	CHN	Zhan Xugang	162.5 WR/OR	195.0 WR/OR	357.5 WR/OR
2	PRK	Myong Kim	160.0	185.0	345.0
3	HUN	Attila Feri	152.5	187.5	340.0
4	BUL	Plamen Zhelyazkov	155.0	180.0	335.0
5	ALG	Abdelmanaame Yahiaoui	150.0	185.0	335.0
6	ARM	Israyel Militosian	152.5	182.5	335.0
7	CHN	Wan Jianhui	152.5	180.0	332.5
8	CUB	Idalberto Aranda	145.0	187.5	332.5
14	USA	Tim McRae	145.0	177.5	322.5

76 KG (167 LBS)

Final: July 24

RANK	CTRY	ATHLETE	SNATCH	C & J	TOTAL KG
1	CUB	Pablo Lara	162.5	205.0	367.5
2	BUL	Yoto Yotov	160.0	200.0	360.0
3	PRK	Chol Jon	162.5	195.0	357.5
4	GRE	Viktor Mitrou	162.5	195.0	357.5
5	CHN	Lin Shoufeng	157.5	195.0	352.5
6	GER	Ingo Steinhoefel	160.0	187.5	347.5
7	RUS	Sergey Filimonov	160.0	185.0	345.0
8	ARM	Hovhannes Barsegian	155.0	190.0	345.0

no USA entry

83 KG (183 LBS)

Final: July 26

RANK	CTRY	ATHLETE	SNATCH	C & J	TOTAL KG
1	GRE	Pyrros Dimas	180.0 WR/OR	212.5 OR	392.5 WR/OR
2	GER	Marc Huster	170.0	212.5 WR	382.5
3	POL	Andrzej Cofalik	170.0	202.5	372.5
4	AUS	Kiril Kounev	170.0	200.0	370.0
5	MDA	Vadim Vacarciuc	165.0	202.5	367.5
6	ARM	Sergo Chakhoian	170.0	195.0	365.0
7	TUR	Dursun Sevinc	165.0	197.5	362.5
8	BUL	Krastu Milev	160.0	200.0	360.0

no USA entry

91 KG (201 LBS)

Final: July 27

RANK	CTRY	ATHLETE	SNATCH	C & J	TOTAL KG
1	RUS	Aleksey Petrov	187.5 WR/OR	215.0	402.5
2	GRE	Leonidas Kokas	175.0	215.0	390.0
3	GER	Oliver Caruso	175.0	215.0	390.0
4	TUR	Sunay Bulut	177.5	212.5	390.0
5	RUS	Igor Alekseev	182.5	205.0	387.5
6	CUB	Carlos Alexis Hernandez	175.0	207.5	382.5
7	UKR	Oleh Chumak	167.5	212.5	380.0
8	BUL	Plamen Bratoychev	175.0	205.0	380.0
14	USA	Tom Gough	167.5	200.0	367.5

99 KG (218 LBS)

Final: July 28

RANK	CTRY	ATHLETE	SNATCH	C & J	TOTAL KG
1	GRE	Akakide Kakhiashvilis	185.0	235.0 WR/OR	420.0 WR/OR
2	KAZ	Anatoli Khrapaty	187.5	222.5	410.0
3	UKR	Denis Gotfrid	187.5	215.0	402.5
4	UKR	Stanislav Rybalchenko	182.5	212.5	395.0
5	RUS	Vyacheslav Rubin	175.0	215.0	390.0
6	RUS	Dmitry Smirnov	175.0	215.0	390.0
7	GER	Igor Sadykov	177.5	207.5	385.0
8	ARM	Aghvan Grigorian	175.0	205.0	380.0
14	USA	Pete Kelley	160.0	197.5	357.5

108 KG (238 LBS)

Final: July 29

RANK	CTRY	ATHLETE	SNATCH	C & J	TOTAL KG
1	UKR	Timur Raimazov	195.0	235.0 WR/OR	430.0
2	RUS	Sergey Syrtsov	195.0	225.0	420.0
3	ROM	Nicu Vlad	197.5	222.5	420.0
4	BLR	Vladimir Emelyanov	187.5	220.0	407.5
5	CHN	Cui Wenhua	190.0	215.0	405.0
6	USA	Wes Barnett	175.0	220.0	395.0
7	ARM	Ara Vardanian	180.0	215.0	395.0
8	POL	Dariusz Osuch	177.5	215.0	392.5
12	USA	Konstantine Starikovitch	177.5	210.0	387.5

+108 KG (+238 LBS)

Final: July 30

RANK	CTRY	ATHLETE	SNATCH	C & J	TOTAL KG
1	RUS	Andrey Chemerkin	197.5	260.0 WR/OR	457.5 WR/OR
2	GER	Ronny Weller	200.0	255.0	455.0
3	AUS	Stefan Botev	200.0	250.0	450.0
4	KOR	Kim Tae-hyun	190.0	247.5	437.5
5	BLR	Aleksandr Kurlovich	195.0	230.0	425.0
6	GER	Manfred Nerlinger	185.0	237.5	422.5
7	GRE	Pavlos Saltsidis	185.0	235.0	420.0
8	HUN	Tibor Stark	187.5	227.5	415.0
14	USA	Mark Henry	175.0	202.5	377.5
16	USA	Tom Ingalsbe	165.0	200.0	365.0

WRESTLING

48 KG (105.5 LBS) FREESTYLE

Final: July 31

RANK	CTRY	ATHLETE
1	PRK	Il Kim
2	ARM	Armen Mkrchyan
3	CUB	Alexis Vila Perdomo
4	RUS	Vugar Orudzhov
5	KOR	Jung Soon-won
6	MDA	Vitaliy Railean
7	ROM	Gheorghe Corduneanu
8	USA	Rob Eiter

52 KG (114.5 LBS) FREESTYLE

Final: August 2

RANK	CTRY	ATHLETE
1	BUL	Valentin Jordanov
2	AZE	Namik Abdullayev
3	KAZ	Maulen Mamyrov
4	RUS	Chechenol Mongush
5	IRI	Gholamreza Mohammadi
6	TUR	Metin Topaktas
7	UZB	Adkhamjon Achilov
8	CAN	Greg Woodcroft
11	USA	Lou Rosselli

57 KG (125.5 LBS) FREESTYLE

Final: July 31

RANK	CTRY	ATHLETE
1	USA	Kendall Cross
2	CAN	Giuvi Sissaouri
3	PRK	Yong Sam Ri
4	TUR	Harun Dogan
5	MKD	Saban Trstena
6	IRI	Mohammad Talaei
7	BLR	Aleksandr Guzov
8	UZB	Damir Zakhartdinov

62 KG (136.5 LBS) FREESTYLE

Final: August 2

RANK	CTRY	ATHLETE
1	USA	Tom Brands
2	KOR	Jang Jae-sung
3	UKR	Elbrus Tedeyev
4	JPN	Takahiro Wada
5	RUS	Magomed Azizov
6	ITA	Giovanni Schillaci
7	CAN	Marty Calder
8	UZB	Ramil Islamov

68 KG (149.5 LBS) FREESTYLE

Final: July 31

RANK	CTRY	ATHLETE
1	RUS	Vadim Bogiyev
2	USA	Townsend Saunders
3	UKR	Zaza Zazirov
4	CUB	Yosvany Sanchez Larrude
5	ARM	Arayik Gevorgyan
6	KOR	Hwang Sang-ho
7	EST	Kullo Koiv
8	SYR	Ahmad Alaosta

74 KG (163 LBS) FREESTYLE

Final: August 2

RANK	CTRY	ATHLETE
1	RUS	Buvaysa Saytyev
2	KOR	Park Jang-soon
3	JPN	Takuya Ota
4	BUL	Plamen Paskalev
5	GER	Alexander Leipold
6	USA	Kenny Monday
7	MDA	Victor Peicov
8	AZE	Mohamed Salam Gadzhiyev

82 KG (180.5 LBS) FREESTYLE

Final: July 31

RANK	CTRY	ATHLETE
1	RUS	Khadzhimurad Magomedov
2	KOR	Yang Hyun-mo
3	IRI	Amir Reza Khadem Azghadi
4	TUR	Sebahattin Ozturk
5	AZE	Magomed Ibragimov
6	KAZ	Elmadi Jabrailov
7	USA	Les Gutches
8	CUB	Ariel Ramos Wilson

90 KG (198 LBS) FREESTYLE

Final: August 2

RANK	CTRY	ATHLETE
1	IRI	Rasull Khadem Azghadi
2	RUS	Makharbek Khadartsev
3	GEO	Eldari Kurtanidze
4	SVK	Jozef Lohyna
5	UKR	Dzambolat Tyedyeyev
6	NGR	Victor Kodei
7	USA	Melvin Douglas
8	KOR	Kim Ik-hee

100 KG (220 LBS) FREESTYLE

Final: July 31

RANK	CTRY	ATHLETE
1	USA	Kurt Angle
2	IRI	Abbas Jadidi
3	GER	Arawat Sabejew
4	BLR	Sergey Kovalevskiy
5	POL	Marek Garmulewicz
6	KGZ	Konstantin Aleksandrov
7	UKR	Sahid Murtazaliyev
8	CAN	Oleg Ladik

130 KG (286 LBS) FREESTYLE

Final: August 2

RANK	CTRY	ATHLETE
1	TUR	Mahmut Demir
2	BLR	Aleksey Medvedev
3	USA	Bruce Baumgartner
4	RUS	Andrey Shumilin
5	KGZ	Aleksandr Kovalevskiy
6	GER	Sven Thiele
7	UKR	Merabi Valiyev
8	GRE	Petros Bourdoulis

48 KG (105.5 LBS) GRECO-ROMAN — Final: July 21

RANK	CTRY	ATHLETE
1	KOR	Sim Kwon-ho
2	BLR	Aleksandr Pavlov
3	RUS	Zafar Gulyov
4	PRK	Yong Kang
5	CUB	Wilber Sanchez Amita
6	GEO	Gela Papashvili
7	JPN	Hiroshi Kado
8	GRE	Varntan Ioann Agakatzanian
13	**USA**	**Mujaahid Maynard**

52 KG (114.5 LBS) GRECO-ROMAN — Final: July 23

RANK	CTRY	ATHLETE
1	ARM	Armen Nazaryan
2	**USA**	**Brandon Paulson**
3	UKR	Andriy Kalashnikov
4	RUS	Samvel Danielyan
5	CUB	Lazaro Rivas Scull
6	BUL	Yordan Anev
7	KOR	Ha Tae-yeon
8	POL	Dariusz Jablonski

57 KG (125.5 LBS) GRECO-ROMAN — Final: July 21

RANK	CTRY	ATHLETE
1	KAZ	Yuriy Melnichenko
2	**USA**	**Dennis Hall**
3	CHN	Sheng Zetian
4	UKR	Ruslan Khakymov
5	GER	Rifat Yildiz
6	CUB	Luis Sarmiento Hernandez
7	GRE	Sarkis Elgkian
8	JPN	Kenkichi Nishimi

62 KG (136.5 LBS) GRECO-ROMAN — Final: July 23

RANK	CTRY	ATHLETE
1	POL	Wlodzimierz Zawadzki
2	CUB	Juan Luis Maren Delis
3	TUR	Mehmet Pirim
4	GEO	Koba Guliashvili
5	BUL	Ivan Ivanov
6	UKR	Hryhoriy Kamyshenko
7	ARM	Mkhitar Manukyan
8	RUS	Sergey Martynov
10	**USA**	**David Zuniga**

68 KG (149.5 LBS) GRECO-ROMAN — Final: July 21

RANK	CTRY	ATHLETE
1	POL	Ryszard Wolny
2	FRA	Ghani Yolouz
3	RUS	Aleksandr Tretyakov
4	BLR	Kamandar Madzhidov
5	BUL	Biser Georgiev
6	UZB	Grigoriy Pulyayev
7	CUB	Liubal Colas Oris
8	EST	Valeri Nikitin
9	**USA**	**Rodney Smith**

74 KG (163 LBS) GRECO-ROMAN — Final: July 23

RANK	CTRY	ATHLETE
1	CUB	Feliberto Ascuy Aguilera
2	FIN	Marko Asell
3	POL	Jozef Tracz
4	GER	Erik Hahn
5	RUS	Mnatsakan Iskandaryan
6	HUN	Tamas Berzicza
7	KOR	Kim Jin-soo
8	JPN	Takamitsu Katayama
9	**USA**	**Gordy Morgan**

82 KG (180.5 LBS) GRECO-ROMAN — Final: July 21

RANK	CTRY	ATHLETE
1	TUR	Hamza Yerlikaya
2	GER	Thomas Zander
3	BLR	Valeriy Tsilent
4	KAZ	Daulet Turlykhanov
5	ISR	Gotcha Tzitzuashvily
6	SWE	Martin Lidberg
7	ARM	Levon Geghamyan
8	KGZ	Raatbek Sanatbayev
12	**USA**	**Dan Henderson**

90 KG (198 LBS) GRECO-ROMAN — Final: July 23

RANK	CTRY	ATHLETE
1	UKR	Vyacheslav Oleynyk
2	POL	Jacek Fafinski
3	GER	Maik Bullmann
4	BLR	Aleksandr Sidorenko
5	TUR	Hakki Basar
6	GRE	Iordanis Konstantinidis
7	**USA**	**Derrick Waldroup**
8	CZE	Marek Svec

100 KG (220 LBS) GRECO-ROMAN — Final: July 21

RANK	CTRY	ATHLETE
1	POL	Andrzej Wronski
2	BLR	Sergey Lishtvan
3	SWE	Mikael Ljungberg
4	RUS	Teymuraz Edisherashvili
5	CUB	Hector Milian Perez
6	MDA	Igor Grabovetski
7	UKR	Heorhiy Soldadze
8	BUL	Todor Manov
12	**USA**	**Jason Gleasman**

130 KG (286 LBS) GRECO-ROMAN — Final: July 23

RANK	CTRY	ATHLETE
1	RUS	Aleksandr Karelin
2	**USA**	**Matt Ghaffari**
3	MDA	Serguei Moureiko
4	UKR	Petro Kotok
5	GRE	Panayiotis Poikilidis
6	GER	Rene Schiekel
7	SWE	Tomas Johansson
8	JPN	Kenichi Suzuki

YACHTING

MEN'S 470 — Final: August 1

RANK	CTRY	ATHLETES	NET PTS.
1	UKR	Yevhen Braslavets / Ihor Matviyenko	40.00
2	GBR	Ian Walker / John Merricks	61.00
3	POR	Vitor Rocha / Nuno Barreto	62.00
4	FIN	Petri Leskinen / Mika Aarnikka	65.00
5	RUS	Dmitriy Beryozkin / Yevgeniy Burmatnov	67.00
6	FRA	Jean-Franáois Berthet / Gwenael Berthet	72.00
7	ARG	Martin Billoch / Martin Rodriguez	74.00
8	**USA**	**Morgan Reeser / Kevin Burnham**	**75.00**

MEN'S MISTRAL — Final: July 29

RANK	CTRY	ATHLETE	NET PTS.
1	GRE	Nikolaos Kaklamanakis	17.00
2	ARG	Carlos Espinola	19.00
3	ISR	Gal Fridman	21.00
4	NZL	Aaron McIntosh	27.00
5	FRA	Jean-Max De Chavi	37.00
6	**USA**	**Mike Gebhardt**	**41.00**
7	POR	Joao Rodrigues	42.00
8	AUS	Brendan Todd	48.00

FINN — Final: July 29

RANK	CTRY	ATHLETE	NET PTS.
1	POL	Mateusz Kusznierewicz	32.00
2	BEL	Sebastien Godefroid	45.00
3	NED	Roy Heiner	50.00
4	AUT	Hans Spitzauer	54.00
5	SWE	Fredrik Loof	57.00
6	AUS	Paul McKenzie	67.00
7	ESP	Jose Maria van der Ploeg	69.00
8	RSA	Ian Ainslie	72.00
23	**USA**	**William Martin III**	**136.00**

LASER — Final: July 31

RANK	CTRY	ATHLETE	NET PTS.
1	BRA	Robert Scheidt	26.00
2	GBR	Ben Ainslie	37.00
3	NOR	Peer Moberg	46.00
4	AUS	Michael Blackburn	48.00
5	GER	Stefan Warkalla	54.00
6	SWE	John Harrysson	55.00
7	POR	Vasco Serpa	74.00
8	FIN	Thomas Johanson	78.00
21	**USA**	**Nick Adamson**	**164.00**

TORNADO — Final: July 30

RANK	CTRY	ATHLETES	NET PTS.
1	ESP	Jose Luis Ballester / Fernando Leon	30.00
2	AUS	Mitch Booth / Andrew Landenberg	42.00
3	BRA	Kiko Pellicano / Lars Grael	43.00
4	AUT	Andreas Hagara / Florian Schneeberg	44.00
5	ITA	Marco Pirinoli / Walter Pirinoli	45.00
6	FRA	Franck Citeau / Frederic Le Peutrec	46.00
7	GER	Roland Gabler / Frank Parlow	48.00
8	**USA**	**John Lovell III / Charlie Ogletree**	**48.00**

STAR — Final: July 29

RANK	CTRY	ATHLETES	NET PTS.
1	BRA	Marcelo Ferreira / Torben Grael	25.00
2	SWE	Bobbie Lohse / Hans Wallen	29.00
3	AUS	Colin Beashel / David Giles	32.00
4	GRE	Dimitrios Boukis / Anastassios Bountouris	45.00
5	NZL	Roderick Davis / Donald Cowie	46.00
6	ITA	Roberto Sinibaldi / Enrico Chieffi	52.00
7	ESP	Javier Hermida / Jose Luis Doreste	57.00
8	**USA**	**Mark Reynolds / Hal Haenel**	**58.00**

SOLING — Final: August 2

RANK	CTRY	ATHLETES
1	GER	Thomas Flach / Bernd Jaekel / Jochen Schuemann
2	RUS	Dmitriy Shabanov / Georgiy Shayduko / Igor Skalin
3	**USA**	**Jeff Madrigali / Kent Massey / Jim Barton**
4	GBR	Andrew Beadsworth / Barry Parkin / Adrian George Stead
5	CAN	Joanne Abbott / William Abbott / Brad Boston
6	DEN	Jan Andersen / Jens Bojsen-Moeller / Stig Westergaard
7	UKR	Serhiy Khayndrava / Volodymyr Korotkov / Serhiy Pichugin
8	ESP	Luis Doreste / Domingo Manrique / David Vera

WOMEN'S 470 — Final: August 1

RANK	CTRY	ATHLETES	NET PTS.
1	ESP	Theresa Zabell / Begona Via Dufresne	25.00
2	JPN	Yumiko Shige / Alicia Kinoshita	36.00
3	UKR	Olena Pakholchik / Ruslana Taran	38.00
4	**USA**	**Kristina Stookey / Louise Van Voorhis**	**47.00**
5	GER	Kathrin Adlkofer / Susanne Bauckholt	49.00
6	DEN	Susanne Ward / Lise Michaela Ward	56.00
7	ITA	Federica Salva / Emanuela Sossi	64.00
8	AUS	Jennifer Lidgett / Addy Bucek	64.00

WOMEN'S MISTRAL — Final: July 29

RANK	CTRY	ATHLETE	NET PTS.
1	HKG	Lai Shan Lee	16.00
2	NZL	Barbara Kendall	24.00
3	ITA	Alessandra Sensini	28.00
4	CHN	Li Ke	29.00
5	NOR	Jorunn Horgen	31.00
6	POL	Dorota Staszewska	38.00
7	GBR	Penny Wilson	44.00
8	FRA	Maud Herbert	46.00
11	**USA**	**Lanee Butler**	**53.00**

WOMEN'S EUROPE — Final: July 31

RANK	CTRY	ATHLETES	NET PTS.
1	DEN	Kristine Roug	24.00
2	NED	Margriet Matthijsse	30.00
3	**USA**	**Courtenay Becker-Dey**	**39.00**
4	GBR	Shirley Robertson	41.00
5	NZL	Sharon Ferris	73.00
6	GER	Sibylle Powarzynski	75.00
7	NOR	Linda Konttorp	81.00
8	ART	Serena Amato	81.00

U.S. Olympic Committee
USA Team Summary

XIIth Pan American Games
Mar del Plata, Buenos Aires, Parana, Argentina
March 11-26, 1995

Juegos Deportivos Panamericanos | Mar del Plata '95 Argentina

Games of the XXVIth Olympiad
Atlanta, Ga.
July 19-August 4, 1996

Atlanta 1996

TM © 1992 ACOG

Xth Paralympic Games
Atlanta, Ga.
August 15-25, 1996

1996 ATLANTA PARALYMPIC GAMES

U.S. Olympic Committee

Officers

Dr. LeRoy T. Walker
President

Dr. Ralph W. Hale
Vice President

Michael B. Lenard
Vice President

George Steinbrenner
Vice President

Charles U. Foster
Secretary

Sandra Baldwin
Treasurer

Executive Director

Richard D. Schultz

Executive Committee

Name, Affiliation

Sandra Baldwin, Phoenix, Ariz.
USOC Treasurer

Gen. Howard Buxton, Richmond, Vt.
Olympic/Pan Am Sports Organization
U.S. Biathlon Association

Chris Campbell, Fayetteville, N.Y.
Athletes' Advisory Council

Anita DeFrantz, Los Angeles, Calif.
International Olympic Committee Member

Cedric Dempsey, Overland Park, Kan.
Education-Based Multisport Organization
NCAA

Chris Dorst, Menlo Park, Calif.
Athletes' Advisory Council

Jim Easton, Van Nuys, Calif.
International Olympic Committee Member

Charles Foster, Duxbury, Mass.
USOC Secretary

Paul George, Wellesley, Mass.
Olympic/Pan Am Sports Organization
USA Hockey

*George Gowen, Esq., New York, N.Y.
USOC Counselor

Dr. Ralph Hale, Herndon, Va.
USOC Vice President

Sarah Josephson, Concord, Calif.
Athletes' Advisory Council

George Killian, Colorado Springs, Colo.
International Olympic Committee Member

Andrew Kostanecki, Darien, Conn.
Olympic/Pan Am Sports Organization
U.S. Sailing

Michael B. Lenard, Los Angeles, Calif.
USOC Vice President

Marty Mankamyer, Colorado Springs, Colo.
Olympic/Pan Am Sports Organization
U.S. Soccer Federation

Terry McCann, Mission Viejo, Calif.
Olympic/Pan Am Sports Organization
USA Wrestling

Edwin Moses, Atlanta, Ga.
Athletes' Advisory Council

*John Ruger, Boulder, Colo.
Athletes' Advisory Council

George Schaefer, London, England
Armed Forces

*Richard D. Schultz , Colorado Springs, Colo.
USOC Executive Director

George M. Steinbrenner,
Tampa, Fla./New York, N.Y.
USOC Vice President

Dr. LeRoy T. Walker, Durham, N.C.
USOC President

*Non-voting member

Howard Buxton   **Chris Campbell**

Cedric Dempsey   **Chris Dorst**

Paul George   **George Gowen**

Sarah Josephson   **Andrew Kostanecki**

Marty Mankamyer   **Terry McCann**

Edwin Moses   **John Ruger**

George Schaefer

U.S. Olympic Committee

Board of Directors

(Voting members: 103* as of 7/96)
Name, Hometown (Affiliation)

Therese Abair-Wilson, N. Palm Beach, Fla.
   Athletes' Advisory Council
Brig. Gen. Patrick Adams, Arlington, Va.
   Armed Forces
Dr. Alpha Alexander, New York, N.Y.
   YWCA of the USA
Sandra Baldwin, Phoenix, Ariz.
   USOC Treasurer
Dwight Bell, Atlanta, Ga.
   U.S. Luge Association
Warren Brown, Colorado Springs, Colo.
   USA Basketball
Edward Burke Jr., Los Gatos, Calif.
   National Exploring Division,
   Boy Scouts of America
Gen. Howard Buxton, Richmond, Vt.
   U.S. Biathlon Association
John (Jack) Byrne, Sun City Center, Fla.
   U.S. Speedskating
Keith Calkins, Mission Viejo, Calif.
   American Amateur Racquetball Association
Chris Campbell, Fayetteville, N.Y.
   Athletes' Advisory Council
Lynn Cannon, Oroville, Calif.
   USA Track & Field
Richard Case, Trenton, N.J.
   USA Baseball
Gary Castro, Oklahoma City, Okla.
   U.S. Amateur Confederation of
   Roller Skating
Dr. James R. Chasteen, Tulsa, Okla.
   National Association of
   Intercollegiate Athletics
Hwa Chong, Detroit, Mich.
   U.S. Taekwondo Union
Jane Forbes Clark, New York, N.Y.
   American Horse Shows Association
Philip Cota, Alexandria, Va.
   Armed Forces
Anita DeFrantz, Los Angeles, Calif.
   International Olympic Committee Member
Brian Derwin, Burnsville, Minn.
   U.S. Weightlifting Federation
Bobby Dodd, Memphis, Tenn.
   Amateur Athletic Union
Chris Dorst, Menlo Park, Calif.
   Athletes' Advisory Council
Jerry Dusenberry, Portland, Ore.
   USA Boxing
Jim Easton, Van Nuys, Calif.
   International Olympic Committee Member
Marian Wright Edelman, Washington, D.C.
   Public Sector
Larry Ellis, Skillman, N.J.
   USA Track & Field
Jonathan Fish, New York, N.Y.
   Athletes' Advisory Council

Charles Foster, Duxbury, Mass.
   USOC Secretary
Richard Foster, Irvine, Calif.
   U.S. Water Polo
Ann French, La Jolla, Calif.
   Athletes' Advisory Council
James E. Fuchs, New York, N.Y.
   Public Sector
Frank Fullerton, El Paso, Texas
   U.S. Judo
Mark Fusco, Arlington, Mass.
   Athletes' Advisory Council
Paul George, Wellesley, Mass.
   USA Hockey
Thomas Gompf, Fort Lauderdale, Fla.
   U.S. Diving, Inc.
Dr. Ralph Hale, Herndon, Va.
   USOC Vice President
Eric Haught, Crownsville, Md.
   U.S. Canoe and Kayak Team
Robert H. Helmick, Des Moines, Iowa
   USOC Past President
Judith Holland, Culver City, Calif.
   National Collegiate Athletic Association
William J. Hybl, Colorado Springs, Colo.
   USOC Immediate Past President
Carol Heiss Jenkins, Akron, Ohio
   U.S. Figure Skating Association
Tom Jernstedt, Overland Park, Kan.
   National Collegiate Athletic Association
Peggy Johnston, Oakland, Calif.
   Athletes' Advisory Council
Nancy Johnstone, Jackson, Wyo.
   Athletes' Advisory Council
Richard Jones, Columbus, Ohio
   YMCA of the USA
Sarah Josephson, Concord, Calif.
   Athletes' Advisory Council
Jim R. Joy, Quantico, Va.
   Armed Forces
Robert Kanaby, Kansas City, Mo.
   National Federation of
   State High School Associations
Richard Katz, Cincinnati, Ohio
   Jewish Community Centers Association
Cynthia Dryden Kelly, Wellesley Hills, Mass.
   U.S. Badminton Association
Gene Keluche, Colorado Springs, Colo.
   Native American Sports Council
Terry Kent, Lake Placid, N.Y.
   Athletes' Advisory Council
George Killian, Colorado Springs, Colo.
   National Junior College Athletic Association
   International Olympic Committee Member
Sandy Knapp, Austin, Texas
   USA Gymnastics
Gerald Koenig, Colorado Springs, Colo.
   USA Bowling
Andrew Kostanecki, Darien, Conn.
   U.S. Sailing
Michael B. Lenard, Los Angeles, Calif.
   USOC Vice President

U.S. Olympic Committee

Serge Lussi, Lake Placid, N.Y.
  U.S. Skiing
Tina Lux, North Palm Beach, Fla.
  National Association of Police
  Athletic Leagues
Marty Mankamyer, Colorado Springs, Colo.
  U.S. Soccer Federation
Connie Mara, Belvidere, Ill.
  USA Trampoline and Tumbling
Robert Marbut, San Antonio, Texas
  U.S. Modern Pentathlon Association
Frank Marshall, Santa Monica, Calif.
  Public Sector
Terry McCann, Mission Viejo, Calif.
  USA Wrestling
Jimmy McClure, Indianapolis, Ind.
  USA Table Tennis
Charles H. Moore Jr., Ithaca, N.Y.
  Public Sector
James S. Morris, White Plains, N.Y.
  U.S. Bobsled and Skeleton Federation
Edwin Moses, Atlanta, Ga.
  Athletes' Advisory Council
Dale Neuburger, Indianapolis, Ind.
  U.S. Swimming
Dr. Carole Oglesby, Glenside, Pa.
  American Alliance for Health,
  Physical Education, Recreation and Dance
Tom Osborne, Billings, Mont.
  National Congress of State Games
Joseph Panepinto, New York, N.Y.
  Catholic Youth Organization

Wilbur Peck, Indianapolis, Ind.
  U.S. Volleyball Association
Dave Peterson Sr., Vero Beach, Fla.
  State Olympic Organizations
Mary Plant, Peachtree City, Ga.
  Athletes' Advisory Council
Don Porter, Oklahoma City, Okla.
  Amateur Softball Association
Ernesto Ramos, Santa Fe, N.M.
  U.S. National Senior Sports Organization
Col. Stevan Richards, San Antonio, Texas
  USA Shooting
Tim Richardson, Atlanta, Ga.
  Boys and Girls Clubs of America
Dr. Thomas Rosandich, Daphne, Ala.
  U.S. Team Handball Federation
Thomas Satrom, Cambridge, Mass.
  USA Curling
George Schaefer, London, England
  Armed Forces
Lewis Siegel, New York, N.Y.
  U.S. Fencing Association
William E. Simon, Morristown, N.J.
  USOC Past President
Barbara Smith, Austin, Texas
  U.S. Tennis Association
Cokey Smith, Gregory, Mich.
  Athletes' Advisory Council
Robert C.W. Smith, Bethlehem, Pa.
  National Archery Association
Bill Stapleton, Austin, Texas
  Athletes' Advisory Council

George M. Steinbrenner,
  Tampa, Fla./New York, N.Y.
  USOC Vice President
Sharon Taylor, Lock Haven, Pa.
  U.S. Field Hockey Association
Perry Toles, Roswell, N.M.
  Athletes' Advisory Council
Ernie Vande Zande, Vancouver, Wash.
  Athletes' Advisory Council
Lisa Voight, Colorado Springs, Colo.
  USA Cycling
Dr. LeRoy T. Walker, Durham, N.C.
  USOC President
Bonny Warner, Byron, Calif.
  Athletes' Advisory Council
Thomas K. Welch, Salt Lake City, Utah
  Public Sector
Peter Westbrook, New York, N.Y.
  Athletes' Advisory Council
Leo White, Newport News, Va.
  Athletes' Advisory Council
Nancy Wightman, Petersburg, N.Y.
  U.S. Synchronized Swimming
(Alexander) Sandy Williams, New York, N.Y.
  Athletes' Advisory Council
Christopher "Tiff" Wood, Lake Oswego, Ore.
  USRowing Association
Duncan Wyeth, Lansing, Mich.
  Disabled Sports USA
Hon. Andrew Young, Atlanta, Ga.
  Public Sector

Medal Milestones

USA athletes in Argentina signalled their readiness for the Olympic Games, medalling in 35 of 37 sports at the Pan Am Games en route to a record total.

Erin Hartwell, Pan Am Cycling Silver Medalist

Peter Westbrook, Opening Ceremonies Flagbearer

It seems only fitting that the largest contingent of American athletes ever sent to the Pan American Games came home with the largest medal haul.

The U.S. delegation—more than 750 athletes in 36 sports—demonstrated both its talent and depth by surpassing all its previous all-time marks for overall medals (424), golds (169), silvers (146) and bronzes (109). The previous bests were 369 total medals (1987), 168 gold (1987), 125 silver (1991) and 97 bronze (1991).

The U.S. continued its mastery at the Pan Am Games, winning the overall country medal count for the 11th time in 12 tries among the countries of North, Central and South America. The Pan Am Games, which attracted nearly 5,000 athletes from 42 countries in March, are held every four years. The 1995 version in the Argentine cities of Mar del Plata, Buenos Aires, Parana and Santa Fe were the largest ever in terms of sports and participating nations.

U.S. record-breaking honors initially went to freestyle wrestler Zeke Jones whose gold medal broke the mark for most overall medals ever won by a country at the Pan Am Games. Then on the final day of competition, light heavy-weight boxer Antonio Tarver captured a gold medal to establish the record for most gold medals.

"I was just one of the 169 gold-medal winners that stood on the medal stand for our great country," Tarver said. "I guess it is easy for me to stand here and talk about my gold medal, but my respect goes out to every athlete that wore a U.S. uniform. This medal is something we can all be proud of."

Metal detectors at airports around the country probably went haywire with all the medals that American athletes brought home. In the team sports, the U.S. women's softball team ran its unprecedented international winning streak to 105 games with its third Pan Am gold medal; the water polo team dominated outscoring its opponents by a 69-22 margin; women's team handball maintained its perfect all-time Pan Am record at 9-0.

There was a silver (medal) lining in basketball, men's and women's volleyball, men's softball and women's field hockey while the men's field hockey team took bronze. With its delirious crowds singing in support, host Argentina won gold medals in six of the 13 team sports on the way to its most

Pan American Games Review

successful Pan Am performance.

Impressive U.S. performances also came in freestyle wrestling, with seven of 10 golds; swimming (22 of 32 golds, including all relays), shooting (19 of 32 golds); roller speed skating (17 of 24 golds); artistic roller skating (5 of 6 golds); fencing (5 of 10 golds); cycling (9 of 14 golds); bowling (5 of 8 golds), racquetball (6 of 6 golds); women's gymnastics (6 of 6 golds) and archery (9 of 12 golds).

As the American flag was passed from fencer Peter Westbrook at Opening Ceremonies to wrestler Bruce Baumgartner at Closing Ceremonies, the Games also witnessed the emergence of 19-year-old archer Vic Wunderle, the return of hurdler Roger Kingdom, the longevity of Bruce Davidson, who medalled again in equestrian after a 20-year hiatus, the domination of roller skater Derek Parra, who won eight gold medals, the sweep of Becky Dyroen-Lancer in synchronized swimming, the consistency of Mike Herbert, the only canoe/kayak athlete to win two medals in each of his three Pan Am appearances, and the command of swimmer Angel Martino, who won four gold medals.

The U.S. also excelled in first-time Pan Am sports as racquetball and water skiing each captured eight medals followed by karate with seven, badminton with six, squash with five and women's taekwondo with four. The Americans also garnered a medal of each color in the men's and women's triathlon competition.

The 1995 Games marked a homecoming of the event for Argentina which had hosted the initial Games in 1951. U.S. athletes will be looking for another home away from home in 1999 when the Pan American Games are next in Winnipeg, Canada, the same city that hosted the 1967 Games.

1995 Pan Am Games Medal Chart

Country	G	S	B	T
USA	169	146	109	424
Cuba	112	66	60	238
Canada	48	60	69	177
Argentina	40	45	74	159
Brazil	18	27	37	82
Mexico	23	20	37	80
Venezuela	9	14	25	48
Colombia	5	15	28	48
Puerto Rico	1	9	12	22
Chile	2	6	10	18
Uruguay	1	4	3	8
Guatemala	1	1	6	8
Dominican Republic	1	1	5	7
Peru	0	3	4	7
Netherlands Antilles	1	1	4	6
Trinidad & Tobago	0	0	6	6
Ecuador	1	1	3	5
Jamaica	0	2	2	4
Nicaragua	0	2	2	4
Virgin Islands	0	3	0	3
Bahamas	0	2	1	3
Paraguay	0	1	2	3
Costa Rica	0	1	1	2
Honduras	0	0	2	2
Surinam	0	0	2	2
Dominica	0	1	0	1
El Salvador	0	1	0	1
Panama	0	1	0	1
Antigua & Barbuda	0	0	1	1
Bermuda	0	0	1	1
St. Vincent	0	0	1	1
Totals	**432**	**433**	**507**	**1372**

Pan American Games

Year	Site	Nations	Sports	Athletes
1951	Buenos Aires, ARG	21	19	2,513
1955	Mexico City, MEX	22	17	2,583
1959	Chicago, Ill., USA	24	18	2,263
1963	Sao Paulo, BRA	22	19	1,165
1967	Winnipeg, CAN	29	19	2,361
1971	Cali, COL	32	17	2,935
1975	Mexico City, MEX	33	19	3,146
1979	San Juan, PUR	34	22	3,700
1983	Caracas, VEN	36	25	3,426
1987	Indianapolis, Ind., USA	38	27	4,453
1991	Havana/Santiago, CUB	39	31	5,200
1995	Mar del Plata/	42	37	5,000
	Buenos Aires/Parana, ARG			
1999	Winnipeg, CAN			

Antonio Tarver, Pan Am Boxing Gold Medalist

1995 Pan American Team Roster

ARCHERY

Men (4)
Athlete, Birthdate, Birthplace, Hometown/Current Residence
Edwin Eliason, 1/5/38, Port Gamble, Wash., Stansbury Park, Utah
Butch Johnson, 8/30/55, Worcester, Mass., Woodstock, Conn.
(Richard) Rick McKinney, 10/12/53, Decatur, Ind., Gilbert, Ariz.
(Victor) Vic Wunderle, 3/4/76, Lincoln, Ill., Bryan, Texas

Women (4)
Athlete, Birthdate, Birthplace, Hometown/Current Residence
Judi Adams, 7/12/59, Phoenix, Ariz., Scottsdale, Ariz.
Janet Dykman, 1/17/54, Monterey Park, Calif., El Monte, Calif.
Denise Parker, 12/12/73, Hilldale, Utah, South Jordan, Utah
Ruth Rowe, 11/3/47, Pittsburgh, Pa., McLean, Va.
Team Leader: (Robert) Bob Sonoda, Honolulu, Hawaii
Coaches: Mike King, Grand Rapids, Mich.; Sheri Rhodes, Atlanta, Ga.

ATHLETICS (Track & Field)

Men (45)
Athlete, Birthdate, Birthplace, Hometown/Current Residence
(Orrin) Tony Barton, 10/17/69, Washington, D.C., Fairfax, Va.
Dion Bentley, 8/26/71, Pittsburgh, Pa., Stone Mountain, Ga.
Bryan Bridgewater, 9/7/70, Los Angeles, Calif., Los Angeles, Calif.
LaMark Carter, 4/18/68, Shreveport, La., Natchitoches, La.
Andrzej Chylinski, 12/5/60, New York, N.Y., Colo. Springs, Colo.
Ron Clark, 11/1/69, Lake Charles, La., Garland, Texas
Mark Coogan, 5/1/66, Manhaset, N.Y., Boulder, Colo.
Terril Davis, 4/21/68, Austin, Texas, Austin, Texas
Lance Deal, 8/21/61, Riverton, Wyo., Eugene, Ore.
(William) Bill Deering, 7/20/71, St. Joseph, Ind., Miami Beach, Fla.
Brian Diemer, 10/10/61, Grand Rapids, Mich., Caledonia, Mich.
(James) Jim Driscoll, 8/15/65, St. Paul, Minn., Eugene, Ore.
Chris Fox, 10/22/58, Washington, D.C., Hagerstown, Md.
(Steven) Steve Fritz, 11/1/67, Salina, Kan., Manhattan, Kan.
Wendell Gaskin, 1/7/73, Kansas City, Kan., Edwardsville, Kan.
(Timothy) Tim Hacker, 12/27/62, Milwaukee, Wis., Madison, Wis.
Ronnie Harris, 5/16/65, San Antonio, Texas, Arlington, Va.
Courtney Hawkins, 7/11/67, W. Palm Beach, Fla., Houston, Texas
Randy Heisler, 8/7/61, Warsaw, Ind., Bloomington, Ind.
Vince Henderson, 10/20/72, Pine Bluff, Ark., Fayetteville, Ark.
Terrance Herrington, 7/31/66, Hartsville, S.C., Portsmouth, Va.
(Cottrell) C.J. Hunter, 12/14/68, Washington, D.C., Arvada, Colo.
Allen James, 4/14/64, Sacramento, Calif., La Grange, Ga.
Kip Janvrin, 7/8/65, Guthrie Center, Iowa, Warrensburg, Minn.
(Christopher) Chris Jones, 10/8/73, Dallas, Texas, Houston, Texas
(Edward) Ed Kaminski, 3/26/68, Kansas City, Kan., La Grange, Ga.
Roger Kingdom, 8/26/62, Vienna, Ga., Monroesville, Pa.
Gerald Lawson, 7/2/66, Syracuse, N.Y., Jacksonville, Fla.
Kevin Lyles, 6/23/73, New Brunswick, N.J., South Orange, N.J.
Patrick Manson, 11/29/67, West Point, N.Y., Baldwin, Kan.
Jonathan Matthews, 7/2/56, New York, N.Y., Palo Alto, Calif.
Tony Miller, 2/12/71, Mount Pleasant, Texas, Waco, Texas
Marco Morgan, 4/14/71, Youngstown, Ohio, Raleigh, N.C.
(Dionicio) Dino Napier, 11/24/69, El Paso, Texas, El Paso, Texas
Steve Plasencia, 10/28/56, Minneapolis, Minn., Eugene, Ore.
Jason Pyrah, 4/6/69, Willard, Mo., Provo, Utah
Robert Reading, 6/9/67, Buffalo, N.Y., Los Angeles, Calif.
Daniel Reese, 10/15/63, Salt Lake City, Utah, Littleton, Colo.
Todd Riech, 10/24/70, Polson, Mont., Fresno, Calif.
Carlos Scott, 7/2/60, Hempstead, Texas, Spring, Texas
Steve Smith, 1/11/71, Indianapolis, Ind., Terre Haute, Ind.
(William) Brad Sumner Jr., 8/4/70, Waverly, N.Y., Bryn Mawr, Pa.
Gregg Tafralis, 4/9/68, San Francisco, Calif., San Bruno, Calif.
Richard Thompson Jr., 6/16/69, Bronx, N.Y., Atlanta, Ga.
Tony Walton, 6/3/69, Paris, Texas, College Station, Texas
Team Leaders: Fred Newhouse, Houston, Texas; Leo Williams II, Los Angeles, Calif.

Head Coach: Fred Samara, Pennington, N.J.
Assistant Coaches: Charles Harris, Sanford, Fla.; John Moon, Somerset, N.J.; Doug Nordquist, La Habra, Calif.

Women (39)
Athlete, Birthdate, Birthplace, Hometown/Current Residence
(Jane) Kim Batten, 3/29/69, McRae, Ga., Tallahassee, Fla.
Paula Berry, 2/18/69, John Day, Ore., Redding, Calif.
Angela Bradburn, 9/4/68, Fort Wayne, Ind., Austin, Texas
Tonja Buford, 12/13/70, Dayton, Ohio, Urbana, Ill.
Dawn Burrell, 11/1/73, Philadelphia, Pa., Houston, Texas
(Gwynneth) Gywn Coogan, 8/21/65, Trenton, N.J., Boulder, Colo.
Tamara Cuffee, 6/16/71, Norfolk, Va., Fairfax, Va.
Karol Damon, 12/20/69, Austin, Texas, Spring City, Tenn.
Misti Demko, 10/18/67, Valparaiso, Ind., Hershey, Pa.
Terri Dendy, 5/8/65, Wilmington, Del., Norfolk, Va.
Sonja Fitts, 10/4/70, Rochester, N.Y., Cambria Heights, N.Y.
Chryste Gaines, 9/14/70, Lawton, Okla., Ennis, Texas
Alexandria Givan, 4/25/70, Stamford, Conn., New Haven, Conn.
Kimberly Graham, 3/26/71, Durham, N.C., Charlottesville, Va.
Flirtisha Harris, 12/21/72, Calvert County, Md., S. Orange, N.J.
Crystal Irving, 5/26/70, Long Beach, Calif., Las Vegas, Nev.
Omegia Keeys, 6/25/75, Michigan City, Ind., Michigan City, Ind.
Kristin Kuehl, 7/30/70, Windom, Minn., Fargo, N.D.
Laura La Mena-Coll, 10/10/66, Niskayuna, N.Y., Eugene, Ore.
Lynda Lipson, 12/13/71, Lynn, Mass., Hillsborough, N.C.
Kendra Mackey, 1/14/69, Rock Hill, S.C., Durham, N.C.
Jennifer Martin, 10/23/61, Buffalo, N.Y., Erie, Pa.
Jamie McNeair, 6/26/69, Buffalo, N.Y., Lafayette, Ind.
(LeShundra) DeDee Nathan, 4/20/68, Birmingham, Ala., Bloomington, Ind.
Ramona Pagel, 11/10/61, Los Angeles, Calif., San Diego, Calif.
Connie Price-Smith, 6/3/62, St. Charles, Mo., Bloomington, Ind.
Kelly Rabush, 10/22/67, Lakewood, N.J., Arlington, Va.
Meredith Rainey, 10/15/68, New York, N.Y., Silver Spring, Md.
Michelle Rohl, 11/12/65, Madison, Wis., La Grange, Calif.
Carla Shannon, 2/13/68, Atlanta, Ga., Syracuse, N.Y.
Ceci St. Geme, 4/13/63, New York, N.Y., Menlo Park, Calif.
Sarah (Renk) Thorsett, 3/18/70, Winona, Minn., Madison, Wis.
Maria Trujillo, 10/19/59, Mexico City, Mexico, Marina, Calif.
Shantel Twiggs, 10/4/72, St. Louis, Mo., St. Louis, Mo.
Teresa Vaill, 11/20/62, Torrington, Conn., Brooksville, Fla.
Richelle Webb, 10/8/71, Cleveland, Ohio, Ann Arbor, Mich.
Amy Wickus, 6/25/72, Baraboo, Wis., Madison, Wis.
(Mary) Allison Williams, 6/1/71, E. Meadow, N.Y., Pittsburgh, Pa.
Trevaia Williams, 9/7/68, Houston, Texas, Las Vegas, Nev.
Team Leaders: Henley Gibble, Alexandria, Va.; Rita Somerlot, Centerville, Ohio
Head Coach: Dave Rodda, Long Beach, Calif.
Assistant Coaches: (Canyetta) Candy Young (Sanders), Dublin, Ohio; (Anthony) Tony Veney, Inglewood, Calif.

BADMINTON

Men (4)
Athlete, Birthdate, Birthplace, Hometown/Current Residence
(Michael) Mike Edstrom, 2/22/73, Denver, Colo., Tempe, Ariz.
(Christopher) Chris Hales, 9/29/76, Pomona, Calif., Wooster, Ohio
Kevin Han, 11/25/72, Shanghai, China, Colorado Springs, Colo.
Tom Reidy, 11/26/68, Brooklyn, N.Y., Colorado Springs, Colo.

Women (4)
Athlete, Birthdate, Birthplace, Hometown/Current Residence
Ann French, 7/25/60, Oak Park, Ill., La Jolla, Calif.
Linda French, 3/4/64, Oak Park, Ill., Colorado Springs, Colo.
Erika Von Heiland, 12/24/65, Angeles City, Phillipines, Colorado Springs, Colo.
(Katherine) Kathy Zimmerman, 10/8/72, Denver, Colo., Colorado Springs, Colo.
Team Leader: Bill Pickthorn, Palo Alto, Calif.
Coach: Goran Sterner, Colorado Springs, Colo.

1995 Pan American Team Roster

BASEBALL

Athlete, Birthdate, Birthplace, Hometown/Current Residence
Derek Adair, 8/25/75, Astoria, N.Y., Albertson, N.Y.
Charles Alben, 6/5/76, Huntington, N.Y., Kings Park, N.Y.
John Aramento, 11/16/75, Worcester, Mass., Worcester, Mass.
Anthony D'Esposito, 8/9/74, Staten Island, N.Y., Staten Is, N.Y.
Jason Dellaero, 12/17/76, Mount Kisco, N.Y., Brewster, N.Y.
William Dinkelacker, 10/4/74, Manhasset, N.Y., Mineola, N.Y.
Brian Fitzsimmons, 6/11/74, Suffern, N.Y., Monsey, N.Y.
Matt Hannon, 11/16/72, Queens, N.Y., Ozone Park, N.Y.
Michael Hughes, 12/5/75, Bethpage, N.Y., East Meadow, N.Y.
Michael Johnson, 10/16/73, Plainview, N.Y., Miller Place, N.Y.
Chris Lemonis, 8/21/73, Brooklyn, N.Y., New City, N.Y.
(Jeffrey) Jeff Love, 11/25/73, New Haven, Conn., Seymour, Conn.
(Michael) Mike Maerten, 12/13/72, Philadelphia, Pa., Delran, N.Y.
Todd Montesano, 6/2/75, Bronxville, N.Y., Scarsdale, N.Y.
Matthew Mushorn, 12/24/74, Manhatten, N.Y., Bethpage, N.Y.
Edvard Olsen, 1/31/75, Brooklyn, N.Y., Staten Island, N.Y.
Derek Pasolini, 1/30/75, Farmingdale, N.Y., Farmingdale, N.Y.
Anthony Sagnelli, 8/14/74, Brooklyn, N.Y., Staten Island, N.Y.
Vincent Schuster, 7/18/75, Trenton, N.J., Bordentown, N.J.
(Thomas) Tom Tuttle, 1/17/73, Syosset, N.Y., Levittown, N.Y.
Gary Villacres, 1/30/75, Guyaquil, Ecuador, Astoria, N.Y.
Edward Wennerholm, 12/29/74, Bayshore, N.Y., Lynbrook, N.Y.
Team Leader: (Richard) Dick Bergquist, Amherst, Mass.
Head Coach: (Joseph) Joe Russo, Trenton, N.J.
Assistant Coaches: (Gregory) Greg Sabat, Bellmore, N.Y.; (Donald) Don Landolphi, Baldwin Harbor, N.Y.
Team Administrator: Cecilia Russo, Flushing, N.Y.

BASKETBALL

Men (12)

Athlete, Birthdate, Birthplace, Hometown/Current Residence
Brian Davis, 6/21/70, Atlantic City, N.J., Durham, N.C.
Sean Gay, 11/30/66, Dallas, Texas, Houston, Texas
(John) Dave Jamerson, 8/13/67, Clarksburg, W.Va., Minerva, Ohio
Larry Lewis, 11/14/69, Los Angeles, Calif., Los Angeles, Calif.
Erik Martin, 5/26/71, Cambridge, Mass., West Covina, Calif.
Scott Paddock, 12/29/68, Yorktown Heights, N.Y., Tinley Park, Ill.
Rumeal Robinson, 11/13/66, Mandeville, Jamaica, Cambridge, Mass.
Carl Thomas, 10/3/69, Dayton, Ohio, Lansing, Mich.
Kelsey Weeks, 9/16/67, Atlanta, Ga., Moline, Ill.,
Chuckie White, 3/6/68, Monrovia, Calif., Monrovia, Calif.
(Michael) Mike Williams, 8/14/63, Chicago, Ill., Chicago, Ill.
A.J. Wynder, 9/11/64, Bronx, N.Y., Newport News, Va.
Team Leader: (James) Jim Tooley, Colorado Springs, Colo.
Head Coach: (Michael) Mike Thibault, Omaha, Neb.
Assistant Coaches: John Pariseau, Seattle, Wash.; (Milton) Sharm Scheuerman, Denver, Colo.

Women (12)#

(#The women's basketball tournament was cancelled by COPAN, the local organizing committee, and PASO, the Pan American Sports Organization, due to insufficient entries. The USA team selected prior to that decision, however, is considered part of the official delegation.)
Athlete, Birthdate, Birthplace, Hometown/Current Residence
Edna Campbell, 11/26/68, Philadelphia, Pa., Pittsburgh, Pa.
Sylvia Crawley, 9/27/72, Stebenville, Ohio, Wintersville, Ohio
Karen Deden, 9/23/69, Sandpoint, Idaho, Missoula, Mont.
Dena Evans, 10/11/70, Pasadena, Texas, Deer Park, Texas
Molly Goodenbour, 2/8/72, Waterloo, Iowa, Waterloo, Iowa
Melody Howard, 4/2/72, Springfield, Mo., Lebanon, Mo.
Carla McGhee, 3/6/68, Peoria, Ill., Decatur, Ga.
Tari Phillips, 3/6/68, Orlando, Fla., Winter Park, Fla.
Dawn Staley, 5/4/70, Philadelphia, Pa., Philadelphia, Pa.
(Kathryn) Katy Steding, 12/11/67, Portland, Ore., Tualatin, Ore.
Sheryl Swoopes, 3/25/71, Brownfield, Texas, Lubbock, Texas

Valeria Whiting, 4/9/72, Orange, N.J., Wilmington, Del.
Team Leader: Lynn Barry, Colorado Springs, Colo.
Head Coach: Paula Edney, Gainesville, Fla.
Assistant Coaches: Tonya Edwards, Flint, Mich.; Cindy Noble-Hauserman, Danville, Ky.

BOWLING

Men (4)

Athlete, Birthdate, Birthplace, Hometown/Current Residence
Chris Barnes, 2/25/70, Topeka, Kan., Wichita, Kan.
John Eiss, 8/16/53, n/a, Minn., Brooklyn Park, Minn.
Patrick Healey Jr., 10/9/68, Niagara Falls, N.Y., Niagara Falls, N.Y.
Mark Van Meter, 1/17/53, n/a, Ill., Albuquerque, N.M.

Women (4)

Athlete, Birthdate, Birthplace, Hometown/Current Residence
Lisa Bishop, 2/9/71, n/a, Mich., Belleville, Mich.
Missy Howard, 10/16/68, Alton, Ill., Coon Rapids, Minn.
(Elizabeth) Liz Johnson, 5/2/74, n/a, N.Y., Niagara Falls, N.Y.
Lesia Stark, 9/23/66, Lancaster, Calif., Lancaster, Calif.
Team Leader: Mark Lewis, Wichita, Kan.
Coaches: Fred Borden, Akron, Ohio; Jerrylin Edwards, Akron, Ohio

BOXING

Athlete, Birthdate, Birthplace, Hometown/Current Residence
Datris Biagas, 1/14/69, Lawtell, La., Fayetteville (Fort Bragg), N.C.
Lamon Brewster, 6/5/73, Indianapolis, Ind., Los Angeles, Calif.
Diego Corrales Jr., 8/25/77, Columbia, S.C., Sacramento, Calif.
Albert Guardado Jr., 7/11/73, Red Lands, Calif., Topeka, Kan.
(Arturo) Eric Morel, 10/1/75, San Juan, Puerto Rico, Madison, Wis.
Carlos Navarro, 9/11/76, Los Angeles, Calif., Los Angeles, Calif.
David Reid, 9/17/73, Philadelphia, Pa., Philadelphia, Pa.
Ronald Simms, 12/16/63, Washington, D.C., Newport News, Va.
Antonio Tarver, 11/21/68, Orlando, Fla., Orlando, Fla.
Fernando Vargas, 12/7/77, Oxnard, Calif., Oxnard, Calif.
Rhoshii Wells, 12/30/76, Austin, Texas, Riverdale, Ga.
Lance Whitaker, 5/29/71, Granada Hills, Calif., Granada Hills, Calif.
Team Leader: Peter Balcunas, Lauderdale Lakes, Fla.
Head Coach: Tom Mustin, Tacoma, Wash.
Assistant Coaches: (Alfred) Al Mitchell, Marquette, Mich.; Israel Acosta, Milwaukee, Wis.

CANOE/KAYAK

Men (10)

Athlete, Birthdate, Birthplace, Hometown/Current Residence
Curt Bader, 1/5/61, Bloomfield, Iowa, Bloomfield, Iowa
Chris Ball, 3/21/72, Arlington, Va., Costa Mesa, Calif.
(Neil) Chris Barlow, 12/12/61, Oxfordshire, GBR, San Diego, Calif.
Michael Harbold, 5/22/68, Oakland, Calif., Washington, D.C.
Joseph Harper, 1/13/66, Ventura, Calif., Ventura, Calif.
(Michael) Mike Herbert, 9/30/60, Belleville, Ill., Rogers, Ark.
Stein Jorgensen, 7/12/62, Arcadia, Calif., San Diego, Calif.
Martin Lowenfish, 8/27/68, New York, N.Y., Costa Mesa, Calif.
Peter Newton, 6/3/70, Kailua, Hawaii, Bellevue, Wash.
(James) Jim Terrell, 4/20/65, Cincinnati, Ohio, Costa Mesa, Calif.

Women (4)

Athlete, Birthdate, Birthplace, Hometown/Current Residence
Alexandra Harbold (Bernhart), 3/4/65, New York, N.Y., Washington, D.C.
DeAnne Hemmens, 7/2/64, San Francisco, Calif., Costa Mesa, Calif.
Kate Henrickson-Borg, 7/14/67, Cooperstown, N.Y., James Island, S.C.
Traci Phillips, 8/1/64, Honolulu, Hawaii, Honolulu, Hawaii
Team Leaders: (Emily) Kay Dambach, Crownsville, Md.; Karen Lunsford, Indianapolis, Ind.
Coach: (Reginald) Reg Hatch, Chula Vista, Calif.

1995 Pan American Team Roster

Assistant Coach: (Jerzy) George Dziadkowiec, Chula Vista, Calif.
Boat Handler: John Puakea, Honolulu, Hawaii

CYCLING

Men (14)
Athlete, Birthdate, Birthplace, Hometown/Current Residence
Kent Bostick, 6/27/53, Lowell, Mass., Corrales, N.M.
Zachary Conrad, 10/11/75, Ft. Collins, Colo., Colo. Springs, Colo.
Mariano Friedick, 1/9/75, Tarzana, Calif., Colorado Springs, Colo.
Erin Hartwell, 6/1/69, Philadelphia, Pa., Colorado Springs, Colo.
(David) "Tinker" Juarez, 3/4/61, Los Angeles, Calif., Norwalk, Calif.
Adam Laurent, 7/6/71, Santa Cruz, Calif., Arroyo Grande, Calif.
(William) Chann McRae, 10/11/71, Albany, Ga., Plano, Texas
Scott Mercer, 2/21/67, Dubugue, Iowa, Boulder, Colo.
(Thomas) Clay Moseley, 12/5/71, Denver City, Texas, Albuquerque, N.M.
Marty Nothstein, 2/10/71, Allentown, Pa., Wescosville, Pa.
Fred Rodriguez, 9/3/73, Bogata, Columbia, Westminster, Colo.
Jeff Solt, 9/13/62, Redwood City, Calif., Hermosa Beach, Calif.
Carl Sundquist, 11/24/61, Indianapolis, Ind., Colo. Springs, Colo.
Christian Vande Velde, 5/22/76, Hindsdale, Ill., Lemont, Ill.

Women (7)
Athlete, Birthdate, Birthplace, Hometown/Current Residence
(Deirdre) "Dede" Demet, 10/8/72, Milwaukee, Wis., Colorado Springs, Colo.
Alison Dunlap, 7/27/69, Denver, Colo., Colorado Springs, Colo.
Janie Eickhoff (Quigley), 6/15/70, Long Beach, Calif., Topton, Pa.
Juliana Furtado, 4/4/67, New York, N.Y., Durango, Colo.
Jeanne Golay, 4/16/62, Miami, Fla., Glenwood Springs, Colo.
Connie Paraskevin-Young, 7/4/61, Detroit, Mich., Corona Del Mar, Calif.
Julie Young, 4/7/66, Sacramento, Calif., Sacramento, Calif.
Team Leader: *(Jon) Chris Carmichael, Colorado Springs, Colo.
Coaches: Andrzej Bek, Colorado Springs, Colo. (sprint); David Farmer, Durango, Colo. (mountain biking); Craig Griffin, Colorado Springs, Colo. (endurance/track); Roy Knickman, Boulder, Colo. (men's road); (Hendrikj)i "Henny" Top, Denver, Colo. (women's road)

DIVING

Men (6)
Athlete, Birthdate, Birthplace, Hometown/Current Residence
Mark Bradshaw, 5/12/62, Happy Camp, Calif., Galloway, Ohio
Christopher Devine, 2/29/72, Allentown, Pa., Breinigsville, Pa.
Kent Ferguson, 3/9/63, Cedar Rapids, Iowa, Miami Beach, Fla.
Bryan Gillooly, 2/29/76, Auburn, N.Y., Kissimmee, Fla.
Patrick Jeffrey, 6/24/65, Morristown, N.J., Fort Lauderdale, Fla.
Dean Panaro, 7/15/71, Knoxville, Tenn., Cincinnati, Ohio

Women (5)
Athlete, Birthdate, Birthplace, Hometown/Current Residence
Kristen Kane, 12/16/71, Oxnard, Calif., Kingston, Wash.
Melisa Moses, 2/28/72, Jacksonville, Fla., Orange Park, Fla.d
Becky Ruehl, 12/23/77, Covington, Ky., Lakeside Park, Ky.
(Angela) Angie Trostel, 2/23/77, Oxford, Ohio, Oxford, Ohio
Carrie Zarse, 6/24/74, Libertyville, Ill., Ann Arbor, Mich.
Team Leader: (Colleen) Cokey Smith, Gregory, Mich.
Coaches: David Ardey, Murphysboro, Ill.; Kongzheng Li, Orlando, Fla.; Allan Spreen, Jacksonville, Fla.

EQUESTRIAN

Dressage (4)
Athlete, Birthdate, Birthplace, Hometown/Current Residence
Elizabeth Ball, 7/12/64, Lexington, Ky., Menlo Park, Calif.
Anne Gribbons, 9/26/46. Stockholm, Sweden, Brentwood, N.Y.
Guenter Seidel, 9/23/60, Oberstdorf, W. Germany, Encinitas, Calif.
Leslie Webb, 10/30/56, Denver, Colo., Bakersfield, Calif.
Team Leader: (Elizabeth) Beth Clarke, Gladstone, N.J.

Chef de Equipe: Jessica Ransehousen, Unionville, Pa.
Grooms: Paul Breneman, n/a; Tamara Brown, n/a; Katherine Ryan, n/a; James Higdon, n/a
Show Jumping (5)
Athlete, Birthdate, Birthplace, Hometown/Current Residence
Nona Garson, 9/30/58, Westfield, N.J., Lebanon, N.J.
(Dorothy) DD Matz, 2/6/63, Coatesville, Pa., Collegeville, Pa.
Michael Matz, 1/23/51, Reading, Pa., Collegeville, Pa.
(Douglas) Doug Russell, 2/24/5, n/a, Wellington, Fla.
(Deborah) Debbie Stephens, 6/17/50, Joliet, Ill., Ambler, Pa.
Team Leader: (Sarah) Sally Ike, Oldwick, N.J.
Chef de Equipe: George Morris, West Palm Beach, Fla.
Grooms: Juan Hernandez Angelar, n/a; Martha Bowen, n/a; Susan Pinney, n/a; Brigid Schirk, n/a
Three-Day Event (5)
Athlete, Birthdate, Birthplace, Hometown/Current Residence
Bruce Davidson, 12/31/49, Newburg, N.Y., Unionville, Pa.
Mara Depuy, 7/30/73, Hanover, N.H., Millwood, Va.
Virginia Jenkins, 3/4/72, Tarboro, N.C., Tarboro, N.C.
Missy Ransehousen, 7/14/69, Hanover, N.H., Unionville, Pa.
Denise Rath, 7/23/56, Jacksonville, Fla., Great Falls, Va.
Team Leader: Jim Wolf, Gladstone, N.J.
Chef de Equipe: Capt. Mark Phillips, Tetbury Glos, England
Grooms: Deborah Furnas, n/a; Jennifer Shuck, n/a; Eric Stauffer, n/a; Hannah Whitehouse, n/a; Alexandra Zaeske, n/a

FENCING

Men (12)
Athlete, Birthdate, Birthplace, Hometown/Current Residence
Tamir Bloom, 12/24/71, New York, N.Y., Millburn, N.J.
(Eric) Nick Bravin, 5/28/71, New York, N.Y., Sunnyvale, Calif.
James Carpenter, 4/14/62, Canton, Conn., Hasbrouck Hgts., N.J.
Michael D'Asaro II, 11/2/64, Brooklyn, N.Y., New York, N.Y.
John Friedberg, 3/9/61, Baltimore, Md., New York, N.Y.
Zaddick Longenbach, 10/27/71, Philadelphia, Pa., New York, N.Y.
Michael Marx, 7/7/58, Portland, Ore., Pittsford, N.Y.
Sean McClain, 9/13/75, Kettering, Ohio, Round Rock, Texas
James O'Neill, 10/1/66, Concord, Mass., Greenwich, Conn.
(Tomasz) Thomas Strazalkowski, 12/30/70, Krakow, Poland, State College, Pa.
Alan Weber, 8/29/69, Bethpage, N.Y., Philadelphia, Pa.
Peter Westbrook, 4/16/52, St. Louis, Mo., New York, N.Y.

Women (8)
Athlete, Birthdate, Birthplace, Hometown/Current Residence
Olga Chernyak, 7/30/72, Kiev, Ukraine, Tenexa, Kan.
Monique De Bruin, 5/12/77, Portland, Ore., Wilsonville, Ore.
Rachel Haugh, 2/17/70, Portland, Ore., Portland, Ore.
Ann Marsh, 6/30/71, Royal Oak, Mich., Royal Oak, Mich.
Leslie Marx, 4/24/67, Ft. Belvoir, Va., Pittsford, N.Y.
Margo Miller, 5/01/49, San Francisco, Calif., Santa Monica, Calif.
Donna Stone, 1/17/57, Wahawkin, N.J., Lincoln Park, N.J
Felicia Zimmermann, 8/16/75, Rochester, N.Y., Rush, N.Y.
Team Leader: Sherry Posthumus, San Jose, Calif.
Coach: Carl Borack, Los Angeles, Calif.
Assistant Coaches: Dr. Aladar Kogler, New York, N.Y.; Anthony Leach, Rochester, N.Y.; Zoran Tulum, East Palo Alto, Calif.
Armorer: Jeffrey Rosen, Colorado Springs, Colo.

FIELD HOCKEY

Men (16)
Athlete, Birthdate, Birthplace, Hometown/Current Residence
Larry Amar, 2/24/72, Ventura, Calif., Camarillo, Calif.
Nicholas Butcher, 5/7/76, Pasadena, Calif., Imperial Beach, Calif.
Steven Danielson, 3/15/72, Honolulu, Hawaii, Chula Vista, Calif.
Jeff Horrocks, 2/3/71, Fullerton, Calif., Chula Vista, Calif.
Steve Jennings, 7/24/69, Washington, D.C., Washington, D.C.
Paul Lewis, 8/25/71, Denver, Colo., Oceanside, Calif.
Olaf Maack, 8/26/67, Centralia, Wis., Colorado Springs, Colo.

1995 Pan American Team Roster

Ben Maruquin, 2/26/70, Ventura, Calif., Ventura, Calif.
Marq Mellor, 3/5/68, Bayshore, N.Y., Mount Vernon, N.Y.
Jonathan (Sumberg) O'Haire, 7/24/59, Brooklyn, N.Y., Long Island City, N.Y.
John O'Neill, 11/23/68, Detroit, Mich., Chula Vista, Calif.
Otto Steffers, 10/19/72, Louisville, Ky., Chula Vista, Calif.
Phil Sykes, 7/24/70, Tacoma, Wash., Chula Vista, Calif.
Nigel Traverso, 11/18/58, n/a, New York City
Taylor Trickle, 8/10/72, Thief River Falls, Minn., Imperial Beach, Calif.
Steven Wagner, 11/5/67, Philadelphia, Pa., Mount Laurel, N.J.
Team Leader: Jay Patel, Colorado Springs, Colo.
Coach: Lenny McCaigue, San Diego, Calif.
Assistant Coaches: David McMichael, Colorado Springs, Colo.; Jeff Woods, Radford, Va.
Women (16)
Athlete, Birthdate, Birthplace, Hometown/Current Residence
Pam Bustin, 4/24/67, Providence, R.I., Haslett, Mich.
(Kristen) Kris Fillat, 11/7/70, San Diego, Calif., San Diego, Calif.
Tracey Fuchs, 11/3/66, Smithtown, N.Y., Mansfield, Conn.
Kelli James, 3/16/70, n/a, Pa., Medford, N.J./Norfolk, Va.
Antoinette Lucas, 10/27/68, Richmond, Va., Willington, Conn.
Leslie Lyness, 8/7/68, Bryn Mawr, Pa., Paoli, Pa.
(Barbara) Barb Marois, 3/1/63, Worcester, Mass., Dover, N.H.
Laurel Martin, 6/8/69, Hershey, Pa., Virginia Beach, Va.
Pamela Neiss, 11/10/69, Lancaster, Pa., Norfolk, Va.
Marcia Pankratz, 10/1/64, Wakefield, Mass., San Diego, Calif.
Jill Reeve, 11/1/69, Bennington, Vt., Hoosick Falls, N.Y.
(Patricia) Patty Shea, 9/15/62, Boston, Mass., Iowa City, Iowa
Eleanor Stone, 11/19/70, Lowell, Mass., Cheshire, Conn.
Liz Tchou, 9/25/66, Camden, N.J., Medford Lakes, N.Y.
Cindy Werley, 2/26/75, Allentown, Pa., Allentown, Pa.
Andrea Wieland, 7/25/69, Philadelphia, Pa., White River Jct., Vt.
Team Leader: Beth Vasta, Colorado Springs, Colo.
Coach: Pam Hixon, Amherst, Mass.
Assistant Coaches: Charlene Morett, University Park, Pa.; (Margaret) "Missy" Meharg, North Bethesda, Md.

GYMNASTICS

Men, Artistic (7)
Athlete, Birthdate, Birthplace, Hometown/Current Residence
Mihai Bagiu, 4/10/71, Timisoara, Romania, Albuquerque, N.M.
Steve McCain, 1/9/74, Houston, Texas, Missouri City, Texas
John Roethlisberger, 6/21/70, Fort Atkinson, Wis., Minneapolis, Minn.
Bill Roth, 8/21/70, Yonkers, N.Y., Philadelphia, Pa.
Kip Simons, 9/11/72, Media, Pa., Columbus, Ohio
(Albert) Chainey Umphrey, 8/2/70, Albuquerque, N.M., Albuquerque, N.M.
Chris Waller, 9/20/68, Evanston, Ill., Albuquerque, N.M.
Team Leader: Ron Galimore, Indianapolis, Ind.
Coaches: Edward Burch, Albuquerque, N.M.; Yefim Furman, Los Angeles, Calif.
Women, Artistic (7)
Athlete, Birthdate, Birthplace, Hometown/Current Residence
Mary Beth Arnold, 7/11/81, Reno, Nev., Sparks, Nev.
Amanda Borden, 5/10/77, Cincinnati, Ohio, Cincinnati, Ohio
Amy Chow, 5/15/78, San Jose, Calif., San Jose, Calif.
Shannon Miller, 3/10/77, Rolla, Mo., Edmond, Okla.
Kristy Powell, 2/13/80, Stuart, Fla., Colorado Springs, Colo.
Katherine Teft, 9/2/81, Grand Rapids, Mich., Grand Rapids, Mich.
(Donielle) Doni Thompson, 2/17/81, Wheatridge, Colo., Colorado Springs, Colo.
Team Leader: Kathy Kelly, Indianapolis, Ind.
Coach: Steve Nunno, Oklahoma City, Okla.
Assistant Coach: Mary Lee Tracy, Fairfield, Ohio
Women, Rhythmic (9)
Athlete, Birthdate, Birthplace, Hometown/Current Residence
Jessica Davis, 4/10/78, Greenbrae, Calif., San Anselmo, Calif.

Mandy James, 12/09/78, Jacksonville, Fla., Orange Park, Fla.
Tamara Levinson, 11/17/76, Buenos Aires, Argentina, Silver Spring, Md.
Aliane Mata (Baquerot), 11/23/78, New York, N.Y., N.Y., N.Y.
Nicole Sengstock, 12/26/77, West Allis, Wis., West Allis, Wis.
Brandi Siegel, 8/04/79, Miami, Fla., Miami, Fla.
Challen Sievers, 4/19/79, Downers Grove, Ill., Downers Grove, Ill.
(Rebecca) Becky Turner, 9/17/77, Marietta, Ga., Kennesaw, Ga.
Team Leader: Nora Campbell, Indianapolis, Ind.
Coaches: Efrossina Anguelona, Indianapolis, Ind.; (Yekaterina) Catherine Yakhimovich, Gaithersburg, Md.

JUDO

Men (8)
Athlete, Birthdate, Birthplace, Hometown/Current Residence
(Jacob) Jake Flores, 7/22/78, Glendale, Calif., Temecula, Calif.
Orlando Fuentes, 11/19/74, Rapid City, S.D., Hialeah, Fla.
Rafael Hueso, 10/30/71, Miami, Fla., Colorado Springs, Colo.
Damon Keeve, 8/27/60, San Francisco, Calif., San Francisco, Calif.
Jason Morris, 2/3/67, Schenectady, N.Y., Scotia, N.Y.
Brian Olson, 3/6/73, Tallahassee, Fla., Colorado Springs, Colo.
James Pedro, 10/30/70, Lawrence, Mass., Danvers, Mass.
Clifton Sunada, 5/18/71, Honolulu, Hawaii, Colo. Springs, Colo.
Women (8)
Corinna Broz, 3/13/74, Garberville, Calif., Colorado Springs, Colo.
Grace Jividen, 6/12/64, Buffalo, N.Y., Lakewood, Colo.
Colleen McDonald, 10/3/74, Hollywood, Fla., Covina, Calif.
Liliko Ogasawara, 5/21/72, Englewood, N.Y., Montvale, N.J.
Sherrie Phillips, 7/15/63, New Guinea, Australia, Colorado Springs, Colo.
JoAnne Quiring, 10/8/63, Littleton, Colo., Westcliffe, Colo.
Colleen Rosensteel, 3/13/67, S. Greensburg, Pa., Gainesville, Fla.
Hillary Wolf, 2/7/77, Chicago, Ill., Chicago, Ill.
Team Leaders: Ralph Reyes, Greenwich, Conn.; Darlene Montgomery, Pleasant Valley, Calif.
Coaches: Michael Swain, (men), San Jose, Calif.; Corinne Shigemoto, Tres Pinos, Calif. (women)

KARATE

Men (6)
Athlete, Birthdate, Birthplace, Hometown/Current Residence
Ferdie Allas, 9/12/68, Manila, Phillipines, San Diego, Calif.
(Wyatt) Hiroshi Allen, 9/16/72, Iwakumi, Japan, Monroe, La.
Dustin Baldas, 5/2/69, Pittsburgh, Pa., Sewickley, Pa.
William Chadrow, 9/23/72, San Diego, Calif., Seattle, Wash.
Tommy Hood Jr., 9/17/75, Columbia, S.C., Columbia, S.C.
Doug Selchan, 5/15/73, McKeesport, Pa., Pittsburgh, Pa.
Women (4)
Athlete, Birthdate, Birthplace, Hometown/Current Residence
Townsend Carr, 2/12/62, Mineral Wells, Texas, Superior, Colo.
Tracey Day, 2/23/67, Mount Vernon, N.Y., Selden, N.Y.
Melanie Genung, 1/14/74, Seattle, Wash., Seattle, Wash.
Christina Muccini, 4/16/73, Manhasset, N.Y., Douglastown, N.Y.
Team Leader: Robert Fujimura, Colorado Springs, Colo.
Coach: Chuck Merriman, Waterford, Conn.

RACQUETBALL

Men (5)
Athlete, Birthdate, Birthplace, Hometown/Current Residence
Michael Bronfeld, 4/12/67, Fremont, Calif., Carmel Valley, Calif.
John Ellis, 10/4/72, Stockton, Calif., Stockton, Calif.
(Walter) "Sudsy" Monchik (nee Klugewicz), 10/12/74, Staten Island, N.Y., Staten Island, N.Y.
Derek Robinson, 5/20/69, Kennewicks, Wash., Muncie, Ind.
Tim Sweeney, 6/3/67, Chicago, Ill., Glendale, Ill.
Women (5)
Athlete, Birthdate, Birthplace, Hometown/Current Residence
Michelle Gould, 12/22/70, Ontario, Ore., Boise, Idaho

1995 Pan American Team Roster

Cheryl Gudinas, 5/11/67, Chicago, Ill., Lisle, Ill.
Robin Levine, 6/21/69, Poughkeepsie, N.Y., Sacramento, Calif.
Joy (Paraiso) MacKenzie, 9/14/66, Fort Bragg, N.C., Santee, Calif.
(Jacqueline) Jackie Paraiso GIbson, 9/14/66, Fort Bragg, N.C., El Cajon, Calif.
Team Leader: Van Dubolsky, Gainesville, Fla.
Coach: (Stewart) Jim Winterton, Syracuse, N.Y.
Assistant Coaches: Francine Davis, San Francisco, Calif.; John Foust, Aurora, Colo.

ROLLER SKATING

Artistic (13)
Men (6)
Athlete, Birthdate, Birthplace, Hometown/Current Residence
Eric Anderson, 12/31/74, La Mesa, Calif., El Cajon, Calif.
Shawn Coover, 4/7/71, Coatesville, Pa., Kinzer, Pa.
Steven Findlay, 5/29/70, Farmington Hills, Mich., Dayton, Ohio
Heath Medeiros, 12/1/72, Fall River, Mass., Westport, Mass.
Tim Patten, 1/8/66, Everett, Wash., Taunton, Mass.
Brian Richardson, 4/18/75, Davney, Calif., Wildomar, Calif.
Women (7)
Athlete, Birthdate, Birthplace, Hometown/Current Residence
April Dayney, 8/12/75, Isup, N.Y., Maumee, Ohio
Jennifer Denton, 10/7/78, Long Branch, N.J., Howell, N.J.
Lisa Friday, 6/14/70, Pasadena, Texas, Double Oak, Texas
Tara Graney, 5/20/70, Norwood, Mass., Medfield, Mass.
Jennifer Rodriguez, 6/8/76, Miami, Fla., Miami, Fla.
Dezera Salas, 5/15/72, Santa Barbara, Calif., Goleta, Calif.
Amy York, 7/5/77, Santa Ana, Calif., Vorba Linda, Calif.
Team Leader: Betty Ann Danna, Sarasota, Fla.
Coach: Delores Dunn, Bakersfield, Calif.

Hockey (10)
Athlete, Birthdate, Birthplace, Hometown/Current Residence
Keith Berard, 4/11/76, Sacramento, Calif., Elk Grove, Calif.
Randy Erickson, 5/20/72, Bremerton, Wash., Bremerton, Wash.
Jeff Gibson, 10/21/67, Michigan City, Ind., Bremerton, Wash.
Nick Grassia, 4/22/76, Philadelphia, Pa., Woodbury, N.J.
Shane Hayden, 2/7/76, Huntsville, Ala., Colorado Springs, Colo.
David Jones, 7/17/61, Lubbock, Texas, Wolfforth, Texas
Michael Knowles, 5/10/69, Stratford, N.J., Gibbsboro, N.J.
(Aaron) Frankie Lee, 10/1/60, Olympia, Wash., Poulsbo, Wash.
Taylor Sisson, 6/7/75, Lubbock, Texas, Waxahchie, Texas
Mike Stevenson, 12/17/72, Olympia, Wash., Bremerton, Wash.
Team Leader: (Oris) Lester Burkett, Gainesville, Fla.
Coach: Dick Sisson, Lubbock, Texas

Speed (10)
Men (5)
Athlete, Birthdate, Birthplace, Hometown/Current Residence
Chad Hedrick, 4/17/77, Houston, Texas, Spring, Texas
(Anthony) Tony Muse, 4/30/68, Ames, Iowa, Des Moines, Iowa
Derek Parra, 3/15/70, San Bernardino, Calif., Dover, Del.
Keith Turner, 8/21/75, Blacksburg, Va., Vinton, Va.
James Weiderhold Jr., 2/29/72, Westchester, Pa., Honey Brook, Pa.
Women (5)
Athlete, Birthdate, Birthplace, Hometown/Current Residence
Theresa Cliff, 6/19/78, Grand Rapids, Mich., Cedar Springs, Mich.
Cheryl Ezzell, 1/12/79, Houston, Texas, Houston, Texas
Vicci King, 3/11/72, Laurel, Miss., Cheyenne, Wyo.
Heather Laufer, 7/13/72, Willingboro, N.J., Kansas City, Mo.
Gypsy Lucas, 11/5/74, Memphis, Tenn., Lewisville, Texas
Team Leader: Sue Dooley, Dover, Del.
Coach: Doug Ingles, Hillsdale, Mich.

ROWING

Men (38)
Athlete, Birthdate, Birthplace, Hometown
Cyrus Beasley, 2/29/72, Rome, N.Y., Atlanta, Ga.
Jonathan Brown, 11/28/68, New York, N.Y., New York, N.Y.

William Carlucci, 6/03/67, Minneapolis, Minn., Philadelphia, Pa.
Pete Cipollone, 2/5/71, Marietta, Ohio, Oakland, Calif.
David Collins, 10/12/69, Bethpage, N.Y., Tacoma, Wash.
Mike Dreher, 1/26/65, Grosse Pointe, Mich., Durham, N.H.
Andrew Finch, 3/07/72, Annapolis, Md., Hanover, Mass.
Ross Flemer, 10/8/65, San Francisco, Calif., Newport Beach, Calif.
Jason Gailes, 3/28/70, Tauntou, Mass., Dighton, Mass.
Stephen Gantz, 5/12/68, San Jose, Costa Rica, Cambridge, Mass.
David Gleeson, 6/19/57, Norwich, Great Britain, Milwaukee, Wis.
Tom Grace, 12/2/70, Columbus, Ohio, Philadelphia, Pa.
Edward Grose, 3/28/67, Portsmouth, Va., Philadelphia, Pa.
Michael (Sean) Hall, 8/20/67, Williamsburg, Va., Shepherdstown, W.Va.
Ed Hewitt, 3/30/62, Ventnor, N.J., Philadelphia, Pa.
Fred Honebein, 1/14/68, San Francisco, Calif., Laguna Nigual, Calif.
Brian Jamieson, 3/7/69, Livingston, N.J., Augusta, Ga.
Bob Kaehler, 4/5/64, Burlingame, Calif., Bala Cynwyd, Pa.
Chris Kerber, 7/23/68, Philadelphia, Pa., Collingswood, N.J.
Barry Klein, 2/4/66, Grand Rapids, Mich., Macomb Township, Mich.
Jeffrey Klepacki, 12/17/68, Kearny, N.J., Kearny, N.J.
Gregg Klingsporn, 12/9/69, Morristown, N.J., Watertown, Mass.
Jamie Koven, 4/18/73, Morristown, N.J., Green Village, N.J.
Kane Larin, 9/12/67, White Plains, N.Y., Cambridge, Mass.
(John) Chip McKibben, 6/23/65, Escondido, Calif., Newport Beach, Calif.
Jonathan Moss, 11/22/68, New York, N.Y., Somerville, Mass.
Tom Murray, 1/20/69, Buffalo, N.Y., Buffalo, N.Y.
Jim Neil, 5/15/68, Buffalo, N.Y., Buffalo, N.Y.
John Paynich, 12/12/68, Madison, Wis., Hull., Mass.
Jeffrey Pfaendtner, 2/28/67, Detroit, Mich., Philadelphia, Pa.
Steve Robinson, 2/17/72, Washington, D.C., Arlington, Va.
Chris Schulten, 4/8/72, Hartford, Conn., Guilford, Conn.
Steven Segaloff, 7/21/70, New Haven, Conn., New Haven, Conn.
Donald Smith, 4/07/68, North Tonawanda, N.Y., North Tonawanda, N.Y.
Chris Swan, 9/24/67, New Haven, Conn., Old Saybrook, Conn.
John Velyvis, 1/25/66, North Adams, Mass., North Adams, Mass.
Greg Walker, 2/18/64, Mount Clemens, Mich., Paradise Hills, Calif.
Tim Young, 4/9/69, Philadelphia, Pa., Augusta, Ga.
Women (16)
Athlete, Birthdate, Birthplace, Hometown, Ht., Wt., Event(s)
Andrea Bonaccorsi, 1/14/68, Philadelphia, Pa., Augusta, Ga.
Molly Brock, 7/05/68, Walnut Creek, Calif., Augusta, Ga.
Lindsay Burns, 1/06/65, Billings, Mont., Cambridge, Mass.
Barbara Byrne, 2/11/67, East Orange, N.J., Princeton, N.J.
Julia Chilicki, 8/1/71, Hartford, Conn., Somers, Conn.
Ruth Davidon, 3/20/64, New York, N.Y., Baltimore, Md.
(Elizabeth) "Izzie" Gordon, 4/1/65, Clinton, N.Y., S. Hadley, Mass.
Michelle Knox-Zaloom, 11/17/64, Portland, Ore., Washington, D.C.
Elizabeth McCagg, 4/29/67, Seattle, Wash., Chattanooga, Tenn.
Mary McCagg, 4/29/67, Seattle, Wash., Chattanooga, Tenn.
Ellen Minzner, 3/3/66, Lawrence, Mass., Brookline, Mass.
Lisa Schlenker, 10/7/64, Spokane, Wash., Lake Oswego, Ore.
Christine Smith, 9/9/69, n/a, Darien, Conn.
Barbara Spitz, 8/10/56, New York, N.Y., Bloomfield, N.J./Philadelphia, Pa.
Catherine Symon, 12/16/71, Kingston, Jamaica, Augusta, Ga.
Andrea Thies, 9/21/67, Irvington, N.Y., Arlington, Va.
Team Leaders: Elise Lindborg, Indianapolis, Ind.; Laura Darby, Concord, Mass.; Bill Zack, Long Beach, Calif.
Head Coach: Mike Spracklen, Chula Vista, Calif.
Assistant Coaches: John Bannan, Philadelphia, Pa.; Hartmut Buschbacher, Chattanooga, Tenn.; Ken Dreyfus, Washington, D.C.; Igor Grinko, Augusta, Ga.; Bruce Konopka, Philadelphia, Pa.; Ted Nash, Medford, N.J.; Tom Tehaar, Chattanooga, Tenn.
Boat Handler: Brooks Dagman, San Diego, Calif.

1995 Pan American Team Roster

SHOOTING

Men (29)

Athlete, Birthdate, Birthplace, Hometown/Current Residence

Ben Amonette, 10/8/54, Richmond, Va., Radford, Va.
Terry Anderson, 6/12/45, Sydney, Australia, Dallas, Texas
Lance Bade, 2/6/71, Vancouver, Wash., Ridgefield, Wash.
Brian Ballard, 11/18/70, Bakersfield, Calif., Coto De Caza, Calif.
Ken Corwin, 3/6/75, Columbus, Ohio, Grove City, Ohio
Glenn Dubis, 2/5/59, Lincoln, Neb., Columbus, Ga.
Bret Erickson, 9/26/60, Blair, Neb., Buena Vista, Calif.
Bob Foth, 7/3/58, Buffalo, N.Y., Colorado Springs, Colo.
Steve Goff, 4/29/58, Leavenworth, Kan., Columbus, Ga.
(James) Todd Graves, 3/27/63, Rustin, La., Columbus, Ga.
Rob Harbison, 6/27/66, Philadelphia, Pa., Phenix City, Ala.
(Roy) "Rusty" Hill, 12/27/70, Orange, Calif., Sun City, Calif.
Koby Holland, 9/24/74, Dillon, Mont., Dillon, Mont.
Dan Iuga, 11/12/45, Tg. Oena, Romania, Colorado Springs, Colo.
David Johnson, 5/29/64, Mount Holly, N.J., Colo. Springs, Colo.
Ken Johnson, 11/24/68, Quincy, Mass., Columbus, Ga.
Michael Johnson, 3/31/67, Denver, Colo., Columbus, Ga.
John McNally, 1/20/56, Naha, Japan, Heath, Texas
Don Nygord, 6/13/36, Pocatello, Idaho, La Crescenta, Calif.
Steve Puls, 1/27/72, Redlands, Calif., Cushing, Okla.
Bill Roy, 12/4/58, Chicago, Ill., Alamogordo, N.M.
Adam Saathoff, 5/25/75, Tuscon, Ariz., Hereford, Ariz.
Lonn Saunders, 9/13/71, Helena, Wash., Colorado Springs, Colo.
Patrick Saunders, 9/3/59, Los Angeles, Calif., Colo. Springs, Colo.
Mike Schmidt Jr., 4/15/58, Decatur, Ill., Eagan, Minn.
Ed Suarez, 10/27/66, San Jose, Calif., Minneapolis, Minn.
Daryl Szarenski, 3/14/68, Saginaw, Mich., Seale, Ala.
Web Wright III, 3/19/67, Annapolis, Md., Columbus, Ga.
Darius Young, 4/2/38, Anaheim, Calif., Winterburn, Canada

Women (14)

Athlete, Birthdate, Birthplace, Hometown/Current Residence

Shari LeGate (Aitken), 9/30/55, Chicago, Ill., Peyton, Colo.
Elizabeth Bourland, 8/13/63, San Jose, Costa Rica, Wichita Falls, Texas
(Elizabeth) "Libby" Callahan, 2/25/52, Columbia, S.C., Upper Marlboro, Md.
Roxane Conrad, 9/7/64, Sandpoint, Idaho, St. Helena, S.C.
Wanda Jewell, 6/19/54, Havre, Mont., Columbus, Ga.
Deena Julin, 12/21/55, Omaha, Neb., Colorado Springs, Colo.
(Katherine) Kate Kelemen, 11/8/72, Detroit, Mich., Livonia, Mich.
Denise Morrison, 11/26/61, Phoenix, Ariz., Stafford, Va.
Connie Petracek, 12/25/47, Chambersburg, Pa., Nashville, Tenn.
Ann-Marie Pfiffner, 5/13/69, Dubuque, Iowa, Colo. Springs, Colo.
Kim Rhode, 7/16/79, Whittier, Calif., El Monte, Calif.
Sandra Utasy, 4/12/71, n/a, Singapore, Columbus, Ga.
(Theresa) Terry Wentzel, 4/16/63, Fort Bragg, N.C., Seale, Ala.
Deena Wigger, 8/27/66, Great Falls, Mont., Colo. Springs, Colo.

Team Leader: Willis Platt, Conklin, N.Y.
Assistant Coaches: Erich Buljung, Colorado Springs, Colo. (pistol); Martin Edmondson, Colorado Springs, Colo. (running target); Robert Mitchell, Englewood, Colo. (rifle); Lloyd Woodhouse, Colorado Springs, Colo. (shotgun)
Gunsmith: Scott Pilkington, Monteagle, Tenn.

SOCCER (Football)

Athlete, Birthdate, Birthplace, Hometown/Current Residence

Imad Baba, 3/15/74, Humble, Texas, Houston, Texas
Gregg Berhalter, 8/1/73, Englewood, N.J., Tenafly, N.J.
Jeffrey Cassar, 2/2/74, Livonia, Mich., Livonia, Mich.
(Donovahnn) Mike DuHaney, 4/5/74, New Haven, Conn., San Diego, Calif.
Brian Johnson, 3/7/74, Carmichael, Calif., Livermore, Calif.
Andrew Lewis, 9/10/74, Plainfield, N.J., New Providence, N.J.
#Brian Maisonneuve, 6/28/73, Mount Clemens, Mich., Warren, Mich. (#Injured and did not compete.)

Matt McKeon, 9/24/74, St. Louis, Mo., Florissant, Mo.
Obi Moneme, 3/2/75, Enugu, Awambra, Nigeria, Crestline, Ohio
Jason Moore, 4/4/78, Atlanta, Ga., Atlanta, Ga.
Clint Peay, 9/6/73, Columbia, Md., Columbia, Md.
Brandon Pollard, 10/9/73, Richmond, Va., Richmond, Va.
(George) Eddie Pope, 12/24/73, Greensboro, N.C., High Point, N.C.
Damian Silvera, 7/27/74, Flushing, N.Y., Huntington, N.Y.
(Robert) Rob Smith, 8/20/73, Wilmington, Del., Wilmington, Del.
(Cuauhtemoc) "Temoc" Suarez, 4/19/75, Greenwood, S.C., Mount Pleasant, S.C.
Zach Thornton, 10/10/73, Baltimore, Md., Edgewood, Md.
(Anthony) A.J. Wood, 8/17/73, Pittsburgh, Pa., Rockville, Md.

Team Leader: John Martin, Chicago, Ill.
Coach: Timo Liekoski, Solon, Ohio
Assistant Coach: (Siegfried) Sigi Schmid, Los Angeles, Calif.
Equipment Manager: John Cope, Titusville, Fla.

SOFTBALL

Men (18)

Athlete, Birthdate, Birthplace, Hometown/Current Residence

Raymond Atkinson, 4/12/64, Logan, Utah, Kent, Wash.
William Boyer, 6/10/60, Renton, Wash., Enumclaw, Wash.
David Boys, 7/22/64, Decatur, Ill., Decatur, Ill.
Daniel Cronkright, 5/15/63, Midland, Mich., Midland, Mich.
Rick Dohogne, 3/29/59, Cape Girandeau, Mo., Kelso, Mo.
Vondel Edgar, 3/27/66, Decatur, Ill., Decatur, Ill.
Steven Kerian, 8/7/61, Waverly, Iowa, Sioux City, Iowa.
(Adolphus) Avon Meacham, 10/8/56, Washington, D.C., Mitcheville, Md.
Peter Meredith, 3/2/60, Ranfuly, New Zealand, Salt Lake City, Utah
Mitch Munthe, 10/21/59, Modesto, Calif., Modesto, Calif.
Scott Plangger, 1/26/66, Benton Harbor, Mich., Bloomington, Ill.
Alan Rebling, 8/19/60, Fairfield, Iowa, Fairfield, Iowa
Shawn Rychcik, 5/12/68, Oleam, N.Y., Salamanca, N.Y.
Steve Schott, 5/17/65, Cape, Mo., Kelso, Mo.
Todd Schultz, 5/1/64, St. Joseph, Mich., Webberville, Mich.
Peter Turner, 10/19/56, French Camp, Calif., Stockton, Calif.
Tim Wahl, 12/22/60, Spokane, Wash., Grayland, Wash.
Michael White, n/a, Wellington, New Zealand, Sioux City, Iowa

Team Leader: Cliff Warrick, Georgetown, Texas
Head Coach: Tom Wagner, Federal Way, Wash.
Assistant Coaches: Russell Boice, Oakville, Mo.; Steven Kaiser, Dickeyville, Wis.

Women (18)

Athlete, Birthdate, Birthplace, Hometown/Current Residence

(Patricia) Pat Benedict, 3/3/71, Hart, Mich., Wyoming, Mich.
Jenny Condon, 5/2/68, Minneapolis, Minn., Las Vegas, Nev.
Sheila Cornell, 2/26/62, Encino, Calif., Diamond Bar, Calif.
Debbie Doom, 2/12/63, Charleston, Ill., Pasadena, Calif.
(Patricia) Pat Dufficy, 7/2/61, Westerly, R.I., Stratford, Conn.
Michele Granger, 1/15/70, Anaheim, Calif., Anchorage, Alaska
Lori Harrigan, 9/5/70, Anaheim, Calif., Las Vegas, Nev.
Barbara Jordan, 8/23/65, Mount Vernon, N.Y., Agoura, Calif.
Jill Justin, 10/23/67, Oaklawn, Ill., Oaklawn, Ill.
Kim Maher, 9/5/71, Siagon, Vietnam, Fresno, Calif.
Martha O'Kelley, 12/4/67, Santa Ana, Calif., Las Vegas, Nev.
Susie Parra, 12/8/72, Phoenix, Ariz., Scottsdale, Ariz.
Dot Richardson, 9/22/61, Orlando, Fla., Los Angeles, Calif.
Ann Rowan, 3/24/69, Phoenix, Ariz., Phoenix, Ariz.
Karen Sanchelli, 11/19/65, Morristown, N.J., W. Columbia, S.C.
Julie Smith, 5/10/68, Glendora, Calif., Glendora, Calif.
Michele Smith, 6/21/67, Califon, N.J., Redding, Calif.
Shelly Stokes, 10/26/67, Sacramento, Calif., Fresno, Calif.

Team Leader: Kathy Arendsen, Warwick, R.I.
Head Coach: Ralph Raymond, Worcester, Mass.
Assistant Coaches: Shirley Topley, Anaheim, Calif.; Ralph Weekly, Chattanooga, Tenn.

1995 Pan American Team Roster

SQUASH

Men (4)
Athlete, Birthdate, Birthplace, Hometown/Current Residence
(Antony) Tony Brettkelly, 11/2/60, Parapara VMV, New Zealand, Corte Madera, Calif.
(Alexander) Marty Clark, 1/9/72, Edina, Minn., McLean, Va.
Moshen Mir, 3/3/75, New York, N.Y., Portland, Ore.
Mark Talbott, 4/30/60, Dayton, Ohio, Wakefield, R.I.

Women (4)
Athlete, Birthdate, Birthplace, Hometown/Current Residence
Demer Holleran, 3/17/67, Philadelphia, Pa., Wynnewood, Pa.
Shabana Khan, 6/24/68, n/a, Seattle, Wash.
Alicia McConnell, 6/15/63, Manhattan, N.Y., Brooklyn, N.Y.
Ellie Pierce, 5/29/66, New Bedford, Mass., New York, N.Y.
Team Leader: Craig Brand, Bala-Cynwyd, Pa.
Coaches: Craig Thorpe-Clark, Bala-Cynwyd, Pa.; Richard Millman, Atlanta, Ga.

SWIMMING

Men (21)
Athlete, Birthdate, Birthplace, Hometown/Current Residence
Brian Alderman, 4/10/69, Santa Barbara, Calif., Fort Lauderdale, Fla.
Ryan Berube, 12/26/73, Tequesta, Fla., Tequesta, Fla.
Brad Bridgewater, 3/29/73, Charleston, W.Va., Los Angeles, Calif.
Carlton Bruner, 2/1/72, Dunnoody, Ga., Ann Arbor, Mich.
Greg Burgess,1/11/72, Baltimore, Md., Jacksonville, Fla.
Ryan Cox, 4/20/73, Mission Viejo, Calif., Mission Viejo, Calif.
Josh Davis, 9/1/72, San Antonio, Texas, Austin, Texas
Gary Hall, 9/26/74, Cincinnati, Ohio, Phoenix, Ariz.
Mark Henderson, 11/14/69, Washington, D.C., Colorado Springs, Colo.
Tom Jager, 10/6/64, East St. Louis, Ill., Tijeras, N.M.
Tom Malchow, 8/18/76, St. Paul, Minn., St. Paul, Minn.
Tyler Mayfield, 4/26/72, San Carlos, Calif., Las Vegas, Nev.
Ian Mull, 2/15/74, Lansing, Mich., Auburn, Ala.
Eric Namesnik, 8/7/70, Butler, Pa., Butler, Pa.
Jon Olsen, 4/25/69, New Britian, Conn., Colorado Springs, Colo.
Bill Pilczuk, 9/14/71, Cape May County, N.J., Auburn, Ala.
Joey Rossetti, 8/27/71, Santa Rosa, Calif., Santa Rosa, Calif.
Jeff Rouse, 2/6/70, Petersburg, Va., Palo Alto, Calif.
(Jonathan) Jon Sakovich, 6/26/70, Hilo, Hawaii, Gainesville, Fla.
Tripp Schwenk, 6/17/71, Sarasota, Fla., Colorado Springs, Colo.
Seth van Neerden, 8/7/68, Wilmington, Del., Fort Lauderdale, Fla.

Women (18)
Athlete, Birthdate, Birthplace, Hometown/Current Residence
Barbara Bedford, 11/9/72, Hanover, N.H., Etna, N.H.
Kelli King Bednar, 5/22/70, Silver Springs, Md., Tuscon, Ariz.
Brooke Bennett, 5/6/80, Tampa, Fla., Plant City, Fla.
Lindsey Farella, 6/6/79, Chicago, Ill., Elk Grove Village, Ill.
Alison Fealey, 4/10/78, Cincinnati, Ohio, Cincinnati, Ohio
Catherine Fox, 12/15/77, Washington, D.C., Santa Clara, Calif.
Michelle Griglione, 6/12/69, Ames, Iowa, Gainesville, Fla.
Kristin Heydanek, 11/21/72, Royal Oak, Mich., Los Angeles, Calif.
Trina Jackson, 2/16/77, Plantation, Fla., Jacksonville, Fla.
Rachel Joseph, 1/28/77, Eugene, Ore., Springfield, Ore.
(Jennifer) Jenny Kurth, 3/21/77, Toledo, Ohio, North Wales, Pa.
Angel Martino, 4/25/67, Tuscaloosa, Ala., Tuscaloosa, Ala.
Anita Nall, 7/21/76, Harrisbury, Pa., Hummelstown, Pa.
Buffy Nelson, 11/27/74, Brunswick, Ga., Brunswick, Ga.
Cristina Teuscher, 3/12/78, Bronx, N.Y., New Rochelle, N.Y.
Amy Van Dyken, 2/15/73, Denver, Colo., Englewood, Colo.
(Daedre) Dady Vincent, 10/6/69, Gainesville, Fla., Gainesville, Fla.
Angie Wester-Krieg, 10/28/64, Los Gatos, Calif., Campbell, Calif.
Team Leader: Rich DeSelm, Charlotte, N.C.
Assistant Team Leaders: Alice Kempthorne, Fort Lauderdale, Fla.; Greg Werner, Dallas, Texas
Head Coaches: Gregg Troy, Jacksonville, Fla. (men); John Collins, Larchmont, N.Y. (women) [Unable to travel with team]
Assistant Coaches: Jay Fitzgerald, Santa Clara, Calif. (men); Larry Liebowitz, Santa Barbara, Calif. (men); Steve Lochte, Bloomfield, N.Y. (women); Bill Rose, Mission Viejo, Calif. (women)

SYNCHRONIZED SWIMMING

Athlete, Birthdate, Birthplace, Hometown/Current Residence
Suzannah Bianco, 5/15/73, San Jose, Calif., Saratoga, Calif.
Tammy Cleland, 10/26/75, Sanford, Fla., Walnut Creek, Calif.
Becky Dyroen-Lancer, 2/19/71, San Jose, Calif., Campbell, Calif.
Emily Porter (LeSueur), 11/7/72, Glendale, Calif., Mesa, Ariz.
Heather Pease, 9/29/75, Monterey, Calif., Lafayette, Calif.
Jill Savery, 5/2/72, Fort Lauderdale, Fla., Concord, Calif.
Nathalie Schneyder, 5/25/68, San Francisco, Calif., Walnut Creek, Calif.
Heather Simmons, 5/25/70, Mount View, Calif., Santa Clara, Calif.
Jill Sudduth, 9/9/71, Baltimore, Md., Morgan Hill, Calif.
Margot Thien, 12/29/71, San Diego, Calif., Berkeley, Calif.
Team Leader: Laura LaCursia, Walnut Creek, Calif.
Coaches: Gail Emery, Lafayette, Calif.; Christine Carver, Saratoga, Calif.

TABLE TENNIS

Men (4)
Athlete, Birthdate, Birthplace, Hometown/Current Residence
Jim Butler, 2/15/71, Iowa City, Iowa, Augusta, Ga.
Chi-Sun Chui, 8/8/73, Winchester, Mass., San Mateo, Calif.
Derek May, 5/31/68, Augusta, Ga., Augusta, Ga.
Sean O'Neill, 7/31/67, Toledo, Ohio, McLean, Va.

Women (4)
Athlete, Birthdate, Birthplace, Hometown/Current Residence
(Thu Ai) "Tawny" Banh, 12/12/74, Bac Lieu, Vietnam, Alhambra, Calif.
Diana Gee, 12/21/68, Burlingame, Calif., North Brunswick, N.J.
Wei Wang, 3/21/61, Beijing, China, Pasadena, Calif.
Lily Yip, 8/22/63, Canton, China, Metuchen, N.J.
Team Leader: Bob Fox, St. Paul, Minn.
Coaches: Zhenshi Li, Colorado Springs, Colo. (men); Zhang Li, Colorado Springs, Colo. (women)

TAEKWONDO

Men (8)
Athlete, Birthdate, Birthplace, Hometown/Current Residence
Paris Amani, 4/30/65, Chicago, Ill., Colorado Springs, Colo.
Clayton Barber, 5/16/68, Dallas, Texas, Colorado Springs, Colo.
(Panagiotas) Peter Bardatsos, 4/27/71, Astoria, N.Y., Woodside, N.Y.
Garth Cooley, 6/27/67, Phoenix, Ariz., Indianapolis, Ind.
(Seoil) Steven Lee, 10/7/71, Seoul, Korea, Colorado Springs, Colo.
Jean Lopez, 8/31/73, New York, N.Y., Colorado Springs, Colo.
Steven Lopez, 9/11/78, New York, N.Y., Sugarland, Texas
Sammy Pejo, 9/18/69, New York, N.Y., Colorado Springs, Colo.

Women (8)
Athlete, Birthdate, Birthplace, Hometown/Current Residence
Yoon Kyung Chaing, 5/1/79, Torrance, Calif., Rancho Palos Verdes, Calif.
Elizabeth Evans, 3/30/62, Seattle, Wash., Marysville, Wash.
Sharon Hough, 2/18/75, Palo Alto, Calif., Wayne, Mich.
Barbara Kunkel, 9/17/69, Tacoma, Wash., Federal Way, Wash.
Dana Martin, 7/3/77, Paramount, Calif., Norwalk, Calif.
Diane Murray, 12/26/56, Palo Alto, Calif., Rocklin, Calif.
Kelly Thorpe, 6/5/77, St. Joseph, Mo., Edmond, Okla.
Robin Umphrey, 4/21/65, Garden Grove, Calif., Irvine, Calif.t
Team Leader: Sang Chul Lee, Colorado Springs, Colo.
Coaches: Sun Ki Chong, Getzville, N.Y.; Byung Won Kang, Laguna Niguel, Calif.; Lynnette Love, Waldorf, Md.

1995 Pan American Team Roster

TEAM HANDBALL

Men (16)
Athlete, Birthdate, Birthplace, Hometown/Current Residence
Derek Brown, 4/8/70, Washington, D.C., Washington, D.C.
Gregory Caccia, 1/17/67, Bayshore, N.Y., Bayshore, N.Y.
Dave DeGraaf, 3/26/71, Lansing, Mich., Macon, Ga.
Denny Fercho, 10/28/69, Ventura, Calif., Camarillo, Calif.
Tom Fitzgerald, 3/31/66, Brooklyn, N.Y., Atlanta, Ga.
Darrick Heath, 10/12/64, New York, N.Y., Hempstead, N.Y.
Danny Hennessy, 9/24/74, Queens, N.Y., Floral Park, N.Y.
Michael Jones, 12/6/68, Oakland, Calif., Union Gap, Wash.
John Keller, 10/5/65, Toledo, Ohio, Atlanta, Ga.
Robert Mayfield, 11/22/63, Statesville, N.C., Smyrna, Ga.
Rick Oleksyk, 3/10/63, Parma, Ohio, Gulf Breeze, Fla.
Steve Penn, 11/19/69, Brevard, N.C., Atlanta, Ga.
Matt Ryan, 2/19/66, Port Jefferson, N.Y., Mille Place, N.Y.
Mark Schmocker, 5/17/66, Unterseen, Switzerland, Riggenberg, Switzerland
(George) "Chip" Van Os, 2/13/70, Houston, Texas, Houston, Texas
Kevin Withrow, 9/19/63, Santa Monica, Calif., Thousand Oaks, Calif.
Team Leader: Tom Rosandich, Daphne, Ala.
Head Coach: Javier Garcia Cuesta, Marietta, Ga
Assistant Coach: Laszlo Jurak, Hempstead, N.Y.; Donal O'Shea, Greene, N.Y.

Women (16)
Athlete, Birthdate, Birthplace, Hometown/Current Residence
Dawn Allinger, 9/3/68, Salt Lake City, Utah, Bozeman, Mon.
Sharon Cain, 1/31/64, San Antonio, Texas, Smyna, Ga.
Kim Clarke, 1/31/65, Tulsa, Okla., Atlanta, Ga.
Laura Coenen, 10/16/62, Neenah, Wis., Peyton, Colo.
Kristin Danihy, 1/27/69, Lawton, Okla., Atlanta, Ga.
Lisa Eagen, 3/1/71, Harlan, Iowa, Atlanta, Ga.
Laurie Fellner, 1/15/68, Appleton, Wis., Atlanta, Ga.
Jennifer Horton, 8/10/68, Dover, N.J., Stone Mountain, Ga.
Tami Jameson, 4/13/68, Minneapolis, Minn., Marietta, Ga.
Toni Jameson, 4/13/68, Minneapolis, Minn., Marietta, Ga.
Dannette Leininger, 6/6/63, Kaillia, Hawaii, Atlanta, Ga.
Dawn Marple, 11/1/70, Salem, Ohio, Atlanta, Ga.
Patricia Neder, 12/14/66, Waukesha, Wis., Waukesha, Wis.
Carol Peterka, 12/23/63, Little Falls, Minn., Atlanta, Ga.
Tonia Stubbs, 8/31/63, Warren, Ohio, Fort McPherson, Ga.
Chryssandra Watts, 11/27/66, Bristol, Conn., Stone Mountain, Ga.
Team Leader: Mary Phyl Dwight, Raytown, Mo.
Head Coach: Claes Hellgren, Marietta, Ga.
Assistant Coaches: Leora "Sam" Jones, Marietta, Ga.; Jan O'Shea, Marietta, Ga.

TENNIS

Men (3)
Athlete, Birthdate, Birthplace, Hometown/Current Residence
(Jimmy) J.J. Jackson, 5/10/75, Durham, N.C., Chapel Hill, N.C.
Don Johnson, 9/9/68, Allentown, Pa., Chapel Hill, N.C.
(Robert) Jack Waite, 5/1/69, Madison, Wis., Waukesha, Wis.

Women (4)
Athlete, Birthdate, Birthplace, Hometown/Current Residence
Erika Delone, 10/14/72, Boston, Mass., Lincoln, Mass.
Ann Grossman, 10/13/70, Columbus, Ohio, Grove City, Ohio
Chanda Rubin, 2/18/76, Lafayette, La., Lafayette, La.
Shaun Stafford,12/13/68, Ocala, Fla., Gainesville, Fla.
Team Leader: Sally Etterbeek, Key Biscayne, Fla.
Coaches: Stan Smith, Hilton Head, S.C.; Sue Burke, Miami Beach, Fla.

TRIATHLON

Men (3)
Athlete, Birthdate, Birthplace, Hometown/Current Residence
Andrew Carlson, 12/8/66, San Diego, Calif., Boulder, Colo.
Timothy DeBoom, 11/4/70, Cedar Rapids, Iowa, Denver, Colo.
Nate Llerandi, 12/1/68, Schaumburg, Ill., Boulder, Colo.

Women (3)
Athlete, Birthdate, Birthplace, Hometown/Current Residence
Gail Laurence Garci, 12/18/63, Montreal, Canada, Denver, Colo.
Kelley Kwiatkowski, 9/21/62, Fremont, Ohio, Hollywood, Fla.
Karen Smyers, 9/1/61, Corry, Pa., Lincoln, Mass.
Team Leaders: Michael Scannell, Tempe, Ariz.; Steven Locke, Colorado Springs, Colo.

VOLLEYBALL

Men (12)
Athlete, Birthdate, Birthplace, Hometown/Current Residence
Lloy Ball, 2/17/72, Fort Wayne, Ind., Woodburn, Ind.
Duncan Blackman, 5/21/70, Pasadena, Calif., San Diego, Calif.
Bob Ctvrtlik, 7/8/63, Long Beach, Calif., Long Beach, Calif.
Daniel Greenbaum, 3/12/69, Torrance, Calif., Rancho Palos Verdes, Calif.
Brent Hilliard, 4/13/70, San Gabriel, Calif., San Diego, Calif.
Bryan Ivie, 5/5/69, Manhattan Beach, Calif., Manhattan Beach, Calif.
Daniel Landry, 1/15/70, San Diego, Calif., Lakeside, Calif.
Dexter Rogers, 4/30/69, St. Petersburg, Fla., Encinitas, Calif.
Patrick Sinclair, 5/3/72, Tacoma, Wash., Walnut Creek, Calif.
Thomas Sorensen, 4/6/71, Racine, Wis., San Diego, Calif.
Chris Underwood, 11/27/70, Los Angeles, Calif., Los Angeles, Calif.
Ethan Watts, 5/4/72, Philadelphia, Pa., San Diego, Calif.
Team Leader: Eric Daly, San Diego, Calif.
Head Coach: Fred Sturm, San Diego, Calif.
Assistant Coaches: Rudy Suwara, San Diego, Calif.; Rod Wilde, Santee, Calif.

Women (12)
Athlete, Birthdate, Birthplace, Hometown/Current Residence
Tara Cross-Battle, 9/16/68, Houston, Texas, San Diego, Calif.
Lori Endicott, 8/1/67, Kansas City, Mo., San Diego, Calif.
Kristin Klein, 3/20/70, Santa Monica, Calif., San Diego, Calif.
Tammy Liley, 3/6/65, Long Beach, Calif., San Diego, Calif.
Alicia Mills (Polzin), 9/6/71, Houston, Texas, San Diego, Calif.
Beverly Oden, 3/9/71, Millington, Tenn., San Diego, Calif.
Elaina Oden, 3/21/67, Orange, Calif., San Diego, Calif.
Danielle Scott, 10/1/72, Baton Rouge, La., La Mesa, Calif.
Samantha Shaver, 7/20/69, Stanford, Calif., San Diego, Calif.
Tonya "Teee" Williams, 3/28/68, Los Angeles, Calif., San Diego, Calif.
Elaine Youngs, 2/14/70, Orange, Calif., San Diego, Calif.
Yoko Zetterlund, 3/24/69, San Francisco, Calif., San Diego, Calif.
Team Leader: Kent Miller, San Diego, Calif.
Head Coach: (Taras) Terry Liskevych, Leucadia, Calif.
Assistant Coaches: Aldis Berzins, San Diego, Calif.; Dave Fleming, San Diego, Calif.

WATER POLO

Athlete, Birthdate, Birthplace, Hometown/Current Residence
Gavin Arroyo, 5/10/72, Orange, Calif., Orange, Calif.
Chris Duplanty, 10/21/65, Palo Alto, Calif., Honolulu, Hawaii
Kirk Everist, 4/12/67, Houston, Texas, Newport Beach, Calif.
Dan Hackett, 9/11/70, Syracuse, N.Y., Manhattan Beach, Calif.
Chris Humbert, 12/27/69, Modesto, Calif., Lodi, Calif.
Colin Keely, 2/12/69, Buffalo, N.Y., Seal Beach, Calif.
Doug Kimbell, 6/22/60, Long Beach, Calif., Long Beach, Calif.
Kyle Kopp, 11/10/66, San Bernardino, Calif., Long Beach, Calif.
(Craig) Chi Kredell, 2/16/71, Long Beach, Calif., Seal Beach, Calif.
Jeremy Laster, 2/24/74, Fullerton, Calif., Capistrano Beach, Calif.
(John) Rick McNair, 9/4/68, Berkeley, Calif., Lafayette, Calif.
Chris Oeding, 9/10/71, Santa Ana, Calif., Newport Beach, Calif.
Alex Rousseau, 11/4/67, Paris, Fra., Seal Beach, Calif.
Team Leader: Terry Wong, Augoura Hills, Calif.

1995 Pan American Team Roster

Head Coach: Richard Corso, North Hollywood, Calif.
Assistant Coaches: Richard Azevedo, Long Beach, Calif.; Ed Reed, Tuscaloosa, Ala.

WATER SKIING

Men (3)
Athlete, Birthdate, Birthplace, Hometown/Current Residence
(Michael) Tory Baggiano, 1/10/67, Denver, Colo., Montgomery, Ala.
Sammy Duvall, 8/9/62, Greenville, S.C., Windermere, Fla.
Carl Roberge, 2/8/64, Montreal, Canada, Winter Springs, Fla.
Women (3)
Athlete, Birthdate, Birthplace, Hometown/Current Residence
Tawn Larsen, 11/1/69, Madison, Wis., Tampa, Fla.
Deena Mapple, 3/2/60, Sacramento, Calif., Orlando, Fla.
Sherri Slone, 5/6/66, Russell, Kan., Baton Rouge, La.
Team Leader: Tony Baggiano, Alexandria, Va.
Head Coach: Jack Travers, Okahumpka, Fla.

WEIGHTLIFTING

Athlete, Birthdate, Birthplace, Hometown/Current Residence
Wes Barnett, 4/1/71, St. Joseph, Mo., Colorado Springs, Colo.
Dean Goad, 3/29/68, Seattle, Wash., Sumner, Wash.
Tom Gough, 2/20/72, San Francisco, Calif., Colo. Springs, Colo.
Mark Henry, 6/12/71, Silsbee, Texas, Austin, Texas
Bryan Jacob, 2/1/69, Daytona Beach, Fla., Alpharetta, Ga.
Peter Kelley, 5/9/74, St. Joseph, Mo., Colorado Springs, Colo.
Mario Martinez, 7/6/57, Salinas, Calif., Salinas, Calif.
Tim McRae, 8/4/70, Daytona Beach, Fla., Colorado Springs, Colo.
David Santillo, 7/15/70, Norristown, Pa., Colorado Springs, Colo.
Rich Schutz, 12/21/65, Chicago, Ill., River Forest, Ill.
Team Leader: Leo Totten, Littlestown, Pa.
Head Coach: Dragomir Cioroslan, Colorado Springs, Colo.
Assistant Coach: Dennis Snethen, St. Joseph, Mo.

WRESTLING

Freestyle (10)
Athlete, Birthdate, Birthplace, Hometown/Current Residence
Bruce Baumgartner, 11/2/60, Haledon, N.J., Cambridge Spgs., Pa.
Terry Brands, 4/9/68, Omaha, Neb., Iowa City, Iowa
Tom Brands, 4/9/68, Omaha, Neb., Iowa City, Iowa
Melvin Douglas, 8/21/63, Topeka, Kan., Mesa, Ariz.
Kevin Jackson, 11/25/64, Highland Falls, N.Y., Ames, Iowa
(Larry) Zeke Jones Jr., 12/2/66, Ypsilanti, Mich., Chandler, Ariz.
Mark Kerr, 12/21/68, Toledo, Ohio, Syracuse, N.Y.
Townsend Saunders, 4/20/67, White Sands, N.M., Phoenix, Ariz.
David Schultz, 6/6/59, Palo Alto, Calif., Newton Square, Pa.
Tim Vanni, 2/2/61, Van Nuys, Calif., Porterville, Calif.
Team Leader: John Graham, Poquoson, Va.
Head Coach: Joe Seay, Oklahoma City, Okla.
Assistant Coach: Gene Davis, Colorado Springs, Colo.
Greco-Roman (10)
Athlete, Birthdate, Birthplace, Hometown/Current Residence
Michial Foy, 2/24/62, Chicago, Ill., Brooklyn Park, Minn.
Matt Ghaffari, 11/11/61, Tehran, Iran, Colorado Springs, Colo.
Dennis Hall, 2/5/71, Milwaukee, Wis., Stevens Point, Wis.
Dan Henderson, 8/24/70, Downey, Calif., Huntington Beach, Calif.
Jerry Jackson, 9/8/64, Fitzgerald, Ga., Columbus, Ga.
Mujaahid Maynard, 4/9/71, Brooklyn, N.Y., Colo. Springs, Colo.
Gordy Morgan, 8/12/66, Minneapolis, Minn., Bloomington, Minn.
Andy Seras, 12/4/62, New York, N.Y., Schenectady, N.Y.
Shawn Sheldon, 11/18/64, Norwich, Conn., Colo. Springs, Colo.
David Zuniga, 3/1/68, Worland, Wyo., New Brighton, Minn.
Team Leader: Van Stokes, Clarksville, Tenn.
Head Coach: Rob Hermann, Pensacola, Fla.
Assistant Coach: Pavel Katsen, Brooklyn, N.Y.

YACHTING (Sailing)

Athlete, Birthdate, Birthplace, Hometown/Current Residence
John Bartlett, 1/7/57, Austin, Texas, Austin, Texas
(Carrie) Lanee Butler, 6/3/70, Manhasset, N.Y., Dana Point, Calif.
Jennifer Coolidge, 5/23/70, Salem, Mass., Marblehead, Mass.
Brenda Crane, 5/14/59, Buffalo, N.Y., Newark, Conn.
Jim Crane, 10/12/46, Miami, Fla., Darien, Conn.
(William) Bill Crane, 2/4/58, Stamford, Conn., Norwalk, Conn.
Paul Foerster, 11/19/63, Rangely, Colo., Dallas, Texas
Mike Gebhardt, 11/25/65, Columbus, Ohio, Fort Pierce, Fla.
Doug Hart, 10/30/53, Bloomington, Ind., Chula Vista, Calif.
Debbie Hopkins, 12/17/67, Dayton, Ohio, Fort Wayne, Ind.
Rob Johnston, 11/20/65, Palo Alto, Calif., Dallas, Texas
Troy Lawson, 9/7/61, San Antonio, Texas, Austin, Texas
Tom Lihan, 5/29/60, Fort Lauderdale, Fla., Fort Lauderdale, Fla.
Robert Little, 2/14/67, Boston, Mass., Santa Monica, Calif.
Kimberly Logan, 4/14/70, Coral Gables, Fla., Miami, Fla.
Steve Stewart, 1/28/57, San Diego, Calif., San Diego, Calif.
Michael Sturman, 12/17/66, Glendale, Calif., Newport Beach, Calif.
Jody Swanson, 2/24/65, Buffalo, N.Y., Buffalo, N.Y.
Team Leader: Norm Freeman, Stuart, Fla.
Coach: Roland "Skip" Whyte, Lynn, Mass.
Assistant Coach: Eric Krebs, San Diego, Calif.
Boatwright: Carl Eichenlaub Jr., San Diego, Calif.

MISSION STAFF

Chef de Mission: Sandra Baldwin
Asst. Chef de Mission (Buenos Aires): Gary Castro
Asst. Chef de Mission (Mar del Plata): Charlie Greene
Games Preparation and Services Committee Chair: Joe Kearney
Deputy Secretary General and Interim Executive Director: John Krimsky
Government Liaison/Security Director: Larry Buendorf
Attache/ International Games Preparation Director: Greg Harney
Delegation Director: Doug Ingram
Assistant Delegation Director (Mar del Plata): Nancy Gonsalves
Assistant Delegation Director (Buenos Aires): Steve Saye
Delegation Spokesperson: Mike Moran
Local Liaison: Jenny Storms

USA MEDICAL STAFF

Medical Coordinators: Ed Ryan, Kevin Moody
Physicians: L. George Hershey, John Reasoner, Sean Hanley, Barry Jordan, Margaret Karg, Bruce Moseley Jr., Herbert Parris, Len Scarpinato, Arnold Scheller Jr., Brock Schnebel, Robert Terrell
Athletic Trainers: Martin Anderegg, Donald Bagnall, William Bandy, Kim Barrett, Richard Burr, Byron Craighead, William Ford, Joseph Fritz, Kerry Gatch, Kim Gottshall, Ray Gray, Emery Hill, Jim Hillis, Lisa Jesberg, Tim Kelly, William Kulju, Larry "Chip" Ladd, Gina Konin, Donna McPartland, James Miller, Frank Novakoski, Catherine Ortega, Margaret Peter, Dan Pickett, Marcia Roschke, Steve Simpson, Chris Smalley, Kent Timm, Cynthia Wall, Cathi Yayac

USA MEDIA SERVICES STAFF

Mike Moran, Bob Condron, Frank Zang, Gayle Bodin, J. Michael Wilson, Jim Fox, Craig Bohnert, Craig Cotton, Jeff Dimond, Steve Dittmore, Matt Farrell, Terry Friel, Jim Froslid, John Halpin, Liz Hoskinson, Carolyn Koch, Christie Krebs, Cheryl Kvasnicka, Laura LaMarca, Colleen Walker Mar, Craig Miller, Linda Mojer, Nancy Moore, Leona Perry, Bill Plummer, Ramonna Robinson, Andy Seeley, Eileen Sexton, Dave Shatkowski, Craig Smith, Kurt Stenerson, Doug Walker, Rich Wanninger, Hazel White-Jones, Marc Whitney, Mike Wolf

1995 Pan American Games Results

ARCHERY

Men's 30 Meters
1, Vic Wunderle, (USA/Mason City, Ill.), 354 (Pan Am Games record; old record, Darrell Pace, 353); 2, Ed Eliason, (USA/Stansbury Park, Utah), 350; *3, Butch Johnson, (USA/Woodstock, Conn.), 346; (*Bronze medal was awarded to fourth place due to PASO rule of a maximum of two medals per country per event.); 4, Rob Rusnod (CAN), 345; 15, Rick McKinney, (USA/Gilbert, Ariz.), 339.

Women's 30 Meters
1, Denise Parker, (USA/South Jordan, Utah), 346; 2, Janet Dykman, (USA/El Monte, Calif.), 337; 3, Maria Reyes, (PUR), 333. 7, Ruth Rowe, (USA/McLean, Va.), 328. 9, Judi Adams, (USA/Scottsdale, Ariz.), 327.

Men's 50 Meters
1, Vic Wunderle, (USA/Mason City, Ill.), 332 points; 2, Ed Eliason, (USA/Stansbury Park, Utah), 330; *3, Butch Johnson, (USA/Woodstock, Conn.), 327 (*Bronze medal was awarded to fourth place due to PASO rule of a maximum of two medals per country per event.); 4, Rob Rusnod, (CAN), 323; 7, Rick McKinney, (USA/Gilbert, Ariz.), 318.

Women's 50 Meters
1, Denise Parker, (USA/South Jordan, Utah), 313; 2, Janet Dykman, (USA/El Monte, Calif.), 312; 3, Marisol Breton, (MEX), 310. 7, Judi Adams, (USA/Scottsdale, Ariz.), 297; 8, Ruth Rowe, (USA/McLean, Va.), 296.

Women's 60 Meters
1, Denise Parker, (USA/South Jordan, Utah), 330. 2,. Ruth Rowe, (USA/McLean, Va.), 318. 3,. Marisol Breton, (MEX), 315. 6, Janet Dykman, (USA/El Monte, Calif.), 305. 8.. Judi Adams, (USA/Scottsdale, Ariz.), 304.

Men's 70 Meters
1, Robert Rusnov, (CAN), 316; 2, Butch Johnson, (USA/Woodstock, Conn.), 315; 3, Ed Eliason, (USA/Stansbury Park, Utah), 313; 5, Rick McKinney, (USA/Gilbert, Ariz.), 313; 7, Vic Wunderle, (USA/Mason City, Ill.), 309.

Women's 70 Meters
1, Jacquelin Fernandez, (CUB), 314; 2, Denise Parker, (USA/South Jordan, Utah), 314. 3, Marisol Breton, (MEX), 306; 4, Janet Dykman, (USA/El Monte, Calif.), 304. 5, Ruth Rowe, (USA/McLean, Va.), 303. 14, Judi Adams, (USA/Scottsdale, Ariz.), 277.

Men's 90 Meters
1, Robert Rusnov, (CAN), 290 points. 2, Jeannot Robitaile, (CAN), 282. 3, Pablo Basgall, (ARG), 280. 5, Ed Eliason, (USA/Stansbury Park, Utah), 279. 7, Butch Johnson, (USA/Woodstock, Conn.), 275. 9, Rick McKinney, (USA/Gilbert, Ariz.), 272. 13, Vic Wunderle, (USA/Mason City, Ill.), 264.

Men's Team
1, USA, 243 (Ed Eliason/Stansbury Park, Utah; Rick McKinney/Gilbert, Ariz.; Vic Wunderle/Mason City, Ill.); 2, ARG, 230; 3, CAN, 237

Women's Team
1, USA, 232 (Janet Dykman/El Monte, Calif.; Denise Parker/S. Jordan, Utah; Ruth Rowe/McLean, Va.); 2, CUB; 215. 3, CAN, 224.

Men's Individual
1, Ed Eliason, (USA/Stansbury Park, Utah), 109; 2, Vic Wunderle, (USA/Mason City, Ill.), 104. 3, Rob Rusnov, (CAN), 110*; 4, Rick McKinney (USA/Gilbert, Ariz.), 103. *Pan American Games men's record for 12 arrows.

Women's Individual
1, Janet Dykman, (USA/ El Monte, Calif.), 104; 2, Ruth Rowe, (USA/McLean, Va.), 103 3#, Marisol Breton, (MEX), 100-110; 3, Denise Parker, (USA/South Jordan, Utah), 110*-100. *Pan American Games women's record for 12 arrows. # No bronze medal awarded to Parker due to PASO rule of a maximum of two medals per country per event. Bronze medal went to Breton.

ATHLETICS (TRACK & FIELD)

Men's 100 Meters (Wind: +3.40)
1, Glenroy Gilbert, (CAN), 10.21w. 2, Yoel Isasi Gonzalez, (CUB), 10.23w. 3, A. DeSilva (BRA), 10.23. 4, Andre Henderson, (USA/Fayetteville, Ark.), 10.25w. Dino Napier, El Paso, Texas, elim. semifinals.

Women's 100 Meters (Wind: 0.00)
1, Chryste Gaines, (USA/Ennis, Texas), 11.05 (ties Pan American Games record, 11.05, Evelyn Ashford, (USA), 1979). 2, Liliana Allen Doll, (CUB), 11.16. 3, Heather Samuel, (ANT), 11.33.

Men's 200 Meters (Wind: +1.10)
1, Ivan Garcia Sanchez, (CUB), 20.29 seconds. 2, Andrew Tynes, (BAH), 20.33. 3, Sebastian Keitel Bianchi, (CHI), 20.55. 6, Ron Clark, (USA/Garland, Texas), 20.84. 8, Bryan Bridgewater, (USA/Stone Mountain, Ga.), 21.22.

Women's 200 Meters (Wind: +0.70)
1, Liliana Doll, (CUB), 22.73 seconds. 2, Dahlia Duhaney, (JAM), 23.03. 3, Omegia Keeys, (USA/Michigan City, Ind.), 23.24. DNS - Richelle Webb, Ann Arbor, Mich.

Men's 400 Meters
1, Norberto Tellez Santana, (CUB), 45.30 seconds. 2, Omar Mena Abreu, (CUB), 45.64. 3, Eswort Coombs, (VIN), 45.68. 5, Chris Jones, (USA/Houston, Texas), 45.82. 6, Wendell Gaskin, (USA/Edwardsville, Kan.), 45.86.

Women's 400 Meters
1, Julia Duporte Torres, (CUB), 50.77 seconds. 2, Nancy McLean Ferrera, (CUB), 51.81. 3, Flirtisha Harris, (USA/South Orange, N.J.), 52.51. 4, Crystal Irving, (USA/Las Vegas, Nev.), 52.69.

Men's 800 Meters
1, Jose Luiz Barbosa, (BRA), 1:46.02 (Pan American Games record; old record: 1:46.29, Jose Barbosa, BRA, 1995); 2, Alain Miranda Truste, (CUB), 1:46.88; 3, Brad Sumner, (USA/Terre Haute, Ind.), 1:47.58; 8, Terril Davis, (USA/Austin, Texas), 1:51.21.

Women's 800 Meters
1, Meredith Rainey, (USA/Silver Springs, Md.), 1:59.44; 2, Luciana De Paul Mendes, (BRA), 2:01.71. 3, Letitia Alma Vriesde, (SUR), 2:02.25. DNC - Amy Wickus, Madison, Wis.

Men's 1,500 Meters
1, Joaquim Cruz, (BRA), 3: 40.26 seconds (Pan American Games record, old record: 3:40.5, Don Paige, USA, 1979). 2, Terrance Herrington, (USA/Portsmouth, Va.), 3:40.97. 3, Jason Pyrah, (USA/Provo, Utah), 3:42.34.

Women's 1,500 Meters
1, Sarah Renk-Thorsett, (USA/Madison, Wis.), 4:21.84. 2, Sarah Howell, (CAN), 4:22.10. 3, Marta Orellana, (ARG), 4:22.44. 5, Kelly Rabush, (USA/Arlington, Va.), 4:25.04.

3,000-Meter Steeplechase
1, Wander Do Prado Moura, (BRA), 8:14.41; 2, Brian Diemer, (USA/Caledonia, Mich.), 8:30.58. 3, Richard Reese, (USA/Littleton, Colo.), 8:31.58.

Men's 5,000 Meters
1, Armando Quintanilla, (MEX), 13:30.35 (Pan American Games record; old record: 13:31.40, Arturo Barrios, MEX, 1987); 2, Wander Do Prado Moura, (BRA), 13:45.53; 3, Silvio Burbano, (ECU), 13:52.29; 4, Tim Hacker, (USA/Madison, Wis.), 13:52.42; 6, Ronnie Harris, (USA/ Arlington, Va.), 14:00.39.

Women's 5,000 Meters
1, Adriana Fernandez, (MEX), 15:46.32 (Pan American Games record; first time event held at PAG); 2, Maria Dian Mancilla, (MEX), 15:46.43; 3, Carol Ellen Montgomery, (CAN), 15:46.80; 5, Misti Demko, (USA/Arlington, Va.), 16:04.56. 10, Ceci St.Geme, (USA/Madison, Wis.), 16:43.15.

Men's 10,000 Meters
1, Armando Quintanilla, (MEX), 28:57.41. 2, Valdenor Dos Santos, (BRA), 29:04.79. 3, Ronaldo Dos Santos, (BRA), 29:07.68. 5, Steve Plasencia, (USA/Eugene, Ore.), 29:10.33. 8, Chris Fox, (USA/Hagerstown, Md.), 29:56.54.

Women's 10,000 Meters
1, Carmen Furtado, (BRA), 33:10.19. 2, Carol Ellen Montgomery,

1995 Pan American Games Results

(CAN), 33:13.58. 3, Maria Del Carmen Diaz Mancilla, (MEX), 33:14.94. 5, Laura LaMena-Coll, (USA/Eugene, Ore.), 33:16.15. 7, Gwyn Coogan, (USA/Boulder, Colo.), 33:32.49.

Men's 110-meter Hurdles (Wind: +0.80)
1, Roger Kingdom (USA/Monroeville, Pa.), 13.39; 2, Emilio Valle Alvarez (CUB), 13.40; 3, Courtney Hawkins (USA/Houston, Texas) 13.54.

Women's 100-meter Hurdles (Wind: +2.10)
1, Aliuska Lopez Pedroso, (CUB) 12.68w; 2, Donalda Duprey, (CAN), 13.16; 3, Odalys Adams Castillo (CUB) 13.17; 4, Allison Williams, (USA/Pittsburgh, Pa.), 13.30.

Men's 400-meter Hurdles
1, Eron Nunes Araujo, (BRA), 49.29; 2, Everson Teixeira, (BRA), 50.24; 3, Llimi Rivas Carabali, (COL), 50.37; 5, Marco Morgan, (USA/Raleigh, N.C.), 52.67.

Women's 400-meter Hurdles
1, Kim Batten, (USA/Tallahassee, Fla.), 54.74; 2, Tonja Buford, (USA/Urbana, Ill.), 55.05. 3, Lency Montelier Ulaci, (CUB), 55.74.

Men's 4x100-meter Relay
1, CUB,, 38.67; 2, USA (Dino Napier/El Paso, Texas; Ron Clark/Garland, Texas; Wendell Gaskin/Edwardsville, Kan.; Robert Reading/Los Angeles, Calif.), 39.12; 3, MEX, 39.77.

Women's 4x100-meter Relay
1, USA (Shantel Twiggs/St. Louis, Mo.; Richelle Webb/Ann Arbor, Mich.; Flirtisha Harris/S. Orange, N.J.; Chryste Gaines/Ennis, Texas), 43.55; 2, CUB, (M. Fernandez Ferrer, A. Lopez Pedroso, D. Perez Sanchez, Liliana Allen Doll), 44.08; 3, COL (E. Mera Chara, F. Palacios Hinest, L. Rodriguez Orjue, M. Brock Forbes), 44.10.

Men's 4x400-meter Relay
1, CUB, (Sanchez, Crusellas, Mena Abreu, Tellez Santana) 3:01.53; 2, JAM, (Taylor, Blake, Martin, McDonald), 3:02.11; 3, TRI, (Guy, De Silva, Stephens, Morris), 3:02.24. USA, (Dino Napier, El Paso, Texas; Tony Miller, Waco, Texas; Wendell Gaskin, Edwardsville, Kan.; Kevin Lyles, South Orange, N.J.), disqualified.

Women's 4x400-meter Relay
1, CUB, (Morales Rosillo, McLean Ferrera, Bonne Rouseauk, DuPorte Torres), 3:27.45; 2, USA (Trevaia Williams/Las Vegas, Nev.; Flirtisha Harris/S. Orange, N.J.; Crystal Irving/Las Vegas, Nev.; Terri Dendy/Norfolk, Va.), 3:31.22. 3. COL, (Mera Chara, Rodriguez Orjue, Palacios Hinest, Brock Forbes), 3:38.54.

Women's 10-Kilometer Walk
1, Graciela Mendoza, MEX, 46:31.93. 2, Michelle Rohl, USA/La Grange, Calif., 46:36.52. 3, Francisca Martinez, MEX, 47:44.78. Teresa Vaill, USA/Brooksville, Fla., DQ.

Men's 20-Kilometer Walk
1, Jefferson Leona Perez Quezada, (ECU), 1:22:52.80 seconds (Pan American Games record; old record: 1:24:50.00, Carlos Mercenario, (MEX), 1987). 2, Daniel Garcia Cordova, (MEX), 1:22:56.40. 3, Julio Rene Martinez Sican, (GUA), 1:23:49.70. Allen James, (USA/La Grange, Ga.), DNF. Jonathan Matthews, (USA/Palo Alto, Calif.), DNF.

Men's 50-kilometer Walk
1, Carlos Moreno, (MEX), 3:47.55 (Pan American Games record; old record: 3:58.54, Carlos Bermudez, MEX, 1987). 2, Miguel Rodriguez Gall, (MEX), 3:48:22. 3, Julio Urias Meda, (GUA), 3:49:37; 6, Allen James, (USA/La Grange, Ga.), 3:59:27. 9, Andrzej Chylinski, (USA/Colorado Springs, Colo.), 4:12:39.

Men's Marathon
1, Benjamin Paredes Martin, (MEX), (2:14:44); 2, Mark Coogan, (USA/Boulder, Colo.), 2:15:21; 3, Luiz Carlos Da Silva, (BRA), 2:15:46; Gerald Lawson, (USA/Jacksonville, Fla.), did not finish.

Women's Marathon
1, Maria Trujillo, (USA/Marina, Calif.), 2:43:56; 2, Jennifer Martin, (USA/Erie, Pa.), 2:44:10; 3, Emma Cabrera Palafox, (MEX), 2:46:36.

Decathlon
1, Kip Janvrin, (USA/Warrensburg, Minn.), 8,049. 2, Eugenio Balanque Llopiz, (CUB), 7,948. 3, Alejandro Cardenas Robles, (MEX), 7,387. Did Not Start: Steve Fritz, (USA/Manhattan, Kan.).

Heptathlon - Exhibition Only
1, Jamie McNeair, (USA/Lafayette, Ind.), 6,266 points (Pan American Games record; old record: 6,184, Cindy Greiner, USA, 1987). 2, Magaly Garcia Leibra, (CUB), 6,055. 3, DeDee Nathan, (USA/Bloomington, Ind.), 5,879.

Men's Long Jump
1, Ivan Pedroso, (CUB), 27-10 3/4 (8.50 meters). 2, Jaime Jefferson, (CUB), 27-0 (8.23). 3, Elmer Williams, (PUR), 26-0 (8.00). 4, Tony Walton, (USA/College Station, Texas), 25-10 3/4 (7.89). 6, Dion Bentley, (USA/Stone Mountain, Ga.), 25-2 1/2 (7.68).

Women's Long Jump
1, Niurka Montalvo Amro (CUB), 22-7 1/4 (6.89 meters); 2, Andrea Avila (ARG), 21-4 3/4 (6.52); 3, Jackie Edwards (BAH), 21-4 (6.50); 5, Dawn Burrell (USA/Houston, Texas) 20-2 1/4 (6.15); 6, Tamara Cuffee (USA/Fairfax, Va.), 19-11 3/4 (6.09).

Men's High Jump
1, Javier Sotomayor, (CUB), 7-10 1/2 (2.40 meters) (Pan American Games record; old record: 7-8 1/2 (2.35), Sotomayor, CUB, 1991; 2, Stephen Smith, (USA/Terre Haute, Ind.), 7-6 (2.29); 3, Gilmar Mayo Lozano, (COL), 7-5 (2.26); 4, Tony Barton, (USA/Fairfax, Va.), 7-3 3/4 (2.23).

Women's High Jump
1, Ioamnet Quintero Alvare, (CUB), 6- 4 1/4 (1.94 meters). 2, Silvia Costa Acosta, (CUB), 6-3 1/4 (1.91). 3, Angela Bradburn, (USA/Austin, Texas), 6-3 1/4 (1.91). 4, Karol Damon, (USA/Spring City, Tenn.), 6-2 (1.88).

Men's Triple Jump
1, Yoelbi Luis Quesada Fernandez, (CUB), 57-11 3/4 inches (17.67 meters); 2, Jerome Romain, (DMA), 56-6 3/4 (17.24); 3, Yoel Garcia Luis, (CUB), 56-5 3/4 (17.21). 4, LaMark Carter, (USA/Natchitoches, La.), 55-0 1/4 (16.77); 6, Richard Thompson, Jr., (USA/Atlanta, Ga.), 53-0 1/4 (16.16).

Women's Triple Jump
1, Leiza Milagro Carrillo Mesa, (CUB), 46 feet, 6 inches (wind: +3.4 meters per second) (14.09 meters). 2, Niurka Montalvo Amro, (CUB), 45-3 (13.90m) (wind: +3.4). 3, Andrea Veronica Avila, (ARG), 44-10 1/2 (13.84m) (wind: +3.2). 5, Carla Shannon, (USA/Syracuse, N.Y.), 41-10 1/2w (13.36m) (wind: +3.6).

Pole Vault
1, Pat Manson, (USA/Baldwin, Kan.), 18-10 1/2 (5.75 meters). 2, Bill Deering, (USA/Miami Beach, Fla.), 18-4 (5.65). 3, Tape Manzano, (CUB), 16- 8 1/2 (5.40).

Men's Shot Put
1, C.J. Hunter, (USA/Arvada, Colo.), 66-11 1/2, (20.52 meters) (Pan American Games record, old record: 66-4 (20.22), Dave Laut, (USA), 1979). 2, Greg Tafralis, (USA/San Bruno, Calif.), 64-11 (19.85). 3, Jorge Montenegro Fun, (CUB), 61-7 1/2 (18.94).

Women's Shot Put
1, Connie Price Smith (USA/Bloomington, Ind.), 62-10 3/4 (19.17 meters); 2, Ramona Pagel (USA/San Diego, Calif.) 60-8 1/2 (18.50); 3, Yumileidis Cumba Jay (CUB) 60-7 1/4 (18.47).

Men's Discus
1, Roberto Sandoval, (CUB), 208-7 (63.58 meters). 2, Alexis Elizarde, (CUB), (203-5 (62.00). 3, Randy Heisler, (USA/Bloomington, Ind.), 197-3 (60.12). 6, Carlos Scott, (USA/Spring, Texas), 179-1 (54.58).

Women's Discus
1, Maritza Marten Garcia, (CUB), 200-10 (61.22 meters); 2, Barbara Hechvarria, (CUB), 197-6 (60.20); 3, Kristin Kuehl, (USA/Fargo, N.D.), 186-9 (56.92). DNC - Ramona Pagel, San Diego, Calif.

Men's Javelin
1. Emeterio Silva, CUB, 260-1 (79.28 meters). 2. Edgar Bauman, PAR, 258-2 (78.70). 3, Todd Riech, USA/Fresno, Calif., 255-4 (77.82). 6, Ed Kaminski, USA/LaGrange, Ga., 237-2 (72.30).

Women's Javelin
1, Xiomara Azcuy, (CUB), 209 feet, 8 inches (63.92 meters). 2, Laverne Eve, (BAH), 201-0 (61.28). 3, Valerie Tulloch, (CAN), 198-9 (60.58). 5, Paula Berry, (USA/Redlands, Calif.), 177-5 (54.08). 7, Lynda Lipson, (USA/Hillsboro, N.C.), 166-9 (50.82).

Men's Hammer Throw
1, Lance Deal, (USA/Eugene, Ore.), 248-2 (75.64 meters); 2, Alberto Sanchez Escobar, (CUB), 242-7 (73.94); 3, Andres Charadia, (ARG), 235-6 (71.78); 6, Jim Driscoll, (USA/Eugene, Ore.), 224-4 (68.38).

Women's Hammer Throw
1, Alexandria Givan, (USA/New Haven, Conn.), 193 feet, 4 inches (58.92 meters)(Pan American Games record: first time event held at Games). 2, Maria Eugenia Villamizar Amad, (COL), 184-2 (56.14m). 3, Sonja Fitts, (USA/Cambria Heights, N.Y.), 183-11 (56.06m).

BADMINTON

Men's Singles
1, Jaimie Dawson, (CAN); 2, Iain Sydie, (CAN); 3T, Kevin Han, (USA/Colorado Springs, Colo.), and Mario Carulla, (PER). Tom Reidy, Colorado Springs, Colo., elim. quarterfinals.

Women's Singles
1, Denyse Julien, (CAN); 2, Sian Deng, (CAN); 3T, Beverly Tang Choon, (TRI) and Kathy Zimmerman, (USA/Colorado Springs, Colo.).

Men's Doubles
1, CAN, (Iain Sydie/Anil Kaul); 2, USA (Kevin Han/Colorado Springs, Colo. and Thomas Reidy/ Colorado Springs, Colo.); 3T, JAM, (Paul Leyow/Roy Paul) and CAN, (Jaimie Dawson/D. Yung). Michael Edstrom/Tempe, Ariz., and Christopher Hales/Wooster, Ohio, elim. quarterfinals.

Women's Doubles
1. CAN, (Sian Deng/Denyse Julien); 2, CAN (Melanie Cloutier/ Robbyn Hermitage); 3T. USA (Linda French/Colorado Springs, Colo., Erika Von Heiland/Colorado Springs, Colo.), and USA, (Ann French/La Jolla, Calif., Kathy Zimmerman/Colorado Springs, Colo).

Mixed Doubles
1, CAN, (Yeng/Julien); 2, CAN (Anil Kaul/Sian Deng); 3T, USA, (Michael Edstrom/Tempe, Ariz., and Linda French/Colorado Springs, Colo.), and JAM (P. Leyow/T. Leyow). Christopher Hales/Wooster, Ohio, and Ann French/La Jolla, Calif., elim. first round.

BASEBALL

1, CUB; 2, NIC; 3, PUR; 9T, USA, (Derek Adair/Albertson, N.Y.; Charles Alben/Kings Park, N.Y; John Aramento/Worcester, Mass.; Anthony D'Esposito/Staten Island, N.Y.; Jason Dellaero/Brewster, N.Y.; William Dinkelacker/Mineola, N.Y.; Brian Fitzsimmons/ Monsey, N.Y.; Matt Hannon/Ozone Park, N.Y.; Michael Hughes/ East Meadow, N.Y.; Michael Johnson/Miller Place, N.Y.; Chris Lemonis/New City, N.Y.; Jeff Love/Seymour, Conn.; Mike Maerten/Delran, N.Y.; Todd Montesano/Scarsdale, N.Y.; Matthew Mushorn/Bethpage, N.Y.; Edvard Olsen/Staten Island, N.Y.; Derek Pasolini/Farmingdale, N.Y.; Anthony Sagnelli/Staten Island, N.Y.; Vincent Schuster/Bordentown, N.J.; Tom Tuttle/ Levittown, N.Y.; Gary Villacres/Astoria, N.Y.; Edward Wennerholm/Lynbrook, N.Y.).

> USA Results (0-6)
> ARG 6, USA 4
> MEX 7, USA 2
> PUR 8, USA 1
> GUA 14, USA 4
> AHO 9, USA 2
> BRA 4, USA 2

BASKETBALL (Men only)

1, ARG; 2, USA, (Brian Davis, Durham, N.C.; Sean Gay, Houston, Texas; Dave Jamerson,, Minerva, Ohio; Larry Lewis, Los Angeles, Calif.; Erik Martin, West Covina, Calif.; Scott Paddock, Tinley Park, Ill.; Rumeal Robinson, Cambridge, Mass.; Carl Thomas, Lansing, Mich.; Kelsey Weeks, Moline, Ill.; Chuckie White, Monrovia, Calif.; Mike Williams, Chicago, Ill.; A.J. Wynder, Newport News, Va.; 3, BRA.

> USA Results (4-3)
> ARG 68, USA 67
> BRA 101, USA 98
> USA 97, PUR 78

USA 104, URU 96 (OT)
USA 104, MEX 80
USA 89, BRA 85
ARG 90, USA 86 (gold medal game)

BOWLING

Men's Team
1, USA (Pat Healey, Jr., Niagara Falls, NY, Mark VanMeter, Albuquerque, N.M., John Eiss, Brooklyn Park, Minn., and Chris Barnes, Wichita, Kan.), 4923; 2, VEN (Agustin De Farias, Pedro Avendano, Arturo Hernandez, Pedro Carreyo), 4684; 3, CAN (Mark Doi, Douglas Schatz, Paul Gyarnati, William Rowe), 4677.

Women's Team
1, CAN (Sandra Lowe, Anne Saasto, Deborah Ship, Catharine Willis), 4676; 2, USA (Lisa Bishop/Belleville, Mich., Lesia Stark/ Lancaster, Calif., Missy Howard/Coon Rapids, Minn., Elizabeth Johnson/Niagara Falls, N.Y.), 4557; 3, VEN (Margalit Mizrachi, Marianela Lista, Mirella Trasolini, Mariela Alarza), 4547.

Men's Division Individual
1, Bill Rowe, (CAN), 1295; 2, Pat Healey, Jr., (USA/Niagara Falls, N.Y.), 1260; 3, Marco Zepeda, (MEX), 1237; 6, Chris Barnes, (USA/ Wichita, Kan.), 1222; 10, Mark VanMeter, (USA/Albuquerque, N.M.), 1204; 22, John Eiss, (USA/Brooklyn Park, Minn.), 1161.

Women's Division Individual
1, Catharine Willis, (CAN), 1305; 2, Mariela Alarza, (VEN), 1266; 3, Lisa Bishop, (USA/Belleville, Mich.), 1212; 10, Liz Johnson, (USA/ Niagara Falls, N.Y.), 1162; 15, Missy Howard, (USA/Coon Rapids, Minn.), 1133; 17, Lesia Starck, (USA/Lancaster, Calif.), 1124.

Men's Division Doubles
1, USA (Pat Healey, Jr./Niagara Falls, N.Y. and Chris Barnes/ Wichita, Kan., USA), 2559; 2, AHO, (Samir Daou and Carlos Finx Jr.), 2545; 3. CAN, (Mark Doi and Bill Rowe), 2463; 4, USA, (John Eiss, /Brooklyn Park, Minn. and Mark Van Meter/Albuquerque, N.M.), 2445.

Women's Division Doubles
1, USA, (Missy Howard/Coon Rapids, Minn. and Lesia Starck/ Lancaster, Calif.), 2548; 2, MEX, (Georgina Serratos and Gabriela Sandoval), 2463; 3, VEN, (Margalit Mizrachi and Mariela Alarza), 2445. 4. USA (Liz Johnson/Niagara Falls, N.Y. and Lisa Bishop/ Belleville, Mich.), 2397.

Men's Final Masters
16 game totals (Scratch Total, match play record, total score)
1, Pat Healey, Jr., (USA/Niagara Falls, N.Y.), (3354, 11-5, 3464); 2, Pedro Carreyo, (VEN), (3300, 11-5, 3410); 3 Agustin De Farias, (VEN), (3334, 7-9, 3405. 5. Chris Barnes, (USA/Wichita, Kan.), (3257, 8- 8, 3337).

Women's Final Masters
6 game totals (Scratch total, match play record, total score)
1, Liz Johnson, (USA/ Niagara Falls, N.Y.), (2636, 9-3, 2726); 2, Edda Piccini, (MEX), (2510, 8-4, 2590); 3, Luz Leal, (COL), (2395, 9-3, 2485). 7, Missy Howard, (USA/Coon Rapids, Minn.), (2342, 7-5, 2412).

BOXING

106 lbs/Light Flyweight
1, Edgar Alexander Velazquez (VEN); 2, Juan Ramirez (CUB); 3T, Oscar Jeovanny Back Oliva (HON) and Albert Guardado Jr., (USA/ Topeka, Kan.).

112 lbs/Flyweight
1, Juan Guzman (DOM); 2, Raul Gonzalez (CUB); 3T, Jose Lopez (VEN) and Jose Cotto (PUR); Arturo Morel, (USA/Madison, Wis.), injured, did not fight.

119 lbs/Bantamweight
1, Juan Antonio Despaigne (CUB); 2, Jose Cotto Vazquez (PUR); 3T, Jhonny Vasquez (DOM) and Claude Lambert (CAN); Carlos Navarro, (USA/Los Angeles, Calif.) elim. in quarterfinals.

125 lbs/Featherweight
1, Arnaldo Mesa (CUB); 2, Alexander Trujillo (PUR); 3T, Luis Jose (DOM) and Cristian Rodriguez (ARG); Diego Corrales Jr., (USA/

1995 Pan American Games Results

Sacramento, Calif.), elim. first round.

132 lbs/Lightweight
1, Julio Gonzalez (CUB); 2, Acelino Freitas (BRA); 3T, Francisco Osorio Gary (COL) and Michael Strange (CAN); Datris Biagas, (USA/Fayetteville (Fort Bragg), N.C.), elim. in quartefinals.

139 lbs/Light Welterweight
1, Walter Cruce (ARG); 2, Luis Perez (PUR); 3T, Fernando Vargas, (USA/Oxnard, Calif.) and Hector Vinent (CUB).

147 lbs/Welterweight
1, David Reid, (USA/Philadelphia, Pa.); 2, Daniel Santos Pena (PUR); 3T, Hercules Kyvelos (CAN) and Tomas Enrique Leiva Hernandez (GUA).

156 lbs/Light Middleweight
1, Alfredo Duvergel (CUB); 2, Derbys Alvarez (VEN); 3T, Kirt Sinnette (TRI) and Jason Smith (CAN); Rhoshii Wells, (USA/ Riverdale, Ga.) did not compete due to injury.

165 lbs/Middleweight
1, Ariel Hernandez Azicy (CUB); 2, Ricardo Anibal Araneda Aviles (CHI); 3T, Jhon Eduardo Arroyo Esocbar (COL) and Ronald Simms, (USA/Newport News, Va.).

178 lbs/Light Heavyweight
1, Antonio Tarver, (USA/Orlando, Fla.), ; 2, Thompson Garcia (ECU); 3T, Edgardo Santos (PUR) and Gabriel Hernandez (DOM).

201 lbs/Heavyweight
1, Fleix Savon Fabre (CUB); 2, Lamon Brewster, (USA/Los Angeles, Calif.); 3T, Moises Rolon Rodriguez (PUR) and Santiago Felipe Palavecino (ARG).

+201 lbs/Super Heavyweight
1, Leonardo Martinez (CUB); 2, Jean Bergeron (CAN); 3T, Lance Whitaker, (USA/Granada Hills, Calif.) and Romulo Cuarez (VEN).

CANOE/KAYAK

Men's Single Kayak 500 Meters
1, Peter Newton, (USA/Bellevue, Wash.), 1:42.63; 2, Emmanuel Auger, (CAN), 1:44.65; 3, Sergio Mangin, (ARG), 1:44.84.

Women's Single Kayak 500 Meters
1, Alexandra Harbold, (USA/Rockaway Beach, N.Y.), 2:02.37; 2, Erika Duron Miranda, (MEX), 2:02.81; 3, Anmary Lopez Cabrera, (CUB), 2:03.23.

Men's Single Kayak 1,000 Meters
1, Abelardo Andres Sztrum, (ARG), 3:46.72; 2, Peter Newton, (USA/Bellevue, Wash.), 3:48.53; 3, Sebastian Ariel Cuattrin, (BRA), 3:48.63.

Men's Double Kayak 500 Meters
1, USA (Peter Newton/Bellevue, Wash., Stein Jorgensen/San Diego, Calif.), 1:35.51; 2, CUB, (Marcelino Cipriano Pinon, Luis Perez Ramos), 1:35.93; 3, ARG (Diego Canepa, Sergio Mangin), 1:38.22.

Women's Double Kayak 500 Meters
1, USA (DeAnne Hemmens/Costa Mesa, Calif., Traci Phillips/ Honolulu, Hawaii), 1:46.55; 2, CAN, (Kelly O'Leary, Marie-Jose Gibeau), 1:48.06; 3, MEX, (Renata Hernandez, Sandra Rojas Gutierrez), 1:51.56.

Men's Double Kayak 1,000 Meters
1, ARG (Abelardo Andres Sztrum/Javier Andres Correa), 3:24.37; 2, CUB, (Luis Enrique Perez Ramos /Marcelino Cipriano Pinon), 3:26.67; 3, BRA (Sebastian Ariel Cuattrin/Alvaro Acco Koslowski), 3:27.47; 5, USA (Chris Ball/Costa Mesa, Calif., and Curt Bader/ Bloomfield, Iowa), 3:36.20.

Four-Man Kayak 500 Meters
1, CUB (Marcelino Cipriano Pinon, Luis Perez Ramos, Rafael Varona Reyes and Toani Ventura Cruz), 1:27.06; 2, USA (Chris Ball/ Costa Mesa, Calif., Curt Bader/Bloomfield, Iowa, Michael Harbold/ Honolulu, and Mike Herbert/Rogers, Ark.), 1:27.92; 3, ARG, (Abelrado Sztrum, Diego Canepa, Ariel Basualto and Javier Correa), 1:29.25.

Four-Woman Kayak 500 Meters
1, CAN (Catharine Breckenridge, Jessica Ferguson, Marie- Jose Gibeau and Danica Rice), 1:37.55; 2, USA (Traci Phillips/Honolulu, DeAnne Hemmens/Costa Mesa, Calif., Alexandra Harbold/

Rockaway Beach, N.Y., and Kate Hendrickson Borg/Charleston, S.C.), 1:39.62; 3, CUB (Mirlenis Aguilera, Anmary Lopez Cabrera, Mariela Suarez Resino and Yamile Ley Alvarez), 1:41.50.

Four-Man Kayak 1,000 Meters
1, CUB (Marcelino Cipriano Pinon, Rafael Varona Reyes, Luis Enrique Perez Ramos, Yoani Ventura Cruz), 3:02.87; 2, USA, (Mike Herbert/Rogers, Ark., Michael Harbold/Honolulu, Hawaii; Chris Barlow/San Diego, Calif.; Stein Jorgensen/San Diego, Calif.), 3:03.06; 3, ARG, (Javier Andres Correa, Juan De La Cruz Labrin, Fernando Gabriel Ortiz, Sergio Alejandro Mangin), 3:08.72.

Men's Single Canoe 500 Meters
1, Jim Terrell, (USA/Milford, Ohio), 1:55.00; 2, Attila Buday, (CAN), 1:55.133; 3, Juan Martinez Santan, (MEX), 1:57.90.

Men's Single Canoe 1,000 Meters
1, Ledy Frank Balceiro Pajon, (CUB), 4:12.98; 2, Juan Martinez Santan, (MEX), 4:13.60; 3, Danny Howe, (CAN), 4:14.53. 4, Jim Terrell, (USA/Milford, Ohio), 4:20.49.

Men's Double Canoe 500 Meters
1, CAN, (Mike Oryschak, Danny Howe), 1:47.54. 2, MEX, (Juan Antonio Romero Casalez, Ramon Ferrer Cruz), 1:47.77; 3, CUB, (Juan Aballi Delgado, Fernando Zamora Machado), 1:47.91;. 4, USA, (Martin Lowenfish/Dobbs Ferry, N.Y., Joseph Harper/ Ventura, Calif.), 1:59.31.

Men's Double Canoe 1,000 Meters
1, CUB, (Jose Yordi Calcines/Ibrahim Rojas Blanco), 3:34.42;. 2, CAN, (Tamas/Attila Buday), 3:34.92; 3, MEX (Juan Martinez Santan/ Ramon Ferrer Cruz), 3:43.46; 4, USA, (Joseph Harper/ Ventura, Calif., Martin Lowenfish/Dobbs Ferry, N.Y.), 4:01.20.

CYCLING

Women's 25-Kilometer Individual Time Trial
1, Dede Demet (USA/Colorado Springs, Colo.), 34:11; 2, Yacel Ojeda, (CUB), 35:02; 3, Clara Hughes, (CAN), 36:04.

Men's 50-Kilometer Individual Time Trial
1, Clay Moseley (USA/Albuquerque, N.M.), 1:04:36; 2, Jesus Zarate, (MEX), 1:05:53; 3, Servando Figueredo, (URU), 1:06:12.

Men's 4,000-Meter Individual Pursuit
1, Kent Bostick (USA/Corralles, N.M.), 4:35.839, (Pan American record, old record, Walter Perez, ARG, 4:37.089, March 14, 1995); 2, Walter Perez, (ARG), 4:36.831; 3, Brian Walton (CAN) 4:40.050 (semifinal time).

Women's 3,000-Meter Individual Pursuit
1, Janie Eickhoff (USA/Wilmington, Del.), 3:47.199, (Pan American record, old record, Janie Eickhoff, USA, 3:50.296, March 15, 1995); 2, Yoanka Gonzalez, (CUB), caught in final; 3, Belem Guerrero, MEX, 4:03.144, (semifinal time).

Men's 39.5-kilometer Cross-Country Mountain Bike Race
1, David "Tinker" Juarez (USA/Sugarloaf, Calif.), 1:47:14; 2, Andres Brenes, (CRC), @ 0:10; 3, Sandro Miranda, (ARG), @ 1:50.

Women's 26.3-kilometer Cross-Country Mountain Bike Race
1, Alison Sydor, (CAN), 1:21:13; 2, Juliana Furtado (USA/Durango, Colo.), @ 3:45; 3, Jimena Florit, (ARG), @ 8:25.

One Kilometer Time Trial
1, Gil Cordoves, (CUB), 1:05.688; 2, Erin Hartwell (USA/Indianapolis, Ind.), 1:06.269; 3, Gene Samuel, (TRI), 1:07.630.

4,000-meter Team Pursuit
1, USA, (Carl Sundquist/Colorado Springs, Colo., Zach Conrad/ Colorado Springs, Colo., Mariano Friedick/Colorado Springs, Colo., Adam Laurent/Arroyo Grande, Calif.). NOTE: Christian Vande Velde (Lemont, Ill.) replaced Conrad in the semifinal; 2, CUB, (Ivan Dominguez, Reinaldo Rodriguez, Eugenio Castro, Hector Ajete); 3, BRA, (Hernandez Quadri, Mauro Ribeiro, Marcio May, Jamil Suaiden).

Men's Sprint
1, Marty Nothstein, (USA/Trexlertown, Pa.); 2, Christian Arrue (CHI); 3. Gil Cordoves (CUB).

Women's Sprint
1, Tanya Dubnicoff (CAN); 2, Connie Paraskevin-Young (USA/ Detroit, Mich.); 3, Nancy Contreras (MEX).

1995 Pan American Games Results

Men's Points Race
1, Brian Walton (CAN), 26 pts.; 2, Milton Wynants (URU), 22 pts., 2 laps; 3, Juan Merheb (PUR), 21 pts., 2 laps; 8, Christian Vande Velde (USA/Lemont, Ill.), 29 pts., 4 laps.

Women's Points Race
1, Janie Eickhoff (USA/Wilmington, Del.), 45 pts.; 2, Belem Guerrero (MEX), 27 pts.; 3, Dania Perez (CUB), 22 pts.

Men's Road Race (169.4 km)
1, Brian Walton, (CAN), 3 hours, 49 minutes, 33 seconds (3:49.33); 2, Mariano Friedick, (USA,/ Colorado Springs, Colo.), :47 back; 3, Fred Rodriguez, (USA/Charlotte, N.C.), 1:29 back; 10, (William) Chann McRae, (USA/Plano, Texas), 4:33 back; 16, Scott Mercer, (USA/Boulder, Colo.), 4:45 back.

Women's Road Race (61 km)
1, Jeanne Golay, (USA/Glenwood Springs, Colo.), 1 hour, 30 minutes, 12 seconds (1:30:12); 2, Clara Hughes, (CAN), :01 back; 3, Yacel Ojeda, (CUB), :12 back; 4, Julie Young, (USA/Sacramento, Calif.), 1:09 back; 7, Alison Dunlap, (USA/ Colorado Springs, Colo.), 2:54 back; 13, (Deirdre) Dede Demet, (USA/Colorado Springs, Colo.), 5:32 back.

DIVING

Men's One-meter Springboard
1, Dean Panaro, (USA/Miami, Fla.), 404.82; 2, Fernando Platas, (MEX), 395.70; 3, Abel Ramirez, (CUB), 375.84; 7, Chris Devine, (USA/Breinigsville, Pa.), 338.67.

Women's One-meter Springboard
1, Mayte Garbey (CUB), 270.15; 2, Annie Pelletier, (CAN), 269.34; 3, Carrie Zars, (USA/Rockford, Ill.), 268.29; 4, Melisa Moses, (USA/Orange Park, Fla.), 261.2.

Men's Three-meter Springboard
1, Fernando Platas, (MEX), 661.80; 2, Mark Bradshaw, (USA/Galloway, Ohio), 624.93; 3, David Bedard, (CAN), 609.63; 4, Kent Ferguson, (USA/Miami Beach, Fla.), 609.21.

Women's Three-meter Springboard
1, Annie Pelletier, (CAN), 519.81; 2, Melisa Moses, (USA/Orange Park,Fla.), 483.54; 3, Bobbi-Anne Mapherson, (CAN), 477.57; 6, Kristen Kane, (USA/Austin, Texas), 435.03.

Men's Platform Results
1, Fernando Platas, (MEX), 617.52; 2, Alberto Acosta, (MEX), 546.18; 3, Patrick Jeffrey, (USA/Fort Lauderdale, Fla.), 543.93; 6, Bryan Gillooly, (USA/Kissimmee, Fla.), 504.06.

Women's Platform Results
1, Anne Montminy, (CAN), 492.39; 2, Angie Trostel, (USA/Oxford, Ohio), 456.96; 3, Becky Ruehl, (USA/Lakeside Park, Ky.), 454.35.

EQUESTRIAN

Team Show Jumping
1, BRA (Andre Johannpeter, on Calei Joter; Nelson Pessoa, on Special Envoy; Rodrigo Pessoa, on Tomboy Loropiano; Victor Alves Texeira, on Attack 2), 23.25 faults. 2, MEX (Jaime Romandia Azcarraga, on Kashim; Jaime Guerra Piedra, on Murphy Brown; Luis Flyvier Ximinez, on Airborne Montecillo; Gerardo Valencia Tazzer, on Caviar), 25.07 faults. 3, USA (Nona Garson/Lebanon, N.J., on Derrek; D.D. Matz/ Collegeville, Pa., on Tashiling; Michael Matz/ Collegeville, Pa., on The General; Debbie Stephens/ Glenmoore, Pa., on Blind Date), 27.45 faults.

Team Dressage Final
1, MEX (Lourdes Ariza, on Dante; Patric Burssens, on Emir Telcel; Cristobal Egerstron, on Romantic Dream; Antonio Rivera, on Aczidos) 4,341 points. 2, USA (Elizabeth Ball/ Menlo Park, Calif., on Bolshoj; Anne Gribbons/ Brentwood, N.Y., on Metallic; Guenter Seidel/Encinitas, Calif., on Batido; Leslie Webb/ Bakersfield, Calif., on Hannabal) 4,304 points. 3, CAN (Nancy MacLachlan, on Davis Cup; Louise Miechowsky, on Tambourin; Stefan von Schalburg, on Asnavour 2; Victoria Winter, on Wedgwood) 4,121 points.

Individual Dressage Final
1, Patric Burssens, (MEX), on Emir Telcel, 1,379 points. 2, Leslie Webb, (USA/Bakersfield, Calif.), on Hannabal, 1,329 points. 3, Victoria Winter, (CAN), on Wedgwood, 1,315 points. 5, Guenter Seidel, (USA/Encinitas, Calif.), on Batido, 1,282 points. 6, Anne Gribbons, (USA/Brentwood, N.Y.), on Metallic, 1,272 points. Elizabeth Ball, Menlo Park, Calif., won consolation.

Individual Show Jumping Final
1, Michael Matz, (USA/Collegeville, Pa.), on The General, 6.30 faults. 2, Jaime Romandia Azcarraga, (MEX), on Kashim, 7.88 faults. 3, Luis Fyver Ximinex, (MEX), on Airborne Montecillo, 12.00 faults. 11, D.D. Matz, (USA/Collegeville, Pa.), on Tashiling, 32.78 faults. 12, Nona Garson, (USA/Lebanon, N.J.), on Derrek, 32.87 faults. Debbie Stephens, (USA/Glenmoore, Pa.), on Blind Date, no score.

Team Three-Day Event
1, BRA, (Luciano Drubi, on Xilena, 110.4 penalties; Serguei Fofanoff, on Kaiser Eden, 133.4 penalties; Filho Ruy Leme da Fonseca, on Man Friday, 284.2 penalties), 348.40 penalties. 2, USA, (Bruce Davidson/Unionville, Pa., on Heyday, 94.0 penalties; Mara DePuy/ S. Strafford, Vt., on Hopper, 147.8 penalties; Missy Ransehousen/ Unionville, Pa., on Pacific Lion, 118.8 penalties; Denise Rath/ Great Falls, Va., on Galliard) 360.60 penalties. No bronze medal awarded.

Individual Three-Day Event
1, Bruce Davidson, (USA/Unionville, Pa.), on Heyday, 94.0 penalties. 2, Federico Castaing, (ARG), on Nippur, 94.6 penalties. 3, Andre Giovanni, (BRA), on Aldo Beto, 104.6 penalties. 5, Missy Ranshousen, Unionville, Pa., on Pacific Lion, 113.8. 10, Mara DePuy, South Strafford, Vt., on Hopper, 147.8. 11, Denise Rath, Great Falls, Va., on Galliard, 221.4. DNF - Virginia Jenkins, Tarboro, N.C., on Rumours in the Air.

FENCING

Men's Team Foil
1, CUB (Rolando Tucker Leon, Elvis Gregory Gil, Ignacio Gonzalez Rimont, Oscar Garcia Perez); 2, USA (Nick Bravin, Sunnyvale, Calif., Zaddick Longenbach, New York, N.Y., Sean McClain, Round Rock, Texas, Alan Weber, Philadelphia, Pa.); 3. ARG.

Men's Individual Foil
1, Elvis Gregory Gil, (CUB); 2, Rolando Tucker Leon, (CUB); 3T, Nick Bravin, (USA/Sunnyvale, Calif.) and Leandro Marchetti (ARG); 7, Zaddick Longenbach, (USA/New York, N.Y.).

Women's Individual Foil
1, Ann Marsh, (USA/Royal Oak, Mich.), 2, Isadoris Diaz, (CUB); 3T, Felicia Zimmermann, (USA/Rush, N.Y.), and Barbara Hernandez , (CUB).

Men's Team Epee
1, CUB (Aguilara, Castro, Trevejo); 2. USA (Tamir Bloom/Milburn, N.J., Michael Marx/Rochester, N.Y., James Carpenter/Hasbrouck Heights, N.J.); 3. COL (Rivas, Carrasquilla, Paz).

Women's Team Epee
1, USA (Leslie Marx/Rochester, N.Y., Margo Miller/Santa Monica, Calif./Donna Stone, Lincoln Park, N.J., Rachel Haugh/Portland, Ore.); 2, CUB (Palma, Garcia, Suarez, Ortiz); 3, CAN (Griffin, Schalm, Landymore).

Men's Individual Epee
1, Carlos Pedroso, (CUB); 2, Tamir Bloom, (USA/Millburn, N.J.), 3T, Perez Trevejo, (CUB) and Paris Inostroza (CHI). Michael Marx, Rochester, N.Y., lost first round.

Women's Individual Epee
1, Leslie Marx (USA/Rochester, N.Y.); 2, Milagros Palma, (CUB); 3T, Yolitzin Martinez (MEX) and Milagros Palma Gonzalez (CUB). Margo Miller/Santa Monica, Calif., lost in quarterfinals.

Women's Team Foil
1, CUB (Hernandez, Estrada, Diaz); 2. USA (Olga Chernyak/ Lafayette, Calif., Monique de Bruin/ Wilsonville, Ore., Ann Marsh/ Royal Oak, Mich., Felicia Zimmermann/Rush, N.Y.); 3, ARG (Ianuzzi, Giancola, Carbone).

Men's Team Sabre
1, USA (Peter Westbrook/ New York, N.Y., Michael D'Ansaro/ New York, N.Y., John Friedberg/New York, N.Y., Thomas Strzalkowski/Richmond, Va.); 2, CUB, (Faure, Cabezaz, Garcia); 3, CAN (Banos, Plourde, Mowosielski).

Men's Individual Sabre
1, Peter Westbrook, (USA/New York, N.Y.); 2, Aristides Faure, (CUB); 3T, Alexis Leyva, (CUB) and Carlos Jose Bravo Lopez (VEN). 10, Thomas Strzalkowski (USA/Richmond, Va.).

FIELD HOCKEY

Men
1, ARG; 2, CAN; 3, USA, (Larry Amar/Camarillo, Calif.; Nick Butcher/Simi Valley, Calif.; Steve Danielson/ Livermore, Calif.; Jeff Horrocks/Newbury Park, Calif.; Steve Jennings/Bethesda, Md.; Paul Lewis/ Livermore, Calif.; Olaf Maack/San Diego; Ben Maruquin/Ventura, Calif.; Marq Mellor/Mt. Vernon, N.Y.; John O'Haire/Coram, N.Y.; John O'Neill/Newbury Park, Calif.; Otto Steffers/San Diego, Calif.; Phil Sykes/Pleasanton, Calif.; Nigel Traverso/New York, N.Y.; Taylor Trickle/Camarillo, Calif.; Steve Wagner/ Mt. Laurel, N.J.).

USA Results (5-2)
USA 3, CUB 3
CAN 3, USA 1
USA 8, TRI 1
ARG 2, USA 1
USA 11, PAR 0
USA 2, CHI 0
USA 3, CUB 2 (bronze medal game)

Women
1, ARG; 2, USA, (Pam Bustin/Somerset, Mass.; Kris Fillat/ San Diego; Tracey Fuchs, Centereach, N.Y.; Kelli James/Medford, N.J.; Antoinette Lucas/Willington, Conn.; Leslie Lyness/Paoli, Pa.; Barb Marois/Auburn, Mass.; Laurel Martin/Hummelstown, Pa.; Pam Neiss/Lancaster, Pa.; Marcia Pankratz/Wakefield, Mass.; Jill Reeve/ Norfolk, Va.; Patty Shea/Belmont, Mass.; Eleanor Stone/ Cheshire, Conn.; Liz Tchou/Medford Lakes, N.J.; Cindy Werley/Alletown, Pa.; Andrea Wieland/ Atlanta); 3, CAN.

USA Results (5-1-1)
USA 2, CAN 0
USA 4, CUB 0
USA 4, JAM 0
USA 1, ARG 1
USA 11, PAR 0
USA 6, TRI 0
ARG 3, USA 2 (gold medal game)

GYMNASTICS — Artistic

Men's Team
1, USA, (Mihai Bagiu/Albuquerque, N.M.; Steve McCain/Houston, Texas; John Roethlisberger/ Minneapolis, Minn.; Bill Roth/ Mohegan Lake, N.Y.; Kip Simons/Bloomsburg, Pa.; Chainey Umphrey/ Albuquerque, N.M.; Chris Waller/Mt. Prospect, Ill.), 551.150; 2, CUB (Felix Anguilera, Francisco Diaz, Abel Driggs, Yoel Gutierrez, Lazaro Lamelas, Erick Lopez, Damian Merino), 550.900; 3, CAN (Kristan Burley, Peter Schmid, Travis Romagnoli, Alan Nolet, Jason Hardabura, Jason Papp, Richard Ikeda), 546.100.

Men's All-Around
1, Erick Lopez, (CUB), 56.375; 2, John Roethlisberger, (USA/Minneapolis, Minn.), 55.725; 3, Lazaro Lamelas, (CUB), 55.400. 7, Stephen McCain, (USA/Houston, Texas), 54.300; 8, Mihai Bagiu, (USA/Albuqerque, N.M.), 54.150.

Men's Floor Exercise
1, Damian Merino, (CUB), 9.625; 2, Bill Roth, (USA/Mohegan Lake, N.Y.), 9.500; 3, Kristan Burley, (CAN), 9.487. 8, John Roethlisberger, (USA/Minneapolis, Minn.), 8.750.

Men's Pommel Horse
1, Erick Lopez, (CUB), 9.450; 2, Mihai Bagiu, (USA/Albuquerque, N.M.), 9.350; 3, Richard Ikeda, (CAN), 9.300; 4, John Roethlisberger, (USA/Minneapolis, Minn.), 9.275.

Men's Still Rings
1, Damian Merino, (CUB), 9.725; 2, John Roethlisberger, (USA/Minneapolis, Minn.), 9.550; 3, Erick Lopez, (CUB), 9.500. 7, Chris Waller, (USA/Mt. Prospect, Ill.), 9.075.

Men's Vault
1, Victor Solorzano, (VEN), 9.593; 2, Lazaro Lamelas, (CUB), 9.462; 3, Kristan Burley, (CAN), 9.450; 4, Steve McCain, (USA/Houston, Texas), 9.387; 6, John Roethlisberger, (USA/Minneapolis, Minn.), 9.087.

Men's Parallel Bars
1, Erick Lopez, (CUB), 9.425; 2, Lazaro Lamelas, (CUB), 9.275; 3, Isidro Ibarrondo, (ARG), 9.250. 7, Bill Roth, (USA/Mohegan Lake, N.Y.), 8.900; 8, John Roethlisberger, (USA/Minneapolis, Minn.), 8.425.

Men's High Bar
1, John Roethlisberger, (USA/Minneapolis, Minn.), 9.275; 2T, Bill Roth, (USA/Mohegan Lake, N.Y.), 9.200; 2T, Victor Colon Ortiz, (PUR), 9.200.

Women's Team
1, USA, (Amanda Borden/Cincinnati, Ohio; Amy Chow/San Jose, Calif.; Shannon Miller/ Edmond, Okla.; Kristy Powell/Colorado Springs, Colo.; Katie Teft/Grand Rapids, Mich.; Doni Thompson/ Colorado Springs, Colo.; Mary Beth Arnold/Sparks, Nev.), 388.475 (Pan American Games record, old record, 385.95, USA, 1987); 2,. ARG (Ana Destefano, Aldana Simone, Laura Alvarez, Romina Mazzoni, Romina Plataroti, Nancy Diorio, Ariadna Argoitia), 369.125; 3, CAN (Natalie Barrington, Shanyn Maceachern, Lena Deteva, Jennifer Ellen Exaltac), 368.450.

Women's All-Around
1, Shannon Miller, (USA/Edmond, Okla.), 38.587; 2, Amanda Borden, (USA/Cincinnati, Ohio), 38.575; 3, Amy Chow, (USA/San Jose, Calif.), 38.375.

Women's Vault
1, Amy Chow, (USA/San Jose, Calif.), 9.718; 2, Shannon Miller, (USA/Edmond, Okla.), 9.706; 3, Annia Portuondo, (CUB), 9.662.

Women's Uneven Bars
1, Shannon Miller, (USA/Edmond, Okla.), 9.812; 2, Amy Chow, (USA/San Jose, Calif.), 9.725; 3, Annia Portuondo, (CUB), 9.650.

Women's Balance Beam
1, Amanda Borden, (USA/Cincinnati, Ohio), 9.612; 2, Annia Portuondo, (CUB), 9.600; 3, Leyanet Gonzalez, (CUB), 9.500.

Women's Floor Exercise
1, Shannon Miller, (USA/Edmond, Okla.), 9.812; 2, Amanda Borden, (USA/Cincinnati, Ohio), 9.787; 3, Leyanet Gonzalez, (CUB), 9.387.

GYMNASTICS — Rhythmic

Team
1, USA, (Tamara Levinson/Silver Spring, Md. and Jessica Davis/ San Anselmo, Calif.), 71.250; 2. CUB, (Yordaniana Corrales, Yamile Sotolongo, Kirenia Ruiz), 70.700; 3, ARG (Cecilia Schtutman, Luciana Eslava, Alejandra Unsain), 70.400.

All-Around
1, Yordania Corrales, (CUB), 36.675; 2, Tamara Levinson, (USA/ Silver Spring, Md.), 36.200; 3, Jessica Davis, (USA/San Anselmo, Calif.), 35.850.

Group
1, CUB; 2, USA (Mandy James/; Aliane Baquerot/; Brandi Siegel/ ; Challen Sievers/; Becky Turner/;); 3, BRA 18.500.

Rope
1, Yordania Corrales (CUB), 9.266; 2, Kireniz Cruz, (CUB), 9.066; 3, Tamara Levinson, (USA/Silver Spring, Md.), 9.033; 7, Jessica Davis (USA/San Anselmo, Calif.), 8.855.

Ball
1, Alejandro Unsam (ARG), 9.233; 2, Cecilia Schtutman (ARG), 9.150; 3, Tamara Levinson (USA/Silver Spring, Md.), 9.033; 4T, Jessica Davis (USA/San Anselmo, Calif.), 9.033.

Clubs
1, Yordania Corrales (CUB), 9.233; 2, Jessica Davis (USA/San Anselmo, Calif.), 9.116; 3, Tamara Levinson (USA/Silver Spring, Md.), 9.082.

Ribbon
1, Tamara Levinson (USA/Silver Spring, Md.), 9.166; 2, Jessica Davis (USA/San Anselmo, Calif.), 9.10; 3, Luciana Eslava (ARG), 9.082

JUDO

Men's 56 kg
1, Ismady Alonso, (CUB); 2, Luis Vizcaino, (DOM); 3T, Jake Flores, (USA/Temecula, Calif.) and Rodolfo Yamaiose, (BRA).

Men's 60 kg
1, Ewan Beaton, (CAN); 2, Manolo Poulot, (CUB); 3T, Jorge Lencina, (ARG) and Carlos Bortole, (BRA); 9, Clifton Sunada, (USA/Colorado Springs, Colo.).

Men's 65 kg
1, Israel Hernandez, (CUB); 2, Francisco Morales, (ARG); 3T, Enrique Guimaraes, (BRA) and Taro Tan, (CAN); 9, Orlando Fuentes, (USA/Hialeah, Fla.).

Men's 71 kg
1, Jim Pedro, (USA/Danvers, Mass.); 2, Erick De La Paz, (CUB); 3T, Sergio Oliveira, (BRA) and Jean Pierre Cantin, (CAN).

Men's 78kg
1, Dario Garcia (ARG); 2, Jason Morris, (USA/Scota, N.Y.); 3T, Colin Morgan (CAN) and Flavio Canto (BRA).

Men's 86kg
1, Nicolas Gill (CAN); 2, Carlos Matt (BRA); 3T, Bryan Olson (USA/Colorado Springs, Colo.) and Pablo Elisii (ARG).

Men's 95 kg
1, Keith Morgan, (CAN); 2, Daniel Dell'Aquila, (BRA); 3T, Rafael Hueso, (USA/Colorado Springs, Colo.) and Belarmino Salgado, (CUB).

Men's +95 kg
1, Jose Mario Tranquilini, (BRA); 2, Frank Moreno, (CUB). 3T, Damon Keeve, (USA/San Francisco, Calif.) and (ARG).

Women's 45 kg
1, Milredis Turro, (CUB); 2, Sherrie Phillips, (USA/Colorado Springs, Colo.); 3, Evelyn Matias, (PUR) and Dora Maldonado, (HON).

Women's 48 kg
1, Amarylis Savon, (CUB); 2, Carolyne LePage, (CAN); 3T, Andrea Rodrigues, (BRA) and Maria Villapol, (VEN). Hilary Wolf, Chicago, Ill., elim. first round.

Women's 52 kg
1, Legna Verdecia, (CUB); 2, Claudia Mariani, (ARG); 3T, JoAnne Quiring, (USA/Westcliffe, Colo.) and Nathalie Gosselin, (CAN).

Women's 56 kg
1, Driulis Gonzalez, (CUB); 2, Corinna Broz, (USA/Colorado Springs, Colo.); 3T, Renee Hock, (CAN) and Danielle Zangrando, (BRA).

Women's 61 kg
1, Ileana Beltran (CUB); 2, Michelle Buckingham (CAN); 3T, Colleen McDonald (USA/Covina, Calif.) and Xiomara Griffith (VEN).

Women's 66 kg
1, Odalis Reve (CUB); 2, Liliko Ogasawara (USA/Montvale, N.J.); 3T, Dulce Pina D'Oleo (DOM) and Vania Ishii (BRA).

Women's 72 kg
1, Diandenys Luna, (CUB); 2, Francis Gomez, (VEN); 3T, Gracie Jividen, (USA/Lakewood, Colo.) and Valeria Brandino, (BRA).

Women's +72 kg
1, Daima Beltran, (CUB); 2, Edilene Andrade, (BRA); 3T, Colleen Rosensteel, (USA/Gainesville, Fla.) and (CAN)..

KARATE

Women's Kata
1, Melanie Genung (USA/Bellevue, Wash.); 2, Kim (PER); 3, Chaves (ARG).

Men's Kata
1, Chuhurru (ARG); 2, Arevalo (PUR); 3, Ferdie Allas (USA/San Diego, Calif.).

Women's Team Kumite
1, CUB; 2, BRA; 3, USA (Townsend Carr, Superior, Colo,; Tracey Day, Selden, N.Y.; Christina Muccini, Douglastown, N.Y.).

Men's Team Kumite
1, ARG; 2, BRA; 3, USA (William Chadrow, Seattle, Wash.; Doug Selchan, Pittsburgh, Pa.; Tommy Hood Jr., Columbia, S.C.)

Women's -52kg
1, V. Sosa (CUB); 2, F. Oliveira (BRA); 3T, M. Ling (CAN) and J. Seclea (PER). Christina Muccini, Douglastown, N.Y., lost bronze playoff.

Women's +52kg
1, N. Poirier (CAN); 2, Tracey Day (USA/Selden, N.J.); 3T. L. How (AHO) and L. Silvera (URU).

Men's -66kg
1, P. Torres (CUB); 2, S. Gavrelof (ARG); 3T, C. Espaja (COL) and H. Niebe (AHO). William Chadrow, Seattle, Wash., lost bronze play-off.

Men's +66kg
1, J. Vilela Gay (CUB); 2, J. Strohmeier (PER); 3T, Dustin Baldis (USA/Manor, Pa.) and J. Barreto (AHO).

Men's -80kg
1, N. Hernandez Cuni (CUB); 2, D. Tesoro (ARG); 3T, Tommy Hood, Jr. (USA/W. COlumbia, S.C.) and A. Leyto (AHO).

Men's +80kg
1, E. Obispo (AHO); 2, A. Rossi (ARG); 3T, B. Cartagena (PUR) and A. Oliverira (BRA). Doug Selchan, Pittsburgh, Pa., lost in first round.

Men's Open
1, J. Gomez (BRA); 2, L. Montano Garcia (CUB); 3T, E. Albino (PUR) and R. Pietersz (AHO). Hiroshi Allen, Monroe, La., lost in quarterfinals.

PELOTA

Fronton 30m Men
1, MEX; 2, ARG; 3, CUB.

Handball Trinq.
1, MEX; 2, CUB; 3, VEN.

Fronton Men's Individual 30 meters
1, MEX; 2, VEN; 3, CUB.

Fronton Pairs Trinq.
1, MEX; 2, VEN; 3, CUB.

Fronton Women's 30 meters
1, MEX; 2, CUB; 3, ARG.

RACQUETBALL

Women's Singles
1, Michelle Gould, (USA/Boise, Idaho); 2, Cheryl Gudinas, (USA/Lisle, Ill.); *3, Robin Levine (USA/Sacramento, Calif.); 4, Carol McFetridge, (CAN), (*PASO rules do not allow one country to sweep medals. Fourth-place finisher awarded bronze medal.)

Men's Singles
1, John Ellis, (USA/Stockton, Calif.); 2, Mike Bronfeld, (USA/Sacramento, Calif.); *3, Derek Robinson, (USA/Muncie, Ind.); 4, Sherman Greenfeld, (CAN), (*PASO rules do not allow one country to sweep medals. Fourth-place finisher awarded bronze medal.)

Women's Doubles
1. USA, (Jackie Gibson/San Diego, Calif., and Joy MacKenzie/San Diego, Calif.); 2, CAN, (Vicky Shanks Brown and Debbie Hope Ward); 3, MEX (Guadalupe Torres and Rosy Torres).

Men's Doubles
1. USA, (Sudsy Monchik/Staten Island, N.Y., and Tim Sweeney/Chicago, Ill.); 2, CAN, (Chris Brumwell and Jacques Demers); 3. VEN (Fabian Balmori and Jorge Hirsekorn).

Women's Team
1, USA, (Michelle Gould/Boise, Idaho; Cheryl Gudinas/Lisle, Ill.;

1995 Pan American Games Results

Robin Levine/Sacramento, Calif.; Jackie Gibson/San Diego, Calif.; Joy MacKenzie/San Diego, Calif.); 2. CAN; 3. MEX.

Men's Team

1, USA (Mike Bronfeld/Sacramento, Calif.; John Ellis/Stockton, Calif.; Derek Robinson/Muncie, Ind.; Sudsy Monchik/Staten Island, N.Y.; Tim Sweeney/Chicago, Ill.); 2. CAN; 3. VEN.

ROLLER SKATING

Speed, Road — Women's 500 meters

1, Lina Zapata, (COL), 58.80; 2, Heather Laufer, (USA/Kansas City, Mo.); 3, Gypsy Lucas, (USA/ Lewisville, Texas).

Speed, Road — Men's 500 meters

1, Tony Muse, (USA/Des Moines, Iowa), 47.51; 2, Julian Fernandez, (COL); 3, Sergio McCargo, (ARG).

Speed, Road — Women's 1,500 meters

1, Heather Laufer, (USA/Kansas City, Mo.), 3:17.81; 2, Andrea Gonzalez, (ARG); 3, Eva Richardson, (ARG).

Speed — Men's 1,500 meters

1, Derek Parra, (USA/Dover, Del.), 2:31.060; 2, Jorge Botero, (COL); 3, Chad Hedrick, (USA/ Spring, Texas).

Women's 5,000-meter road

1, Cheryl Ezzell, (USA/Spring, Texas), 9:13.66; 2, Rosana Sastre, (ARG); 3, Marcela Caceres, (CHI).

Men's 10,000-meter road

1, Chad Hedrick, (USA/Spring, Texas), 17:22.22; 2, Martin Escobar, (ARG); 3, Jose Botero, (COL).

Women's 300 meters

1, Nora Vega, (ARG), 31.315; 2, Gypsy Lucas, (USA/ Lewisville,Texas), 31.460; 3, Lina Zapapta, (COL), 31.77; 4, Vicci King, (USA/Puyallup, Wash.), 32.259.

Men's 300 meters

1, Derek Parra, (USA/Dover, Del.), 29.535; 2, Tony Muse, (USA/ Des Moines, Iowa), 29.564; 3, Sergie McCarge, (ARG), 29.791.

Women's 10,000-meter elimination

1, Cheryl Ezzell, (USA/Spring, Texas), 19:26.72; 2, Marcela Cazeres, (CHI); 3, Natalia Martinez, (ARG). 6, Heather Laufer, (USA/ Kansas City, Mo).

Men's 20,000-meter elimination

1, Chad Hedrick, (USA/Spring, Texas), 39:13.01; 2, Jorge Botero, (COL); 3, Derek Parra, (USA/Dover, Del.).

Women's 300-meter sprint

1, Gypsy Lucas, (USA/Lewisville, Texas), 30.140; 2, Nora Vega, (ARG), 30.149; 3, Heather Laufer, (USA/Kansas City, Mo.), 30.508.

Men's 300-meter sprint

1, Tony Muse, (USA/Des Moines, Iowa), 27.600; 2, Derek Parra, (USA/Dover, Del.), 2.010; 3, Sergio McCargo, (ARG), 28.167.

Women's 10,000-meter elimination race

1, Vicci King, (USA/Puyallup, Wash.), 16:03.95; 2, Rosana Sastre, (ARG); 3, Marcela Caceres, (CHI).

Men's 20,000-meter elimination race

1, Derek Parra, (USA/Dover, Del.); 2, Jorge Botero, (COL); 3, Chad Hedrick, (USA/Spring, Texas).

Men's 500 meters

1, Tony Muse, (USA/Des Moines, Iowa), 50.210; 2, Derek Parra, (USA/Dover, Del.); 3, Adrian Victor Villegas, (ARG).

Women's 500 meters

1, Heather Laufer, (USA/Kansas City, Mo.), 52.590; 2, Gypsy Lucas, (USA/Lewisville, Texas); 3, Nora Vega, (ARG).

Men's 10,000-meter points race

1, Chad Hedrick, (USA/Spring, Texas), 18:23.3; 2, Jorge Botero, (COL); 3, Martin Escobar, (ARG). 7, Jimmy Weiderhold, Honey Brook, Pa.

Women's 5,000-meter points race

1, Rosana Sastre, (ARG), 9:29.030; 2, Vicci King, (USA/Puyallup, Wash.); 3, Isabel Henao, (COL). 6, Theresa Cliff, Cedar Springs, Mich.

Women's 1,500 meters

1, Isabel Henao, (COL), 3:17.920; 2, Rosana Sastre, (ARG); 3, Cheryl Ezzell, (USA/Spring, Texas).

Men's 1,500 meters

1, Julian Fernandez, (COL), 3:05.410; 2, Tony Muse, (USA/Des Moines, Iowa); 3, Adrian Villegas, (ARG).

Women's 5,000-meter relay

1, ARG (Sastre, Vega, Gonzalez), 8:47.16; 2, CHI (Aburto, Caceres, Castro); 3, COL (Escobar, Henao, Gutierrez). 4, USA (Cheryl Ezzell, Houston, Texas; Vicci King, Cheyenne, Wyo.; Heather Laufer, Kansas City, Mo.)

Men's 10,000-meter relay

1, USA (Tony Muse/Des Moines, Iowa, Derek Parra/Dover, Del., Chad Hedrick/Spring, Texas), 16:28.01; 2, COL (Botero, Fernandez, Yepes); 3, ARG (Escobar, McCargo, Villegas).

Men's Marathon, 42 kilometers

1, Derek Parra, (USA/Dover, Del.); 2, Chad Hedrick, (USA/Spring, Texas); 3, Guillermo Trinaroli, (ARG).

Women's Marathon, 21 kilometers

1, Marcela Carceras, (CHI); 2, Rosana Sastre, (ARG); 3, Cheryl Ezzell, (USA/Spring, Texas).

ARTISTIC

Dance

1, USA, (Lisa Frida/Double Oak, Texas, and Tim Patten/Taunton, Mass.), 2, CAN, (Sally Geen/Keith Hickman); 3, ARG, (Monica Lazzerini/Marcelo Porce).

Men's Freestyle Singles

1, Eric Anderson, (USA/El Cajon, Calif.); 2, Edwin Guevara, (COL); 3, Heath Medeiros, (USA/ Westport, Mass.).

Women's Singles Freestyle

1, Dezera Salas, (USA/Goleta, Calif.); 2, Canela Emede, (ARG); 3, Maria Rodriguez, (ARG).

Men's Artistic Figures

1, Steven Findlay, (USA/Farmington Hills, Mich.); 2, Ernesto Tamagnon, (ARG); 3, Jason Moreton, (CAN).

Women's Artistic Figures

1, April Dayney, (USA/Maumee, Ohio); 2, Jennifer Rodriguez, (USA/Miami, Fla.); 3, Carolina Pogliano, (ARG).

Freestyle Pairs

1, ARG, (Flavio Fissolo/Gabriela Mugica); 2, USA, (Shawn Coover, Kinzer, Pa./Jennifer Denton, /Howell, N.J.); 3. USA, (Brian Richardson/Wildomar, Calif., Amy York/Yorba Linda, Calif.).

ROLLER HOCKEY

1, ARG, BRA 3, COL;. 4, USA, (Berard/Elk Gorve, Calif; Randy Erickson/Bremerton, Wash; Jeff Gibson/Bremerton, Wash; Nicholas Grassia/Woodbury, N.J.; Shane Hayden/Colorado Springs, Colo.; David Jones/Wolfforth, Texas; Michael Knowles/Gibbsboro, N.J.; Aaron Lee/Poulsbro, Wash.; Taylor Sisson/Waxahcie, Texas; Mike Stevenson/Bremerton, Wash.).

> USA Results (2-2)
> ARG 5, USA 0
> BRA 5, USA 3
> USA 7, CAN 1
> COL 4, USA 2 (bronze medal game)

ROWING

Lightweight Men's Single Sculls

1, Osmani Martin, (CUB), 7:14.79; 2, Adam Oliver, (ESA), 7:17.09; 3, James Brambell, (CAN), 7:17.66; 6, Ross Flemer, (USA), 7:30.64.

Lightweight Women's Single Sculls

1, Maria Garisoain, (ARG), 9:20.80; 2, Wendy Wiebe, (CAN), 9:30.65; 3, Andrea Bradstret, (MEX), 9:35.81; 4, Lindsay Burns, (USA/Big Timber, Mont.), 9:44.66.

Men's Single Sculls

1, Sergio Fernandez, (ARG), 6:03.43; 2, Cyrus Beasley, (USA/Atlanta, Ga.), 6:14.81; 3, Leonides Same Sanchez, (CUB), 6:23.65.

Women's Single Sculls

1, Silken Laumann, (CAN), 8:34.09; 2, Ruth Davidon, (USA/Baltimore, Md.), 8:46.63; 3, Maria Garisoain, (ARG), 8:54.70.

Men's Double Sculls

1, ARG, 7:23.17; 2, BRA, 7:32.63; 3, CAN, 7:34.46; 4, USA (David Gleeson/Milwaukee, Wis.; Jason Gailes/Dighton, Mass.), 7:35.90.

Women's Double Sculls
1, CAN, 7:57.95; 2. USA, (Michelle Knox Zaloom/Annapolis, Md.; Andrea Thies/Irvington, N.Y.), 8:05.80; 3, CUB, 8:22.73.

Lightweight Men's Double Sculls
1, USA, (Barry Klein/Grand Rapids, Mich., Christopher Schulten/Guilford, Conn.), 6:33.94; 2, CUB, 6:38.98; 3, CAN, 6:40.95.

Lightweight Women's Double Sculls
1, ARG, 8:06.13; 2, USA, (Barbara Spitz/Philadelphia, Pa.; Elizabeth Gordon/S. Hadley, Mass.), 8:10.54; 3, MEX, 8:17.50.

Men's Quadruple Sculls
1, ARG, 5:51.73; 2, USA, (David Gleeson/Milwaukee, Wis., Jason Gailes/Dighton, Mass.; Brian Jamieson/Livingston, N.J.; Tim Young/Moorestown, N.J.), 5:55.17; 3, CUB, 6:03.00.

Women's Quadruple Sculls
1, CUB, 6:39.83; 2, USA, (Ruth Davidon/Baltimore, Md.; Cathy Symon/Washington, D.C.; Julia Chilicki/Somers, Conn.; Lindsay Burns/Big Timber, Mont.), 6:43.34; 3, ARG. *Note: Canada won the event, however, one of its participants failed the drug test.*

Lightweight Men's Quadruple Sculls
1, CUB, 6:36.54; 2, USA, (Jeffrey Pfaendtner/Grosse Point, Mich.; Ed Hewitt/Ventnor, N.J.; William Carlucci/Rye Brook, N.Y.; Michael Dreher/Durham,N.H.), 6:39.62; 3, MEX, 6:43.73.

Lightweight Women's Quadruple Sculls — Exhibition Event
1, USA, (Molly Brock/Sacramento, Calif.; Lisa Schlenker/Lake Oswego, Ore.; Andrea Bonaccorsi/ Augusta, Ga.; Barbara Byrne/ Princeton, N.J.), 6:48.73 ; 2, ARG, 6:58.03.

Men's Pair without Coxswain
1, USA, (Don Smith/N. Tonawonda, N.Y.; Fred Honebein/Laguna Niguel, Calif.), 6:41.19; 2, ARG, 6:47.75; 3, BRA, 6:49.01.

Women's Pair without Coxswain
1, USA, (Mary McCagg/Kirkland, Wash., Betsy McCagg/Kirkland, Wash.), 7:33.92; 2, CUB, 7:51.89; 3, ARG, 7:57.81.

Lightweight Men's Pair without Coxswain
1, USA, (Chris Kerber/Collingswood, N.J.; Andrew Finch/Boston, Mass.), 7:38.50; 2, CAN, 7:52.58; 3, MEX, 7:52.58.

Lightweight Women's Pair without Coxswain
1, USA, (Ellen Minzner/Lawrence, Mass.; Christine Smith/Darien, Conn.), 7:42.30; 2, MEX, 8:04.88; 3, ARG, 8:10.59.

Men's Pair with Coxswain
1, CUB, 8:08.34; 2, USA, (Chris Swan/Old Saybrook, Conn.; Tom Murray/Buffalo, N.Y.; Peter Cipollone/Ardmore, Pa.), 8:11.33; 3, ARG, 8:19.18.

Lightweight Men's Four without Coxswain
1, USA, (Kane Larin/Newtown, Conn.; John Velyvis/N. Adams, Mass.;Greg Klingsporn/Morristown, N.J.;Jonathan Moss/Tenafly, N.J.), 6:13.66; 2, CAN, 6:14.07; 3, GUA, 6:17.64.

Men's Four without Coxswain
1, USA, (Jamie Koven/Green Village, N.J.; Jon Brown/New York City, N.Y.; Bob Kaehler/Huntington, N.Y.; Sean Hall/Arlington, Va.), 6:36.80; 2, CAN, 6:39.84; 3, CUB, 6:48.31.

Men's Four with Coxswain
1, USA, (Steven Segaloff/New Haven, Conn.; Jeff Klepacki/Kearny, N.J.; Tom Murray/Buffalo, N.Y.; Chris Swan/Old Saybrook, Conn.; Jim Neil/Buffalo, N.Y.), 6:15.86; 2, CAN, 6:16.37; 3, CUB, 6:18.75.

Lightweight Men's Eight
1, USA, (Peter Cipollone/Ardmore, Pa.; Steve Gantz/McLean, Va.; John Velyvis/N. Adams. Mass.; David Collins/Thousand Oaks, Calif.; Steve Robinson/Arlington, Va.; Kane Larin/Newtown, Conn.; Jonathan Moss/Tenafly, N.J.; Ed Grose/Juneau, Alaska, Tom Grace/Dallas, Texas), 6:24.70; 2, ARG, 6:27.76; 3, CUB, 6:34.58.

Men's Eight
1, USA, (Steven Segaloff/New Haven, Conn.; Jeff Klepacki/Kearny, N.J., Jamie Koven/Green Village, N.J.; Jon Brown/New York, N.Y., Don Smith/N. Tonawonda, N.Y., Bob Kaehler/Huntington, N.Y.; Chip McKibben/Balboa Island, Calif.; Fred Honebein/Laguna Niguel, Calif., Sean Hall/Arlington, Va.), 5:39.80; 2, CAN, 5:44.24; 3, CUB, 5:47.19.

SHOOTING

Men's Trap
(out of 200 possible points)
1, Lance Bade (USA/Ridgefield, Wash.), 143 (119 + 24) 2, Bret Erickson, (USA/Bennington, Neb.), 142 (119 + 23; shoot-off: 1). 3, George Leary, (CAN), 142 (120 + 22; shoot-off: 0). 4, Brian Ballard, (USA/Coto de Caza, Calif.), (117 +).

Men's Trap Team
1, USA (Lance Bade, Ridgefield, Wash.; Bret Erickson, Bennington, Neb.; Brian Ballard, Coto de Caza, Calif.), 355. 2, CAN, 339. 3, COL 334.

Men's Double Trap
(top six out of 200 possible points; others out of 150)
1, Alex Gyori, (CAN), 177 (131 + 46). 2, Kirk Reynolds, (CAN), 176 (133 + 43). 3.*, Rodney Boll, (CAN), 174 (132 + 42). 4., Steve Puls, (USA/Cushing, Okla.), 172 (125 + 47); Bret Erickson, (USA/ Bennington, Neb.), 122.

Women's Double Trap - Exhibition Only
(out of 160 possible points)
1, Terry Wentzel, (USA/Cincinnati, Ohio), 131 (99 + 32). 2, Susan Nattrass, (CAN), 123 (91 + 32). 3, Deena Julin, (USA/Omaha, Neb.), 114 (84 + 30). 4, Shari LeGate (Aiken), (USA/Peyton, Colo.), 106 (78 + 28).

Men's Double Trap Team
1, CAN, 397. 2, USA (Steve Puls, Cushing, Okla.; Lance Bade, Ridgefield, Wash.; Bret Erickson, Bennington, Neb.), 374. 3, PER, 370.

Running Target 30 + 30
(top eight out of 709 possible points; others out of 600)
1, Atila Solti, (GUA), 676.8 (580 + 96.8). 2, Lonn Saunders, (USA/ Billings, Mont.), 666.7 (568 + 98.7). 3, Andre Torres, (COL), 665.4 (565 + 100.4). 5, Mike Johnson, (USA/Norman, Okla.), 661.4 (567 + 94.4). 9, Adam Saathoff, (USA/Hereford, Ariz.), 560.

Individual Center Fire Pistol
1. Dan Iuga, (USA/Colorado Springs, Colo.), 581. 2. Julio Almeida, (BRA), 580. 3. Ed Suarez, (USA /Minneapolis, Minn.), 579. 11. Darius Young, (USA/Grangeville, Idaho), 567.

Team Center Fire Pistol
1. USA (Dan Iuga, Colorado Springs, Colo., Ed Suarez, Colorado Springs, Colo.; Darius Young, Grangeville, Idaho), 1,726. 2, BRA, 1,716. 3. ARG, 1,703.

Men's Free Rifle Prone
(top three out of 709 possible points; others out of 600)
1, Rob Harbison, (USA/Fallston, Md.), 693.5 (591 + 102.5). 2, Bruce Meredith, (ISV), 692.0 (591 + 103.0; shoot-off: 10.6). 3, Michel Dion, (CAN), 692. 0 (591.0 + 101.0; shoot-off: 10.5). 10, Bob Foth, (USA/ Colorado Springs, Colo.), 584. 15, Web Wright, (USA/Annapolis, Md.), 581.

Women's Standard Rifle 3x20
(out of 709 possible points)
1, Deena Wigger, (USA/Colorado Springs, Colo.), 662.7 (568 + 94.7). 2, Sharon Bowes, CAN, 655.4 (564 + 91.4). 3, Wanda Jewell, (USA/Great Falls, Mont.), 654.7 (562 + 92.7). 6, Ann-Marie Pfiffner, (USA/Dubuque, Iowa), 648.5 (555 + 93.5).

Men's Free Rifle 3x40
(out of 1309 possible points)
1, Ricardo Rusticucci, (ARG), 1248.0 (1154 +94.0). 2, David Johnson, (USA/Hampton, Va.), 1247.3 (1148 + 99.3). 3, Bob Foth, (USA/ Colorado Springs, Colo.), 1243.8 (1149 + 94.8). 8, Web Wright, (USA/Annapolis, Md.), 1221.9 (1127 + 94.9).

Men's Air Rifle (out of 709 possible points)
1, Ken Johnson (USA/Marshfield, Mass.), 690.1 (588 +102.1). 2, J. Senacal, (CAN), 687.7 (589 + 98.7). 3, Glenn Dubis (USA/Bethel Park, Pa.), 685.7 (586 + 99.7). 6, Rob Harbison (USA/Fallston, Md.), 680.9 (579 + 101.9).

Women's Air Rifle (out of 509 possible points)
1, Elizabeth Bourland, (USA/Wichita Falls, Texas), 491.7 (392 + 99.7). 2, Amelia Rosa Fournel, (ARG), 491.0 (389 + 102.0). 3,

Ann-Marie Pfiffner (USA/Dubuque, Iowa), 490.0 (389 + 101.0). 4, Kate Kelemen (USA/Livonia, Mich., 488.3 (388 + 100.3).

Men's Air Rifle Team
1, USA (Ken Johnson, Marshfield, Mass.; Glenn Dubis, Bethel Park, Pa.; Rob Harbison, Fallston, Md.), 1753. 2, CAN, 1746. 3, CUB, 1743.

Women's Air Rifle Team — exhibition
1, USA (Elizabeth Bourland/Wichita Falls, Texas; Ann-Marie Pfiffner/Dubuque, Iowa; Kate Kelemen, / Livonia, Mich.), 1169. 2, ARG, 1141. 3, CUB, 1139.

300-Meter Standard Rifle 3x40
(out of 600 possible points)
1, Rob Harbison (USA/Fallston, Md..), 588*. 2, Bob Foth (USA/ Colorado Springs, Colo.), 582. #3. Steve Goff (USA/Leavenworth, Kan.), 581. 4, Edgardo Peragallo, (ARG), 554.

300-Meter Standard Rifle 3x40 Teams - exhibition
1, USA (Rob Harbison, Fallston, Md..; Bob Foth, Colorado Springs, Colo.; Steve Goff, Leavenworth, Kan.), 1751. 2, ARG, 1656. 3, BRA, 1574.

Women's Standard Rifle Prone
(out of 600 possible points)
1, Cecilia Zeid Jan, (ARG), 584. 2, Elizabeth Bourland, (USA/ Wichita Falls, Texas), 579. 3, Kate Kelemen, (USA/Livonia, Mich.), 578. 8, Wanda Jewell, (USA/Great Falls, Mont.), 571.

Women's Standard Rifle Prone Team - exhibition
1, ARG, 1729. 2, USA (Elizabeth Bourland/Wichita Falls, Texas; Kate Kelemen/Livonia, Mich,; Wanda Jewell/Great Falls, Mont.), 1728. 3, CUB, 1714.

300-Meter Free Rifle 3x40 (out of 1200 possible points) -- 1, Ken Johnson (USA/ Marshfield, Mass.), 1169*. 2, Steve Goff (USA/ Leavenworth, Kan.), 1163. 3, Ricardo Rusticucci, (ARG), 1154. 5, Bob Foth (USA/Colorado Springs, Colo.), 1143.

300-Meter Free Rifle Prone (out of 600 points) -- 1, Web Wright (USA/Annapolis, Md.), 592. 2, Angel Velarte, (ARG), 591. 3, Bob Foth (USA/Colorado Springs, Colo.), 590. 4, Glenn Dubis (USA/ Bethel Park, Pa.), 583.

Standard Pistol (out of 600 possible points)
1, Rafael Alberto Olivera, (ARG), 570. 2, Don Nygord, (USA/ LaCrescenta, Calif.), 569. 3, Ben Amonette (USA/Radford, Va.), 566. 10, Terry Anderson (USA/Dallas, Texas), 556.

Standard Pistol Team
1, USA (Don Nygord/LaCrescenta, Calif.; Ben Amonette/Radford, Va., Terry Anderson/Dallas, Texas), 1691. 2, ARG, 1684. 3, CUB, 1683.

Men's Air Pistol
(out of 709 possible points)
1, Norbelis Barzaga Vazquez, (CUB), 672.3 (577 + 95.3). 2, Ben Amonette, (USA/Radford, Va.), 670.5 (574 + 93.5). 3, Vicente De La Cruz, (CUB), 668.7 (571 + 97.7). 4, Patrick Saunders (USA/Simi, Calif.), 668.6 (571 + 97.6). 5, Don Nygord, (USA/LaCrescenta, Calif.), 667.1 (568 + 99.1).

Women's Air Pistol
(top three out of 509 possible points; others out of 400).
1, Connie Petracek, (USA/Nashville, Tenn.), 475.1 (379 + 96.1). 2, Lorena Guado, (ARG), 472.5 (377 + 95.5). 3, Lilia Perez, CUB, 470.9 (371 + 99.9). 11, Libby Callahan (USA/Upper Marlboro, Md.), 369. 13, Sandra Utasy (USA/Los Angeles, Calif.), 363.

Men's Air Pistol Team
1, USA (Ben Amonette/Radford, Va.; Patrick Saunders/ Simi, Calif.; Don Nygord/LaCrescenta, Calif.), 1713. 2, CUB, 1710. 3, CAN, 1704.

Women's Air Pistol Team
1, USA (Connie Petracek/Nashville, Tenn.; Libby Callahan/ Upper Marlboro, Md.; Sandra Utasy/Los Angeles, Calif.), 1111. 2, COL, 1109. 3, ARG, 1109.

Women's Sport Pistol
(top eight out of 709 possible points, others out of 600)
1, Connie Petracek, (USA/Nashville, Tenn.), 685.8 (585 + 100.8). 2, Margarita Tarradel, (CUB), 675.4 (577 + 98.4). 3, Lorena Guardo,

(ARG), 671.1 (575 + 96.1). 8, Roxane Conrad, (USA/Sandpoint, Idaho), 667.3 (569 + 98.3). 9, Libby Callahan, (USA/Upper Marlboro, Md.), 569.

Women's Sport Pistol Team
1, USA (Connie Petracek/Nashville, Tenn.; Roxane Conrad/ Sandpoint, Idaho, Libby Callahan/Upper Marlboro, Md.), 1723. (Pan American Games record) 2, CUB, 1714. 3, ARG, 1699.

Men's Free Pistol (out of 709 possible points)
1, Abel Juncosa, (CUB), 652.6 (556 + 96.6). 2, Ben Amonette, (USA/ Radford, Va.), 651.1 (555 + 96.1). 3, Jodson Edington, (BRA), 650.9 (561 + 99.9). 5, Daryl Szarenski, (USA/Saginaw, Mich.), 646.8 (551 + 95.8). 8, Darius Young, (USA/Grangeville, Idaho), 640.0 (546 + 94).

Men's Free Pistol Team
1, CUB, 1655. 2, USA (Ben Amonette/Radford, Va.; Daryl Szarenski/ Saginaw, Mich; Darius Young/ Grangeville, Idaho), 1652. 3, GUA, 1621.

Rapid Fire Pistol (out of 709 possible points) -- 1, Guido Arbona, (CUB), 682.6 (582 + 100.6). 2, Dan Iuga (USA/Colorado Springs, Colo.), 681.5 (583 + 98.5). 3, Bernardo Tobar, (COL), 680.3 (580 + 100.3) 5, Terry Anderson (USA/Dallas, Texas), 677.9 (578 + 99.9). 6, John McNally, (USA/Heath, Texas), 676.9 (579 + 98.9).

Rapid Fire Pistol Team -- 1, USA (Dan Iuga/Colorado Springs, Colo.; John McNally/Heath, Texas; Terry Anderson/Dallas, Texas), 1739. 2, CUB, 1737. 3, ARG, 1717.

Running Target Mixed Runs
(out of 400 possible points)
1, Andres Torres, (COL), 382. 2, Jose Hernandez, (CUB), 380. 3, Lonn Saunders, (USA/Billings, Mont.), 379. 5, Koby Holland, (USA/Dillon, Mont.), 373. 6, Adam Saathoff, (USA/ Hereford, Ariz.), 370.

Skeet (top six out of 150, others out of 125) -- 1, Sevenano Puldon Reyes, (CUB), 146 (121 + 25). 2, Juan Rodriguez Marti, (CUB), 144 (121 + 23; shoot-off: 14) 3, J.F. Nixon, (CAN), 144 (121 +23; shoot-off: 12). 4, Bill Roy (USA/Alamogordo, N.M.), Mt. Sterling, Ill., 144 (121 +23; shoot-off: 9). 5, Mike Schmidt (USA/Eagan, Minn.), 144 (119 + 25; shoot-off: 0). 28, Ken Corwin, (USA/Grove City, Ohio), 108.

Skeet Team -- 1, CUB, 361. 2, CAN, 352. 3, GUA, 352. 4, USA (Bill Roy/ Alamogordo, N.M.; Mike Schmidt/Eagan, Minn.; Ken Corwin/Grove City, Ohio), 348.

 # Bronze medal awarded to fourth-place finisher by PASO rules.

SOCCER

1, ARG; 2, MEX; 3, COL; 12, USA, (Imad Baba/Dallas, Texas; Gregg Berhalter/Tenafly, N.J.; Jeffrey Cassa/Livonia, Mich.; Donovahnn DuHaney/San Diego, Calif.; Brian Johnson/Livermore, Calif.; Andrew Lewis/New Providence, N.J.; Brian Maisonneuve/Warren, Mich.; Matt McKeon/Florissant, Mo.; Obi Moneme/ Crestline, Ohio; Jason Moore/Atlanta, Ga.; Clint Peay/Columbia, Md.; Brandon Pollard/Richmond, Va.; George Pope/High Point, N.C.; Damian Silvera/Huntington, N.Y.; Robert Smith/Wilmington, Del.; Cuauhtemoc Suarez/Mount Pleasant, S.C.; Zach Thornton/ Edgewood, Md.; Anthony Wood,/Rockville, Md.).

USA Results (0-3)
ARG 3, USA 0
PAR 2, USA 0
HON 2, USA 0

SOFTBALL

Men
1, CAN; 2, USA, (Raymond Atkinson/Kent, Wash.; William Boyer/ Enumclaw, Wash.; David Boys/Decatur, Ill.; Daniel Cronkright/ Midland, Mich.; Richard Dohogne/Kelso, Mo.; Vondel Edgar/ Decatur, Ill.; Steven Kerian/Sioux City, Iowa; Adolphus Meacham/ Mitcheville, Md.; Peter Meredith/Salt Lake City, Utah; Mitch Munthe/Modesto, Calif.; Scott Plangger/Bloomington, Ill.; Alan Rebling/Fairfield, Iowa; Shawn Rychcik/Salamanca, N.Y.; Steve

Schott/Kelso, Mo.; Todd Schultz/Webberville, Mich.; Peter Turner/Stockton, Calif.; Tim Wahl/Grayland, Wash.; Michael White/Sioux City, Iowa); 3, CUB.

USA Results (14-2)
USA 4, CUB 0
USA 5, VEN 1
USA 1, CAN 0 (10 inn.)
USA 4, DOM 3
USA 10, ARU 0 (5 inn.)
USA 8, ARG 0
USA 10, GUA 0 (5 inn.)
USA 3, CUB 2
CAN 5, USA 4 (10 inn.)
USA 10, VEN 0
USA 4, DOM 0
USA 11, ARU 1 (6 inn.)
USA 7, ARG 0
USA 7, GUA 1
USA 4, CAN 1
CAN 2, USA 1 (gold medal game)

Women

1, USA, (Patricia Benedict/Wyoming, Mich.; Jennifer Condon/Las Vegas, Nev.; Sheila Cornell/Diamond Bar, Calif.; Debbie Doom/Pasadena, Calif.; Patricia Dufficy/Stratford, Conn.; Michele Granger/ Anchorage, Alaska; Lori Harrigan/Las Vegas, Nev.; Barbara Jordan/Agoura, Calif.; Jill Justin/ Oaklawn, Ill.; Kim Maher/Fresno, Calif.; Martha O'Kelley/Las Vegas, Nev.; Susie Parra/Scottsdale, Ariz.; Dorothy Richardson/Los Angeles, Calif.; Ann Rowan/Phoenix, Ariz.; Karen Sanchelli/W. Columbia, S.C.; Julie Smit/Glendora, Calif.; Michele Smith/Redding, Calif.; Shelly Stoke/Fresno, Calif.); 2, PUR; 3, CUB.

USA Results (12-0)
USA 6, PUR 0
USA 11, AHO 0 (5 inn.)
USA 6, CAN 1
USA 1, CUB 0
USA 11, ARG 0 (5 inn.)
USA 14, PUR 0 (5 inn.)
USA 10, AHO 0 (6 inn.)
USA 2, CAN 0
USA 2, CUB 0
USA 11, ARG 0 (5 inn.)
USA 5, CUB 0
USA 4, PUR 0 (gold medal game)

SQUASH

Men's Singles

1, Gary Waite, (CAN); 2, Jonathan Power, (CAN); 3T, Jamie Crombie, (CAN) and Sabir Butt (CAN); #5, Federico Usandizaga (ARG); 6, Mark Talbott (USA/Wakefield, R.I.); 9, Marty Clark (USA/McLean, Va.); 11T, Tony Brettkelly (USA/San Francisco, Calif.); Mohsen Mir (Portland, Ore.), elim. in first round.

Women's Singles

1, Heather Wallace, (CAN); 2. Demer Holleran, (USA/Wynnewood, Pa.); 3. Ellie Pierce, (USA/New York, N.Y.) and Alicia McConnell, (USA/Brooklyn, N.Y); 9, Shabana Khan, (USA/Seattle, Wash.).

Men's Team

1, CAN; 2. ARG; 3T. BRA and USA (Marty Clark/McLean, Va., Tony Brettkelly/San Francisco, Calif., Mark Talbott/Wakefield, R.I., Mohsen Mir/Portland, Ore.).

Women's Team

1, CAN; 2, USA (Ellie Pierce/New York, N.Y., Demer Holleran/Wynnewood, Pa, Alicia McConnell/Brooklyn, N.Y., Shabana Khan, Seattle, Wash.); 3T, BRA and COL.

Grand Champion

1, CAN; 2, USA, (Marty Clark/McLean, Va., Tony Brettkelly/San Francisco, Calif., Mark Talbott/ Wakefield, R.I., Mohsen Mir/Portland, Ore, Ellie Pierce/New York, N.Y., Demer Holleran/

Wynnewood, Pa, Alicia McConnell/Brooklyn, N.Y., Shabana Khan, Seattle, Wash.); 3, BRA.

received bronze medals according to PASO rules

SWIMMING

Men's 50-Meter Freestyle

1, Fernando De Queiroz, (BRA), 22.65; 2, Bill Pilczuk, (USA/Cape May Point, N.J.), 22.71; 3, Tom Jager, (USA/Tijeras, N.M.), 22.75.

Women's 50-Meter Freestyle

1, Angel Martino (USA/Americus, Ga.), 25.40 (Pan American Games record, old record, 26.01, Kristen Topham, (CAN), 1991); 2, Shannon Shakespeare, (CAN), 26.19; 3, Andrea Leigh Moody, (CAN), 26.54; 4, Lindsey Farella (USA/Elk Grove Village, Ill.), 26.63.

Men's 100-Meter Freestyle

1, Gustavo Franco Borges, (BRA), 49.31, (Pan American Games record, old record, 49.48, Gustavo Franco Borges, (BRA), 1991); 2, Jon Olsen, (USA/Jonesboro, Ark.), 49.39; 3, Fernando De Quieroz, (BRA), 49.79; 4, Gary Hall, (USA/Phoenix, Ariz.), 50.08.

Women's 100-Meter Freestyle

1, Angel Martino, (USA/Americus, Ga.), 55.62; 2, Amy Van Dyken (USA/Englewood, Colo.), 55.92; 3, Marianne Limpert, (CAN), 56.80.

Men's 200-Meter Freestyle

1, Gustavo Franca Borges, (BRA), 1:48.49; 2, Greg Burgess (USA/Jacksonville, Fla.), 1:51.69; 3, Josh Davis (USA/San Antonio, Texas), 1:51.92.

Women's 200-Meter Freestyle

1, Cristina Teuscher (USA/New Rochelle, N.Y) 2:01.49; 2, Marianne Limpert, (CAN), 2:02.05; 3, Dady Vincent (USA/Gainesville, Fla.), 2:03.37.

Men's 400-Meter Freestyle

1, Josh Davis (USA/San Antonio, Texas), 3:55.59; 2, Luis Carneiro Silva, (BRA), 3:56.33; 3, Jon Sakovich, (USA/Gainesville, Fla.), 3:57.37.

Women's 400-Meter Freestyle

1, Brooke Bennett, (USA/Brandon, Fla.), 4:11.78; 2, Cristina Teuscher (USA/New Rochelle, N.Y.), 4:13.97. 3, Katie Brambley, (CAN), 4:18.74.

Women's 800-Meter Freestyle

1, Trina Jackson (USA/Jacksonville, Fla.), 8:35.42; 2, Brooke Bennett (USA/Brandon, Fla.), 8:47.99; 3, Alicia Barrancos, (ARG), 8:49.57.

Men's 1,500-Meter Freestyle

1, Carlton Bruner (USA/Atlanta, Ga.), 15:13.90; 2, Luiz Eduardo Carneiro Silva, (BRA), 15:19.53; 3, Ryan Cox, (USA/Mission Viejo, Calif.), 15:37.28.

Men's 100-Meter Backstroke

1, Jeff Rouse (USA/Fredericksburg, Va.), 54.74 (Pan American Games record, old record, 1:02.18, Sylvia Poll, (CRC), 1987); 2, Tripp Schwenk (USA/Sarasota, Fla.), 55.60; 3, Rodolfo Falcon Cabrera, (CUB), 56.13.

Women's 100-Meter Backstroke

1, Barbara Bedford (USA/Etna, N.H.), 1:01.71 (Pan American Games record, old record, 1:02.18, Sylvia Poll (CRC) 1987); 2, Kristy Heydanek (USA/Midland, Mich.), 1:03.10; 3, Fabiola Pulga Molina, (BRA), 1:04.85.

Men's 200-Meter Backstroke

1, Brad Bridgewater (USA/Dallas, Texas), 2:00.79; 2, Rodolfo Falcon Cabrera, (CUB), 2:00.98; 3, Rogerio Aoki Romero, (BRA), 2:01.13; 6, Greg Burgess (USA/Jacksonville, Fla.), 2:02.13.

Women's 200-Meter Backstroke

1, Barbara Bedford, (USA/Mt. Etna, N.H.), 2:12.98 (Pan American Games record, old record, 2:13.65, Katie Welch, USA, 1987); 2, Rachel Joseph, (USA/Springfield, Ore.), 2:14.74; 3, Joanne Malar, (CAN), 2:16.67.

Men's 100-Meter Breaststroke

1, Seth van Neerden (USA/Wilmington, Del.), 1:02.48; 2, Jon T. Cleveland, (CAN), 1:03.01; 3, Tyler Mayfield (USA/Las Vegas, Nev.) 1:03.17.

1995 Pan American Games Results

Women's 100-Meter Breaststroke
1, Lisa Flood, (CAN), 1:10.36; 2, Guylaine Cloutier, (CAN), 1:10.44; 3, Kelli King Bednar (USA/Tucson, Ariz.), 1:11.44; 4, Buffy Nelson (USA/Americus, Ga,.), 1:12.19.

Men's 200-Meter Breaststroke
1, Seth van Neerden (USA/Wilmington, Del.), 2:16.08; 2, Eric Namesnik (USA/Butler, Pa.), 2:17.70; 3, Curtis Myden, (CAN), 2:19.00.

Women's 200-Meter Breaststroke
1, Lisa Flood, (CAN), 2:31.33; 2. Guylaine Cloutier, (CAN), 2:32.42; 3, Anita Nall (USA/ Hummelstown, Pa.) 2:32.83; 4, Alison Fealey (USA/Cincinnati, Ohio) 2:35.02.

Men's 100-Meter Butterfly
1, Mark Henderson (USA/Fort Washington, Md.), 54.11; 2, Becca Piccini, (BRA), 54.63; 3, Brian Alderman (USA/Santa Barbara, Calif.) 54.75.

Women's 100-Meter Butterfly
1, Amy Van Dyken (USA/Englewood, Colo.), 1:00.71; 2, Rose Franco, (BRA), 1:01.67; 3, Angie Wester-Krieg (USA/Campbell, Calif.), 1:02.79.

Men's 200-Meter Butterfly
1, Nelson Mora Molina, (VEN), 200.38; 2, Tom Malchow (USA/St. Paul, Minn.), 2:00.49; 3, Andre Castro Teixeira, (BRA), 2:01.95; 6, Joey Rossetti (USA/Santa Rosa, Calif.), 2:06.26.

Women's 200-Meter Butterfly
1, Trina Jackson (USA/Jacksonville, Fla.), 2:12.37; 2, Michelle Griglione (USA/Alexandria, Va.), 2:14.94; 3, Maria Pereyra, (ARG), 2:18.52.

Men's 200-Meter Individual Medley
1, Curtis Myden, (CAN), 2:01.70; 2, Greg Burgess (USA/Jacksonville, Fla.), 2:03.62; 3, Eric Namesnik (USA/Butler, Pa.), 2:03.70.

Women's 200-Meter Individual Medley
1, Joanne Malar, CAN, 2:15.66 (Pan American Games record, old record, 2:16.11, Tracy Caulkins, (USA), 1979); 2, Marianne Limpert, (CAN), 2:16.13; 3, Alison Fealey (USA/Cincinnati, Ohio), 2:17.14; 4, Catherine Fox (USA/Shawnee Mission, Kan.), 2:19.04.

Men's 400-Meter Individual Medley
1, Curtis Myden, (CAN), 4:18.55; 2, Eric Namesnik (USA/Butler, Pa.) 4:19.00; 3. Lian Mull (USA/East Lansing, Mich.) 4:26.32.

Women's 400-Meter Individual Medley
1, Joanne Malar, (CAN), 4:43.64; 2, Alison Fealey (USA/Cincinnati, Ohio), 4:48.31; 3, Jenny Kurth (USA/Toledo, Ohio), 4:57.24.

Men's 400-Meter Freestyle Relay
1, USA (Gary Hall/Phoenix, Ariz., Tom Jager/Tijeras, N.M., Josh Davis/San Antonio, Texas, Jon Olsen/Jonesboro, Ark.), 3:18.60 (Pan American Games record, old record, 3:19.97, USA, 1991); 2, BRA, 3:20.33; 3, VEN, 3:25.43.

Women's 400-Meter Freestyle Relay
1, USA (Angel Martino/Americus, Ga., Amy Van Dyken/Englewood, Colo., Lindsey Farella/Elk Grove Village, Ill., Cristina Teuscher/New Rochelle, N.Y.), 3:44.71 (Pan American Games record, old record, 3:45.82, USA, 1979); 2, CAN, 3:49.26; 3, BRA, 3:52.85.

Men's 800-Meter Freestyle Relay
1, USA (Jon Olsen/Jonesboro, Ark.; Josh Davis/San Antonio, Texas; Ryan Berube/Tequesta, Fla.; Greg Burgess/Jacksonville, Fla.) 7:21.61 (Pan American Games record, old record,); 2, BRA, 7:28.70; 3, MEX, 7:39.56.

Women's 800-Meter Freestyle Relay
1, USA (Trina Jackson/Jacksonville, Fla., Dady Vincent/ Gainesville, Fla., Catherine Fox/Shawnee Mission, Kan., Cristina Teuscher/New Rochelle, N.Y.), 8:07.30; 2, CAN, 8:08.25; 3, ARG, 8:27.87.

Men's 4x100-Meter Medley Relay
1, USA (Jeff Rouse/Fredericksburg, Va.; Seth van Neerden/Wilmington, Del.; Mark Henderson/Fort Washington, Md.; Jon Olsen/Jonesboro, Ark.), 3:41.24; 2, BRA, 3:43.93; 3, CAN, 3:45.10.

Women's 4 x 100-Meter Medley Relay
1, USA (Barbara Bedford/Etna, N.H.; Kelli King Bednar/Tucson, Ariz.; Amy Van Dyken/Englewood, Colo.; Angel Martino/ Americus, Ga.), 4:08.17 (Pan American record, old record, 4:12.51, USA, 1991); 2, CAN, 4:19.06; 3, BRA, 4:22.08.

SYNCHRONIZED SWIMMING

Solo
1, Becky Dyroen-Lancer, (USA/San Jose, Calif.), 97.090. 2, Karen Clark, (CAN), 95.595. 3, Maria Elena Giusti, (VEN), 95.381. 4, Liliam Leal Ramirez, (MEX), 91.226. 5, Paula Oliveira, (BRA), 88.750. 6, Maria Ximena Pardinas Boivin, (URU), 85.385. 7, Julieta Yelin, (ARG), 85.190.

Duet
1, USA, (Becky Dyroen-Lancer/San Jose, Calif. and Jill Sudduth/ Morgan Hill, Calif.), 96.451; 2, CAN; 3, MEX.

Team
1, USA, (Suzannah Bianco/San Jose, Calif.; Tammy Cleland/Walnut Creek, Calif.; Becky Dyroen-Lancer/San Jose, Calif.; Jill Savery/Concord, Calif.; Nathalie Schneyder/Walnut Creek, Calif.; Heather Simmons/Santa Clara, Calif.; Jill Sudduth/Morgan Hill, Calif.; Margot Thein/Spring Valley, Calif.), 96.164. 2, CAN, 95.059. 3, MEX, 92.997.

TABLE TENNIS

Men's Team
1. BRA; 2. USA, (Jim Butler/Iowa City, Iowa; Chi-Sun Chui/Winchester, Mass.; Derek May/Augusta, Ga.; Sean O'Neill/McLean, Va.); 3. CAN.

Women's Team
1. CAN; 2. USA, (Tawny Banh/Bac Lieu, Vietnam; Diana Gee/Burlingame, Calif.; Wei Wang/Beijing, China; Lily Wip/Canton, China). 3. CUB.

Men's Singles
1, Hugo Hoyama (BRA); 2, Claudio Kano (BRA); 3T, Jim Butler (USA/Augusta, Ga.) and Horatio Pintea (CAN). Sean O'Neill, McLean, Va., and Chi-Sun Chui, San Mateo, Calif., elim. first round; Derek May, Augusta, Ga., elim. pool play.

Women's Singles
1, Lijuan Geng (CAN); 2, Lily Yip (USA/Metuchen, N.J.); 3T, Diana Gee (USA/San Carlos, Calif.) and Barbara Chiu (CAN). Wei Wang, Pasadena, Calif., and Tawny Banh, Alhambra, Calif., lost in quarterfinals.

Men's Doubles
1, Hoyama/Kano, (BRA). 2, Tabachnik/Paradela, (ARG). 3, Pintea/Ng, (CAN) and Salamanca/Papic, CHI. Jim Butler, (USA/Augusta, Ga.)., and Sean O'Neill, (McLean, Va.), elim. quarterfinals. Derek May, (Augusta, Ga.), and Chi-Sun Chui, (San Mateo, Calif.)., elim. first round.

Women's Doubles
1, Geng/Chiu, (CAN). 2, Tepes Cancino/Diaz Caro, (CHI). 3T Tawny Banh, (USA/Alhambra, Calif.), and Wei Wang, (Pasadena, Calif) and Macaya/Rodriguez, (CHI). Lily Yip (USA/Metuchen, N.J.), and Diana Gee, (San Carlos, Calif.), elim. quarterfinals.

Mixed Doubles Final
1, Geng/Pintea, (CAN); 2, Arado de Armas/Armas Nunez, (CUB); 3T, Chiu/Ng, (CAN) and Kawai /Kosaka, (BRA); USA (Sean O'Neill, McLean, Va., and Diana Gee, San Carlos, Calif.), elim. quarterfinals. USA, (Derek May, Augusta, Ga., and Tawny Banh, Alhambra, Calif.), elim. quarterfinals. USA, (Jim Butler, Augusta, Ga., and Lily Yip, Metuchen, N.J., elim. second round);. USA, (Chi-Sun Chui, San Mateo, Calif, and Wei Wang, Pasadena, Calif., elim. first round).

TAEKWONDO

Women's Finweight (under 43 kg)
1, Liliana Aguirre (MEX); 2, Yanet Puerto Pimentel, (CUB); 3T, Yoon Kyung Chaing, (USA/Rancho Palos Verdes, Calif.), and Patricia Santana, (ARG).

1995 Pan American Games Results

Women's Flyweight (47 kg)
1, Betsy Ortiz, (PUR); 2, Yunia Cruz, (CUB); 3T, Miranda Hall Mitchell, (CAN), and Mariela Valenzuela, (ARG). DNC - Sharon Hough, Wayne, Mich., injured.

Women's Bantamweight (51 kg)
1, Eliana Maria Pantoja, (VEN); 2, Roxanne Forget, (CAN); 3T, Cheryl Ann Sankar, (TRI) and Patricia Mariscal, (MEX). Diane Murray, Rocklin, Calif., lost in first round.

Women's Featherweight (55 kg)
1, Oly Pardon, (VEN). 2, Alejandra Chancalay, (ARG). 3T, Yenny Conreras Loyol, (CUB), and Veronica Marquez Montes, (MEX). Kelly Thorpe, Edmond, Okla., lost in first round.

Women's Lightweight (60 kg)
1, Zonayi Mayan Ramos, (CUB); 2, Elizabeth Evans, (USA/Marysville, Wash.); 3T, Paola Raquel Viveros, (PAR), and Maria Carolina Bejarano, (COL).

Women's Welterweight (65 kg)
1, Vanina Paola Sanchez, (ARG); 2, Lazara Cristina Zayas, (CUB); 3T, Dana Martin, (USA/Norwalk, Calif.), and Cecilia Malpica Herrera, (VEN).

Women's Middleweight (70 kg)
1, Monica Del Real Jaime, (MEX); 2, Natalia Susana Acciaio, (ARG); 3T, Ursula Guimet, (PER), and Marcia King, (CAN). Barbar Kunkel, Federal Way, Wash., lost in first round.

Women's Heavyweight (over 70 kg)
1, Adriana Carmona, (VEN); 2, Robin Umphrey, (USA/Irvine, Calif.); 3T, Domonique Bosshart, (CAN), and Yudelkis Pupo Aviles, (CUB).

Men's Finweight (under 50 kg)
1, Carlos Ayala Yee, (MEX); 2, Luis Eliseo Pinto, (ARG); 3T, Reinaldo Ross Chivas, (CUB), and Sherland Flores, (TRI). Steven Lopez, Sugarland, Texas, lost in first round.

Men's Flyweight (54 kg)
1, Ruben Palafox, (MEX); 2, Sammy Pejo, (USA/Colorado Springs, Colo.); 3T, Manuel Chamorro, (ARG), and Alexei Pedroso, (CUB).

Men's Bantamweight (58 kg)
1, Rafael Zuniaga, (MEX); 2, Yosuany Perez, (CUB); 3T, Pedro Carazo, (CRC), and Fernando Jose Luna, (ARG). Steve Lee, Colorado Springs, Colo., eliminated in quarterfinals.

Men's Featherweight (65 kg)
1, Alejandro Hernando, (ARG); 2, Clay Barber, (USA/Colorado Springs, Colo); 3T, Agostinho Do Santos, (CAN), and Armando Valladares Herr, (CUB).

Men's Lightweight (70 kg)
1, Roberto Lazaro Abreu, (CUB); 2, Quidio Quero, (VEN); 3T, Sergio Curdenas, (CHI), and Sebastian Zapata, (ARG). Jean Lopez, Colorado Springs, Colo., lost in quarterfinals.

Men's Welterweight (76 kg)
1, Arturo Utria Estevez, (CUB); 2, Mario Guillermo Bonilla, (GUA); 3T, Stephen Goodwin, (CAN), and Regillio Iwan Goedhoop, (SUR). Garth Colley, Indianapolis, Ind., lost in quarterfinals.

Men's Middleweight (83 kg)
1, Victor Estrada Garibay, (MEX); 2, Alfredo Martin Peterson, (PAN); 3T, Milton Casiro, (COL), and Anibal Cintron Torres, (PUR). Peter Bardatsos, Woodside, N.Y., lost in quarterfinals.

Men's Heavyweight (over 83 kg)
1, Nelson Saenz Miller, (CUB); 2, Lucio Aurelio De Frietas, (BRA); 3T, Julio Vasquez, (DOM), and Paris Amani, (USA/Colorado Springs, Colo.).

TEAM HANDBALL

Men
1, CUB; 2, BRA; 3, ARG; 4, USA, (Derek Brown/Atlanta; Greg Caccia/Bayshore, N.Y.; Dave DeGraaf/Lansing, Mich.; Denny Fercho/Camarillo, Calif.; Tom Fitzgerald/Brooklyn, N.Y.; Darrick Heath/Hempstead, N.Y.; Danny Hennessy/Floral Park, N.Y.; Michael Jones/Union Gap, Wash.; John Keller/Toledo, Ohio; Robert Mayfield/Statesville, N.C.; Rick Oleksyk/Gulf Breeze, Fla.; Steven Penn/ Brevard, N.C.; Matt Ryan/Miller Place, N.Y.; Mark

Schmocker/Riggenberg, Switzerland; Chip Van Os/ Houston; Kevin Withrow/Thousand Oaks, Calif.)

> USA Results (2-4)
> USA 27, PAR 13
> USA 26, PUR 9
> BRA 27, USA 21
> CUB 20, USA 15
> ARG 20, USA 16
> ARG 22, USA 13 (bronze medal match)

Women
1, USA, (Dawn Allinger, Bozeman, Mont.; Sharon Cain, San Antonio, Texas; Kim Clarke, Tulsa, Okla.; Laura Coenen, Peyton, Colo.; Kristin Danihy, Lawton, Okla.; Lisa Eagen, Harlan, Iowa; Laurie Fellner, Appleton, Wis.; Jennifer Horton, Dover, N.J.; Tami Jameson, Minneapolis; Toni Jameson, Minneapolis; Dannette Leininger, Kaillia, Hawaii; Dawn Marple, Salem, Ohio; Pat Neder, Waukesha, Wis.; Carol Peterka, Little Falls, Minn.; Tonia Stubbs, Warren, Ohio; Chryss Watts, Bristol, Conn.); 2, CAN; 3, BRA.

> USA Results (5-0)
> USA 22, ARG 12
> USA 30, CUB 26
> USA 29, BRA 26
> USA 17, CAN 16
> USA 24, CAN 18 (gold medal game)

TENNIS

Men's Singles
1, Hernan Gumy (ARG) def. Javier Frana (ARG) 7-6, 7- 6; 3T, Jimy Szymanski (VEN) and Nicholas Pereira (VEN); Don Johnson (USA/Chapel Hill, N.C) elim. quarterfinals; J.J. Jackson (USA/Chapel Hill, N.C.) elim. third round.

Women's Singles
1, Florencia Labat (ARG) def. Ann Grossman (USA/Grove City, Ohio), 6-3, 6-3; 3T, Chandra Rubin (USA/Lafayette, La.) and Bettina Fulco (ARG).

Men's Doubles
1, Javier Frana/Luis Lobo (ARG) def. Juan Bianchi/Nicolas Pereira (VEN) 6-4, 6-1; 3T, Ricardo Herrera/Mario Pacheco (MEX) and Gabriel Silberstein/Sergio Cortez (CHI); Don Johnson and J.J. Jackson (USA/Chapel Hill, N.C.) elim. quarterfinals.

Women's Doubles
1, Mercedes Paz/Patricia Tarabini (ARG) def. Chanda Rubin (USA/Lafayette, La.)/Ann Grossman (Grove City, Ohio), 6-3, 6-2; 3T. Lucila Becerra/Xochiti Escobedo (MEX) and Andrea Vieira/Luciana Tella (BRA).

Mixed Doubles
1, USA, (Shaun Stafford/Gainesville, Fla. and Jack Waite/Waukesha, Wis.) def. Patricia Tarabini/Luis Lobo (ARG) 1-6, 6-2, 6-4; 3T, VEN, (Jimy Szymanski /Ninfa) and CUB, (Aramndo Perez/Belkis Rodriguez).

Men's Nation Cup Results
1, ARG; 2, URU; 3T, USA (Don Johnson/Chapel Hill, N.C. and J.J. Jackson/Chapel Hill, N.C.) and CHI.

Women's Nation Cup Results
1, ARG; 2, CHI; 3T, USA (Shaun Stafford/Gainesville, Fla. and Erika DeLone/Lincoln, Mass.) and BRA.

TRIATHLON

Men's Individual
1, Leandro Macedo (BRA), 1:52.14; 2. Mark Daryl Bates (CAN), 1:51.36; 3. Oscar Saul Galindez (ARG), 1:52.10; 4. Ricardo Glez Davila (MEX), 1:52.24; 5. Andrew Carlson (USA/Boulder, Colo.), 1:53.33. 12. Nate Llerandi, Schaumburg, Ill. DNS - Timothy DeBoom (USA/Denver, Colo.).

Men's Team
1, MEX, (Ricardo Glez Davila and Carlos Probert); 2, ARG, (Oscar Saul Galindez and Ariel Oscar Garrigo); 3, USA, (Andrew Carlson/Boulder, Colo. and Nathaniel Llerandi/Boulder, Colo.).

1995 Pan American Games Results

Women's Individual
1, Karen Smyers (USA/Lincoln, Mass.), 2:04.52; 2, Kristie Otto (CAN), 2:07.17. 3, Fiona Dorothy Cribb (CAN), 2:08.14; 4, Gail Laurence-Garcia (USA/currently resides in Belgium), 2:08.51; 5, Maria Luisa Martinez (MEX), 2:09.42. DNS - Kelly Kwiatkowski (USA/Hollywood, Fla.)

Women's Team
1, CAN, (Kristie Otto and Fiona Dorothy Cribb); 2, USA, (Karen Smyers/Lincoln, Mass. and Gail Laurence-Garcia/Denver, Colo.). 3, MEX, (Maria Luisa Martinez and M. Del Carmen Ochoa Duran).

VOLLEYBALL

Men
1, ARG; 2, USA, (Lloy Ball/Woodburn, Ind.; Duncan Blackman/Santa Monica, Calif.; Bob Ctvrtlik/ Long Beach, Calif.; Dan Greenbaum/Rolling Hills, Calif.; Brent Hilliard/Dana Point, Calif.; Bryan Ivie/Manhattan Beach, Calif.; Dan Landry/San Diego; Dexter Rogers/St. Petersburg, Fla.; Pat Sinclair/Walnut Creek, Calif.; Tom Sorensen/Racine, Wis.; Chris Underwood/Los Angeles; Ethan Watts/Tulsa, Okla.; 3. CUB.

> USA Results (2-2)
> USA 3, PUR 0 (15-12, 15-12, 15-5)
> ARG 3, USA 0 (15-6, 15-12, 15-8)
> USA 3, CUB 2 (16-14, 10-15, 15-13, 11-15, 16-14)
> ARG 3, USA 2 (15-6, 15-11, 13-15, 8-15, 20-18) (gold medal match)

Women
1, CUB; 2, USA, (Tara Cross-Battle/Long Beach, Calif.; Lori Endicott/Springfield, Mo; Kristin Klein/ Pacific Palisades, Calif.; Tammy Liley/Westminster, Calif.; Alicia Mills-Potzin/Houston, Texas; Bev Oden/Irvine, Calif.; Elaina Oden/Irvine, Calif.; Danielle Scott/Baton Rouge, La.; Samantha Shaver/ Mountain View, Calif.; Teee Williams/Long Beach, Calif.; Elaine Youngs/El Toro, Calif.; Yoko Zetterlund/San Francisco); 3. CAN.

> USA Results (5-2)
> USA 3, ARG 0 (15-6, 15-10, 15-3)
> USA 3, BRA 0 (15-2, 15-0, 15-4)
> USA 3, CAN 0 (15-8, 15-7, 15-6)
> USA 3, PER 0 (15-2, 15-4, 15-1)
> CUB 3, USA 1 (15-7, 8-15, 16-14, 15-7)
> USA 3, CAN 0 (15-5, 15-5, 15-3)
> CUB 3, USA 1 (15-10, 13-15, 15-11, 15-4) (gold medal match)

WATER POLO

Men
1, USA, (Gavin Arroyo, Orange, Calif.; Chris Duplanty, Honolulu; Kirk Everist, Orinda, Calif.; Dan Hackett, Irvine, Calif.; Chris Humbert, Lodi, Calif.; Colin Keely, Orinda, Calif.; Doug Kimbell, Orange, Calif.; Kyle Kopp, San Bernadino, Calif.; Craig Kredell, Seal Beach, Calif; Jeremy Laster, San Clemente, Calif.; Rick McNair, Pt. Richmond, Calif.; Chris Oeding, Newport Beach, Calif.; Alex Rousseau, Santa Monica, Calif.); 2. BRA; 3, CUB.

> USA Results (5-0)
> USA 10, BRA 5
> USA 14, MEX 5
> USA 17, ARG 4
> USA 12, CAN 3
> USA 16, BRA 5 (gold medal match)

WATER SKIING

Women's Slalom
1, Deena Mapple (USA/Orlando, Fla.), 5 @ 12 meters; 2, Susi Graham (CAN), 2.5 @ 12 meters. 3, Kim DeMacedo (CAN), 4 @ 13 meters. 9T. (prelims) Sherri Slone, Baton Rouge, La.

Men's Slalom
1, Carl Roberge (USA/Winter Springs, Fla.), 5 @ 12 meters; 2, Kreg Llewellyn (CAN), 4 @ 12 meters; 3, Jorge Renosto (ARG), 3 @ 12

meters. 13T. (prelims) Sammy Duvall, Windermere, Fla.

Women's Tricks
1, Tawn Larsen (USA/Tampa, Fla.), 6,650 points; 2, Kim DeMacedo (CAN), 6,020 points; 3, Lorena Botana (ARG), 5,390 points; 5, Sherri Slone (USA/Baton Rouge, La.), 4,690 points. 9. (prelims) Deena Mapple, Orlando, Fla.

Men's Tricks
1, Jaret Llewellyn (CAN), 9,960 points; 2, Tory Baggiano (USA/Montgomery, Ala.), 8,920 points; 3, Sergio Font (MEX), 8,800 points.

Women's Jumping
1, Sherri Slone (USA/Baton Rouge, La.), 137 feet; 2, Kim DeMacedo (CAN), 134 feet; 3, Andrea Gaytan (MEX), 109 feet.

Men's Jumping
1, Jaret Llewellyn (CAN), 197 feet; 2, Carl Roberge (USA/Winter Springs, Fla.), 195 feet; 3, Sammy Duvall (USA/Windermere, Fla.), 192 feet. **Team**
1, CAN, 8,426.2 points; 2, USA (Tory Baggiano, Montgomery, Ala., Sammy Duvall, Windermere, Fla., Carl Roberge, Winter Springs, Fla.), 7,741.8 points; 3, ARG, 6,900.2 points. 98.2 points.

WEIGHTLIFTING

54 kg Snatch
1, Jesus Aparicio, (COL), 110.0 kg (242 1/2 lbs.) (Pan American Games record); 2, Orlando Vasquez, (NIC), 107.5 kg (236 3/4 lbs.); 3, Juan Fernandez, (COL), 105.0 (231 1/4 lbs.). No USA participant.

54 kg Clean-and-Jerk
1, Juan Fernandez, (CUB), 142.5 kg (314 lbs.) (Pan American Games record); 2, Jesus Aparicio, (CUB), 142.5 kg (314 lbs.); 3, Orlando Vasquez, (NIC), 135 kg (297 1/2 lbs.). No USA participant.

54 kg Total
1, Jesus Aparicio, (CUB), 252.5 kg (556 1/2 lbs.) (Pan American Games record); 2, Juan Fernandez, (COL), 247.5 kg (545 lbs.); 3, Orlando Vasquez, (NIC), 242.5 kg (534 lbs.). No USA participant.

59 kg Snatch
1. William Vargas, (CUB), 127.5 kg (281 lbs.); 2. Bryan Jacob (USA/Alpharetta, Ga.), 120 kg (264 1/2 lbs.); 3. Roger Berrio, (COL), 112.5 kg (248 lbs.).

59 kg Clean-and-Jerk
1. William Vargas, (CUB), 157.5 kg (347 lbs.); 2. Bryan Jacob (USA/Alpharetta, Ga.), 147.5 kg (325 lbs.); 3. Jonny Gonzales, (COL), 142.5 kg (314 lbs.).

59 kg Total
1. William Vargas, (CUB), 285 kg (628 1/4 lbs.); 2. Bryan Jacob (USA/Alpharetta, Ga.), 267.5 kg (589 1/2 lbs.); 3. Roger Berrio, (COL), 252.5 kg (556 1/2 lbs.).

64 kg Snatch
1. Idalberto Aranda, (CUB), 127.5 kg (281 lbs.); 2. Gustavo Majauskas, (ARG), 125 kg (275 1/2 lbs.); 3. Marcelo Gandolfo, (ARG), 122.5 kg (270 lbs.).

64 kg Clean-and-Jerk
1. Idalberto Aranda, (CUB), 175 kg (385 3/4 lbs.) (Junior World Record); 2. Gustavo Majauskas, (ARG), 160 kg (352 1/2 lbs.); 3. Henry Blanco, (VEN), 157.5 kg (347 lbs.).

64 kg Total
1. Idalberto Aranda, (CUB), 302.5 kg (666 3/4 lbs.); 2. Gustavo Majauskas, (ARG), 285 kg (628 1/4 lbs.); 3. Henry Blanco, (VEN), 277.5 kg (611 3/4 lbs.).

70 kg Snatch
1. Rafael Gomez, (CUB), 137.5 kg (303 lbs.); 2. Tim McRae (USA/Daytona Beach, Fla.), 137.5 kg (303 lbs.); 3. Gabriel Lemme, (ARG), 135 kg (297 1/2 lbs.); 4. Eyne Acevedo, Columbia, 135 kg (297 1/2 lbs.). (Note: Gomez wins tie for gold medal with McRae because his bodyweight is lighter, 69.50 kg to 70.00 kg; Lemme wins tie for bronze medal with Acevedo because his bodyweight is lighter, 69.30 kg to 69.80 kg).

70 kg Clean-and-Jerk
1. Rafael Gomez, (CUB), 175 kg (385 3/4 lbs.); 2. Eyne Acevedo, (COL), 175 kg (385 3/4 lbs.); 3. Jose Medina, (VEN), 172.5 kg (380 1/

1995 Pan American Games Results

4 lbs.); 4. Tim McRae (USA/Daytona Beach, Fla.), 172.5 kg (380 1/4 lbs.). (Note: Gomez wins tie for gold medal with Acevedo because his bodyweight is lighter, 69.5 kg to 69.8 kg; Medina wins tie for bronze medal with McRae because his bodyweight is lighter, 69.9 kg to 70.00 kg).

70 kg Total
1. Rafael Gomez, (CUB), 312.5 kg (688 3/4 lbs.); 2. Eyne Acevedo, (COL), 310 kg (683 1/4 lbs.); 3. Tim McRae (USA/Daytona Beach, Fla.), 310 kg (683 1/4 lbs.) (Note: Acevedo wins tie for silver medal with McRae because of lower bodyweight, 69.80 kg to 70.00 kg).

76 kg Snatch
1. Pablo Lara, (CUB), 155 kg (341 1/2 lbs.); 2. Alvaro Velazco, (COL), 147.5 kg (325 lbs.); 3. Walter Llerena, (ECU), 142.5 kg (314 lbs.) 6. Dave Santillo (USA/Runnemede, N.J.), 132.5 kg (292 lbs.).

76 kg Clean-and-Jerk
1. Pablo Lara, (CUB), 207.5 kg (457 1/4 lbs.) (world record; old record: 205 kg, set by Lara Nov. 25, 1993 in Ponce, Puerto Rico; 2. Alvaro Velazco, (COL), 180 kg (396 3/4 lbs.); 3. Dave Santillo (USA/Runnemede, N.J.), 170 kg (374 3/4 lbs.) (Note: Lara also lifted a world record of 205.5 kg on his second attempt before lifting 207.5 on his third)

76 kg Total
1. Pablo Lara, (CUB), 362.5 kg (799 lbs.); 2. Alvaro Velazco, (COL), 327.5 kg (722 lbs.); 3. Walter Llerena, (ECU), 310 kg (683 1/4 lbs.); 5. Dave Santillo (USA/Runnemede, N.J.), 302.5 kg (666 3/4 lbs.).

83 kg Snatch
1. Julio Luna, (VEN), 150 kg (330 1/2 lbs.); 2. Gustavo Stasiukiewicz, (ARG), 145 kg (319 1/2 lbs.); 3. Eduardo Moreno, (CUB), 145 kg (319 1/2 lbs.); 7. Dean Goad (USA/Sumner, Wash.), 137.5 kg (303 lbs.).

83 kg Clean-and-Jerk
1. Julio Luna, (VEN), 192.5 kg (424 1/4 lbs.); 2. Eduardo Moreno, (CUB), 190 kg (418 3/4 lbs.); 3. Erlyn Mena, (COL), 182.5 kg (402 1/4 lbs.); 4. Dean Goad (USA/Sumner, Wash.), 180 kg (396 3/4 lbs.).

83 kg Total
1. Julio Luna, (VEN), 342.5 kg (755 lbs.); 2. Eduardo Moreno, (CUB), 335 kg (738 1/2 lbs.); 3. Erlyn Mena, (COL), 322.5 kg (710 3/4 lbs.); 5. Dean Goad (USA/Sumner, Wash.), 317.5 kg (699 3/4 lbs.).

91 kg Snatch
1. Carlos Hernandez, (CUB), 165 kg (363 3/4 lbs.); 2. Dario Lecman, (ARG), 162.5 kg (358 lbs.); 3. Tom Gough (USA/Fairfax, Calif.), 155 kg (341 1/2 lbs.).

91 kg Clean-and-Jerk
1. Dario Lecman, (ARG), 202.5 kg (446 1/4 lbs.); 2. Carlos Hernandez, (CUB), 200 kg (440 3/4 lbs.); 3. Tom Gough (USA/Fairfax, Calif.), 192.5 kg (424 1/4 lbs.).

91 kg Total
1. Carlos Hernandez, (CUB), 365 kg (804 1/2 lbs.); 2. Dario Lecman, (ARG), 365 kg (804 1/2 lbs.); 3. Tom Gough (USA/Fairfax, Calif.), 347.5 kg (766 lbs.) (American record; old record of 345 kg set by Paul Fleschler, May 9, 1993, in Peoria, Ill.) (Note: Hernandez and Lecman had identical bodyweights of 90.20 kg, so Hernandez was awarded the gold medal because he performed the total first).

99 kg Snatch
1. Pete Kelley (USA/St. Joseph, Mo.), 157.5 kg (347 lbs.); 2. Claudio Henschke, (ARG), 155 kg (341 1/2 lbs.); 3. Edmilson Dantas, (BRA), 155 kg (341 1/2 lbs.); 4. Rich Schutz (USA/River Forest, Ill.), 155 kg (341 1/2 lbs.) (Note: Three-way tie for silver medal was broken on bodyweight, with Henschke weighing 97.4 kg, Dantas 98.2 kg and Schutz 98.7 kg).

99 kg Clean-and-Jerk
1. Alexander Fonseca, (CUB), 200 kg (440 3/4 lbs.); 2. Claudio Henschke, (ARG), 190 kg (418 3/4 lbs.); 3. Edmilson Dantas, (BRA), 187.5 kg (413 1/4 lbs.); 4. Pete Kelley (USA/St. Joseph, Mo.), 187.5 kg (413 1/4 lbs.); 7. Rich Schutz (USA/River Forest, Ill.), 182.5 kg (402 1/4 lbs.) (Note: Dantas was awarded the bronze medal over Kelley because his bodyweight was lower, 98.20 kg to 98.80 kg).

99 kg Total
1. Alexander Fonseca, (CUB), 352.5 kg (777 lbs.); 2. Claudio Henschke, (ARG), 345 kg (760 1/2 lbs.); 3. Pete Kelley (USA/St. Joseph, Mo.), 345 kg (760 1/2 lbs.); 5. Rich Schutz (USA/River Forest, Ill.), 337.5

kg (744 lbs.) (Note: Henschke was awarded the silver medal over Kelley because his bodyweight was lower, 97.40 kg to 98.80 kg).

108 kg Snatch
1. Osvaldo Bango, (CUB), 165 kg (363 3/4 lbs.); 2. Wes Barnett (USA/St. Joseph, Mo.), 165 kg (363 3/4 lbs.) (American record; old record of 162.5 kg set by Barnett, April 3, 1994, in Colorado Springs, Colo.); 3. Ramon Alvarez, (PUR), 152.5 kg (336 lbs.) (Note: Bango was awarded the gold medal over Barnett because his bodyweight was lower, 101.0 kg to 107.2 kg).

108 kg Clean-and-Jerk
1. Wes Barnett (USA/St. Joseph, Mo.), 210 kg (462 3/4 lbs.) (American record; old record of 207.5 kg set by Barnett, April 3, 1994, in Colorado Springs, Colo.); 2. Osvaldo Bango, (CUB), 190 kg (418 3/4 lbs.); 3. Pedro Marin, (VEN), 190 kg (418 3/4 lbs.) (Note: Bango was awarded the silver medal over Marin because his bodyweight was lower, 101.0 kg to 107.2 kg).

108 kg Total
1. Wes Barnett (USA/St. Joseph, Mo.), 375 kg (826 1/2 lbs.) (American record; old record of 370 kg set by Barnett, April 3, 1994, in Colorado Springs, Colo.); 2. Osvaldo Bango, (CUB), 355 kg (782 1/2 lbs.); 3. Pedro Marin, (VEN), 342.5 kg (755 lbs.) (Note: Barnett set two American records in the total. After making his second snatch attempt of 207.5 kg, Barnett's total was 372.5 kg).

108+ kg Snatch
1. Mark Henry (USA/Silsbee, Texas), 177.5 kg (391 1/4 lbs.) (American record; old record of 175 kg by Henry, May 9, 1993, in Peoria, Ill.); 2. Modesto Sanchez, (CUB), 175 kg (385 3/4 lbs.); 3. Mario Martinez (USA/Salinas, Calif.), 160 kg (352 1/2 lbs.).

108+ kg Clean-and-Jerk
1. Modesto Sanchez, (CUB), 215 kg (473 3/4 lbs.); 2. Mario Martinez (USA/Salinas, Calif.), 202.5 kg (446 1/4 lbs.); 3. Mark Henry (USA/Silsbee, Texas), 192.5 kg (424 1/4 lbs.).

108+ kg Total
1. Modesto Sanchez, (CUB), 390 kg (859 3/4 lbs.); 2. Mark Henry (USA/Silsbee, Texas), 370 kg (815 1/2 lbs.); 3. Mario Martinez (USA/Salinas, Calif.), 362.5 kg (799 lbs.).

WRESTLING

Freestyle

48 kg
1, Alexis Vila, (CUB); 2, Paul Ragusa, (CAN); 3, Tim Vanni,(USA/Porterville, Calif.).

52 kg
1, Zeke Jones, (USA/Chandler, Ariz.); 2, Carlos Varela, (CUB); 3, Selwyn Tam, (CAN).

57 kg
1, Terry Brands, (USA/Iowa City, Iowa); 2, Rob Dawson, (CAN); 3, Alejandro Puerto, (CUB).

62 kg
1, Tom Brands, (USA/Iowa City, Iowa); 2, Anibal Nieves, (PUR); 3, Carlos Ortiz, (CUB).

68 kg
1, Townsend Saunders, (USA/Phoenix, Ariz.); 2, Craig Roberts, (CAN); 3, Jesus Rodriguez, (CUB).

74 kg
1, Alberto Rodriguez, (CUB); 2, David Hohl, (CAN); 3, Dave Schultz, (USA/Newtown Square, Pa.).

82 kg
1, Kevin Jackson, (USA/Ames, Iowa); 2, Luis Varela, (VEN); 3, Arriel Ramos, (CUB).

90 kg
1, Melvin Douglas, (USA/Mesa, Ariz.); 2, Evelio Suarez, (VEN); 3, Miguel Molina, (CUB).

100 kg
1, Wilfredo Morales, (CUB); 2, Mark Kerr, (USA/Syracuse, N.Y.); 3, Gavin Carrow, (CAN).

130 kg
1, Bruce Baumgartner, (USA/Cambridge Springs, Pa.); 2, Angel Amaya, (CUB); 3, Andy Borodow, (CAN).

1995 Pan American Games Results

Greco-Roman

48 kg
1, Mujaahid Maynard (USA/ Colorado Springs, Colo.); 2, Enrique Aguilar, (MEX); 3, Wilber Sanchez (CUB).

52 kg
1, Raul Martinez (CUB); 2, Shawn Sheldon, (USA/Colorado Springs, Colo.); 3, Joel medina (VEN).

57 kg
1, Dennis Hall, (US/Stevens Point, Wis.); 2, WIlliam Lara (CUB); 3, Armando Fernandez (MEX).

62 kg
1, Juan Mare (CUB); 2, Winston Santos (VEN); 3, David Zuniga, (USA/New Brighton, Minn.)

68 kg
1, Liubal Colas (CUB); 2, Andy Seras, (USA/Niskayuna, N.Y.); 3, Alberto Diaz (VEN).

74 kg
1, Filberto Azcuy (CUB); 2, Antonio Garcia (VEN); 3, Gordy Morgan, (USA/Bloomington, Minn.).

82 kg
1, Alexis Banes (CUB); 2, Jose Betancourt (PUR); 3, Dan Henderson, (USA/Huntington Beach, Calif.).

90 kg
1, Reynaldo Pena (CUB); 2, Michial Foy, (USA/Brooklyn Park, Minn.); 3, Mario Gonzales (MEX).

100 kg
1, Hector Milhan (CUB); 2, Jerry Jackson, (USA/Columbus, Ga.); 3, Emilio Suarez (VEN).

130 kg
1, Matt Ghaffari, (USA/Colorado Springs, Colo.); 2, Edwin Millet (PUR); 3, Andy Borodow (CAN).

YACHTING (Sailing)

Europe *(6 boats)*
1. Marcia Pellicano (BRA), 1-2-(3)-2-2-3-1-1-1-1; 12.75. 2. Kim Logan (USA/Miami, Fla.), 2-1-1-1-1-2-2-(2)-2-2; 13. 3. Paula Lewin (BER), 3-(5)-2-4-4-1-5-3-3-3; 27.75.

470 Men's *(5 boats)*
1. Pedro Fernandez/Angel Jimenez (CUB), 3-1-4-3-(5)-3-1-1-2- 1; 18. 2. Mike Sturman/Bob Little (USA/Newport Beach/Santa Monica, Calif.), 4-3-3-1-2-1-3-(5)-1-2; 19.25. 3. Martin Billoch/Juan Zizzi (ARG), 1-2-1-2-3-4-4-3-(5)-3; 22.5.

470 Women's *(4 boats)*
1. Penny Davis/Leigh Pearson (CAN), 1-1-(2)-2-1-1-1-1-1-DNF; 9.25. 2. Jody Swanson/Debbie Hopkins (USA/Rochester, N.Y./Ft. Wayne, Ind.), 2-(DNF)-1-1-2-2-2-2-2-1; 14.25. 3. Maria Sesto/Consuelo Monsegur (ARG), (3)-2-3-3-3-3-3-3-3- 2; 25.

J/24 Match Racing *(12 boats)*
(scores are win-loss records) 1. Paul Foerster/Rob Johnston/John Bartlett/Troy Lawson (USA/Dallas/Dallas/Austin/Austin, Texas), prelims 9-2/semis 3- 0/finals 4-0. 2. Peter Holmberg/Morgan Avery/Maurice Krug/Chris Rosenberg (ISV), prelims 9-2/semis 3-0/finals 0-4. 3. Gonzalo Campero/Francisco Campero, Santiago Morixe, Ezequiel Mendoca (ARG), prelims 9-2/semis 0-3/finals 4-1.

Laser Men's *(15 boats)*
1. Robert Scheidt (BRA), 1-1-1-2-1-1-1-1-1-(DNS); 8. 2. Santiago Lange (ARG), 2-(3)-2-1-3-3-3-3-3-2; 21.75. 3. Jason Rhodes (CAN), 4-2-3-(9)-4-5-2-2-4-4; 30. 4. Tom Lihan (USA/Fort Lauderdale, Fla.), 5-4-4-3-6-2-(7)-5-5-3; 37.

Laser Women's *(7 boats)*
1. Maria Marcone (ARG), 4-1-1-2-1-1-(4)-1-1-DNF; 14.5. 2. Jennifer Coolidge (USA/Marblehead, Mass.), 1-3-(6)-3-4-3-1-3- 2-1; 20.25. 3. Maria Krahe (BRA), 3-2-2-(7)-2-7-2-4-3-2; 27.

Lightning *(6 boats)*
1. German Schacht/Christian Herman/Albertos Gonzalez (CHI),1-3-2-(6)-3-1-5-1-1-1; 16.75. 2. Biekarck, Ficker Silva (BRA), 3-2-(6)-5-4-2-2-2-2-2; 24. 3. Diego Rudoy/Alejandro Noe, Alejandro Colla (ARG), 2-1-3- 3-1-(5)-4-5-4-4; 25.5. 3. Jim Crane/Bill Crane/

Brenda Crane (USA/Darien, Conn.), 6-6-4- 1-2-3-1-3-5-(DNF); 30.5.

Mistral Men's *(12 boats)*
1. Carlos Espinola (ARG), 1-1-1-2-1-2-2-1-1-(DNS); 10.5. 2. Mike Gebhardt (USA/Ft. Pierce, Fla.), 2-2-3-1-2-1-1-5-2- (DNS); 18.25. 3. Murray McCaig (CAN), 3-4-2-3-4-3-4-4-(8)-1; 27.75.

Mistral Women's *(7 boats)*
(one throwout) 1. Caroll-Anne Alie (CAN), 2-1-1-2-2-2-1-1-1-(DNF); 11.75. 2. Lisa Neuburger (ISV), 1-2-2-3-(4)-4-2-2-2-2; 19.75. 3. Lanee Butler (USA/Aliso Viejo, Calif.), (3)-3-3-1-1-3-3-3-3- 1; 20.25.

Snipe *(8 boats)*
1. Octavio Lorenzo/Nelido Manso (CUB), 1-1-1-3-1-3-1-12- (DNF); 12.5. 2. Ricardo Fabiani/Roberto Fabiani (URU), 2-2-4-2-3-2-5-(6)-1-1; 21.5. 3. Guillermo Parada/Gonzalo Martinez (ARG), 3-(DSQ)-2-1-4-1- 4-2-3-2; 21.5. 5. Doug Hart/Steven Stewart (USA/San Diego, Calif.), 5-(DSQ)-5- 6-5-4-2-5--3; 39.

1996 U.S. Olympic Team Roster

ARCHERY

Men (3)

Athlete, Birthdate, Birthplace, Hometown/Current Residence

Justin Huish, 1/9/75, Fountain Valley, Calif., Simi Valley, Calif./Chula Vista, Calif.

(Richard) "Butch" Johnson, 8/30/55, Worcester, Mass., Woodstock, Conn.

Rod White, 3/1/77, Sharon, Pa., Hermitage, Pa.

Women (3)

Judi Adams, 7/12/59, Phoenix, Ariz., Scottsdale, Ariz.

(Adrienne) "Janet" Dykman, 1/17/54, Monterey Park, Calif., El Monte, Calif./Chula Vista, Calif.

Lindsay Langston, 2/2/79, Modesto, Calif., Mesa, Ariz.

Team Leader: Teresa Brothers, Loveland, Ohio

Head Coach: Mike King, Grand Rapids, Mich.

Assistant Coaches: Lloyd Brown, San Diego, Calif.

Auxiliary Staff: Tim Strickland, Aurora, Ind.

ATHLETICS

Men (68)

Athlete, Birthdate, Birthplace, Hometown/Current Residence

Derrick Adkins, 7/2/70, Brooklyn, N.Y., Atlanta, Ga.

Charles Austin, 12/19/67, Bay City, Texas, San Marcos, Texas

Randy Barnes, 6/16/66, Charleston, W.Va., S. Charleston, W.Va.

Brad Barquist, 2/24/68, Portland, Ore., Seattle, Wash.

Keith Brantly, 5/23/62, Scott AFB, Ill., Scott AFB, Ill./Fort Lauderdale, Fla.

(John) Bryan Bronson, 9/9/72, Jasper, Texas, Houston, Texas, Rice

Ed Broxterman, 11/28/73, Baileysville, Kan., Manhattan, Kan.

LeRoy Burrell, 2/21/67, Philadelphia, Pa., Houston, Texas

Andrzej Chylinski, 12/5/60, New York, N.Y., Colo. Springs, Colo.

Curt Clausen, 10/9/67, Trenton, N.J., Durham, N.C.

Mike Conley, 10/5/62, Chicago, Ill., Fayetteville, Ark.

Mark Coogan, 5/1/66, New York, N.Y., Manhasset, N.Y./Boulder, Colo.

Mark Crear, 10/2/68, San Francisco, Calif., Valencia, Calif.

Mark Croghan, 1/8/68, Akron, Ohio, Columbus, Ohio

Calvin Davis, 4/2/72, Eutaw, Ala., Boston, Mass.

Marc Davis, 12/17/69, Oceanside, Calif., Portland, Ore./Boulder, Colo.

Lance Deal, 8/21/61, Riverton, Wyo., Eugene, Ore.

Jon Drummond, 9/9/68, Philadelphia, Pa., Culver City, Calif.

Steve Fritz, 11/1/67, Salina, Kan., Manhattan, Kan.

Robert Gary, 4/5/73, Chicago, Ill., Columbus, Ohio/Evanston, Ill.

Matt Giusto, 10/25/66, San Francisco, Calif., Albuquerque, N.M.

John Godina, 5/31/72, Fort Sill, Okla., Los Angeles, Calif.

Johnny Gray, 6/19/60, Los Angeles, Calif., Los Angeles, Calif.

Joe Greene, 2/17/67, Dayton, Ohio, Westerville, Ohio

Tim Harden, 1/27/74, Kansas City, Mo., Grandview, Mo.

Alvin Harrison, 1/20/74, Orlando, Fla., Salinas, Calif.

(Kerry) "Kenny" Harrison, 2/13/65, Milwaukee, Wis., Bridgeton, Mo.

Jeff Hartwig, 9/25/67, St. Louis, Mo., Jonesboro, Ark.

Robert Howard, 11/26/76, Brooklyn, N.Y., Fayetteville, Ark.

Chris Huffins, 4/15/70, Brooklyn, N.Y., Oakland, Calif.

Scott Huffman, 11/30/64, Quinter, Kan., Lawrence, Kan.

(Cottrell) "C.J." Hunter, 12/14/68, Hyde Park, N.Y., Durham, N.C.

Brian Hyde, 10/13/72, Grand Rapids, Mich., Williamsburg, Va.

Allen James, 4/14/64, Sacramento, Calif., Sacramento, Calif./LaGrange, Ga.

Allen Johnson, 3/1/71, Washington, D.C., Chapel Hill, N.C.

Lawrence Johnson, 5/7/74, Norfolk, Va., Chesapeake, Va.

Michael Johnson, 9/13/67, Dallas, Texas, Rockwell, Texas

(Robert) Bob Kempainen, 6/18/66, Minneapolis, Minn., Minnetonka, Minn.

(Robert) Bob Kennedy Jr., 8/18/70, Bloomington, Ind., Indianapolis, Ind.

(Frederick) Carl Lewis, 7/1/61, Birmingham, Ala., Houston, Texas

Michael Marsh, 8/4/67, Los Angeles, Calif., Houston, Texas

Anthuan Maybank, 12/30/69, Georgetown, S.C., Los Angeles, Calif.

Kevin McMahon, 5/26/72, San Jose, Calif., Washington, D.C.

Paul McMullen, 2/19/72, Cadillac, Mich., Ypsilanti, Mich.

Dan Middleman, 10/19/69, Brooklyn, N.Y., Raleigh, N.C.

Derek Mills, 7/9/72, Washington, D.C., Marietta, Ga.

Dennis Mitchell, 2/20/66, Havelock, N.C., Gainesville, Fla. Timothy Montgomery, 1/28/75, Gaffney, S.C., Gaffney, S.C.

Herm Nelson, 9/20/61, Renton, Wash., Pontiac, Mich.

Dan O'Brien, 7/18/66, Portland, Ore., Moscow, Idaho

Jose Parrilla, 3/31/72, Ancon, Canal Zone, Panama, Knoxville, Tenn.

Dave Popejoy, 2/15/72, San Francisco, Calif., Monte Serveo, Calif./La Jolla, Calif.

(Michael) Mike Powell, 11/10/63, Philadelphia, Pa., Rancho Cucamoga, Calif.

Tom Pukstys, 5/28/68, Glen Ellyn, Ill., Providence, R.I.

Jason Pyrah, 4/6/69, Willard, Mo., Springfield, Mo., Provo, Utah

(Harry) "Butch" Reynolds, 6/8/64, Akron, Ohio, Westerville, Ohio

Todd Riech, 10/24/70, Polson, Mont., Cloud, Calif.

Brandon Rock, 7/8/72, Las Vegas, Nev., Fayetteville, Ark./Rogers, Ark.

Jason Rouser, 3/22/70, Tucson, Ariz., Norman, Okla.

Adam Setliff, 12/19/69, El Dorado, Ariz., Houston, Texas/Seattle, Wash.

Lamont Smith, 12/11/72, Philadelphia, Pa., Houston, Texas

Jim Spivey, 3/7/60, Franklin Park, Ill., Glen Ellyn, Ill.

Dave Stephens, 2/8/62, Chico, Calif., Herndon, Va.

Eugene Swift, 9/14/64, Berkeley, Calif., Richmond, Calif./Oakland, Calif.

Anthony Washington, 1/16/66, Glascow, Mont., Aurora, Colo.

Jeff Williams, 12/31/64, Los Angeles, Calif., San Fernando, Calif.

Todd Williams, 3/7/69, Knoxville, Tenn., Knoxville, Tenn.

Cameron Wright, 11/7/72, Murphysboro, Ill., Carbondale, Ill./Creal Springs, Ill.

Team Leader: Al Baeta, Carmichael, Calif.

Assistant Team Leaders: Charlie Greene, Washington, D.C.; Edward Levy, New York, N.Y.

Head Coach: Erv Hunt, El Sobrante, Calif.

Assistant Coaches: Douglas Brown, Knoxville, Tenn.; Charles Craig, Bakersfield, Calif.; Chick Hislop, Ogden, Utah; Tony Naclerio, Rockaway, N.J.; George Williams, Raleigh, N.C.

Women (55)

Athlete, Birthdate, Birthplace, Hometown/Current Residence

Amy Acuff, 7/14/75, Port Arthur, Texas, Robstown, Texas

Valeyta Althouse, 1/7/74, Moberly, Mo., Blue Springs, Mo.

Olga Appell, 8/2/63, Duranago, Mexico, Albuquerque, N.M.

(Lenora) "Lacy" Barnes-Mileham, 12/23/64, Ridegcrest, Calif., Fresno, Calif.

(Kimberly) Kim Batten, 3/29/69, McRae, Ga., Tallahassee, Fla.

Kelly Blair, 11/24/70, Prosser, Wash., Eugene, Ore.

Tonya Buford-Bailey, 12/13/70, Dayton, Ohio, Overland Park, Kan./Champaign, Ill.

Nicole Carroll, 4/18/68, San Francisco, Calif., San Francisco, Calif.

Joetta Clark, 8/1/62, East Orange, N.J., Somerset, N.J.

Gail Devers, 11/19/66, Seattle, Wash., Bridgeton, Mo.

Cheryl Dickey, 12/12/66, Houston, Texas, Houston, Texas

Sandra Farmer-Patrick, 8/18/62, Kingston, Jamaica, Austin, Texas

Katherine Fonshell, 10/10/69, Kinsasha, Zaire, Africa, Ardmore, Pa.

Chryste Gaines, 9/14/70, Lawton, Calif., San Leandro, Calif.

Lynda Tolbert Goode, 10/3/67, Washington, D.C., Phoenix, Ariz.

(Kimberly) Kim Graham, 3/26/71, Durham, N.C., Austin, Texas

Carlette Guidry, 9/4/68, Houston, Texas, Austin, Texas

Suzy Hamilton, 8/8/68, Stevens Point, Wis., Eugene, Ore.

Sharon Hanson, 9/24/65, Lake Charles, La., Fairfax Station, Va.

Juli Speights Henner, 5/13/70, El Paso, Texas, Harrisonburg, Va.

Victoria Herazo, 6/2/59, West Palm Beach, Fla., Lilburn, Ga.

Aretha Hill, 8/14/76, Seattle, Wash., Seattle, Wash.

1996 U.S. Olympic Team Roster

D'Andre Hill, 4/19/73, Cincinnati, Ohio, Cincinnati, Ohio/Baton Rouge, La.

Vicki Huber, 5/29/67, Wilmington, Del., Eugene, Ore.

Sheila Hudson, 6/30/67, Wurzburg, Germany, Elverta, Calif./Fayetteville, Ark.

Regina Jacobs, 8/28/63, Los Angeles Calif., Oakland, Calif.

Lynn Jennings, 7/1/60, Princeton, N.J., Newmarket, N.H.

Jackie Joyner-Kersee, 3/3/62, East St. Louis, Ill., Canoga Park, Calif./Bridgeton, Mo.

Natasha Kaiser-Brown, 5/14/67, Des Moines, Iowa, Columbia, Mo.

Anne Marie Lauck, 3/7/69, Rochester, N.Y., Glen Gardner, N.J./Marietta, Ga.

Debbi Lawrence, 10/15/61, Columbus, Ind., Kenosha, Wis.

Maicel Malone, 6/12/69, Indianapolis, Ind., Gainesville, Fla.

Jearl Miles, 9/4/66, Gainesville, Fla., Gainesville, Fla.

Inger Miller, 6/12/72, Los Angeles, Calif., Altadena, Calif.

Joan Nesbit, 1/20/62, Fort Wayne, Ind., Carrboro, N.C.

(Elexa) Diana Orrange, 8/9/67, Orange, Texas, Sugar Land, Texas

Ramona Pagel, 11/10/61, Los Angeles, Calif., Kent, Ohio

(Suzanne) "Suzy" Powell, 9/3/76, Modesto, Calif., Modesto, Calif.

Connie Price-Smith, 6/3/62, St. Charles, Mo., Bloomington, Ind.

Meredith Rainey, 10/15/68, Brooklyn, N.Y., Brooklyn, N.Y./Silver Springs, Md.

Cynthea Rhodes, 9/30/68, Terrell, Texas, Austin, Texas

Michelle Rohl, 11/12/65, Madison, Wis., Kenosha, Wis./LaGrange, Ga.

Amy Rudolph, 9/18/73, Ridgeway, Pa., Providence, R.I.

Mary Slaney, 8/4/58, Plemington, N.J., Eugene, Ore.

Linda Somers, 5/7/61, Bitburg, Germany (USAF), Oakland, Calif.

Jenny Spangler, 7/20/63, Monroe, Wis., Gurnee, Ill.

Rochelle Stevens, 9/8/66, Memphis, Tenn., Memphis, Tenn.

Connie Teaberry, 8/15/70, St. Louis, Mo., Toledo, Ohio

Gwen Torrence, 6/12/65, Atlanta, Ga., Lithonia, Ga.

Marieke Veltman, 9/18/71, Charlotte, N.C., Los Angeles, Calif.

Tisha Waller, 12/1/70, South Boston, Va., Decatur, Ga.

Erica Wheeler, 11/28/67, Pretoria, South Africa, Sequim, Wash.

Shana Williams, 4/7/72, Bridgeton, N.J., Eugene, Ore.

Linetta Wilson, 10/11/67, Los Angeles, Calif., Hawthorne, Calif.

Dannette Young, 10/6/64, Jacksonville, Fla., Lithonia, Ga.

Team Leader: Martha Watson, Las Vegas, Nev.

Assistant Team Leaders: Stephanie Hightower, Columbus, Ohio; Robert Myers, Vacaville, Calif.

Head Coach: Deanne Vochatzer, Dixon, Calif.

Assistant Coaches: John Babington, Cambridge, Mass.; Sue Humphrey, Austin, Texas; Bob Kersee, Los Angeles, Calif.; Mamie Rollins, Port Clinton, Ohio

Auxiliary Staff: Thomas Bynum, Greensboro, N.C.; Janice Daniels, Rocklin, Calif.; Donna DeBerry, n/a; Rick McGuire, Columbia, Mo.; James Reardon, Worthington, Ohio; Ashland Whitfield, Indianapolis, Ind.

ATHLETICS/DISABLED (Exhibition Wheelchair)

Men (2)

Athlete, Birthdate, Birthplace, Hometown/Current Residence

Jacob Heiveil, 3/11/70, Cheju-do, Korea, Bothell, Wash.

Scot Hollonbeck, 11/5/69, Fort Benning, Ga., Champaign, Ill./Atlanta, Ga.

Women (3)

Athlete, Birthdate, Birthplace, Hometown/Current Residence

Cheri Becera, 9/27/76, Omaha, Neb., Nebraska City, Neb.

#Jean Driscoll, 11/18/66, Milwaukee, Wis., Champaign, Ill.

LeAnn Shannon, 12/17/82, Jacksonville, Fla., Orange Park, Fla.

Team Leader/Assistant Coach: Maureen Mausser, Savoy, Ill.

Head Coach: (Martin) "Marty" Morse, Champaign, Ill.

BADMINTON

Athlete, Birthdate, Birthplace, Hometown/Current Residence

Linda French, 3/4/64, Oak Park, Ill., Elmhurst, Ill./Colorado Springs, Colo.

Kevin Han, 11/25/72, Shanghai, China, Colorado Springs, Colo./Colorado Springs, Colo.

Erika Von Heiland, 12/24/65, Angeles City, Philippines, Anaheim, Calif.

Team Leader: Ann French, San Diego, Calif.

Coach: Goran Stenner, Colorado Springs, Colo.

Auxiliary Staff: Ignatius Rusli, Colorado Springs, Colo.

BASEBALL

Athlete, Birthdate, Birthplace, Hometown

Chad Allen, 2/6/75, Dallas, Texas, DeSoto, Texas

Kris Benson, 11/7/74, Duluth, Minn., Kennesaw, Ga.

(Robert Allen) "R.A." Dickey, 10/29/74, Nashville, Tenn., Nashville, Tenn.

Troy Glaus, 8/3/76, Tarzana, Calif., Oceanside, Calif.

Chad Green, 6/28/75, Dunkirk, N.Y., Cincinnati, Ohio

Seth Greisinger, 7/29/75, Kansas City, Kan., McLean, Va.

Kip Harkrider, 9/16/75, Carthage, Texas, Carthage, Texas

(Andrew Jay) "A.J." Hinch, 5/15/74, Waverly, Iowa, Midwest City, Okla.

Jacque Jones, 4/25/75, San Diego, Calif., San Diego, Calif.

Billy Koch, 12/14/74, West Babylon, N.Y.

Mark Kotsay, 12/2/75, Whittier, Calif., Santa Fe Springs, Calif.

Matt LeCroy, 12/13/75, Anderson, S.C., Belton, S.C.

Travis Lee, 5/26/75, San Diego, Calif., Olympia, Wash.

Braden Looper, 10/28/74, Weatherford, Okla., Mangum, Okla.

Brian Loyd, 12/3/73, Lynwood, Calif., Yorba Linda, Calif.

Warren Morris, 1/11/74, Alexandria, La., Alexandria, La.

Augie Ojeda, 12/20/74, Los Angeles, Calif., Southgate, Calif.

Jim Parque, 2/8/76, n/a, Crescenta, Calif.

Jeff Weaver, 8/22/76, n/a, Simi Valley, Calif.

Jason Williams, 12/18/73, Baton Rouge, La., Gonzales, La.

Team Leader: Scott Carnahan, McMinnville, Ore.

Head Coach: Skip Bertman, Baton Rouge, La.

Assistant Coaches: Ron Polk, Starkville, Miss.; Ray Tanner, Raleigh, N.C.; Jerry Weinstein, Sacramento, Calif.

Auxiliary Staff: Pamela Case, Trenton, N.J.

BASKETBALL

Men (12)

Athlete, Birthdate, Birthplace, Residence

Charles Barkley, 2/20/63, Leeds, Ala., Phoenix, Ariz.

Anfernee "Penny" Hardaway, 7/18/72, Memphis, Tenn., Orlando, Fla.

Grant Hill, 10/5/72, Dallas, Texas, Detroit, Mich.

Karl Malone, 7/24/63, Summerfield, La., Salt Lake City, Utah

Reggie Miller, 8/24/65, Riverside, Calif., Indianapolis, Ind.

Hakeem Olajuwon, 1/21/63, Lagos, Nigeria, Houston, Texas

Shaquille O'Neal, 3/6/72, Newark, N.J., Orlando, Fla.

Gary Payton, 7/23/68, Oakland, Calif., Seattle, Wash.

Scottie Pippen, 9/25/65, Hamburg, Ark., Chicago, Ill.

Mitch Richmond, 6/30/65, Fort Lauderdale, Fla., Sacramento, Calif.

David Robinson, 8/6/65, Key West, Fla., San Antonio, Texas

John Stockton, 3/26/62, Spokane, Wash., Salt Lake City, Utah

Team Leader: Clem Haskins, Minneapolis, Minn.

Head Coach: Lenny Wilkens, Atlanta, Ga.

Assistant Coaches: Bobby Cremins, Atlanta, Ga.; Jerry Sloan, Salt Lake City, Utah

Auxiliary Staff: JoAn Scott, Colorado Springs, Colo.; Jim Tooley, Colorado Springs, Colo.

1996 U.S. Olympic Team Roster

Women (12)
Athlete, Birthdate, Birthplace, Hometown, Residence
Jennifer Azzi, 8/31/68, Oak Ridge, Tenn., Oak Ridge, Tenn., Oak Ridge, Tenn.
(Alice) Ruthie Bolton, 5/25/67, Lucedale, Miss., McClain, Miss., Gainesville, Fla.
Teresa Edwards, 7/19/64, Cairo, Ga., Smyrna, Ga., Atlanta, Ga.
Venus Lacey, 2/9/67, Chattanooga, Tenn., Chattanooga, Tenn., Ruston, La.
Lisa Leslie, 7/7/72, Gardena, Calif., Inglewood, Calif., Hawthorne, Calif.
Rebecca Lobo, 10/6/73, Hartford, Conn., Southwick, Mass., Southwick, Mass.
Katrina McClain, 9/19/65, Washington, D.C., Charleston, S.C., Atlanta, Ga.
Nikki McCray, 12/17/71, Collierville, Tenn., Memphis, Tenn., Memphis, Tenn.
Carla McGhee, 3/6/68, Peoria, Ill., Peoria, Ill., Stone Mountain, Ga.
Dawn Staley, 5/4/70, Philadelphia, Pa., Philadelphia, Pa., Philadelphia, Pa.
(Kathryn) "Katy" Steding, 12/11/67, Portland, Ore., Lake Oswego, Ore., Tualatin, Ore.
Sheryl Swoopes, 3/25/71, Brownfield, Texas, Brownfield, Texas, Lubbock, Texas
Team Leader: Ceal Barry, Boulder, Colo.
Head Coach: Tara VanDerveer, Menlo Park, Calif.
Assistant Coaches: Nancy Darsch, Columbus, Ohio; Marian Washington, Lawrence, Kan.
Auxiliary Staff: Lynn Barry, Colorado Springs, Colo.; Carol Callan, Colorado Springs, Colo.

BOXING

Athlete, Birthdate, Birthplace, Hometown
Terrance Cauthen, 5/14/76, Trenton, N.J., Philadelphia, Pa.
Lawrence Clay-Bey, 12/14/65, Hartford, Conn., Hartford, Conn.
David Diaz, 6/7/76, Chicago, Ill., Chicago, Ill.
Albert Guardado Jr., 7/11/73, Redlands, Calif., Topeka, Kan.
Nate Jones, 8/18/72, Chicago, Ill., Chicago, Ill.
Floyd Mayweather, 2/24/77, Grand Rapids, Mich., Grand Rapids, Mich.
Eric Morel, 10/1/75, Puerto Rico, Madison, Wis.
Zahir Raheem, 11/7/76, Philadelphia, Pa., Philadelphia, Pa.
David Reid, 9/17/73, Philadelphia, Pa., Philadelphia, Pa.
Antonio Tarver, 11/21/68, Orlando, Fla., Orlando, Fla.
Fernando Vargas, 12/7/77, Oxnard, Calif., Oxnard, Calif.
Rhoshii Wells, 12/30/76, Austin, Texas, Riverdale, Calif.
Team Leader: Gerald Smith, Portland, Ore.
Head Coach: Al Mitchell, Philadelphia, Pa., Marquette, Mich.
Assistant Coaches: Patrick Burns, Miami, Fla.; Jesse Ravelo, Fort Huachuca, Ariz.
Auxiliary Staff: John Anderson, Colorado Springs, Colo.; Tom Coulter, Syracuse, N.Y.

CANOE/KAYAK

Sprint (Flatwater) (16)
Men (11)
Athlete, Birthdate, Birthplace, Hometown and/or Current Residence
Curt Bader, 1/5/61, Bloomfield, Iowa, Bloomfield, Iowa
Philippe Boccara, 6/7/59, LeMans, France, San Diego, Calif.
Mark Hamilton, 2/6/58, Louisville, Ky., Louisville, Ky.
(Michael) Mike Harbold, 5/22/68, Oakland, Calif., Honolulu, Hawaii, Chula Vista, Calif.
Joseph Harper, 1/13/66, Ventura, Calif., Ventura., Calif., Ventura, Calif.
Mike Herbert, 9/30/60, Belleville, Ill., Mascoutah, Ill., Rogers, Ark.
Stein Jorgensen, 7/12/62, Arcadia, Calif., San Diego, Calif.
Cliff Meidl, 3/6/66, Hollywood, Calif., Redondo Beach, Calif., Manhattan Beach, Calif.

John Mooney, 9/6/64, Seattle, Wash., Eugene, Ore.
Peter Newton, 6/3/70, Kailua, Hawaii, Bellevue, Wash./Chula Vista, Calif.
(James) Jim Terrell, 4/20/65, Cincinnati, Ohio, Milford, Ohio/Chula Vista, Calif.
Women (5)
Athlete, Birthdate, Birthplace, Hometown/Current Residence
Alexandra Harbold, 3/4/65, New York, N.Y., Rockaway Beach, N.Y./Chula Vista, Calif.
DeAnne Hemmens, 7/2/64, San Francisco, Calif., Costa Mesa, Calif./Costa Mesa, Calif.
Traci Phillips, 8/1/64, Honolulu, Hawaii, Honolulu, Hawaii/Honolulu, Hawaii
Lia Rousset, 10/5/77, Alhambra, Calif., Newport Beach, Calif./Newport Beach, Calif.
(Drusilla) "Dru" van Hengel, 9/9/63, Tarrytown, N.Y., Tarrytown, N.Y./Santa Barbara, Calif.
Team Leader: (Emily) Kay Dambach, Crownsville, Md.
Head Coach: (Reginald) "Reg" Hatch, Chula Vista, Calif.
Assistant Coach: Jerzy Dziadkowiec, Chula Vista, Calif.
Boathandler: Georg Kissner, Honolulu, Hawaii
Slalom (Whitewater) (9)
Men (7)
Athlete, Birthdate, Birthplace, Hometown/Current Residence
Adam Clawson, 12/28/72, Salt Lake City, Utah, Bryson City, N.C./Bryson City, N.C.
Wayne Dickert, 12/8/58, Chattanooga, Tenn., Bryson City, N.C., Bryson City, N.C.
Eric Giddens, 5/8/73, Atlanta, Ga., Atlanta, Ga.
David Hearn, 4/17/59, Washington, D.C., Bethesda, Md./Bethesda, Md.
Horace Holden Jr., 5/24/63, Atlanta, Ga., Bryson City, N.C./Bryson City, N.C.
Scott Shipley, 5/15/71, Bremerton, Wash., Poulsbo, Wash./Poulsbo, Wash.
Rich Weiss, 9/18/63. Munich, Germany, Steamboat Springs, Colo./Atlanta, Ga.
Women (2)
Athlete, Birthdate, Birthplace, Hometown/Current Residence
Dana Chladek, 12/27/63, Decin, Czech Republic, Kensington, Md./Kensington, Md.
Cathy Hearn, 6/1/58, Washington, D.C., Garrett Park, Md./Bethesda, Md.
Team Leader: Lisa Riblet, Decatur, Ga.
Head Coach: Jiri Pultera, Atlanta, Ga.
Assistant Coach: Silvan Poberaj, Bethesda, Md.
Auxiliary Staff: Robert Campbell, Carbondale, Colo.; Mike Larimer, Kennesaw, Ga.; Don Whittle, Indianapolis, Ind.

CYCLING

Men (16)
Athlete, Birthdate, Birthplace, Hometown, Current Residence
Frankie Andreu, 9/26/66, Dearborn, Mich., Dearborn, Mich., Dearborn, Mich.
Lance Armstrong, 9/18/71, Plano, Texas, Austin, Texas, Austin, Texas
Kent Bostick, 6/27/53, Lowell, Mass., Corrales, N.M., Corrales, N.M.
Bill Clay, 12/27/73, Yokosuka, Japan, Vernon Hills, Ill., Indianapolis, Ind.
Dirk Copeland, 9/5/72, Los Angeles, Calif., San Diego, Calif., San Diego, Calif.
Mariano Friedick, 1/9/75, Tarzana, Calif., Santa Monica, Calif., Colorado Springs, Colo.
Erin Hartwell, 6/1/69, Philadelphia, Pa., Indianapolis, Ind., Colorado Springs, Colo.
(Cregg) Steve Hegg, 12/3/63, Dana Point, Calif., Dana Point, Calif., Dana Point, Calif.

1996 U.S. Olympic Team Roster

George Hincapie, 6/29/73, Queens, N.Y., Charlotte, N.C., Charlotte, N.C.
David "Tinker" Juarez, 3/4/61, Los Angeles, Calif., Sugarloaf, Calif., Sugarloaf, Calif.
Adam Laurent, 7/6/71, Santa Cruz, Calif., Arroyo Grande, Calif., Shell Beach, Calif.
Mike McCarthy, 6/20/68, Brooklyn, N.Y., New York, N.Y., New York, N.Y.
Brian McDonough, 8/16/65, Long Beach, Calif., Winston-Salem, N.C., Winston-Salem, N.C.
Don Myrah, 1/17/66, Oakland, Calif., Saratoga, Calif.
Marty Nothstein, 2/10/71, Allentown, Pa., Trexlertown, Pa., Trexlertown, Pa.
Greg Randolph, 12/12/72, Denver, Colo., McCall, Idaho, McCall, Idaho

Women (7)
Athlete, Birthdate, Birthplace, Hometown, Current Residence
Linda Brenneman, 10/13/65, Wheat Ridge, Colo., Des Moines, Iowa, Dana Point, Calif.
Susan DeMattei, 10/15/62, San Francisco, Calif., Fairfax, Calif., Gunnison, Colo.
Alison Dunlap, 7/27/69, Denver, Colo., Denver, Colo., Colorado Springs, Colo.
Juliana "Juli" Furtado, 4/4/67, New York, N.Y., New York, N.Y., Durango, Colo.
Jeanne Golay, 4/16/62, Coral Gables, Fla., Hollywood, Fla., Glenwood Springs, Colo.
Connie Paraskevin-Young, 7/4/61, Detroit, Mich., Detroit, Mich., Corona del Mar., Calif.
Rebecca Twigg, 3/26/63, Honolulu, Hawaii, Seattle, Wash., Colorado Springs, Colo.
Team Leader: (Jon) Chris Carmichael, Colorado Springs, Colo.
Mountain Bike Coach: Doug Martin, Seal Beach, Calif.
Road Coaches: (Clarence) Roy Knickman, Colorado Springs, Colo. (men); Henny Top, Denver, Colo. (women)
Track Coaches: Andrzej Bek, Colorado Springs, Colo. (sprint); Craig Griffin, Colorado Springs, Colo. (endurance)
Auxiliary Staff: Edward Balcerzak, n/a; David Bolch, Pflugerville, Texas; D. Scott Daubert, Durango, Colo.; Matthew Driskell, Colorado Springs, Colo.; Stephanie Graham, n/a; Stephen Kent, Colorado Springs, Colo.; Jiri Mainus, Colorado Springs, Colo.; Lauri McKnight, Mill Valley, Calif.; (John) "Sean" Thomson, Colorado Springs, Colo.

DIVING

Men (4)
Athlete, Birthdate, Birthplace, Hometown, Current Residence
Scott Donie, 10/10/68, Vicenza, Italy, Houston, Texas, Miami, Fla.
Patrick Jeffrey, 6/24/65, Madison, N.J., Morristown, N.J., Orlando, Fla.
Mark Lenzi, 3/9/63, Huntsville, Ala., Bloomington, Ind., Bloomington, Ind.
David Pichler, 9/3/68, Butler, Pa., Fort Lauderdale, Fla., Columbus, Ohio

Women (4)
Mary Ellen Clark, 12/25/62, Abington, Pa., Fort Lauderdale, Fla., Fort Lauderdale, Fla.
Jenny Keim, 6/17/78, Cincinnati, Ohio, Cincinnati, Ohio, Fort Lauderdale, Fla.
Melisa Moses, 2/28/72, Jacksonville, Fla., Orange Park, Fla., Scottsdale, Ariz.
Becky Ruehl, 12/23/77, Lakeside Park, Ky., Lakeside Park, Ky., Cincinnati, Ohio
Team Leader: Micki King, Lexington, Ky.
Coaches: Randy Ableman, Miami, Fla.; Ron O'Brien, Fort Lauderdale, Fla.
Auxiliary Staff: Charlie Casuto, Crestview Hill, Ky.; Kongzheng Li, Orlando, Fla.; Vincent Panzano, Columbus, Ohio; Alan Spreen, Mesa, Ariz.

EQUESTRIAN

Dressage (4)
Athlete, Birthdate, Birthplace, Hometown/Current Residence
Robert Dover, 6/7/56, Chicago, Ill., Lebanon, N.J./Wellington, Fla.
(Lois) Michelle Gibson, 2/25/69, Takoma Park, Md., Roswell, Ga.
Steffen Peters, 9/18/64, Wesel, Germany, Escondido, Calif.
Guenter Seidel, 9/23/60, Oberstdorf, Germany, Encinitas, Calif.
Team Leader: Kathy Roberts, Oxford, N.J.
Chef de equipe: (Anne) Jessica Ransehousen, Unionville, Pa.
Grooms: Katherine Bateson, Wellington, Fla.; Beate Dutsch, Weidin, Germany; Sofia Lovequist, Solana Beach, Calif.; Allyson Rogers, Coto de Caza, Calif.
Auxiliary Staff: Paul Goodness, n/a; Dr. Midge Leitch, n/a

Show Jumping (4)
Athlete, Birthdate, Birthplace, Hometown/Current Residence
Leslie Burr-Howard, 10/1/56, Morristown, N.J., Westport, Conn.
Anne Kursinski, 4/16/59, Pasadena, Calif., Flemington, N.J.
Peter Leone, 8/1/60, Paterson, N.J., Greenwich, Conn.
Michael Matz, 1/23/51, Reading, Pa., Collegeville, Pa.
Team Leader: (Sara) "Sally" Ike, Oldwick, N.J.
Chef de equipe: Frank Chapot, Neshanic Station, N.J.
Grooms: Mary Albarello, Ocala, Fla.; Valerie Huckstepp, Greenwich, Conn.; Margaret Mulligan, Collegeville, Pa.; Melvin Borrego, Flemington, N.J.; Lucinda Somers, n/a
Auxiliary Staff: Dr. Richard Mitchell, Easton, Conn.

Three-Day Event (6)
Athlete, Birthdate, Birthplace, Hometown/Current Residence
Bruce Davidson, 12/31/49, Newburgh, Pa., Unionville, Pa.
Mara DePuy, 7/30/73, Hanover, N.H., South Strafford, Vt./Millwood, Va.
Jill Henneberg, 9/22/74, Lakewood, N.J., Pottersville, N.J.
Kerry Millikin, 12/10/61, n/a, Westport, Mass.
David O'Connor, 1/18/62, Washington, D.C., The Plains, Va.
Karen O'Connor, 2/17/58, Concord, Mass., The Plains, Va.
Team Leader: James Wolf, Gladstone, N.J.
Chef de equipe: Mark Phillips, Tetbury, Great Britain
Grooms: Samantha Buckley, Kildare, Ireland; Deborah Furnas, Upperville, Va.; Edmund Gibney, The Plains, Va.; Petra James, Pembrokeshire, Dyfed, Great Britain; Megan McCaffrey, Medford Lakes, N.J.; Hannah Whitehouse, Leesburg, Va.
Auxiliary Staff: Dr. Brendan Furlong, Oldwick, N.J.; Eric Stauffer, Middleburg, Va.

FENCING

Men (9)
Athlete, Birthdate, Birthplace, Hometown, Current Residence
Cliff Bayer, 6/24/77, New York N.Y., New York, N.Y., New York, N.Y.
Tamir Bloom, 12/24/71, New York, N.Y., Millburn, N.J., Millburn, N.J.
(Eric) "Nick" Bravin, 5/28/71, New York, N.Y., New York, N.Y., Los Angeles, Calif.
James Carpenter, 4/14/62, Canton, Conn., Canton, Conn., Fort Lee, N.J.
Peter Cox Jr., 1/18/67, Bronxville, N.Y., Concord, Mass., Overland Park, Kan.
Peter Devine, 5/17/76, New York, N.Y., New York, N.Y., New York, N.Y.
Michael Marx, 7/7/58, Portland, Ore., Portland, Ore., Pittsford, N.Y.
Thomas Strzalkowski, 12/30/71, Krakow, Poland, Richmond, Va., State College, Pa.
Peter Westbrook, 4/16/52, St. Louis, Mo., New York, N.Y., New York, N.Y.

Women (6)
Athlete, Birthdate, Birthplace, Hometown, Current Residence
Elaine Cheris, 1/8/46, Dotham, Ala., Denver, Colo., Denver, Colo.
Nhi Lan Le, 5/30/64, Vietnam, Atlanta, Ga., Atlanta, Ga.

1996 U.S. Olympic Team Roster

Ann Marsh, 6/30/71, Rochester, N.Y., Royal Oak, Mich., Rochester, N.Y.

Leslie Marx, 4/24/67, Fort Belvoir, Va., Houston, Texas, Pittsford, N.Y.

(Margaret) Suzanne Paxton, 12/27/69, Baltimore, Md., East Lansing, Mich., Rochester, N.Y.

Felicia Zimmermann, 8/16/75, Rochester, N.Y., Rush, N.Y., Rochester, N.Y.

Team Leader: Sherry Posthumus, San Jose, Calif.
Team Captain: Carl Borack, Beverly Hills, Calif.
Coaches: Aladar Kogler; New York, N.Y.; Buckie Leach, Rochester, N.Y.; Zoran Tulum, Stanford, Calif.
Armorer: Carl Oberg, North Hills, Calif.
Auxiliary Staff: Wieslaw Glon, State College, Pa.; Yefim Litvan, Millburn, N.J.

FIELD HOCKEY

Men (16)
Athlete, Birthdate, Birthplace, Hometown, Current Residence

Larry Amar, 2/24/72, Camarillo, Calif., Camarillo, Calif., San Diego, Calif.

(Nicholas) "Nick" Butcher, 5/7/76, Los Angeles, Calif., Simi Valley, Calif., San Diego, Calif.

Steve Danielson, 3/15/72, Honolulu, Hawaii, Livermore, Calif., San Diego, Calif.

Ahmed Elmaghraby, 4/26/68, Suez, Egypt, Lodgewood, N.J., Parsippany, N.J.

Steve Jennings, 7/24/69, Washington, D.C., Bethesda, Md., Washington, D.C.

(Benjamin) Ben Maruquin, 2/26/70, Ventura, Calif., Ventura, Calif., San Diego, Calif.

Marq Mellor, 3/5/68, Long Island, N.Y., Mount Vernon, N.Y., Mount Vernon, N.Y.

John O'Neill, 11/23/68, Detroit, Mich., Newbury Park, Calif., San Diego, Calif.

(Mark) "Otto" Steffers, 10/10/72, Louisville, Ky., Hockessin, Del., San Diego, Calif.

(Philip) "Phil" Sykes, 7/24/70, Tacoma, Wash., Pleasanton, Calif., San Diego, Calif.

Thomas Vano, 10/26/70, Plainfield, N.J., Simi Valley, Calif., San Diego, Calif.

Steven Van Randwijck, 8/27/69, Washington, D.C., Leiden, The Netherlands, Chula Vista, Calif.

Steven Wagner, 11/5/67, Philadelphia, Pa., Mount Laurel, N.J., Mount Laurel, N.J.

Eelco Wassenaar, 12/14/73, Groningen, The Netherlands, Utrecht, The Netherlands, Chula Vista, Calif.

Mark Wentges, 6/22/74, Walnut Creek, Calif., Rotterdam, The Netherlands, Chula Vista, Calif.

Scott Williams, 1/16/71, Orange, Calif., Thousand Oaks, Calif., Chula Vista, Calif.

Team Leader: Jay Patel, Colorado Springs, Colo.
Head Coach: Jon Clark, Brentwood, Essex, England/Chula Vista, Calif.
Assistant Coaches: Lenny McCaigue, Brookline, N.H.; Dave McMichael, Flourtown, Pa.
Auxiliary Staff: Jeffery Woods, Radford, Va.

Women (16)
Athlete, Birthdate, Hometown, Current Residence

Pam Bustin, 4/24/67, Somerset, Mass., Haslett, Mich.

(Kristen) "Kris" Fillat, 11/7/70, San Diego, Calif., San Diego, Calif.

Tracey Fuchs, 11/3/66, Centereach, N.Y., Mansfield Center, Conn.

Kelli James, 3/16/70, Medford, N.J., Atlanta, Ga.

Katie Kauffman, 9/26/74, West Lawn, Pa., Atlanta, Ga.

Antoinette Lucas, 10/27/68, Crozier, Va., Atlanta, Ga.

Leslie Lyness, 8/7/68, Paoli, Pa., Chapel Hill, N.C.

Diane Madl, 8/31/67, Mountain Top, Pa., Bangor, Maine

(Barbara) "Barb" Marois, 3/1/63, Auburn, Mass., Dover, N.H.

Laurel Martin, 6/8/69, Hummelstown, Pa., Virginia Beach, Va.

Marcia Pankratz, 10/1/64, Wakefield, Mass., Atlanta, Ga.

Jill Reeve, 11/1/69, Hoosick Falls, N.Y., Atlanta, Ga.

(Patricia) Patty Shea, 9/15/62, Belmont, Mass., Iowa City, Iowa

Liz Tchou, 9/25/66, Medford Lakes, N.J., Durham, N.C.

Cindy Werley, 2/26/75, Allentown, Pa., Austell, Ga.

Andrea Wieland, 7/25/69, Atlanta, White River Junction, Vt.

Team Leader: Beth Vasta, Merchantville, N.J.
Head Coach: Pam Hixon, Amherst, Mass. (Univ. of Mass.)
Assistant Coach: Margaret "Missy" Meharg, North Bethesda, Md.
Manager: Bruce Dick, Del Mar, N.Y.
Auxiliary Staff: Michele Madison, Haslett, Mich.; Terry Walsh, Perth, Australia

GYMNASTICS

Artistic

Men (7)
Athlete, Birthdate, Birthplace, Hometown, Current Residence

Mihai Bagiu, 4/10/71, Timisuara, Romania, Albuquerque, N.M., Albuquerque, N.M.

Jair Lynch, 10/2/71, Amherst, Mass., Washington, D.C., Stanford, Calif.

John Macready, 4/29/75, Los Angeles, Calif., Los Angeles, Calif., Colorado Springs, Colo.

John Roethlisberger, 6/21/70, Fort Atkinson, Wis., Minnespolis, Minn., Minneapolis, Minn.

Kip Simons, 9/11/72, Media, Pa., Bloomsburg, Pa., Columbus, Ohio

(Albert) Chainey Umphrey, 8/2/70, Albuquerque, N.M., Albuquerque, N..M., Los Angeles, Calif.

Blaine Wilson, 8/3/74, Columbus, Ohio, Columbus, Ohio, Columbus, Ohio

Team Leader: Ron Galimore, Tallahassee, Fla.
Head Coach: Peter Kormann, Columbus, Ohio (Ohio State Univ.)
Assistant Coach: Mark Williams, Stillwater, Okla. (Univ. of Oklahoma)
Auxiliary Staff: Gary Alexander, Indianapolis, Ind.; Miles Avery, Columbus, Ohio; (John) Ed Burch, Albuquerque, N.M.; Sadao Hameda, Stanford, Calif.; Vitaly Marmich, Colorado Springs, Colo.; Fred Roethlisberger, Minneapolis, Minn.; Art Shurlock, Los Angeles, Calif.

Women (7)
Athlete, Birthdate, Birthplace, Hometown, Current Residence

Amanda Borden, 5/10/77, Cincinnati, Ohio, Cincinnati, Ohio, Cincinnati, Ohio, Cincinnati, Ohio

Amy Chow, 5/15/78, San Jose, Calif., San Jose, Calif., San Jose, Calif.

Dominique Dawes, 11/20/76, Silver Spring, Md., Silver Spring, Md., Gaithersburg, Md.

Shannon Miller, 3/10/77, Rolla, Mo., Edmond, Okla., Edmond, Okla.

Dominique Moceanu, 9/30/81, Hollywood, Calif., Hollywood, Calif., Hollywood, Calif.

Jaycie Phelps, 9/26/79, Indianapolis, Ind., Greenfield, Ohio, Cincinnati, Ohio

Kerri Strug, 11/19/77, Tucson, Ariz., Tucson, Ariz., Houston, Texas

Team Leader: Kathy Kelly, Indianapolis, Ind.
Head Coach: Martha Karolyi, Houston, Texas
Assistant Coach: Mary Lee Tracy, Cincinnati, Ohio
Auxiliary Staff: Diane Amos, Campbell, Ga.; Kelly Hill, Gaithersburg, Md.; Bela Karolyi, Houston, Texas; (Elizabeth) "Peggy" Liddick, Oklahoma City, Okla.; Steve Nunno, Oklahoma City, Okla.; Mark Young, Campbell, Ga.

Rhythmic (7)
Athlete, Birthdate, Birthplace, Hometown, Current Residence

Aliane Baquerot, 11/23/78, New York, N.Y., Manhattan, N.Y,. Downers Grove, Ill.

Jessica Davis, 4/10/78, Greenbrae, Calif., San Anselmo, Calif., San Anselmo, Calif.

1996 U.S. Olympic Team Roster

Mandy James, 12/9/78, Jacksonville, Fla., Orange Park, Fla., Downers Grove, Ill.
Kate Nelson, 12/27/77, Evanston, Ill., Arlington Heights, Ill., Downers Grove, Ill.
Brandi Siegel, 8/4/79, Miami, Fla., Miami, Fla., Downers Grove, Ill.
Challen Sievers, 4/19/79, Downers Grove, Ill., Downers Grove, Ill., Downers Grove, Ill.
Becky Turner, 9/17/77, Marietta, Ga., Atlanta, Ga., Downers Grove, Ill.
Team Leader: Tracey Callahan-Molnar, Downers Grove, Ill.
Head Coach: Jan Exner, Fairfax, Calif.
Auxiliary Staff: Rossitza Todoroza, Downers Grove, Ill.

JUDO

Men (7)
Athlete, Birthdate, Birthplace, Current Residence
Rene Capo, 5/9/61, Pinal del Rio, Cuba, Minneapolis, Minn.
Orlando Fuentes, 11/19/74, Ellsworth AFB, S.D., Hialeah, Fla.
Damon Keeve, 8/27/60, San Francisco, Calif., San Francisco, Calif.
Jason Morris, 2/3/67, Schenectady, N.Y., Scotia, N.Y.
Brian Olson, 3/6/73, Tallahassee, Fla., Colorado Springs, Colo.
James Pedro, 10/30/70, Danvers, Mass., Danvers, Mass.
Cliff Sunada, 5/18/71, Honolulu, Hawaii, Colorado Springs, Colo.
Team Leader: David Matsumoto, El Cerrito, Calif.
Coach: Michael Swain, San Jose, Calif.
Auxiliary Staff: Patrick Burris, Norman, Okla.

Women (7)
Athlete, Birthdate, Birthplace, Current Residence
Sandra Bacher, 5/28/68, Long Island, N.Y., San Jose, Calif.
Corinna Broz, 3/13/74, Garberville, Calif., Colorado Springs, Colo.
Liliko Ogasawara, 5/21/72, Englewood, N.J., San Jose, Calif.
Marisa Pedulla, 4/25/69, Bellefonte, Pa., Pittsburgh, Pa.
Colleen Rosensteel, 3/13/67, South Greensburg, Pa., Colorado Springs, Colo.
Celita Schutz, 2/17/68, Rivervale, N.J., Rivervale, N.J.
Hillary Wolf, 2/7/77, Chicago, Ill., Chicago, Ill.
Team Leader: Darlene Montgomery, Pleasant Valley, Calif.
Coach: Corinne Shigemoto, Tres Pinos, Calif. (women)
Auxiliary Staff: Eddie Liddie, Colorado Springs, Colo.

MODERN PENTATHLON

Athlete, Birthdate, Birthplace, Current Residence
Michael Gostigian, 2/21/63, Philadelphia, Pa., Newtown Square, Pa.
Team Leader: Dolph Lundgren, New York, N.Y.
Head Coach: Jan Bartu, San Antonio, Texas

ROWING

Men (26)
Athlete, Birthdate, Birthplace, Hometown/Current Residence
Thomas Auth, 9/9/68, Orange, N.J., Maplewood, N.J.
Cyrus Beasley, 2/29/72, Rowe, N.Y., Newburyport, Mass., Augusta, Ga.
Jonathan Brown, 11/28/68, New York, N.Y., New York, N.Y., Chula Vista, Calif.
(William) Doug Burden, 7/29/65, Rutland, Vt., Pawlet, Vt./Washington, D.C.
William Carlucci, 6/3/67, Minneapolis, Minn., Rye Brook, N.Y., Philadelphia, Pa.
David Collins, 10/12/69, BethPage, N.Y., Thousand Oaks, Calif., Princeton, N.J.
(Atwood) Porter Collins, 6/27/75, New York, N.Y., Darien, Conn., Chula Vista, Calif.
Jason Gailes, 3/28/70, Taunton, Mass., Webster, Mass. & Dighton, Mass., Augusta, Ga.
(Michael) Sean Hall, 8/20/67, Williamsburg, Va., Arlington, Va.
(Jonathan) Adam Holland, 9/14/71, Austin, Texas, Philadelphia & Glenside, Pa., Chula Vista, Calif.

Fredric Honebein, 1/14/68, San Francisco, Calif., Tiburon, Calif., Chula Vista, Calif.
Brian Jamieson, 3/7/69, Livingston, N.J., Livingston, N.J., Augusta, Ga.
Robert Kaehler, 4/5/64, Burlingame, Calif., Holland, Pa., Chula Vista, Calif.
Jeffrey Klepacki, 12/17/68, Kearny, N.J., Kearny, N.J., Chula Vista, Calif.
Jamie Koven, 4/18/73, Morristown, N.J., Green Village, N.J.
Eric Mueller, 11/6/70, Cedarburg, Wis., Cedarburg, Wis., Augusta, Ga.
(Edward) Ted Murphy, 10/30/71, Boston, Mass., West Newton, Mass., Chula Vista, Calif.
Thomas Murray, 1/20/70, Buffalo, N.Y., Kenmore, N.Y., Chula Vista, Calif.
Michael Peterson, 1/4/67, Washington, D.C., Gulph Mills, Pa., Chula Vista, Calif.
Stephen Peterson, 6/27/63, Detroit, Mich., Glastonbury, Conn., Morganville, N.J.
Jeffrey Pfaendtner, 2/28/67, Detroit, Mich., Detroit, Mich., Philadelphia, Pa.
Marcus Schneider, 4/28/73, Lubbock, Texas, Everett, Wash., Princeton, N.J.
Jason Scott, 2/11/70, Iowa City, Iowa, Seattle, Wash., Chula Vista, Calif.
Steven Segaloff, 7/21/70, New Haven, Conn., Chula Vista, Calif.
Donald Smith, 4/7/68, North Tonawanda, N.Y., Chula Vista, Calif.
Timothy Young, 4/9/69, Philadelphia, Pa., Moorestown, N.J., Augusta, Ga.

Women (20)
Athlete, Birthdate, Birthplace, Hometown/Current Residence
Teresa Z. Bell, 8/28/66, n/a, Washington Crossing, N.J., Philadelphia, Pa.
Lindsay Burns, 1/6/65, Billings, Mont., Big Timber, Mont., Cambridge, Mass.
Julia Chilicki, 8/1/71, Hartford, Conn., Somers, Conn.
Ruth Davidon, 3/20/64, New York, N.Y., Haverford, Pa./Arlington, Va.
Jennifer Devine, 12/19/68, Portland, Ore., Portland, Ore./Philadelphia, Pa.
Jennifer Dore, 12/19/71, Montclair, N.J., Kearny, N.J./Chattanooga, Tenn.
Catriona Fallon, 8/8/70, Burlingame, Calif., Burlingame, Calif., Chattanooga, Tenn.
Yaz Farooq, 11/25/65, Minneapolis, Minn., Waupun, Wis./Chattanooga, Tenn.
Amy Fuller, 5/30/68, Inglewood, Calif., Westlake Village, Calif./Chattanooga, Tenn.
Anne Kakela, 6/22/70, Steamboat Springs, Colo., Steamboat Springs, Colo., Chattanooga, Tenn.
Laurel Korholz, 6/10/70, New York, N.Y., La Jolla, Calif./Chattanooga, Tenn.
Karen Kraft, 5/3/69, Fremont, Calif., San Mateo, Calif./Newport, Wash.
Elizabeth McCagg, 4/29/67, Seattle, Wash., Kirkland, Wash., Chattanooga, Tenn.
Mary McCagg, 4/29/67, Seattle, Wash., Kirkland, Wash./Chattanooga, Tenn.
Monica Tranel Michini, 5/4/66, Sheridan, Wyo, Billings, Mont./Philadelphia, Pa.
Melissa (Missy) Schwen, 7/17/72, Bloomington, Ind., Bloomington, Ind.
Catherine Symon, 12/16/71, Kingston, Jamaica, Villanova, Pa.
Andrea Thies, 9/21/67, Freeport, N.Y., Irvington, N.Y., Washington, D.C.
Cecile Tucker, 5/19/69, Wellesley, Mass., Warren, Maine/Philadelphia, Pa.
Michelle Knox Zaloom, 11/17/64, Portland, Ore., Edgewater, Md./Washington, D.C.
Team Leader: Juan Anzaldo, Indianapolis, Ind.

1996 U.S. Olympic Team Roster

Assistant Team Leaders: Elise Lindborg, Seattle, Wash.; Bill Zack, Rochester, N.Y.
Head Coaches: Mike Spracklen, Chula Vista, Calif. (men); Hartmut Buschbacher, Chattanooga, Tenn. (women)
Sculling Coach: Igor Grinko, Augusta, Ga.
Assistant Coaches: Richard "Dick" Garrard, Bells Beach, Victoria, Australia; Jan Harville, Edmonds, Wash.; (Ralph) Curtis Jordan, Hopewell, N.J.; (Katherine) "Kathy" Keeler, Winchester, Mass.; Mike Teti, Princeton, N.J.
Boat Manager: Mike Davenport, Centreville, Md.
Auxiliary Staff: Eric Beinhocker, Arlington, Va.; Charles Butt Jr., Belmont, Mass.; Peter Cipollone, Ardmore, Pa.; Ted Nash, Medford, N.J.

SHOOTING

Men (21)
Athlete, Birthdate, Birthplace and/or Hometown, Current Residence
David Alcoriza, 10/13/68, Lodi, Calif., Columbus, Ga.
Ben Amonette, 10/8/54, Radford, Va., Radford, Va., Radford, Va.
Terry Anderson, 6/12/45, Sydney, Australia, Dallas, Texas
Lance Bade, 2/6/71, Vancouver, Wash., Ridgefield, Wash., Colorado Springs, Colo.
Neal Caloia, 4/9/70, Torrance, Calif., Cottage Grove, Ore., Colorado Springs, Colo.
Greg Derr, 10/13/60, Marshfield, Mass., Marshfield, Mass.
Glenn Dubis, 2/5/59, Lincoln, Neb., Bethel Park, Pa., Columbus, Ga.
Bret Erickson, 9/26/60, Bennington, Neb., Buena Vista, Ga.
Robert Foth, 7/3/58, Clarence, N.Y., Colorado Springs, Colo.
(James) Todd Graves, 3/27/63, Laurel, Miss., Columbus, Ga.
(Robert) "Rob" Harbison, 6/27/66, Fallston, Md., Phenix City, Ala.
Ken Johnson, 11/24/68, Marshfield, Mass., Columbus, Ga.
Josh Lakatos, 3/24/73, Pasadena, Calif., Pasadena, Calif., Colorado Springs, Colo.
Roger Mar, 4/30/68, Seattle, Wash., Seattle, Wash., Colorado Springs, Colo.
John McNally, 1/20/56, Naha, Okinawa, Japan, Columbus, Ga., Heath, Texas
(William) "Bill" Meek, 5/14/53, Upland, Pa., Riverside, Calif., Colorado Springs, Colo.
John Oppio, 3/29/73, Sparks, Nev., Colorado Springs, Colo.
George Quigley Jr., 2/1/68, Cincinnati, Ohio, Cincinnati, Ohio, Cincinnati, Ohio
(William) "Bill" Roy, 12/4/58, Versailles, Ill., Alamagordo, N.M.
Adam Saathoff, 5/25/75, Tucson, Ariz., Hereford, Ariz., Colorado Springs, Colo.
Eric Uptagrafft, 2/16/66, Spokane, Wash., Spokane, Wash., Lakewood, Colo.

Women (10)
Athlete, Birthdate, Birthplace and/or Hometown, Current Residence
Elizabeth Bourland, 8/13/63, Costa Rica, Wichita Falls, Texas, Wichita Falls, Texas
(Elizabeth) "Libby" Callahan, 2/25/52, Columbia, S.C., Upper Marlboro, Md.
(Teresa) "Terry" Wentzel DeWitt, 4/15/63, Fort Bragg, N.C., Cincinnati, Ohio, Seale, Ala.
Jayme Dickman, 7/30/77, South Bend, Ind., Columbus, Ga.
Jean Foster, 10/13/72, Columbus, Ga., Bozeman, Mont., Colorado Springs, Colo.
Nancy Napolski, 1/14/74, Hinsdale, Ill., Downers Grove, Ill., Lexington, Ky.
Connie Petracek, 12/25/47, Chambersburg, Pa., Nashville, Tenn.
Kimberly Rhode, 7/16/79, Whittier, Calif., El Monte, Calif., El Monte, Calif.
JoAnn Sevin, 4/5/77, Dubois, Pa., Brockway, Pa., Colorado Springs, Colo.
Rebecca Snyder, 7/15/76, Grand Junction, Colo., Colorado Springs, Colo.
Team Leader: Ernie Vande Zande, Vancouver, Wash.

Coaches: Erich Buljung, Colorado Springs, Colo. (pistol); Sergey Luzov, Colorado Springs, Colo. (running target); Robert Mitchell, Englewood, Colo. (rifle); Lloyd Woodhouse, Colorado Springs, Colo. (shotgun)
Gunsmith: David Mattice, Nashville, Tenn.
Auxiliary Staff: Thomas Krcmar, San Antonio, Texas

SOCCER

Men (18)
Athlete, Birthdate, Birthplace, Hometown
Imad Baba, 3/15/74, Humble, Texas, Humble, Texas
Frank Hejduk, 8/5/74, La Mesa, Calif., Cardiff, Calif.
Miles Joseph, 5/2/74, West Springfield, Mass., Clifton Park, N.Y.
Kasey Keller, 11/19/69, Olympia, Wash., Lacey, Wash.
Jovan Kirovski, 3/18/76, Escondido, Calif., Escondido, Calif.
Alexi Lalas, 6/1/70, Birmingham, Mich., Detroit, Mich.
Brian Maisonneuve, 6/28/73, Detroit, Mich., Warren, Mich.
(Matthew) "Matt" McKeon, 9/24/74, Florissant, Mo., St. Louis, Mo.
Clint Peay, 9/16/73, Columbia, Md., Columbia, Md.
Brandon Pollard, 10/9/73, Richmond, Va., Richmond, Va.
(George) Eddie Pope, 12/24/73, Greensboro, N.C., High Point, N.C.
Claudio Reyna, 7/20/73, Livingston, N.J., Springfield, N.J.
Damian Silvera, 7/27/74, Flushing, N.Y., Huntington, N.Y.
Rob Smith, 8/20/73, Wilmington, Del., Wilmington, Del.
Chris Snitko, 1/24/73, Anaheim, Calif., Anaheim, Calif.
Nelson Vargas, 8/6/74, 8-6-74 Miami, Fla., Miami, Fla.
(William) "Billy" Walsh, 10/7/75, Summitt, N.J., Chatham, N.J.
(Anthony) "A.J." Wood, 8/17/73, Pittsburgh, Pa., Rockville, Md.
Team Leader: John Martin, Chicago, Ill.
Head Coach: Bruce Arena, Charlottesville, Va.
Assistant Coach: Glenn Myernick, Colorado Springs, Colo.
Equipment Manager: Charles Raycroft, Titusville, Fla.
Auxiliary Staff: (Robert) "Bob" Bradley, Pennington, N.J.

Women (16)
Athlete, Birthdate, Birthplace, Hometown
Michelle Akers, 2/1/66, Santa Clara, Calif., Oviedo, Fla.
Brandi Chastain, 7/21/68, San Jose, Calif., San Jose, Calif.
Joy Fawcett, 2/8/68, Inglewood, Calif., Huntington Beach, Calif.
Julie Foudy, 1/23/71, San Diego, Calif., Mission Viejo, Calif.
Carin Gabarra, 1/9/65, East Orange, N.J., Annapolis, Md.
(Mariel) Mia Hamm, 3/17/72, Selma, Ala., Chapel Hill, N.C.
Mary Harvey, 6/4/65, Palo Alto, Calif., Los Altos Hills, Calif.
Kristine Lilly, 7/22/71, New York, N.Y., Wilton, Conn.
Shannon MacMillan, 10/7/74, Syosset, N.Y., Escondido, Calif.
Tiffeny Milbrett, 10/23/72, Portland, Ore., Portland, Ore.
Carla Overbeck, 5/9/69, Pasadena, Calif., Dallas, Texas
Cindy Parlow, 5/8/78, Memphis, Tenn., Memphis, Tenn.
Tiffany Roberts, 5/5/77, Petaluma, Calif., San Ramon, Calif.
Briana Scurry, 9/7/71, Minneapolis, Minn., Dayton, Minn.
Tisha Venturini, 3/3/73, Modesto, Calif., Modesto, Calif.
Staci Wilson, 7/8/76, Livingston, N.J., Herndon, Va.
Team Leader: (Pamela) "Pam" Perkins, Orlando, Fla.
Head Coach: (Anthony) "Tony" DiCicco, Wethersfield, Conn.
Assistant Coach: Lauren Gregg, Wellesley, Mass.; April Heinrichs, Silver Springs, Md.
Auxiliary Staff: Michelle Jolicoeur, Marblehead, Mass.; Steven Slain, Oviedo, Fla.

SOFTBALL

Women (15)
Athlete, Birthdate, Birthplace, Hometown
Laura Berg, 1/6/75, Whittier, Calif., Santa Fe Springs, Calif.
Gillian Boxx, 9/1/73, Fontana, Calif., Torrance, Calif.
Sheila Cornell, 2/26/62, Encino, Calif., Diamond Bar, Calif.
Lisa Fernandez, 2/22/71, Lakewood, Calif., Long Beach, Calif.
Michele Granger, 1/15/70, Anaheim, Calif., Anchorage, Alaska

1996 U.S. Olympic Team Roster

Lori Harrigan, 9/5/70, Anaheim, Calif., Las Vegas, Nev.
Dionna Harris, 3/4/68, Wilmington, Del., Wilmington, Del.
Kim Ly Maher, 9/5/71, Saigon, Vietnam, Fresno, Calif.
Leah O'Brien, 9/9/74, Garden Grove, Calif., Chino, Calif.
Dot Richardson, 9/22/61, Orlando, Fla., Sherman Oaks, Calif.
Julie Smith, 5/10/68, Glendora, Calif., Glendora, Calif.
Michele Smith, 6/21/67, Califon, N.J., Plainfield, N.J.
Shelly Stokes, 10/26/67, Sacramento, Calif., Carmichael, Calif.
(Daniale) "Dani" Tyler, 10/23/74, Denver, Colo., Des Moines, Iowa
Christa Williams, 2/8/78, Houston, Texas, Houston, Texas
Team Leader: Ronnie Isham, Stephenville, Texas
Head Coach: Ralph Raymond, Worcester, Mass.
Assistant Coaches: Ralph Weekly Jr., Chattanooga, Tenn.; Margie Wright, Fresno, Calif.
Auxiliary Staff: Timothy O'Toole, Oklahoma City, Okla.

SWIMMING

Men (24)
Athlete, Birthdate, Birthplace, Hometown/Current Residence
Ryan Berube, 12/26/73, Palm Beach Gardens, Fla., Tequesta, Fla./ Dallas, Texas
Brad Bridgewater, 3/29/73, Charleston, W.Va., Dallas, Texas/Los Angeles, Calif.
(Thomas) Carlton Bruner, 2/1/72, Atlanta, Ga., Atlanta, Ga./Ann Arbor, Mich.
Greg Burgess, 1/11/72, Baltimore, Md., Jacksonville, Fla.
Ray Carey, 6/1/73, Kinchlow, Mich., Marblehead, Mass., Palo Alto, Calif.
Josh Davis, 9/1/72, San Antonio, Texas, San Antonio, Texas/ Austin, Texas
Tom Dolan, 9/15/75, Arlington, Va., Arlington, Va., Ann Arbor, Mich.
David Fox, 2/25/71, Raleigh, N.C., Raleigh, N.C./Colorado Springs, Colo.
Kurt Grote, 8/3/73, La Jolla, Calif., San Diego, Calif., Palo Alto, Calif.
Gary Hall, 9/26/74, Cincinnati, Ohio, Paradise Valley, Ariz.
John Hargis, 7/3/75, Little Rock, Ark., Clinton, Ark./Auburn, Ala.
Mark Henderson, 11/14/69, Washington, D.C., Fort Washington, Md./Colorado Springs, Colo.
Joe Hudepohl, 11/16/73, Cincinnati, Ohio, Cincinnati, Ohio
Jeremy Linn, 1/6/76, Harrisburg, Pa., Harrisburg, Pa., Knoxville, Tenn.
Tom Malchow, 8/18/76, St. Paul, Minn., St. Paul, Minn.
Eric Namesnik, 8/7/70, Butler, Pa., Butler, Pa./Ann Arbor, Mich.
Jon Olsen, 4/25/69, New Britain, Conn., Jonesboro, Ark./Colorado Springs, Colo.
John Piersma, 1/25/75, Huntsville, Ala., Huntsville, Ala./Ann Arbor, Mich.
Jeff Rouse, 2/6/70, Petersburg, Va., Fredericksburg, Va., Palo Alto, Calif.
Brad Schumacher, 3/5/74, Washington, D.C., Bowie, Md./Stockton, Calif.
(William) Tripp Schwenk, 6/17/71, Sarasota, Fla., Sarasota, Fla., Colorado Springs, Colo.
Scott Tucker, 2/18/75, Birmingham, Ala., Birmingham, Ala., Auburn, Ala.
Peter Wright, 12/3/72, York, Pa., Delran, N.J.
Eric Wunderlich, 5/22/70, Atlanta, Ga., Atlanta, Ga./Ann Arbor, Mich.
Head Coach: Skip Kenney, Menlo Park, Calif.
Assistant Coaches: Eddie Reese, Austin, Texas; Jon Urbanchek, Ann Arbor, Mich.

Women (20)
Athlete, Birthdate, Birthplace, Hometown/Current Residence
Amanda Beard, 10/29/81, Newport Beach, Calif., Irvine, Calif.
Brooke Bennett, 5/6/80, Tampa, Fla., Plant City, Fla.
Beth Botsford, 5/21/81, Baltimore, Md., Timonium, Md.
Janet Evans, 8/28/71, Fullerton, Calif., Placentia, Calif./Pasadena, Calif.
Catherine Fox, 12/15/77, Detroit, Mich., Shawnee Mission, Kan.
Whitney Hedgepeth, 3/19/71, Charlottesville, Va., Rocky Mount, N.C./Austin, Texas
Trina Jackson, 2/16/77, Plantation, Fla., Jacksonville, Fla.
Lisa Jacob, 5/13/74, St. Louis, Mo., Mission Viejo, Calif./Stanford, Calif.
Angel Martino, 4/25/67, Tuscaloosa, Ala., Americus, Ga./Hattiesburg, Miss.
Whitney Metzler, 4/19/78, York, Pa., Glen Rock, Pa.
Kristine Quance, 4/1/75, Whittier, Calif., Northridge, Calif./Los Angeles, Calif.
Annette Salmeen, 12/7/74, Detroit, Mich., Ann Arbor, Mich./Los Angeles, Calif.
Jilen Siroky, 11/20/81, Winter Park, Fla., Matthews, N.C.
Sheila Taormina, 3/18/69, Dearborn, Mich., Livonia, Mich.
Cristina Teuscher, 3/12/78, Bronx, N.Y., New Rochelle, N.Y.
Jenny Thompson, 2/26/73, Danvers, Mass., Dover, N.H./Stanford, Calif.
Melanie Valerio, 5/7/69, Youngstown, Ohio, Campbell, Ohio/Tucson, Ariz.
Amy Van Dyken, 2/15/73, Denver, Colo., Englewood, Colo.
Allison Wagner, 7/21/77, Gainesville, Fla., Gainesville, Fla.
Ashley Whitney, 8/21/79, Nashville, Tenn., Nashville, Tenn./ Augustine, Fla.
Head Coach: Richard Quick, Menlo Park, Calif.
Assistant Coaches: Mark Schubert, Surfside, Calif.; Gregg Troy, Jacksonville, Fla.
Team Leader: Susan Teeter-Eggert, Flemington, N.J.
Assistant Team Leaders: Joke Schubert, Surfside, Calif.; (John) Jack Jackson, Omaha, Neb.
National Team Director: Dennis Pursley, Colorado Springs, Colo.
Auxiliary Staff: David Marsh, Auburn, Ala.; Brian Schrader, Colorado Springs, Colo.; Jonty Skinner, Colorado Springs, Colo.; (Harold) Murray Stephens, Baltimore, Md.; Jim Wood, n/a

SYNCHRONIZED SWIMMING

Athlete, Birthdate, Birthplace, Hometown/Current Residence
Suzannah Bianco, 5/15/73, San Jose, Calif., Saratoga, Calif.
Tammy Cleland, 10/26/75, Sanford, Fla., Walnut Creek, Calif.
Becky Dyroen-Lancer, 2/19/71, San Jose, Calif., Campbell, Calif.
Heather Pease, 9/29/75, Monterey, Calif., Lafayette, Calif.
Emily Porter-LeSueur, 11/7/72, Glendale, Calif., Mesa, Ariz.
Jill Savery, 5/2/72, Fort Lauderdale, Fla., Concord, Calif.
Nathalie Schneyder, 5/25/68, San Francisco, Calif., Walnut Creek, Calif.
Heather Simmons-Carrasco, 5/25/70, Mount View, Calif., Santa Clara, Calif.
Jill Sudduth, 9/9/71, Baltimore, Md., Morgan Hill, Calif.
Margot Thien, 12/29/71, San Diego, Calif., Berkeley, Calif.
Team Leader: Laura Lacursia, Walnut Creek, Calif.
Coaches: Gail Emery, Lafayette, Calif.; Chris Carver, Saratoga, Calif.
Auxiliary Staff: Charlotte Davis, Seattle, Wash.

TABLE TENNIS

Men (3)
Athlete, Birthdate, Birthplace or Hometown, Current Residence
Jim Butler, 2/15/71, Iowa City, Iowa., Augusta, Ga.
Todd Sweeris, 5/28/73, Grand Rapids, Mich., Potomac, Md.
David Zhuang, 9/1/63, China, East Brunswick, N.J.

Women (3)
Amy Feng, 4/9/69, Tianjin, China, Wheaton, Md.
Wei Wang, 3/21/61, Beijing, China, Pasadena, Calif.
Lily Yip, 8/22/63, Canton, China, Metuchen, N.J.
Team Leader: Bob Fox
Head Coaches: Zhenshi Li, Colorado Springs, Colo. (men); Jonice Bosika, Davison, Mich.(women)

1996 U.S. Olympic Team Roster

TEAM HANDBALL

Men (16)

Athlete, Birthdate, Birthplace, Hometown

Derek Brown, 4/8/70, Washington, D.C., Washington, D.C.
Gregory Caccia, 1/17/67, Bayshore, N.Y., Bayshore, N.Y.
Yaro Dachniwsky, 1/15/63, Chicago, Ill., Chicago, Ill.
David DeGraaf, 3/26/71, Lansing, Mich., Spring Arbor, Mich.
Robert Dunn, 1/7/73, Glen Cove, N.Y., Glen Cove, N.Y.
Dennis "Denny" Fercho, 10/28/69, Ventura, Calif., Camarillo, Calif.
Joseph Fitzgerald, 8/30/71, Brooklyn, N.Y., North Babylon, N.Y.
Thomas Fitzgerald, 3/31/66, Brooklyn, N.Y., North Babylon, N.Y.
Darrick Heath, 10/12/64, Hempstead, N.Y., Hempstead, N.Y.
John Keller Jr., 10/5/65, Toledo, Ohio, Toledo, Ohio
(Frank) Clifton "Cliff" Mannon, 1/7/70, Amarillo, Texas, Amarillo, Texas
Steven Penn, 11/19/68, Brevard, N.C., Brevard, N.C.
Matthew Ryan, 2/19/66, Port Jefferson, N.Y., Miller Place, N.Y.
Mark Schmocker, 5/17/66, Interlaken, Switzerland, Ringgenberg, Switzerland
Michael Thornberry, 8/16/72, Virginia Beach, Va., Suffolk, Va.
(George) "Chip" Van Os Jr., 2/13/70, Houston, Texas, Houston, Texas
Team Leader: Jim Miller, Edmond, Okla.
Head Coach: Rick Oleksyk, Gulf Breeze, Fla.
Assistant Coach: Rhett Nichol, Cerrios, Calif.
Team Manager: Don O'Shea, Marietta, Ga.
Auxiliary Staff: James Thome, Stockton, Calif.

Women (16)

Athlete, Birthdate, Birthplace, Hometown

Cheryl Abplanalp, 6/1/72, Bryn Mawr, Pa., Malvern, Pa.
Dawn Allinger, 9/3/68, Salt Lake City, Utah, Bozeman, Mont.
Sharon Cain, 1/31/64, San Antonio, Texas, San Antonio, Texas
Kim Clarke, 1/31/65, Tulsa, Okla., Muscatine, Iowa
Laura Coenen, 10/16/62, Neenah, Wis., Peyton, Colo..
Kristen Danihy, 1/27/69, Lawton, Okla., Waldick, N.J.
Lisa Eagan, 3/1/70, Harlan, Iowa, Oskaloosa, Iowa
Laurie Fellner, 1/15/68, Appleton, Wis., Muskego, Wis.
Chryssandra Hires, 11/27/66, Bristol, Conn., Bristol, Conn.
Jennifer Horton, 8/10/68, Dover, N.J., Wharton, N.J.
Tami Jameson, 4/13/68, Minneapolis, Minn., St. Paul, Minn.
Toni Lee Jameson, 4/13/68, Minneapolis, Minn., St. Paul, Minn.
Dannette Leininger, 6/6/63, Kailua, Hawaii, Bloomington, Minn.
Dawn Marple, 11/1/70, Salem, Ohio, Lisbon, Ohio
Pat Neder, 12/18/66, Waukesha, Wis., Waukesha, Wis.
Carol Peterka, 12/23/63, Little Falls., Minn., St. Cloud, Minn.
Team Leader: Sandra DeLaRiva, Encino, Calif.
Head Coach: Claes Hellgren, Marietta, Ga.
Assistant Coach: Reita Clanton, Indianapolis, Ind.
Team Manager: Jan O'Shea, Marietta, Ga.

TENNIS

Men (3)

Athlete, Birthdate, Birthplace, Current Residence

Andre Agassi, 4/29/70, Las Vegas, Nev., Las Vegas, Nev.
Richey Reneberg, 10/5/65, Phoenix, Ariz., Minneapolis, Minn.
MaliVai Washington, 6/20/69, Glen Cove, N.Y., Ponte Verde Beach, Fla.
Coach: Tom Gullikson, Palm Coast, Fla.

Women (5)

Athlete, Birthdate, Birthplace, Current Residence

Lindsay Davenport, 6/8/76, Palos Verdes, Calif., Newport Beach, Calif.
Gigi Fernandez, 2/22/64, San Juan, Puerto Rico, Aspen, Colo.
Mary Joe Fernandez, 8/19/71, Santo Domingo, Dominican Republic, Miami, Fla.
Chanda Rubin, 2/18/76, Lafayette, La., Lafayette, La.
Monica Seles, 12/2/73, Novi Sad, Yugoslavia, Sarasota, Fla.

Coach: Billie Jean King, Chicago, Ill.
Team Leader: Sally Etterbeek, Key Biscayne, Fla.
Auxiliary Staff: Ron Woods, Key Biscayne, Fla.

VOLLEYBALL

Indoor

Men (12)

Athlete, Birthdate, Birthplace, Hometown/Current Residence

Lloy Ball, 2/17/72, Fort Wayne, Ind., Woodburn, Ind./San Diego, Calif.
(Robert) "Bob" Ctvrtlik, 7/8/63, Long Beach, Calif., Long Beach, Calif./Encinitas, Calif.
Scott Fortune, 1/23/66, Newport Beach, Calif., Laguna Beach, Calif./Del Mar, Calif.
John Hyden, 10/7/72, Pensacola, Fla., San Diego, Calif./San Diego, Calif.
Bryan Ivie, 5/5/69, Manhattan Beach, Calif., Manhattan Beach, Calif./San Diego, Calif.
Michael Lambert, 4/14/74, Honolulu, Hawaii, Kaneohe, Hawaii/La Jolla, Calif.
Dan Landry, 1/15/70, San Diego, Calif., San Diego, Calif./Lakeside, Calif.
Jeff Nygaard, 8/3/72, Madison, Wis., Madison, Wis./San Diego, Calif.
(Thomas) "Tom" Sorensen, 4/6/71, Racine, Wis., Racine, Wis./San Diego, Calif.
Jeffrey Stork, 7/8/60, Topanga, Calif., Topanga Canyon, Calif., El Cajon, Calif.
Ethan Watts, 5/4/72, Philadelphia, Pa., Tulsa, Okla./San Diego, Calif.
Brett Winslow, 9/8/67, Santa Barbara, Calif., Irvine, Calif./San Diego, Calif.
Team Leader: Eric Daly, San Diego, Calif.
Head Coach: Fred Sturm, San Diego, Calif.
Assistant Coaches: Rudy Suwara, San Diego, Calif.; Rod Wilde, Santee, Calif.
Auxiliary Staff: Darrell Akimoto, San Diego, Calif.; Carl McGown, San Diego, Calif.

Women (12)

Athlete, Birthdate, Birthplace, Hometown

Tara Cross-Battle, 9/16/68, Houston, Texas, Long Beach, Calif./San Diego, Calif.
Lori Endicott, 8/1/67, Kansas City, Mo., Springfield, Mo./San Diego, Calif.
Caren Kemner, 4/16/65, Quincy, Ill., Quincy, Ill./San Diego, Calif.
Kristin Klein, 3/20/70, Santa Monica, Calif., Pacific Palisades, Calif./San Diego, Calif.
Tammy Liley, 3/6/65, Long Beach, Calif., Westminster, Calif./Poway, Calif.
Beverly Oden, 3/9/71, Millington, Tenn., Irvine, Calif./San Diego, Calif.
Elaina Oden, 3/21/67, Orange, Calif., Irvine, Calif./San Diego, Calif.
Danielle Scott, 10/1/72, Baton Rouge, La., Baton Rouge, La./San Diego, Calif.
Paula Weishoff, 5/1/62, Hollywood, Calif., Torrance, Calif.
(Tonya) "Teee" Williams, 3/28/68, Los Angeles, Calif., Long Beach, Calif./San Diego, Calif.
Elaine Youngs, 2/14/70, Orange, Calif., El Toro, Calif./San Diego, Calif.
Yoko Zetterlund, 3/24/69, San Francisco, Calif., San Francisco, Calif./San Diego, Calif.
Team Leader: David Fleming, El Cajon, Calif.
Head Coach: (Taras) "Terry" Liskevych, Leucadia, Calif.
Assistant Coaches: Aldis Berzins, San Diego, Calif.; Jeanne Reeves, San Diego, Calif.
Auxiliary Staff: Dan McDonough, San Diego, Calif.; William Parham, n/a

1996 U.S. Olympic Team Roster

Beach
Men (6)
Athlete, Birthdate, Birthplace, Current Residence
Mike Dodd, 8/20/57, Los Angeles, Calif., El Segundo, Calif.
Carl Henkel, 8/16/69, Torrance, Calif., Redondo Beach, Calif.
Karch Kiraly, 11/3/60, Jackson, Mich., San Clemente, Calif.
Sinjin Smith, 5/7/57, Los Angeles, Calif., Pacific Palisades, Calif.
Kent Steffes, 6/23/68, Ann Arbor, Mich., Santa Monica, Calif.
Mike Whitmarsh, 5/18/62, San Diego, Calif., Del Mar, Calif.
Women (6)
Athlete, Birthdate, Birthplace, Current Residence
Gail Castro, 11/12/57, Glendale, Calif., Carlsbad, Calif.
Linda Hanley, 6/8/60, Whittier, Calif., Pacific Palisades, Calif.
Barbra Fontana Harris, 9/8/65, Manhattan Beach, Calif., Laguna Beach, Calif.
Holly McPeak, 5/15/69, Hollywood, Calif., Manhattan Beach, Calif.
Nancy Reno, 12/24/65, Glen Ellyn, Ill., Encinitas, Calif.
Debra Richardson, 2/17/61, Minneapolis, Minn., Santa Barbara, Calif.
Team Leader: Kerry Klostermann, Colorado Springs, Colo.
Technical Manager: Jim Coleman, Chula Vista, Calif.
Administrative Manager: Carla Hall, Colorado Springs, Colo.
Auxiliary Staff: Ed Garrett, San Diego, Calif.

WATER POLO

Athlete, Birthdate, Birthplace, Hometown/Current Residence
Gavin Arroyo, 5/10/72, Orange, Calif., Orange, Calif.
Troy Barnhart, 5/22/71, Hanford, Calif., Hanford, Calif.
Chris Duplanty, 10/21/65, Palo Alto, Calif., Honolulu, Hawaii
Mike Evans, 3/26/60, Fontana, Calif., Orem, Utah
Kirk Everist, 4/12/67, Houston, Texas, Orinda, Calif.
Dan Hackett, 9/11/70, Syracuse, N.Y., Irvine, Calif.
Chris Humbert, 12/27/69, Modesto, Calif., Lodi, Calif.
Kyle Kopp, 11/10/66, San Bernardino, Calif., San Bernardino, Calif.
Jeremy Laster, 2/24/74, Fullerton, Calif., San Clemente, Calif.
(John) Rick McNair, 9/4/68, Berkeley, Calif., San Francisco, Calif.
Chris Oeding, 9/10/71, Santa Ana, Calif., Newport Beach, Calif.
Alex Rousseau, 11/4/67, Paris, France, Santa Monica, Calif.
(Wolfgang) "Wolf" Wigo, 5/8/73, Abington, Pa., New York, N.Y.
Team Leader: Terry Wong, Agoura Hills, Calif.
Head Coach: Richard "Rich" Corso, Van Nuys, Calif.
Assistant Coaches: Ricardo Azevedo, Long Beach, Calif.; John Vargas, Hacienda Heights, Calif.
Auxiliary Staff: Ken Ravizza, Redondo Beach, Calif.; Ed Reed, Tuscaloosa, Ala.

WEIGHTLIFTING

Athlete, Birthdate, Birthplace, Hometown, Current Residence
(Wesley) "Wes" Barnett, 4/1/70, St. Joseph, Mo., St. Joseph, Mo., Colorado Springs, Colo.
Thomas Gough, 2/20/72, Fairfax, Calif., Fairfax, Calif., Colorado Springs, Colo.
Mark Henry, 6/12/71, Galveston, Texas, Silsbee, Texas, Austin, Texas
Thomas Ingalsbe, 11/16/69, Marietta, Ga., Marietta, Ga., Powder Springs, Ga.
Bryan Jacob, 2/1/69, Daytona Beach, Fla., Palatka, Fla., Alpharetta, Ga.
Peter Kelley, 5/9/74, St. Joseph, Mo., St. Joseph, Mo., Colorado Springs, Colo.
Thanh Nguyen, 6/18/64, Saigon, Vietnam, Pacifica, Calif., Pacifica, Calif.
(Timothy) "Tim" McRae, 8/4/70, Daytona Beach, Fla., Daytona Beach, Fla., Colorado Springs, Colo.
Vernon Patao, 2/13/70, Wailuku, Hawaii, Wailuku, Hawaii
Konstantine Starikovitch, 3/20/68, Podolsk, Russia, Podolsk, Russia, White Plains, N.Y.
Team Leader: Leo Totten, Littlestown, Pa.
Head Coach: Dragomir Cioroslan, Colorado Springs, Colo.
Auxiliary Staff: Dennis Snethen, St. Joseph, Mo.

WRESTLING

Freestyle (10)
Athlete, Birthdate, Birthplace, Hometown/Current Residence
Kurt Angle, 12/9/68, Pittsburgh, Pa., Pittsburgh, Pa.
Bruce Baumgartner, 11/2/60, Haledon, N.J., Cambridge Springs, Pa.
Tom Brands, 4/9/68, Omaha, Neb., Iowa City, Iowa
Kendall Cross, 2/24/68, Hardin, Mont., Raleigh, N.C.
Melvin Douglas, 8/21/63, Topeka, Kan., Mesa, Ariz.
Rob Eiter, 9/12/67, Chicago, Ill., Clarion, Pa.
Les Gutches, 2/21/73, Medford, Ore., Corvallis, Ore.
Kenny Monday, 11/25/61, Tulsa, Okla., Tulsa, Okla.
Lou Rosselli, 7/13/70, New York, N.Y., Edinboro, Pa.
Townsend Saunders, 4/20/67, White Sands, N.M., Phoenix, Ariz.
Team Leader: John Graham, Poquoson, Va.
Head Coach: Joe Seay, Phoenix, Ariz.
Assistant Coach: Greg Strobel, Bethlehem, Pa.
Auxiliary Staff: Bruce Burnett, Colorado Springs, Colo.; Bobby Douglas, Ames, Iowa; Roye Oliver, Colorado Springs, Colo.
Greco-Roman (10)
Athlete, Birthdate, Birthplace, Hometown/Current Residence
Matt Ghaffari, 11/11/61, Tehran, Iran, Colorado Springs, Colo.
Jason Gleasman, 3/27/75, Wilmington, Del., Boonville, N.Y.
Dennis Hall, 2/5/71, Milwaukee, Wis., Stevens Point, Wis.
Dan Henderson, 8/24/70, Downey, Calif., Huntington Beach., Calif.
Mujaahid Maynard, 4/9/71, Brooklyn, N.Y., Colo. Springs, Colo.
Gordy Morgan, 8/12/66, Minneapolis, Minn., Richfield, Minn.
Brandon Paulson, 11/22/73, Anoka, Minn., Anoka, Minn.
Rodney Smith, 4/13/66, Washington, D.C., Fort Benning, Ga.
Derrick Waldroup, 10/22/62, Chicago, Ill., Columbus, Ga.
Dave Zuniga, 3/1/68, Worland, Wyo., New Brighton, Minn.
Team Leader: Al Kastl, Clinton Township, Mich.
Head Coach: Rob Hermann, Pensacola, Fla.
Assistant Coach: Bill Martell, Walnut Creek, Calif.
Auxiliary Staff: Bob Anderson, San Clemente, Calif.; Dan Chandler, Minneapolis, Minn.; Steve Fraser, Colorado Springs, Colo.

YACHTING

Men (2)
Athlete, Birthdate, Birthplace, Hometown/Current Residence
Mike Gebhardt, 11/25/65, Columbus, Ohio, Fort Pierce, Fla.
William Martin III, 4/29/70, Charleston, S.C., Charleston, S.C.
Mixed (10)
Athlete, Birthdate, Birthplace, Hometown/Current Residence
(James) "Nick" Adamson, 4/11/69, Freeport, Bahamas, Newport Beach, Calif.
Jim Barton, 3/3/56, Lincoln, Neb., Fairfax, Calif.
Kevin Burnham, 12/21/56, Hollis, N.Y., Coral Gables, Fla.
Hal Haenel, 10/18/58, St. Louis, Mo., St. Louis, Mo./Los Angeles, Calif.
John Lovell, 10/11/67, Baton Rouge, La., New Orleans, La.
Jeff Madrigali, 5/8/56, Walnut Creek, Calif., San Anselmo, Calif.
Kent Massey, 4/2/52, Oklahoma City, Okla., Santa Barbara, Calif.
Charles Ogletree, 10/11/67, Greenville, N.C., Columbia, N.C.
Morgan Reeser, 11/14/62, Fort Lauderdale, Fla., Wilton Manors, Fla.
Mark Reynolds, 11/2/55, San Diego, Calif., San Diego, Calif.

1996 U.S. Olympic Team Roster

Women (4)

Athlete, Birthdate, Birthplace, Hometown/Current Residence

Courtenay Becker-Dey, 4/27/65, Greenwich, Conn., The Dalles, Ore.

Lanee Butler, 6/3/70, Manhasset, N.Y., Dana Point, Calif.

Kristina Farrar Stookey, 6/30/69, Martha's Vineyard, Mass., Darien, Conn.

Louise Van Voorhis, 7/4/70, Rochester, N.Y., Rochester, N.Y.

Team Leader: William Shore, Newport, R.I.

Boatwright: Carl Eichenlaub, San Diego, Calif.

Assistant Coaches: Luther Carpenter; Rollin "Skip" Whyte

Auxiliary Staff: Chris Bedford, n/a; Jerry May, Reno, Nev.; Michael Zani, n/a

MISSION STAFF

President: Dr. LeRoy T. Walker, Durham, N.C.

Executive Director: Richard D. "Dick" Schultz, Colorado Springs, Colo.

Chef de Mission/Vice President: Dr. Ralph Hale, Herndon, Va.

Assistant Chefs de Mission: Lynn Cannon, Oroville, Calif.; Herman Frazier, Phoenix, Ariz.; Andy Kostanecki, Darien, Conn.

Delegation Supervisors: Jack Favro, Lake Placid, N.Y.; Jonathan Harley, Portsmouth, R.I.; Vicky Holmberg, Colorado Springs, Colo.; Marty Mankamyer, Colorado Springs, Colo.; Terry McCann, Mission Viejo, Calif.; Cindy Munro, Colorado Springs, Colo.

Attache: Maynard Jackson, Atlanta, Ga.

Games Preparation and Services Committee Chair: Joe Kearney, Tucson, Ariz.

International Games Preparation Director: Greg Harney, Colorado Springs, Colo.

Delegation Director: Doug Ingram, Colorado Springs, Colo.

Assistant Delegation Director/Village Operations: Nancy Gonsalves, Colorado Springs, Colo.

Assistant Delegation Director/Envoy: Steve Saye, Colorado Springs, Colo.

Associate Envoys: Addy Choi, Atlanta, Ga.; Jay Greaves, Atlanta, Ga.

Official Spokesperson: Mike Moran, Colorado Springs, Colo.

Athlete Services Coordinators: Benita Fitzgerald, Chula Vista, Calif.; Peggy Johnston, Oakland, Calif.; Bryan Leturgez, Atlanta, Ga.; Leslie Milne, La Jolla, Calif.; Leo White, Newport News, Va.

USA MEDICAL STAFF

Title: Name, Hometown, Sport Assignment(s)

Head Physician (1): John Lehtinen, M.D., Marquette, Mich., boxing

Medical Coordinator (1): Ed Ryan, ATC, Colorado Springs, Colo., all sports

Physicians (10): Mark A. Adams, M.D., Columbia, Mo., women's soccer; Daniel E. Carr, M.D., Williamsburg, Va., field hockey, gymnastics; M. Craig Ferrell, M.D., Franklin, Tenn., aquatics, equestrian; Sean T. Hanley, M.D., Portland, Maine, men's soccer; John C. Lalonde, M.D., Greensboro, N.C., yachting; Lawrence M. Magee, M.D., Lawrence, Kan., athletics (track & field), judo; J. Bruce Mosely Jr., M.D., Houston, Texas, basketball; Herbert Parris, M.D., Denver, Colo., weightlifting, wrestling; Brock Schnebel, M.D., Oklahoma City, Okla., team handball, volleyball; Carlan Yates, M.D., Oklahoma City, Okla., canoe/kayak, rowing

Chiropractor (1): Steven Horwitz, D.C., Silver Spring, Md., all sports

Athletic Trainers (31): Rufi Alday, ATC, Los Gatos, Calif., canoe/kayak (sprint); William Bandy, ATC, Conway, Ark., rowing; Wayne Barger, ATC, Durango, Colo., men's field hockey; Kim Barrett, ATC, Cobleskill, N.Y., softball; Steven Brace, ATC, Omaha, Neb., men's basketball; (Joe) "Rigo" Carbajal, ATC, Phoenix, Ariz., men's gymnastics; Joe Fritz, ATC, Irving, Texas, wrestling; Kerry Gatch, ATC, Columbus, Ohio, canoe/kayak (slalom); Ernest Golin, ATC, Richmond, Va., baseball; (William) "Woody" Graham, ATC, San Diego, Calif., men's volleyball; (Anthony) "Tony" Harris, ATC, Phoenix, Ariz., boxing; Emery Hill Jr., ATC, Colorado Springs, Colo., diving, swimming; Lisa Jesberg, ATC, Virginia Beach, Va., women's field hockey; Gina Konin, ATC, Lewes, Del., women's basketball; Thomas Koto Jr., ATC, Boise, Idaho, wrestling; (Charlene) "Dawn" Kurihara, ATC, Laie, Hawaii, fencing; (Larry) "Chip" Ladd, ATC, Knoxville, Tenn., men's team handball; Patty Marchak, ATC, Sanford, Fla., women's soccer; (Patricia) "Skippy" Mattson, ATC, Decatur, Ga., swimming, synchronized swimming; Sally Mays, ATC, Minneapolis, Minn., women's volleyball; Karen McClellan, ATC, Colorado Springs, Colo., rhythmic gymnastics; Tyrone McSorley, ATC, Manilla, Iowa, cycling; James Miller, ATC, Hobbs, N.M., swimming, water polo; Frank Novakoski, ATC, Jacksonville, Fla., athletics (track & field); Dave Pawlowski, ATC, Richmond, Va., weightlifting; Barbara Pearson, ATC, Madison, Wis., women's artistic gymnastics; Margaret Peter, ATC, Colorado Springs, Colo., women's team handball; Richard Quincy Jr., ATC, Colorado Springs, Colo., men's soccer; Denise Richardson, ATC, Huntington Beach, Calif., athletics (track & field); Marcia Roschke, ATC, New York, N.Y., judo; Rene Revis Shingles, ATC, Mount Pleasant, Mich., tennis

USA PRESS SERVICES & BROADCASTING STAFF

Official USA Spokesperson/Media Director (1): Mike Moran, Colorado Springs, Colo.

Press Operations Director (1): Bob Condron, Colorado Springs, Colo.

Other USOC Staff (2): Frank Zang, Colorado Springs, Colo.; Gayle Bodin, Colorado Springs, Colo.

Village Press Coordinator (1): J. Michael Wilson, Colorado Springs, Colo.

Broadcasting Liaison (1): Jim Fox, Colorado Springs, Colo.

Press Officers (31): Gary Abbott, Colorado Springs, Colo. (USA Wrestling); Ron Babb, Oklahoma City, Okla. (Amateur Softball Association); Anthony Bartkowski, Colorado Springs, Colo. (U.S. Weightlifting Federation); Marty Baumann, Sharon, Mass. (U.S. Equestrian Team); Craig Bohnert, Indianapolis, Ind. (U.S. Canoe & Kayak Team); Amy Early, Colorado Springs, Colo. (USA Basketball); Terry Friel, Indianapolis, Ind. (USRowing); Jim Froslid, Chicago, Ill. (U.S. Soccer Federation); Bill Hancock, Overland Park, Kan. (NCAA); Leslie King, Atlanta, Ga. (Goodwill Games); Cheryl Kvasnicka, Colorado Springs, Colo. (USA Cycling, Inc.); Laura LaMarca, Indianapolis, Ind. (U.S. Synchronized Swimming, Inc.); Tom Lange, Chicago, Ill. (U.S. Soccer Federation); Ken Lee, Trenton, N.J. (USA Baseball); Barby MacGowan, Newport, R.I. (United States Sailing Association); Mike Mahon, Des Moines, Iowa (Drake Univ.); Colleen Walker Mar, Colorado Springs, Colo. (National Archery Association; U.S. Fencing Association); Dan McDonald, Lafayette, La. (Univ. of Southwestern Louisiana); Craig Miller, Colorado Springs, Colo. (USA Basketball); Nancy Moore, Colorado Springs, Colo. (USA Shooting); Paul Pawlaczyk, Colorado Springs, Colo. (U.S. Badminton Association); Luan Peszek, Indianapolis, Ind. (USA Gymnastics); Mary Ann Rinehart, Indianapolis, Ind. (United States Water Polo); Dave Shatkowski, Indianapolis, Ind. (United States Diving, Inc.); Tommy Sheppard, Denver, Colo. (Denver Nuggets); Charlie Snyder, Colorado Springs, Colo. (U.S. Swimming, Inc.); Kurt Stenerson, Colorado Springs, Colo. (USA Boxing); Lenny Vangilder, New Orleans, La. (Tulane Univ.); Marc Whitney, Colorado Springs, Colo. (U.S. Field Hockey Association); Mike Wolf, St. Louis, Mo. (Washington Univ.); Phil Worth, Golden, Colo. (USA Volleyball)

1996 U.S. Olympic Team

Archery

Judi Adams

Janet Dykman

Lindsay Langston

Justin Huish

Butch Johnson

Rod White

Mike King

Lloyd Brown

Teresa Brothers

Athletics

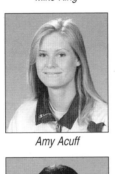
Amy Acuff

Valeyta Althouse

Olga Appell

Lacy Barnes-Mileham

Kim Batten

Kelly Blair

Tonya Buford-Bailey

Nicole Carroll

Joeta Clark

Gail Devers

Cheryl Dickey

Sandra Farmer-Patrick

Katherine Fonshell

Chryste Gaines

Lynda Tolbert Goode

Kim Graham

Carlette Guidry

Suzy Hamilton

Sharon Hanson

Juli Speights Henner

Victoria Herazo

Aretha Hill

D'Andre Hill

Vicki Huber

Sheila Hudson

Regina Jacobs

Lynn Jennings

Jackie Joyner-Kersee

1996 U.S. Olympic Team

Natasha Kaiser-Brown

Anne Marie Lauck

Debbi Lawrence

Maicel Malone

Jearl Miles

Inger Miller

Joan Nesbit

Diana Orrange

Ramona Pagel

Suzy Powell

Connie Price-Smith

Meredith Rainey

Cynthea Rhodes

Michelle Rohl

Amy Rudolph

Mary Slaney

Linda Somers

Jenny Spangler

Rochelle Stevens

Connie Teaberry

Gwen Torrence

Marieke Veltman

Tisha Waller

Erica Wheeler

Shana Williams

Linetta Wilson

Dannette Young

Deanne Vochatzer

John Babington

Sue Humphrey

Bob Kersee

Mamie Rollins

Martha Watson

Stephanie Hightower

Robert Myers

Derrick Adkins

Charles Austin

Randy Barnes

Brad Barquist

Keith Brantly

Bryan Bronson

Ed Broxterman

1996 U.S. Olympic Team

LeRoy Burrell

Andrzej Chylinski

Curt Clausen

Mike Conley

Mark Coogan

Mark Crear

Mark Croghan

Calvin Davis

Marc Davis

Lance Deal

Jon Drummond

Steve Fritz

Robert Gary

Matt Giusto

John Godina

Johnny Gray

Joe Greene

Tim Harden

Alvin Harrison

Kenny Harrison

Jeff Hartwig

Robert Howard

Chris Huffins

Scott Huffman

C.J. Hunter

Brian Hyde

Allen James

Allen Johnson

Lawrence Johnson

Michael Johnson

Bob Kempainen

Bob Kennedy

Carl Lewis

Michael Marsh

Anthuan Maybank

Kevin McMahon

Paul McMullen

Dan Middleman

Derek Mills

Dennis Mitchell

Timothy Montgomery

Herm Nelson

1996 U.S. Olympic Team

Dan O'Brien

Jose Parrilla

Dave Popejoy

Mike Powell

Tom Pukstys

Jason Pyrah

Butch Reynolds

Todd Riech

Brandon Rock

Jason Rouser

Adam Setliff

Lamont Smith

Jim Spivey

Dave Stephens

Eugene Swift

Anthony Washington

Jeff Williams

Todd Williams

Cameron Wright

Erv Hunt

Douglas Brown

Charles Craig

Chick Hislop

Tony Naclerio

George Williams

Al Baeta

Charlie Greene

Edward Levy

Athletics--Disabled

Atlanta 1996
TM, © 1992 ACOG

Cheri Becera

Jean Driscoll

LeAnn Shannon

Jacob Heiveil

Scot Hollonbeck

Marty Morse

Maureen Mausser

Badminton

Atlanta 1996
TM, © 1992 ACOG

Linda French

Kevin Han

Erika Von Heiland

1996 U.S. Olympic Team

Goran Stenner

Ann French

Baseball

Chad Allen

Kris Benson

R.A. Dickey

Troy Glaus

Chad Green

Seth Greisinger

Kip Harkrider

A.J. Hinch

Jacque Jones

Billy Koch

Mark Kotsay

Matt LeCroy

Travis Lee

Braden Looper

Brian Loyd

Warren Morris

Augie Ojeda

Jim Parque

Jeff Weaver

Jason Williams

Skip Bertman

Ron Polk

Ray Tanner

Jerry Weinstein

Scott Carnahan

Basketball

Jennifer Azzi

Ruthie Bolton

Teresa Edwards

Venus Lacey

Lisa Leslie

Rebecca Lobo

Katrina McClain

Nikki McCray

Carla McGhee

Dawn Staley

1996 U.S. Olympic Team

Katy Steding

Sheryl Swoopes

Tara VanDerveer

Nancy Darsch

Marian Washington

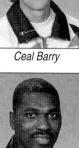
Ceal Barry

Charles Barkley

Penny Hardaway

Grant Hill

Karl Malone

Reggie Miller

Hakeem Olajuwon

Shaquille O'Neal

Gary Payton

Scottie Pippen

Mitch Richmond

David Robinson

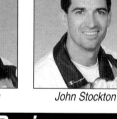
John Stockton

Lenny Wilkens

Bobby Cremins

Jerry Sloan

Clem Haskins

Terrance Cauthen

Lawrence Clay-Bey

David Diaz

Albert Guardado Jr.

Nate Jones

Floyd Mayweather

Eric Morel

Zahir Raheem

David Reid

Antonio Tarver

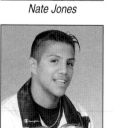
Fernando Vargas

Rhoshii Wells

Al Mitchell

Patrick Burns

Jesse Ravelo

Gerald Smith

1996 U.S. Olympic Team

Alexandra Harbold

DeAnne Hemmens

Traci Phillips

Lia Rousset

Dru van Hengel

Curt Bader

Philippe Boccara

Mark Hamilton

Mike Harbold

Joseph Harper

Mike Herbert

Stein Jorgensen

Cliff Meidl

John Mooney

Peter Newton

Jim Terrell

Reg Hatch

Jerzy Dziadkowiec

Georg Kissner

Kay Dambach

Dana Chladek

Cathy Hearn

Adam Clawson

Wayne Dickert

Eric Giddens

David Hearn

Horace Holden Jr.

Scott Shipley

Rich Weiss

Jiri Pultera

Silvan Poberaj

Lisa Riblet

Cycling

Atlanta 1996
TM, © 1992 ACOG

Linda Brenneman

Susan DeMattei

Alison Dunlap

Juli Furtado

Jeanne Golay

C. Paraskevin-Young

Rebecca Twigg

Frankie Andreu

1996 U.S. Olympic Team

Lance Armstrong

Kent Bostick

Bill Clay

Dirk Copeland

Mariano Friedick

Erin Hartwell

Steve Hegg

George Hincapie

Tinker Juarez

Adam Laurent

Mike McCarthy

Brian McDonough

Don Myrah

Marty Nothstein

Greg Randolph

Doug Martin

Roy Knickman

Henny Top

Andrzej Bek

Craig Griffin

Chris Carmichael

Diving

Mary Ellen Clark

Jenny Keim

Melisa Moses

Becky Ruehl

Scott Donie

Patrick Jeffrey

Mark Lenzi

David Pichler

Randy Ableman

Ron O'Brien

Micki King

Equestrian

Robert Dover

Michelle Gibson

Steffen Peters

Guenter Seidel

Jessica Ransehousen

Kathy Roberts

1996 U.S. Olympic Team

Leslie Burr-Howard

Anne Kursinski

Peter Leone

Michael Matz

Frank Chapot

Sally Ike

Bruce Davidson

Mara DePuy

Jill Henneberg

Kerry Millikin

David O'Connor

Karen O'Connor

Mark Phillips

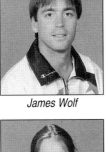
James Wolf

Fencing

Atlanta 1996
TM, © 1992 ACOG

Elaine Cheris

Nhi Lan Le

Ann Marsh

Leslie Marx

Suzanne Paxton

Felicia Zimmermann

Cliff Bayer

Tamir Bloom

Nick Bravin

James Carpenter

Peter Cox Jr.

Peter Devine

Michael Marx

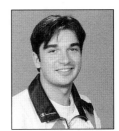
Thomas Strzalkowski

Peter Westbrook

Carl Borack

Aladar Kogler

Buckie Leach

Zoran Tulum

Carl Oberg

Field Hockey

Sherry Posthumus

Atlanta 1996
TM, © 1992 ACOG

Pam Bustin

Kris Fillat

Tracey Fuchs

1996 U.S. Olympic Team

Kelli James

Katie Kauffman

Antoinette Lucas

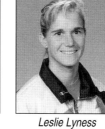
Leslie Lyness

Diane Madl

Barb Marois

Laurel Martin

Marcia Pankratz

Jill Reeve

Patty Shea

Liz Tchou

Cindy Werley

Andrea Wieland

Pam Hixon

Missy Meharg

Bruce Dick

Beth Vasta

Larry Amar

Nick Butcher

Steve Danielson

Ahmed Elmaghraby

Steve Jennings

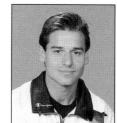
Ben Maruquin

Marq Mellor

John O'Neill

Otto Steffers

Phil Sykes

Thomas Vano

Steven Van Randwijck

Steven Wagner

Eelco Wassenaar

Mark Wentges

Scott Williams

Jon Clark

Lenny McCaigue

Dave McMichael

Jay Patel

Gymnastics

Atlanta 1996
TM, © 1992 ACOG

Aliane Baquerot

Jessica Davis

Mandy James

1996 U.S. Olympic Team

Kate Nelson

Brandi Siegel

Challen Sievers

Becky Turner

Jan Exner

Tracey Callahan-Molnar

Amanda Borden

Amy Chow

Dominique Dawes

Shannon Miller

Dominique Moceanu

Jaycie Phelps

Kerri Strug

Martha Karolyi

Mary Lee Tracy

Kathy Kelly

Mihai Bagiu

Jair Lynch

John Macready

John Roethlisberger

Kip Simons

Chainey Umphrey

Blaine Wilson

Peter Kormann

Mark Williams

Ron Galimore

Atlanta 1996
TM, © 1992 ACOG

Sandra Bacher

Corinna Broz

Liliko Ogasawara

Marisa Pedulla

Colleen Rosensteel

Celita Schutz

Hillary Wolf

Corinne Shigemoto

Darlene Montgomery

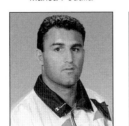
Rene Capo

Orlando Fuentes

Damon Keeve

Jason Morris

Brian Olson

1996 U.S. Olympic Team

James Pedro

Cliff Sunada

Michael Swain

David Matsumoto

Michael Gostigian

Jan Bartu

Dolph Lundgren

Teresa Z. Bell

Lindsay Burns

Julia Chilicki

Ruth Davidon

Jennifer Devine

Jennifer Dore

Catriona Fallon

Yaz Farooq

Amy Fuller

Anne Kakela

Laurel Korholz

Karen Kraft

Elizabeth McCagg

Mary McCagg

Monica Tranel Michini

Missy Schwen

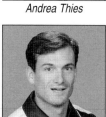
Catherine Symon

Andrea Thies

Cecile Tucker

Michelle Knox Zaloom

Thomas Auth

Cyrus Beasley

Jonathan Brown

Doug Burden

William Carlucci

David Collins

Porter Collins

Jason Gailes

Sean Hall

Adam Holland

Fredric Honebein

1996 U.S. Olympic Team

Brian Jamieson

Robert Kaehler

Jeffrey Klepacki

Jamie Koven

Eric Mueller

Ted Murphy

Thomas Murray

Michael Peterson

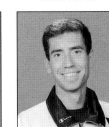
Stephen Peterson

Jeffrey Pfaendtner

Marcus Schneider

Jason Scott

Steven Segaloff

Donald Smith

Timothy Young

Mike Spracklen

Hartmut Buschbacher

Igor Grinko

Dick Garrard

Jan Harville

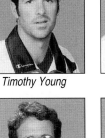
Curtis Jordan

Kathy Keeler

Mike Teti

Mike Davenport

Juan Anzaldo

Elise Lindborg

Bill Zack

Shooting

Atlanta 1996
TM, © 1992 ACOG

Elizabeth Bourland

Libby Callahan

Terry Wentzel DeWitt

Jayme Dickman

Jean Foster

Nancy Napolski

Connie Petracek

Kim Rhode

JoAnn Sevin

Rebecca Snyder

David Alcoriza

Ben Amonette

Terry Anderson

1996 U.S. Olympic Team

Lance Bade

Neal Caloia

Greg Derr

Glenn Dubis

Bret Erickson

Robert Foth

Todd Graves

Rob Harbison

Ken Johnson

Josh Lakatos

Roger Mar

John McNally

Bill Meek

John Oppio

George Quigley Jr.

Bill Roy

Adam Saathoff

Eric Uptagrafft

Erich Buljung

Sergey Luzov

Robert Mitchell

Lloyd Woodhouse

David Mattice

Ernie Vande Zande

Soccer

Atlanta 1996
TM, © 1992 ACOG

Michelle Akers

Brandi Chastain

Joy Fawcett

Julie Foudy

Carin Gabarra

Mia Hamm

Mary Harvey

Kristine Lilly

Shannon MacMillan

Tiffeny Milbrett

Carla Overbeck

Cindy Parlow

Tiffany Roberts

Briana Scurry

Tisha Venturini

Staci Wilson

1996 U.S. Olympic Team

 Tony DiCicco

 Lauren Gregg

 April Heinrichs

 Pam Perkins

 Imad Baba

 Frank Hejduk

 Miles Joseph

 Kasey Keller

 Jovan Kirovski

 Alexi Lalas

 Brian Maisonneuve

 Matt McKeon

 Clint Peay

 Brandon Pollard

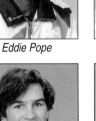 Eddie Pope

 Claudio Reyna

 Damian Silvera

 Rob Smith

 Chris Snitko

 Nelson Vargas

 Billy Walsh

 A.J. Wood

 Bruce Arena

 Glenn Myernick

 Charles Raycroft

 John Martin

Softball

Atlanta 1996
TM, © 1992 ACOG

 Laura Berg

Gillian Boxx

 Sheila Cornell

 Lisa Fernandez

Michele Granger

Lori Harrigan

 Dionna Harris

 Kim Ly Maher

 Leah O'Brien

 Dot Richardson

Julie Smith

Michele Smith

 Shelly Stokes

 Dani Tyler

1996 U.S. Olympic Team

Christa Williams

Ralph Raymond

Ralph Weekly Jr.

Margie Wright

Ronnie Isham

Amanda Beard

Brooke Bennett

Beth Botsford

Janet Evans

Catherine Fox

Whitney Hedgepeth

Trina Jackson

Lisa Jacob

Angel Martino

Whitney Metzler

Kristine Quance

Annette Salmeen

Jilen Siroky

Sheila Taormina

Cristina Teuscher

Jenny Thompson

Melanie Valerio

Amy Van Dyken

Allison Wagner

Ashley Whitney

Richard Quick

Mark Schubert

Gregg Troy

Ryan Berube

Brad Bridgewater

Carlton Bruner

Greg Burgess

Ray Carey

Josh Davis

Tom Dolan

David Fox

Kurt Grote

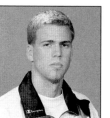

Gary Hall Jr.

John Hargis

1996 U.S. Olympic Team

Mark Henderson

Joe Hudepohl

Jeremy Linn

Tom Malchow

Eric Namesnik

Jon Olsen

John Piersma

Jeff Rouse

Brad Schumacher

Tripp Schwenk

Scott Tucker

Peter Wright

Eric Wunderlich

Skip Kenney

Eddie Reese

Jon Urbanchek

Susan Teeter-Eggert

Joke Schubert

Jack Jackson

Dennis Pursley

Suzannah Bianco

Tammy Cleland

Becky Dyroen-Lancer

Heather Pease

Emily Porter-LeSueur

Jill Savery

Nathalie Schneyder

H. Simmons-Carrasco

Jill Sudduth

Margot Thien

Gail Emery

Chris Carver

Laura Lacursia

Amy Feng

Wei Wang

Lily Yip

Jim Butler

1996 U.S. Olympic Team

Todd Sweeris

David Zhuang

Zhenshi Li

Jonice Bosika

Bob Fox

Team Handball

Cheryl Abplanalp

Dawn Allinger

Sharon Cain

Kim Clarke

Laura Coenen

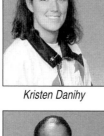
Kristen Danihy

Lisa Eagan

Laurie Fellner

Chryssandra Hires

Jennifer Horton

Tami Jameson

Toni Lee Jameson

Dannette Leininger

Dawn Marple

Pat Neder

Carol Peterka

Claes Hellgren

Reita Clanton

Jan O'Shea

Sandra DeLaRiva

Derek Brown

Gregory Caccia

Yaro Dachniwsky

David DeGraaf

Robert Dunn

Denny Fercho

Joseph Fitzgerald

Thomas Fitzgerald

Darrick Heath

John Keller Jr.

Cliff Mannon

Steven Penn

Matthew Ryan

Mark Schmocker

1996 U.S. Olympic Team

Michael Thornberry

Chip Van Os Jr.

Rick Oleksyk

Rhett Nichol

Don O'Shea

Jim Miller

Lindsay Davenport

Gigi Fernandez

Mary Joe Fernandez

Chanda Rubin

Monica Seles

Billie Jean King

Sally Etterbeek

Andre Agassi

Richey Reneberg

MaliVai Washington

Tom Gullikson

Tara Cross-Battle

Lori Endicott

Caren Kemner

Kristin Klein

Tammy Liley

Beverly Oden

Elaina Oden

Danielle Scott

Paula Weishoff

Teee Williams

Elaine Youngs

Yoko Zetterlund

Terry Liskevych

Aldis Berzins

Jeanne Reeves

David Fleming

Lloy Ball

Bob Ctvrtlik

Scott Fortune

John Hyden

Bryan Ivie

1996 U.S. Olympic Team

Michael Lambert

Dan Landry

Jeff Nygaard

Tom Sorensen

Jeffrey Stork

Ethan Watts

Brett Winslow

Fred Sturm

Rudy Suwara

Ron Wilde

Eric Daly

Gail Castro

Linda Hanley

Barbra Fontana Harris

Holly McPeak

Nancy Reno

Debra Richardson

Mike Dodd

Jim Coleman

Carl Henkel

Karch Kiraly

Sinjin Smith

Kent Steffes

Mike Whitmarsh

Jim Coleman

Carla Hall

Kerry Klostermann

Water Polo

Atlanta 1996
TM, © 1992 ACOG

Gavin Arroyo

Troy Barnhart

Chris Duplanty

Mike Evans

Kirk Everist

Dan Hackett

Chris Humbert

Kyle Kopp

Jeremy Laster

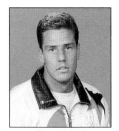
Rick McNair

Chris Oeding

Alex Rousseau

Wolf Wigo

Rich Corso

1996 U.S. Olympic Team

Ricardo Azevedo

John Vargas

Terry Wong

Wes Barnett

Thomas Gough

Mark Henry

Thomas Ingalsbe

Bryan Jacob

Peter Kelley

Tim McRae

Thanh Nguyen

Vernon Patao

Konstantine Starikovitch

Dragomir Cioroslan

Leo Totten

Matt Ghaffari

Jason Gleasman

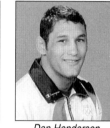
Dennis Hall

Dan Henderson

Mujaahid Maynard

Gordy Morgan

Brandon Paulson

Rodney Smith

Derrick Waldroup

Dave Zuniga

Rob Hermann

Bill Martell

Al Kastl

Kurt Angle

Bruce Baumgartner

Tom Brands

Kendall Cross

Melvin Douglas

Rob Eiter

Les Gutches

Kenny Monday

Lou Rosselli

1996 U.S. Olympic Team

Townsend Saunders

Joe Seay

Greg Strobel

John Graham

Nick Adamson

James Barton

Courtenay Becker-Dey

Kevin Burnham

Lanee Butler

Mike Gebhardt

Hal Haenel

John Lovell

Jeff Madrigali

William Martin

Kent Massey

Charles Ogletree

Morgan Reeser

Mark Reynolds

Kristina Farrar Stookey

Louise Van Voorhis

Carl Eichenlaub

Luther Carpenter

Skip Whyte

William Shore

Headshots of 1996 U.S. Olympic Team members provided by Long Photography, Inc., Los Angeles, Calif.

Triumph Of Human Spirit

An amazing 225 world records were set at the Paralympics as the participants proved they were athletes, first, and human interest stories, second.

The Olympic flame had scarcely been extinguished when Atlanta opened its doors and hearts again to yet another international celebration. Representing cerebral palsy, visually impaired, amputees and les autres, wheelchair and mentally disabled athletes, more than 3,300 athletes from around the world gathered for 10 days to celebrate the 1996 Paralympic Games, saluting the triumph of the human spirit.

But these Games were not only a celebration—the athletes of the Xth Paralympiad came to Atlanta on Aug. 15-25 with something to prove. Tired of being classified as human interest stories, the Paralympic competitors sought to prove that they were athletes, first and foremost. They sought to remove the focus from their disabilities and rather emphasize their achievements. And for anyone who saw them, for anyone who witnessed just one of the 225 world records set at these Games, it would be safe to say that the athletes made their point.

The spirit of the event was kindled at the Opening Ceremonies. The evening's festivities, which were hosted by Master of Ceremonies Christopher Reeve, began with the national anthem by Teddie Pendergrass. Following the tradi-

tional March of Athletes, the ceremony was highlighted by performances from Carly Simon, Daryl Hall & John Oates, Liza Minelli and concluded with the Paralympic theme song, "What's Your Excuse?", performed by Aretha Franklin.

With 157 total medals over 19 sports, Team USA was chock full of success stories. From the Olympic Stadium to the Georgia International Horse Park, the 320 Paralympians who comprised Team USA were a tribute both to their country and to the spirit of the Games. The athletes were celebrated by more than 700,000 spectators who came out to witness the competition, as well as a host of political figures, including President Bill Clinton, the Honorary Paralympic Chairman, Vice President Al Gore, Bob Dole and runningmate Jack Kemp, Ross Perot, Janet Reno and Georgia Lieutenant Governor Pierre Howard.

And while each had a story of their own to be told, there were a number of athletes whose stories and accomplishments won't be forgotten.

The Olympic Stadium was host to a number of spectacular moments, including those belonging to 13-year-old LeAnn Shannon of Orange Park, Fla., the youngest athlete at the

1996 Paralympic Games Review

Paralympic Games. Shannon broke two world records in the T52 wheelchair class during the Games, winning three gold medals, and a silver.

Heptathlete Marla Runyan of El Cajon, Calif., was no stranger to Olympic Stadium, having competed in the 1996 Olympic Trials. As a T12 visually-impaired Paralympian, she came to Atlanta on a quest for gold and she found it. Runyan set a world record in the heptathlon, in addition to winning a silver medal in the shot put.

Double-amputee Tony Volpentest, born without hands and feet, set a world record in the 100-meter class T43-44, in a time of 11.36 seconds, besting the previous mark by .27 seconds.

The Georgia Tech Aquatic Center, site of the swimming competition, was also the birthplace of champions. One of the Games most well-known competitors, four-time Paralympian Trischa Zorn, 32, of Indianapolis, Ind., earned medals in Atlanta, raising her career total to 47. For Zorn, classified as a B2 athlete for her visual impairment, the silver and bronze that she won were the first medals of a color other than gold to make it into her trophy case.

Among the other swimmers who joined Zorn in her success was Karen Norris of Van Nuys, Calif. Norris was "tickled pink" by the silver medal she won in the women's 100-meter backstroke class S10. Norris, who had won six medals in Barcelona, had come close to not competing when she lost her father last fall, only six months after having broken her shoulder.

"That really made me question my goals and motivations for swimming," Norris said. "I was ready to throw in the towel." But she did not, and after her event, a tearful Norris said of her win, "All the hurdles that I had to overcome made this one much sweeter."

One of the world records which were set at these Games belonged to U.S. powerlifter Kim Brownfield of Dewar, Okla. Brownfield, who had won a gold medal at the 1992 Paralympic Games in Barcelona, lifted 237.5 kilograms in the 100+ kilogram weight division to claim his Atlanta gold. Afterward, Brownfield said, "This is a dream come true. I've worked 19 years for this single moment."

Cyclist Dory Selinger of Oakland, Calif., not only won a medal for the mixed omnium, in a world-record performance, but he also won the award for the most memorable medal ceremony of the Games. Selinger, who finished first in each of three events which comprise the omnium—the 200-meter sprint, the kilometer time trial and the individual pursuit—had been awarded his gold medal and was awaiting the national anthem when the technology gods struck and the sound system went down. Fortunately for all, the American crowd was not about to let the ceremony commence without Selinger hearing the Star-Spangled Banner. So they sang it to him—a cappella.

Table tennis players Tahl Leibovitz of Woodhaven, N.Y., and Jennifer Johnson, of Port Chester, N.Y., each collected gold medals for Team USA in the individual events. Both athletes came from behind to take their wins, deriving their strength from the cheers of the enthusiastic crowd which gathered at the Gwinnett Civic Center. Johnson said, "Seoul was good, but here I had the crowd cheering, and I was pumped. I really won the medal for the crowd. If it wasn't for them, I wouldn't have been so determined."

One of the most popular events of the Games won't join the official program until 2000 in Sydney, but went a long way toward developing a following in Atlanta. The wheelchair rugby competition was tough, the competitors were fierce, and the crowds loved it. Team USA dominated the field and brought home a gold medal for this demonstration event, scoring a total of 288 goals. The other demonstration sport featured at the Games, yachting, brought home a bronze medal.

As the curtain fell on the 1996 Paralympic Games, both the fans and athletes reflected on the success of the 10 days, and looked forward with great anticipation to the next meeting of these athletes in Sydney. But as the competitors moved on, the legacy of these Atlanta Paralympic Games was the recognition—at long last—that these were, in fact, great athletes. And there was no one who could overlook that any longer.

1996 Paralympic Games Medal Chart

Country	G	S	B	T
USA	46	46	65	157
Germany	40	58	51	149
Great Britain	39	42	41	122
Australia	42	37	27	106
Spain	39	31	36	106
France	35	29	31	95
Canada	24	21	24	69
Italy	11	20	15	46
Netherlands	17	11	17	45
Denmark	7	17	17	41
People's Republic of China	16	13	10	39
Japan	14	10	13	37
Poland	13	14	8	35
Sweden	12	14	10	36
Korea	13	2	15	30
Egypt	8	11	11	30
South Africa	10	8	10	28
Russia	9	7	11	27
Belgium	8	10	7	25
Austria	6	6	10	22
Switzerland	9	6	6	21
Brazil	2	6	13	21
Norway	9	7	4	20
New Zealand	9	6	3	18
Islamic Republic of Iran	9	5	3	17
Hong Kong	5	5	5	15
Portugal	6	4	4	14
Iceland	5	4	5	14
Finland	4	5	4	13
Belarus	3	3	7	13
Mexico	3	5	4	12
Cuba	8	3	0	11
Slovakia	2	4	5	11
Lithuania	3	2	6	11
Hungary	5	2	3	10
Czech Republic	2	7	1	10
Ireland	1	3	6	10
Estonia	3	4	2	9
Argentina	2	5	2	9
Israel	0	4	5	9
Nigeria	3	2	3	8
Algeria	2	2	3	7
Ukraine	1	4	2	7
Greece	1	1	3	5
Slovenia	0	2	3	5

1996 Paralympic Team Roster

ARCHERY

Athlete, Birthdate, Hometown/Current Residence
Aaron Cross, 6/28/75, Waterloo, Iowa/St. Cloud, Minn.
Robert Norvelle, 12/11/61, Columbus, Ga./Tucson, Ariz.
Sid Williams, 8/20/56, Ogden, Utah/Roy, Utah
Team Leader/Coach: Robert Szyman, 6/1/47, St. Louis, Mo.

ATHLETICS

Men (81)
Athlete, Birthdate, Hometown/Current Residence
Andre Asbury, 10/28/64, Belle Harbor, N.Y.
Arnold Astrada, 12/23/45, San Jose, Calif.
Robert Balk, 3/7/66, Rochester, N.Y.
Larry Banks, 12/27/73, Decatur, Ga.
Tom Becke, Crown Point, Ind.
Ryan Blankenship, 12/30/74, Tampa, Fla.
Thomas Bougeois, 10/9/67, San Antonio, Texas
William Brady, 2/28/59, Harrisburg, N.C.
Willard Brooks, 5/6/68, Huntsville, Ala.
Shawn Brown, 9/23/71, San Diego, Calif.
Matt Bulow, 4/22/68, Nashville, Tenn.
Garland Burress, 5/13/64, Valley Park, Mo.
Marvin Campbell, 10/16/76, Jacksonville, Fla.
Michael Castle, 7/9/63, Ann Arbor, Mich.
Roger Charter, 8/7/55, Bethany, Okla.
Joe Christmas, 8/4/41, Mt. Sidney, Va.
John (Wiley) Clark, 3/5/56, Pasacagoula, Miss.
Tico Clawson, 4/30/77, Baltimore, Md.
Kurt Collier, 1/6/66, Tucson, Ariz.
David Collins, 1/19/62, Vista, Calif.
Patrick Cottini, 6/11/72, Champaign, Ill.
William Covington, 2/5/53, Washington, D.C.
William "Ross" Davis, 11/16/68, Amarillo, Texas
Jerry Deets, 11/1/49, Santa Cruz, Calif.
Gabriel Diaz deLeon, 3/10/63, San Antonio, Texas
Paul Dietrich, 2/5/65, Fairborn, Ohio
Barton Dodson, 4/17/58, Murfreesboro, Tenn.
Marc Fenn, 3/28/70, Indianapolis, Ind.
Arthur Foote, 10/17/65, Waterbury, Conn.
Brian (Timothy) Frasure, 2/2/73, Kerry, N.C.
Wardell Gadson, 12/13/71, Philadelphia, Pa.
Winford Haynes, 2/12/55, Alamogordo, N.M.
Jacob Heilveil, 3/11/70, Bothell, Wash.
Douglas Heir, 2/27/60, Cherry Hill, N.J.
Kelvin Hogans, 8/9/68, Janesville, Wis.
Scot Hollenbeck, 11/5/69, Smyrna, Ga.
Larry Hughes, 12/12/48, Columbia, Md.
Scott (Asa) Ison, 6/9/65, Mansfield, Ohio
Denton Johnson, 10/2/56, Port Chester, N.Y.
Mike Keohane, 4/4/65, New York, N.Y.
Al Kovach, 1/12/65, San Diego, Calif.
David Larson, 11/2/69, Carlsbad, Calif.
Arthur Lewis, 6/5/72, Los Angeles, Calif.
Aaron Little, 5/2/60, Allegon, Mich.
William Locke, 5/2/67, Glen Shaw, Pa.
Richard Lowe, 8/13/55, Follansbee, W.Va.
Norman Lyduch, 7/4/72, Champaign, Ill.
Craig Mallinckrodt, 10/13/58, Fort Collins, Colo.
Vince Martin, 11/22/64, Atlanta, Ga.
Jim Martinson, 10/27/46, Puyallup, Wash.
Jim Mastro, 7/22/48, Fridley, Minn.
Shawn Meredith, 3/25/64, Champaign, Ill.
Robert Molinatti, 9/10/58, Huntington Beach, Calif.
Don Mott, 12/2/52, Carpentersville, Ill.
Edward Munroe, St. Augustine, Fla.
Eric Neitzel, 11/25/75, San Diego, Calif.
Paul Nitz, 3/9/69, Avon, Conn.
Dennis Oehler, 4/13/60, East Hampton, N.Y.

Joseph Parker, 9/21/78, Goose Creek, S.C.
Matt Parry, 4/30/74, Chandler, Ariz.
Nathan Perkins, 2/14/67, Menlo Park, Calif.
Joe Quintanilla, 6/8/76, Cambridge, Mass.
Brad Ramage, 1/8/68, Mechanicsville, Va.
Freeman Register, 10/14/72, Starke, Fla.
Christopher Ridgway, 9/26/64, Bryn Mawr, Pa.
Rich Ruffalo, 9/28/51, Bloomfield, N.J.
Todd Schaffhauser, 6/16/69, Coram, N.Y.
Lincoln Scott, Tampa, Fla.
Tom Sellers, 12/26/65, Ormond Beach, Fla.
John Siciliano, 3/11/71, New York, N.Y.
Eric Stenback, 9/13/67, Derby, Kan.
Hugo Storer, 9/29/63, Garland, Texas
Kevin Szott, 4/14/63, State College, Pa.
Greg Taylor, 4/8/65, Tampa, Fla.
Jason Tercey, Kansas City, Mo.
Tony Volpentest, 10/3/72, Federal Way, Wash.
Chris Waddell, 9/28/68, Granby, Mass.
Lynn Watchell, 1/4/69, Cincinnati, Ohio
James Weidner, 3/19/61, Tampa, Fla.
Tim Willis, 3/30/71, Tucker, Ga.
Dana Zimmerman, 8/31/79, St. Paul, Minn.

Women (27)
Athlete, Birthdate, Hometown/Current Residence
Jennifer Barrett, Gonzalez, Calif.
Cheri Becerra, 9/27/76, Nebraska City, Neb.
Candace Cable, 7/5/54, Truckee, Calif.
Katheryne "Lyn" Carlton, 1/27/55, Cupertino, Calif.
Jean Driscoll, 11/18/66, Champaign, Ill.
Susan Edwards, 8/17/56, Trenton, Mich.
Ellen Hyman, 4/14/70, Chicago, Ill.
Angel James, 9/25/74, Orangeburg, S.C.
Susan Katz, 11/12/78, North Potomac, Md.
Melissa "Missy" Lehman, 12/20/78, Watertown, Wis.
Karen Lewis, 3/24/64, Steilacoom, Wash.
Peggy Martin, 8/30/68, Shakopee, Minn.
Linda Mastandrea, 6/10/64, Elmhurst, Ill.
Pam McGonigle, 3/12/68, Pittsburgh, Pa.
Tracy Miller, 11/9/62, Mukilteo, Wash.
Aimee Mullins, 7/20/75, Washington, D.C.
Sheila O'Neil, Libertyville, Ill.
Jacqueline Payne, 11/25/68, Fruita, Colo.
Marla Runyan, 1/4/69, El Cajon, Calif.
Laura Schwanger, 11/15/68, Williamstown, N.J.
LeAnn Shannon, 12/17/82, Orange Park, Fla.
Judy Siegle, 12/9/60, Fargo, N.D.
Deanna Sodoma, 5/23/67, Carlsbad, Calif.
Mary Thompson, 1/26/61, San Diego, Calif.
Ann Walters, 5/19/69, Savoy, Ill.
Jeanie Waters, 10/2/58, Rockeville Centre, N.Y.
Rose Winand, 2/21/60, Boston, Mass.
Team Leader: Paul Tetreault, 7/17/52, North Kingstown, R.I.
Head Coaches: Dr. John Kernan (field events), 6/17/51, Alamosa, Colo.; Tamara Larson (WC track), 6/6/62, Lino Lakes, Minn.; Stan Narewski (ambulatory track), 6/22/49, Gardendale, Ala.; Bill Wegehaupt (SOI coach)
Assistant Coaches: Randy Frommater, 1/22/52, Park City, Utah; Kevin Hansen, 10/28/52, Eugene, Ore.; Ellen Jelinek, 10/6/63, Chicago, Ill.; Maureen Mausser, 5/5/65, Champaign, Ill.; Philip Roberts, 12/3/35, Forestville, Conn.; Caryl Senn, n/a, Massapequa, N.Y.; Jim Vargo, 3/26/60, Statesboro, Ga.; Rick Wolfley, 7/9/62, Westbrry, N.Y.

BASKETBALL

Men (12)
Athlete, Birthdate, Hometown/Current Residence
Reggie Colton, 11/28/64, Gainesville, Fla.
Chuck Gill, 12/28/63, San Francisco, Calif.

1996 Paralympic Team Roster

Larry "Trooper" Johnson, 12/6/63, Santa Cruz, Calif.
Melvin Juette, 5/18/69, Whitewater, Wis.
Tim Kazee, 7/15/65, Little Rock, Ark.
Rob Knight, 11/25/70, Savoy, Ill.
Jim Miller, 11/7/53, Fresno, Calif.
Mike Schlappi, 12/14/62, Sandy, Utah
Mark Shepherd, 2/2/54, Colorado Springs, Colo.
Craig Shewmake, 8/9/56, Long Beach, Calif.
Randy Snow, 5/24/59, Heath, Texas
Darryl Waller, 1/13/58, Antioch, Texas
Team Leader: Marv Lapicola, n/a, Schaumburg, Ill.
Head Coach: Brad Hedrick, 8/29/52, Urbana, Ill.
Assistant Coaches: Lew Shaver; 1/27/37, Canby, Minn.; Rick Swauger, 12/28/56, Columbus, Ohio
Women (12)
Athlete, Birthdate, Hometown/Current Residence
Jamie Danskin, 1/24/73, Lawson, Mo./Manhattan Beach, Fla.
Pam Fontaine, 12/16/64, North Brunswick, N.J./Richardson, Texas
Susan Hagel, 2/5/54, Minneapolis, Minn.
Sharon Herbst, 4/23/67, Townsend, Mont./Fresno, Calif.
Ronda Jarvis, 7/6/67, Santa Fe, N.M./Birmingham, Ala.
Josie Johnson, 7/31/74, Gary, Minn.
Kim Martin, 1/11/68, Columbus, Ohio
Ruth Nunez, 9/11/74, Austin, Texas/Champaign, Ill.
Margaret Stran, 4/25/73, Shorewood, Ill./Champaign, Ill.
Jana Stump, 2/11/75, Belleville, Kan./Champaign, Ill.
Tiana Tozer, 4/22/68, Boise, Idaho/Reno, Nev.
Renee Tyree-Gross, 7/23/65, Racine, Wis./Tucson, Ariz.
Team Leader: Perry Hendricks, n/a, Minneapolis, Minn.
Head Coach: Deb Sundeman, 9/6/56, Savage, Minn.
Assistant Coaches: (Paula) Susie Grimes, 9/15/54, Eugene, Ore.; Frank Brasile, 1/16/45, Omaha, Neb.

BOCCIA

Athlete, Birthdate, Hometown/Current Residence
Austin Hanson, 1/4/74, Topeka, Kan.
James "Jason" Hilborn, 3/25/71, Lilburn, Ga.
Kenny Johnson, 8/23/66, Chicago, Ill.
Gary Ragland, 11/5/63, Fort Worth, Texas
James Thomson, 3/1/66, N. Babylon, N.Y.
Steve Thompson, 8/24/63, Overland Park, Kan.
Team Leader/Head Coach: Debbie Akins, 8/28/57, Fort Worth, Texas
Assistant Coach: Patrick Oliver, 6/23/56, Fort Worth, Texas

CYCLING

Men (20)
Athlete, Birthdate, Hometown/Current Residence
Stephen Aukward, 7/7/49, Roanoke, Va.
John Asquini, 11/13/67, Redford, Mich.
Pier Angelo Beltrami, 2/17/50, Hagerstown, Md.
Raymond Collins, 8/13/60, Plymouth, Mass.
Steve Cook, 7/11/68, Salt Lake City, Utah
Steve (John) Hermanson, 7/5/64, Yucaipa, Calif.
Corey Huntley, 8/15/74, Springfield, Mass.
Ron Irvine, 12/2/56, Vienna, Calif.
Matthew King, 11/2/65, Breinigsville, Pa.
Jake (Jacob) Klementich, 4/14/68, Houston, Texas
Mark Lindsey, 10/30/61, Riverside, Calif.
Tom (Hendrick) Neal, Hosham, Pa.
Daniel Nicholson, 11/3/70, Richmond, Va.
Rex Patrick, 3/14/60, Englewood, Colo.
Christopher Pyrkosz, 10/19/70, Livonia, Mich.
Lawrence Schultz, 4/4/66, Seville, Ohio
Gary Seghi, n/a, Austin, Texas
Dory Selinger, 10/13/71, Oakland, Calif.
John Theobald, 1/3/57, Syracuse, N.Y.
Bob Whitford, 3/4/68, Wichita Falls, Texas

Women (2)
Athlete, Birthdate, Hometown/Current Residence
Julia Haft, 12/18/56, Kensington, Md.
Mary Pirrallo, 7/10/62, Clinton Township, Mich.
Mixed (3)
Athlete, Birthdate, Hometown/Current Residence
Cara Dunne, 3/17/70, Los Angeles, Calif.
Pamela Fernandes, 6/24/61, Brighton, Mass.
Kathleen Urschel, 3/3/64, Baldwinsville, N.Y.
Team Leader: Peter Paulding, 1/12/48, Plymouth, Mass.
Head Coach: Jose Alcala, 11/30/60, Bronx, N.Y.
Assistant Coaches: Karen Fitzgerald, 1/30/54, Feeding Hills, Mass.; Tina Russo, 2/11/60, Tampa, Fla.
Mechanic: Steve Lasand

EQUESTRIAN

Athlete, Birthdate, Hometown/Current Residence
Gerald Hoff, 10/16/65, Ballwin, Mo.
Tony Hojnacki, 5/27/47, Bloomfield, N.J./Plano, Texas
Lauren McDevitt, 9/25/72, Atlanta, Ga./Carrboro, N.C.
Vicki Sweigart, 1/29/56, Denver, Colo./Reinholds, Pa.
Schoena Townsend, 1/30/71, St. Louis, Mo./Chesterfield, Mo.
Janie Zukas, 3/30/61, Hastings, N.Y.
Team Leader: Lisa Gatti, 8/20/67, Lindenhurst, N.Y.
Head Coach: Sandy Rafferty, 5/7/44, Troy, Mo.
Assistant Coaches: Gloria Hamblin, 9/19/51, Chatsworth, Calif.; (Elizabeth) Lili Kellogg, 9/24/53, Wylie, Texas; Gail Pace, 4/17/45, Dallas, Texas

FENCING

Men (5)
Athlete, Birthdate, Hometown/Current Residence
David Baker, 6/25/53, Hackensack, N.J.
Robert Davis, 4/4/59, Louisville, Ky.
John Loechle, 5/30/69, Newcastle, Ky.
Joe Mueller, 6/12/50, Marietta, Ga.
Mario Rodriguez, 3/6/59, Sugar Land, Texas
Women (3)
Athlete, Birthdate, Hometown/Current Residence
Terri Cecil-Ramsey, 2/9/66, Louisville, Ky.
Ella Chafee, 3/4/45, Oak Lawn, Ill.
Kathleen Rose Winter, 9/10/56, Chicago Ill.
Team Leader: James R. James, Jr. 9/20/58, Louisville, Ky.
Head Coach: Leszek Stawicki, 2/24/36, Louisville, Ky.

GOALBALL

Men (6)
Athlete, Birthdate, Hometown/Current Residence
Walter Blackmon, 3/15/73, Tallahassee, Fla.
Shawn Donaldson, 2/3/74, Livonia, Mich.
Daniel Foppiano, 5/9/68, Massapequa, N.Y.
David Hacker, 3/31/61, Nashville, Tenn.
Ed McInnis, 1/21/63, Saginaw, Mich.
George Morris, 2/27/61, St. Louis, Mo.
Team Leader: Gay Clement-Atkinson, 8/26/40, Gaston, S.C.
Head Coach: Tom Parrigin, 3/24/37, St. Augustine, Fla.
Assistant Coach: Walt Lawrence, 4/20/32, Greenville, Mich.
Women (6)
Athlete, Birthdate, Hometown/Current Residence
Jeni Armbruster, 2/12/75, Colorado Springs, Colo.
Irene Davis-Sparks, 9/28/70, Austin, Texas
Patty Egensteiner-Asbury, 5/16/61, Belle Harbor, N.Y.
Sheryl Gordon, 7/28/60, Kalamazoo, Mich.
Margaret "Maggi" Ostrowski, 4/7/55, Pittsburgh, Pa.
Maureen Ryan-Esposito, 4/16/64, Tampa, Fla.
Head Coach: Ken Armbruster, 8/15/46, Colorado Springs, Colo.
Assistant Coach: Wendy Fagan, 4/15/63, Fort Worth, Texas

1996 Paralympic Team Roster

JUDO

Athlete, Birthdate, Hometown/Current Residence
Ray Dunmeyer, 9/12/58, Newark, N.J.
Brett Lewis, 8/2/66, Santa Monica, Calif.
Marlon Lopez, 12/13/75, Los Angeles, Calif.
Jim Mastro, 7/22/48, Fridley, Minn.
Stephen "Scott" Moore, 11/10/69, Lafayette, La.
Kevin Szott, 4/14/63, State College, Pa.
Team Leader: Walter Dean, 6/10/42, Stuart, Fla.
Head Coach: Larry Lee, 1/25/63, Aurora, Colo.

LAWN BOWLS

Athlete, Birthdate, Hometown/Current Residence
Carolyn Nobbe, 11/29/46, Milwaukee, Wis./Libertyville, Ill.
Rob Patterson, 9/5/48, Charlotte, N.C./Pemberville, Ohio
Team Leader/Head Coach: James Copeland, 5/6/39, Ripon, Wis.

POWERLIFTING

Athlete, Birthdate, Hometown/Current Residence
Tim Babinec, 2/18/64, Tavares, Fla.
Kim Brownfield, 4/26/64, Dewar, Okla.
Pernell Cooper, 6/28/63, Atlanta, Ga.
Doug Farrell, 5/6/58, Healdsburg, Calif.
Jerry Millhouse, 5/12/66, Lexington, Ky.
Normez Schulz, 7/16/62, Chicago, Ill.
Jaronnie Smith, 10/14/67, Houston, Texas
William "Mitch" Strickland, 10/1/58, Tuscaloosa, Ala.
Rob Wills, 9/10/67, Osseo, Minn.
Team Leaders: William Hens, n/a, Levittown, Pa.
Head Coach: Michael McDevitt, 1/24/60, Upper Darby, Pa.
Assistant Coach: Alan Goldstein, 1/24/60, Chicago, Ill.

QUAD RUGBY

Athlete, Birthdate, Hometown/Current Residence
Dave Ceruti, 10/21/64, Southington, Conn.
Cliff Chunn, 10/10/78, Brentwood, Tenn.
Eddie Crouch, 2/14/64, Antioch, Tenn.
David Gould, 9/17/63, Newport Richey, Fla.
Bill Renje, n/a, Tinley Park, Ill.
Joe Soares, 8/13/59, Tampa, Fla.
Brad Updegrove, 3/19/66, Houston, Texas
Mike Wyatt, 11/28/67, Oceanside, Calif.
Team Leader: Judy Pfiester
Head Coach: Terry Vinyard
Assistant Coach: Reggie Richner

SHOOTING

Athlete, Birthdate, Hometown/Current Residence
Ron Davis, 12/28/57, Middletown, Pa.
Barbaro Ponce, 12/15/67, Atlanta, Ga.
Bob Shields, 3/22/65, North Brunswick, N.J.
Alex Smith, 11/25/27, Vero Beach, Fla.
Mike Stovall, 9/4/62, Dunwoody, Ga.
Team Leader: Peggy Turner, 11/10/59, Houston, Texas
Head Coach: Robert Robertson

SOCCER

Athlete, Birthdate, Hometown/Current Residence
Elias "Eli" Abarbanel-Wolff, 4/22/77, Washington, D.C.
Adolfo Aguilar, 4/15/76, Garland, Texas
Craig Baker, 1/31/55, Moultrie, Ga.
Tim Kistner, 5/10/76, Houston, Texas
Matt Lavin, 12/30/59, Grand Prairie, Texas
John McCullough, 11/29/65, Washington, D.C.
Josh McKinney, 1/18/79, Hilton Head, S.C.
Daniel Nicholson, 11/3/70, Richmond, Va.

Mike Peters, 2/3/69, Tucson, Ariz.
Brian Robinson, 2/15/74, Sparta, N.J.
John Theobald, 1/3/57, Syracuse, N.Y.
Team Leader/Head Coach: Alistair Young, 1/8/62, Dallas, Texas
Assistant Coach: Lori Goldenberg, 5/31/64, Athens, Ga.; Rick Moss; Phil Rose

SWIMMING

Men (18)
Athlete, Birthdate, Hometown/Current Residence
Dana Adam Albrycht, 11/23/77, Canton, Conn.
Luis Alicea, 4/6/73, Ontario, Calif.
Doug Bell, 2/6/77, Brazil, Ind.
Gregory Burns, 9/30/57, Singapore/Washington, D.C.
Dan Butler, 2/22/55, Falls Church, Va.
Dennis Calonico, 5/3/51, San Mateo, Calif.
Michael Doyle, 10/17/55, Warrington, Pa.
Nick Karris, 8/22/78, Portage, Ind.
Dan Kelly, 7/13/76, Golden Valley, Minn.
Craig Laufenberg, 1/14/74, Whitewater, Wis.
Travis Mohr, 5/1/81, Northampton, Pa.
Martin Parker, 9/24/64, Tucson, Ariz.
Aaron Paulson, 4/4/77, Portland, Ore.
John Register, 3/9/65, Springfield, Va.
Jay Styperk, 10/5/80, Pittsburgh, Pa.
Mike Taber, 6/9/57, Albany, N.Y.
Jim Thompson, 11/20/65, Cherry Hill, N.J.
Jason Wening, 9/27/74, Jefferson City, Mo.
Women (24)
Athlete, Birthdate, Hometown/Current Residence
Julie Atwell, 12/27/79, Endwell, N.Y.
Stephanie Brooks, 6/24/81, Algonquin, Ill.
Aimee Bruder, 8/3/74, Lawrenceburg, Ind.
Colleen Dailey, 3/15/61, Houston, Texas
Colleen Dougherty, 2/26/69, Bend, Ore.
Dawn Duffy, 10/5/76, Moore, Okla.
Katie Edgar, 12/21/77, Wilmington, Del.
Sandy Hanebrink, 5/4/65, Mount Pleasant, S.C.
Jenn Hazen, 11/28/77, Bloomfield, N.J.
Anne Herman, 7/10/49, San Diego, Calif.
Brenda Levy, 10/30/57, Rockville, Md.
Joyce Luncher, 6/19/75, Pittsburgh, Pa.
Susan Moucha, 1/28/58, Brandon, Fla.
Jill Nelson, 5/9/78, Pampa, Texas
Karen Norris, 6/22/65, Van Nuys, Calif.
Allison Pittman, 5/13/76, San Diego, Calif.
Elizabeth Scott, 6/25/74, Rockville, Md.
Jenny Skinner, 1/30/71, Huntington Beach, Calif.
Mandy Sommer, 9/16/78, Omaha, Neb.
Diane Straub, 6/5/68, Cambridge, Mass.
Kelly Sutton, 6/5/76, Lexington, Ky.
Camille Waddell-Black, 10/23/61, Pensacola, Fla.
Julie Wolfe, 9/25/72, Tucson, Ariz.
Trisha Zorn, 6/1/64, Indianapolis, Ind.
Team Leader: Bill Priest, 6/17/48, North Yarmouth, Maine
Head Coach: Mark Maxwell, 5/12/58, Canby, Ore.; Jan Krekel (SOI Coach)
Assistant Coaches: Tom Calomeris, 9/16/42, Beltsville, Md.; Rob Hale, 11/19/59, Cumberland, Maine; Joan Karpuk, n/a, Glastonbury, Conn.; (Katherine) Martie McKinney, 2/18/65, La Jolla, Calif.; Pam Redding

TABLE TENNIS

Men (8)
Athlete, Birthdate, Hometown/Current Residence
Gary Blanks, 2/4/59, Virginia Beach, Va.
Ken Brooks, 1/21/48, Lebanon, N.J.
Sebastian DeFrancisco, n/a, n/a (n/a)

1996 Paralympic Team Roster

Mike Dempsy, 9/8/56, Oxnard, Calif.
James Hall, 2/14/57, Colton, Calif.
Tahl Liebovitz, 6/1/75, Woodhaven, N.Y.
Andre (Anderson) Scott, 6/14/65, Elizabeth, N.J.
Mitch Siedenfeld, 3/18/63, Minneapolis, Minn.
Women (4)
Athlete, Birthdate, Hometown/Current Residence
Jackie DiLorenzo, 2/24/49, Hastings-on-Hudson, N.Y.
Jennifer Johnson, 10/25/48, Port Chester, N.Y.
Ruth Rosenbaum, 4/18/44, Hackensack, N.J.
Teresa Terranova, 5/21/47, Fort Lauderdale, Fla.
Team Leader: Rong Li Lillieroos, n/a, Oklahoma City, Okla.
Head Coach: Christopher Lehman, 3/13/50, Somerset, N.J.
Assistant Coach: Pei-Zhen Shao, 7/16/49, Flushing, N.Y.

TENNIS

Men (3)
Athlete, Birthdate, Hometown/Current Residence
Jim Black, 5/6/62, Oceanside, Calif.
Scott Douglas, 12/12/63, Birmingham, Ala.
Vance "Chip" Parmelly, 10/11/56, Diamond Bar, Calif.
Steve Welch, n/a, Arlington, Texas
Team Leader/Coach (M): Wayne Leavitt
Women (2)
Athlete, Birthdate, Hometown/Current Residence
Hope Lewellen, 4/20/67, Palos Park, Ill.
Nancy Olson, 3/8/57, Daytona Beach, Fla.
Coach (W): David Crowe, n/a, Palm Beach, Fla.

VOLLEYBALL

Sitting (10)
Athlete, Birthdate, Hometown/Current Residence
Lloyd Bachrach, n/a, Chicago, Ill.
Larry Chloupek, 1/24/61, Potomac, Md.
Bill Demby, 9/8/50, Mitchellville, Md.
Steve Doudt, 11/6/69, Indianapolis, Ind.
Jim Dugan, 7/16/47, Bethalto, Ill.
Jim Kessler, 6/1/61, Sabetha, Kan.
Paul Kramer, 12/11/46, San Jose, Calif.
Tracey Lange, 3/11/67, Waunakee, Wis.
Paul Moran, 12/31/66, Chicago, Ill.
Kurt Smith, 12/21/63, Elmhurst, Ill.
James Terpenning, 10/26/68, Cornwall, N.Y.
Edward Tuthill, 11/7/63, Montauk, N.Y.
Team Leader: Kelly Finger, 12/13/70, Chicago, Ill.
Head Coach: Mike Hulett, 2/13/55, Des Plaines, Ill.
Assistant Coach: Ron Stahl, 8/10/66, Dallas, Texas
Standing (12)
Athlete, Birthdate, Hometown/Current Residence
Barry Hammer, 9/23/59, Lebanon, Tenn.
Dennis Lee, 3/11/61, Greensboro, N.C.
Jeff Munn, 5/4/57, Sugar Hill, Ga.
David Newkirk, 8/22/73, Lubbock, Texas
Robert Osbahr, 6/8/64, Freehold, N.J.
Douglas "Ray" Ragsdale, 9/19/75, Lubbock, Texas
Chris Seilkop, 11/8/69, Deland, Fla.
Thomas Sestanovich, n/a, Manhatten Beach, Calif.
Joe Sullivan, 9/21/69, Richmond, Va.
Dwight Van Tassell, 3/24/68, Alpharetta, Ga.
Mike Walters, 5/11/65, Hudson, Wis.
Jeff Werner, 8/9/73, Reading, Pa.
Team Leader: Andrea Kelliher
Head Coach: Jill Mushett, 10/9/59, Norwalk, Ohio
Assistant Coach: Jim Luna, 6/27/48, Murfreesboro, Tenn.

YACHTING

Athlete, Birthdate, Hometown/Current Residence
James Leatherman, n/a, Baltimore, Md.
Chris Murphy, 6/18/71, Annapolis, Md.
John Ross-Duggan, 8/2/55, Orlando, Fla.
Waldo Esparza, (alternate), 9/30/56, Seffner, Fla.
Team Leader: Sergo Jorgensen

MISSION STAFF

Chef de Mission: Duncan Wyeth, Lansing, Mich.
Attache: Greg Harney, Colorado Springs, Colo.
AAC Representatives: Nancy Kinnier; Lynn Manning
Delegation Director: Nancy Gonsalves, Colorado Springs, Colo.

MEDICAL STAFF

Medical Coordinator (1): Sue Snouse, ATC, Lake Placid, N.Y. (USOC)
Head Physician (1): Greg Palutsis, M.D., Lake Bluff, Ill.
Physicians (6): David Garrison, M.D., State College, Pa.; Henry Goitz, M.D., St. Clair Shores, Mich.; Douglas Henry, M.D., St. Clair Shores, Mich.; Marcy Millar, M.D., Evanston, Ill.; Kevin Murphy, M.D., Duluth, Minn.; Jim Sterling, M.D., Dallas, Texas
Orthotist/Prosthetist: James McElhiney, Brentwood, Tenn.
Athletic Trainers/Physical Therapists (16): Mark Anderson, ATC/RPT, Oklahoma City, Okla.; David Balsley, RPT, New York, N.Y.; DeLane Davidson, ATC, North Brunswick, N.J.; Mary Donahue, ATC/RPT, Grosse Pointe Park, Mich.; Suzan Frovik, ATC, Maple Grove, Minn.; Robert Gailey, RPT, Coral Gables, Fla.; (William) Darren Hammond, ATC/RPT, Philadelphia, Pa.; (Patricia) Trish Kelly, ATC, Muncie, Ind.; John Knarr, RPT, Wilmington, Del.; David Lawrence, ATC/RPT, Richmond, Va.; Renee Lehman, ATC, Cranston, R.I.; Robert Loll, ATC, Dublin, Ohio; Laine Murret, ATC/RPT, Hattiesburg, Miss.; John Nyland, ATC/RPT, Lexington, Ky.; Laureen Ouellette, ATC, San Diego, Calif.; Debra Runkle, ATC, North Mankato, Minn.

PERSONAL CARE ATTENDANTS

Gary Barraclough; Jim Beckford; Corey Bell; Kelly Kowan; Pedro Gneiting; Connie Hansen; Kathy Nelligan; Kim Pittman; Biran Reeves; Brenna Richmond; Eugene Sloan; Kim Speer; Troy Stewart, Tim Thompson

MEDIA SERVICES STAFF

Eric Bacher; Anthony Black; Michael Braughton; Wendy Day; Steve Dittmore; Barbara Gresham; Kathy Harper; Ed Harrison; Christy McAllister; Paul Meznarich

1996 Paralympic Games Results

ARCHERY

Individual Men Standing
1. Ryszard Olejnik, POL; 2. Jean F. Garcia, FRA; 3. Tae AHN, KOR; No USA entries.

Individual Men W1
1. Martti Rantavuori, FIN; 2. Kurt Maccaferri, SUI; 3. Koichi Minami, JPN; 4. Aaron Cross, Waterloo, Iowa; 8. Sid Williams, Ogden, Utah.

Individual Men W2
1. Ouk Lee, KOR; 2. Jacob Walstra, NED; 3. Udo Wolf, GER; 15. Robert Norvelle, Columbus, Ga.

Individual Women Standing
1. Malgorzata Olejnik, POL; 2. Anita Chapman, GBR; 3. Marie F. Hybois, FRA; No USA entries.

Individual Women W2
1. Hifumi Suzuki, JPN; 2. Sandra Truccolo, ITA; 3. Paola Fantato; No USA entries.

Team Men Standing
1. KOR; 2. POL; 3. JPN; No USA entry.

Team Men W1/W2
1. GER; 2. ITA; 3. KOR; 7. USA (Aaron Cross, Waterloo, Iowa/St. Cloud, Minn; Robert Norvelle, Columbus, Ga./Tucson, Ariz.; Sid Williams, Ogden, Utah/Roy, Utah).

Team Women Open
1. ITA; 2. JPN; 3. GBR; No USA entry

ATHLETICS

100m Men T10
1. Julio Requena, ESP, 11.66 PR; 2. Jose Rodriguez, ESP, 11.70; 3. Andrew Curtis, GBR, 11.73; Marvin Campbell, Jacksonville, Fla., USA, elim. in semifinal; Winford Haynes, Alamogordo, N.M., USA, elim. in semifinal; Vincent Martin, Atlanta, Ga., USA, elim. in semifinal.

100m Women T10
1. Puri Santamarta, ESP, 12.59; 2. Adria Santos, BRA, 12.92; 3. Raquel Diaz, ESP, 12.99; No USA entries.

100m Men T11
1. Juan Preto, ESP, 11.38; 2. Miroslaw Pych, POL, 11.39; 3. Jorge Nunez, ESP, 11.51; Andre Asbury, Belle Harbor, N.Y., USA, elim. in heat.

100m Women T11
1. Beatriz Mendoza, ESP, 13.02; 2. Claire Brunotte, GER, 13.19; 3. Maria Jose Alves, BRA, 13.38; No USA entries.

100m Men T12
1. Aldo Mmanganaro, ITA, 11.01, PR; 2. Enrique Caballero, CUB, 11.38; 3. Leroi Court, AUS, 11.48; Arthur Lewis, Los Angeles, Calif., USA, elim. in semifinal.

100m Men T32
1. Lachlan Jones, AUS, 19.90; 2. Joseph Radmore, CAN, 21.59; 3. Paul Williams, GBR, 21.86; No USA entries.

100m Women T32-33
1. Noriko Arai, JPN, 19.89; 2. Linda Mastandrea, Elmhurst, Ill., USA, 20.02; 3. Sheila O'Neil, Libertyville, Ill., USA, 21.80.

100m Men T33
1. William Davis, Amarillo, Texas, USA, 16.46; 2. Gunnar Krantz, SWE, 16.52; 3. David Larson, Carlsbad, Calif., USA, 16.86; 7. Christopher Ridgway, Bryn Mawr, Pa., USA, 19.22.

100m Men T34
1. Suarez Nestor, ARG, 14.34; 2. Jaime Romaguera, AUS, 14.96; 3. Paul Hughes, GBR, 15.23; No USA entries.

100m Women T34-35
1. Caroline Innes, GBR, 15.78; 2. Maria Alvarez, ESP, 16.11; 3. Cornelia Teubner, GER, 16.54; 4. Angel James, Orangeburg, S.C., USA, 16.69.

100m Men T35
1. Du Kim, KOR, 13.22; 2. Fernando Gomez, ESP, 13.23; 3. Freeman Register IV, Starke, Fla., USA, 13.31; 8. Eric Stenback, Derby, Kan., USA, 14.10; James Weidner, Tampa, Fla., USA, elim. in semifinal.

100m Men T36
1. Mohamed Allek, ALG, 12.03, WR; 2. Peter Haber, GER, 12.45;

Ahmed Mahmoud, EGY, 12.65; No USA entries.

100m Women T36-37
1. Katrina Webb, AUS, 14.79; 2. Isabelle Foerder, GER, 15.08; 3. Alison Quinn, AUS, 15.31; No USA entries.

100m Men T37
1. Stephen Payton, GBR, 11.90; 2. Lincoln Scott, Tampa, Fla., USA, 12.29; 3. Douglas Amador, BRA, 12.31; 6. Ryan Blankenship, Tampa, Fla., USA, 13.09.

100m Men T42
1. Lukas Christen, SUI, 13.55; 2. Paul Gregori, FRA, 14.05; 3. Todd Schaffhauser, Coram, N.Y., USA, 14.60; John Siciliano, New York, N.Y., USA, 15.70.

100m Women T42-46
1. Annely Ojastu, EST, 12.78; 2. Jessica Sachse, GER, 12.86; 3. Amy Winters, AUS, 12.89; Aimee Mullins, Washington, D.C., USA, elim. in semifinal.

100m Men T43-44
1. Anthony Volpentest, Federal Way, Wash., USA, 11.36, WR; 2. Neil Fuller, AUS, 11.97; 3. Bradley Thomas, AUS, 12.02; Timothy Frasure, Kerry, N.C., DNF final.

100m Men T45-46
1. Adeoye Ajibola, NGR, 11.11; 2. Geir Sverrisson, ISL, 11.23; 3. Klaus Felser, AUT, 11.28.

100m Men T51
1. Paul Nitz, Avon, Conn., USA, 17.62, WR; 2. Anrea Beaudoin, CAN, 17.80; 3. Dean Bergeron, CAN, 17.83; 4. Bradley Ramage, Mechanicsville, Pa., USA, 17.99; 8. Patrick Cottini, Quincy, Calif., USA, 19.18.

100m Men T52
1. John Lindsay, AUS, 15.22; 2. Yasuhiro Une, JPN, 15.37; 3. Mattew Parry, Chandler, Ariz., USA, 15.41; 7. Christopher Waddell, Granby, Mass., USA, 16.13; Paul Dietrich Jr., Fairborn, Ohio., USA, elim. in semifinal.

100m Women T52
1. LeAnn Shannon, Orange Park, Fla., USA, 16.62, WR; 2. Tanni Grey, GBR, 17.18; 3. Colette Bourgonje, CAN, 18.35.

100m Men T53
1. David Holding, GBR, 14.45; 2. Hakan Eriksson, SWE, 14.60; 3. Claude Issorat, FRA, 14.79; Eric Neitzel, San Diego, Calif., USA, elim. in heat.

100m Women T53
1. Chantal Petitclerc, CAN, 16.70; 2. Cheri Becerra, Nebraska City, Neb., USA, 16.74; 3. Nicola Jarvis, GBR, 17.93; 6. Tracy Miller, Mukiliteo, Calif., USA, 18.53.

200m Men T10
1. Julio Ruquena, ESP, 23.80 PR; 2. Andrew Curtis, GRB, 23.89; 3. Jorge Llerena, URU, 24.38; Marvin Campbell, Jacksonville, Fla., elim. in semi; Winford Haynes, Alamogordo, N.M., elim. in heat.

200m Women T10
1. Puri Santamarta, ESP, 25.45 WR; 2. Adria Santos, BRA, 26.15; 3. Maria Ligorio, ITA, 26.23; No USA entries.

200m Women T11
1. Beatriz Mendoza, ESP, 26.32 WR; 2. Claire Brunotte, GER, 26.80; 3. Maria Jose Alves, BRA, 26.87; No USA entries.

200m Men T11
1. Omar Moya, CUB, 22.89 WR; 2. Juan Prieto, ESP, 23.10; 3. Holger Geffers, GER, 23.10; Kelvin Hogans, Jamesville, Wis., USA, elim. in heat; Andre Asbury, Belle Harbor, N.Y., USA, elim. in heat.

200m Men T12
1. Robert Jimenez, DOM, 22.57; 2. Aldo Manganaro, ITA, 22.74; 3. Arthur Lewis III, Los Angeles, Calif., USA, 23.13.

200m Men T20 (Exhibition)
1. Nigel Bourne, GBR, 22.20, WR; 2. Tico Clawson, Baltimore, Md., USA, 22.24; 3. Kenneth Colaine, GBR, 22.65; 4. Wardell Gadson, Philadelphia, Pa., USA, 23.56.

200m Women T20 (Exhibition)
1. Sharon Rackham, AUS, 26.79, WR; 2. Tracey Melesko, CAN, 26.79; 3. Lisa Llorens, AUS, 27.32; No USA entries.

200m Women T32-33
1. Linda Mastandrea, Elmhurst, Ill., USA, 35.30, WR; 2. Noriko,

Arai, JPN, 37.18; 3. Mary Rice, IRL, 39.96.

200m Men T34-35

1. Freeman Register IV, Starke, Fla., USA, 26.96; 2. Fernando Gomez, ESP, 27.04; 3. Du Kim, KOR, 27.26.

200m Women T34-37

1. Katrina Webb, AUS, 30.7; 2. Isabelle Foerder, GER, 31.14; 3. Alicia Martinez, ESP, 31.73; Angel James, Orangeburg, S.C., USA, elim. in semifinal.

200m Men T36

1. Mohamed Allek, ALG, 24.32, WR; 2. Peter Haber, GER, 25.30; 3. Ahmed Mahmoud, EGY, 25.50; Gregory Taylor, Tampa, Fla., USA, elim. in semifinal.

200m Men T37

1. Stephen Payton, GBR, 24.34; 2. Douglas Amador, BRA, 25.18; 3. Darren Thrupp, AUS, 25.52; 4. Lincoln Scott, Tampa, Fla., 25.83.

200m Men T42

1. Lukas Christen, SUI, 27.62; 2. Paul Gregori, FRA, 30.16; 3. Lothar Overesch, GER, 30.79; 7. John Siciliano, New York, N.Y., USA, 57.80; Todd Schaffhauser, Coram, N.Y., USA, disqualified in final.

200m Women T42-46

1. Amy Winters, AUS, 25.97, WR; 2. Annely Ojastu, EST, 26.26; 3. Irina Leontiouk, BLS, 26.34; No USA entries.

200m Men T43-44

1. Anthony Volpentest, Federal Way, Wash., USA, 23.28; 2. Neil Fuller, AUS, 24.72; 3. Patrick Stoll, SUI, 25.86.

200m Men T45-46

1. Adeoye Ajibola, NGR, 21.89; 2. Geir Sverrisson, ISL, 22.24; 3. Daniel Louw, RSA, 22.76; No USA entries.

200m Men T51

1. Dean Bergeron, CAN, 31.44; 2. Shawn Meredith, Champaign, Ill., USA, 31.83; 3. Bradley Ramage, Mechanicsville, Va., USA, 31.90; 6. Paul Nitz, Avon, Conn., USA, 33.18.

200m Women T51

1. Cristeen Smith, NZE, 41.11 PR; 2. Leticia Torres, MEX, 42.08; 3. Ursina Greuter, SUI, 42.73; 4. Jean Waters, Rockville Center, N.Y., USA, 42.96; 8. Mary Thompson, San Diego, Calif., USA, 45.99.

200m Men T52

1. Yasuhiro Une, JPN, 26.90, WR; 2. John Lindsay, AUS, 27.38; 3. Wolfgang Petersen, GER, 27.72; 4. Matthew Parry, Chandler, Ariz., USA, 27.99; 5. Chris Waddell, Granby, Mass., USA, 28.15; 8. Paul Dietrich, Jr., Fairborn, Ohio, USA, 29.15.

200m Women T52

1. LeAnn Shannon, Orange Park, Fla., USA, 29.76, WR; 2. Tanni Grey, GBR, 30.38; 3. Colette Bourgonjoe, CAN, 33.18; 5. Ann Walters, Savoy, Ill., USA, 33.50.

200m Men T53

1. Claude Issorat, FRA, 26.07; 2. Hakan Eriksson, SWE, 26.21; 3. David Holding, GBR, 26.52; Eric Neitzel, San Diego, Calif., elim. in semifinal.

200m Women T53

1. Chantal Petitclerc, CAN, 29.41; 2. Cheri Becerra, Nebraska City, Neb., USA, 29.64; 3. Nicola Jarvis, GBR, 31.27; Tracy Miller, Mukilteo, Wash., USA, 32.66; Rose Winand, Boston, Mass., USA, elim. in semifinal.

400m Men T10

1. Donmingos Ramiao Game, POR, 52.92; 2. J. Tovar, ESP, 52.99; 3. Da Conceicao Lopes, POR, 53.64; No USA entries.

400m Women T10

1. Puri Santamarta, ESP, 58.16; 2. Adria Santos, BRA, 59.97; 3. Maria Ligorio, ITA, 1:00.11; No USA entries.

400m Men T11

1. Omar Moya, CUB, 50.02; 2. Sergio Sanchez, ESP, 51.40; 3. Ingo Geffers, GER, 52.67; Kelvin Hogans, Jamesville, Wis., USA, elim. in heat; Craig Mallinckrodt, Fort Collins, Colo., USA, elim. in heat.

400m Women T11

1. Rima Batalova, RUS, 59.39 PR; 2. Maria Ortega, ESP, 1:02.94; 3. Elena Jdanova, RUS, 1:03.06; Pam McGonigle, Pittsburgh, Pa., USA, elim. in semifinal.

400m Men T12

1. Ambrosio Zaldivar, CUB, 50.72; 2. Youcef Boudjeltia, ALG, 51.09;

3. Aldo Manganaro, ITA, 52.11; No USA entries.

400m Men T32-33

1. David Larson, Carlsbad, Calif., USA, 54.60 WR; 2. Gunnar Krantz, SWE, 55.78; 3. William Davis, Amarillo, Texas, USA, 55.97; 6. Christopher Ridgway, Bryn Mawr, Pa., USA, 1:01.62.

400m Men T34-35

1. Du Kim, KOR, 1:00.25, WR; 2. Fernando Gomez, ESP, 1:02.15; 3. Richard Collins, GBR, 1:02.91; Eric Stenback, Derby, Kan., elim. in heat.

400m Men T36

1. Ahmed Mahmoud, EGY, 56.15, WR; 2. Lamouri Rahmouni, FRA, 56.83; 3. Yiu Cheung Cheng, HKG, 57.37; No USA entries.

400m Men T37

1. Stephen Payton, GBR, 54.23, WR; 2. Malcolm Pringle, RSA, 55.34; 3. Jose Gonzales, ESP, 56.83; 5. Jason Tercey, Jefferson, Mo., USA, 58.62.

400m Men T42-46

1. B. Kone Oumar, CIV, 50.23; 2. Geir Sverrisson, ISL, 50.25; 3. Patrice Gerges, FRA, 50.62; No USA entries.

400m Men T44-46

1. B. Kone Oumar, CIV, 1:55.46, WR; 2. David Evans, AUS, 1:55.81; 3. Bachir Zergoune, ALG, 1:57.05; No USA entries.

400m Men T50

1. Alvise De Vidi, ITA, 1:22.16; 2. Tim Johansson, SWE, 1:22.40; 3. Giuseppe Forni, SUI, 1:22.56; 4. Barton Dodson, Murfreesboro, Tenn., USA, 1:27.78; 5. Norman Lyduch, Carpentersville, Ill., USA, 1:29.41.

400m Women T51

1. Ursina Greuter, SUI, 1:21.99, WR; 2. Jean Waters, Rockville Center, N.Y., 1:22.29; 3. Leticia Torres, MEX, 1:22.55; 4. Judith Siegle, Fargo, N.D., 1:23.57; Mary Thompson, San Diego, Calif., USA, elim. in semifinal.

400m Men T51

1. Shawn Meredith, Champaign, Ill., USA, 1:01.9; 2. Dean Bergeron, CAN, 1:01.93; 3. Andre Beaudoin, CAN, 1:02.5; 6. Paul Nitz, Avon, Conn., USA, 1:06.9; 7. Bradley Ramage, Mechanicsville, Va., USA, 1:07.52.

400m Men T52

1. Winfried Sigg, GER, 52.43; 2. Markus Pilz, GER, 52.61; 3. John Lindsay, AUS, 52.93; Thomas Sellers, Ormond Beach, Fla., USA, elim. in semifinal; Christopher Waddell, Granby, Mass., USA, elim. in semifinal.

400m Women T52

1. LeAnn Shannon, Orange Park, Fla., USA, 57.55; 2. Tanni Grey, GBR, 58.09; 3. Joelle Vogel, FRA, 1:03.52; 4. Ann Walters, Rockvillle Centre, N.Y., USA, 1:04.77. Linda Mastandrea, Elmhurst, Ill., USA, elim. in semifinal.

400m Men T53

1. Claude Issorat, FRA, 48.67; 2. Jeffrey Adams, CAN, 48.95; 3. Jeffrey Muralt, NZL, 49.08; Eric Neitzel, San Diego, Calif., elim. in heat.

400m Women T53

1. Louise Sauvage, AUS, 54.96, PR; 2. Chantal Petitclerc, CAN, 56.83; 3. Cheri Becerra, Nebraska City, Neb., USA, 57.15; 4. Candace Cable, Truckee, Calif., USA, 57.15; Rose Winand, Boston, Mass., USA, elim. in semifinal.

800m Men T10

1. Domingos Ramiao Game, POR, 2:05.48; 2. Coelho De Almeida, POR, 2:06.02; 3. Pedro Delgado, ESP, 2:06.40; No USA entries.

800m Women T10-11

1. Rima Batalova, RUS, 2:15.65, WR; 2. Claudia Meier, GER, 2:21.77; 3. Sigita Markeviciene, LTU, 2:22.17; 4. Pam McGonigle, Pittsburgh, Pa.; Melissa Lehman, Watertown, Wis., disqualified in semifinal.

800m Men T11

1. Jose Sanchez, ESP, 1:59.9; 2. Jose Saura, ESP, 2:00.94; 3. Ruben Delgado, ESP, 2:01.57; 5. Craig Mallinckrodt, Fort Collins, Colo., USA, 2:08.01.

800m Men T34-36

1. Joseph Parker, Goose Creek, S.C., USA, 2:09.67, WR; 2. Andrzej Wrobel, POL, 2:10.79; 3. Faouzi Bellele, ALG, 2:12.00; 4. Dana

1996 Paralympic Games Results

Zimmerman, St. Paul, Minn., USA, 2:15.36.

800m Men T37
1. Malcolm Pringle, RSA, 2:06.78, WR; 2. John Nethercott, GBR, 2:11.13; 3. Manfred Koody, NED, 2:12.25; 4. Jason Tercey, Kansas City, Mo., USA, 2:16.93.

800m Men T44-46
1. B. Kone Oumar, CIV, 1:55.45, WR; 2. David Evans, AUS, 1:55.81; 3. Bachir Zergoune, ALG, 1:57.05; No USA entries.

800m Men T50
1. Alvise De Vidi, ITA, 2:46.34; 2. Fabian Blattman, AUS, 2:46.67; 3. Barton Dodson, Murfreesboro, Tenn., USA, 2:47.63; 8. Norman Lyduch, Champaign, Ill., USA, 3:07.22.

800m Men T51
1. Shawn Meredith, Champaign, Ill., USA, 2:09.57; 2. Dean Bergeron, CAN, 2:09.91; 3. Per Vesterlund, SWE, 2:11.45; 4. John Clark, Pascagoula, Miss., USA, 2:11.57; Paul Nitz, Avon, Conn., USA, elim. in semifinal.

800m Women T51
1. Teruyo Tanaka, JPN, 2:43.17, WR; 2. Cristeen Smith, NZL, 2:43.28; 3. Ursina Greuter, SUI, 2:43.85; 4. Judy Siegle, Fargo, N.D., USA, 2:44.28; 6. Jean Waters, Rockeville Centre, N.Y., USA, 2:44.55.

800m Men T52
1. Steve Orens, BEL, 1:41.71, WR; 2. Heinz Frei, SUI, 1:41.76; 3. Marc Quessy, CAN, 1:42.13; 8. Christopher Waddell, Granby, Mass., USA, 1:44.68; Robert Molnatti, Huntington Beach, Calif., USA, elim. in semifinal; Thomas Sellers, Ormond Beach, Fla., USA, elim. in semifinal.

800m Women T52
1. Tanni Grey, GBR, 1:55.12, WR; 2. LeAnn Shannon, Orange Park, Fla., USA, 1:55.89; 3. Ann Walters, Savoy, Ill., USA, 2:02.41.

800m Men T53
1. Jeffrey Adams, CAN, 1:38.34 PR; 2. Scot Hollonbeck, Smyrna, Ga., USA, 1:38.43; 3. Mustapha Badid, FRA, 1:38.55; 8. Jacob Heilveil, Bothell, Wash., USA, 1:39.76; James Martinson, Puyallup, Wash., USA, elim. in heat.

800m Women T53
1. Louise Sauvage, AUS, 1:52.80, PR; 2. Chantal Petitclerc, CAN, 1:53.30; 3. Cheri Becerra, Nebraska City, Neb., 1:53.41; 4. Deanna Sodoma, Carlsbad, Calif., 1:55.26; Rose Winand, Boston, Mass., USA, did not start.

1,500m Men T10
1. De Almeida Coehlo, POR, 4:08.52 PR; 2. Robert Matthews, GBR, 4:12.48; 3. Tim Willis, Tucker, Ga., USA, 4:19.25.

1,500m Men T11
1. Jose Sanchez, ESP, 4:01.19; 2. Cesar Carlavilla, ESP, 4:03.61; 3. Saulius Leonavicius, LTU, 4:04.44; No USA entries.

1,500m Women T10-11
1. Rima Batalova, RUS, 4:51.17; 2. Claudia Meier, GER, 4:51.98; 3. Sigita Markeviciene, LTU, 5:00.85; 4. Pam McGonigle, Pittsburgh, Pa., USA, 5:01.45; Melissa Lehman, Watertown, Wis., USA, elim. in semifinal.

1,500m Men T12
1. Said Gomez, PAN, 3:57.53, WR; 2. Stuart McGregor, CAN, 4:03.70; 3. Christophe Carayon, FRA, 4:07.93.

1,500m Men T34-37
1. Andrzej Wrobel, POL, 4:24.82; 2. Malcolm Pringle, RSA, 4:25.61; 3. Faouzi Bellele, ALG, 4:26.78; 5. Joseph Parker, Goose Creek, S.C., USA, 4:26.93; 7. Dana Zimmerman, St. Paul, Minn., USA, 4:42.71.

1,500m Men T44-46
1. David Evans, AUS, 3:59.68; 2. Yanjian Wu, CHN, 4:00.10; 3. Emmanuel Lacroix, 4:01.07, FRA; Michael Keohane, New York, N.Y., USA, did not start final.

1,500m Men T50
1. Fabian Blattman, AUS, 5:09.41 PR; 2. Alvise DeVidi, ITA, 5:09.80; 3. Tim Johansson, SWE, 5:41.73; 5. Barton Dodson, Murfreesboro, Tenn., 6:27.13; Norman Lyduch, Carpentersville, Ind., USA, dns.

1,500m Men T51
1. Per Versterlund, SWE, 4:00.86, WR; 2. Dean Bergeron, CAN, 4:01.02; 3. Clayton Gerein, CAN, 4:03.23; 5. Shawn Meredith, Champaign, Ill., USA, 4:03.48; 9. Albert Kovach Jr., San Diego,

Calif., USA, 4:12.22; 11. Bradley Ramage, Mechanicsville, Va., USA, 4:33.68.

1,500m Men T52-53
1. Heinz Frei, SUI, 3:05.52; 2. Scot Hollonbeck, Smyrna, Ga., USA, 3:05.76; 3. Phillippe Couprie, FRA, 3:05.76; 10. Jacob Heilveil, Bothell, Wash., USA, 3:08.12; Eric Neitzel, San Diego, Calif., USA, elim. in semifinal.

1,500m Women F52-53
1. Louise Sauvage, AUS, 3:30.45, WR; 2. Chantal Petitclerc, CAN, 3:30.63; 3. Jean Driscoll, Champaign, Ill., USA, 3:30.83; 5. LeAnn Shannon, Orange Park, Fla., USA, 3:34.18; 7. Candace Cable, Truckee, Calif., 3:37.05.

3,000m Women T10-11
1. Rima Batalova, RUS, 10:35.67, PR; 2. Claudia Meier, GER, 10:37.39; 3. Samanta Meneghelli, ITA, 11:00; 5. Melissa Lehman, Watertown, Wis., USA, 11:22.47; Pam McGonigle, Pittsburg, Pa., USA, DNF.

5,000m Men T10
1. De Almedia Coehlo, POR, 16:04.28; 2. Alenjandro Guerrero, MEX, 16:07.55; 3. Tim Willis, Tucker, Ga., USA, 16:08.77.

5,000m Men T11
1. Noel Thatcher, GBR, 15:24.66; 2. Kestutis Bartkenas, LTU, 15:25.99; 3. Waldemar Kikolski, POL, 15:33.56; No USA entries.

5,000m Men T12
1. Saud Gomez, PAN, 15:01.49 PR; 2. Diosmany Gonzalez, CUB, 15:54.74; 3. Ildar Pomykalov, RUS, 16:16.93.

5,000m Men T34-37
1. Joseph Parker, Goose Creek, S.C., 16:34.36, WR; 2. Faouzi Bellele, ALG, 16:49.35; 3. Benny Govaerts, BEL, 17:33.42; 5. Dana Zimmerman, St. Paul, Minn., USA, 18:29.14.

5,000m Men T45-46
1. Jose Conde, ESP, 15:02.00; 2. Yanjian Wu, CHN, 15:15.44; 3. Emmanuel Lacroix, FRA, 15:28.97; 11. Michael Keohane, New York, N.Y., USA, 18:00.96.

5,000m Men T51
1. Clayton Gerein, CAN, 13:39.04; 2. Gregory Smith, AUS, 13:39.90; 3. Patrick Cottini, Quincy, Calif., USA, 13:40.44; 4. John (Wiley) Clark, Pascagoula, Miss., USA, 13:40.49.

5,000m Men T52-53
1. Saul Mendoza, MEX, 10:46.83; 2. Steve Orens, BEL, 10:46.92; 3. Franz Nietlispach, SUI,10:47.05; 4. Scot Hollonbeck, Smyrna, Ga., USA, 10:47.43; James Martinson, Puyallup, Wash., USA, elim. in heat; Jacob Heilveil, Bothell, Wash., USA, elim. in heat.

5,000m Women T52-53
1. Louise Sauvage, AUS, 12:40.71, WR; 2. Jean Driscoll, Champaign, Ill., USA, 12:40.80; 3. Kazu Hatanaka, JPN, 12:41.49; 4. Candace Cable, Truckee, Calif., USA, 12:42.21; 5. Deanna Sodoma, Carlsbad, Calif., USA, 12:42.50.

10,000m Men T10
1. Alejandro Guerrero, MEX, 34:53.29; 2. Tim Willis, Tucker, Ga., USA, 35:38.65; 3. C. Amaral Ferreira, POR, 35:41.51.

10,000m Men T11
1. Noel Thatcher, GBR, 32:20.27, WR; 2. Waldemar Kikolski, POL, 33:00.78; 3. Kestutis Bartekenas, LTU, 33:12.78; No USA entries.

10,000m Men T12
1. Diosmany Gonzalez, CUB, 33:34.42, PR; 2. Mark Farnell, GBR, 34:20.57; 3. Nikolai Tchoumak, MLD, 34:36.85; No USA entries.

10,000m Men T52-53
1. Heinz Frei, SUI, 21:58.31; 2. Steve Orens, BEL, 21:58.40; 3. P. Klunngern, THA, 21:58.49; 5. Jacob Heilveil, Bothell, Wash., USA, 21:58.62; James Martinson, Puyallup, Wash., USA, elim. in semi.

10,000m Women T52-53
1. Jean Driscoll, Champaign, Ill., USA, 24:21.64, WR; 2. Kazu Hatanaka, JPN, 24:31.88; 3. Deanna Sodoma, Carlsbad, Calif., USA, 25:22.69; 5. Ann Walters, Savoy, Ill., USA, 26:21.55.

Marathon Men T10
1. Harumi Yanagawa, JPN, 2:54.45; 2. Carlo Durante, ITA, 2:57.32; 3. Nicolas Ledezma, MEX, 3:00.13; 7. Donald Mott, Carpentersville, Ill., USA, 3:32.34.

Marathon Men T11
1. Waldemar Kikolski, POL, 2:39.57; 2. Tomasz Chmurzynski, POL,

1996 Paralympic Games Results

2:46.01; 3. Francisco Perez, ESP, 2:48.24; Joe Quintanilla, Cambridge, Mass., USA, did not start.

Marathon Men T12
1. Anton Sluka, SVK, 2:43.23; 2. Mark Farnell, GBR, 2:56.46; 3. J. Onofre Da Costa, POR, 2:58.04; 5. Michael Castle, Ann Arbor, Mich., USA, 3:00.15; 6. Lynn Wachtell, Cincinnati, Ohio, USA, 3:05.51.

Marathon Men T50
1. Heinrich Koeberle, GER, 2:52.11; 2. Barton Dodson, Murfreesboro, Tenn., USA, 3:11.26; 3. Tim Johansson, SWE, 3:39.41.

Marathon Men T51
1. Brent McMahon, CAN, 2:09.08; 2. Clayton Gerein, CAN, 2:09.08; 3. Patrick Cottini, Quincy, Calif., USA, 2:10.31; 4. Albert Kovach Jr., San Diego, Calif., USA, 2:10.51; 7. John Clark, Pasacagoula, Miss., 2:22.01; 8. Bradley Ramage, Mechanicsville, Va., USA, 2:25.27.

Marathon Men T52-53
1. Franz Nietlispach, SUI, 1:29.44 PR; 2. Kazuya Murozuka, JPN, 1:31.56; 3. Heinz Frei, SUI, 1:32.24; 4. Scot Hollonbeck, Smyrna, Ga., USA, 1:32.53; 10. Jacob Heilveil, Bothell, Wash., USA, 1:37.29; 39. Thomas Sellers, Ormond Beach, Fla., USA, 1:48.07; 40. James Martinson, Puyallup, Wash., USA, 1:48.25; Robert Molinatti, Huntington Beach, Calif., USA, did not start.

Marathon Men T42, 44-46
1. Javier Conde, ESP, 2:35.15 WR; 2. Joseba Larringa, ESP, 2:47.23; 3. Mark Brown, GBR, 2:59.33.

Marathon Women T52-53
1. Jean Driscoll, Champaign, Ill., USA, 1:52.54; 2. Kazu Hantanaka, JPN, 1:52.56; 3. Deanna Sodoma, Carlsbad, Calif., USA, 1:57.16; Candace Cable, Truckee, Calif., USA, did not start.

4x100m Men T10-12
1. ESP; 2. GER; 3. USA (Arthur Lewis, Los Angeles, Calif.; Marvin Campbell, Jacksonville, Fla.; Andre Asbury, Belle Harbor, N.Y.; Kelvin Hogans, Jamesville, Wis.).

4x100m Men T52-53
1. Germany, 56.05; dq: United States, Eric Neitzel, San Diego, Calif.; Chris Waddell, Granby, Mass.; Scot Hollonbeck, Smyrna, Ga.; Matt Parry, Chandler, Ariz.); France; Canada.

4x400m T10-12
1. ESP, 3:28.65; 2. GER, 3:33.61; 3. USA (Edward Munro, St. Augustine, Fla.; Winford Haynes, Alamogordo, N.M.; Kelvin Hogans, Jamesville, Wis.; Craig Mallinkcrodt, Fort Collins, Colo.).

4x400m Men T52-53
1. FRA, 3:14.45, WR; 2. SUI, 3:16.46; 3. CAN, 3:21.63; USA disqualified in semifinal.

4x100m Men T42-46
1. AUS, 45.40; 2. AUT, 46.55; 3. USA (Kurt Collier, Tucson, Ariz.; Dennis Oehler, East Hampton, N.Y.; Thomas Bourgeois, San Antonio, Texas; Matt Bulow, Nashville, Tenn.), 49.72.

4x100m Men T34-37
1. HKG, 50.46 WR; 2. USA (Freeman Register IV, Starke, Fla.; Lincoln Scott, Tampa, Fla.; Ryan Blankenship, Tampa, Fla; Jason Tercey, Kansas City, Mo.; Lincoln Scott, Tampa, Fla.), 50.94; 3. GBR, 52.18.

Club Men F50
1. Stephen Miller, GBR, 25.84, WR; 2. James Richardson, GRB, 22.75; 3. Aaron Little, Allegon, Mich., USA, 20.65.

High Jump Men F10-11
1. Oleg Chepel, BLS, 1.85; 2. Alejo Velez, ESP, 1.82; 3. Shigeo Yoshihara, JPN, 1.73; No USA entries.

High Jump Men F42-44
1. Bin Hou, CHN, 1.92; 2. Alan Earle, GBR, 1.79; 3. Juergen Kern, GER, 1.79; No USA entries.

Long Jump Men F10
1. Jose Rodriguez, ESP, 6.67; 2. Serguei Sevostainov, RUS, 6.21; 3. Sen Wang, CHN, 5.96; No USA entries.

Long Jump Women F10-11
1. Magdalena Amo, ESP, 5.22, PR; 2. Rosalia Lazaro, ESP, 5.22, EPR; 3. Purificacion Ortiz, ESP, 5.07; No USA entries.

Long Jump Men F11
1. Stephane Bozzolo, FRA, 6.74, PR; 2. Moises Esmeralda, ESP, 6.61;

3. Juan Viedma, ESP, 6.59; 15. Andre Asbury, Belle Harbor, N.Y., USA, 5.75.

Long Jump Men F12
1. Enrique Caballero, CUB, 7.17, PR; 2. Igor Fortounov, BLS, 7.02; 3. Kurt Van Raefelghem, BEL, 6.83; No USA entries.

Long Jump Women F34-37
1. A. Grigaliuniene, LTU, 4.49; 2. Katrina Webb, AUS, 4.46; 3. Carmen Storch, GER, 3.92; 7. Angel James, Orangeburg, S.C., USA, 3.13.

Long Jump Men F42
1. Lukas Christen, SUI, 5.20, WR; 2. Gunther Belitz, GER, 4.55; 3. Andreas Siegl, AUT, 4.32; No USA entries.

Long Jump Women F42-46
1. Irina Leontiouk, BLS, 5.70, WR; 2. Annely Ojastu, EST, 5.37; 3. Alice Basford, GBR, 4.35; 8. Aimee Mullins, Washington, D.C., USA, 3.14.

Long Jump Men F44
1. Urs Kolly, SUI, 5.80, WR; 2. Patrick Stoll, SUI, 5.75; 3. Bradley Thomas, AUS, 5.74; 7. Matthew Bulow, Nashville, Tenn., USA, 5.61; 10. Timothy Frasure, Kerry, N.C., USA, 5.49; 11. Dennis Oehler, East Hampton, N.Y., USA, 5.31.

Long Jump Men F45, 46
1. Ruben Alvarez, ESP, 6.75, WR; 2. Adeoye Ajibola, NGR, 6.64; 3. Georgios Toptsis, GRE, 6.36; No USA entries.

Long Jump Men MH (exhibition)
1. Nigel Bourne, GBR, 6.81, PR; 2. Wissem Ben Bahri, TUN, 6.42; 3. Wardell Gadson, Philadelphia, Pa., USA, 6.24; 5. Tico Clawson, Baltimore, Md., USA, 6.13.

Long Jump Women MH (exhibition)
1. Lisa Llorens, AUS, 4.95, WR; 2. Tracey Melesko, CAN, 4.80; 3. Malle Jukham, EST, 4.76; No USA entries.

Triple Jump Men F10
1. Jose Rodriguez, ESP, 12.93; 2. Sen Wang, CHN, 12.06; 3. Victor Joukovski, BLS, 11.56; No USA entries.

Triple Jump Men F12
1. Enrique Caballero, CUB, 14.87; 2. Igor Fourtounov, BLS, 14.30; 3. Ulrich Striegel, GER, 13.29; No USA entries.

Triple Jump Men F45, 46
1. Xueen Zhao, CHN, 13.39, WR; 2. Florian Boehl, GER, 13.28; 3. Ruben Alvarez, ESP, 13.24; No USA entries.

Javelin Men F10
1. Mineho Ozaki, JPN, 42.60; 2. Vytautas Girnius, LTU, 42.46; 3. Richard Ruffalo, Bloomfield, N.J., USA, 39.20.

Javelin Men F11
1. Miroslaw Pych, POL, 58.48; 2. Siegmund Hegeholz, GER, 48.84; 3. Mark Whiteley, GBR, 43.52; No USA entries.

Javelin Men F12
1. Haitao Sun, CHN, 51.80, PR; 2. France Gagne, CAN, 48.88; 3. Thomas Validis, GER, 48.54; No USA entries.

Javelin Men F34, 37
1. Brian Harvey, AUS, 34.70; 2. Paul Williams, GBR, 34.42; 3. James Shaw, CAN, 32.54; 5. William Locke, Glen Shaw, Pa., USA, 31.46; 7. Thomas Becke, Crown Point, Ind., USA, 28.04.

Javelin Men F35
1. Fahed Al-Murairi, KUW, 31.74; 2. Keith Gardner, GBR, 29.12; 3. Yeon Choi, KOR, 28.50; No USA entries.

Javelin Men F36
1. Kenneth Churchill, GBR, 45.54, WR; 2. Jacobus Jonker, RSA, 43.80; 3. J. Janse Van Vuuren, RSA, 41.24; No USA entries.

Javelin Men F41
1. Christopher Moori, KEN, 44.44; 2. Ahmed Dahy, EGY, 41.20; 3. Ahmed Abd Elgawad, EGY, 40.48; No USA entries.

Javelin Men F42
1. Guilermo Perez, CUB, 49.70, WR; 2. Jakob Mathiasen, DEN, 43.38; 3. Roberto Simonazzi, GER, 42.00; No USA entries.

Javelin Women F42-44, 46
1. Andrea Schnerney, AUT, 31.98, WR; 2. Tatiana Mezinova, RUS, 30.60; 3. Natalia Kletskova, RUS, 30.28; 11. Karen Lewis, Steilacoom, Wash., USA, 25.08.

Javelin Men F43-44

1996 Paralympic Games Results

1. Silao Ha, CHN, 53.54, WR; 2. Lutivico Halagahu, FRA, 50.00; 3. Dirk Mimberg, GER, 49.72; Brian Frasure, Cary, N.C., USA, dns.

Javelin Men F46
1. Joerg Schiedek, GER, 53.58, PR; 2. Patita Tuipoloto, FRA, 52.50; 3. Tomasz Rebisz, POL, 49.70.

Javelin Men F51
1. Ghader Modebberraz, IRI, 15.68; 2. David Maccalman, NZL, 14.78; 3. Douglas Heir, Cherry Hill, N.J., USA, 13.86.

Javelin Men F52
1. Adrian Paz, MEX, 16.72, WR; 2. Peter Martin, NZL, 15.80; 3. A. Loreh Jokar, IRI, 15.08; 7. Gabriel Diaz deLeon, San Antonio, Texas, USA, 13.94; 8. Richard Lowe, Follansbee, W.Va., 13.14.

Javelin Men F53
1. Mokhtar Nourafshan, IRI, 25.78, PR; 2. Rauno Sunavarra, FIN, 24.42; 3. Bruce Wallrodt, AUS, 23.68; 4. Jerry Deets, Santa Cruz, Calif., USA, 21.78.

Javelin Women F53-54
1. Martina Willing, GER, 22.10, WR; 2. Laura Schwanger, Williamston, N.J., USA, 20.20; 3. M. Buggenhagen, GER, 18.04.

Javelin Men F54
1. Mikael Saleva, FIN, 29.32, PR; 2. Jacques Martin, CAN, 27.22; 3. Janez Roskar, SLO, 25.88; 5. Arnold Astrada, San Jose, Calif, USA, 23.36.

Javelin Men F55
1. Stefan Danko, CZE, 26.00; 2. Robert Balk, Rochester, N.Y., USA, 25.28; 3. Mashal Al-Otaibi, KUW, 24.80.

Javelin Women F55-57
1. Zakia Abdin, EGY, 23.40, WR; 2. Mary Nakhumicha, KEN, 19.82; 3. Sylvia Grant, JAM, 18.98; 10. Susan Katz, North Potomac, Md., USA, 11.36; 11. Kathryne Carlton, Cupertino, Calif., USA, 10.56.

Javelin Men F56
1. Jaberi Mirzaei, IRI, 40.42, PR; 2. Rostislav Pohlmann, CZE, 37.98; 3. Steyn Humphries, RSA, 30.96; 6. Larry Hughes, Columbia, Md., USA, 27.42.

Javelin Men F57
1. Stephanus Lombaard, RSA, 51.06, WR; 2. Ali Mohammad, KUW, 41.42; 3. Mohammed Hassan, EGY, 41.28; 6. Roger Charter, Bethany, Okla., USA, 27.62.

Discus F10
1. Alfonso Fidalgo, ESP, 40.12, PR; 2. S. Turteltaube, GER, 35.96; 3. N. Denissevitch, BLS, 35.14; 9. Vincent Martin, Atlanta, Ga., USA, 26.96; 10. James Mastro, Fridley, Minn., USA, 24.36; Richard Ruffalo, Bloomfield, N.J., did not start.

Discus Women F10-11
1. Liiudys Beliser, CUB, 45.96, WR; 2. Hongyan Xu, CHN, 41.32; 3. Ljilijana Ljubisic, CAN, 37.20; No USA entries.

Discus Men F11
1. Serguei Khodakov, RUS, 43.10, WR; 2. Vasyl Lischynsky, UKR, 39.60; 3. Gueorgia Sakelarov, BUL, 38.56; No USA entries.

Discus Men F12
1. Haitao Sun, CHN, 47.56, WR; 2. Russell Short, AUS, 42.56; 3. Jason Delesalle, CAN, 42.36; 6. Garland Burress, Valley Park, Mo., USA, 36.02; 9. Kevin Szott, State College, Pa., USA, 33.86.

Discus Women F12
1. Bridie Lynch, IRL, 37.14; 2. Courtney Knight, CAN, 36.98; 3. Tamara Sivakova, BLS, 35.48; No USA entries.

Discus Men F32-33
1. Andreas Mueller, GER, 31.56, WR; 2. Antoine Delaune, FRA, 27.50; 3. Stephen Eaton, AUS, 27.42; No USA entries.

Discus Men T34-37
1. James Shaw, CAN, 41.24; 2. Denton Johnson, Port Chester, N.Y., USA, 27.00; 3. Paul Williams, GBR, 26.78.

Discus Women F34-35
1. Ellen Hyman, Chicago, Ill., USA, 19.62, WR; 2. Maria Rodriguez, ARG, 18.80; 3. Kris Hodgins, CAN, 18.38; 6. Angel James, Orangeburg, S.C., USA, 14.22; 9. Jacquelyn Payne, Fruita, Colo., USA, 9.18.

Discus Men F35
1. Hossein Barghchi, IRI, 35.92, WR; 2. Milan Kubala, CZE, 34.76; 3. Willem Noorduin, NED, 32.86; 11. Eric Stenback, Derby, Kan. USA, 18.70.

Discus Men F36
1. Damien Burroughs, AUS, 38.40, WR; 2. A. Ben Dhifallah, TUN, 37.90; 3. Anderson Santos, BRA, 37.46.

Discus Women F41
1. Malda Baumgarte, LIT, 30.80; 2. Araceli Castro, MEX, 25.82; 3. Catalina Rosales, MEX, 25.68; No USA entries.

Discus Men F41
1. Ahmed Dahy, EGY, 51.12, WR; 2. Nachman Wolf, ISR, 45.54; 3. Ahmed Abd Elgawad, EGY, 43.94; No USA entries.

Discus Men F42
1. Gino De Keersmaeker, BEL, 43.26; 2. Horst Beyer, GER, 42.12; 3. John Eden, AUS, 41.14; No USA entries.

Discus Women F42-44, 46
1. Jennifer Barrett, Gonzales, Calif., USA, 38.92, WR; 2. Hongping Wu, CHN, 37.56; 3. Britta Jaenicke, GER, 32.28; 5. Karen Lewis, Steilacoom, Wash., USA, 30.42.

Discus Men F43-44
1. Shawn Brown, San Diego, Calif., USA, 53.08, WR; 2. Xiuqing CHN, 43.48; 3. Klaus Kulla, GER, 42.96; 7. Thomas Bourgeois, San Antonio, Texas, USA, 40.16; 11. Douglas Collier, Tucson, Ariz., USA, 38.52.

Discus Men F46
1. Jerzy Dabrowski, POL, 45.20; 2. Tomasz Rebisz, POL, 45.08; 3. Ayman Abou Elata, EGY, 40.08; No USA entries.

Discus Men F51
1. Ghader Modabberaz, IRI, 16.48, PR; 2. Horacio Bascioni, ARG, 14.54; 3. Douglas Heir, Cherry Hill, N.J., 13.88.

Discus Men F52
1. A. Loreh Jokar, IRI, 20.34; 2. Imad Gharbawi, JOR, 17.14; 3. Gabriel Diaz deLeon, San Antonio, Texas, 17.05; 4. Willard Brooks Jr., Huntsville, Ala., USA, 16.16; 9. Richard Lowe, Follansbee, W.Va., USA, 16.16.

Discus Men F53
1. L. Labuschagne, RSA, 28.04, PR; 2. Mokhtar Nourafshan, IRI, 27.12; 3. Francisco Norafshan, ESP, 24.56; No USA entries.

Discus Women F53-54
1. M. Buggenhagen, GER, 23.76; 2. Laura Schwanger, Williamston, N.H., USA, 21.04; 3. Martina Willing, GER, 20.92.

Discus Men F54
1. Jacques Martin, CAN, 33:24; 2. Marc Fenn, Indianapolis, Ind., USA, 28.24; 3. Sean O'Grady, IRL, 28.24.

Discus Men F55
1. Steyn Humphries, RSA, 36.06; 2. M. Sadeghi Mehryar, IRI, 35.52; 3. Kevan Baker, GBR, 34.40; 7. Nathan Perkins, Menlo Park, Calif., USA, 28.40.

Discus Women, F55-57
1. K. Feleifal, EGY, 26.84; 2. Mervat Omar, EGY, 24.52; 3. S. Guimares, BRA, 24.54; 12. Kathryne Carlton, Cupertino, Calif., USA, 19.74; 14. Susan Katz, North Potomac, Md., USA, 18.88.

Discus Men F56
1. Larry Hughes, Columbia, Md., USA, 41.34; 2. Maurizio Nalin, ITA, 40.70; 3. H. Abdel Latif, EGY, 40.68.

Discus Men F57
1. Mohamed Gawad, EGY, 50.66, WR; 2. Hany Elbehiry, EGY, 49.42; 3. Stephanus Lombaard, RSA, 47.95.

Shot Put Men F10
1. Alfonso Fidalgo, ESP, 13.30; 2. N. Denissevitch, BLS, 12.27; 3. Andres Martinez, ESP, 12.08; 7. James Mastro, Fridley, Minn., 9.42.

Shot Put Women, F10-11
1. Hongyan Xu, CHN, 12.12; 2. Jodi Willis-Roberts, AUS, 11.46; 3. Ljiljana Ljubisic, CAN, 10.99; No USA entries.

Shot Put Men F11
1. Vasyl Lishchynsky, UKR, 13.66, PR; 2. Karl Mayr, AUT, 13.62; 3. Serguei Khodakov, RUS, 13.54.

Shot Put Men F12
1. Haitao Sun, CHN, 15.66; 2. Russell Short, AUS, 14.94; 3. Rolandas Urbonas, LTU, 14.02.

Shot Put Women F12
1. Tamara Sivakova, BLS, 12.51; 2. Marla Runyan, El Cajon, Calif.,

USA, 11.40; 3. Bridie Lynch, IRL, 10.72.

Shot Put Men F32-33

1. Hamish MacDonald, AUS, 10.45, WR; 2. Andreas Mueller, GER, 9.25; 3. Daniel West, GBR, 8.80; No USA entries.

Shot Put Women, F32-33

1. Birgit Pohl, GER, 8.36; 2. Janice Lawton, GBR, 6.12; 3. Sharon Rice, IRL, 5.41; No USA entries.

Shot Put Men F34, 37

1. James Shaw, CAN, 11.55; 2. Miroslav Janecek, CZE, 11.36; 3. Roman Kolek, CZE, 11.21; 5. Thomas Becke, Crown Point, Ind., USA, 9.86; 8. William Locke, Glen Shaw, Pa., USA, 9.16; 9. Denton Johnson, Port Chester, N.Y., USA, 8.98.

Shot Put Men F35

1. Willem Noorduin, NED, 13.74, PR; 2. Alex Hermans, BEL, 13.73; 3. Wolfgang Dubin, AUT, 11.82; No USA entries.

Shot Put Men F36

1. Gert Van Der Merwe, RSA, 12.65; 2. Franjo Izlakar, SLO, 11.68; 3. Kenneth Churchill, GBR, 10.98; No USA entries.

Shot Put Men F41

1. Ahmed Abd Elgawad, EGY, 13.91; 2. Ashraf Elsafi, EGY, 13.18; 3. Juan Lebrero, ESP, 12.20; No USA entries.

Shot Put Women F41

1. Malda Baumgarte, LIT, 9.07; 2. Catalina Rosales, MEX, 8.86; 3. G. Barrett-Condron, IRl, 8.07; No USA entries.

Shot Put Men F42

1. Thierry Daubresse, BEL, 11.79; 2. Detlef Eckert, GER, 11.68; 3. Hort Beyer, GER, 11.46; 8. Hugo Storer, Dallas, Texas, USA, 10.73.

Shot Put Women F42-46

1. Hongping Wu, CHN, 11.06; 2. Britta Jaenicke, GER, 10.98; 3. Jennifer Barrett, Gonzales, Calif., USA, 10.88; 10. Karen Lewis, Steilacoom, Wash., USA, 8.67.

Shot Put Men F43-44

1. Lutovico Halagahu, FRA, 14.23, PR; 2. Joerg Frischmann, GER, 14.21; 3. Asa Ison, Mansfield, Ohio, USA, 13.83; 5. Arthur Foote, Waterbury, Conn., USA, 13.50; 7. Shawn Brown, San Diego, Calif., USA, 13.12.

Shot Put Men F46

1. Jerzy Dabrowski, POL, 14.50, PR; 2. Tomas Rebisz, POL, 13.84; 3. Hongru Liu, CHN, 13.35; No USA entries.

Shot Put Men F51

1. Ghader Modabberraz, IRI, 7.17; 2. Douglas Heir, Cherry Hill, N.J., USA, 7.05; 3. Hal Merrill, CAN, 6.75.

Shot Put Men F52

1. Peter Martin, NZL, 7.69; 2. Josias Lima, BRA, 7.11; 3. Mauro Maximo, MEX, 6.56; 8. Gabriel Diaz deLeon, San Antonio, Texas, USA, 5.46.

Shot Put Men F53

1. Bruce Wallrodt, AUS, 9.12; 2. Mokhtar Nourafshan, IRI, 8.77; 3. Jerry Deets, Santa Cruz, Calif., USA, 8.22; 9. William Brady, Harrisburg, N.C., USA, 7.38.

Shot Put Women F53-54

1. M. Buggenhagen, GER, 8.39, WR; 2. Laura Schwanger, Williamston, N.J., USA, 8.29; 3. Martina Willing, GER, 7.51.

Shot Put Men F54

1. Arnold Astrada, San Jose, Calif., USA, 10.90; 2. David Dudley, GBR, 10.24; 3. Stefanos Anargyroy, GRE, 9.55; 12. Marc Fenn, Indianapolis, Ind., USA, 7.99.

Shot Put Men F55

1. D. Konstantangas, GRE, 9.78; 2. M. Sadeghi Mehryar, IRI, 9.77; 3. Terence Giddy, AUS, 9.44; No USA entries.

Shot Put Women F55-57

1. Mervat Omar, EGY, 7.83, PR; 2. Zakia Abdin, EGY, 7.54; 3. Sohir Elkoumy, EGY, 7.49; 15. Susan Katz, North Potomac, Md., USA, 5.41; 16. Kathryne Carlton, Cupertino, Calif., USA, 5.05.

Shot Put Men F56

1. Michael Louwrens, RSA, 12.86, WR; 2. Steyn Humphries, RSA, 12.05; 3. Maurizio Nalin, ITA, 12.05; 7. Larry Hughes, Columbia, Md., USA, 10.60.

Shot Put Men F57

1. Stephanus Lombaard, RSA, 14.28, WR; 2. Hany Elbehiry, EGY,

13.06; 3. Shaaban El Khatib, EGY, 12.30; 7. Roger Charter, Bethany, Okla., USA, 10.01.

Pentathlon Men P10

1. Seguei Sevostianov, RUS, 2,597 pts.; 2. Rayk Haucke, GER, 2,135 pts.; 3. Victor Joukovski, BLS, 2,051 pts.; 5. Vincent Martin, Atlanta, Ga., USA, 1,441 pts.

Pentathlon Women P10-12

1. Marla Runyan, El Cajon, Calif., 3,661 pts., WR; 2. Olga Tchourkina, RUS, 2,830 pts.; 3. Helena Silm, EST, 2,713 pts.

Pentathlon Men P11

1. Miroslaw Pych, POL, 3,118 pts.; 2. Stephane Bozzolo, FRA, 2,826, pts.; 3. Frantisek Godri, SVK, 2,738 pts.; No USA entries.

Pentathlon Men P12

1. Jason DeLaSalle, CAN, 3,050 pts., PR; 2. Kurt Van Raefelghem, BEL, 3,040 pts.; 3. Igor Fortounov, BLS, 2,896 pts.; 5. Edward Munro, St. Augustine, Fla., USA, 2,592 pts.

Pentathlon P44

1. Urs Kolly, URS, 4,947 pts.; 2. Thomas Bourgeois, San Antonio, Texas, USA, 4,761 pts.; 3. Kirk Collier, Tucson, Ariz., USA, 4,693 pts.

Pentathlon P53-57

1. Maurizo Nalin, ITA, 5,130 pts.; 2. Robert Balk, Rochester, N.Y., 4,947 pts.; 3. Jerry Deets, Santa Cruz, Calif., USA, 4,792 pts.; 12. William Brady, Harrisburg, N.C., USA, 4,354 pts.

BASKETBALL

Men

1. AUS; 2. GBR, 3. USA (Reggie Colton, Gainesville, Fla.; Chuck Gill, San Francisco, Calif.; Larry "Trooper" Johnson, Santa Cruz, Calif.; Melvin Juette, Whitewater, Wis.; Tim Kazee, Little Rock, Ark.; Rob Knight, Savoy, Ill.; Jim Miller, Fresno, Calif.; Mike Schalappi, Sandy, Utah; Mark Shepherd, Colorado Springs, Colo.; Craig Shewmake, Long Beach, Calif.; Randy Snow, Heath, Texas; Darryl Waller, Denver, Colo.).

Women

1. CAN; 2. NED; 3. USA (Jamie Danskin, Lawson, Mo.; Pam Fontaine, North Brunswick, N.J.; Susan Hagel, Minneapolis, Minn.; Sharon Herbst, , Townsend, Mont.; Ronda Jarvis, Sante Fe, N.M.; Josie Johnson, Gary, Minn.; Kim Martin, Columbus, Ohio; Ruth Nunez, Austin, Texas; Margaret Stran, Shorewood, Ill.; Jana Stump, Belleville, Kan.; Tiana Tozer, Boise, Idaho; Renee Tyree-Gross, Racine, Wis.).

BOCCIA

C1 Individual

1. Hae Kim, KOR; 2. Henrik Jorgensen, DEN; 3. Steven Thompson, Overland Park, Kan., USA.

C1 Wad Individual

1. Jose Macedo, POR; 2. Yolanda Martin, ESP; 3. Paul Driesen, BEL; 5T. Austin Hanson, Topeka, Kan., USA.

C2 Individual

1. Maria Rodriguez, ESP; 2. Thomas Leahy, IRL; 3. Jesus Fraile, GBR; No USA entry.

C1/C2 Team

1. ESP; 2. POR; 3. KOR; No USA entry.

C1 Wad Pairs

1. POR; 2. GBR; 3. AUS; 4. USA (Austin Hanson, Topeka, Kan.; Gary Ragland, Fort Worth, Texas).

CYCLING

Tandem Kilo Men Open - N1

1. Thierry Gintrand (Pilot) and Patrice Senmartin, FRA, 1:06.858; 2. Eric Guezo (Pilot) and Vincent Mignon, FRA, 1:07.092; 3. Paolo Botti (Pilot) and Giancarlo Galli, ITA, 1:07.474; 10. Michael Buttrey (Pilot) and Raymond Collins, Plymouth, Mass., USA, 1:09.529; 12. Frederick Stanage (Pilot) and Mark Lindsey, Riverside, Calif., USA, 1:10.331; 20. Gregory Combs (Pilot) and Stephen Aukward, Roanoke, Va., USA, 1:13.631.

Tandem Kilo Women Open - N1

1996 Paralympic Games Results

1. Sandra Smith (Pilot) and Teresa Poole, AUS, 1:13.473; 2. Elfriede Ranz (Pilot) and Ursula Egner, GER, 1:16.612; 3. Guylaine LaRouche (Pilot) and Julie Cournoyer, CAN, 1:18.346; 4. Tiffany Tretschoik (Pilot) and Julia Haft, Kensington, Md., USA, 1:18.724.

Tandem Kilo Mixed Open - N1

1. Patrizia Spadaccini (Pilot) and Claudio Costa, ITA, 1:11.467; 2. Scott Evans (Pilot) and Cara Dunne, Los Angeles, Calif., USA, 1:12.094; 3. Michael Rosenberg (Pilot) and Pamela Fernandes, Brighton, Mass., USA, 1:12.915; 7. Michael Hopper (Pilot) and Kathleen Urschel, Baldwinsville, N.Y., USA, 1:14.173.

Mixed LC1 Omnium (200m Sprint/Kilo Time Trial/Individual Pursuit)

1. Wolfgang Eibck AUT, 5 points (3rd 12.045/1st 1:11.301/1st 4:54.296); 2. Matthew Gray, AUS, 10 pts. (4th 12.165/3rd 1:12.955/ 3rd 5:05.563); 3. Aage Joensberg NOR, 11 pts. (5th 12:420/4th 1:131.171/2nd 5:04.258); 4. Tom Neal, Horsham, Pa., 11 pts. (2nd 12.033/2nd 1:12.680/7th 5:07.049); 6. Bob Whitford, Wichita Falls, Texas, USA, 17 pts. (1st 11.830 5th 1:13.313; 11th 5:24.299) 11. Steve Hermanson, Yucaipa. Calif., USA, 31 pts. (12th, 13.291; 13th, 1:18.063; 6th, 5:18.551).

Mixed LC2 Omnium

1. Dory Selinger, Oakland, Calif., 3 points (1st 12.304/1st 1:12.914/ 1st 5:09.328); 2. Paul Lake, AUS, 7 pts. (2nd 12.908/3rd 1:16.906/ 2nd 5:10.854); 3. Patrick Ceria, FRA, 9 pts.,, (3rd 13.073/2nd 1:16.892/ 4th 5:23.439); 5. Steve Cook, Salt Lake City, Utah, USA, 19 pts. (9th 13.812/5th 1:17.887/5th 5:29.250).

Mixed LC3

1. Miguel Perez ESP, 9 points (7th 15.002/1st 1:22.322/1st 5:30.483); 2. Rex Patrick, Englewood, Colo., 9 pts. (2nd 14.528/2nd 1:26.947/ 5th 5:59.816); 3. Norbert Zettler, NOR, 10 pts. (1st 14.084/5th 1:29.909/4th, 5:59.450); 6. Pier Beltram, Hagerstown, Md., USA, 12 pts. (3rd 14.574/3rd 1:29.081/6th 6:00.311).

Men's Individual Pursuit

1. Pascal Schoots (Pilot) and Jan Mulder, NED, 4:37.598; 2. Eddy Hollands (Pilot) and Paul Clohessy, AUS, 4:38.901; 3. Guy Rouchovze (Pilot) and Herve Dechamp, FRA, 4:37.497; 4. Spencer Yates (Pilot) and Matthew King, Breinigsville, Pa., USA, 4:42.198.

Women's Individual Pursuit

1. Sandra Smith (Pilot) and Teresa Poole, AUS, 3:54.563; 2. Guylaine Larouch (Pilot) and Julie Cournoyer, CAN, 4:01.323; 3. Tiffany Tretschoik (Pilot) and Julia Haft, Kensington, Md., USA, 4:01.327.

Mixed Individual Pursuit

1. Patrizia Spadaccini (Pilot) and Claudio Costa, ITA, 3:43.534; 2. Michael Hopper (Pilot) and Kathy Urschel, Baldwinsville, N.Y., 3:48.860; 3. Francisco Lara (Pilot) and Belen Perez, ESP, 3:47.057; 4. Scott Evans (Pilot) and Cara Dunne (Los Angeles, Calif.) 3:51.378; 5. Michael Rosenberg (Pilot) and Pamela Fernandes, Brighton, Mass., USA, 3:48.754.

Men's 200 Meter Tandem Sprint (ride 1, ride 2, ride 3)

1. Paolo Botti (Pilot) and Giancarlo Galli ITA, 2-0, (11.474, 11.912); 2. Pavel Takac (Pilot) and Miroslav Jamor SVK, 0-2; 3. Eric Guezo (Pilot) and Vincent Mignon FRA, 2-0, (11.553, 11.725); 4. Michael Buttrey (Pilot) and Raymond Collins, Plymouth,Mass., 0-2.

Mixed 200 Meter Tandem Sprint

1. Kerry Golding (Pilot) and Kieran Modra, AUS, 2-0 (12.720, 12.521); 2. Manuela Agnese (Pilot) and Damiano Zanotti, ITA, 0-2; 3. Scott Evans (Pilot) and Cara Dunne (Los Angeles, Calif.) 2-0, (13.301, 12.139); 4. Michael Rosenberg (Pilot) and Pamela Fernandes (Brighton, Mass.) 0-2.

50/60 Tandem Road Women Open

1. Guylaine LaRouche (Pilot) and Julie Cournoyer, CAN, 1:30.49; 2. Tiffany Tretschoik (Pilot) and Julia Haft, Kensington, Md., USA, 1:30.50; 3. Rosario Corral (Pilot) and Maria Chaves, ESP, 1:30.54.

20km Bicycle Road Mixed Div. 3

1. Daniel Nicholson, Richmond, Va., USA, 34:58; 2. Jong Kim, KOR, 35:00; 3. Gary Longhi, CAN, 36:20; 8. Jacob Klementich, Houston, Texas, USA, 41:10.

20km Bicycle Road Mixed Div. 4

1. Peter Homann, AUS, 31:05; 2. Christopher Scott, AUS, 32.41; 3. Lawrence Schultz, Seville, Ohio, 33:36; 7. John Asquini, Redford, Mich., USA, 40:35; 8. John Theobald, Syracuse, N.Y., USA, 41:42.

1,500m Tricycle T.T. Mixed Div.

1. Guy Culot, BEL, 2:47.00; 2. Andreas Hillers, GER, 2:51.00; 3. Mutsuhiko Ogawa, JPN, 2:56.00; 4. Corey Huntley, Springfield, Mass., USA, 3:03.00; 7. Christopher Pyrkosz, Livonia, Mich., USA, 3:36.00; 8. Mary Pirrallo, Clinton Township, Mich., USA, 3:44.00.

100/120 Tandem Road Men Open

1. Jean Bertrand (Pilot) and Franck Miquard, FRA, 2:26:35; 2. Pasquale Campedelli (Pilot) and Giancarlo Galli, ITA, 2:26:35; 3. Martin Boesch (Pilot) and Frank Hoefle, GER; 17. Michael Buttrey (Pilot) and Raymond Collins, Plymouth, Mass., USA, 2:35:22; 20. Gregory Combs (Pilot) and Stephen Aukward, Roanoke, Va., USA, 2:47.02; Spencer Yates (Pilot) and Matthew King, Breinigsville, Pa., USA, withdrew.

45/55km Bicycle Road Mixed LC3

1. Luc Raoul, FRA, 1:46:16; 2. Beat Schwarzenbach, SUI, 1:46:16; 3. Norbert Zettler, AUT, 1:46:16; 9. Rex Patrick, Englewood, Colo., USA, 1:46:39; 10. Pier Beltram, Hagerstown, Md., USA, 1:54:02.

55/65km Bicycle Road Mixed LC2

1. Patrick Ceria, FRA, 1:44:00; 2. Lubomir Simovec, CZE, 1:45:09; 3. Patrice Bonneau, CAN, 1:45:15; 7. Gary Seghi, Austin, Texas, USA, 1:45:15; 8. Steve Cook, Salt Lake City, Utah, USA, 1:45:15; Dory Selinger, Oakland, Calif., USA, did not start.

65/75km Bicycle Road Mixed LC1

1. David Mercier, FRA, 1:48:09; 2. Wolfgang Mahler, GER, 1:48:22; 3. Aage Joensberg, NOR, 1:48:48; 5. Hendrick Neal, Hosham, Pa., USA, 1:49:06; 11. Ronne Irvine, Vienna, Calif., USA, 1:49:06; 12. Steve Hermanson, Yucaipa, Calif., USA, 1:49:28.

5,000m Bicycle T.T. Mixed Div. 2

1. Mutsuhiko Ogawa, JPN, 10:15.00; 2. Guy Culot, BEL, 10:24.00; 3. Corey Huntley, Springfield, Mass., USA, 11:32.00; 6. Christopher Pyrkosz, Livonia, Mich., USA, 12:43.00; 8. Mary Pirrallo, Clinton Township, Mich., USA, 13:51.00

5,000m Bicycle T.T. Mixed Div. 3

1. Gary Longhi, CAN, 8:24.14; 2. Daniel Nicholson, Richmond, Va., USA, 8:25. 34; 3. Shojiro Maeda, JPN, 8:29.31; 8. Jacob Klementich, Houston, Texas, 9:47.27.

5,000m Bicycle T.T. Mixed Div. 4

1. Christopher Scott, AUS, 7:13.76; 2. Peter Homann, AUS, 7:56.06; 3. Lawrence Schultz, Seville, Ohio, 7:56.57; 7. John Asquini, Redford, Mich., USA, 10:51.83; 8. John Theobald, Syracuse, N.Y., USA, 11:26.84.

60/70 Tandem Road Mixed Open

1. Alexandre Cloutier (Pilot) and Julie Cournoyer, CAN, 1:31.42; 2. Francisco Lara (Pilot) and Belen Perez, ESP, 1:31.42; 3. Jose Santiago (Pilot) and Elena Padrones, ESP, 1:31.50; 4. Michael Rosenberg (Pilot) and Pamela Fernandes, Brighton, Mass., 1:31.52; 10. Michael Hopper (Pilot) and Kathleen Urschel, Baldwinsville, N.Y., USA, 1:32.01; 12. Scott Evans (Pilot) and Cara Dunne, Los Angeles, Calif., USA, 1:32.01.

EQUESTRIAN

Kur Trot Grade I

1. Birgit Dreszis/Miss Jane Marple GER 423.00; 2. Brita Andersen/ Midlands Carousel, DEN, 406.00; 3. Dianne Tubbs/Music, GBR, 385.00; 4. Tony Hojnacki/Eraf Aisha, Bloomfield N.J., USA, 373.20.

Kur Trot Grade II

1. Vicki Sweigart/Miss Jane Marple, Denver,Colo., USA; 389.20; 2. Angelika Trabert/Amber, GER, 388.80; 3. Anne Dunham/Doodle-bug, GBR, 357.80; 4. Lauren McDevitt/Dilettante, Atlanta, Ga., USA, 353.20; 5. Gerald Hoff/Scruples Pistol Pete, Ballwin, Mo., USA, 333.00.

Kur Canter Grade III

1. Anne Cecilie Ore/Victor Victoria, NOR, 400.60; 2. Frederic Aguillaume/Vabanque, FRA, 377.00; 3. Joan Salmon/Schimmel Haasan, IRL, 376.20; 7. Schoena Townsend/Black Tie Affair, St. Louis Mo., USA, 331.60.

Kur Canter Grade IV

1. Jo Jackson/Irish Classic, GBR, 396.20; 2. Charlotte Jensen/The Anvil Baraque, DEN, 376.40; 3. Britta Sorensen/Doctor Thomiss, DEN, 372.20; 6. Janie Zucas/Tre Awain Rising Sun, Hastings-on-Hudson, N.Y., USA, 333.60.

Dressage Grade I
1. Brita Andersen/Midlands Carousel, DEN, 318; 2. Dianne Tubbs/Music, GBR, 276; 3. Sara Rydh/Royal Aristar, SWE, 270; 5. Tony Hojnacki/Eraf Aisha Bloomfield, N.J., USA, 246.

Dressage Grade II
1. Vicki Sweigert/Miss Jane Marple Denver, Colo., USA, 375; 2. Angelika Trabert/Amber, GER, 359; 3. Lauren McDevitt/Dilet-tante, Atlanta, Ga., USA,335; 6. Gerald Hoff/Scruples Pistol Pete, Bloomfield, Pa., USA, 286.

Dressage Grade III
1. Anne Cecilie/Victor Victoria, NOR, 67 points; 2. Elizabeth Stone/Irish Classic, GBR 67 pts.; 3. Joop Stokkel/Noel's Maximilliam, NED, 65 pts.; 15. Schoena Townsend/Black Tie Affair, 57 pts.

Dressage Grade IV
1. Joanna Jackson/Goldoni, GBR, 67 points; 2. Patricia Straughan/Not A Penny More, GBR, 63 pts.; 3. Britta Sorensen/Doctor Thomiss, DEN, 63 pts.; 11. Jane Zucas/Venture, 49 pts.

FENCING

Individual Foil Men A
1. Wai Leung, HKG; 2. Alberto Pellegrini, ITA; 3. Kam Loi Chan, HKG; 13. David Baker, Hackensack, N.J., USA; 17. Joseph Mueller, Marietta, Ga., USA; 18. Mario Rodriguez, Sugar Land, Texas, USA.

Individual Foil Women A
1. Josette Bourgain, FRA; 2. Belgodere-Paralitici, FRA; 3. Patricia Picot, FRA; No USA Entries.

Individual Foil Men B
1. Pal Szekeres, HUN; 2. Jean Rosier, FRA; 3. Pascal Durand, FRA; 11. John Loechle, Newcastle, Ky., USA.

Individual Foil Women B
1. M. Van De Cappelle, FRA; 2. Judit Palfi, HUN; 3. Esther Weber-Kranz, GER; 8. Ella Chafee, Oak Lawn, Ill., USA; 9. Kathleen Winter, Chicago, Ill., USA; 10, Terri Cecil-Ramsey, Louisville, Ky., USA.

Individual Epee Men A
1. Wai Leung Cheung, HKG; 2. Alberto Pellegrini, ITA; 3. Wilfried Lipinski, GER; 18. Mario Rodriguez, Sugar Land, Texas, USA; 19. David Baker, Hackensack, N.J., USA.

Individual Epee Women A
1. Silke Schwarz, GER; 2. Jadwiga Polasik, POL; 3. Belgodere-Paralitici, FRA; No USA entries.

Individual Epee Men B
1. Jean Rosier, FRA; 2. Soriano Ceccanti, ITA; 3. Tae Hoon Park, KOR; 14. Robert Davis, Louisville, Ky., USA.

Individual Epee Women B
1. Mariella Bertini, ITA; 2. Rosalba Vettraino, ITA; 3. Esther Weber-Kranz, GER; 10. Ella Chafee, Oak Lawn, Ill., USA; 11. Kathleen Winter, Chicago, Ill., USA.

Team Epee Men A&B
1. HKG; 2. ITA; 3. FRA; 7. USA (David Baker, Hackensack, N.J.; Robert Davis, Louisville, Ky.; Mario Rodriguez, Sugar Land, Texas).

Team Epee Women A&B
1. FRA; 2. GER; 3. ESP; 5. USA (Terri Cecil-Ramsey, Louisville, Ky., USA; Ella Chafee, Oak Lawn, Ill., USA; Kathleen Winter, Chicago, Ill., USA).

Individual Sabre Men A
1. Yvon Pacault, FRA; 2. Wilfried Lipinski, GER; 3. Yan Yun Tai, HKG; 13. Joseph Mueller, Marietta, Ga., USA.

Individual Sabre Men B
1. Pal Szekeres, HUN; 2. Gerardo Mari, ITA; 3. Pascal Durand, FRA; 12. Robert Davis, Louisville, Ky., USA; John Loechle, Newcastle, Ky., USA.

Team Sabre Men A&B
1. FRA; 2. HKG; 3. GER; 6. USA (Robert Davis, Louisville, Ky.; John Loechle, Newcastle, Ky.; Joe Mueller, Marietta, Ga.).

FOOTBALL
1. NED; 2. RUS; 3. ESP; 4. USA (Elias Abarbanel-Wolff, Washington, D.C., Adolfo Aguilar, Garland, Texas; Craig Baker, Moultrie, Ga.; Tim Kistner, Houston, Texas; Matt Lavin, Grand Prairie, Texas; John McCullough, Washington, D.C.; Josh McKinney, Hilton Head, S.C.; Dan Nicholson, Richmond, Va.; Mike Peters, Tucson, Ariz.; Brian Robinson, Sparta, N.J.; John Theobald, Syracuse, N.Y.).

GOALBALL

Men
1. FIN; 2. CAN; 3. ESP; 11. USA (Walter Blackman, Tallahasse, Fla.; Shawn Donaldson, Livonia, Mich.; Daniel Foppiano, North Massapequa, N.Y.; David Hacker, Nashville, Tenn.; Ed McInnis, Saginaw, Mich.; George Morris, Jr., St. Louis, Mo.).

Women
1. GER; 2. FIN; 3. USA (Jeni Armbruster, Colorado Springs, Colo.; Irene Davis-Sparks, Fort Worth, Texas; Patty Egensteiner-Asbury, Belle Harbor, N.Y.; Sheryl Gordon, Kalamazoo, Mich.; Maggi Ostrowski, Pittsburgh, Pa.; Maureen Ryan-Esposito, Tampa, Fla.).

JUDO

Up to 60 kg
1. Ching-Chung Lee, TPE; 2. Nobuhiro Kanki, JPN; 3T. Il Kim, KOR; 3T. V. Mitchourine, RUS; No USA entry.

Up to 65 kg
1. Satoshi Fujimoto, JPN; 2. A. Gazemagomedova, RUS; 3T. Marlon Lopez, Los Angeles, Calif., USA; 3T. Cyril Morel, FRA.

Up to 71 kg
1. Takio Ushikubo, JPN; 2. Gerald Rollo, FRA; 3T. Stephen (Scott) Moore, Lafayette, La.; 3T. Baoji Cui, BRA.

Up to 78 kg
1. Simon Jackson, GBR; 2. Fabian Ramirez; 3T. Jonas Stoskus, LTU; 3T. Eugenio Santana, ESP; Ray Dunmeyer, Newark, N.J., elim. in repechage.

Up to 86 kg
1. Antonio Da Silva, BRA; 2. Francisco Boedo, ESP; 3T. You An, KOR; 3T. Ian Rose, GBR; No USA entries (Brett Lewis withdrew Aug. 15 with herniated neck).

Up to 95 kg
1. Anthony Clarke, AUS; 2. Runming Men, CHN; 3T. Terence Powell, GBR; 3T. James Mastro, Fridley, Minn., USA.

Over 95 kg
1. Walter Hanl, AUT; 2. Kevin Szott, State College, Pa., USA; 3T. Osamu Takagaki, JPN; 3T. Eric Censier, FRA.

LAWN BOWLS

Men LB2
1. William Curran, GBR; 2. Willem Neimann, RSA; 3. Chul Lim, KOR; No USA entries.

Men LB3/4/5
1. Samuel Shaw, GBR; 2. David Heddle, GBR; 3. Lun Chiu; 9. Rob Patterson, Charlotte, N.C./Pemberville, Ohio, USA.

Men LB7/8
1. Alan Lyne, GBR; 2. George Wright, GBR; 3. Keith Brenton, GBR; No USA entries.

Women LB7/8
1. Rosa Crean, GBR; 2. Lai Tang, HKG; 3. Mary Elias; No USA entries.

POWERLIFTING

Up to 48 kg
1. Jung Kwak, KOR, 165.0, WR; 2. Abraham Obaretin, NGR, 160.0; 3. Anthony Peddle, GBR, 160.0.

Up to 52 kg
1. Kum Jung, KOR, 179.0, WR; 2. Jian Wang, CHN, 162.5; 3. Johnson Sulola, NGR, 150.0.

1996 Paralympic Games Results

Up to 56 kg
1. Ahmed Ahmed, EGY, 177.5, WR; 2. Ferydon, Karimipour, IRI, 170.0; 3. Sang Yoon, KOR, 165.0; 10. Normez, Schulz, Chicago, Ill., USA, 125.0.

Up to 60 kg
1. Monday Emoghavwe, NGR, 195.0, WR; 2. Metwaly Mathna, EGY, 177.5; 3. Allahbakhsh Akbari, IRI, 177.5; No USA entries.

Up to 67.5 kg
1. Haildong Zhang, CHN, 195.0, WR; 2. Emadeldin Mohamed, EGY, 187.5; 3. Siavoshani Zeynal, IRI, 185.0; 10. Doug Farrell, Healdsburg, Calif., USA, 165.0; Jerry Millhouse, Lexington, Ky., USA, no lift.

Up to 75 kg
1. Ryszard Fornalczyk, POL, 207.5, WR; 2. Jong Park, KOR, 205.0; 3. Abd Elmonem Farag, EGY, 197.5; 11. Jaronnie Smith, USA, 150.0.

Up to 82.5 kg
1. Bernd Vogel, GER, 205, PR; 2. Mostafa Hamed, EGY, 200; 3. Jiahua Zhou, CHN, 190; Timothy Babinec, Tavares, Fla., no lift.

Up to 90 kg
1. Ryszard Tomaszewski, POL, 220.5, WR; 2. Brian McNicholl, AUS, 202.5; 3. Frank Gyland, NOR, 200.0; No USA entries.

Up to 100 kg
1. Zhiqiang Luo, CHN, 232.5, WR; 2. Sherif Bakr, EGY, 222.5; 3. Patrick Akutaekwe, NGR, 220.0.

100+ kg
1. Kim Brownfield, USA, 237.5, WR; 2. Leszek Hallmann, POL, 225.0; 3. Pernell Cooper, Atlanta, Ga., USA, 225.0.

RUGBY (Demonstration)

1. USA (Dave Ceruti, Southington, Conn.; Cliff Chunn, Brentwood, Tenn.; Eddie Crouch, Antioch, Tenn.; David Gould, Newport Richey, Fla.; Bill Renje, Tinsley Park, Ill.; Joe Soares, Tampa, Fla.; Brad Updegrove, Houston, Texas; Michael Wyatt, Oceanside, Calif.); 2. CAN; 3. NZL.

SHOOTING

Air Rifle Standing Mixed SH2
1. Thomas Johansson, SWE, 703.2; 2. Santo Managano, ITA, 700.8; 3. Lotta Helsinger, SWE, 698.9; 24. Barbaro Ponce, Atlanta, Ga., USA, 561.

Free Rifle 3x40 Men SH1
1. Josef Neumaier, GER, 1,238.3, WR; 2. Doron Sheziri, ISR, 1,237.0; 3. Oscar De Pellegrin, ITA, 1,231; 19. Mike Stovall, Dunwoody, Ga., USA, 1,075; 20. Robert Shields, North Brunswick, N.J., USA, 1,044; 22. Alexander Smith, Vero Beach, Fla., USA, 1,036.

10m Air Rifle Standing Men SH1
1. Tae Han, KOR, 687.8, PR; 2. Franc Pinter, SLO, 686.1; 3. Franz Falke, GER, 683.1; 26. Robert Shields, North Brunswick, N.J., USA, 542; 27. Mike Stovall, Dunwoody, Ga., USA, 537; Alexander Smith, Vero Beach, Fla., USA, withdrew.

10m Air Rifle Prone Mixed SH2
1. Thomas Johansson, SWE, 705.8, EWR; 2. Lotta Helsinger, SWE, 703.5; Santo Managano, ITA, 700.9; 24. Barbaro Ponce, Atlanta, Ga., USA, 563.

10m Air Rifle Standing Women SH1
1. Deanna Coates, GBR, 491.3, PR; 2. Nan Zhang, CHN, 490.5; 3. Im Kim, KOR, 489.1; No USA entries.

Air Rifle Prone Mixed SH1
1. E. Bokharaei, IRI, 705.8, WR; 2. Kazimierz Mechula, DEN, 704.7; 3. Jonas Jakobsson, SWE, 704.7; 45. Robert Shields, North Brunswick, N.J., USA, 581; 47. Mike Stovall, Dunwoody, Ga., USA, 578; Alexander Smith, Vero Beach, Fla., USA, did not start.

Air Rifle 3x20 Women SH1
1. Im Kim, KOR, 690.1; 2. Deana Coates, GBR, 689.7; 3. Sabine Brogle, GER, 686.4; No USA entrires.

Air Rifle 3x40 Men SH1
1. Jonas Jacobsson, SWE, 1,289.7 pts., PR; 2. Josef Neumaier, GER, 1,282.2; 3. Alfred Beringer, GER, 1,280.9; 25. Mike Stovall, Dunwoody, Ga., USA, 1,136; 27. Robert Shields, North Brunswick, N.J., USA, 1,122; 30. Alexander Smmith, Vero Beach, Fla., USA, 1,095.

Air Pistol Men SH1
1. Andrei Lebedinski, RUS, 662.2, PR; 2. Hubert Aufschnaiter, AUT, 659.6; 3. Antonio Martella, ITA, 659; 11. Ronald Davis, Middletown, Pa., USA, 553.

Air Rifle 3x40 Mixed SH2
1. Thomas Johansson, SWE, 1,302.0, PR; 2. Lotta Helsinger, SWE, 1,301.8; 3. Santo Mangano, ITA, 1,298.4; 24. Barbaro Ponce, Atlanta, Ga., USA, 1,131.

Air Pistol Women SH1
1. Ruzica Aleksov, YUG, 456.9, PR; 2. Lone Overbye, DEN, 454.3; 3. Rosabelle Riese, RSA, 448.2; No USA entries.

Sport Pistol Mixed SH1
1. Andrei Lebedinski, RUS, 682.3, WR; 2. James Nomarhas, AUS, 660.7; 3. Valeri Ponomarenko, RUS; 16. Ronald Davis, Middletown, Pa., USA, 525.

Standard Rifle 3x20 Women SH1
1. Im Kim, KOR, 661.8, WR; 2. Michele Amiel, FRA, 653; 3. Sabine Brogle, GER, 651.6; No USA entries.

English Match Mixed SH1
1. Jonas Jacobsson, SWE, 691.4, WR; 2. Doron Sheziri, ISR, 691.0 3. Oscar De Pelligrin, ITA, 690.7; 31. Mike Stovall, Dunwoody, Ga., USA, 559; 34. Bob Shields, North Brunswick, N.J., USA, 545.

Free Pistol .22 Mixed SH1
1. Francisco Soriano, ESP, 620.9, PR; 2. Ruzica Aleksov, YUG, 617.1; 3. Andrei Lebedinski, RUS, 613.9; 18. Ron Davis, Middletown, Pa., USA, 505.

SWIMMING

150m Individual Medley Men SM3
1. Petter Edstrom, SWE, 3:30.54; 2. Genezi Andrade, BRA, 3:34.32; 3. Stig Morten Sandvik, NOR, 3:38.23; No USA entry.

150m Individual Medley Men SM4
1. Javier Torres, ESP, 2:38.64; 2. Krzysztof Sleczka, POL, 2:43.17; 3. John Petersson, DEN, 2:53.88; 8. James Thompson, Cherry Hill, N.J., USA, 3:20:64.

150m Individual Medley Women SM4
1. Kay Espenhayn, GER, 3:00.39; 2. Margaret McEleny, GBR, 3:04.24; 3. Mayumi Narita, JPN, 3:08.63; 4. Aimee Bruder, Lawrenceburg, Ind., USA, 3:17.91; 6. Jennifer Hazen, Bloomfield, N.J., USA, 4:01.28; 7. Colleen Dougherty, Bend, Ore., 4:20.45.

200m Individual Medley Men SM5
1. Arkadiusz Pawlowski, POL, 3:13.90, WR; 2. Pascal Pinard, FRA, 3:19.17; 3. Peter Andersen, DEN, 3:19.32; No USA entry.

200m Individual Medley Women SM5
1. Beatrice Hess, FRA, 3:35.94, WR; 2. Jennifer Newstead, NZL, 3:39.08; 3. Katalin Englehardt, HUN, 4:14.83; 7. Susan Moucha, Brandon, Fla., 4:50.05.

200m Individual Medley Men SM6
1. Sebastian Xhrouet, BEL, 3:00.41; 2. Thomas Grimm, GER, 3:06.26; 3. Tadhg Slattery, RSA, 3:09.48; 7. Gregory Burns, Singapore/Washington, D.C., 3:20.96.

200m Individual Medley Women SM6
1. Eva Nesheim, NOR, 3:24.87, WR; 2. Maria Gotze, GER, 3:41.84; 3. Ludivine Loiseau, FRA, 3:42.35; 4. Camille Waddell, Pensacola, Fla., USA, 3:55.13; Colleen Dailey, Houston, Texas, USA, elim. heat.

200m Individual Medley Men SM7
1. Eric Lindmann, FRA, 2:52.05; 2. Simon Ahlstad, SWE, 2:52.80; 3. Gledson Soares, BRA, 2:54.10; Aaron Paulson, Portland, Ore., USA, elim. in heat.

200m Individual Medley Women SM7
1. Kristin Hakonard, ISL, 3:15.16, WR; 2. Malgorzata Okupniak, POL, 3:23.66; 3. Hadda Guerchouche, FRA, 3:26.78; Julie Wolfe, Tucson, Ariz., USA, elim in heat.

200m Individual Medley Men SM8
1. J. Terblanche, RSA, 2:40.83, WR; 2. Holger Kimmig, GER, 2:44.04; 3. Giles Long, GBR, 2:45.80; Jason Wening, Jefferson City, Mo.,

USA, disqualified in final; Travis Mohr, Northampton, Pa., USA, disqualified in heat.

200m Individual Medley Women SM8
1. Priya Cooper, AUS, 3:05.32, WR; 2. S. Van Amelsvoort, NED, 3:11.30; 3. Silvia Vives, ESP, 3:12.65; No USA entries.

200m Individual Medley Men SM9
1. Helge Bjornstad, NOR, 2:30.55, WR; 2. Rutger Sturkenboom, NED, 2:30.96; 3. Olafur Eiriksson, ISL, 2:32.89; 8. Dana Albrycht, Canton, Conn., USA, 2:42.19; Michael Doyle, Warrington, Pa., USA, elim. in heat; Luis Alicea, Ontario, Calif., USA, elim. in heat.

200m Individual Medley Women SM9
1. Emily Jennings, GBR, 2:49.60; 2. Joyce Luncher, Pittsburgh, Pa., USA, 2:49.62; 3. Ricka Stenger, DEN, 2:53.00; Allison Pittman, San Diego, Calif., USA, elim. in heat.

200m Individual Medley Men SM10
1. Alwin De Groot, NED, 2:19.75, WR; 2. Jurjen Engelsman, NED, 2:21.12; 3. Stefan Loeffler, GER, 2:26.94; No USA entries.

200m Individual Medley Women SM10
1. Sarah Bailey, GBR, 2:38.38, WR; 2. Gemma Dashwood, AUS, 2:38.93; 3. Claudia Hengst, GER, 2:42.60; 7. Karen Norris, Van Nuys, Calif., USA, 2:57.50.

100m Butterfly Women B1
1. Tracey Cross, AUS, 1:27.53; 2. E. Fingerroos, FIN, 1:28.83; 3. Janice Burton, GBR, 1:35.25; No USA entries.

100m Butterfly Men B2
1. Jeffrey Hardy, AUS, 1:06.42; 2. Kingsley Bugarin, AUS, 1:07.13; 3. Daniel Kelly, Golden Valley, Minn., USA, 1:07.85.

100m Butterfly Men B3
1. Walter Wu, CAN, 1:02.64; 2. Ian Sharpe, GBR, 1:03.58; 3. Ivan Nielsen, DEN, 1:04.83; No USA entries.

100m Butterfly Women B3
1. Elizabeth Scott, Rockville, Md., USA, 1:06.58; 2. Daniela Henke, GER, 1:08.22; 3. Marie Claire Ross, CAN, 1:09.66; 4. Trischa Zorn, Indianapolis, Ind., USA, 1:16.46; Dawn Duffy, Moore, Okla., USA, 1:23.39, elim. in heat; Elizabeth Scott, Rockville, Md., USA, 1:07.38.

200m Individual Medley Men B1
1. Daniel Kelly, Golden Valley, Minn., USA, 2:30.94; 2. Timothy Reddish, GBR, 2:33.27; 3. Junichi Kawai, JPN, 2:36.27; Michael Taber, Albany, N.Y., disqualified in final.

200m Individual Medley Women B1
1. Tracey Cross, AUS, 3:07.76; 2. Danela Roehle, GER, 3:11.79; 3. E. Fingerroos, FIN, 3:15.89; No USA entries.

200m Individual Medley Men B2
1. Kingsley Bugarin, AUS, 2:22.45, WR; 2. Christopher Holmes, GBR, 2:22.84; 3. Jeffrey Hardy, AUS, 2:32.42; No USA entries.

200m Individual Medley Women B2
1. Trischa Zorn, Indianapolis, Ind., USA, 2:47.99; 2. Maria Fernandez, ESP, 2:56.82; 3. Birgit Beeker, GER, 2:59.35.

200m Individual Medley Men B3
1. Walter Wu, CAN, 2:20.68, PR; 2. Noel Pederson, NOR, 2:21.56; 3. Flemming Berthelsen, DEN, 2:30.84; No USA entries.

200m Individual Medley Women B3
1. Marie Claire Ross, CAN, 2:31.86, WR; 2. Yvonne Hopf, GER, 2:35.53; 3. Elizabeth Scott, Rockville, Md., 2:36.90.

50m Butterfly Men S3
1. Andrej Zatko, SVK, 1:11.23, PR; 2. Kenneth Cairns, GBR, 1:22.27; 3. Vallehos Contreras, CHI, 1:29.03; No USA entries.

50m Butterfly Men S4
1. Luca Pancalli, ITA, 49.86, PR; 2. Christian Fritsche, GER, 52.35; 3. John Petersson, DEN, 53.46; No USA entries.

50m Butterfly Men S5
1. Dan Butler, Falls Church, Va., 42.20; 2. Qiwen Mao, CHN, 42.26; 3. Pascal Pinard, FRA, 42.34.

50m Butterfly Women S5
1. Beatrice Hess, FRA, 47.35, WR; 2. Monika Jaromi, HUN, 47.48; 3. Katalin Engelhardt, HUN, 50.88; 6. Aimee Bruder, Lawrenceburg, Ind., USA, 1:09.38; Colleen Dougherty, Bend, Ore., USA, disqualified in final; Susan Moucha, Brandon, Fla., elim. in heat.

50m Butterfly Men S6
1. Duane Kale, NZL, 34.37, EWR; 2. Kai Xia, CHN, 34.35; 3. Peter

Andersen, DEN, 37.44; Dennis Calonico, San Mateo, Calif., USA, elim. in heat.

50m Butterfly Women S6
1. Maria Gotze, GER, 49.11; 2. Beate Schretzmann, GER, 49.41; 3. Elizabeth Wright, AUS, 51.20; 4. Camille Waddell, Pensacola, Fla., 51.69; Jill Nelson, Pampa, Texas, USA, elim. in heat; Stephanie Brooks, Algonquin, Ill., USA, elim. in heat; Colleen Dailey, Houston, Texas, disqualified in heat.

50m Butterfly Men S7
1. Jose Medieros, BRA, 33.78; 2. Daniel Kunzi, SUI, 34.47; 3. W. El-Kader Aly, EGY, 35.19; Aaron Paulson, Portland, Ore., USA, elim. in heat.

50m Butterfly Women S7
1. Eva Nesheim, NOR, 41.55, WR; 2. Margita Prokeinova, SVK, 41.64; 3. Malgorzata, POL, 41.96; Julie Wolfe, Tucson, Ariz., USA, disqualified in final.

100m Butterfly Men S8
1. Giles Long, GBR, 1:09.80 PR; 2. Emil Brondum, DEN, 1:10.24; 3. J. Terblance, RSA, 1:11.24; Jason Wening, Jefferson City, Mo., USA, disqualified in heat.

100m Butterfly Women S8
1. S. Van Amelsvoort, NED, 1:25.71 WR; 2. Silvia Vives, ESP, 1:28.55; 3. Priya Cooper, AUS, 1:30.42.

100m Butterfly Men S9
1. Olafur Eiriksson, ISL, 1:05.02; 2. Alexey Kapura, RUS, 1:06.88; 3. Andrew Haley, CAN, 106.90; 4. Dana Albrycht, Canton, Conn., USA, 1:08.02; Luis Alicea, Ontario, Calif., USA, elim. in heat; Michael Doyle, Warrington, Pa., elim. in heat.

100m Butterfly Women S9
1. Joyce Luncher, Pittsburgh, Pa., 1:14.40, WR; 2. Melissa Carlton, AUS, 1:16.21; 3. Marina Tozzini, ITA, 1:19.63.

100m Butterfly Men S10
1. Jody Cundy, GBR, 1:02.44, WR; 2. Alwin De Groot, NED, 1:03.02; 3. Scott Brockenshire, AUS, 1:04.59; No USA entries.

100m Butterfly Women S10
1. Gemma Dashwood, AUS, 1:08.88, WR; 2. Judith Young, AUS, 1:12.64; 3. Ana Bernardo, ESP, 1:13.55.

400m Freestyle Men S7
1. Eric Lindmann, FRA, 5:04.96; 2. Sebastian Xhrouet, BEL, 5:08.45; 3. Frederic Delpy, FRA, 5:09.49; No USA entries.

400m Freestyle Women S7
1. Rebeccah Bornemann, CAN, 5:59.82; 2. Julie Wolfe, Tucson, Ariz., USA, 6:00.55; 3. Mireia Riera, ESP, 6:03.11.

400m Freestyle Men S8
1. Jason Wening, Jefferson City, Mo., USA, 4:49.87, WR; 2. Holger Kimmig, GER, 4:52.04; 3. Emil Brondum, DEN, 4:53.85; Jay Styperk, Pittsburgh, Pa., USA, elim. in heat.

400m Freestyle Women S8
1. Priya Cooper, AUS, 5:11.47, WR; 2. Petra Reuvekamp, NED, 5:55.08; 3. Janelle Falzon, AUS, 5:57.28; No USA entries.

400m Freestyle Men S9
1. Enrique Tornero, ESP, 4:34.04; 2. Luis Alicea III, Ontario, Calif., USA, 4:39.78; 3. Andrew Haley, CAN, 4:39.94.

400m Freestyle Women S9
1. Melissa Carlton, AUS, 5:01.22; 2. Marina Tozini, ITA, 5:01.96; 3. Sabrina Bellavia, BEL, 5:05.25; 6. Diane Straub, Cambridge, Mass., USA, 5:30.24.

400m Freestyle Men S10
1. Alwin De Groot, NED, 4:26.55, WR; 2. Stefan Loeffler, GER, 4:30.72; 3. Marc Woods, GBR, 4:31.87; No USA entries.

400m Freestyle Women S10
1. Gemma Daswood, AUS, 4:40.94, WR; 2. Sarah Bailey, GBR, 4:50.98; 3. Claudia Hengst, GER, 4:54.34; 6. Julie Atwell, Endwell, N.Y., USA, 5:24.40; 7. Karen Norris, Van Nuys, Calif., USA, 5:28.00.

100m Breaststroke Men B1
1. Christian Bundgaard, DEN, 1:13.84; 2. Daniel Kelly, Golden Valley, Minn., USA, 1:19.79; 3. Panom Lagsanaprim, THA, 1:21.76; Michael Taber, Albany, N.Y., disqualified in final.

100m Breaststroke Men B2
1. Kingsley Bugarin, AUS, 1:10.81, WR; 2. Jose Arribas, ESP, 115.36;

3. Vitali Krylov, RUS, 1:17.92; No USA entries.

100m Breaststroke Women B2
1, Carine Van Puyvelde, BEL, 1:31.00; 2. Elaine Barrett, GBR, 1:31.84; 3. Trischa Zorn, Indianapolis, Ind., USA, 1:32.27.

100m Breaststroke Men B3
1. Noel Pedersen, NOR, 1:08.18; 2. Ivan Nielsen, DEN, 1:12.84; 3. Jurgen Lentink, NED, 1:16.09; No USA entries.

100m Breaststroke Women B3
1. Marie Claire Ross, CAN, 1:20.45, WR; 2. Daniela Henke, GER, 1:24.37; 3. Elizabeth Scott, Rockville, Md., USA, 1:26.48.

100m Freestyle Men S2
1. James Anderson, GBR, 2:41.94, WR; 2. Alan McGregor, GBR, 2:44.18; 3. Adriano Pereira, BRA, 2:54.50; No USA entries.

100m Freestyle Women S2
1. Betiana Basualdo, ARG, 3:09.00, WR; 2. A. Perezlido, ARG, 3:11.02; 3. Sara Carracelas, ESP, 3:17.28; No USA entries.

400m Freestyle Men B2
1. Jeffrey Hardy, AUS, 4:33.85; 2. Francisco Segarra, ESP, 4:35.36; 3. Kingsley Bugarin, AUS, 4:35.52; 6. Daniel Kelly, Golden Valley, Minn., USA, 4:51.14; Michael Taber, Albany, N.Y., elim. in heat.

400m Freestyle Women B2
1. Melanie Easter, GBR, 5:11.32; 2. Trischa Zorn, Indianapolis, Ind., USA, 5:17.57; 3. Maria Fernandez, ESP, 5:17.97; Mandy Sommer, Omaha, Neb., elim. in heat.

400m Freestyle Men B3
1. Walter Wu, CAN, 4:21.08, WR; Ivan Nielsen, DEN, 4:40.03; 3. Christopher Fox, GBR, 4:41.56; No USA entries.

200m Freestyle Men S3
1. Palmar Gudmundsson, ISL, 4:10.17, WR; 2. Petter Edstrom, SWE, 4:10.82; 3. Genezi Andrade, BRA, 4:15.76; No USA entries.

200m Freestyle Men S4
1. Ricardo Oribe, ESP, 3:11.00, WR; 2. Luca Pancalli, ITA, 3:26.16; 3. James Thompson, Cherry Hill, N.J., USA, 3:29.18; 8. Craig Laufenberg, Whitewater, Wis., USA, 3:59.68.

200m Freestyle Women S4
1. Kay Espenhayn, GER, 3:21.82, WR; 2. Mayumi Narita, JPN, 3:22.47; 3. Aimee Bruder, Lawrenceburg, Ind., USA, 3:53.19.

200m Freestyle Men S5
1. Lars Luerig, GER, 2:54.31; 2. Juan Fuertes, ESP, 2:59.70; 3. Krzysztof Sleczka, POL, 3:02.94; No USA entries.

200m Freestyle Women S5
1. Beatrice Hess, FRA, 3:01.18, WR; 2. Olena Akopyan, UKR, 3:17.71; 3. Margaret Mceleny, GBR, 3:20.51; No USA entries.

200m Freestyle Men S6
1. Duane Kale, NZL, 2:28.33, WR; 2. Peter Andersen, DEN, 2:33.96; 3. Danijel Pavlinec, SLO, 2:43.85; Martin Parker, Tucson, Ariz., USA, elim. in heat.

200m Freestyle Women S6
1. Jennifer Newstead, NZL, 2:55.15, WR; 2. Ludivine Loiseau, FRA, 2:58.44; 3. Jeanette Esling, GBR, 3:04.73; Colleen Dailey, Houston, Texas, USA, elim. in heat; Jill Nelson, Pampa, Texas, elim. in heat.

100m Freestyle Men MH
1. Alwin Houtsma, NED, 56.40, WR; 2. Grant Fitzpatrick, AUS, 59.32; 3. Craig Groenewald, RSA, 1:01.09; Nicholas Karris, Portage, Ind., USA, elim. in heat; Douglas Bell, Brazil, Ind., USA, elim. heat.

100m Freestyle Women MH
1. Tracy Wiscombe, GBR, 1:05.31, WR; 2. Carla Sullivan, AUS, 1:10.53; 3. Petra Barker, AUS, 1:10.91; Kelly Sutton, Lexington, Ky., USA, elim. in heat; Jenny Skinner, Huntington Beach, Calif., USA, elim. in heat.

50m Breaststroke Men SB2
1. James Thompson, Cherry Hill, N.J., USA, 1:03.59, WR; 2. Nenad Krisanovic, 1:03.67; 3. Andrej Zatko, SLO, 1:07.51.

50m Breaststroke Men SB3
1. Christian Fritsche, GER, 50.07, WR; 2. John Petersson, DEN, 58.33; 3. Garth Harris, CAN, 1:00.22; No USA entries.

50m Breaststroke Women SB3
1. Noriko Kajiwara, JPN, 54.21, WR; 2. Margaret McEleny, GR, 57.03; 3. Kay Espenhayn, GER, 1:04.91; 5. Aimee Bruder, Lawrenceburg, Ind., USA, 1:10.90; 4. Colleen Dougherty, Bend,

Ore., USA, elim. in heat; 5. Jennifer Hazen, Bloomfield, N.J., USA, elim. in heat.

100m Backstroke Men S7
1. Eric Lindmann, FRA, 1:19.28; 2. Andrew Lindsey, GBR, 1:19.37; 3. Soo Kim, KOR, 1:20.78; Aaron Paulson, Portland, Ore., USA, disqualified in heat.

100m Backstroke Women S7
1. Kristin Hakonard, ISL, 1:26.41, WR; 2. Eva Nesheim, NOR, 1:30.65; 3. Elisabeth Walker, CAN, 1:33.22; 4. Julie Wolfe, Tucson, Ariz., USA, 1:36.31.

100m Backstroke Men S8
1. Holger Kimmig, GER, 1:11.06, PR; 2. Kasper Hansen, DEN, 1:12.55; 3. Geert Jaehrig, GER, 1:12.70; 5. Travis Mohr, Northampton, Pa., 1:16.72.

100m Backstroke Women S8
1. Priya Cooper, AUS, 1:23.43 PR; 2. Silvia Vives, ESP, 1:31.73; 3. Janelle Falzon, AUS, 1:32.48; No USA entries.

100m Backstroke Men S9
1. Helge Bjornstad, NOR, 1:08.23, PR; 2. David Malone, IRL, 1:08.98; 3. Detlef Schmidt, GER, 1:09.33; 6. Luis Alicea III, Ontario, Calif., USA, 1:10.63; 8. Dana Albrycht, Canton, Conn., USA, 1:12.84.

100m Backstroke Women S9
1. J. Nannenbert, NED, 1:18.13; 2. K. Michalczyk, POL, 1:20.33; 3. Melissa Carlton, AUS, 1:20.42; No USA entries.

100m Backstroke Men S10
1. Alwin De Groot, NED, 1:04.10, WR; 2. Marc Woods, GBR, 1:06.48; 3. Jurjen Engelsman, NED, 1:07.11.

100m Backstroke Women S10
1. Sarah Bailey, GBR, 1:15.74; 2. Karen Norris, Van Nuys, Calif., USA, 1:16.23; 3. Judith Young, AUS, 1:17.41; 4. Julie Atwell, Endwell, N.Y., USA, 1:19.74.

100m Freestyle Men B1
1. Junichi Kawai, JPN, 1:01.18; 2. Daniel Kelly, Golden Valley, Minn., USA, 1:01.47; 3. Timothy Reddish, GBR, 1:03.82; Michael Taber, Albany, N.Y., USA, elim. in heat.

100m Freestyle Women B1
1. Eila Nilsson, SWE, 1:17.50; 2. Daniela, Roehle, GER, 1:18.69; 3. E. Fingerroos, FIN, 1:19.34; Mandy Sommer, Omaha, Neb., USA, elim. in heat.

100m Freestyle Men B2
1. Christopher Holmes, GBR, 58.42; 2. Kingsley Bugarin, AUS, 59.08; 3. Ziv Better, ISR, 1:00.01; No USA entries.

100m Freestyle Women B2
1. Marge Korkjas, EST, 1:07.43; 2. Maria Fernandez, ESP, 1:07.75; 3. Trischa Zorn, Indianapolis, Ind., USA, 1:08.34.

100m Freestyle Men B3
1. Walter Wu, CAN, 57.63, PR; 2. Ebert Kleynhans, RSA, 58.77; 3. Vladimir, Tchesnov, RUS, 59.27; No USA entries.

100m Freestyle Women B3
1. Yvonne Hopf, GER, 59.88, WR; 2. Daniela Henke, GER, 1:01.90; 3. Marie Claire Ross, CAN, 1:02.37; 4. Elizabeth Scott, Rockville, Md., USA, 1:02.62.

4x50m Freestyle Men S1-S6
1. USA (Dan Butler, Falls Church, Va.; Aaron Paulson, Portland, Ore.; Greg Burns, Singapore/Washington, D.C.; Marty Parker, Tucson, Ariz.; Jim Thompson, Cherry Hill, N.J., competed in prelim. only), 2:38.13, WR; 2. ESP, 2:41.33; 3. CHN, 2:42.02.

4x50m Freestyle Women S1-S6
1. GBR, 2:52.36, WR; 2. FRA, 2:53.55; 3. USA (Stephanie Brooks, Algonquin, Ill.; Aimee Bruder, Lawrenceburg, Ind.; Sandy Hannebrink, Mount Pleasant, S.C.; Camille Waddell, Pensacola, Fla.), 3:08.27.

50m Backstroke Men S2
1. James Anderson, GBR, 1:13.66, WR; 2. Miroslaw Piesak, POL, 1:15.37; 3. Alan McGregor, GBR, 1:19.36; No USA entries.

50m Backstroke Women S2
1. Sara Carracelas, ESP, 1:30.89, WR; 2. Mairead Berry, IRL, 1:31.45; 3. Betiana Basualdo, ARG, 1:33.12; No USA entries.

50m Backstroke Men S3
1. Albert Bakaev, RUS, 56.21; 2. Claude Badie, FRA, 56.34; 3. Petter

1996 Paralympic Games Results

Edstrom, SWE, 57.52; No USA entries.

50m Backstroke Women S3
1. Aranzazu Gonzlez, ESP, 1:02.82, WR; 2. S. Barroso, POR, 1:06.45; 3. Annke Conradi, GER, 1:07.78; 7. Anne Herman, San Diego, Calif., 1:42.24

50m Backstroke Men S4
1. Luca Pancalli, ITA, 49.23; 2. Pierre Bellot, FRA, 49.83; 3. Craig Laufenberg, Whitewater, Wis., USA, 54.01.

50m Backstroke Women S4
1. Kay Espenhayn, GER, 51.48, WR; 2. Mayumi Narita, JPN, 54.87; 3. Karen Braeumso, DEN, 1:03.21; 4. Jennifer Hazen, Bloomfield, N.J., USA, 105.54.

50m Backstroke Men S5
1. Zsolt Vereczkei, HUN, 39.95, WR; 2. Essam Attia, EGY, 41.40; 3. Pascal Pinard, FRA, 42.63; No USA entries.

50m Backstroke Women S5
1. Beatrice Hess, FRA, 45.86, WR; 2. Corine D'Urzo, FRA, 49.09; 3. Jane Stidever, GBR, 52.40; 4. Susan Moucha, Brandon, Fla., USA, 1:01.81; Colleen Dougherty, Bend, Ore., USA, elim. in heat; Sandra Hanebrink, Mount Pleasant, S.C., USA, elim. in heat.

100m Backstroke Men S6
1. Weiming Zhu, CHN, 1:21.12; 2. Gregory Burns, Singapore/Washington, D.C., 1:21.19; 3. Duane Kale, NZL, 1:23.51.

100m Backstroke Women S6
1. Jennifer Newstead, NZL, 1:37.96; 2. Polina Djourova, BUL, 1:40.43; 3. Xiangrong Zhou, CHN, 1:42.31

100m Freestyle Men S7
1. Eric Lindmann, FRA, 1:07.13, PR; 2. Tony Alexander, CAN, 1:08.29; 3. Yuriy Andryushyn, UKR, 1:08.60; No USA entries.

100m Freestyle Women S7
1. Daniela Pohl, GER, 1:19.76; 2. Mireia Riera, ESP, 1:20.84; 3. Kristin Hakonard, ISL, 1:22.87; 8. Julie Wolfe, Tucson, Ariz., USA, 1:25.76.

100m Freestyle Men S8
1. Emil Brondum, DEN, 1:03.87, WR; 2. Holger Kimmig, GER, 1:04.06; 3. Kasper Hansen, DEN, 1:05.34; 8. Jason Wening, Jefferson City, Mo., 1:08.09; Travis Mohr, Northampton, Pa., USA, elim. in heat; Jay Styperk, Pittsburgh, Pa., USA, elim. in heat.

100m Freestyle Women S8
1. Priya Cooper, AUS, 1:12.08 PR; 2. Pernille Thomsen, DEN, 1:18.76; 3. Petra Reuvekamp, NED, 1:20.32; 6. Brenda Levy, Rockville, Md., USA, 1:22.38.

100m Freestyle Men S9
1. Luis Alicea III, Ontario, Calif., USA, 1:01.04; 2. Rutger Sturkenboom, NED, 1:01.09; 3. Olafur Eiriksson, ISL, 1:01.69; Dana Albrycht, Canton, Conn., USA, elim. in heat.

100m Freestyle Women S9
1. Joyce Luncher, Pittsburgh, Pa., USA, 1:08.16, WR; 2. Melissa Carlton, AUS, 1:08.35; 3. Sabrina Bellavia, BEL, 1:08.52; 6. Allison Pittman, San Diego, Calif., USA, 1:10.98; Diane Straub, Cambridge, Mass., USA, elim. in heat.

100m Freestyle Men S10
1. Alwin De Groot, NED, 57.26, WR; 2. Stefan Loeffler, GER, 57.86; 3. Jurjen Engelsman, NED, 58.13; No USA entries.

100m Freestyle Women S10
1. Claudia Hengst, GER, 1:04.68 PR; 2. Gemma Dashwood, AUS, 1:05.82; 3. Sarah Bailey, GBR, 1:06.04; 6. Karen Norris, Van Nuys, Calif., USA, 1:09.55; Julie Atwell, Endwell, N.Y., USA, 1:15.83.

4x100m Freestyle Relay Women B1-3
1. GER, 4:33.52, WR; 2. GBR, 4:49.65; 3. USA (Trischa Zorn, Indianapolis, Ind.; Mandy Sommer, Omaha, Neb.; Dawn Duffy, Moore, Okla.; Beth Scott, Rockville, Md.), 4:57.32.

100m Freestyle Men S3
1. Petter Edstrom, SWE, 1:59.21, PR; 2. Palmar Gudmundsson, ISL, 1:59.82; 3. Genezi Andrade, BRA, 2:01.97.

100m Freestyle Women S3
1. Aranzazu Gonzalez, ESP, 2:16.03, WR; 2. Annke Conradi, GER, 2:19.78; 3. S. Barroso, POR, 2:23.18; 7. Anne Herman, San Diego, Calif., USA, 3:25.11.

100m Freestyle Men S4
1. Ricardo Oribe, ESP, 1:31.35, WR; 2. Luc Pancalli, ITA, 1:33.44; 3.

John Petersson, DEN, 1:39.94; 6. James Thompson, Cherry Hill, N.J., USA, 1:44.56; Craig Laufenberg, Whitewater, Wis., USA, elim. in heat.

100m Freestyle Women S4
1. Mayumi Narita, JPN, 1:36.23, WR; 2. Kay Espenhayn, GER, 1:37.58; 3. Aimee Bruder, Lawrenceburg, Ind., USA, 1:53.27; 8. Jennifer Hazen, Bloomfield, N.J., USA, 2:28.71.

100m Freestyle Men S5
1. Juan Fuertes, ESP, 1:21.61, WR; 2. Lars Luerig, GER, 1:22.51; 3. Krzysztof Sleczka, POL, 1:25.91; No USA entries.

100m Freestyle Women S5
1. Beatrice Hess, FRA, 1:23.84, WR; 2. Olena Akopyan, UKR, 1:28.59; 3. Margaret Mceleny, GBR, 1:34.82; 7. Sandra Hanebrink, Mount Pleasant, S.C., USA, 1:56.67.

100m Freestyle Men S6
1. Duane Kale, NZL, 1:08.45, WR; 2. Peter Andersen, DEN; 1:09.96; 3. Danijel Pavlinec, SLO, 1:14.55; 8. Martin Parker, Tucson, Ariz., 1:21.66.

100m Freestyle Women S6
1. Jeanette Esling, GBR, 1:23.63, WR; 2. Ludivine Loiseau, FRA, 1:23.98; 3. Jennifer Newstead, NZL, 1:24.19; 7. Stephanie Brooks, Algonquin, Ill., USA, 1:32.81; Colleen Dailey, Houston, Texas, elim. in heat; Jill Nelson, Pampa, Texas, USA, elim. in heat; Camille Waddell, Pensacola, Fla., USA, elim. in heat.

200m Breaststroke Men B2
1. Kingsley Bugarin, AUS, 2:35.21, WR; 2. Christian, DEN, 2:42.56; 3. Vitali Krylov, RUS, 2:44.08; Michael Taber, Albany, N.Y., USA, elim. in heat.

200m Breaststroke Women B2
1. Carine Van Puyvelde, BEL, 3:17.28; 2. Elaine Barrett, GBR, 3:18.57; 3. Garcia-Arcicollar, ESP, 3:23.04; Trischa Zorn, Indianapolis, Ind., USA, disqualified in heat.

200m Breaststroke Men B3
1. Noel Pedersen, NOR, 2:33.82, WR; 2. Ivan Nielsen, DEN, 2:37.51; 3. Andrei Nefedov, RUS, 2:46.73; No USA entries.

50m Freestyle Men MH (exhibition)
1. Alwin Houtsma, NED, 26.18, WR; 2. Grant Fitzpatrick AUS, 27.01; 3. Craig Groenewald, RSA, 27.32; Douglas Bell, Brazil, Ind., USA, elim. in heat; Nicholas Karris, Portage, Ind., USA, elim. in heat.

50m Freestyle Women MH (exhibition)
1. Tracy Wiscombe, GBR, 31.73; 2. Eela Kokk, EST, 33.14; 3. Sigrun Hrafnsdottir, ISL, 33.29; Jenny Skinner, Huntington Beach, Calif., USA, elim. in heat.

4x100m Freestyle Men S7-10
1. GER, 4:08.50, WR; 2. AUS, 4:12.11; 3. ESP, 4:14.36; 5. USA (Dana Albrycht, Canton, Conn.; Jason Wening, Jefferson City, Mo.; John Register, Springfield, Va.; Luis Alicea, Ontario, Calif.), 4:16.15

4x100m Freestyle Women S7-10
1. AUS, 4:45.65, WR; 2. USA (Brenda Levy, Rockville, Md.; Karen Norris, Van Nuys, Calif.; Allison Pittman, San Diego, Calif.; Joyce Luncher, Pittsburgh, Pa.), 4:47.87; 3. GER, 449.63.

50m Freestyle Men S2
1. Miroslaw Piesak, POL, 1:14.59, WR; 2. James Anderson, GBR, 1:17.63; 3. Adriano Pereira, BRA, 1:19.19

50m Freestyle Women S2
1. Sara Carracelas, ESP, 1:29.77, WR; 2. Betiana Basualdo, ARG, 1:31.66; 3. Victoria Broadribb, GBR, 1:31.72

50m Freestyle Men S3
1. Jaime Eulert, PER, 51.95, WR; 2. Albert Bakaev, RUS, 57.78; 3. Petter Edstrom, SWE, 57.80

50m Freestyle Women S3
1. Aranzazu Gonzalez, ESP, 1:05.56, WR; 2. S. Barroso, POR, 1:06.38; 3. Annke Conradi, GER, 1:07.47; 8. Anne Herman, San Diego, Calif., USA, 1:38.38.

50m Freestyle Men S4
1. Ricardo Oribe, ESP, 41.85, PR; 2. Luca Pancalli, ITA, 42.62; 3. Akinobu Aoki, JPN, 44.83; 4. James Thompson, Cherry Hill, N.J., USA, 47.56; Craig Laufenberg, Whitewater, Wis., USA, elim. heat.

50m Freestyle Women S4

1996 Paralympic Games Results

1. Mayumi Narita, JPN, 44.47, WR; 2. Kay Espenhayn, GER, 47.55; 3. Karen Braeumso, DEN, 54.16; 5. Aimee Bruder, Lawrenceburg, Ind., USA, 54.35

50m Freestyle Men S5
1. Juan Fuertes, ESP, 37.52, WR; 2. Lars Luerig, GER, 38.73; 3. Krzysztof Sleczka, POL, 39.86; 4. Daniel Butler, Falls Church, Va., USA, 40.36.

50m Freestyle Women S5
1. Beatrice Hess, FRA, 39.47, PR; 2. Olena Akoan, UKR, 40.82; 3. Margaret Mceleny, GBR, 43.81; 8. Sandra Hanebrink, Mount Pleasant, S.C., 54.06.

100m Breaststroke Men SB4
1. Pascal Pinard, FRA, 1:42.20, WR; 2. Ricardo Ten, ESP, 1:43.33; 3. I. Vasconcelos, BRA, 1:46.55; 5. Dan Butler, Falls Church, Va., USA, 1:58.79.

100m Breaststroke Women SB4
1. Jennifer Newstead, NZL, 1:55.49; 2. Sara Olofsson, SWE, 2:07.92; 3. Maria Vikgren, SWE, 209.50; 7. Sandra Hanebrink, Mount Pleasant, S.C., USA, 2:48.33

100m Breaststroke Men SB5
1. Kasper Engel, NED, 1:31.50, WR; 2. Tadhg Slattery, RSA, 1:38.59; 3. Aaron Paulson, Portland, Ore., USA, 1:39.70; 5. Gregory Burns, Singapore/Washington, D.C., USA, 1:41.24; Martin Parker, Tucson, Ariz., USA, elim. in heat.

100m Breaststroke Women SB5
1. Camille Waddell, Pensacola, Fla., USA, 1:53.48, WR; 2. Eva Nesheim, NOR, 2:01.66; 3. Gitta Raczko, HUN, 2:03.07; 5. Collen Dailey, Houston, Texas, USA, 2:11.73; 7. Susan Moucha, Brandon, Fla., 2:22.31.

100m Breaststroke Men SB6
1. Jesus Iglesias, ESP, 1:31.78; 2. Aaron Bidois, NZL, 1:33.62; 3. Mathias Schlubeck, GER, 1:34.92.

100m Breaststroke Women SB6
1. Malgorzata Okupniak, POL, 1:56.65; 2. Edyta Okoczuk, POL, 1:57.95; 3. Gerda Lampers, NED, 2:01.58.

100m Breaststroke Men SB7
1. Baoren Gong, CHN, 1:25.92, WR; 2. Sascha Kidred, GBR, 1:28.86; 3. Laurentius Van Geel, NED, 1:31.17; 6. Travis Mohr, Northampton, Pa., 1:40.77; Jay Styperk, Pittsburgh, Pa., USA, elim. in heat.

100m Breaststroke Women SB7
1. Kristin Hakonard, ISL, 1:39.34, WR; 2. Beate Schretzmann, GER, 1:53.14; 3. Petra Reuvekamp, NED, 1:59.45.

100m Breaststroke Men SB8
1. Rune lvang, NOR, 1:19.96, WR; 2. Helge Bjornstad, NOR, 122.80; 3. Yongzhong Guo, CHN, 1:23.70; 6. Michael Doyle, Warrington, Pa., USA, 1:31.97

100m Breaststroke Women SB8
1. Tieyin Shi, CHN, 1:38.10; 2. Laura Tramuns, ESP, 1:38.25; 3. S. Van Amelsvoort, NED, 1:39.38; 7. Diane Straub, Cambridge, Mass., USA, 1:45.19.

100m Breaststroke Men SB9
1. Jurjen Engelsman, NED, 1:14.63, WR; 2. Alwin De Groot, NED, 1:18.19; 3. Sergey Bestuchev, RUS, 1:19.04.

100m Breaststroke Women SB9
1. Katerina Coufalova, CZE, 1:25.84; 2. Joyce Luncher, Pittsburgh, Pa., 1:29.21; 3. Begona Reina, ESP, 1:30.22; Karen Norris, Van Nuys, Calif., USA, elim. in heat.

100m Breaststroke Men SB10
1. Stefan Loeffler, GER, 1:13.50, WR; 2. Tomas Kjellqvist, SWE, 1:18.41; 3. Mario Kofler, GER, 1:18.93.

100m Breaststroke Women SB10
1. Sarah Bailey, GBR, 1:26.97; 2. Judith Young, AUS, 1:29.89; 3. Ricka Stenger, DEN, 1:30.38.

100m Backstroke Men B1
1. Daniel Kelly, Golden Valley, Minn., USA, 1:09.92; 2. Junichi Kawai, JPN, 1:13.43; 3. Birkir Gunnarsson, ISL, 1:17.74.

100m Backstroke Women B1
1. Raquel Saavedra, ESP, 1:24.68, WR; 2. E. Fingerroos, FIN, 1:25.50; 3. Qiming Dong, CHN, 1:26.37.

100m Backstroke Men B2

1. Christopher Holmes, GBR, 1:07.29; 2. Francisco Segarra, ESP, 1:11.08; 3. Ziv Better, ISR, 1:12.31.

100m Backstroke Women B2
1. Trischa Zorn, Indianapolis, Ind., 1:15.43; 2. Marge Korkjas, EST, 1:22.43; 3. Garcia-Arcicollar, ESP, 1:23.82.

100m Backstroke Men B3
1. Walter Wu, CAN, 1:04.80, WR; 2. Noel Pedersen, NOR, 1:07.47; 3. Jurgen Lentink, NED, 111.30.

100m Backstroke Women B3
1. Yvonne Hopf, GER, 1:09.28, WR; 2. Marie Claire Ross, CAN, 1:13.50; 3. Elizabeth Scott, Rockville, Md., USA, 1:15.03.

50m Freestyle Men S6
1. Peter Andersen, DEN, 31.26, WR; 2. Duane Kale, NZL, 31.41; 3. Adriano Lima, BRA, 33.22; 8. Martin Parker, Tuscon, Ariz., USA, 39.16.

50m Freestyle Women S6
1. Ludivine Loiseau, FRA, 36.73, WR; 2. Jeanette Esling GBR, 38.63; 3. Karni Liddell, AUS, 39.56; 8. Stephanie Brooks, Algonquin, Ill., USA, 43.31; Jill Nelson, Pampa, Texas, USA, elim. in heat.

50m Freestyle Men S7
1. Tony Alexnander, CAN, 30.81; 2. Eric Lindmann, FRA, 31.23; 3. Jesus Iglesias, ESP, 31.28; No USA entries.

50m Freestyle Women S7
1. Daniela Pohl, GER, 36.85; 2. Tracey Oliver, AUS, 37.18; 3. Margita Prokeinova, SLO, 37.34; 7. Julie Wolfe, Tucson, Ariz., USA, 40.83.

50m Freestyle Men S8
1. Emil Brondum, DEN, 28.84, WR; 2. Konstantinos Fyas, GRE, 29.83; 3. Holger Kimmig, GER, 29.85; Jay Styperk, Pittsburgh, Pa., USA, elim. in heat.

50m Freestyle Women S8
1. Pernille Thomsen, DEN, 33.03, WR; 2. Priya Cooper, AUS, 34.17; 3. Brenda Levy, Rockville, Md., USA, 35.38

50m Freestyle Men S9
1. Brendan Burkett, AUS, 28.09; 2. Rutger Sturkenboom, NED, 28.12; 3. Luis Alicea III, Ontario, Calif., USA, 28.16

50m Freestyle Women S9
1. Joyce Luncher, Pittsburg, Pa., 31.36, WR; 2. Sabrina Bellavia, BEL, 31.56; 3. Ricka Stenger, DEN, 32.02; 4. Allison Pittman, San Diego, Calif., USA, 32.49; John Register, Springfield, Va., USA, elim. in heat; Dana Albrycht, Canton, Conn., USA, elim. in heat; Diane Straub, Cambridge, Mass., elim. in heat.

50m Freestyle Men S10
1. Alwin De Groot, NED, 26.52; 2. Stefan Loeffler, GER, 26.60; 3. Scott Brockenshire, AUS, 26.82; No USA entries.

50m Freestyle Women S10
1. Claudia Hengst, GER, 29.90; 2. Judith Young, AUS, 30.22; 3. Elizabeth Prinsloo, RSA, 31.01; 4. Karen Norris, Van Nuys, Calif., USA, 31.62; 8. Julie Atwell, Endwell, N.Y., USA, 34.16.

50m Freestyle Men B1
1. Junichi Kawai, JPN , 27.24; 2. Izhar Cohen, ISR, 27.78; 3. Daniel Kelly, Golden Valley, Minn., 28.10; 7. Michael Taber, Albany, N.Y., USA, 29.89.

50m Freestyle Women B1
1. Elia Nilsson, SWE, 32.02, WR; 2. Tracey Cross, AUS, 34.41; 3. Janice Burton, GBR, 35.16; Mandy Sommer, Omaha, Neb., USA, elim. in heat.

50m Freestyle Men B2
1. Christopher Holmes, GBR, 26.61; 2. Pablo Corral, ESP, 26.77; 3. Ziv Better, ISR, 26.93; No USA entries.

50 m Freestyle Women B2
1. Marge Korkjas, EST, 29.90; 2. Trischa Zorn, Indianapolis, Ind., USA, 30.93; 3. Maria Fernandez, ESP, 31.28.

50m Freestyle Men B3
1. Ebert Kleynhans, RSA, 26.06, PR; 2. Noel Pedersen, NOR, 26.41; 3. Walter Wu, CAN, 26.64; No USA entries.

50m Freestyle Women B3
1. Yvonne Hopf, GER, 27.38, WR; 2. Daniela Henke, GER, 28.72; 3. Marie Claire Ross, CAN, 28.87; 4. Elizabeth Scott, Rockville, Md., USA, 29.33.

4x50m Medley Men S1-6

1. USA (Greg Burns, Singapore/Washington D.C.; Aaron Paulson, Portland, Ore.; Dan Butler, Falls Church, Va.; Marty Parker, Tucson, Ariz.), 2:39.28, WR; 2. CHN, 2:46.35; 3. ESP, 2:50.27.

4x50m Medley Women S1-6
1. HUN, 3:22.65, PR; 2. USA (Susan Mocha, Bradon, Fla.; Camille Waddell, Pensacola, Fla.; Jill Nelson, Pampa, Tex.; Stephanie Brooks, Algonquin, Ill.), 3:27.99; 3. GBR, 3:28.60

4x100m Medley Men S7-10
1. GER, 4:41.50; 2. GBR, 4:41.62; 3. NED, 4:46.06; USA, withdrew due to injury.

4x100m Medley Women S7-10
1. USA (Karen Norris, Van Nuys, Calif.; Diane Straub, Cambridge, Mass.; Joyce Luncher, Pittsburgh, Pa.; Allison Pittman, San Diego, Calif.), 5:27.46, WR; 2. GER, 5:28.39; 3. ESP, 5:30.27.

4x100m Medley Women B1-3
1. GER, 5:11.58; 2. USA (Trischa Zorn, Indianapolis, Ind.; Katie Edgar, Wilmington, Del.; Elizabeth Scott, Rockville, Md.; Mandy Sommer, Omaha, Neb.), 5:29.71; 3. ESP, 5:37.55.

TABLE TENNIS

Individual Men 1
1. Hae Lee, KOR; 2. Matti Launonen, FIN; 3T. Daniel Haylan, ARG; 3T. Sun Kang, KOR; 5T. Sebastian DeFrancisco, USA.

Individual Men 2
1. Kyung Kim, KOR; 2. Vincent Boury, FRA, 3T. Gerhard Scharf, AUT; 3T. Jari Kurkinen, FIN; 5T. Gary Blanks, Virginia Beach, Va., USA.

Individual Men 3
1. Zlatko Kesler, YUG; 2. Neil Robinson, GBR; 3T. F. Altendorfer, AUT; 3T. James Rawson.

Individual Men 4
1. Bruno Benedetti, FRA; 2. Michal Stefanu, CZE; 3T. Christian Sutter, AUT; 3T. Thomas Kreidel, GER.

Individual Men 5
1. Guy Tisserant, FRA; 2. Kam Kwong, HKG; 3T. Ernst Bollden, SWE; 3T. Chang-Shen Chou, TPE; 5T. Andre Scott, Elizabeth, N.J., USA.

Indivudal Men 6
1. Brian Nielsen, DEN; 2. Mattias Karlsson, SWE; 3. Harold Kersten, NED.

Individual Men 7
1. Tahl Leibovitz, Woodhaven, N.Y., USA; 2. Jochen Wollmert, GER; 3. Thomas Kurfess, GER.

Individual Men 8
1. Magnus Andree, SWE; 2. Mitchell Seidenfeld, Minneapolis, Minn., USA; 3. Vladimir Polkanov, MOL.

Individual Men 9
1. Stanislaw Fraczyk, AUT; 2. Olivier Chateigner, FRA; 3T. Alain Pichon, FRA; 3T. Ladislav Gaspar, SLO.

Individual Men 10
1. De La Bourdonnaye, FRA; 2. Robert Bader, SWE; 3T. Enrique Agudo, ESP; 3T. Kwant Jeong, KOR.

Individual Women 1-2
1. Isabelle Lafaye, FRA; 2. Anne-Marie Gibelin, FRA; 3. Baerbel Rode, GER; 4. Ruth Rosenbaum, Hackensack, N.J., USA.

Individual Women 3
1. Paulik Sasvarine, HUN; 2. Monika Bartheidel, GER, 3. Marie-LIne Pollet, BEL.

Individual Women 4
1. Jennifer Johnson, Port Chester, N.Y., USA; 2. Christiane Pape, GER; 3. Gertrudis Laemers, NED.

Individual Women 5
1. Susanne Schwendtner, AUT; 2. Maria Hoffman, MEX; 3T. Gisela Pohle, GER; 3T. Maria Nardelli, ITA; 5T. Terese Terranova, Fort Lauderdale, Fla., USA.

Individual Women 6-8
1. Ingrid Borre, BEL; 2. Martine Thierry, FRA; 3. Xiaoling Zhang, CHN.

Individual Women 9
1. Fuqun Luo, CHN; 2. M. Odeide-Simian, FRA; 3. Michiyo Nuruki, JPN.

Individual Women 10
1. Michelle Sevin, FRA; 2. Jolana Davidkova, CZE; 3. K. Jagodzinska, POL.

Team Men 1-2
1. FIN; 2. AUT; 3T. GER; 3T. KOR; USA (Sebastian DeFrancisco, Santa Cruz, Calif.; Ken Brooks, Lebanon, N.J.; Gary Blanks, Virginia Beach, Va.) elim. in pool play

Team Men 3
1. KOR; 2. AUT; 3T. GBR; 3T GER; No USA entry.

Team Men 4-5
1. SWE; 2. FRA; 3T. AUT; 3T. BEL; USA (Andre Scott, Elizabeth, N.J.; Michael Dempsey, Oxnard, Calif.), elim. in quarterfinals

Team Men 6-8
1. GER; 2. SWE; 3. USA (Tal Leibovitz, Woodhaven, N.Y., and Mitch Seidenfeld, Minneapolis, Minn.).

Team Men 9-10
1. FRA; 2. AUT; 3T. GER; 3T. SLO.

Team Women 3-5
1. GER; 2. HKG; 3. USA (Jackie DiLorenzo, Hastings-on-Hudson, N.Y.; Terese Terranova, Fort Lauderdale, Fla., and Jennifer Johnson, Port Chester, N.Y.).

Team Women 6-10
1. CHN; 2. CZE; 3. FRA.

TENNIS

Men's Singles
1. Ricky Molier, NED; 2. Stephen Welch, Arlington, Texas, USA; 3. David Hall, AUS.

Men's Doubles
1. Stephen Welch, Arlington, Texas and Chip Parmelly, Diamond Bar, Calif., USA; 2. David Hall and Mica Connell, AUS, 3. Ricky Molier and Eric Stuurman, NED.

Women's Singles
1. Maaike Smit, NED; 2. Monique Kalkman, NED, 3. Chantal Vandierendonck, NED.

Women's Doubles
1. Chantal Vandierendonck and Monique Kalkman, NED; 2. Nancy Olson, Daytona Beach, Fla. and Hope Lewellen, Palos Park, Ill., USA; 3. Oristelle Marx and Arlette Racineux, FRA.

VOLLEYBALL

Sitting
1. IRI; 2. NOR; 3. FIN; 11. USA (Kenneth Bode, New Brunswick, N.J.; Lloyd Bacharach, Chicago, Ill.; Larry Chloupek, Potomac, Md.; Bill Demby, Mitchville, Md.; Steve Doubt, Indianapolis, Ind.; Jim Dugan, Bethalto, Ill.; Jim Kessler, Sebetha, Kan.; Paul Kramer, San Jose, Calif.; Tracey Lange, Waunakee, Wis.; Paul Moran, Chicago, Ill.; Kurt Smith, Elhurst, Ill.; Bryan Tabler, Winter Park, Fla.; James Terpenning, Cornwall, N.Y.; Edward Tuthill, Montauk, N.Y.).

Standing
1. GER; 2. SVK; 3. POL; 4. USA (Barry Hammer, Lebanon, Tenn.; Dennis Lee, Greensboro, N.C.; Jeffery Munn, Sugar Hill, Ga.; David Newkirk, Lubbock, Texas; Robert Osbahr, Freehold, N.J.; Douglas (Ray) Ragsdale, Lubbock, Texas; Chris Seilkop, Deland, Fla.; Thomas Sestanovich, Manhattan Beach, Calif.; Joe Sullivan, Richmond, Va.; Dwight Van Tassell, Alpharetta, Ga.; Michael Walters, Hudson, Wis.; Jeffery Werner, Reading, Pa.).

YACHTING (Demonstration)

1. GBR, 18.50 points; 2. CAN, 22.50 pts.; 3. USA (Waldo Esparza, Seffner, Fla.; James Leatherman, Baltimore, Md.; Chris Murphy, Annapolis, Md.; John Ross-Duggan, Orlando, Fla.) 27.00 pts.